WESTERN IMP
THE MIDDLE E.

Western Imperialism in the Middle East 1914–1958

D. K. FIELDHOUSE

OXFORD
UNIVERSITY PRESS

OXFORD
UNIVERSITY PRESS

Great Clarendon Street, Oxford OX2 6DP

Oxford University Press is a department of the University of Oxford.
It furthers the University's objective of excellence in research, scholarship,
and education by publishing worldwide in

Oxford New York

Auckland Cape Town Dar es Salaam Hong Kong Karachi
Kuala Lumpur Madrid Melbourne Mexico City Nairobi
New Delhi Shanghai Taipei Toronto

With offices in

Argentina Austria Brazil Chile Czech Republic France Greece
Guatemala Hungary Italy Japan Poland Portugal Singapore
South Korea Switzerland Thailand Turkey Ukraine Vietnam

Oxford is a registered trade mark of Oxford University Press
in the UK and in certain other countries

Published in the United States
by Oxford University Press Inc., New York

© D. K. Fieldhouse 2006

British Library Cataloguing in Publication Data
Data available

Library of Congress Cataloging in Publication Data
Data available

Typeset by Laserwords Private Limited, Chennai, India
Printed in Great Britain
on acid-free paper by
Biddles Ltd., King's Lynn, Norfolk

ISBN 978–0–19–928737–6 (Hbk.)   978–0–19–954083–9 (Pbk.)

3 5 7 9 10 8 6 4 2

For Roger Louis, who suggested, read, and improved it

Preface

This book is a by-product of *Kurds, Arabs and Britons: The Memoir of Wallace Lyon in Iraq 1918–1944* (I. B. Tauris, 2002), which I edited for publication. I did so initially as an act of family piety, since Lyon was my father-in-law and the book was written for and dedicated to his daughter, my wife Sheila. I did it reluctantly, because, though an imperial historian by profession, I knew very little about the Middle East and that highly specialized and over-crowded historical field. But in the process of reading about Iraq I became fascinated by the complexities of the whole Middle Eastern situation during the earlier twentieth century. As a result, when Professor Wm Roger Louis, after reading my draft, suggested that I go on to write a more general history of the five post-1918 League of Nations mandates in the Middle East, I decided to do so. This book is the result.

I confess that I am still intimidated by the scale of the subject and by my own ignorance of its finer points. Each of the five countries covered—Iraq, Palestine, Jordan, Syria, and Lebanon—has its own extensive body of specialist literature: Palestine by far the largest and most controversial due to the very intensive work by Israeli historians. Any outsider who enters these labyrinths does so at risk. Moreover, I know no Arabic, Turkish, or Hebrew, so my sources were necessarily limited to material published in English or French. This relates to a further problem: how to spell Arabic or Turkish or Jewish names when transliterated into English: virtually no two of the published sources I have used adopted the same spelling. Moreover, spelling conventions have changed over time. I have therefore attempted to adopt a consistent rather than a correct approach, using accepted anglicized spellings where possible.

The aim of the book is to provide a comparative overview of how Britain and France came to rule these five portions of the Ottoman empire and how they dealt with them. In one sense, therefore, it is a survey of contrasting imperial techniques for controlling these temporary dependencies. In another it is an investigation of the interaction between western imperialism in its final phase and the power of nascent Arab nationalism. Essentially these European powers converted what had been relatively quiescent provinces of the Ottoman empire into some of the least stable and internationally explosive states in the world. This was certainly not the intention of the mandatory powers, and the reasons for this outcome are specific to each of the five territories. It is a main aim of this book to investigate why it happened. Since this study is limited to these Middle Eastern territories it excludes both Egypt—occupied informally by the British since 1882 and declared a protectorate in 1914—and Cyprus, under British protection from 1878 and made a colony in 1914. But a wider study would draw many parallels between these two and the five mandates studied here.

The book is divided into three parts. Part One contains two introductory chapters on the decline of the Ottoman empire and the process by which after 1914 the western powers (initially also Russia) planned to divide up its remaining possessions in the Middle East. Part Two then has separate chapters on Iraq, Palestine (two chapters because of the greater complexity of the material), Jordan, Syria, and Lebanon. In each study the emphasis is laid on the special features of the imperial approach and the reaction of the indigenous people. In the final part an attempt is made to pull all the material together and to assess how far these particular forms of alien rule can be held responsible for the fact that two of these countries, Iraq and Syria, have long been under military dictatorship; one, Palestine, divided into violently hostile camps by religion; one other, Lebanon, fundamentally unstable and under the aegis of Syria; and only one, Jordan, that appears to be a stable monarchy, though surviving only by use of autocratic royal authority and an effective military force.

The book is intended to be a contribution to imperial history in the broad, which for decades has concerned itself with the indigenous populations of empires not merely with imperial achievement, rather than to Arabian or Israeli history more narrowly defined. I hope that it will be useful to a general readership and in particular to university students who want a broad introductory overview of this region and its continuing problems. It may also provide a useful insight into western motives for, and Arab reactions to, the Coalition occupation of Iraq in 2003.

D. K. Fieldhouse

Jesus College
Cambridge
June 2005

Acknowledgements

I am grateful to the following who have in various ways given advice or have read and commented on all or parts of the book in draft. Professor Wm Roger Louis read and made very useful comments on the whole draft. Dr Metin Kunt read the early material on the Ottomans, pointed me to sources I had ignored, and corrected points of detail and spellings. David McDowall read the whole manuscript and pointed to many errors and inadequacies. An anonymous reader listed a number of books I should have read, mainly relating to the Ottomans. I read all of these I could lay my hand on and was able to make improvements. Dr Dorothy McCarthy copy-edited the book with meticulous care. All residual errors and omissions are, of course, my own responsibility.

I spent three periods of three months between 2001 and 2003 as a Visiting Fellow at the Humanities Research Centre at the Australian National University while working on this book and I am very grateful for the excellent facilities and the friendly welcome I was given there.

Contents

Glossary of Arabic and Turkish Words used in the Text

alim	Muslim religious scholar (pl. ulama)
aliyah	Jewish migration to Palestine
awqaf	Muslim pious endowments
fatwa	formal opinion by an expert in the Sharia
liwa	Ottoman administrative district within a province
millet	recognized autonomous non-Islamic religious community within the Ottoman empire
mufti	Islamic legal official able to deliver an expert legal opinion
mutasarrifiya	Ottoman regional governor (a sanjaq)
nahiya	Ottoman local government unit
Naqib	senior Islamic cleric in charge of a shrine
qadha	Ottoman local government unit
qadi	Muslim legal official
sadah	tribal chief or descendant of the Prophet
sanjaq	sub-division of an Ottoman vilayet
ulama	Islamic religious specialists
vali	Ottoman provincial governor
vilayet	Ottoman province

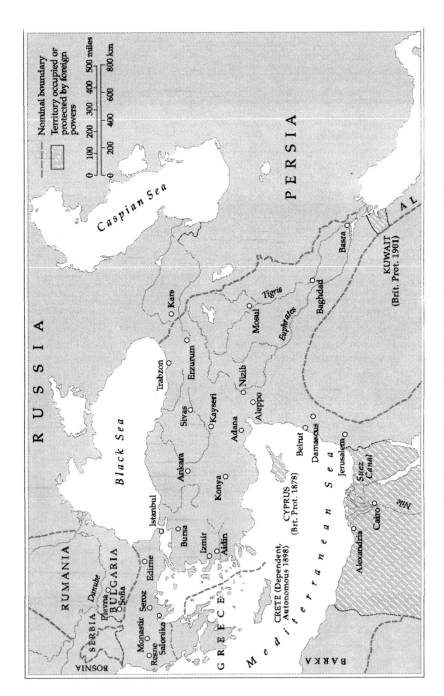

Map 1. The Ottoman Empire in the Middle East in the Early Twentieth Century

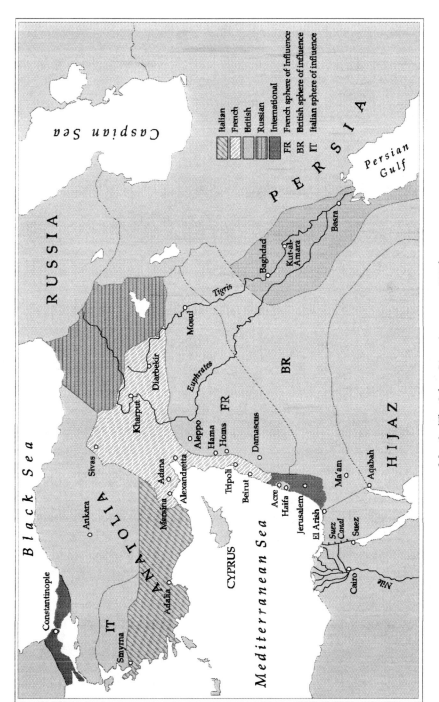

Map 2. The Sykes–Picot Agreement 1916

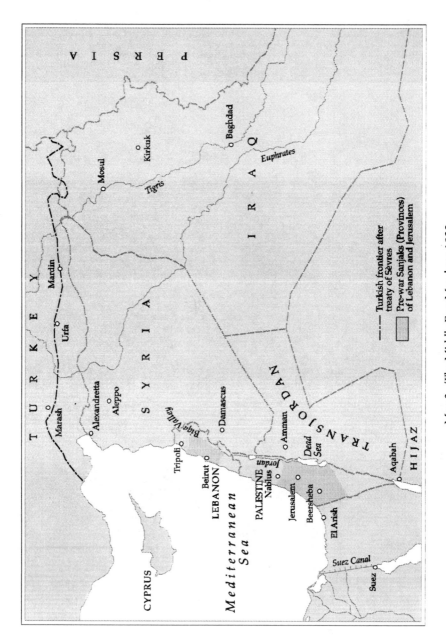

Map 3. The Middle East Mandates 1922

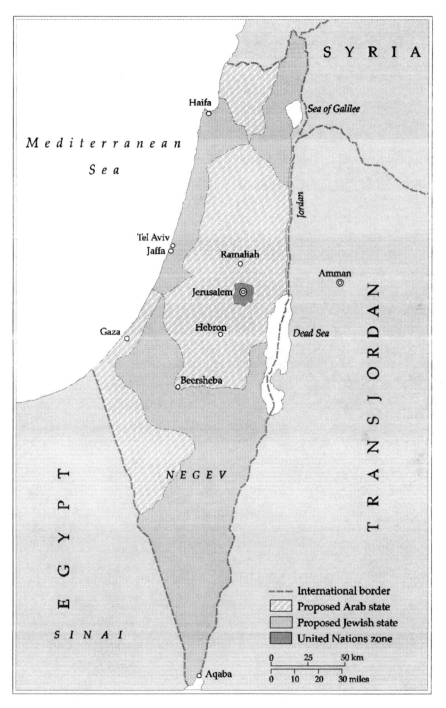

Map 4. The United Nations Partition Plan for Palestine 1947

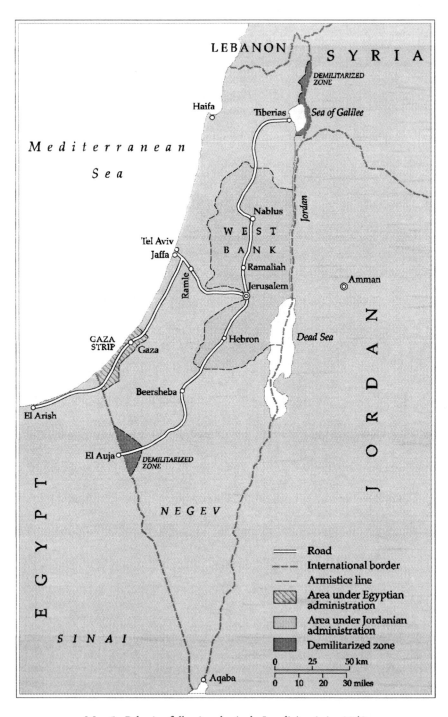

Map 5. Palestine following the Arab–Israeli Armistice 1949

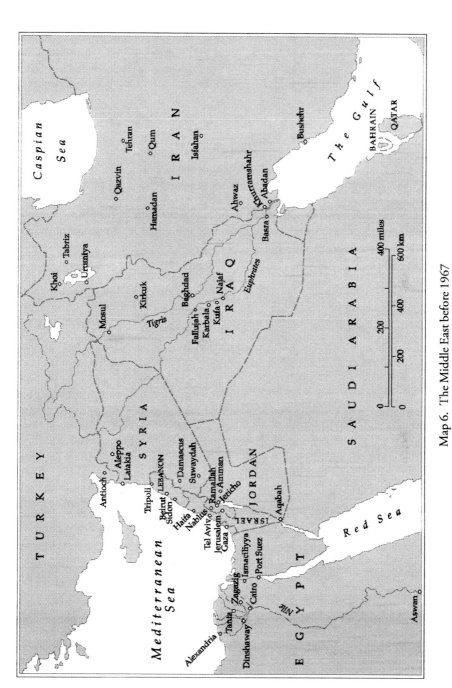

Map 6. The Middle East before 1967

PART ONE

BEFORE THE MANDATES, 1900–1922

1

The Decline of the Ottoman
Empire in the Middle East and the
'Arab Awakening' before 1914

There were two historic developments that had to take place before the Arab Middle East took its post-1914 shape. The first was the decline of the power of the Ottoman empire that had ruled this area from varying dates in the sixteenth century. So long as Istanbul retained its imperial control no new state system in the region was possible. In 1914 there seemed no prospect of loss of Ottoman control in this part of the empire, whatever happened in the Balkans and North Africa. By 1918 the empire was in process of destruction. The first question, therefore, is how far this dissolution of empire was due to imperial decay and how far to extraneous forces.

The second and closely related question is how far hostility to Ottoman rule by the subject peoples contributed to this process. In modern historical analysis of decolonization in other parts of the world there is always tension between, on the one hand, growing weakness of will or capacity to rule on the part of the imperial power and, on the other, growing demand for independence of the part of the dependencies. In the mid-twentieth century, historians and commentators placed greater emphasis on colonial resistance and 'nationalism'. Later interpretations have tended to underline either imperial decline or imperial choice. For the Middle East the critical question is how far the dissolution of empire was due to a new and explosive awakening of Arab nationalism, a desire to caste off Turkish rule and form new nation states. In short, was there an 'Arab Awakening' (a phrase associated with George Antonius, as will be seen) before 1914 and between then and 1918, how strong was it, and could it, by itself, have brought about the dissolution of the Ottoman Arab empire? The function of this chapter is to survey evidence on these two points. Chapter 2 will then examine the 'extraneous' factors from November 1914 that changed the whole pattern.

1. OTTOMAN 'DECLINE'

There should, in fact, also be a question mark against the phrase 'Ottoman decline'. It is not at all certain that such a thing existed. It is equally possible to argue that by 1914 the Ottoman empire was in full revival, although in a much reduced form.

The fact that it had by then lost most of the Balkans and effective control over North Africa might simply have been the result of defeat by militarily superior European forces, not of less capacity at the centre of the empire. In short, what had for nearly a century been described as 'the sick man of Europe'[1] may well have been on the mend by 1914 and due for a further lease of life. The function of this section is to summarize the evidence for Ottoman reform and recovery before 1914.[2]

In the later eighteenth century the empire may loosely be described as a typical 'traditional' autocracy of a type common throughout Asia. Its heyday had been in the sixteenth and seventeenth centuries, when Europe was too concerned with its internal conflicts to challenge its power. A symbolic turning point had been the failure of the siege of Vienna in 1683, but that marked the high-water mark of Ottoman ambitions, not the decline of the empire. It was only during the eighteenth century, with the growth of a centralized Russian state and the rise in the effective military power of Austria, that Ottoman power in the Balkan region was first seriously threatened.

In common with other comparable states, such as that of the Mughal emperors in India before the British conquest, the Ottoman governmental and administrative system was a palimpsest of archaic practices. The Sultan in his palace claimed absolute authority subject only to the laws of Islam. He ruled through bureaucrats headed by the Grand Vizier, based in the Sublime Porte. Imperial edicts were called *irade*. There was no representative body. Law for all Muslims was Islamic, in the hands of the ulama, experts in canon law. The empire was necessarily highly decentralized. In some areas government was in the hands of feudal lords, in others of governors appointed by the Porte. Taxation was for the most part farmed out, as it was in most of Europe, with the invariable result that the heavy burden on the peasantry did not result in large transfers to Istanbul. The army consisted mainly of the Janissaries, a professional force that had been the scourge of Europe in the sixteenth century but by the end of the eighteenth was hopelessly inefficient and, moreover, largely a law to itself. In time of crisis the Porte had to rely on levies raised by its greater subjects. One great virtue of the Ottoman system, and a significant reason for its long survival, was that it provided religious tolerance for non-Muslims. From early days the system of millets allowed each of the very many religious groups to practise its own confession. These groups were also left the responsibility of education, welfare, and civil law. Non-Muslims were not subject to military conscription, but had to pay additional taxes in lieu. A major

---

[1] The description was first made by Tsar Nicholas I in 1853.

[2] This account is based mainly on the following: A. Hourani, 'The Ottoman Background of the Modern Middle East', in K. H. Karpat (ed.), *The Ottoman State and its Place in World History* (Leiden, 1974); J. McCarthy, *The Ottoman Peoples and the End of Empire* (London, 2001); A. L. Macfie, *The End of the Ottoman Empire, 1908–1923* (London and New York, 1998); A. Palmer, *The Decline and Fall of the Ottoman Empire* (London, 1992); S. J. and E. K. Shaw, *History of the Ottoman Empire and Modern Turkey.* Vol. 2: *Reform, Revolution and Republic: The Rise of Modern Turkey 1808–1970* (Cambridge, 1977).

inconvenience in the imperial structure was the system of 'Capitulations' or agreements between the Sultan and foreign states. These had started in the Middle Ages with arrangements made with Italian city states for trade and the protection of their nationals, but had since the sixteenth century been widely extended to most western powers. The effect was that Istanbul could not fix import duties beyond certain agreed levels, and that expatriates in Ottoman territories were subject only to special courts and had other special privileges.

In retrospect all this gives the impression of an imperial structure in serious decline. But taken in isolation it was probably quite viable. Had the Ottoman territories lain as far from a resurgent Europe as China, the empire might, as did the Chinese empire, have remained largely intact and safely unreformed until late in the nineteenth century.

In fact, however, Istanbul was aware of the dangers long before then. The main external threat during the later eighteenth century had been from Russia. The external danger was then greatly increased by the aggression of Austria and the threat from other western powers, particularly after Napoleon's invasion of Egypt in 1798. It remained the chief concern and motive for radical domestic reform until 1914. But there was another serious threat to the imperial system, from within its frontiers, which provided a parallel stimulus to innovation. This can best be seen in the broader context of the three main Islamic agricultural empires of the period: the Ottomans, the Safavids, replaced by the Qajars, of Iran, and the Mughals of India. In his seminal overview of these three empires, as a preliminary to explaining the expansion of British imperialism in the period before 1830, C. A. Bayly suggests that all three empires faced comparable problems, many of them domestic, during the later seventeenth and eighteenth centuries. It was to deal with these internal threats as much as with external dangers that the Ottomans began the process commonly called 'reform' early in the nineteenth century.[3]

Bayly starts with the proposition that at their peak in the sixteenth century all three empires had 'rested on three great pillars'. First, they were able, by diplomacy or the use of force, to subordinate their internal magnates and protect their territories from attacks by external forces, particularly armed tribesmen. Second, the emperors were able to offer provincial elites and some of these outer 'barbarians' rewards in the form of service and a share in the culture of the great cities. Third, by protecting and tolerating minorities of other religious and ethnic groups, they laid the basis for international and sea-borne commercial systems, which irrigated the imperial economies. 'It was the slow erosion of these three pillars which was to bring down the house of the Muslim empires.'[4]

In the Ottoman empire the first of these 'pillars' was being eroded during the eighteenth century by the growing strength of provincial elites. Increasingly, local magnates acquired something approaching freehold in land previously held as

---

[3] C. A. Bayly, *Imperial Meridian: The British Empire and the World 1780–1830* (London, 1989), esp. chs. 1 and 2. [4] Ibid. 19.

part of a bargain with the central government, that is as prebends. Large noble estates sprang up throughout the empire, held by men who no longer felt bound to provide any service or loyalty in return. This not only reduced imperial authority, leading to a quasi-feudal social and land-holding structure, but also reduced the military resources of the Sultan and made him more dependent on the Janissaries or other professional (and expensive) troops.[5] Parallel with this was the increasing use of the tax farm rather than collection of taxes by imperial officers. Since many of these tax-farmers were also the rising landed notables, they were able to increase their power and wealth at the expense both of the peasantry and the imperial treasury. The general effect of these trends, probably increased by the expanding role of western European trade and finance, was to 'hollow out' these empires, and certainly the Ottoman empire, by the later eighteenth century.

While this process of internal weakening was proceeding, and largely as a result of it, the third 'pillar' also was cracking. 'Tribal break-outs', or attacks by groups outside the imperial frontiers, became more common. The most significant in the eighteenth century were those by the 'Franks' in the Balkans and in Arabia those of Ibn Saud of Najd, who adopted the fundamentalist Islamic doctrines of Abd al-Wahhab and whose dynasty was to become increasingly active over the next century and a half. In the later eighteenth century the Wahhabis and other tribes conquered the three important Islamic shrines of Mecca, Medina, and Karbala, with immense destruction and massacre. Weakened by threats in the north and the low quality of the army, Istanbul proved unable for long to reassert authority in this area. It was a pattern which, under different circumstances, was to be repeated endlessly during the nineteenth century, starting with the virtual secession of Muhammad Ali in Egypt.

It would be wrong, however, to suggest that there was any significant trend towards secession from the Ottoman empire, at least in Arabia and the Levant, before the early nineteenth century. While notables in most parts of the empire were establishing quasi-principalities, and some groups began to define themselves in terms of religion (Sunni, Shia, Alawite, etc.) and even as 'Arabs', the principle of allegiance to the Sultan survived, as did the attractions of appointment to imperial offices and the culture of the metropolis, Bayly's second 'pillar'.[6] In short, while the Ottoman empire at the start of the nineteenth century looked increasingly like a collection of partly autonomous fiefdoms, owing allegiance and paying taxes to Istanbul, and not effectively under its control, neither was it in any sense in dissolution.

It was largely to counter this process of imperial disintegration that the successive waves of reforms were undertaken by Ottoman Sultans and their agents from the early nineteenth century. The process was slow, piecemeal, and spasmodic. The question to be considered here is how far 'reform' had gone by 1914 and

---

[5] There were, of course, comparable trends in medieval England and western Europe.

[6] As, indeed, it did to the Emperor in India until 1857.

whether, without the disasters of the First World War, the Ottoman system stood a fair chance of surviving as an empire, at least for the time being.

The process that is generally called 'reform' proceeded over a long period and spasmodically. It is conventionally thought to have begun during the reign of Sultan Selim III (ruled 1789–1807), who concentrated on improving the military and financial position. He was successful in that his new European-type force was able to stand against the French army at Acre in 1799. But the existence of this force was correctly seen by the Janissary Corps as a threat to its existence, and they were supported by many traditionalists in Istanbul. In 1807 these rebelled in Istanbul, Selim was deposed, and the new army disbanded. His successor Mustafa IV lasted only two years. In 1808 ayans (local notables) from the Balkans marched to restore Selim. In the process both Selim and Mustafa were killed, and Mustafa's brother, Mahmud, was installed as Sultan Mahmud II. Although a reformer, he understood that he could only act once he had built up a power-base in the traditional way: by infiltrating supporters into the bureaucracy and manipulating provincial notables. He also propitiated Islamic dignitaries. Instead of creating a new army that was obviously a threat to the Janissaries, he built up the artillery corps.[7] In 1826 he told the Janissaries that they would be reformed. Predictably they revolted, but this time the Istanbul mobs did not support them. The Janissaries in Istanbul retreated to their barracks, and were there bombarded and most killed. The process of disbandment was then taken to the provinces, and the corps eventually ceased to exist. Free from their obstruction, Mahmud was then able to launch a process of modernization that was to be carried on along much the same lines by his successors. A new model army based on western examples was at last established, including conscription for Islamic subjects: a major stimulus for this was the defeat of the army in Syria in 1832 by Ibraham Pasha, son of Muhammad Ali. A postal service was started, some secondary schools along western lines were built for army officers. In the central government ministers amd departments with defined functions were set up for the first time. By Mahmud's death in 1839, change had not gone very far, but it was clearly under way.

The era of modern reform, commonly known as the *Tanzimat* (reordering or reform), is conventionally related to the period 1839 to 1876 under the Sultans Abdulmejid I (1839–61) and Abdulaziz (1861–76). The main architect of the reforming period was Mustafa Resid Pasha, but he had important allies and agents in Mehmed Emin Pasha, Ali Pasha, Kececizade Mehmet Fuat Pasha, Ahmet Cevdet, and Midhat Pasha. Over an extended period major changes took place in both central and local government, but symbolically reform began with a rather grandiose statement of intent by the Sultan in 1839 in the Hatt-i Humayun of Gulhane. In this he declared that his subjects had rights to 'life, honour, and

---

[7] There is an interesting parallel here with European, especially English, monarchical strategy in the sixteenth century.

fortune' and that their property was inviolate. Evils would be remedied. These promises were easier to make than to carry out, but the significance of the declaration was that, for the first time, the Sultan conceded formally that his subjects had secular rights and that these applied to non-Muslims as well as Muslims.

So far as government was concerned, in Istanbul the Supreme Council of Judicial Ordinances, which combined the functions of a privy council and the supreme judiciary, gradually lost most of its administrative functions and became primarily judicial. Meantime the Council of Ministers took over administrative co-ordination. Its membership varied over time, but it included the heads of the main departments and also some Palace officials. The Sultan retained his ultimate power virtually unchanged.

Provincial civil and military administration was radically overhauled. The 1864 Provincial Reform Law established a new universal structure of administrative units—in descending order, vilayets, sanjaqs (Arabic liwas), kazas, and nahiyas— which was to last as long as the empire and was retained in most of the later Middle Eastern mandates. Limited forms of representation were created in some provinces (vilayets) and sanjaqs in the 1840s. Initially these had a majority of officials with some elected local notables; but from 1864 there were to be elected assemblies at local and provincial levels. By 1876 these were obligatory in all parts of the empire except for Egypt. Municipal government also was reformed. From the 1870s municipal councils were set up with between six and twelve members, half of them elected for two years on a property franchise. Mayors, with effective control, were, however, appointed by the Minister of Interior. Overall this was in no sense a democratic structure. Officials controlled work at all levels and were able to influence the electoral choice made by notables who depended on government for patronage. But it was probably well suited to hierarchical societies that had no experience of self-rule and were largely illiterate.

The main failure of the *Tanzimat* lay in taxation. The empire had evolved a wide range of forms of taxation, much as *ancien régime* states had done in Europe. To replace these created the danger of losing income. Urban taxes were collected quite efficiently but rural taxes, essentially a tithe on produce, were not. Again, as in early modern Europe, this and other taxes were farmed out. In the Hatt-i Humayun the Sultan had promised that tax-farming would be replaced by collection by officials. But this took a very long time to happen, due mainly to the shortage of competent officials. In an agricultural empire with limited wealth the result was a totally inadequate tax base. In common with other contemporary Mediterranean Islamic states, and faced with increasing war expenditure during the mid and later nineteenth century, the Ottomans turned to loans from Europe. By 1874–5, nearly 50 per cent of all revenues were required to service the bonded debt. By 1877–8, after renewed warfare, the bonded debt was nearly equal to the whole annual revenue. Much of this was caused by the increasing cost of warfare in the Balkans and the attempt by the Ottomans to adopt modern weapons and strategies, but also by the usurious practices of the European lenders. In 1881 the climax came with the imposition of a Public Debt Commission run by Europeans which collected and took the proceeds of a range of taxes on goods and stamps on official documents and also the entire tribute paid by Bulgaria, Cyprus, Greece, and Montenegro. Even after consolidation of the debt in the later 1880s, service of the debt was still taking 30 per cent of revenues in 1905–6. Finance was thus the Achilles' heel of the Ottoman empire, as it was of many other contemporary and later states.

Poverty did not, however, prevent substantial achievements in many fields during and after the *Tanzimat* era. Education became a major state enterprise, by contrast with the previous dominance of Islamic schools. From the 1840s, a three-level structure of state schools and colleges was created, with a range of teacher and technical colleges at its apex, though a long-projected university in Istanbul did not finally open until 1906. By 1898 some 21 per cent of all in the age-group 5–25 were in some form of education and 90 per cent of boys and 33 per cent of girls had some elementary school education. In 1913 about 300,000 were enrolled in state elementary and secondary schools. Moreover, a similar number were in millet (denominational) schools, and 23,000 in American Missionary schools, which the government approved, despite the fact that they mainly benefited Christians.

Education went hand-in-hand with the growth of a new middle class. Many of these were professionals in the towns and government administration. But there also emerged a new middling landed class of notables. These bought land from the now suppressed feudal estates. In this they were helped by the Land Law of 1858. Its primary purpose was to reassert state ownership and tax rights over imperial (miri) land. The law defined five types of land-ownership: mulk (private, equivalent to freehold in the west), miri (state), vakif (religious endowments), metruk (communal or public), and mevat (idle or barren). A cadastral survey was to be undertaken to provide a full register of all land in the empire, leading to the issue of certificates of owership, tapu senedi. This was to lead to a new land tax of 10 per cent on all crops and livestock. In practice, however, the survey was never completed, and the incoming mandatory governments after 1918 found that land-ownership was extremely uncertain. But for the local notables, registration, coupled with a venal officialdom, enabled many to claim miri land as mulk, and other occupants were able to sell tenanted miri land as if it was mulk. There thus evolved a new class of substantial land-owners, often also closely associated with urban commerce and the professions, who became the dominant ruling class in many parts of the empire, particularly in the Arabian territories.

Related to land and tax reform were legal reforms which provided a more secure environment for trade and investment and, after 1867, allowed non-Ottomans to own real estate for the first time. Communications were another main objective. The telegraph was gradually extended after 1854 and postal services improved. The first railways were built, mostly by European firms operating under guarantee, as in many other parts of the world. Some main roads were improved, but in general roads remained unsealed and many areas had poor communications.

These were substantial achievements for a 'sick man', though they left the empire still far behind western Europe in organizational efficiency and further still in industrialization. In any case the great age of the *Tanzimat* was over by the later 1860s. The Sultan Abdulaziz (1861–76) was less interested in reforms than in the power of the Palace, which had been significantly reduced by the rise of the ministerial system and reformed bureaucracy. So long as Fuat and Ali survived (they died in 1869 and 1871 respectively), the momentum of change was maintained, but governmental efficiency declined as the Sultan constantly changed his ministers to prevent their becoming too powerful. Meantime, Ottoman debts piled up and internal discontent was made worse by revolts in Bosnia-Herzegovina and Bulgaria, leading to intervention by the European powers. In 1876 Abdulaziz was deposed in a military coup, backed by a wide spectrum of reformers, conservative clerics, and students, and was later found dead. He was replaced by his brother Murad V, but he was deemed to be mentally unstable and was confined in comfortable retirement. Yet another brother, Abdulhamid II, became Sultan and reigned until 1909.

Abdulhamid presided over the empire during the last thirty years of its existence in its traditional form. He was, during his lifetime, and remains, the subject of deep disagreements. For long, he was denounced by liberals, democrats, and reformers on the ground that he was deeply conservative, paranoid about his own authority, brutal to minorities such as the Armenians, and dependent on a huge network of spies and secret agents. He agreed to a new representative constitution in 1876, only to suspend it two years later. On the other hand there can be no doubt that during his reign much of the constructive work of the *Tanzimat* was continued and extended. To devout Muslims he was the man who protected their faith and prevented the secularization of the empire. His great misfortune was that his reign coincided with the major Balkan wars of the 1870s, which put impossible pressures on finance and flooded the remaining Ottoman territories with refugees. In 1878, at the Berlin Congress, the Ottomans had to give up two-fifths of the empire's territory and one-fifth of its population, with disastrous effects on their tax revenues.

The reign, however, started with a spurt of liberalism. Under pressure from men aware of western models, and also in response to the threat in the Balkans, Abdulhamid issued a new constitution, largely the work of Midhat. The constitution provided for a western-style departmental executive headed by a cabinet of ministers, though these were appointed by the Sultan rather than chosen by parliament, an elected parliament, extended personal legal rights for all, and improved justice and regional administration. The timing of the announcement was largely to impress the western powers and the Istanbul conference on the future of the Balkans. Conversely, the Balkan crisis enabled the Sultan largely to ignore the principles of parliamentary government. In 1877 he dismissed Midhat as Grand Vizier and dispatched him to exile. The new parliament met in March 1877. It was elected by notables on a limited franchise, operating in two-stage elections, but it was in a sense genuinely representative of the nature of Ottoman society. It proved far too interventionist for Abdulhamid's taste. He suspended it in February 1878 and it did not meet again until 1908. Thereafter government was run from the Palace rather than the Sublime Porte. The leading ministers were all unqualified supporters of the Sultan, who tended to rotate them in the top jobs to prevent any of them becoming too powerful. Apart from the complex bureaucratic structure,[8] most power remained with the Privy Council, the Ministry of Police, the Civil Service Commission, and Press Department, whose collective function was to check criticism and deal with potential troublemakers. Yet there was much progress in many directions. In particular, communications were expanded rapidly, with very extensive construction of railways, telegraph facilities, and roads. By 1908 the state for the first time had the capacity to impose control over quite distant parts of the empire, which became critical during and after the First World War. It was a facility that cut both ways, however: centralization generated provincial demand for local autonomy. This was one seed from which Arabism was to develop.

Despite its physical achievements, the Sultanate could not indefinitely evade the effects of liberal ideas at the centre. There was a lineal descent here from the Young Ottomans, a society founded in 1865. These were mainly sons of the wealthy, some of whom had been educated in Europe and who admired many aspects of European life, particularly representative government and the rule of law. They remained, however, good Muslims who believed that both Islam and a powerful Sultan-Caliph were compatible with democracy. They propagated their ideas partly by sending newspapers through the independent European post offices (protected by the Capitulations) to evade the censorship. By themselves such men could never have created a revolution, but their achievement was to establish a current of reformist thinking in Istanbul. The conditions of 1876, with the Balkan crisis and the installation of a new Sultan, provided their chance. The 1876 constitution was their achievement. This, as has been seen, proved short-lived, but the concept of a constitution in suspension survived and the idea of radical reform gave birth to the so-called Young Turks.

The Young Turk Revolution of 1908 was a major turning point in Ottoman history.[9] On the face of it the Revolution occurred in July 1908 when the Sultan, faced with the threat of a mutinous section of his army in Macedonia, notably at Monastir, announced that the suspended constitution of 1876 would be brought to life with the summoning of parliament. In this sense, therefore, there was no

---

[8] There is a detailed account of the administrative and judicial structure in Shaw and Shaw, *Reform, Revolution and Republic*, 216–21.

[9] A standard detailed account of the revolution and its consequences to 1914 is in F. Ahmad, *The Young Turks: The Committee of Union and Progress in Turkish Politics 1908–1914* (Oxford, 1969). Oddly, in a very careful book based on a wide range of sources, on p. 99 Ahmad resurrects King Edward VII, who died in 1910, to meet Mehmed Kamil at Port Said in November 1911. He presumably meant King George V, then on his way to India for the durbar.

'revolution', merely what the Sultan hoped would be a gesture for defusing army discontent. But in fact there was a lot more behind this than mere concession to mutinous troops. It can best be seen as the product of a longer process of alienation from the Istanbul regime which was brought to a head by army action. This alienation expressed itself in two main forms: the growth of secret societies and an increasing more general alienation from aspects of the regime.

It was typical of the Ottoman empire, as it had been of many European countries during the later nineteenth century, that close governmental control over all forms of publication and collective action should result in the formation of secret societies pledged to reform or even revolution. As will be seen later in this chapter, such societies became common in the Arab provinces before 1914, ironically often in reaction against the policies of the Young Turks. One of these earlier societies, the Ottoman Freedom Society (OFC), renamed Committee of Union and Progress (CUP) in 1907 after a merger with the Young Turk organization, was set up in the military medical school in 1889. In common with other later societies, it was organized in cells, so that if any member was caught and interrogated he could not betray many others. This was a hierarchical society with complicated initiation ceremonies. In the early years, members often met in Masonic lodges (one reason why European commentators and some later Arab critics of the CUP claimed that it was predominantly Masonic or Jewish). Their strategy was to infiltrate all levels of the military and civil administration, but the society was particularly popular among the officer corps of the Second and Third Armies, based in Salonika and Edirne: by 1908 the Salonika branch had 505 members, of whom 319 were army officers and 186 civilians. Early members included those who were to control Istanbul after 1908, such as Mehmet Talat and the then Captain Enver. The CUP's stated aims in 1908 were to remove the allegedly corrupt regime installed by the Sultan and to restore the constitution. This would pave the way for a union of the peoples and social and economic progress. All ethnic groups were to be equal as Ottomans. Meantime there were a number of dispersed reformist and ideological *émigré* groups in Europe and the empire who were in contact with each other and were generically called the Young Turks. These collectively joined with the OFC in 1907, though there was limited contact since the OFC feared that the Young Turks had been infiltrated by government agents.

On this interpretation the 1908 revolution was the work of a relatively small underground revolutionary organization which acted in 1908 because it feared disclosure and also foreign intervention in Macedonia. But this is clearly too narrow an approach. Macfie suggests that, so far as the army was concerned, it was rather the climax of a long series of relatively local military mutinies and discontents, largely due to lack of pay by an imperial Treasury permanently short of funds because of the prior claims of the international debt control. In addition in the early 1900s there were a number of civilian outbreaks, especially tax revolts and major demonstrations, many of which were not suppressed because the military was itself alienated and in sympathy with the rioters. In short, while it was the army's action in 1908 that brought about the notional Young Turk Revolution it seems likely the Abdulhamid recognized the serious growth of widespread hostility to his regime and decided that, by at least going through the motions of reviving the constitution, he would be able to re-establish confidence in himself and his government.[10]

But once this step had been taken, it was not at all clear what would happen next. It was important that it was a threat of action by the army in Macedonia, not an actual military descent on Istanbul, that had sparked things off. The CUP was not, therefore, in physical control of Istanbul. Nor was it technically a political party. Since there had never been a period of constitutional government, the relative roles of Sultan, parliament, and the ministers were uncertain. It was unclear how much support the CUP had in the capital or in the provinces, and there were strong counter forces, led by the Ottoman Liberal Union Party and the Muhammadan Union, which aimed to protect traditional Islamic values and institutions. Thus it was uncertain until 1913 whether the CUP movement would consolidate its power or whether it would seem in retrospect no more than a Fronde or palace revolution. Although nominal supporters of the CUP won a huge majority in elections to the Chamber of Deputies in November–December 1908 (the Senate was appointed by the Sultan) these soon split into factions. Since there was no convention that the Sultan should appoint his Grand Vizier or other ministers in line with the parliamentary majority, these crucial appointments were made by the Sultan according to changing pressures on the Palace. Thus, whereas Kamil Pasha was appointed Grand Vizier in August 1908, under strong CUP pressure, he was forced to resign in February 1909 after a vote of no confidence in the Chamber that was orchestrated and in effect forced by CUP intimidation.

Two months later the instability of politics was demonstrated by the so-called counter-revolution. This was in fact an army mutiny of a type very familiar in Ottoman history. On 13 April 1909, a battalion of disaffected soldiers in the Taskishla barracks in Istanbul, roused by fundamentalist ideas preached by the Muhammadan Union, locked up their officers and marched into the city. As they were joined by other army groups their demands escalated from restoration of the Shariat and dismissal of college-trained officers (as opposed to those promoted from the ranks) to dismissal of the pro-CUP Vizier and senior ministers. The government could easily have suppressed the mutiny. In fact it resigned and its successor quickly restored order. But similar mutinies broke out in eastern Anatolia, Damascus, Mosul, Aleppo, Beirut, and elsewhere. This suggests that, while the rising in Istanbul was essentially a mutiny, partly brought about by the failure of the CUP officers to keep in close contact with their troops, there was a wider backlash against the alleged CUP conspiracy to subvert the traditional Islamic order. In some provinces the counter-revolution gained support from those whose positions seemed threatened by innovations. There is no evidence

[10] Macfie, *The End*, 20–7.

that the 'revolution' was engineered by the Sultan, though he probably remained sympathetic to the conservative aims of the Muhammadan Union. According to the dismissed Grand Vizier, Kamil Pasha, 'He was a broken man . . . and I knew that he could not have engineered this Mutiny, as he was in extreme fear for his life, and would have been very well satisfied if allowed to remain on the throne, no matter how much his power was circumscribed. . . . The Sultan was more frightened than anybody else when the revolt broke out . . . '.[11]

The 'revolution' was in any case short-lived. The CUP central committee in Salonika organized an army, and on 23–24 April occupied Istanbul. The two houses of the parliament assembled in San Stefano, outside Istanbul, passed a resolution approving the army's actions and the punishment of rebels. They declared their intention to obtain the deposition of the Sultan. On 27 April a CUP delegation, led by Talat, armed with a fatwa, went to the palace to inform the Sultan that he had been deposed. He was sent into exile in Salonika, the CUP stronghold, and replaced by his brother, Mehmet V, who ruled until 1918. Meantime a pogrom of supporters of the mutiny and political opponents of the CUP took place under martial law. On 5 May, Huseyin Hilmi Pasha was reappointed Grand Vizier. It seemed that the CUP was now firmly back in the saddle.

But this also proved to some extent an illusion. True, effective power now lay with Mahmud Shevket Pasha, commander of the Action Army that had occupied Istanbul, and he was a CUP man. In the next three years a number of important changes were made along CUP lines. The army was reorganized, and most officers excluded from politics. Non-Muslims were for the first time made liable to conscription to the army, a measure that had important consequences in parts of the Arab world. Government obtained power to control the press and to ban groups or organizations based on ethnic or 'national' groups. At the centre, amendments to the 1876 constitution enabled the Grand Vizier, though still appointed by the Sultan, to appoint to senior ministerial posts, thus creating something like a united cabinet; and ministers were now responsible for both their departments and overall government policy. Cabinets should submit or resign if in conflict with the Chamber of Deputies, whose president, previously appointed by the Sultan, would now be elected by the Deputies. The Sultan himself was forced to swear an oath to respect the constitution. In short, after 1909 the Ottoman constitution, at least superficially, took on the image of a western European model. Many of the CUP's objectives were achieved.

This did not, however, necessarily empower the CUP: it had no monopoly of government posts. Although now for the first time acting as a political party it still lacked cohesion. In February 1910 a splinter group of about 40 CUP supporters broke off and formed the People's Party. The following January another group split off and formed the New Party. In February 1911 both Talat and Javid, the

---

[11] Quoted ibid. 53 from F. McCullagh, *The Fall of Abdul Hamid* (London, 1910), 48–9.

Ministers of Interior and Finance, resigned after disagreements with Shevket. Later that year, after serious defeats by the Italians in Tripolitania, which were deemed to reflect badly on the CUP, the various opposition parties joined in the Liberal Party of Freedom and Understanding, commonly called the Liberal Union or Entente Libérale. In December a Liberal Union candidate defeated a CUP candidate in a by-election in Istanbul. The reaction of the CUP was to organize a dissolution of the Chamber. By intensive and often brutal electioneering methods it obtained all but six of the 275 seats in the 1912 elections. This, however, sparked a last resistance movement. In mid-1912 a group of conservative officers in Istanbul formed a secret society, the Saviour Officers, which was committed to restoring constitutional government and the end of radical policies. They got support among sections of the army in Macedonia, thus replicating the events of 1908, and demanded changes in the government. Under this threat, Shevket resigned followed by the Grand Vizier. The Sultan duly appointed a new cabinet of long-serving Ottoman officials. It was supported by the Liberal Union and many of the more conservative officials and clearly intended to destroy the CUP. On 5 August the Sultan accepted ministerial advice to dissolve the Chamber, and called new elections. Martial law was proclaimed and the CUP's official paper suspended. But before the elections could take place and this scheme carried through, war broke out in the Balkans.

The details of this are not relevant here. Essentially, the one-time Ottoman provinces of Montenegro, Greece, Bulgaria, Romania, and Serbia decided that the moment had come, with the Ottoman defeat in Tripolitania by Italy in 1911, following the earlier loss of Tunis and control of Egypt, to share out Macedonia, the last relic of the once great Ottoman empire in Europe. Between October 1912 and January 1913 the Ottoman armies were decisively defeated on all fronts. The reasons are fairly clear. The Porte could muster only about 25,000 men for this front, so they were heavily outnumbered. More significant was their low fighting ability. According to the German Lieutenant-General Imhoff, who had been reorganizing the Ottoman artillery as a result of an agreement dating from the 1880s that the Germans should advise on military reform, there were three main weaknesses in the quality of the army. Until 1908 only Muslims has served: now minorities also could serve or be conscripted. The old army had been largely untrained. Since 1908, attempts had been made to improve training, but frequent risings in Albania, Syria, and Arabia and the Tripoli war had disrupted this process. Moreover, the mixture of 'races' in the new army had been disastrous, since the army was no longer homogeneous. Then there was the state of the officer corps. This has been seriously politicized since 1908. It was riven by secret societies. Discipline was weak. Finally there was no confidence in the central government, which was constantly changing, and there was serious friction between senior ministers. Imhoff concluded that the reserve troops were 'not acquainted with the handling of their weapons; the artillery did not know how to use their guns. . . . There was a great shortage of officers; the placing of men in position, and their ability when in position, were defective; and finally, the influence of foreign instructors . . . was suppressed.'[12] The most surprising thing is that this was the army that three years later was to defeat the Allies in the Dardanelles, hold British forces for several years in Iraq, and finally eject the French, Greeks, and Italians from Anatolia after 1920. That they could do so reflected the intensive activities of the CUP after 1913 and the efficiency of the German officers who trained and after 1914 led most of the Ottoman troops.

In 1913, however, the immediate effect of the disasters was that they upset the political plans of the Liberal Union and gave the CUP the opportunity to regain power. In December 1912 the Ottomans arranged an armistice, intended to lead to peace talks under the supervision of the powers. This left their enemies a mere 64 km from Istanbul, though the key fortress of Edirne held out until March 1913. Nothing came of the peace talks, and there were accusations that the Porte was ready to concede Edirne as part of a peace deal. This was held to justify the political coup that occurred in Istanbul on 23 January. Indeed, the Treaty of London, concluded on 30 May 1913, did include the cession of most of Macedonia to the Balkan states, including Edirne to Bulgaria; though the subseqent war between Bulgaria and Serbia enabled Ottoman troops, under Enver, to retake Edirne.

Edirne was a critical factor in Ottoman politics because the CUP were able to allege that the government was ready to surrender it to Bulgaria, though still in Ottoman hands, as part of the peace process. This, at least, was the propaganda version put out by the CUP. It was alleged that the Grand Vizier, then Kamil Pasha, inveterate enemy of the CUP, was proposing to send a delegation to London for the peace talks and that Istanbul would cede not only the conquered territories in Europe, but also Edirne. This account suggested that on 23 January a number of disgruntled officers, led by Enver, on the spur of the moment broke into the cabinet room and compelled Kamil to resign. In the process Nazim Pasha, the minister for war, was shot by a CUP member, along with a number of guards.

It is, however, now clear that this was not a spontaneous reaction to concern about Edirne.[13] The so-called Bab-i Ali coup had in fact been planned. As Grand Vizier from October 1912, Kamil had refused to appoint Shevket as Inspector General of the army (which had been the basis of his and CUP power since 1909) after which Nazim as Minister of War had also refused to appoint senior and pro-CUP officers to organize the campaign to save Edirne. Initially the CUP rejected the possibility of a coup to reverse these decisions. But when Kamil summoned a grand council of important people who might be persuaded to accept responsibility for ceding Edirne, the CUP decided to act. They made their move as the cabinet met to decide its response to a note from the powers concerning the peace settlement. In a sense, then, this was a response to circumstances rather than a deliberate political coup.

---

[12] Imhoff Pasha, 'A German View of the Turkish Defeat', *Fortnightly Review*, 93 (1913), quoted Macfie, *The End*, 74–6.   [13] Based on Macfie, *The End*, 78–9.

Perhaps surprisingly, the CUP still did not attempt overtly to take over the government. Shevket became Grand Vizier, but although some CUP men took ministries, they remained in a minority in the cabinet. The aim was to create a sense of national unity in the face of military disaster. But the Liberal Union and other opposition groups within and without the armed forces continued to plan for the downfall of the CUP and possibly the assassination of its leading members. These plots were discovered; but on 15 June 1913 Shevket was killed by assassins. This triggered a coup by the CUP. Many suspects were imprisoned, tried, some condemned to death, others to exile or long prison sentences. A new cabinet was formed with Said Halim as Vizier and Talat as Minister of Interior. In January 1914 Enver was made Minister of War, and in February 1914 Jemal was made Minister of Works, later Minister of Marine. This was the triumvirate that ruled the empire throughout the First World War, and the CUP constituted a single party political system.

The final victory of the CUP has been explained in various ways. It resulted primarily from its dominance in the army officers' corps. It had an efficient central organization, in contrast with other political parties, a large membership, and support from many of the professional and artisan organizations. A key element was the support of the *fedai* units of the army, men pledged to fight to the death. But, once established, CUP rule was enforced as ruthlessly as that of the Sultans before 1908. Parliamentary democracy continued in principle, but most legislation took the form or imperial *irades*, over which parliament had no control. This was, in fact, a virtually totalitarian government, though parliament, elected in 1912 and meeting infrequently, gave it a constitutional veneer. With a compliant Sultan and CUP Grand Vizier, the triumvirate of Talat, Enver, and Jemal took all important decisions.

Their grand strategy was to complete the modernization programme started in 1908, which had been continued thereafter by the bureaucracy despite the changes of government. The key elements of this programme, reflecting continuity from the *Tanzimat* days, were to improve the efficiency of the civil service and tax collection, reform both the educational and legal systems, create a secular state in which millets no longer constituted exceptions to the general rules, and impose effective central control over the remaining Ottoman provinces. Considerable progress was made in improving communications, themselves critical for effective provincial control, though the proposed Istanbul to Baghdad railway was nowhere near completion in 1914. Thus, despite chronic shortage of money, the post-1908 administration was extremely active: change was clearly on the way, whatever the results of palace politics in Istanbul.

There was also a strong element of Turkish, as opposed to generalized Ottoman, nationalism in the make-up of the new regime. This seems to have grown from nineteenth-century European research into the origins of the Turkish language and people and was taken up by a few Turkish intellectuals. To a large extent this was myth-making of the kind typical of nineteenth-century western nationalism, but it fed on the rapid destruction of the Ottoman empire in Europe, with its large Christian population, leaving the question of what it meant to be an Ottoman without a European empire. The movement seems initially to have been strongest in Salonika, the headquarters of the CUP, and was transported to Istanbul. Among those most forcefully promulgating this new brand of Turkish, rather than Ottoman nationalism, Shaw and Shaw highlight Ziya Gokalp, a self-educated Turk who, though not a politician, became the ideologist of the CUP after 1909. He argued for the use of a refined Turkish language as the language of state, in place of Ottoman, which contained a mix of Turkish, Arabic, and Persian. He regarded Islam as central to the Turkish nationality, but argued that it must be modernized and purified: among other things the status of women must be raised.[14] It would not be true to say that Turkish nationalism had replaced Ottomanism. Even Turkish nationalists such as Gokalp believed in the Ottoman empire. Most members of the CUP still remained committed to the idea that all Ottomans, regardless of race, religion, or nationality, were equally members of the same empire. Moreover, Turkish had not become the official language. But many in the Arab provinces of the empire were frightened that this was on the way: that the empire would become Turkish and that Turks would take over all the senior administrative positions. This certainly gave considerable support to the nascent anti-Turkish and pan-Islamic movements in Syria and other parts of the Ottoman Middle East. Conversely, Turkish nationalism was already available for Mustafa Kemal and his supporters after 1918 in their efforts to create a new state called Turkey out of the ruins of the Ottoman empire. Along with language, they inherited the determination to secularize the state, adopt progressive western practices, and throw off European control, particularly as exemplified in the Capitulations.

A key element in the general reform process was modernization of the army, whose limitations had been very obvious in the Balkan Wars. The Ottomans had used German military instructors since the 1880s, since they regarded Germany as the most efficient military power in the West. From 1913 this collaboration was intensified. Berlin was asked to send a military mission to supervise reform and modernization: it was led by General Liman von Sanders; though to balance this the British were invited to send a naval mission, and Istanbul ordered two battleships from British yards, partly paid for by street collections from the patriotic. A remarkable amount was achieved by the Germans in the year and a half before the Ottomans entered the war in November 1914. Moreover, once war had been declared, as an ally of the Central Powers, the German connection proved extremely valuable. Although Enver retained real control over all military matters, the army was effectively run by Germans. Von Sanders was in charge of the First Army, at Istanbul and later in Syria. General von Seeckt was chief of the Ottoman General Staff. General von der Goltz moved to the Sixth Army in Mesopotamia.

14 Shaw and Shaw, *Reform, Revolution and Republic*, 301–3.

General von Falkenhayn commanded very effectively in Palestine. German officers were put in charge of several departments of the Ministry of War, including intelligence, railways, supply, munitions, and fortresses. They appear to have co-operated well with most Ottoman officers, though there were inevitable frictions and disagreements over strategy. Backed by very substantial German financial loans, and helped by the abrogation after 1914 of all payments to Entente bankers, the Ottomans were able to put up a quite unpredictably effective resistance on most of the fronts.

In 1914 the Ottoman empire, despite its recent disasters, was therefore clearly an empire in course of reconstruction. One can even talk of Ottoman 'reconquest' of Arab lands and their reintegration. The dynamic of change was obviously stronger at the centre, in the residual part of Macedonia, western Anatolia, and perhaps in Syria than in more distant parts of the empire, such as the Hijaz. But it is at least arguable that, had there been no war for, say, a decade after 1913, the Ottoman empire might have done what neither of the other old Islamic empires had done: survive in some form into the mid-twentieth century. In terms of Bayly's three pillars of the sixteenth-century Islamic empires, the second and third were still standing. Provincial elites and others could still be bought by offers of office and a place in the larger cosmopolitan culture of empire. Indeed, as will be seen below, one suggested basis of division within Syrian society over relations with Istanbul was precisely the fault line between successful and unsuccessful seekers of Ottoman office. The great majority of Arab Ottoman subjects remained loyal and fought for the empire throughout the First World War. The third pillar also stood. Ottoman trade continued to expand and Ottoman territories were an integral part of the evolving global economy with internal cohesion as well. Thus it was the first of the three pillars that had partly fallen by 1914. While internal control over the Arab provinces was stricter in 1914 than it had ever been before, control had been lost in the Balkan provinces. This in turn was largely due to 'tribal break-outs', or, perhaps more correctly, tribal break-ins. Attacked by Russia and Austria, and faced with rebellion among Christian minorities in the Balkans, the empire had been unable to maintain its grip. In this sense the Russians had played much the same role in the Ottoman empire as had the British, Afghans, and Persians in the Mughal empire. The main difference, of course, was that the Russians and Austrians, while acquiring some Ottoman territories for themselves, had for the most part preferred to set up client states in the Balkans, as had the British in Egypt, whereas in India the British had taken direct control over all but the princely states.

The result was a much truncated Ottoman empire. It had lost its most economically developed areas in the Balkans. It had effectively lost control of Egypt and Cyprus, and Crete was now annexed to Greece. But the Islamic core remained, and this now much more centralized empire seemed likely to establish more effective control over parts of Arabia that were then in varying degrees independent. What Mustafa Kemal was able to achieve in Anatolia he or others might have achieved on a much larger scale. Thus it can be argued that in 1914 what remained of the Ottoman empire was no longer 'sick'. Moreover, it then retained full power to suppress or emasculate any dissident movements, helped immensely by the improvements in communications. Thus, when in 1913 Sayyid Talib, Naqib and city boss of Basra, reacted against the new 1913 Vilayet Law, because it greatly increased the power of the vali, and threatened rebellion, he was eventually bought off by being confirmed in his control over Basra and became an overtly loyal supporter of the empire. How far that capacity to intimidate or persuade would survive during the next decades depended on three things: the continued improvement in imperial efficiency; whether local territorial groups developed a sense of 'national' (in fact mainly denominational) identity comparable to that in the Balkans and demanded autonomy or independence; and whether any of the powers played in the Middle East the role that Russia and Austria had played in the Balkans. Much also depended on the attitude of the remaining and predominantly Arab populations. Was there a powerful 'Arab nationalist movement' in 1914? Did these 'Arab nationalists' want independence or something short of that? How far was Arab 'nationalism' created or manipulated by the British and other interested European parties? These are the questions examined in the following section.

2. 'THE ARAB AWAKENING'

He did not coin the phrase, but George Antonius undoubtedly gave it much of its later significance in his book *The Arab Awakening*, published in 1938. Antonius was an interesting and a symbolically important man.[15] He was born a Greek Orthodox Christian, which underlines the fact that Arab nationalism was not exclusively Islamic. He was educated at Victoria College, Alexandria, and at King's College, Cambridge, where he graduated with a first-class degree in mechanical sciences. He then entered British service. During the First World War he acted as a press censor in Cairo, and was also connected with British Intelligence. He then looked for a career in Palestine and in 1924 was appointed deputy to Humphrey Bowman, Director of Education. In 1927 Antonius was sent on two important diplomatic missions to the Hijaz and Egypt, but on his return found that he had been leap-frogged in the department by a British subordinate. Although he was then given another post in the administration, he now had no faith in the British. He resigned in 1929 and spent the next decade as a researcher in the Chicago-based Institute of Current World Affairs, financed by the Chicago businessman Charles Crane, one-time member of the

[15] There are useful short summaries of his life in N. Shepherd, *Ploughing Sand: British Rule in Palestine* (London, 1999), B. Wasserstein, *The British in Palestine* (1978; rev. edn. Oxford, 1991), 183–9, and M. Kramer, *Arab Awakening and Islamic Revival: The Politics of Ideas in the Middle East* (New Brunswick and London, 1996), ch. 6.

King–Crane commission of 1919.[16] While there he did the research for *The Arab Awakening.*

Antonius may therefore be seen as an example of the way in which able and initially pro-British non-Europeans might be alienated by insensitive and racially based treatment. In its context the book can now be seen as a denunciation of British bad faith in both Palestine and Arabia. It was based not only on published material but also on personal contact with leading actors in the partition of the Middle East, notably the ex-Sharif Husayn, from whom Antonius obtained hitherto unpublished copies of the original correspondence of 1915–16 concerning the future of Arabia, and members of the wartime Arab Bureau in Cairo, including the Oxford professor of archaeology and wartime Royal Naval Commander D. G. Hogarth and Colonel Gilbert Clayton, former Sudan Army officer. But for his information on the genesis of early Arab nationalism Antonius relied very heavily on the recollections of his father-in-law, Faris Nimr, who was the last surviving member of the Secret Society of Beirut, and this may have given a strong Lebanese slant to his treatment of early Arab nationalism.[17] Eliezer Tauber certainly thought that as a result Antonius overstated the importance of the Secret Society. He overlooked the fact that it was more Lebanese-Syrian than Arab, and that 'the idea of Arab nationalism had not even crossed the minds of its founders'.[18]

It is clear that Antonius had a political purpose in mind. He wished to demonstrate that the partition of Arabia into mandates after 1918 was the negation of a spirit of Arab nationalism and unity that had developed from the later nineteenth century and that, in particular, the British had reneged on clear promises made in 1915 that the whole of the Fertile Crescent, including Palestine, would be given to the Sharif Husayn. There were, therefore, two themes: the genesis of Arab nationalism and its subsequent betrayal. The first six chapters are devoted to the origins of Arabism. Antonius argues that it was sparked off by the occupation of Syria and Lebanon by Muhammad Ali and his son Ibrahim in 1830. This was followed by the arrival of Christian, mostly American, Protestant missions who used Arabic in the schools and colleges they established there. The use of classical Arabic was then taken up by some Islamic intellectuals, but more importantly by Christian Arabs, including Nasif Yazeji and Butrus Bustani. By the 1850s there was some sign of Lebanese patriotism, which was helped by Lebanon's new separate status after 1861. It was further stimulated by reaction against what Antonius called 'The Hamidian Despotism' of Abdulhamid II and his techniques of control.

According to Antonius, the origins of organized Arab nationalism lay in the formation in 1875 of the Secret Society of Beirut. Its initial technique was to

[16] For Crane's anti-Semitism and the limitations of the commission's work see I. Friedman, *Palestine: A Twice-Promised Land?* I. *The British, the Arabs and Zionism, 1915–1920* (New Brunswick, 2000). 248–51.

[17] See S. Seikaly, 'Shukri al-Asali: A Case Study of a Political Activist', in R. Khalidi *et al.* (eds.), *The Origins of Arab Nationalism* (New York, 1991), 92 n. 1.

[18] E. Tauber, *The Emergence of the Arab Movements* (London, 1993), 336 n. 1.

distribute placards around the city denouncing Ottoman tyranny. Thus in December 1880 its stated demands were for the creation of an independent Lebanon united with Syria; recognition of Arabic as an official language in Syria; the removal of censorship and freedom of expression; and employment of locally recruited troops only in their locality. Although this campaign was short-lived, Antonius claims that it had helped to create an Arab consciousness: French visitors in the early 1880s spoke of 'a spirit of independence'. The growth of this movement was, however, kept in check by the official clamp-down on publications and secret societies, and also by the fact that Arab Christians educated in English or French tended to be isolated from Muslims who were not. One result was an exodus of Arab intellectuals, particularly Christians, to escape the censorship, some to Cairo, others to Paris.

Antonius then jumps a couple of decades to treat the Arab reaction to the Young Turk and CUP movements after 1908. The initial phase appeared to promise liberalism, and in 1908–9 two Arab parties were founded. Al-Ikha al-Arabi al-Uthmani, designed to have branches everywhere and promote Arab self-awareness, was suppressed in 1909. The following year al-Muntada al-Adabi, the Literary Club, was set up as a general meeting place for Arabs and got a large membership in Syria and Iraq. This seems to have survived. By 1912, however, the centralizing and Turkish nationalist tendencies of the CUP were becoming clear, and this produced a different type of society with more specifically political aims. In 1909 al-Qahtaniya, which aimed at adapting the Austro-Hungarian system of a dual monarchy to the Ottoman empire, was launched, under the leadership of Aziz Ali al-Masri. It was a secret society, but had to be wound up because a member leaked information about it. In 1912 the Decentralization Party was set up, in the safety of Cairo: Antonius said it became 'the best-organised and most authoritative spokesman of Arab aspirations'. As its name implied, its primary aim was autonomy for the Arab provinces. It organized the Paris Congress of 1913, at which an agent from the Porte promised concessions that were never realized. In 1911 another and very secret society was set up, initially in Paris, but moving to Beirut in 1913. This was al-Fatat, whose membership, exclusively Muslim by contrast with most of the earlier societies, was very carefully kept secret and was organized in cells so that disclosure would not implicate many members. It was to have an important future in Syria after 1918. Finally in 1914 al-Masri set up al-Ahd (the Covenant), with the same objectives as al-Qahtaniya, consisting mostly of army officers, many of them Iraqis. It may be regarded as the military equivalent of al-Fatat.

Having described these Arab societies, Antonius had then to demonstrate that they had a significant influence on events, particularly the Arab rising in the Hijaz. This was where his task became more difficult and where the historian has to consider whether his societies were in fact as influential as he makes out. Opinions on this will be considered later. But his link between the two lay in a mission made by Fauzi al-Bakri, a member of al-Fatat, to Mecca in January 1915. Fauzi told the Sharif Husayn that there was much Arab discontent in Syria and that the Arab army officers there would back a revolt if Husayn would lead it. Husayn's third son, Faysal, was then sent to Istanbul via Damascus and there contacted al-Fatat. He was told that, while the society had voted to back an Arab rising, it would back the Ottomans if a foreign state (France was regarded as the most likely) intervened. In May 1915, al-Fatat and al-Ahd prepared a protocol for Faysal to take back to Mecca which suggested that Husayn should negotiate with Britain for support to gain the independence of the whole of Syria (including Iraq and Palestine), after which the Arab state would abolish the Capitulations and form an alliance with Britain. But there must be no foreign rule under any form: Arabia was to be truly independent.

There followed the first publication of details of the correspondence in 1915 between Husayn and Sir Henry McMahon, who had succeeded Lord Kitchener as High Commissioner of Egypt: the key letters were printed as an appendix, in Antonius's own translation from the Arabic. Antonius's central argument was that in these letters Britain had promised independence for the whole of Arabia under Husayn, and that this included Palestine, since it was not explicitly excluded. The argument suggests that it was on this basis that Husayn declared his independence and started the war in 1916. The desert campaign is described in three dramatic chapters which emphasized the importance of the Arab role in forcing the Ottomans to withdraw troops from other fronts: Antonius even claimed that Faysal's army, increasingly led by ex-Ottoman officers, faced more Turkish and German troops than did Allenby's army as it drove through Palestine; indeed, that it was the Arab army that made possible the advance to Damascus.

This section poses two initial questions that have engaged historians. First, how important were these Arab envoys from Damascus in persuading Husayn to declare war, and did he share their allegedly nationalistic objectives? Second, and less important, how significant was the desert campaign in the conquest of Palestine?

From the occupation of Damascus in 1918 Antonius went on to describe the complex negotiations for a Middle East settlement. These will be dealt with in the following chapter; but Antonius deployed the standard Arab argument that the mandate system was incompatible with the Husayn–McMahon correspondence and also with the 1918 Anglo-French declaration that the Arab countries would be allowed to make their own choice of regime. Both statements were later challenged, notably by Elie Kedourie, as will be seen in Chapter 2. Antonius also described the Iraq rebellion of 1920 and the 1921 Cairo conference at which the future of Iraq was decided. In the final two chapters he described events in Arabia, notably the success of Ibn Saud and the admirably puritan characteristics of the Wahhabi movement. He gave a favourable account of the Iraqi settlement and a damning account of events in Palestine.

For the purpose of my argument the three important questions to ask about Antonius's account are, first, how powerful Arab nationalism was before 1914; and second, how influential it was in persuading Husayn to enter the war in alliance with Britain. These questions will be considered in the present chapter on the basis of changes in the historiography over time. The third question concerns the role of the Arabs in the war and whether the eventual territorial settlement was consistent with the McMahon promises. This will be examined in Chapter 2.

Some of the weaknesses and omissions in Antonius are obvious even from a cursory reading. He never really defines 'Arab' or 'Arab Awakening'. This is taken to mean the rediscovery of the virtues of Arabic as a language, and heavy emphasis is therefore placed on the early cultural movement in the most sophisticated of all Arab regions before 1914, Lebanon and Syria. But to leap from a linguistic revival among the literati to widespread desire for Arab independence is comparable to believing that, for example, the Irish nationalist movement of the same period stemmed from the desire of a very small minority to resurrect Gaelic as the national language. Again, the growth of secret societies, once more in Lebanon and Syria, is taken to reflect a widespread Arab consciousness, but no evidence is provided of this wider feeling, nor is there a real definition of what 'Arab nationalism' meant, for example to the beduin in general and Sharif Husayn of Mecca in particular. In short, there were grounds for an eventual revision of Antonius's whole thesis, and this began seriously after the Second World War.

One of the first serious attempts to revise Antonius's arguments was by C. E. Dawn in an essay first published in 1962 called 'The Rise of Arabism in Syria'.[19] After summarizing the standard list of Arab reform societies before 1914 Dawn argued that none spoke openly of possible independence, demanding only reform and greater Arab rights. On the other hand it is likely that some in the two most secret societies, al-Fatat and al-Ahd, did in fact hope for some form of independence from Istanbul. Assuming that membership of these societies was roughly the same as the roll-call of Arab nationalists, Dawn then proceeded to analyse their membership, which totalled 144. Of these 126 were known public advocates of some form of Arab nationalism: 51 Syrians, 1 Egyptian, 21 Lebanese, 18 Iraqis, 22 Palestinians, and 13 other notables. Thirty, however, were doubtful, and they may have had more supporters, as reflected in the Paris Congress of 1913. Nationalists were dominated by Syrians, who were more active than Lebanese or Palestinians. The commitment of these men was tested by later events. Of the 51 Syrians, only 15 were active in the Hashemite crusade. This may have been due to Ottoman repression in Syria: 16 members of the reform societies were sentenced and 13 executed in 1915–16, though it is uncertain how many of these had actually been engaged in anti-Ottoman activities. On the other hand, at least ten pre-war nationalists were either inactive during the war or collaborated with the Turks. So in fact very few Syrian nationalists were involved in the Hashemite rising. The Turks had exiled some of those suspected of anti-Ottoman

---

[19] It was reprinted as ch. 6 in a collection of his work in *From Ottomanism to Arabism: Essays on the Origins of Arab Nationalism* (Urbana, Ill., 1973). References are to this edition.

sympathies to distant areas, and in 1915 moved the predominantly Arab regiments then in Syria to other fronts, thus pre-empting the promised military rising in support of Husayn. Most Arab recruits to Husayn's army were prisoners taken from the Ottoman army who opted to serve the Allies rather than languish in prisoner-of-war camps.

In fact, Dawn argued, the Arab revolt had a far greater impact on Arab nationalism than the converse. It was the eventually successful war that rallied opinion to what looked like a winning cause. By 1919–20 there had been a huge increase in the membership of both al-Fatat and al-Ahd, and in 1920 the Syrian Congress adopted a full independence strategy for the first time, electing Faysal as king. It is important, however, that the pre-war nationalists played a minor part in the Damascus regime in 1918–20. Thirty-nine out of the 44 members of the Congress had not been nationalists before 1914, and of the five others only one had been actively anti-Ottoman during the war. On the other hand, three of the five army senior command had been pre-1914 nationalists and a number of junior officers had also been active against the Ottomans during the war. Two out of the twelve members of the Committee of National Defence were pre-1914 nationalists.

The conclusions suggested by these figures are, first, that the great majority of those dominant in the Syrian regime in 1918–20 were not pre-war nationalists, but had jumped on the band-wagon once the war swung against the Turks; and, second, that the nationalists were in no sense homogeneous. This in turn led Dawn to analyse the social background of the nationalists and what persuaded them to take up an anti-Ottoman position. In particular, were they predominantly members of a 'rising middle class', and what distinguished nationalists from Ottomanists?

On the first question it is clear that the great majority of both pre- and post-1914 nationalists were members of the land-owning and land-owner/scholar class, that mix of roles which characterized most members of the ruling classes in Ottoman provinces. There were few members of the merchant or banking class, though these were in fact more likely to be nationalist than Ottoman in their sympathies. Above all, holders of government offices, especially religious dignitaries, were predominantly pro-Ottoman. In the army, senior officers also were mainly loyal Ottomans, though there was considerable nationalist influence among junior officers, from whom most members of al-Ahd were drawn. Hence 'the principal distinction between Arabist and Ottomanist was holding of office. . . . The conflict between Arab nationalists and Ottomanists in pre-1914 Syria was a conflict between rival members of the Arab elite. . . . The conflict . . . was essentially of the type that was traditional in Near Eastern society. The new element was the ideological definition of the conflict.'[20] But they had a common aim. This was 'defending and justifying the Islamic East in the face of the Christian West. In this, Ottomanism and Arabism were identical. They differed only in the means proposed for the pursuit of the desired goal. In Syria those

[20] Ibid. 170, 173.

members of the Arab elite who had a vested interest in the Ottoman state were Ottomanists. Those who were without such a stake were Arabists. This was a traditional intra-elite conflict defined in terms of the new ideology.'[21] Dawn concluded that

Neither Arabism, the Arab Revolt, nor the Turkish collapse . . . brought about any far-reaching changes in the Arab personnel who ruled Syria. Nor did the growth of Arabism and the Arab Revolt break the allegiance of the dominant faction of the Arab elite to Ottomanism. The collapse of the Ottoman Empire in the Turkish defeat was different however. Although the political position of the Ottomanist Arabs survived the debacle, their ideology, Ottomanism, could not survive the end of the Ottoman Empire.

Arab nationalism as a political force, then, began as a movement within the dissident faction of the Arab elite of the Ottoman Empire. Arabism was its first success, and a complete success, when the failure of the Ottoman Empire in World War I left the dominant faction of the Arab elite with no alternative to Arabism.[22]

Dawn had thus demolished the concept of a dominant and ideologically based Arab nationalist movement before 1914 and reduced ideology to the level of conventional faction politics. His arguments had a huge impact, by no means all favourable. In 1991 he took the opportunity to revisit his argument and make additions to it.[23] He stuck to his basic argument: 'Arab nationalism arose as the result of intra-Arab elite conflict.' 'Arab nationalism remained a minority opposition position until the end of World War I. The majority of Arab notables remained loyal Ottomanists.'[24] The impression that this nationalism grew fast in reaction against CUP strategies was mainly created by foreign commentators and was probably wrong. On the other hand the CUP did have some effect on Arab opinion. The relative liberalism of the new regime may have led to an increase in Arab pressures for change. Arabs moreover attacked the CUP on specific grounds. It was suspected, particularly by Palestinians, of being favourable to Zionism. It was accused of promoting the use of the Turkish language in administration, justice, and education. Dawn considered these charges to be mainly false. The CUP was not making any radical changes in these fields. Nor was Arab resistance to Istanbul policies new. 'The Arab nationalists were not reacting to Young Turk innovations. Indeed, they were continuing a campaign against a system that was established long before the Young Turks.'[25]

Dawn's critique of Antonius and the concept of an Arab Awakening had a dynamic effect on the subject, comparable, in a British context, with that made by Sir Lewis Namier's *The Structure of Politics at the Accession of George III* in 1929. In both cases, detailed analysis of men and their motivations demonstrated that generalized assumptions that politics were based on ideology were over-simplified. In the British case, other historians responded by attempting to reinstate principle

[21] *From Ottomanism to Arabism: Essays on the Origins of Arab Nationalism*, 173.   [22] Ibid.
[23] In Khalidi *et al.* (eds.), *The Origins of Arab Nationalism*, 3–30.   [24] Ibid. 11–12, 16.
[25] Ibid. 21.

and party rather than individual ambition and patronage as the basis of politics. How far did the same thing happen to Dawn's model?

One of the earlier responses was by B. Tibi in 1971.[26] Most of his book is devoted to an account of the rise of cultural and literary expressions of an Arab consciousness, with the major emphasis on the career and writings of the pan-Arabist Sati al-Husri, particularly after 1920. Tibi does not really engage with Dawn's central argument, though neither does he reject it. For the early period he suggests that 'the early Arab nationalists confined themselves to emphasising the existence of an independent Arab cultural nation without demanding a national state'. Most saw no contradiction between being culturally Arab and being Ottoman subjects, even though the Secret Society of the 1870s put up posters demanding a unified Arab state to include all religions.[27] Much the same was true of the multiple societies founded in and after 1911. They wanted liberalization and decentralization within the Ottoman empire and their aims were increasingly secular rather than Islamic. Conversely the Hijaz revolt in and after 1916 was ultra-conservative with no social or humanitarian perspectives, 'monopolized by traditional politicians who were either rich feudalists or their agents'.[28]

Probably the first really considered and widely influential post-Dawn analysis of the Antonius argument was published by Albert Hourani in his book *The Emergence of the Modern Middle East* (London, 1981).[29] In the chapter called 'The Arab Awakening after Forty Years', he first summarized Antonius's career, then underlined the book's virtues. It was written very lucidly and contained excellent sketches of people such as Mark Sykes, the Sharif Husayn, and T. E. Lawrence, all of whom he had known, and was based on sources not then generally available. Its tone was conditioned by its context: the 1936 Arab rising in Palestine, the 1937 Peel Commission recommendation for partition, and the forthcoming conference. It was the first book of its kind and had a huge influence then and later. Hourani suggested that the book raised three main issues: the nature of Arab nationalism before 1914; the role of nationalism during the First World War; and the evolution of Arab thought and action during the mandate period.

On the first of these issues Hourani broadly agreed with Dawn. Asking who were the nationalists and were they men imbued with so great a love of the Arab language and literature that they were determined 'to create a society in which Arabs could live together and rule themselves', he followed Dawn's argument. Most of the early Arab nationalists were members of the elite and integral to

---

[26] B. Tibi, *Arab Nationalism: A Critical Enquiry* (1971; Eng. trans. M. and P. Sluglett, London, 1981). [27] Ibid. 78–9.

[28] Ibid. 89–90. As this quotation suggests, Tibi seems to have written from a Marxist perspective.

[29] But in *British Policy towards Syria and Palestine, 1906–1914* (London, 1980), R. I. Khalidi had argued, in chs. 4 and 5, that Arab nationalism in Syria was more widespread than Dawn had suggested and that it was based mainly on hostility to the CUP's centralizing policies. See also A. Hourani's earlier study, *Arabic Thought in the Liberal Age* (1962; rev. edn. Cambridge, 1983), ch. 11.

the Ottoman system. Disagreement between nationalists and Ottomanists constituted an inter-elite conflict defined in terms of ideologies. The real basis was personal or factional struggles to get or keep power within the Ottoman system. Most nationalists mixed some Arab sentiment with concern for local power and position, which was thought to be threatened by the increasing centralizaton of the Ottoman system. Disagreement stemmed from dispute over the relative value of the traditional Ottoman and Islamic system as contrasted with a constitutional and liberal state.

Hence Antonius had been wrong to place his main emphasis on the origin of Arabist ideas among the Syrian and Lebanese intelligentsia of the later nineteenth century. Most of the ideas impregnated into Arabism before 1914 were a mix of Islamic modernism of the Salafi School, based on an idealized conception of the early Arab society and the Arab Caliphate, with ideas picked up by Arab students in the professional schools of Istanbul. These in turn were often drawn from French books and German military instructors which were restated in an Arab idiom. These emphasized the sense of exclusion felt by many Arabs from the benefits of the Ottoman state. Such ideas were absorbed by the Arab elite, but were mixed with the traditional Islamic concept of the 'just Muslim Sultan'. It was this source of Arabist ideas that Antonius failed to perceive. Hourani summed up his argument on the relative importance of Arabist ideology as follows:

A few individuals apart, the idea that the Arabs should break away from the [Ottoman] Empire scarcely arose until two events brought it to the surface: the entry of the Empire into the War in 1914, at a moment when Arab–Turkish relations were strained: and the collapse of the Empire in 1918, which faced everyone, and in particular the members of the ruling elite, with an inescapable choice.[30]

Hourani's argument therefore incorporates that of Dawn, while placing more weight on the various ideological influences on the attitudes of the Arab nationalists. Hourani then turned to Antonius's account of how such ideas influenced the Hashemites and their entry into the war in 1916. In Hourani's view Antonius endowed Husayn's cause and strategy in the war with 'a unity and solidity which it did not possess'. There was no unity of aims between the beduins and urban supporters of the revolt in Syria and Lebanon. The Hashemite position in fact went through three phases in and after 1914. During the first phase, from 1914 to 1915, Husayn was tempted by the fact that there was a large Arab element in the Ottoman army in Syria, which al-Faruqi alleged was ready to rebel, and by the prospect of a British naval landing at Alexandretta, to consider lining up with the British in the hope of making gains for himself. In the second phase, however, from 1915 to 1916, the failure of the Dardanelles campaign and the danger of an Ottoman and German attack on Suez put the boot on the other foot. It was now the British who wanted a Hashemite alliance while Husayn became afraid of

---

[30] Hourani, *The Emergence of the Modern Middle East*, 203.

direct Ottoman control of the Hijaz. Husayn eventually came down on the British side because it seemed his best defence against this. In the final phase, from 1917 to 1918, the British drive through Palestine left Husayn dependent on the British, but hopeful that his interpretation of the promises made by McMahon of an Arab kingdom would be honoured. Thus Husayn's entry into the war was not the result of his conversion to the concept of Arab identity but of his and his son Abdullah's assessment of how the situation could best be turned to the advantage of the Hashemites. As to the McMahon–Husayn correspondence, Antonius was wrong to regard promises made in October 1915 as incompatible with the Sykes–Picot Agreement (see Chapter 2). 'It seems clear now that the intention of the British government, when it made the Sykes–Picot agreement, was to reconcile the interests of France with the pledge given to the Sharif Husayn', though, since that Agreement was negotiated under stress of war, it could be interpreted otherwise, as it was later by Antonius.[31]

Hourani, therefore, supported recent revisions of the Antonius thesis. Elsewhere in the same book he argued that 'The nationalist movement was led by the urban aristocracy and moulded in their image: the change did not begin until after 1945.' These notables, including Husayn, did not expect or want full independence from Istanbul but an improvement in their status through a shift of power from the centre to the localities. Those who supported the Allies wanted the best terms for themselves that the British and French could obtain for them. They were therefore later shattered to find that foreign rule did not, in most cases, give the notables the status they had hoped for.[32]

The debate over the nature and extent of Arab nationalism before 1914 nevertheless continued. In 1991 a useful collection of essays, edited by R. Khalidi, appeared which surveyed changing assessments since Antonius.[33] These are reflected in the arguments of three of the contributors.

First, Khalidi himself, in an essay called 'Ottomanism and Arabism in Syria before 1914', defined three stages in the debate since Antonius. The first he called the traditional view, as defined by Antonius and other involved contemporaries, including Asad Daghar and Muhammed Izzat Darwazza. The second phase saw the first serious academic analysis of Antonius, by Dawn, Hourani, Tibawi, Khoury, and others. The third phase, then in process, involved the revision of these second-stage revisionists. It is on this third stage that Khalidi's book concentrates.

It was now accepted that Dawn's basic proposition was correct. As Khoury put it in his seminal study *Urban Notables*, Arabism was 'a humble minority position in Damascus and elsewhere, unable to erode the loyalty of the dominant faction of the public political elite in Syria to Ottomanism'.[34] But more now needed to be said. Although the earlier revisions had downplayed the force of Arab national

[31] Ibid. 209–10.   [32] Ibid. 62, 71–2.

[33] Khalidi *et al.* (eds.), *The Origins of Arab Nationalism.*

[34] P. S. Khoury, *Urban Notables and Arab Nationalism: The Politics of Damascus 1880–1920* (Cambridge, 1983), 74.

feeling, in diplomatic reports, the foreign and local press, and the recollections of contemporaries, it was 'a major tendency' before 1914. Certainly the majority of the Arab press in Beirut, Damascus, and Cairo was Arabist in tone. Why was this fact ignored or played down by earlier historians? Khalidi suggests that the Turkification aspect of the CUP had a major impact on many Arabs who were displaced, or feared they would be displaced, from offices traditionally held by members of the provincial elite. Another factor was that Khoury, Dawn, and others may have over-emphasized Damascus, ignoring attitudes elsewhere; so Arabism may have had a much wider impact, particularly in Beirut, Aleppo, and Jerusalem. Thus the paper *al-Mufid* in Beirut, the mouthpiece of the secret al-Fatat society, expressed strong demands for reform, equality between races, and notional self-expression, while still supporting Islam and the historic role of the empire. Lebanon was still more exposed to western ideas, with rapid population growth and a sophisticated elite and middle class. In Palestine, Jerusalem and Jaffa were also rapidly growing cities with widely read newspapers. There the apparently rapid spread of Zionism was a stimulus for debate over Arabism and Ottomanism. More important still were Cairo and Istanbul, the two dominant economic and intellectual centres of the Ottoman Middle East. Cairo was home to the most important Arabist society, the Ottoman Administrative Decentralization Party, and had many Arabic papers and Arab political refugees. Similarly, in Istanbul there was a very large number of Arabs who produced influential Arab newspapers. It was significant that only three of the Arab deputies elected to the first Ottoman parliament in 1908 were supporters of the CUP and that these were the only Arab deputies not re-elected to the parliament of 1912, despite strong CUP pressure on the electors. This suggested at least a strong and widely spread Arab hostility to the CUP's centralizing strategies.

Another weakness in the conventional discourse was the alleged dichotomy between 'Arabism' and 'Ottomanism'. Khalidi argues that Arabism did not necessarily imply a break with Ottomanism. Rather it meant opposing the perceived policies of centralization and Turkification of the CUP, in particular press censorship and manipulation of the electoral system. Most Arabists saw reform as a means of preserving and strengthening the Ottoman system. Thus the difference between Arabists and Ottomanists was one of method rather than over fundamentals. The problem facing Arabs after 1913–14 was that, once the CUP had crushed all opposition parties, there was no legitimate opposition for these reformers and dissidents to support.

Khalidi also questions whether the older definition of the Arab elite needs broadening from the landed notables of Dawn's Damascus model. There were, in fact, many regional differences. Particularly in the coastal regions such as Lebanon and Palestine, these older notables were being challenged by new arrivals and upwardly mobile groups of merchants, speculative landlords, the newly educated in the professions, and others, so the established groups were finding that they had to share power and place. In fact this period saw the genesis of modern mass politics. Older notables tended to side with the CUP, others with more liberal and decentralizing parties. In competing with their rivals the older notables used mass meetings, street demonstrations, and other mobilizing techniques to retain their position. Khalidi's conclusion was that

Arab nationalism arose as an opposition movement in the Ottoman Empire. It was directed quite as much against Ottoman Arabs as against the Ottoman Turks themselves. The conflict was between elements of the Ottoman Arab elite who competed for office. . . . As in every society, the competitors offered themselves as the ones best qualified to realize the ideals of the society and ward off the dangers that threatened it. . . . The movement made progress before 1914, but it remained a minority movement until 1914, when the Arab revolt, the British agreement with the amir Husayn, and the British defeat of the Ottomans left the dominant faction of the Syrian and Iraqi Arab notables with no alternative to Arabism.[35]

In the same volume others dealt with the distinct issue of the connection between Arabism and the Arab revolt in the Hijaz. W. Ochsenwald's essay, 'Arab Nationalism in the Hijaz', supported earlier arguments that there was virtually no Arab nationalism in the Hijaz before 1916 and Husayn's entry into the war. The Hijaz was economically very undeveloped, depending almost entirely on the profits of the Haj and other subsidies from the faithful. There were very few Christians or educated Muslim Arabs. The main issues as seen from Mecca before 1914 related to the post-1908 CUP push for greater control, which involved extension of the railway to Medina and thence to Mecca and the imposition of the standard Ottoman law of the vilayets. This would have given the vali, as governor, dominant control, whereas by convention the vali had a parallel jurisdiction with the Sharif, who had been able to get over-interfering valis removed by appeal to Istanbul. In 1914, however, Husayn was a loyal Ottomanist, and hoped to use Ottoman military power to pursue his ambitions in the Yemen area. Such patriotism as existed was purely local and the concept of being an Arab scarcely existed. The revolt was possible and quite successful (though Medina was never captured) because many in the Hijaz saw it as a means of preserving their existing freedoms. Moreover Ottoman disasters in the Balkans and North Africa had suggested that Istanbul was no longer able to protect the Hijaz. In Britain Husayn believed he had found an alternative and more co-operative protector, who, moreover, could provide the money and guns that alone could make a revolt successful.[36]

Much the same view was taken by Mary Wilson, again in this book. In her essay 'The Hashemites, the Arab Revolt and Arab Nationalism', she argued that there was no Arab nationalism of the Syrian variety in the Hijaz before 1914, though there was much suspicion of the alleged secularism and centralizing tendencies of the CUP regime. The conventional genesis of links between Mecca and the British, Abdullah's talk with Kitchener in Cairo in February 1914, was caused by Abdullah's fear that Istanbul would replace Husayn as part of its centralizing drive. Abdullah's question was simply whether the British would provide support should Husayn be threatened

[35] Khalidi *et al.* (eds.), *The Origins of Arab Nationalism*, 23.   [36] Ibid. ch. 9.

with deposition as Sharif. Istanbul heard of this and became conciliatory; they offered terms about the railway, the Sharif to share the profits, and promised Husayn the right of family succession to the position. Once war broke out these contacts became more significant, leading to the McMahon–Husayn correspondence of 1915–16. It was at this point only that Husayn began deliberately to adopt the terminology of Arab nationalism, probably to justify his position to the British. Hence 'The ideology of Arabism was not espoused by the Hashemites until it became of particular use to them with particular audiences'; that is, outside the Hijaz and in dialogue with Britain. This was made clear in the contrasting roles of Abdullah and Faysal. Abdullah did not use the Arabist discourse extensively, concentrating on his unsuccessful siege of Medina and his larger ambitions in southern Arabia. Faysal, however, did use it during the revolt and in the Paris conference of 1918–19. This contrast was reflected in their later roles. Faysal in Iraq became an avid pan-Arab nationalist, using this as the basis of his claim for an independent state. Abdullah, however, had to adjust to reduced status in Transjordan, while never giving up specifically Hashemite claims to Syria. Wilson concludes that

The Arab revolt first brought the Hashemites and Arab nationalism together. But what was decisive to their reputations as nationalists was the nature of their compromises with Britain after World War I. Hence the development of Arab nationalism rested less on the revolt itself than on the imposition of the mandates just afterwards.[37]

By the early 1990s something approaching a consensus had emerged among historians, though with different emphases. Thus in 1993 Eliezer Tauber, in perhaps the most exhaustive investigation so far of the character and membership of all the known Arab societies before 1914, came to the conclusion that there was then no such thing as a generalized Arab nationalism.[38] Parts I and II of the book are devoted to description and analysis of all the known Arab societies, open and secret, before 1908 and between then and 1914. Tauber argues that most of these had very small memberships and were seldom influential beyond their own circle. Most concentrated on the specific problems of their own territories and argued for amelioration. This implied a bigger and better role for Arabs and the Arabic language along with greater decentralization. There is no evidence that any of these societies would have been important had it not been for the war which gave some of them temporary foreign allies, the British and French. On the other hand, the sense of being Arabs was by 1914 well developed among a small intelligentsia and parts of the Ottoman official classes. It was particularly strong among officers who failed to the get the promotion they expected and blamed this on their being despised as non-Turks. Yet most army officers remained loyal to the Sultan throughout the war: those who fought on the British side, particularly Iraqis, did so for the most part because they had been taken prisoner and preferred to fight as officers rather than be interned. A number of these received their reward after

[37] Khalidi *et al.* (eds.), *The Origins of Arab Nationalism*, ch. 10 and p. 219.
[38] Tauber, *The Emergence of the Arab Movements*.

1920 in Iraq, becoming members of its ruling elite that survived until 1958. Above all, these societies failed to obtain general support.

The societies with Arab tendencies did not gain the backing of the populace for which they worked. This populace was totally unaware of the existence of some of the societies and did not hasten to support those it was aware of. During this period these societies did not have a crystallized and defined ideology that could attract the masses. The pan-Arab societies, which did have such an ideology, were so small that they were practically unnoticed. On the other hand, the local movements attained at least relative success among the Arabs of the Lebanon, Syria and Iraq, because they had specific solutions to offer the local people, solutions which seemed sufficiently realistic that the populace could imagine them a practical alternative to their plight in the Ottoman Empire.

There was a ramifying, and at times very close, network of connections among the societies, even those of different and contradictory trends. This cooperation stemmed from the common cause of all the trends: the struggle against the common enemy, the Turks, and especially the CUP. The evolution in the societies' methods of action reveals a real turning point in the history of the Arab Middle East, as the activists and the ideologists went from speech to action in an attempt to realize in practice the ideologies they believed in.[39]

Three years after Tauber's book came out, M. Kramer expressed agreement with its general findings.[40] He saw the genesis of Arab nationalism in two factors. The first, as Antonius had argued, was the attempt by minority communities of Arabic-speaking people, many of them Christians, to transform Arabic into a medium of missionary work and modern learning. This led to greater interest in Arabic literature and its adaptation to modern literary forms, especially in the press. Centred in Beirut, this did not immediately produce Arab nationalism, but it argued for a secular Arab culture shared by both Christians and Muslims. This concept was used by Christians to erode the prejudice of the Muslim majority and to work for Christian equality.

But, as Dawn had argued, Arabism also rose from the struggles for power and position among the Muslim elite, which for some turned into demand for greater local autonomy or decentralization. This centred in Damascus, but had reverberations in many other major towns. While sharing the love of the Arabic language with the earlier Christian Arabists, these later movements were specifically Islamic. They appealed to Muslims by arguing that Arab greatness, past and present, stemmed from Islam. While these literary and nationalistic movements had a limited frame of reference they were able to shake the confidence of some people in the legitimacy of Ottoman rule. This was exacerbated after 1908 by the twin bugbears of Turkification and Zionism. Nevertheless, that keen observer of Arab society, Gertrude Bell, wrote in 1907:

Of what value are the pan-Arabic associations and inflammatory leaflets that they issue from foreign printing presses? The answer is easy: they are worth nothing at all. There is no

---

[39] Ibid. 331–2.
[40] Kramer, *Arab Awakening*, esp. ch. 1, 'Arab Nationalism: Mistaken Identity'.

nation of Arabs; the Syrian merchant is separated by a wider gulf from the Bedouin than he is from the Osmanli, the Syrian country is inhabited by Arabic speaking races all eager to be at each other's throats, and only prevented from fulfilling their natural desires by the ragged half fed soldier who draws at rare intervals the Sultan's pay.[41]

Kramer concludes:

Arabism thus arose from a growing unease about the pace and direction of change. Yet, while the Ottoman Empire lasted, this Arabism did not develop into full-fledged national-ism. Its adherents pleaded for administrative decentralization, not Arab independence, and they had no vision of a post-Ottoman order. . . . Above all, they were practical. They did not indulge in dreams of Arab power. Their grievances, in the words of a critic of later Arab nationalism, 'were local and specific; they related to the quality of government services or to the proper scope of local administration; and those who sought redress for such grievances were mostly men well known in their communities, able perhaps to conduct a sober constitutional opposition but not to entertain grandiose, limitless ambi-tions'. On the eve of World War I, they were probably still in the minority, outnumbered by Arabic-speaking Muslims and Christians who raised no doubt about the legitimacy of Ottoman rule, and even stood prepared to defend it.[42]

The answers to the two questions posed at the start of this chapter now become clear. First, while the Ottoman empire, the 'sick man of Europe' for so long, had clearly declined from its glorious past and by 1914 had lost almost all of its European and Christian possessions, it was by no means dead. A continuous process of internal reconstruction over the past century left it with considerable potential for becoming, in some respects at least, a western-style state. It was still not economically or militarily competitive with the great states of western Europe, but it was certainly capable of dealing with dissidence within its Middle Eastern possessions. There was, however, one major proviso attached. In the Balkans, so-called nationalist movements for independence had largely been activated and supported by external powers, notably Russia and Austria. Russia remained a seri-ous threat in the Caucasus; and if naval powers such as Britain or France chose to support breakaway or rebel movements, the Ottomans would find it difficult to respond successfully. Thus their best chance of maintaining their residual empire was a long period of external peace.

To the second question the answer has also become clear. By 1914 'nationalist' movements in the Middle East were still in their infancy. While certain aspects of the post-1908 Ottoman drive for greater efficiency through centralization were deeply distasteful to a minority, and although there was a strong ground swell of

---

[41] Quoted ibid. 24. Bell retained her belief that Arabs could not govern themselves for another decade. Thus in 1915 she wrote: 'the Arabs can't govern themselves', and in 1918 [of Iraq]: 'They can't conceive an independent Arab government. Nor, I confess, can I. There is no one here who could run it.' Quoted E. Burgoyne, *Gertrude Bell: From her Personal Papers, 1914–1926* (London, 1961), 31–2, 78. Bell changed her mind in 1919, possibly under persuasion by the Sharifian Yasin al-Hashimi, and then became an ardent supporter of an Iraqi state with Faysal as king.

[42] Kramer, *Arab Awakening*, 24–5.

Arab self-awareness which might eventually demand greater autonomy for the Arab provinces, these did not yet seriously threaten Ottoman rule. They could still have been accommodated by sensible concessions by Istanbul. Moreover, the region that was to become the focus of resistance to Ottoman rule, the Hijaz, paradoxically, was the least affected by nascent Arabist feeling.

Clearly, then, the ultimate destruction of the Ottoman empire in the Middle East was the outcome of factors not present early in 1914. It was war, not Ottoman decline or Arab nationalism, that broke the Ottoman Middle East into fragments under British and French mandates. These fragments then became the modern states of the contemporary Middle East. Chapter 2 will therefore concentrate on two main questions. First, why did the Ottomans join the war on the side of Germany and Austria, with such disastrous consequences? Second, why did the Middle East emerge from the war as a series of French and British 'mandates', in effect temporary colonies, despite promises allegedly made by the British to leading Arabs for one or more independent Arab kingdoms?

2

War and the Partition of the Ottoman Empire, 1914–1922

In November 1914 the Ottoman empire went to war against Russia, Britain, and France. On 31 October 1918, by the Armistice of Mudros, the war ended with almost total defeat of the Ottoman armies. The result was the dismemberment of the empire and, after a further four years of confusion and fighting, the emergence of the state of Turkey in Anatolia and a small part of Eastern Thrace, north of Istanbul, and of five newly defined territories under British or French control called mandates. This chapter will pose and attempt to answer three questions.

First, why did the Ottomans go to war on the side of Germany and against the Entente, and how did they fight their war?

Second, what were the aims and war strategies of the British and French, and how did they fit with the aims of the Arabs, particularly the Hashemites?

Third, how far were these various aims realized during the period of diplomacy and fighting between 1918 and 1922?

1. OTTOMAN POLICIES BEFORE 1914

There is agreement among most historians that there was no certainty that the Ottomans would enter the war at all, or that they would do so on the side of the Central Powers rather than the Entente.[1] Until early August 1914 they had at least three options. They could enter the war at once, either as a German ally or as an ally of the Entente. They could stay neutral initially, but give moral support to either combatant, and delay entry until they saw how the war was developing (as in fact Italy and Greece were to do). Finally, they could remain neutral throughout, as Turkey did during the Second World War. All these options had

[1] The following account of Ottoman policies is based mainly on the following: S. J. and E. K. Shaw, *History of the Ottoman Empire and Modern Turkey*. Vol. 2: *Reform, Revolution and Republic: The Rise of Modern Turkey 1808–1970* (Cambridge, 1977); A. L. Macfie, *The End of the Ottoman Empire, 1908–1923* (London and New York, 1998); A. Palmer, *The Decline and Fall of the Ottoman Empire* (London, 1992); J. McCarthy, *The Ottoman Peoples and the End of Empire* (London, 2001).

their dangers and opportunities. Moreover, the CUP-dominated cabinet was divided on the matter.

The case for joining Germany, immediately or in due course, was strongly backed by Enver Pasha and Sait Halil, the Grand Vizier; and McCarthy argues that in fact there was no choice.[2] Russia had been the main Ottoman enemy for centuries. It was known to aim at taking Istanbul, controlling the Straits, and expanding its Caucasian territories into eastern Anatolia. An alliance with Russia might not prevent these losses. Moreover, Britain and France could not offer support for the Ottoman ambition of regaining lost territories in the Balkans and Russia would certainly block such a strategy. Conversely, the Germans, if victorious, might well provide these benefits. They had no Balkan interests (though Austria did have) and were not thought to have ambitions in the residual parts of the empire in the fertile crescent or southern Arabia. It was important that the Germans had been reorganizing and training the Ottoman army since the 1880s. They were regarded as the strongest military and industrial power in Europe. They were investing heavily in the empire, notably in the projected Berlin to Baghdad railway with its predicted extension to Basra and the Gulf. This implied a risk that the Ottomans would become an economic satellite of Germany, but this seemed to many a small price to pay for major political and economic benefits.

The case for joining the Entente was the obverse of this, providing negative rather than positive benefits. It offered possible safety from Russian attack, assuming the other allies could restrain Russian acquisitiveness. The Allies could not, or obviously would not, offer the return of any lost Ottoman territory. Cyprus, by now a major British naval and military base, was out of the question, as was Egypt, still nominally part of the Ottoman empire though under British control since 1882. The Greeks, whom the Entente hoped to entice into an alliance, would not return western Thrace. But probably the greatest negative benefit from an Entente alliance would have been to safeguard the Levantine littoral and southern Arabia from naval attack. Already in early 1914 the Amir Abdullah, second son of Husayn of Mecca, had been in touch with Kitchener as the British Agent in Cairo. A British alliance might forestall any British support for separatism in that area. These were all negative attractions. But an Entente alliance had some positive elements. Britain was accepted to be the greatest naval power and British naval officers had been training the Ottoman navy for some time. An order had been placed in British shipyards for two battleships. The French were admired for their administration, along with their tradition of liberalism: French agents had been employed to improve Ottoman governmental institutions. Many Ottomans lived in Paris and admired its culture. The French had large investments in railways and other public works, especially in the Levant provinces. The British were a major trading partner.

Those in power in Istanbul were fully aware of these considerations, but they were seriously divided over which way the balance might tilt. The strongest

---

[2] McCarthy, *The Ottoman Peoples*, 97.

supporter of a German alliance was Enver, Minister of War in 1913–14. He had had close links with the Germans since 1909 and necessarily with the German army officers who were remodelling the Ottoman army. He saw Russia as the main threat, and Russia was now for the first time since the early nineteenth century backed by Britain and France. He had ambitions to regain areas to the east of Anatolia then controlled by the Russians. Germany had no Middle East designs and Austria-Hungary was thought to be satiated. Above all Enver was certain that Germany would win the war. He therefore negotiated secretly with the Germans. Relations with Britain were strained by the British decision not to release the two battleships, which were to be 'leased' to the Royal Navy for the duration of the war with Germany. This caused an outcry in Istanbul, since money for the ships had been partly raised by street collections: they were of great symbolic importance. On 2 August, after fighting had begun in Europe, Enver, Talat, and Halil secretly signed a treaty of alliance with Germany, against the opposition of the other leading ministers, Javid and Jemal, and without informing the other members of the cabinet. The treaty was to come into effect only if war between Austria-Hungary and Serbia led to Russian entry. This occurred on 6 August. The Ottoman parliament was suspended until November 1914 once it had passed the budget because opponents of the alliance were demanding that the secret treaty be published and ratified by the Chamber of Deputies.

But it was still uncertain whether Istanbul would in fact act on the alliance and declare war on the Entente. The Ottomans had to be manipulated into war by the war party. The majority of the cabinet was still against war unless the Germans could guarantee Ottoman security, and the British and Russians were attempting to persuade Istanbul to remain neutral, promising the end of the Capitulations as a reward. The trouble was that only a cast-iron Anglo-French guarantee that Russia would not take any territory if the Ottomans remained neutral would have served, and this they could not provide. Nor could they make the promises demanded by Jemal later in August: a defence treaty with each of the Entente powers; the end of the Capitulations (unilaterally abolished by Istanbul on 9 September); immediate delivery of the two Ottoman warships; no Allied intervention in Ottoman affairs; and the return of western Thrace if Bulgaria sided with the Central Powers. The most the Allies could offer was security of the empire at the peace treaties, but not in the indefinite future. The Germans could offer more. Early in October, while the Germans were not prepared to provide the loan of TL5 million in gold which the Ottomans asked for unless and until Istanbul actually declared war, they agreed to an initial loan of TL2 million. This initially swayed the Ottoman cabinet in favour of war, and on 11 October 1914 the German ambassador was told that the German admiral, Souchon, would be instructed to attack the Russian Black Sea fleet. But the next day, several members of the cabinet wanted to draw back and postpone a decision until the spring of 1915.

They were too late. Ever since early August, Enver had been manipulating events so that in the end there was no choice left. One key factor was that on

11 August, two German warships which were being chased by the British Mediterranean fleet were allowed, contrary to the rules of naval warfare, to take refuge in the Straits: they should either have been sent away or impounded. Instead the Ottomans adopted them as Ottoman naval vessels, renamed them, and equipped the German crews with fezzes. On 2 October the first instalment of German gold reached Istanbul. On 21 October Enver agreed a strategy with the German Chief of Staff, B. von Schellendorf. The German/Ottoman warships would enter the Black Sea and attack Russian ships and fortifications. The Ottomans would launch a land attack on the Russians in the Caucasus and on the British at Suez. On 25 October Enver formally authorized the German warships, along with some Ottoman vessels, to attack the Russians in the Black Sea, and on 29 October they bombarded Odessa and Sevastopol. This caused a major dispute in cabinet, several members threatening to resign if the fighting continued. Talat refused to call a full cabinet, but agreed to offer compensation to the Russians for damage done. This was, predictably, rejected by the Russians unless all German officers were got rid of. On 2 November Russia declared war, followed by the British and French on the following day. On 11 November the Sultan in turn declared war and called for a jihad against the infidels.

It is, therefore, clear that the Ottomans entered the war hesitantly, and mainly because of the skill of Enver in outmanœuvring his opponents in the cabinet. But little of this can have been known to the mass of Ottomans, who entered the war on a tide of patriotism that in many ways lasted until 1918.

The empire mobilized for war with an efficiency not seen in previous wars, and largely due to the role of the German military attachments. At the start, although Enver remained Minister of War and always retained effective control over strategy, most of the senior officers were German. Liman von Sanders commanded the First Army in Istanbul and later in Syria. General Hans von Seeckt was Chief of the Ottoman General Staff. General von der Goltz moved from the First Army to the Sixth Army in Mesopotamia. General von Falkenhayn was commander in Palestine. In addition Germans ran most of the central military establishments, including the Ministry of War departments of operations, intelligence, railways, supply, munitions, and fortresses. Varying numbers of German officers and other ranks were attached to the Ottoman forces. This did not transform the Ottoman army into one capable of facing a western European army on equal terms, but it was able to fight effectively in the right circumstances and even the reluctantly conscripted rank and file infantry proved extremely tenacious.[3] The Entente had certainly not expected such tough opposition.

There was, however, an underlying incompatibility between Ottoman war aims, at least as seen by Enver, and the role the Germans wanted them to play as their allies. The Germans saw the Turks as providing distractions to the Russians and

---

[3] Lieut.-Col. Wallace Lyon, who fought on the Somme in 1916 and in Iraq in 1918, thought that the Germans and Turks, in that order, were the most tenacious infantrymen of whom he had experience.

British to force them to draw troops away from more vital fields of battle. They wanted the Ottomans to attack Russia in the Caucasus and the British through Sinai to Egypt and hoped that the Ottoman declaration of jihad would arouse Muslim movements against Britain and France in North Africa and the East.[4] But Enver had much more ambitious plans. He wanted to regain much of Macedonia, Thrace, and Eastern Anatolia. He also hoped to liberate Egypt and Cyprus (which the British transformed respectively into a protectorate and a colony after war was declared). Beyond these he hoped to liberate Turks under Russian rule in the Caucasus and Central Asia, and had even wider hopes of making the Ottoman empire dominant in the whole Muslim world under the Caliph. Economically, Turkey was to be liberated from European domination. Of these aims only those in the Caucasus and Sinai fitted well with more restricted German intentions. Moreover, as if these were not ambitious plans for the assumed 'sick man of Europe', the British opened up a new front in Mesopotamia when they occupied Basra late in 1914 and in the Dardanelles in 1915, then stimulated the Hashemite revolt in 1916, forcing Enver to split his forces between four or five fronts. It was this problem of multiple fronts that eventually broke the Ottoman army. The Ottoman war record can be summarized according to each of these main fronts.

For Enver the Caucasus was the most important. Apart from the historic Russian threat and past losses to Russia there, by late 1914 there was a major revolt by Armenians in eastern Anatolia, which was supported by the Russians. The Armenians believed, wrongly, that once the Ottomans were defeated they would be given their own state by the Russians. Much of 1915 was spent dealing with the Armenian revolt, in which huge numbers were massacred on both sides. The Armenian rising was eventually suppressed, and from May 1915 a policy of ethnic cleansing was adopted to remove the majority of the Armenians from eastern Anatolia to Syria and Mesopotamia, which resulted in countless deaths from disease and starvation. Whether this was due to lack of preparation and administrative incompetence or to a deliberate Ottoman policy of genocide has been much debated.[5] But the need to deal with this very serious threat had a bad effect on the main Ottoman strategy of invading the Russian Caucasus. The attack started late in December 1914 and was a total disaster. The Ottoman armies were defeated at Sarikamish in January and further defeats followed. Later in 1915, a large part of the Third Army was removed to deal with the Dardanelles threat,

---

[4] For a detailed examination of German attitudes to the Ottoman war effort and the relationship between them see U. Trumpener, *Germany and the Ottoman Empire, 1914–1918* (Princeton, 1968), esp. ch. 3, which makes it clear that Enver never allowed the German staff to dictate to him.

[5] The standard Turkish historiography maintains that the massacre and deportation were a response to the Armenian rising in Van which endangered the whole Turkish front against the Russians. Many historians, especially Armenians, have argued that the massacre was the culmination of a long-standing Turkish hatred of the Armenians, stemming from Islamic attitudes to infidels, and was a successor to the 1894–6 massacres. The war merely provided an opportunity when the western powers could not intervene. See e.g. V. N. Dadrian, *Warrant for Genocide: Key Elements of Turko-Armenian Conflict* (New Brunswick and London, 1999). Trumpener, in *Germany and the Ottoman*

leaving only some 150,000 troops in the Caucasus. The major Russian challenge did not come until 1916. In February they captured Erzerum, then Trabzon. It seemed that there was now nothing to prevent a continued Russian advance into Anatolia.

The Ottomans were then saved by the first of the Russian Revolutions in March 1917. The Russian army began to fade away and in early 1918 Enver was able at last to start his drive into the Caucasus. By March the Ottomans had regained what they had lost since 1914 and by the time of the Armistice of Mudros in October 1918 had occupied Baku. That ended the Enver dream. The Ottoman armies retreated to the 1914 frontiers, but were available there to support the Turkish recovery in the following years.[6] To look ahead, the effects of the Russian Revolution of November 1917 on the Middle East were profound. In particular, it made nonsense of the territorial allocations under the Sykes–Picot Agreement, since there was no longer any need for a French presence in the Mosul area as a barrier between the Russians and the British.

Russian Revolution

While the Caucasian enterprise proved a failure, it undoubtedly served German interests by tying up a large number of Allied troops away from the more crucial battlefields to the north. The same is true of the Ottomans' other fronts. Probably the most significant was that in the Dardanelles. This campaign was sparked by Winston Churchill's cherished project of sending the navy to break into the Straits and so open up a route for an Allied invasion of Anatolia and beyond. But with German assistance the Ottomans had prepared the ground with mines and heavy artillery. The navy's first attempt on 19 February was a complete failure with the loss of three battleships. As an alternative the British sent in an Allied force, with many Australasian troops, to Gallipoli, near the entrance to the Sea of Marmora. The first landing was on 25 April 1915. The Allied forces got ashore but were held by Ottoman troops led by Mustafa Kemal behind fortifications planned by von Sanders. A second landing in August at Suvla Bay was also held. The British persisted but never made a significant incursion. Between December 1915 and January 1916 they evacuated. This was the only British success of the campaign. They had 213,980 casualties as compared with 120,000 for the Ottomans. It was the greatest Ottoman military triumph of the war and released troops to operate in other theatres, notably Mesopotamia.

Ottoman military success

Another success was their long holding operation in Mesopotamia. There were insufficient Ottoman troops to prevent the British landing at Basra late in 1914.

Empire, ch. 7, shows that successive German ambassadors in Istanbul and consuls fully supported the accusation that the Turks were set on exterminating the Armenians and pressed for action by Berlin. But the German government was primarily concerned with keeping the Turks in the war and consistently refused to apply sufficient pressure on Istanbul to stop the massacre or to improve conditions for the surviving Armenian deportees. The evidence for Turkish genocidal intentions seems convincing.

[6] For a detailed account of the Caucasus war and the strain it placed on Ottoman–German relations see Trumpener, *Germany and the Ottoman Empire*, ch. 6. For an inside account of the British intervention in Baku in 1918 see L. C. Dunsterville, who led the British force from Persia, *Stalky's Reminiscences* (London, 1928), ch. 18.

But they then held up the British advance to the north for most of the rest of the war. The defence of Baghdad was organized by von der Goltz and in November 1915 his forces defeated British/Indian troops advancing up the Tigris at Ctesiphon. The British then retreated to Kut al-Amara where they were besieged until 1916. They finally surrendered because the British forces in Basra could not get there and the primitive aircraft of the Royal Flying Corps had not the capacity to drop relief supplies. The British troops were marched into captivity and many of them died, though their commander, General Townshend, was well treated.[7] The British built up overwhelming forces during 1916 and eventually took Baghdad in March 1917. The Ottoman army continued to make a fighting retreat and still held Mosul when the Armistice was signed in October 1918. The British nevertheless went on and took the city, which was to cause considerable dispute between 1918 and 1925.

In the Syrian/Palestinian theatre also, the Ottomans proved serious defenders of territory, though not as conquerors of Egypt. In February 1915 a small Ottoman force of 20,000 under German command made a bid to control the canal but was beaten back by a combination of superior British gunfire, naval bombardment, and poor communications from Palestine. Enver had expected support from Egyptian nationalists, but none came and Egyptian forces helped the British defence. A second attempt under Jemal in August 1916 also failed. By then the British had built up their forces in the region and had begun their invasion of Sinai, establishing a forward base at al-Arish. In 1917 they were ready for a serious drive northwards. They were repulsed at Gaza in March/April 1917, but by December had broken through and taken Jerusalem. Thereafter they were able to drive on, and took Damascus and Aleppo in September 1918.

The loss of Palestine and Syria was in effect the result of the Ottomans having to fight on too many fronts at the same time. In 1917 Enver, against the wishes of Mustafa Kemal, Halil, Enver's uncle, the commander of the Sixth Army, and Jemal, created a force he called *Yildirim* (Lightning) under the command of von Falkenhayn, intended to reconquer Baghdad and drive the British out of Mesopotamia. Jemal in particular opposed this plan, and was effectively removed from his command, while remaining in charge of the civilian government of Syria. He later maintained that if Ottoman forces had not been depleted in 1917, after the failure of the British attempts on Gaza, he could have held the Gaza–Beersheba line indefinitely and thus saved the whole of Palestine and Syria for Ottoman occupation until peace was made. The Lightning force was never sent to Mesopotamia, but its formation may seriously have reduced the efficiency of the Palestine defence at a crucial time.

Equally the Arab revolt, which is discussed below, although it led to the occupation of Aqaba in 1917, had limited military importance. The Hashemite army, under the Amir Faysal and organized by T. E. Lawrence, paid for and supplied by the

---

[7] Von der Goltz died in Baghdad in June 1916. There is a memorial to him outside Kut.

British, sustained a guerrilla war along the line of the Hijaz railway from June 1916 onwards, blowing up parts of the track (though these were usually repaired rapidly), and were eventually able to reach Damascus at the same time as Allenby's army from Palestine. But there was no general rising of Arabs anywhere. Ibn Saud, who might have been a major factor in the revolt had he been prepared to side with the Hashemites, refused to do so. He accepted Ottoman sovereignty in 1914, though he refused to fight for them on account of the danger to him from his main local enemy, the Rashidis: in fact he was defeated by them in 1915. He played with both sides, unobtrusively supplying the Ottoman garrison in Medina. This held out until early 1919, even after the Armistice, tying up most of the Hashemite forces under Amir Abdullah.

It would, therefore, seem that the Ottomans had a remarkably successful military record during the First World War. Had they not been forced to disperse their resources over too many fronts, and had Enver not been over-ambitious in his attempts at conquest rather than defence, they might well have held much of their Middle Eastern possessions. Thus Enver's drive into the Caucasus in 1917–18 meant withdrawing many troops from the Palestine and Mesopotamian fronts and made possible the final British victories there. Istanbul's best hope, of course, was that Germany would win the war in Europe and would therefore at the peace be able to restore any losses the Ottomans had sustained as their allies, along with earlier territorial losses. In 1914, and even as late as 1917 or early 1918, this remained a reasonable gamble. Meantime the Ottomans fully justified German expectations. They had tied up very large numbers of British forces which might otherwise have played a critical role on the Western Front or in the Balkans. The war effort had in some degree been made possible by the Germans. They provided some TL250 million in addition to the initial loan, together with some 25,000 German officers and much German military equipment. But the Ottomans had made a huge war effort on their own behalf. The military manpower was largely Ottoman. Some 3 million men were conscripted, of whom about 350,000 were killed and 240,000 died of disease, apart from the wounded. There were other very serious costs. The Ottoman public debt, despite the suspension of all overseas interest payments, had risen from TL171 million in 1914 to three times that amount. The absence of manpower in the army caused serious food shortages and starvation. In 1918 prices rose 25 times. Only a German victory could have compensated for such suffering.

The end of the war came in October 1918 because the Ottoman defence was crumbling on all fronts. The Bulgarian front collapsed in September, leading to an armistice on 5 October, thus breaking the last direct link with German and military supplies. It also opened the way for a British drive through Salonika to Istanbul. This convinced Talat, who had become Grand Vizier in February 1917, that the game was up and that Istanbul must withdraw from the war. His hope was that peace might be arranged through the United States, which was not a party to the Ottoman war, but this was rejected and Talat was referred to Admiral

Calthorpe, Commander-in-Chief of the British Mediterranean fleet. On 8 October Talat and the CUP government resigned and the three leaders went abroad. On 14 October Ahmet Izzet became Grand Vizier and formed a new cabinet which included Cavit and other CUP members. After prolonged negotiation an armistice was signed on 31 October by Husayn Raf Orbay, the new Minister of War. The terms were as follows. The surrender was unconditional, in contrast with that in the German armistice in November. The Straits were to be opened to Allied ships, the forts dismantled, and Allied warships were to be free to enter the Black Sea to operate against the Bolsheviks. All Allied and Armenian prisoners were to be released. All Ottoman armed forces were to surrender. Apart from the British occupation of Mosul on 7 November, which the Ottomans rightly complained was incompatible with the armistice, and the continued resistance of Medina, the war was over. The Allies were in virtually complete control of the Ottoman empire. How they handled their power will be considered in the second section of this chapter.

2. BRITISH, FRENCH, AND HASHEMITE WAR AIMS AND DIPLOMACY, 1914–1922

In November 1914 no one could have forecast the ultimate shape of the Ottoman empire in Asia Minor.[8] Quite apart from the uncertainties of war, none of the participants, and certainly not the Entente Allies, had any clear view of what they wanted. The result was that during the four years of fighting plans were in constant flux and the final result, as determined at the San Remo conference of 1920, bore little relationship to any earlier projects. The most that can be said is that, coming at the end of a period of western European expansion overseas, there was a continuing momentum of expansionist instincts, and that, once the issues were opened, each power was likely to struggle to get whatever territory or advantages seemed to hand. Moreover, to complicate western diplomacy still further, during the war the Allies, more specifically Britain, made commitments to third parties outside the European system that reduced their freedom of action. The first of these was to the Hashemite ruler of Mecca, Sharif Husayn, in 1915; the second was to the World Zionist Organization in 1917. It is unlikely that European powers had ever before tied their hands in this way to a relatively insignificant

[8] The main sources on which this section is based, in addition to those referred to in section 1, are: J. Nevakivi, *Britain, France and the Arab Middle East 1914–1920* (London, 1969); E. Kedourie, *England and the Middle East: The Destruction of the Ottoman Empire, 1914–1921* (London, 1956); Kedourie, *The Chatham House Version and Other Middle Eastern Studies* (London, 1970), esp. ch. 2; Kedourie, *Into the Anglo-Arab Labyrinth: The McMahon–Hussayn Correspondence and its Interpretations, 1914–1939* (1976; 2nd edn. London, 2000); C. M. Andrew and A. S. Kanya-Forstner, *France Overseas: The Great War and the Climax of French Imperial Expansion* (London, 1981); J. Fisher, *Curzon and British Imperialism in the Middle East 1916–1919* (London, 1999); I. Friedman, *The Question of Palestine, 1914–1918: British–Jewish–Arab Relations* (London, 1973).

Ottoman dignitary and to an apparently amorphous international pressure group with no international standing whatever. The details of the Zionist claim to Palestine and its treatment by the Allies will be examined in Chapter 4. In the present section the emphasis will be on the more general diplomatic and strategic patterns and the relevance to them of the Hashemite ambitions.

There is an ambiguity in the initial Entente attitudes towards the future of the Ottoman empire. The long-term tradition of both British and French diplomacy was that it should be protected, in particular against the consistent ambitions of Russia. In Britain the established official view, from the time when Stratford Canning was the long-serving British Ambassador in Istanbul from 1842 to 1858, was that, however much one might dislike aspects of Ottoman practice—and few positively liked this—the empire must be preserved. The condition of this was reform of government along broadly western European lines, and it was this strategy that the British pressed on Istanbul throughout. This basic concept survived to 1914, though there was a minority view, typified by Wilfred Scawen Blunt and, less significantly, David Urquhart later on, that the Ottomans were unreformable and that it would be better for the empire to be split up and the Middle Eastern components to become Arab states.

Nevertheless, while preservation was still the British aim in 1914, as shown by their attempts to prevent the Ottomans from allying with the Germans, there were also thoughts about possible international partition along informal lines. As early as 1904, when the Anglo-French Entente was formed, Britain accepted that France had a prior claim to Syria as part compensation for Paris accepting the British position in Egypt. Although France was a small trading partner she was the leading investor in the Ottoman empire and in particular in utilities in Syria. Between then and 1914 there were covert discussions between Britain, France, and Germany over a possible division of the Middle East into spheres of interest. France would take a dominant position in Syria and Germany in Anatolia, closely connected with the planned Berlin to Baghdad railway. A crucial element here was that the Baghdad to Basra section was to be built and run by an international consortium to prevent German direct access to the Persian Gulf.[9] So, although no precise pattern of partition was agreed, the concept was clearly there and the French had already staked their particular interest. This is one reason why the inter-Allied debate over future territorial allocations was so complicated.[10]

Once war was declared in November 1914, positions had to be adopted. As early as 15 August 1914, while still negotiating to keep the Ottomans neutral,

[9] See S. A. Cohen, *British Policy in Mesopotamia 1903–1914* (London, 1976) for details of these negotiations.

[10] For a detailed examination of British and French attitudes to the Ottoman Near East see R. I. Khalidi, *British Policy towards Syria and Palestine, 1906–1914* (London, 1980), chs. 1–3, which argues that the basic principles of partition, and also of British determination to control Sinai and Palestine for the defence of Egypt, were established by 1912.

Sir Edward Grey, British Foreign Secretary, had written to the British Ambassador in Paris:

The proper course was to make Turkey feel that, should she remain neutral and should Germany and Austria be defeated, we would take care that the integrity of Turkish possessions as they now were would be preserved in any terms of peace affecting the Near East; but that, on the other hand, if Turkey sided with Germany and Austria and they were defeated, of course we could not answer for what might be taken from Turkey in Asia Minor.[11]

And in November he made it clear that the Ottoman empire would be broken up if the Allies were victorious. The question then was who would take what.

On the Allied side two states were clear in their aims. The Russians wanted what they had always wanted: the northern side of the Sea of Marmora, Istanbul, control of the Straits, and the eastern section of Anatolia with its substantial Armenian population. This was to be expected. Also predictable was the French position, though unlike both Russia and Britain France had no territorial stake in the Middle East. Its stake consisted of a complex of 'sentimental', financial, and religious involvements, particularly in the vilayets of Beirut (including the sanjaq of Mount Lebanon), Aleppo, and Suriyya (whose centre was Damascus), and in the sanjaq of Jerusalem. In Lebanon there were close connections between the French Catholic Church and the Maronites, and there were a number of French missionaries there. In Jerusalem the French claimed a protectorate over all Catholic interests. They owned and ran several railways in Palestine, and the silk industry of Lyon had an interest in the silk production of Lebanon.

It had long been recognized in Europe that France had a prior claim to some form of control or influence over Syria should the occasion arise.[12] Yet the French claim to Syria was based also on an amorphous nationalist impulse that was centred on and mobilized by a number of imperialist organizations. None of these was large in membership but they included a number of key politicians who, once war was declared, were able to manipulate French policy.[13] The main umbrella organization was the Parti Colonial, dominated by Eugène Etienne. Those who had most influence on government policy after 1914 were members of the subsidiary organization, Comité de l'Asie Française (CAF): Philippe Berthelot, Robert de Caix, François Georges-Picot. Stephen Pichon, Foreign Minister from 1906–11, 1912–13, and 1917–20, was a member of two other small organizations, the Comité de l'Orient (CO) and the Comité de Défense des Intérêts Français en Orient (CDIFO). Given the weakness of virtually all French governments in this period, a few men at the centre of affairs were able to swing government policy by intrigue and publicity. Already, before 1914, these organizations had been

---

[11] Quoted in Macfie, *The End*, 123.

[12] Elizabeth Monroe, in *The Mediterranean in Politics* (London, 1938), suggested that France aimed to convert the Mediterranean into virtually a French lake: the Near East would complement French control of most of North Africa.

[13] The best account of these is in Andrew and Kanya-Forstner, *France Overseas*, esp. ch. 1.

campaigning for French control of some kind over what they called 'la Syrie intégrale', which would run from the Taurus mountains in the north to the Egyptian borders in the south and would include much of the Arabian desert. They appeared to have received confirmation of these claims at least to a sphere of interest from Sir Edward Grey in 1912, and this was confirmed in the Franco-Turkish accord over railway concessions in April 1914. But even so, many French jingos were dissatisfied because the Germans had obtained the larger share and in particular the area north of Aleppo, including the key port of Alexandretta. War seemed to provide the opportunity to rectify this at the expense of Germany.

Nevertheless, when war broke out, the French government under René Viviani had no clear war aims in the Middle East: its primary objective was to regain Alsace Lorraine, though Gaston Doumergue as Minister for Colonies was an overseas expansionist. The CAF was split, some fearing that partition would only benefit Britain. The main supporters of a strategy to get political control of Syria for France were Albert Defrance, the French minister in Cairo and one-time member of the Quai d'Orsay's Levant section, and Picot, consul in Beirut, who was removed to Cairo before he could organize a Maronite rising against the Turks. By the end of 1914 there were plans for sending a small French detachment to Syria should the British attempt to conquer it. This was approved in principle by Alexandre Millerand as Minister of War and reluctantly accepted by Théophile Delcassé, hero of Morocco and now again Foreign Minister, simply to block a potential British acquisition. In the event no French troops were sent. Early in 1915, when the Dardanelles expedition was under preparation, Paris was horrified that it would be under British control, since the Mediterranean was supposed to be a French naval command, and because it was feared that the British would take Alexandretta and thus dominate the north of Syria. In February 1915 Grey met Delcassé and it was agreed that France should have prior claim on Alexandretta and Syria if the Ottoman empire was partitioned, though what 'Syria' would comprise was not defined. Delcassé, however, remained hostile to formal partition of the Middle East: he preferred spheres of influence.

French ambitions in the Middle East were, therefore, reasonably clear, even if the limits of Syria were not. But it was beyond their capacity to achieve these. Their military commitments in Europe made it impossible for them to take a leading role in the Middle Eastern war. Their recourse was diplomacy and their strongest card the British concern not to alienate them. It was left to the British and Russians to fight the Ottomans, while the French insisted on building their demands into the tortuous negotiations that led to the Sykes–Picot Agreement of 1916. It was appropriate that Picot, as the French negotiator of the Agreement, should have been one of the leading expansionists of the Quai d'Orsay's staff and one who, in common with those operating on the British side from Cairo, saw the issues from a Middle Eastern rather than a European perspective.

The greatest irony of the Middle Eastern war is that the British, who played the greatest part in the defeat of the Ottomans, should have had initially the most limited range of objectives there. This was in one sense because they were already a satisfied power in the region with control of Egypt and the Suez canal and a number of treaties with states in the Persian Gulf. For them Arabia was primarily a route to India and the east that had to be kept open against Ottoman and German threats. It was also an area under the responsibility of the Indian Government and India Office, and only indirectly of the other British departments. By 1914 there was one other primary concern: the British navy had for some years been converting its ships from coal to oil, and the oil of southern Persia and the refinery at Abadan on the Gulf were British controlled and seen as critical for the war effort. The result was that the first significant British action against the Ottomans was the occupation of Basra with an expeditionary force from India in November 1914. The Foreign Office had no larger plans and there were no pressure groups in Britain comparable to those in France. In fact, the British government did not seriously consider its Middle Eastern objectives until March 1915, and then mainly because the Russians were demanding a diversionary British expedition to the Dardanelles to take Ottoman pressure off them in the Caucasus. The British government typically set up the de Bunsen Committee representing the main departments concerned—War Office, Admiralty, Foreign Office, and India Office—to define British war aims in the region.

The de Bunsen Committee came out against formal partition of the Middle East into colonies or protectorates, preferring zones of interest along pre-war lines. They prepared a map showing possible zones of interest, which in some ways resembled the eventual San Remo divisions of 1920, except for the Russian share. Russia was to be dominant in eastern Anatolia and to control Istanbul and the Straits. France was to dominate Syria, the British would have a sphere of interest in Mesopotamia and would control the port of Haifa as a possible terminal for a railway to Baghdad. It was suggested that 'Syria' should stretch across northern Mesopotamia in order to create a barrier between the British zone and the expected Russian zone in eastern Anatolia and the Caucasus. These proposals were, in fact, simply an extension of pre-1914 diplomatic negotiations. They were in no sense binding and would depend on the fortunes of war, in particular the Dardanelles campaign of 1915–16 and British success in defending Egypt against the Ottoman attacks on the canal during 1915 and 1916. A debated issue was whether it was necessary to defend Basra in depth against the determined Ottoman attempts to retake it, which implied that the Indian Expeditionary Force should fight its way up to Baghdad. This was not authorized until April 1915 and was then unsuccessful: the main forward troops had to retreat to Kut-al-Amara, where they were besieged and surrendered in 1916. It was not until late in 1916 that the campaign to take Baghdad was resumed, once more to relieve pressure on the Russians rather than for its own sake; and the city was not taken until August 1917. In short, as seen from London, the Middle East was a sideshow in the war. It was primarily defensive (for Egypt or the Red Sea and Persian Gulf) or a means of distracting Ottoman troops from the Russian front. Final dispositions could be left until the final peace negotiations, and until then there could be no firm commitments.

This conventional scenario was hopelessly confused by what can best be described as the sub-imperialism of the British in Cairo. This was to produce perhaps the most controversial and confused set of British commitments in any war, and what happened remains highly controversial. It is at this point that the two themes of British expansionism and Arab nationalism came together for the first time, with highly problematical results.[14] But before examining the much-debated commitment to the Hashemites of 1915–16 it is proposed to follow through the logic of the earlier partition schemes to the so-called Sykes–Picot Agreement of 1916.

The need for an Anglo-French agreement over the future of Asia Minor was essentially the product of Russian pressure in March 1915 for a formal Allied commitment to satisfy Russian demands, in particular for Istanbul and the Straits. Grey was prepared to accept this, provided British and French 'desiderata' (a term constantly used at the time for war aims) in the Ottoman empire and Persia were satisfied. Delcassé was initially appalled by this but eventually agreed, provided Russia accepted French demands for an extended Syria. In Britain this was reported to cabinet and led to the de Bunsen Committee. But French agreement to Russian demands was not reported to the French cabinet. Thereafter those French expansionists in the know began a campaign to get firm commitments on French demands from Britain. Among these was Georges-Picot (hereafter Picot), now back in Paris from Beirut. In order to overcome Delcassé's dislike of the Syrian project he and his CAF allies mounted a parliamentary campaign to arouse support. In May 1915, with the backing of the Senator Etienne Flandin, of the pressure group Amis de l'Orient, he got parliament to adopt Flandin's report on Syria and partition of the Ottoman empire, to include Mosul in the French sphere. Picot then went to London as adviser to the French Ambassador Paul Cambon and persuaded him to recommend that he should negotiate a partition of the Middle East with Britain. By this time, although few French actually cared about Syria, French public opinion was now determined that it should not go to Britain. As M. Bompard, previously French Ambassador in Istanbul, and no enthusiast for French claims in the area, put it to Picot in September 1915:

Unhappily the die is cast. You and your Syrian enthusiasts have roused public opinion. Henceforth it will be on your side and we shall have no option but to add Syria to the too-numerous lands which we already control. It now remains for those who have been more far-sighted to reduce the burdens of this operation to the minimum possible. There is only one way of achieving this: to extend the limits of Syria from Egypt to the Taurus mountains, and to push its hinterland beyond Mosul to include half the Baghdad railway. This is what I shall work for henceforth in agreement with you.[15]

---

[14] There is a detailed recent analysis of both issues in I. Friedman, *Palestine: A Twice-Promised Land?* I. *The British, the Arabs and Zionism, 1915–1920* (New Brunswick and London, 2000).
[15] Quoted ibid. 77.

Yet it was Britain who actually started the negotiations. In October 1915 Sir Edward Grey, though no enthusiast for the Middle East, took two steps of momentous significance. First he authorized the High Commissioner in Cairo, Sir Henry McMahon, to give 'cordial assurances' to the Sharif Husayn about British support for his ambitions, though ambiguously excluding Mersina, Alexandretta, Lebanon, and Palestine. This was to result in the commitments made by McMahon in his crucial letter of 24 October, which will be considered below. Second, Grey proposed Anglo-French negotiations concerning Syria, and Picot was nominated by Cambon to conduct these. Thus on the French side their negotiator was one of the most enthusiastic 'Syrians' in the French public service. He was instructed from Paris to negotiate for the whole of Syria to the borders of Egypt and east to Mosul and the Persian frontier. On the British side was Sir Mark Sykes. Sykes was the sixth baronet of his line, a land-owner and before-1914 an extensive traveller in the Middle East. He was a member of parliament and after 1914 was attached as adviser on Middle Eastern affairs in the Foreign Office. He was also an adviser to Lord Kitchener, previously High Commissioner in Egypt but now Secretary of State for War and deeply committed to an extension of British power in the Red Sea and Persian Gulf. Sykes had been a member of the de Bunsen Committee, where he pressed Kitchener's ideas. In 1915 Sykes was reluctant to see France get Syria. Having previously been a supporter of continued Ottoman rule, he now believed that the Arabs should have some form of self-government. France should get compensation elsewhere, with rights over industrial and railway enterprises in Syria. Ottoman Asia Minor should come under a sultan of Egypt and the 'spiritual dominion' of the Sharif of Mecca, that is, under effective British over-rule. At the least Britain must have a broad swathe of territory from south Kurdistan to Haifa and Acre and south to Aqaba as a buffer against France in Syria.

The Anglo-French negotiations began on 23 November 1915, Picot and Sykes being supported by permanent officials from the Foreign Office, India Office, and Quai d'Orsay. The positions adopted by the two sides were, in effect, those of Cairo and the French colonial parties. Picot, while knowing about it, ignored the promise made by McMahon to the Sharif the previous month. He, along with Grey, assumed that it would be impossible for Arabs to govern themselves independently. Backed by the Quai d'Orsay, he demanded effective French rule over all western Syria, including Palestine, the interior to be a French sphere of influence with nominal Arab sovereignty, but with French residents to advise the confederated amirs, who were to come from the Hashemite family. This was approved by Paris. The second round of talks started on 21 December 1915. At this point the British position hardened. Sykes, as a Kitchener mouthpiece, was determined to detach Palestine from Syria. He attempted to get Lebanon, Beirut, and Tripoli made a nominal part of the new Arab state of Syria, though under the control of a French governor. This was rejected by Picot. After much haggling, Sykes accepted that Lebanon and the rest of coastal Syria, along with part of south-east Anatolia, would be detached from inland Syria and would come under some form of direct French rule. Inland Syria, stretching to include Mosul, would be an Arab country under French supervision: this was acceptable to Britain to provide a barrier between British-controlled southern Mesopotamia and the prospective Russian territory of Armenia. Sykes's greatest success was in getting Palestine, extended north from the sanjaq of Jerusalem, declared an international zone, though Britain was to occupy the ports of Haifa and Acre to provide access to a conceptual railway to Baghdad. Provisional allocations of parts of Anatolia were made for Italy, which had joined the Entente in April 1915 on the understanding that it would be allowed to retain the Dodecanese and also 'an equitable share' in the Mediterranean region adjoining the province of Adalia (Antalya) in the event of the total or partial partition of Turkey in Asia.[16] Even Greece, which did not enter the war until 1917, was allocated a slice of Anatolia north of Smyrna: this was part of a complex Allied attempt to influence domestic Greek politics. The King, Constantine I, was a German, cousin of the Kaiser, and keen to join the Central Powers. His Prime Minister, Venizelos, was in favour of the Entente. This produced a stalemate and Greece stayed neutral. In 1915 the Allies had invaded Salonika, nominally to help the Serbs. Venizelos went to Salonika and set up a rival Greek government with Allied support. Hence the allocation of part of Anatolia to Greece. Ultimately, Greece was forced to join the Allies after a British naval force attacked the Piraeus in June 1917 and Greece joined the Entente, so justifying her promised reward. This was to cause immense difficulties in Turkey after the end of the war.

Sykes and Picot signed the draft agreement on 31 January 1916. It was then reviewed by the French government and, while some ministers were unhappy with the exclusion of Palestine from the French zone, was finally accepted in modified form early in February by both British and French governments. There were two conditions: it was to come into effect only when and if the Arab revolt started, and it was subject to Russian agreement. Sykes and Picot therefore went to Petrograd and got Russian approval, subject to some frontier modifications in the Mosul region. The Russians also secretly promised to back France in its determination to get all Palestine. In its revised version the Agreement was ratified by all three allies on 15–16 May 1916. On 5 June Husayn formally rebelled against the Ottomans, thus bringing the Agreement into effect.[17]

Although the Sykes–Picot Agreement was now official Allied policy, it was not a treaty. Nor was it public, but what President Wilson denounced as one of the 'secret treaties', though Kedourie maintains that Husayn was made aware of the main elements. Nor was it at all certain that the Allies would be in a position to act on the Agreement. When it was finally ratified they had made very little impact on the Ottomans in the Middle East. The Dardanelles had been evacuated. The Turks were still threatening Egypt. In Mesopotamia the British were only in

---

[16] Quoted Macfie, *The End*, 110.   [17] See map 2.

control of Basra vilayet. It was entirely unclear whether the Arab revolt would come to anything: first indications were unpromising. Kedourie famously declared that the Agreement was 'the last responsible attempt on the part of Europe to cope with the dissolution of the Ottoman Empire, and to prevent the dissolution from bringing disaster'.[18] But its future was entirely unclear. The Agreement was subsequently denounced by Arab nationalists on the grounds that it denied the Arabs the sovereign independence they thought they had been promised, and many historians, following Antonius, agreed with them. Moreover, it never came fully into effect. The Russians withdrew after the Revolution of 1917, publicizing the Agreement for the first time; and the Greeks and Italians were ultimately chased out of Anatolia. The French did not create that confederacy of Arab states in their planned sphere of interest in inland Syria that was predicted in the negotiations. In 1919 the British persuaded the French to transfer the Mosul vilayet to their sphere of influence. The future of Palestine remained uncertain until 1920, and it required ingenious British playing of the Zionist card to ensure that it did not fall under French control and became a British mandate rather than an international zone. Yet in many respects the post-war and long-term shape of the Middle East was determined by the Sykes–Picot Agreement and its repercussions were being felt in the twenty-first century.

By far the most controversial aspect of the Agreement was its alleged incompatibility with the promises being made while it was being prepared to the Sharif Husayn, and it is now necessary to turn to these.[19]

A fundamental fact here is that the Middle East was the joint concern of at least four British departments in London—the Foreign Office, the India Office, the War Office, and the Admiralty. In addition, the High Commission in Cairo, as the only British authority in the region with knowledge of local conditions, was in a position to run what was effectively its own foreign policy in the area, even though it was answerable to the Foreign Office. The outcome was a classic case of continuous administrative confusion in which Cairo commonly played the active role and the various London departments had to react.

The story began before the war in February 1914 when Husayn's second son, Abdullah, was in Cairo. While there he asked if Britain would help the Sharif if, as was then expected, Istanbul removed him or imposed more direct control over the Hijaz. In fact the immediate threat to Husayn disappeared in a compromise worked out with the Porte; but in April 1914 Abdullah was again negotiating with Ronald Storrs, then Oriental Secretary in Cairo and a self-proclaimed expert in Arabic and Arabian affairs. Storrs later claimed that nothing of substance was

---

[18] Kedourie, *England and the Middle East*, 65–6.

[19] The following is based mainly on Kedourie, *Into the Anglo-Arab Labyrinth* (hereafter *Labyrinth*). See also Friedman, *Palestine: A Twice-Promised Land?*, which argues in great detail that there was never any British intention of including Palestine within the area promised to Husayn, with the implication that it was therefore available to be offered to the Zionists. For the origins of the policy of alliance with the Hashemites see T. J. Paris, *Britain, the Hashemites and Arab Rule, 1920–1925: The Sherifian Solution* (London, 2003).

discussed except that Abdullah asked if Britain would supply the Sharif with machine guns in case he was attacked by the Turks. These were refused, but Storrs claimed that they parted 'on the best of terms'.[20] Kedourie, who made Storrs play a leading and confusing role in later developments, suggested, however, that Storrs went further than he reported and told Abdullah that he had been aiming for ten years at some form of British suzerainty over southern Arabia. But by September 1914, with war against Germany in progress and the position of Turkey uncertain, Kitchener, now Secretary of State for War in London but still regarding Cairo as his fief to which he expected to return, instructed Storrs to discover whether the Sharif would be for or against Britain if the Ottomans declared war. Abdullah replied that the Sharif would back Britain provided it would protect him against the Turks. On 31 October, when the Ottomans were on the brink of declaring war against the Allies, Kitchener therefore instructed Cairo that the Sharif should be told that 'If the Arab nation assists England ... England will guarantee that no internal intervention takes place in Arabia, and will give Arabs every assistance against external aggression. It may be that an Arab of true race will assume the Khalifate at Mecca and Medina ...'.[21] This was related by Storrs to Abdullah in an embellished form which included the phrase 'the cause of the Arabs'. This was followed by a proclamation issued on 5 December, possibly also drafted by Storrs, which promised that if the Arabs drove out the Turks Britain would recognize their 'perfect independence'. It also stated that the Arabs had the best claim on the Caliphate. In April 1915, probably to ensure the Sharif's neutrality, these promises were expanded by Cairo by embellishing a telegram from the Foreign Office. Britain now promised the Arabs that 'The Arabian peninsula and its Mahommedan holy places should remain independent. We shall not annex one foot of land in it, nor suffer any other Power to do so.'

These announcements constituted a serious gage to fortune. Cairo might claim that the language was general and the commitment undefined; but to the Arabs in Mecca they seemed a firm commitment by Britain, and it was on that basis that the correspondence between McMahon in Cairo and Husayn in Mecca was conducted. The main initiative was taken by Abdullah, who started a bargaining process to obtain the maximum British offers, possibly influenced by news of British failure in the Dardanelles which made Arab support more significant. In Cairo on 14 July 1915 he claimed for the 'Arab Nation' the whole of the Arabian peninsula bounded by Persia, the Indian Ocean, the Red Sea, and the Mediterranean as far north as Mersina, excepting only the British colony of Aden. He wanted a formal British acceptance both of this and also the Sharif's claim to the Caliphate. There should be a mutual defence treaty, the Capitulations should

---

[20] R. Storrs, *Orientations* (London, 1937), 142–3. A footnote on p. 143 includes an extract from a letter from Kitchener to the Foreign Office in which he said that Storrs, instructed by Kitchener, had told Abdullah that 'the Arabs of the Hejaz [*sic*] could expect no encouragement from us and that our only interest in Arabia was the safety and comfort of Indian pilgrims [to Mecca]'.

[21] Kedourie, *Labyrinth*, 18.

be abolished, and an answer provided within thirty days. Such demands from a puny Arab amirate dependent almost entirely on the profits of the Haj to Mecca (then largely suspended) were extraordinary. It says much about the lack of British confidence after the disastrous experience of that year in both France and the Dardanelles that it was even taken seriously. At that time of crisis Husayn seemed the best option available since he had considerable cachet in the Arab world. As it was, the Foreign Office told McMahon to keep up discussions with Mecca on both Arab rule and the Caliphate. As was to become the norm in this affair, Cairo replied in florid language that raised Husayn's hopes further than London, and especially the India Office, intended. As a result, on 9 September, Husayn went one stage further and demanded an agreement on the boundaries of his claimed Arab state. He even threatened Arab action against the British it nothing acceptable was offered.

It was at this point that pressure was placed on the negotiations by one of the first Ottoman officers to defect, who arrived in Cairo in September claiming the existence of a powerful Arab nationalist organization in Syria which was capable to swinging the Ottoman army there in support of the Arab cause. This was Lieutenant Mohammed Sharif al-Faruqi, born in Mosul and previously ADC to the Ottoman commander of the 12th Army Corps. Conversely he threatened that if Britain did not meet Arab demands the Arab officers would support the Ottomans. In fact any chance of an Arab military rebellion in Syria was already over. Jemal Pasha as commander-in-chief in Syria had information derived from material left in the one-time French consulates in Beirut and elsewhere about anti-Ottoman organizations. He was already transferring Arab army units elsewhere and replacing them with Turkish troops. In August he had hanged eleven local notables and was to hang a further twenty-one in January 1916. Yet Gilbert Clayton, a retired captain in the Egyptian army then in charge of military intelligence in Cairo, seems to have been ignorant of this and to have believed al-Faruqi without properly evaluating his allegations. So did General Sir John Maxwell, commander of British forces in Egypt. Reports accepting al-Faruqi's arguments were sent by McMahon to the Foreign Office and by Maxwell to Kitchener. When Kitchener demanded more detail, Maxwell telegraphed urging quick action. Moreover he assumed at that al-Faruqi, although he had never had any contact with Mecca, was supporting the Sharif's pretensions. Hence he argued that 'unless we make definite and agreeable proposals to the Shereef at once, we may have united Islam against us'. Spelling out what this might entail, Maxwell argued for some definite territorial commitment to the Sharif. In particular, 'even if we insist on retaining the Villayet of [Basra] as British, the rest of Mesopotamia must be included in the negotiation, likewise on the West, the Arab party will, I think, insist on Homs, Aleppo, Hama and Damascus being in their sphere'.[22]

This was the first time that these Syrian cities had been mentioned in correspondence with London and seems to have reflected Clayton's report of al-Faruqi's

[22] Kedourie, *Labyrinth*, 79–80.

demands. They were to play a leading role in later negotiations. But this was by no means all that al-Faruqi was prepared to demand. In November he told Sykes, who was passing through Cairo, that the Arabs wanted the whole of Syria, subject to the French having a monopoly of concessions in the region west of the Euphrates. But it seems likely that al-Faruqi had indicated that this was a bargaining position and that the 'Arab party' would be content with an independent state consisting of these four named places. How they came to be specified remains conjectural. Kedourie says that al-Faruqi claimed that the idea, which had no geographical or political rationale, came from the British side and thinks it likely that it came from Storrs. These four towns were never part of the crusading Latin empire and Storrs, who knew his Gibbon, may have suggested that they form the core of the proposed Arab state as both a means of reducing the Sharif's territorial ambitions and as 'an esoteric and obscure historical allusion'.[23] Whatever its origin, this quartet was to play a crucial role in what followed.

It is clear that McMahon took al-Faruqi's demands at face value, even though the Sharif did not even know of his existence. He sent telegrams to London urging quick acceptance of part at least of the Sharif's demands as interpreted by al-Faruqi. Despite doubts on the part of some senior permanent officials, Grey sent a telegram on 20 October in which, subject to reservations about the claims of France, and the probability of British control in Mesopotamia extending north of Basra, and the preservation of British treaties with Arab rulers, he gave McMahon a remarkably free hand in what he should offer Husayn.

But the important thing is to give our assurances that will prevent Arabs from being alienated, and I must leave you discretion in the matter as it is urgent and there is not time to discuss an exact formula.

The simplest plan would be to give an assurance of Arab independence saying that we will proceed at once to discuss boundaries if they will send representatives for that purpose, but if something more precise than this is required you can give it.[24]

An imperial government with very wide experience of the unreliability of proconsuls in executing British government policies should have known better than to give McMahon so much discretion. The result was that, out of this mélange of reports and unchecked assertions, emerged the famous letter from McMahon to Husayn of 24 October 1915. The key passages are as follows.

The districts of Mersina and Alexandretta and portions of Syria lying to the west of the districts of Damascus, Hama, Homs and Aleppo cannot be said to be purely Arab and should be excluded from the proposed limits and boundaries.

With the above modification, and without prejudice to our existing treaties with Arab chiefs, we accept those limits and boundaries, and in regard to those portions of the territories wherein Great Britain is free to act without detriment to her Ally, France, I am empowered in the name of the Government of Great Britain to give you the following assurances and make the following reply to your letter:-

Subject to the above modifications, Great Britain is prepared to recognize and support the independence of the Arabs within the territories included in the limits and boundaries proposed by the Sherif of Mecca.

Great Britain will guarantee the Holy Places against all external aggression and will recognize their inviolability.

When the situation admits, Great Britain will give to the Arabs her advice and will assist them to establish what may appear to be the most suitable forms of government in those various territories.

On the other hand, it is understood that the Arabs have decided to seek the advice and assistance of Great Britain only, and that such European Advisers and officials as may be required in the formation of a sound form of administration will be British.

With regard to the Vilayets of Baghdad and Basra, the Arabs will recognize that the established position and interests of Great Britain necessitates special measures of administrative control in order to secure these territories from foreign aggression, to promote the welfare of the local populations and to secure our mutual economic interests.[25]

Since this was to become virtually a sacred text, subject to intensive interpretation, it is important to pinpoint some of its main ambiguities and omissions.

First, when it was written the Sykes–Picot negotiations were still a month off, and it was unclear what French pretensions might be, though it was known that they would include the seaboard areas of Syria. Conversely Sykes–Picot had to incorporate the main elements of the McMahon letter into their scheme, thus, in Kedourie's estimation, making them fully compatible.

Second, the phrase excluding territories 'lying to the west of the districts of Damascus, Hama, Homs and Aleppo' was extremely ambiguous. The first three of these were cities within the vilayet (province) of Damascus, which was the capital. Aleppo was the capital of a vilayet which included Alexandretta. Mersin lay in the vilayet of Adana. Clearly McMahon had implied that the four cities should form the western edge of the proposed Arab state, but this was quite uncertain in the text.

Third, as the India Office pointed out, the reference to Basra and Baghdad as requiring only 'special measures' was incompatible with the de Bunsen Committee's proposals and the Indian government's close interest in their future.

Finally, and perhaps most important, the McMahon letter made no mention of Palestine. Did it lie 'to the west' of the Damascus to Aleppo line? If not, it presumably lay within the area designated an Arab state. In that case both France and Russia, with intense concern about its Christian holy places, were likely to object

[25] Kedourie, *Labyrinth*, 97. There is a slightly different version of this letter in G. Antonius, *The Arab Awakening* (London, 1938; 1945), app. 4, pp. 419–20. The main point of difference is that Antonius, translating from the Arabic version, claimed that in the last paragraph the correct reading was 'special administrative arrangements', not 'special measures of administrative control', so refuting the British claim to 'control' Mesopotamia.

strongly. If it was west of the line, then the Arabs would have a grievance, as indeed they did and continued to proclaim for the next decades.[26]

Given these ambiguities and absurdities the most that can be said of the McMahon letter of 24 October 1915 is that it was an attempt to ensure Arab support for the Allied cause at a time when the Gallipoli expedition was clearly on the brink of final disaster and when the British push north from Basra had been repulsed. London clearly did not take the idea of a vast Arab state seriously. Grey told Austen Chamberlain, now Secretary of State for India, later in October 1915 that the disposition of Mesopotamia was unimportant since 'the whole thing was a castle in the air which would never materialize'.[27] Chamberlain in turn insisted that the offer to Husayn was in any case contingent on his starting an Arab revolt against the Turks. Since this did not start until June 1916 the next months were taken up by continuous and highly hypothetical negotiations between Cairo and Mecca over the precise limits of the proposed Arab state, Husayn even having the effrontery to demand a rent from the British for their occupation of Basra and part of the Baghdad vilayet. Meantime the Sykes–Picot negotiations continued and the Agreement was finally ratified ten days after the Arab revolt began on 5 June 1916.

The military significance of the Arab revolt has been much debated. The Arab version, as later codified by Antonius, was that it was heroic, animated by Arab nationalism, and militarily critical for the Allied conquest of Palestine and Syria. Antonius claimed that the Arab army tied up more Turkish troops than faced Allenby in Palestine, perhaps some 30,000, and that they prevented the Turks and Germans from linking Syria with the Red Sea and giving access to the campaign in East Africa. From another angle it was clear by October 1916 that, left to themselves and even with British-supplied equipment and money, the Arabs were unlikely to achieve much. They had taken Jedda and Mecca, but never took Medina. Thereafter control of the revolt was taken by T. E. Lawrence, backed by a number of mostly Iraqi ex-Ottoman officers, who were able to instil some discipline into the beduin troops, themselves fighting mainly for money and loot. Their guerrilla tactics were successful as a distraction for the Turks from the main battlegrounds of Palestine and Mesopotamia and were given romantic popular appeal by Lawrence's later work, *The Seven Pillars of Wisdom*. It was Lawrence who supported Faysal, Husayn's third son, as a worthy Arab leader and led him into Damascus in October 1918: although Australian troops were there already, Allenby allowed Faysal's army symbolically to enter first and made him military governor of Syria.[28]

From 1916 to the end of the war with the Ottomans in October 1918 the main focus on the Middle East, apart from the military campaigns, was the continued

---

[26] Although unstated, an underlying theme of much of Kedourie's text seems to be that Palestine was never intended to lie within the proposed Arab state and that the British support for a Zionist enterprise there was therefore legitimate.   [27] Kedourie, *Labyrinth*, 108.

[28] There is an interesting assessment of Lawrence in Kedourie, *England and the Middle East*, ch. 4. Kedourie suggests that Lawrence knew that Husayn was aware of the Sykes–Picot Agreement before it was publicized by the Soviets in November 1917, and did not expect the whole of Arabia as his

bickering between Britain and France over the interpretation and implementation of the Sykes–Picot Agreement. In France the colonial groups continued to demand 'la Syrie intégrale' but conditions were turning against them. By the end of 1916 the British in Egypt were poised to attack al Arish (ironically partly to support the failing Hijaz campaign) and start their assault on Palestine. The French response, led by Lyautey, now War Minister, was that, to prevent a British takeover, there should be 3,000 French troops in this campaign and that Palestine, once conquered, should be jointly administered by Sykes and Picot as High Commissioners. This proved quite impractical: there were no French troops available, so the Palestine campaign was fought by British imperial forces. This gave Britain a dominant position which was exploited by Lloyd George, the new British Prime Minister from December 1916. Lloyd George, unlike his predecessor Asquith, was determined that Palestine, by which he meant biblical Palestine, should be under British control, and was prepared to outface the French on it. He was also enthusiastic for the Zionist cause; and in conjunction these facts were to prove fatal to French pretensions in Syria.

The year 1917 was to prove critical for the partition of the Middle East. First, the fall of the Tsarist regime in Russia, resulting in the publication by the Bosheviks in November of the Sykes–Picot terms and the withdrawal of Russia from the war, changed the whole situation. Effectively this freed Britain from the Sykes–Picot commitments and made the plan for an extensive west-to-east French sphere of interest to provide a barrier between Russia in the Caucasus and Britain in Mesopotamia irrelevant. Second, the conquest of Jerusalem by December 1917 and the Balfour Declaration of 2 November promising the Zionists 'a home for the Jews' in Palestine gave Britain trump cards. The Zionists, led by Chaim Weizmann and Nahum Sokolov, were determined that Palestine should come under British control. During 1917 Sokolov had acted as emissary for the Zionists in attempting to get Allied approval for a Zionist settlement in Palestine. He obtained vaguely favourable statements from the Italian government and the Vatican, but the most he could obtain from Paris was a letter from Jules Cambon as Secretary-General of the Foreign Ministry in June 1917 which stated that it would be 'a deed of justice and of reparation to assist . . . in the renaissance of the Jewish nationality in that Land from which the people of Israel were exiled so many centuries ago'.[29] That left the question of political control open, since the French might equally have supported a Zionist enterprise. But the Zionists were determined that the protector should be Britain and this, together with British military domination, was fatal to the French claim that Palestine was integral with Syria.

kingdom. But Lawrence pretended that the Allies had offered Husayn all that he had asked for and from 1919 campaigned for an Arab Syria. Yet Lawrence did not really believe in the capacity of Arabs to establish and run such a state: it would have to be created for them, a feeling he shared with Gertrude Bell.

[29] L. Stein, *The Balfour Declaration* (London, 1961), 416. For the details of this and the whole Zionist enterprise see Ch. 4, below.

Almost equally fatal to the survival of Sykes–Picot and French claims to Palestine was the fact that Georges Clemenceau became French Prime Minister in November 1917. Clemenceau had never been an enthusiast for overseas empire: his concern was always for the German frontier and Alsace-Lorraine. In November 1917 he told Lloyd George that he did not want Syria for France but would accept a protectorate if offered, 'to please some reactionaries'.[30] He effectively gave Lloyd George a free hand to determine the future of the Middle East. The result was a gradual undermining of Sykes–Picot in 1918, helped by the influence of Lord Curzon in the Eastern Committee of the British cabinet. In September 1918 Picot signed a new agreement with Sykes, plus Lord Robert Cecil of the Foreign Office and Lord Crewe, a previous Colonial Secretary. Occupied Enemy Territory Administration (OETA) West, which included Lebanon, was to be under Picot as High Commissioner of a French administration. OETA East, the old 'A' zone of Sykes–Picot, including most of inland Syria, was to be under Allenby's military government, but Picot would act as his chief political adviser. This latter proposal was overtaken by the occupation of Damascus and the appointment of Faysal as OETA East's military governor, which led to the creation of a virtually independent Arab state backed by British military forces. Then on 7 November 1918 the British and French governments made a much publicized and eventually ironic commitment to 'the definite emancipation of peoples so long oppressed by the Turks' and to the establishment and recognition of 'national governments . . . deriving their authority from the initiative and free choice of the indigenous populations'. Although in tune with the promises to the Sharif, this was clearly not compatible with the way things were now developing.

With Russia out of the way, the USA not directly involved, and Italy and Greece as mendicant allies out for scraps thrown by the powers, the future of the Middle East now depended on deals between Britain and France. From a British standpoint France was now reverting to being the main enemy it had been before 1904. Much hung on relations between Lloyd George and Clemenceau. While Lloyd George was determined to hold as much as possible of the Middle East, Clemenceau was not really interested in it, though he was infuriated that the British should unilaterally have accepted an Ottoman surrender at Mudros. On 1 December 1918 he verbally assured Lloyd George in London that he accepted British control of the whole of Mesopotamia, including Mosul, along with Palestine. In return France would get Cilicia and Syria. Typically of the French political system, the Quai d'Orsay was not told of this deal, which led to much later misunderstanding and friction. The Foreign Office was not informed either. Thus, when the Versailles peace conference began in January, neither the French nor the British had any clear Middle Eastern policy. Both delegations were divided in their aims. In the British case Lloyd George usually acted independently of his official advisers. The Foreign Office was divided. Balfour, as Foreign Secretary, was in Paris

---

[30] Andrew and Kanya-Forstner, *France Overseas*, 151.

and Curzon, as his understudy in London, had little freedom of action. The War Office was effectively in control of the occupation. T. E. Lawrence operated as a freelance, mostly supporting the Hashemite claims to the whole of Arabia. Faysal, though not accepted as a delegate to the conference, lobbied the various parties for acceptance of his claims to Syria. Meantime President Wilson, representing a deep-rooted American liberal hatred of all forms of imperialism, which many saw as the root of this and most European conflicts, was determined that any annexations by the Allies should be in the form of mandates (temporary trusts) rather than colonies or protectorates. Given these circumstances it was not surprising that the negotiations proved extremely complicated and long-drawn-out.

The main issues, however, were fairly simple. First, would France accept modification of the Sykes–Picot Agreement so that Faysal could establish a more or less autonomous Arab state in inland Syria? Second, would France accept a British mandate in Palestine? Third, would France accept British control over the whole of Mesopotamia, including the projected but not yet developed Mosul oil? Fourth, would the USA be prepared to play an active role, perhaps as a mandatory for Palestine or even the projected Armenia? It would be pointless here to pursue the complicated negotiations over these questions that lasted from early 1919 to July 1920.[31] In practical terms, given French military weakness in the area, most depended on how far the British were prepared to stick by their promises to Husayn and to back Faysal in his claim to be ruler of the whole of Syria. This last point was critical, since once Faysal's Northern Army had been largely dispersed, leaving a group of mostly Iraqi ex-Ottoman officers behind, he depended entirely on British troops and British subsidies. Faysal, negotiating in Paris, wanted a British mandate over a united Syria. He received no support in this, but in July a Syrian Congress, dominated by nationalist members of al-Fatat, rejected a French mandate under any form and demanded an independent Syria including Lebanon. In March 1920 they were to renew this claim and declare Faysal King of Syria.

But this was to ignore the realities of the international system. By August 1919 Clemenceau was becoming hostile to British claims on a number of fronts, and was under pressure from French colonialist groups not to make concessions over oil in Mosul or the boundaries of Syria. For his part, Lloyd George had decided that British military resources were dangerously overstretched with the rebellion in Ireland, troubles in India and Egypt, and discontent in Mesopotamia, which coincided with British demobilization.[32] In London there were fears about Turkish claims to Mosul and about Bolshevik intentions. In September 1919

---

[31] They can be followed in detail in P. C. Heimreich, *From Paris to Sèvres: The Partition of the Ottoman Empire at the Peace Conference of 1919–1920* (Columbus, Ohio, 1974), Andrew and Kanya-Forstner, *France Overseas*, chs. 7–9, and Nevakivi, *Britain, France and the Arab Middle East*, chs. 5–12, among many other accounts.

[32] The argument concerning over-stretch was outlined by Jack Gallagher in his Ford Lectures in 1974, later published as A. Seal (ed.), *The Decline, Revival and Fall of the British Empire* (Cambridge, 1982) and worked out in detail by Gallagher's pupil, John Darwin, in his *Britain, Egypt and the Middle East: Imperial Policy in the Aftermath of War, 1918–1922* (London, 1981).

Lloyd George indicated to the French that British troops would evacuate Syria by November. But the Arabs would be left in control in the areas defined in the Husayn correspondence: that is, in inland Syria. Lloyd George also made it clear that Britain would retain control over Palestine in 'its ancient boundaries', and also Mosul. This provided a flimsy British claim to have honoured at least part of the McMahon promises. It aroused a vehement response from Paris; but in fact it gave France what she really wanted, provided a satisfactory deal was reached over Mosul oil. Once the British were out of Damascus and the French had had time to build up their forces in Beirut, they would be able to deal with Faysal. In October, Clemenceau appointed General Henri Gouraud, a one-time associate of Lyautey in Morocco and a conservative Catholic, as Commander of the Army of the Levant and High Commissioner in Syria, with Robert de Caix, of the Foreign Ministry and a keen Middle East imperialist, as his Secretary-General.[33]

The British withdrawal from Syria, which was accompanied by halving his financial subsidy, left Faysal to make the best terms he could with France. For the moment he was in a relatively strong position since there was no chance of effective French military intervention in Syria. In October, Clemenceau therefore recognized Syria's right to self-government and undertook to guarantee its integrity against foreign intervention. On his side Faysal agreed to accept foreign help only from France. France would handle foreign relations, would advise on administrative and military matters and have priority for economic concessions. This was not very different from the pattern of protected states of the nineteenth and early twentieth centuries, in the French case in Tunis and Morocco. It also resembled the regime set up by the British in Iraq from 1920 to 1932. In many respects also it was consistent with the Sykes–Picot Agreement in that the inland zone A of Syria would be under 'Arab' rule. From the French standpoint this disappointed the keener imperialists since it divided 'la Syrie intégrale', but it would at least enable France to fulfil its promises to the Maronites for a 'Greater Lebanon' and keep Britain out of Syria. Yet this apparent failure over Syria may have contributed to the defeat in January 1920 of Clemenceau as a candidate for the Presidency by Paul Deschanel. Although he had gained huge support in the elections to the Chamber in November 1919, he then resigned as Prime Minister. He was replaced by the much more expansionist Alexandre Millerand and his Bloc National.[34]

This proved another significant turning point for the Middle Eastern settlement. There was a strong, though in the event brief, revival of French interest in the empire which strengthened the government's hands in the key negotiations of 1920. The San Remo conference of the Supreme Council of the Allies tied up many loose ends. It agreed to recommend to the newly established League of

[33] For Gouraud see P. S. Khoury, *Syria and the French Mandate: The Politics of Arab Nationalism, 1920–1945* (London and Princeton, 1987), and esp. for his appointment, 38–9.

[34] Clemenceau allowed his name to be put forward for the Presidential election by the parliament. Straw polls on 16 January showed that he was unlikely to win. He then withdrew and resigned as Prime Minister on 18 January.

Nations that Lebanon and Syria should be French and Mesopotamia and Palestine British mandates. The French still haggled over the Palestine mandate but later accepted the British claim and the Zionist project, privately giving up the French claim to a protectorate over Catholics. The Mosul oil question was settled: France was to get 25 per cent of the crude oil at current market prices, but the concession-holder, the Turkish Petroleum Company (later reconstructed as the Iraq Petroleum Company), was to be under permanent British control. Subsequently the borders between British and French mandates were agreed and completed by a boundary commission. The conference was followed in May 1920 by an armistice between French and Turkish forces under Mustafa Kemal in Cilicia, which freed French troops for Syria.

It is an interesting historical counter-factual to consider what might have happened to Faysal's regime in Syria had he and his supporters there played their hand differently. At San Remo, France had recognized Syria as an 'independent' state and Britain and France agreed on conditions for Faysal's rule. Much therefore depended on whether Faysal and his supporters in Damascus were prepared to play the game according to the rules laid down for them. In the event they did not. Faysal's cabinet in Damascus was dominated by members of al-Fatat, which had aroused great Arabist fervour. They were demanding not only full independence for Syria but the inclusion in it of Palestine and for Mesopotamia to be under the rule of Abdullah: that is, the area allegedly promised by McMahon in 1915. The militant and largely Iraqi organization al-Ahd launched an expedition east towards Mosul and got as far as Tal Afar, before British forces checked them.[35] Meantime the Syrians were sending raiding parties into Lebanon, and there were allegations that they were in league with the Kemalists in Turkey. In other ways also the Syrians showed that they were not willing to accept the role designated for them. They refused to adopt the French franc as their currency and they blocked railways between Syria and Lebanon. In short the minority, predominantly Iraqi, which controlled Damascus demonstrated clearly that they would not accept the French mandate.

Seen from an Arab nationalist standpoint this was understandable and heroic, and has gone down into Arab histories as justifiable defence of promised Syrian independence and unity. But seen in the hard light of European imperialistic attitudes it was suicidal, reflecting the very limited grasp by Syrian nationalists of the realities of the situation. Moreover, while Britain might have supported the Faysal position, this support was forfeited by the al-Ahd attack on Tal Afar during which two British officers and two other ranks were murdered. Faysal's regime thus stood alone. The French waited until 9 July then sent Faysal an ultimatum. He must accept the French mandate unconditionally. France must have control of the Rayyaq–Homs–Hama–Aleppo railway. Conscription for the Syrian army must be

---

[35] For details of this expedition see E. Tauber, *The Formation of Modern Syria and Iraq* (London, 1995), ch. 7.

ended and the military force reduced. The new Syrian franc must be accepted. Faysal appealed to London but got no support. He eventually accepted these conditions but the French held that he had not done so in time. The French army moved up and routed a largely unprofessional Syrian army at Maysalun on 24 July, then occupied Damascus. Faysal was politely invited to leave, which he did, making his way via Palestine to London. The following year he was to be made king of the new Iraq state, to the disgust of the French (see Chapter 3). But for Syria it meant the end of the dream of Arab independence. Syria was not to retain even the trappings of a kingdom, as had Morocco and Tunis. It became in all but name a French colony. The results are described in Chapter 7 below. The French then proceeded to reward their Maronite supporters of the French cause in Lebanon by cutting it off from the rest of Syria and adding the coastal towns of Tripoli, Sidon, Tyre, and Beirut, along with the Biqa valley, to the small sanjaq of Mount Lebanon that was set up in 1861, so as to create a Greater Lebanon. In July 1922 the League of Nations formally recognized Syria and Lebanon as separate 'A' class mandates which France was to prepare for independence. The League also declared Iraq and Palestine to be British mandates, Palestine to include what became Transjordan under the Amir Abdullah.

These arbitrary dispositions ended the Hashemite dream of ruling an undivided Arabia. They left Husayn weaker even than he had been in 1914 to face his local rivals. His main enemy throughout had been Ibn Saud of Riyadh. Their rivalry dated back to 1910 and was part of a purely local power struggle that extended from the Hijaz to the Yemen.[36] A battle between them in 1915 was indecisive. Meantime Ibn Saud grew stronger. He had a treaty with Britain with a subsidy and his army had the religious zeal of the reformist Wahhabist sect. In 1918 trouble flared over the tax obligations of the Shay tribe at the Khurma oasis on the eastern border of the Hijaz, whose local ruler decided to pay to Ibn Saud rather than Husayn. Abdullah, whose personal ambitions were always in this region, detached forces that were supposed to be besieging Medina, still in Turkish hands, After indecisive early battles, in May 1919 Ibn Saud's forces decisively defeated Abdullah's men at Turaba. That proved a turning point in the history of Arabia and of the Hashemites. Thereafter Ibn Saud became progressively stronger. In 1920 his army captured the Asir province between the Hijaz and Yemen. In 1921 he defeated the last of his Arabian rivals, the Rashidi. In 1924 he invaded the Hijaz and took Mecca. Husayn resigned as Sharif in favour of his eldest son, Ali, and retired to Cyprus. Ali had to surrender Medina and Jedda and in 1926 Ibn Saud was proclaimed King of the Hijaz and recognized by Britain. In 1932 he was proclaimed King of Saudi Arabia and controlled the whole peninsula apart from the British-protected shaykhdoms on the Persian Gulf, the British colony of Aden, and the Yemen.

---

[36] There is a useful account of these issues in Mary Wilson, *King Abdullah, Britain and the Making of Jordan* (Cambridge, 1987), ch. 3. For a detailed account of the decline of Husayn and British relations with him see Paris, *Britain, the Hashemites and Arab Rule*, part IV.

This was in a sense the end of the Hashemite dream in its earlier grandiose form. From Husayn's standpoint Britain had dishonestly failed to fulfil its promises. But for his dynasty there were compensations: they came out with a kingdom in Iraq and an amirate, later a kingdom, in Transjordan. Compared with the petty Ottoman province of 1914, Husayn's family had made significant gains. In Iraq they remained rulers until 1958; in Jordan they were still ruling in the twenty-first century.

There remains the future of the rump Ottoman empire in Anatolia and Thrace. Since this did not become part of the post-war mandates system it will be sketched briefly.[37]

It is easy to assume that modern Turkey, as a unitary state consisting of Anatolia and Eastern Thrace, was the natural outcome of a war that had stripped the Ottomans of their remaining Middle Eastern territories. This would be wrong. In 1918 and down to the Treaty of Lausane in July 1923 it was quite uncertain that anything like modern Turkey would emerge. The Armistice of Mudros had, unlike that of 11 November with Germany, specified unconditional surrender by the Ottomans. This, in theory, would leave a demilitarized Ottoman state at the mercy of predators. The Arab provinces, apart from Mosul, were soon recognized in Istanbul as a lost cause and the new Turkey under Mustafa Kemal was to deny any desire to get them back. That left the Turkish heartland of Anatolia plus Thrace, critical for the defence of Istanbul. It was round and within these areas that the wolves continued to prowl.

The key to events after 1918 is that the Allies did not consider that the residual Turkey had the right to determine its own destiny. The mood of the wartime territorial aggrandisement was running fast, and for the moment the remains of the Ottoman state were seen as simply prizes to be taken by the victors, just as they had already seized the Arab provinces and were in process of taking over German colonies in Africa and the Pacific. Of the original Allies only the Russians, now the Soviets, were not territorially ambitious: they wanted only to regain eastern Anatolia with its significant Armenian population, and were to get it by the Treaty of Alexandropol in December 1918, leaving part of the claimed Republic of Armenia within the USSR. But other Allies were more greedy. The ghost of Sykes–Picot still walked. France had then been promised the historic Cilicia, which adjoined Syria, plus a region stretching east to Armenia. The Italians also were greedy. Sykes–Picot had designated south-western Anatolia as an Italian sphere of influence, along with the Dodecanese Islands, which had significant Italian populations. Italy was bought off by gains at Austrian expense on its own north-eastern frontiers and the Dodecanese. That left Greece, which had entered the war at the last moment and had not fought the Ottomans. It was weak and

[37] There are useful accounts in Shaw and Shaw *Reform, Revolution and Republic*, chs. 4 and 5; Macfie, *The End*, chs. 10 and 11; McCarthy, *The Ottoman Peoples and the End of Empire*, chs. 7, 8, and 11; Palmer, *The Decline and Fall of the Ottoman Empire*, ch. 16; and E. Zurcher, *Turkey: A Modern History* (London, 1993).

could have been ignored. But Lloyd George was a strong philhellene and wanted to create a strong Greece as a British ally in the area. Greek claims to territory in western Anatolia, where there was a significant minority Greek population, and in Thrace, were therefore supported by the British.

In addition to these external predators there were two important internal would-be breakaway states. In the east the Armenians wanted a separate state to include areas of Turkish Anatolia and Russian Caucasus. Finally there were the Kurds, whose territory was inconveniently spread between Turkish Anatolia, Persia, and Mesopotamia. There were Kurdish ambitions to be independent and the Kurds, along with the Armenians, were conditionally promised statehood by the Treaty of Sèvres in 1920. Had all these claims been sustained the new Ottoman/Turkish state would have been very small, reduced to a rump in the centre and north of Anatolia and probably excluding even Istanbul.

It was entirely due to the long-awaited Turkish renaissance that this final destruction of the residual Ottoman empire did not happen. The roots of the Turkish national movement are much debated. Very briefly, and to over-simplify, a group of Turkish army commanders, led by Mustafa Kemal, hero of Gallipoli, organized military and political resistance to the Allied Occupation. Making Ankara their capital, they built up a military force which survived a major Greek invasion from Izmir, a French attack on Cilicia, and an Armenian attempt to create a separate state in the eastern Caucasus. Finally, the Lausanne Conference between November 1922 and July 1923 recognized the independence of Turkey much as it was to remain, including Anatolia, Istanbul, and Eastern Thrace. The future of Mosul was not decided until 1926, when it was allocated to Iraq; and in 1939 the French conceded Alexandretta. Turkey renounced all claims to territories once part of the Ottoman empire outside these limits. Some other matters were left to be sorted out later. The Capitulations were abolished, though some contracts under them were maintained: thus customs duties were not entirely free until 1929. The Ottoman public debt was allocated between Turkey and its one-time provinces, though Turkey did not actually pay any interest on it until 1929: the last payments were made in 1944. The foreign and mixed courts set up under the Capitulations were abolished, though foreign suitors were allowed to plead in their own language. There were to be no limits on the size of the Turkish army, but there was a demilitarized zone on the western frontier of Thrace, and the Straits were under an international commission (with a Turkish president) until 1936.

This virtually tied up the loose ends of the Ottoman empire. The Allies evacuated Istanbul in October 1923. Ankara was declared the capital of the new Turkish Republic. In March 1924 the Grand National Assembly abolished the Caliphate, which had seemed a danger to Kemal because its survival encouraged some conservatives to press for the revival of the Sultanate.

So the Ottoman empire ended. It left the Middle East for the first time for many centuries as a collection of states or proto-states: Turkey, Iraq as a state under British mandate until 1932, and four other mandates which did not become independent until 1945–8. The remainder of this book is concerned with the history of these mandates. They were now entirely free of Turkish control, though Turkish influence remained very strong in many spheres. An underlying counter-factual question must therefore be whether they and the general health of the area turned out to be better under mandate and eventually national rule than they might have done had they remained as part of a reformed Ottoman or Turkish empire.

PART TWO

ALIEN RULE AND NATIONALIST REACTIONS, 1918–1958

3

Britain in Mesopotamia/Iraq, 1918–1958

There were two dominant features of the British position in Mesopotamia—hereafter Iraq, an old name for southern Mesopotamia, indicating the cliff or shore of a great river,[1] which was adopted as the name of the new state created in 1920—that were largely to influence its history until, and in fact after, the end of the mandate in 1932.

First, as in the other mandates, Britain's position there was ambiguous. The very concept of a mandate was new and undefined. As it was stated in article 22 of the 1919 Covenant of the new League of Nations, Iraq was one of a group of ex-Ottoman or ex-German dependencies 'which are inhabited by peoples not yet able to stand by themselves under the strenuous conditions of the modern world'. For such territories 'there should be applied the principle that the well-being and development of such peoples form a sacred trust of civilisation and that securities for the performance of this trust should be embodied in this Covenant'. The 'tutelage' of such people should be entrusted to 'advanced nations' and 'should be exercised by them as Mandatories on behalf of the League'. In the case of Iraq, as also of Syria and Lebanon, the Covenant also stated that the mandate should prepare these countries for independence: in that of Palestine only for 'self-government' because of the commitment to the Zionists (see Chapter 4).

Precisely what all this meant, no one was certain. From a British standpoint, it was bound to be taken as a form of words to cloak the fact of British imperial control. But since this was for a limited period leading to independence—a word not found in the British imperial vocabulary since American independence in 1783—it meant that there could be no long-term plans for full incorporation into the imperial system. On the other hand, the mandate did not specify how this 'sacred trust' was to be exercised, so that Britain had in principle a free hand in deciding the appropriate form of government, and had a very wide range of existing models from which to chose. Conversely, seen from an Iraqi standpoint, the very concept of a mandate, with its implication that they were not fit to 'stand by themselves', was an insult. It was entirely inconsistent with the whole thrust of pre-1914 'Arab nationalism', the experience of the Hashemite campaign in the Hijaz, and the Anglo-French Declaration of 5 November 1918 which had promised 'national

[1] Northern Mesopotamia was known as al-Jazira, the island between the Euphrates and the Tigris.

governments as administrators deriving their authority from the initiative and free choice of the indigenous populations'. The key fact of Iraqi history from 1918 onwards was that the great majority did not want any form of alien control. In practice the Iraqis had to put up with it for the time being, but British control, whether in its early administrative form or under the terms of the 1930 treaty after independence in 1932, was anathema. In the end the Hashemite monarchy, which stuck with the British connection, paid for this with their lives in 1958.

→ The second fundamental feature of post-1918 Iraq was that it had no historical, religious, or ethnic homogeneity. Politically it consisted of the three Ottoman vilayets (provinces) of Mosul, Baghdad, and Basra. These had been administered separately, each with its own vali in direct contact with Istanbul. Iraq had no natural capital and no single administrative system or ruling class. If it was to become a unitary state this would have to be imposed, to some extent against the wishes and traditions of the inhabitants of each province. Then in terms of religion there was great diversity. Perhaps half the population were Shiite Muslims, predominantly in Basra vilayet and the southern region but also scattered elsewhere. Spiritually their closest links were with Persia, from which many of their divines came. In the centre and parts of the north-west, the majority were Sunni Muslims. But there were also a large number of Jews, especially in Baghdad; and in the north and north-east the Kurds, though mostly Sunni, were quite distinct. Also mostly in the north there were a variety of Muslim sects and also Christians. The Turcoman were both Sunni and Shiite. At Jabal Sanjar there was a significant Yazidi population, ethnically Kurdish but considered heathen by the Sunnis. Clearly, it would be impossible to found a single society on the basis of religion. Language provided perhaps the nearest to a common denominator. The great majority of Iraqis, even Jews and other minorities, spoke Arabic, though the Kurds did not. Arabic was eventually to become an important basis for a 'nation-building' strategy.

Faced with such diversity of people and options, the British, in common with France and most colonizing powers, naturally reacted by considering the applicability of their own widely varying imperial administrative models. Decision-making was further complicated by the variety of agencies with an interest. At the imperial centre, four major government departments were concerned initially. There was also the Indian government, within whose orbit Iraq lay, and the High Commission in Cairo, which, as has been seen, was deeply involved in the future of the territory from the start of negotiations with Husayn.

The primary concern of the Foreign Office was strategic and political: its objectives during the war were examined in Chapter 2. But it also had considerable experience in managing imperial possessions, notably Egypt since 1882 and the Anglo-Egyptian Sudan; until 1905 it had also controlled the new East African protectorates. Many of those who were involved in the early occupation and administration of Iraq had Egyptian or Sudanese experience and provided much of the expertise in Arabic and Middle Eastern affairs. The Egyptian model was a peculiar form of indirect British rule by which initially the Consul-General (from 1914, when Egypt was declared a protectorate, the High Commissioner) and a large number of British officials controlled most aspects of government in the guise of advisers to the Khedive and Egyptian ministers. This was possible because in 1882 Egypt had a centralized system of government under a single ruler. It might be possible to adopt such a mechanism in Iraq provided it also could be unified administratively with a single indigenous ruler.

The India Office, together with the government of India in Delhi, had a direct interest in Iraq because it fell within the sphere of interest of the Indian government. The conquest of Iraq had been largely the work of the Indian army and many of the early civilian administrators of the areas conquered were drawn from the Indian Political Service, notably Sir Percy Cox, the Civil Commissioner, and his deputy (Sir) Arnold Wilson. Their experience was mainly with the notionally autonomous Indian princely states and in the states of the Persian Gulf and the Red Sea. Again their experience suggested indirect British control through treaties or agreements on the model of those with rulers such as the Shaykh of Kuwait, which provided for varying degrees of British influence through Residents. There was, however, an alternative model, that of direct rule through a hierarchy of British officials, as operated in much of British India. This model approximated more closely to the pattern of Ottoman rule. Its potential relevance to Iraq lay in the fact that as a result of the Ottomans' centralizing policies of the nineteenth century there were no longer any hereditary territorial rulers in Mesopotamia, apart from the partially autonomous shaykhs. There might, therefore, be a case for some form of direct British rule in which Iraqis became employees of an imperial administration rather than at least notionally rulers in their own right. In practice this was the type of administration set up by the British military administration as they advanced north from Basra from November 1914 to the final conquest of Mosul in November 1918. In fact by then there was a working administrative system along British Indian lines. In Baghdad the central government headed by the Civil Commissioner had five major departments under British secretaries. Regional governments consisted initially of sixteen divisions (liwas) into which the three Ottoman provinces had been divided, subdivided into districts (qadhas) and sub-districts (nahiyas). These were run by Political Officers and their subordinates, using indigenous officials in subordinate positions. This was recognizably the British Indian pattern. The question in and after 1918 was whether it would prove sustainable in the longer term.

The third major interest in Iraq was shared between the British War Office and Admiralty, which controlled the armed forces. Their concerns were mainly strategic. Basra was a crucial point for the protection of British interests in the Gulf and for the oil refineries at Abadan, on which the navy now partly depended for its fuel. From the official standpoint Iraq was part of an integrated system of imperial defence stretching from the Mediterranean to the Indian Ocean. Whatever form of government emerged there, it was essential that the British armed forces should have secure bases and that no other power should be able to intrude.

In addition to these British departments, the Treasury was bound to be interested in developments in Iraq. Although the troops there were mostly Indian, the costs were borne by the Treasury; and after 1918 it became a primary aim to reduce such costs, which in 1919–20 amounted to about £35 million and in 1920–1 to £32 million. It was a fundamental principle of British imperial policy that dependencies should cover their own costs, though costs arising from British military activities were met by London. India was an exceptional case in that it was sufficiently large and wealthy to pay not only for indigenous troops but also for the substantial proportion of the army provided by British regiments. Even so, Indian defence costs were a heavy burden. In 1913–14 defence absorbed 25 per cent of total central and provincial government expenditure: in 1917–18 it had risen to 33 per cent, before dropping to below 30 per cent in the 1920s.[2] It would therefore be unacceptable to set up and maintain a regime in Iraq that depended on continued military action for which so poor a country could not afford to pay. This implied that whatever political structures were created must be acceptable to the bulk of the population so that continuous military action was not needed. In 1920–1 this was to prove a critical factor in the choice of regimes.

The point, then, is that the choice of regime in Iraq, as in all European dependencies, depended very heavily on the nature of the society and its response to the unexpected and uninvited British presence. In every colonial situation, alien rule relied very largely on the ability of the imperial power to gain support or at least acquiescence. One way in which this has commonly been expressed is that empire depended on collaborators, without the stigma attached to the word during the Second World War in Europe. Another is to say that control depended on creating or tapping into networks of patron and client, using patronage and patrimonialism as devices to attach a sufficient proportion of the society to the government. Very broadly, European success in this respect was most impressive where there was a hierarchical social structure with its own networks of patrons and clients, provided of course that it was possible to come to terms with the dominant patrons. In this way the imperial power could achieve some degree of control over society at minimum cost and the least disturbance. Conversely, of course, this would imply British commitment to an existing social order; and that, if that order came under attack, the basis of the imperial structure would crumble. In this chapter the British experience will be examined under four heads: first, the indigenous social structure; second, the early British response to 1932; third, Iraqi politics and society from 1920 to 1941; and finally, the revival, decline, and fall of British influence, 1941 to 1958.

1. THE SOCIAL STRUCTURE OF IRAQ

In common with most parts of the Middle East in the early twentieth century, Iraq was a very hierarchical society.[3] Power and wealth were controlled, in different degrees, by three main groups: the landed class, the urban 'aristocracy' of officials,

---

[2] B. R. Tomlinson, *The Economy of Modern India, 1860–1970* (Cambridge, 1993), table 3.9.
[3] The following account is based mainly on H. Batatu, *The Old Social Classes and the Revolutionary Movements of Iraq* (Princeton, 1978).

and the urban commercial classes, with whom these were often linked. In a country where, before the 1940s, the towns were relatively small and weak, the dominant class were the big land-owners, the mallaks. The concentration of land-ownership was in fact very great, even by the standards of nineteenth-century Europe. In 1958, 1 per cent of all land-owners held 55.1 per cent of all privately held land. Forty-nine families owned 16.8 of all privately held land, some with very large estates. These consisted of 22 shaykhs, 12 sadahs (the collective term for sayyids, descendants of the Prophet), and 11 merchants. The paramount shaykh of the Shamar tribe held 259,509 dunums—about 64,877 acres. Conversely, 72.9 per cent of land-owners held less than 50 dunums (*c.* 12 acres). As between the various land-owning groups, the sadahs held 31 per cent of agricultural land, non-sadah shaykhs 3.4 per cent, non-sadah tribal shaykhs 51 per cent, merchants 12.3 per cent, and all others 2.3 per cent.[4]

These great landed groups were not homogeneous. Nor were they strictly classes. At the top socially were the sadahs. They varied widely in wealth and land-owning, but initially at least commanded considerable popular respect. The British valued this and exploited it. Between 1921 and 1932, 69.2 per cent of prime ministers were from the sadah category. This dropped to 37.5 per cent between 1932 and 1941, 11.1 per cent between then and 1946, and to 10.0 per cent between 1947 and 1958. Two very important political figures in the pre-1941 period came from their ranks: Yasim al-Hashimi, who dominated politics in the 1920s, and Rashid Ali al-Gaylani, who was to rise to a peak of power in 1941.

Below these sayyids were a very large number of shaykhs (often called aghas or begs in Kurdish areas). The majority did not claim descent from the Prophet and were essentially tribal chiefs.[5] Historically they were descended from the tribal rulers of the big military confederations of the period before the consolidation of Ottoman control in the mid-nineteenth century. Their tribal connections remained and constituted complex networks of obligation and support throughout their regions. But, taking advantage of the Ottoman Land Law of 1858 and the Vilayet Law of 1864, most shaykhs and aghas had been able to gain control of those state lands within their tribal area, acquiring conditional title deeds and denying the peasants who worked the land the opportunity to acquire stable tenures. Thus by the time of the British occupation the shaykhs and aghas had, for the most part, become large landed proprietors with semi-servile peasantry working their lands. This did not exclude retention of armed supporters, whose numbers varied according to the wealth of the shaykh. In the Kurdish frontier regions, these might be very large and engaged in recurrent conflicts with rivals. Batatu suggests that the largest shaykhdoms were in the lower Tigris, the Gharraf, the Hillah Branch of the mid-Euphrates, and the Sinjar district of the province of

---

[4] There may have been less concentration of ownership in 1918 than in 1958 since lands seen earlier as held collectively by a tribal group were often registered later under the name of a chief, who became the registered owner and landlord.

[5] The following is based mainly on Batatu, *Old Social Classes*, ch. 6.

Mosul: significantly all these had quite recently been restored to cultivation after periods of decline. Significantly also, these bigger landed shaykhs and aghas were the people who were critical for British control in the period after 1918, yet they took no part in the 1920 rising or in tribal rebellions in 1935–7. Conversely, it was the smaller shaykhs of the middle and lower Euphrates who were the backbone of the 1920 and mid-1930s risings. These were also for the most part Shia, and may have been under the influence of the Shii ulama of Najaf and Karbala, who were very hostile to British rule, the monarchy, and Sunni domination from Baghdad.

The British therefore inherited a structure of tribal groups under a wide range of tribal rulers who dominated rural Iraq. Batatu argues that in the later Ottoman period, despite their hold over the land, they were politically enfeebled by the new centralizing Ottoman strategy and by the revival of urban prosperity. It was not therefore inevitable that the British would support and use these quasi-feudal chiefs as a major prop of their regime: they might have adopted the British Indian option, creating an urban-based bureaucracy and minimizing the political influence of the tribal leaders and structures. They did not do so. In fact, the British adopted something approaching an indirect rule policy, preserving shaykhly power and land-ownership and propping up the decaying structures of the tribal societies. Batatu's explanation for this is as follows.

In the early days from 1914 the shaykhs were seen as the only means, in the absence of a proper civil service, to replace that of the Ottomans, by which control could be kept over the localities occupied by the British. The rebellion of 1920 seemed to underline the dangers of not propitiating them. Some British officials thought that the value and strength of the shaykhs was overestimated, but that was a minority opinion. The very influential Gertrude Bell regarded them in 1922 as 'the backbone of the country'.[6] This was a romantic view, based on her long contacts with the shaykhs, but was widely adopted. After the establishment of the state in 1920 and the Hashemite monarchy in 1921, the shaykhs were seen as playing a double role. In their own areas they could, if loyal, preserve order in the absence of any significant British or Iraqi army or police force. But in terms of national politics they could also be used as a makeweight against the new King Faysal, and his central government dominated by the ex-Sharifian officers (discussed below) who wanted to create a strong central state based on a conscript indigenous army. There was, of course, the danger that shaykhs would prove inconveniently strong and a threat to the centre and to British power. This was particularly evident in 1920 and throughout the years of the mandate in the Kurdish area. There the technique was to play one shaykh against another: the technique is vividly described by C. J. Edmonds, who served in the northern

---

[6] Quoted Batatu, *Old Social Classes* from Lady Bell (ed.), *The Letters of Gertrude Bell* (London, 1927), ii. 647.

area in the early 1920s, and by his friend and colleague, W. A. Lyon, who was there until 1932.[7] This strategy was never entirely successful. Tribes in the northern area retained their capacity to create trouble throughout the Hashemite period and beyond, and the Shia tribes of the lower Euphrates also remained largely unsubdued and ready to rebel into the mid-1930s. But on balance the shaykhly order became a source of strength to both the Baghdad regime and British power, later influence, until 1958.

To buttress the regime of landed tribal leaders the British created a special juridical status for the rural areas and their rulers, the Tribal Criminal and Civil Disputes Regulation. This originated in 1915, largely because it would have been impractical to extend the legal organization set up in Basra and the southern cities to the rural areas. Based on the Indian Frontier Crimes Regulations by (Sir) Henry Dobbs, an officer from the Indian Political Service and later High Commissioner,[8] it was later codified and embodied into Iraqi law in 1924, with general effect outside urban areas, under very strong British pressure on the Iraqi government. Under the Regulation tribal leaders appointed by the British had the power to adjudicate in all cases affecting their tribe and were also appointed tax collectors. This separated the countryside from the towns and left the chosen tribal leaders as agents of British influence. There are few clearer examples of the Indian influence on the early history of Iraq.

Batatu assessed the social effect of these British strategies as follows. First, it checked the previous disintegration of the tribal order, forcing villages and minor chiefs to remain under the authority of the designated tribal head. Second, the tribal chief, being responsible for both justice and taxation, might act in ways that did not please British officials. Third, the status of the leading tribal chiefs was raised further by election to the parliament. In the Ottoman Majlis (Chamber of Deputies in Istanbul) of 1914 there was only one from a shaykhly family, but they constituted 34 per cent of the Constituent Assembly of 1924. Their share declined under Faysal, ranging from 14.8 to 20.4 per cent of members of the Iraq parliament, but was always over 30 per cent between 1943 and the end of the monarchy in 1958.[9] This was possible because of the system of election in two stages, inherited from the Ottomans, which allowed great pressure to be placed on the second-stage electors by the administration. This greatly increased the status of the top tribal leaders. Fourth, the policy adopted after 1920 of keeping down the level of the land tax, a main source of revenue in Ottoman days, to be replaced by indirect taxes, was a great benefit to the large land-owners. Finally shaykhs were helped financially by judicious grants and subsidies.

---

[7] See C. J. Edmonds, *Kurds, Turks and Arabs* (London, 1957) and his voluminous papers and diaries held in the Middle East Archive of St Antony's College, Oxford. See also D. K. Fieldhouse (ed.), *Kurds, Arabs and Britons: The Memoir of Wallace Lyon in Iraq 1918–1944* (London, 2002).

[8] Sir Arnold T. Wilson, *Loyalties: Mesopotamia 1914–1917* (London, 1930), 68.

[9] Batatu, *Old Social Classes*, table 6.1, p. 103.

Batatu's conclusion is that, while the British inherited the remnants of a quasi-feudal social structure, it had been in decline as urban wealth and influence and the power of the central government grew.

Life was pumped into it artificially by an outside force that had an interest in its perpetuation. In other words, the shaikhs and aghas, at least for the most part, ruled not by virtue of their own power or the willingness and loyalty of their peasants, but by the desire and sufferance of the English.

However, even while building up the tribal chief, the English unwittingly undermined him, for their presence implied more order, greater security, and improved communications, all of which, along with other factors, rendered him, from the standpoint of the peasant, increasingly superfluous.[10]

In short, while initially British accommodation with the landed elite was probably a necessity, given their own weakness, it became ossified as part of an *ancien régime* that would be destroyed in and after 1958.

Second only in importance to the tribal chiefs in the control of Iraq was the 'aristocracy of officials'. As in the other ex-Ottoman countries examined in this study, the basis of the state lay in an urban elite which traditionally provided the holders of key administrative, judicial, and ecclesiastical offices. As was seen in Chapter 1, such families also formed cohesive networks with long traditions of state service. In Iraq they did not, for the most part, come from the tribal rulers or the sadah. Many were descendants of Turkish soldiers and officials of the seventeenth-century conquest, but they had also drawn in members of the great feudal families. Either by inheritance or the investment of their wealth, these official families held large quantities of land and at the margins merged into the tribal aristocracy. Faced by the British conquest, many of these office holders avoided commitment, holding on to their jobs where possible, but ready to reverse if the Ottomans turned the tide. In the event many lost their positions or found themselves subordinate to British officials who scrutinized their activities in a way no Ottoman administrator had done.

Yet the old official class soon came to terms with the new dispensation and was ready to serve it in their own interests. They also played a leading role in the new politics. During the whole period 1921–58, 110 out of a total of 575 ministerial appointments were held by members of this class, 62.7 per cent of these from a mere five families. They did not, however, become politically dominant. Thus, a leading member of the class, Hikmat Sulayman, an active reformist politician of the early 1930s and briefly Prime Minister 1936–7, rose to the top only as a protégé of the then dominant General Bakr Sidqi and fell with him. For the most part, the official class remained an administrative rather than political class. They did very well out of the opportunities for financial aggrandisement, particularly in acquired land, and became among the richest sections of society. By and large, apart from Shii divines in the south, the British had few problems

[10] Batatu, *Old Social Classes*, 99.

with such men. They used them as the basis of the administrative and judicial systems.

Also in the urban class were the merchants. By western standards these were few and not politically important. There were a number of gentleman merchants—*chalabis*—who had connections with the landed aristocracy. But they were in the minority. Batatu suggests a number of reasons for the relative unimportance of this class. Muslims distrusted collective enterprises and the Koran banned usury. Until the twentieth century, trade via Baghdad to Syria and beyond was slow and expensive, and this trade route had suffered from the opening of the Suez canal in 1869. It was also to be badly affected by the separation of Iraq and Syria, with frontier customs duties and obstacles. Local handcraft industries had suffered from cheaper, mainly British, imports, low tariffs imposed under the Capitulations, and the growing dominance of British shipping and commercial firms. By the 1930s the dominant 'first-class' trading companies were British. As a result the merchants tended to invest their profits in land rather than in commercial or industrial expansion. Within this commercial class, especially in Baghdad, were the Jews. In 1947 there were 77,417 Jews in Baghdad, 15 per cent of the population. These specialized as bankers and lenders. They had close links with India and some, like the Sassoons, were very rich. But the vast majority of the Jews were very poor.

The British period down to 1958 was, however, generally, except for the recession of 1929–31, a period of growth and business expansion for the urban commercial class. Muslims increasingly got over their distrust of collective enterprise and formed partnerships and companies. The two world wars provided huge opportunities for profit. Agricultural exports, particularly of grain and dates, grew fast. Communications were improved, with the completion of the north–south rail link along the Tigris and expanded motorized river transport. Until the 1950s, British firms continued to dominate most commercial and banking sectors, but from about 1950 Muslim business tended to take over. The exodus of the Jews in 1948–9 opened new avenues, higher protective import duties stimulated industrial investment, and the state gave considerable financial help. Iraq was at last evolving a powerful indigenous commercial and business class, both Sunni and Shia.

Seen from a British standpoint the merchants were important, though less so than the landed classes, and certainly not homogeneous. But there was a significant anti-British element among them, stimulated by resentment at the dominance of alien commerce and the decline of local industries. Some of the leading nationalist politicians of the period were from this class, including Jafar Abu al-Timman, involved in both the 1920 rising and the 1936 military coup and leader of the National Party: it collapsed in 1933 when he withdrew his financial support. There were a number of leading pan-Arabists from this class, including men who became army officers. The *Al-Ahali* journal from 1932 was the mouthpiece of a reforming group with mercantile backing. Merchants had linkages with the army in the 1930s via Hikmat Sulayman. Generally, merchants tended to distrust politicians as venal and untrustworthy, but the leading mercantile families were well represented in government in the period before 1958. Sixteen per cent of all ministerial appointments came from their ranks, but only three Prime Ministers. Most merchants were prepared to play ball with the monarchy of 1921 and the British, and did very well out of the collaboration.

This range of social and interest groups would have been replicated in a number of Middle Eastern societies in the early twentieth century. But in Iraq there was one special group that was relatively very small but had a disproportionate influence on the balance of forces and therefore on British policy. This was the group of about 300 ex-Sharifian officers who descended on Baghdad after 1920. Although all had been supporters of Faysal's short-lived regime in Syria from 1918 to 1920, they were not homogeneous. Their core consisted of Iraqis who had either deserted the Ottoman army or civil service or been taken prisoner during the war and had thrown in their lot with Faysal and his Northern Army in the Hijaz. These included men who were to be the mainstay of the regime for more than thirty years, such as Jafar al-Askari, Nuri as-Said, Jamil al-Midfai, and Ali Jawdat al-Ayyubi. In addition there were a number of ex-Ottoman officers and officials who had joined the band-wagon in 1918 and after. Many were members of the pre-war al-Ahd. When the Syrian regime was destroyed by the French in 1920 all found themselves unemployed. Although some of them had been involved in the attempt early in 1920 to mount an invasion of Mosul vilayet in order to bring it within the intended Syrian kingdom, during which two British officers and two private soldiers were murdered, the British later accepted that these Sharifians must be allowed to return to Iraq. They included some who were later to become leading figures in Iraqi politics: Yasim al-Hashimi, twice Prime Minister, Jamil al-Midfai, seven times Prime Minister, Ali Jawdat al-Ayyubi, three times Prime Minister, and Tahsin Ali, later a provincial governor and minister. A general pardon was issued in 1921, though al-Midfai was not pardoned until 1923.[11]

The arrival of these ex-Sharifians in and after 1921 was to be critical for the nature of the Hashemite regime and also for the structure of the British mandate. Had Faysal not been set on the newly created throne of Iraq in 1921 they would have had no future. Many were waiting in Syria in the hope of something favourable turning up. Others were in Palestine or Turkey. Their recall to Iraq reflected the fact that Faysal, and also the British, in the case of some of them, including Nuri as-Said and Jafar al-Askari, felt some obligation for their past support. Equally important, since Faysal had initially no supporters in Iraq, he needed men who would be entirely loyal to him. These men would depend on royal and British backing since almost none of them came from the various classes of notables in Iraq. In common with very many officers in the Ottoman army before 1914, most came from middle- or lower-middle-class backgrounds and had seen a military career via the Istanbul military academy, where most had in fact joined al-Ahd, as their route to preferment and status. Thus, Nuri as-Said, the

---

[11] The details are in E. Tauber, *The Formation of Modern Syria and Iraq* (London, 1995), 226–60.

most influential and durable of them all, was the son of a minor government auditor. Ali Jawdat was the son of a chief sergeant in the gendarmerie. Jafar al-Askari, one of three brothers who played a leading role in Iraq after 1920, was the son of a professional wrestler from Askar in Chamchemal district who had risen to the rank of brigadier. In short they were in social and political terms adventurers. Their arrival and appointment to high positions in the army and administration did not please local notables. Thus in 1922 forty shaykhs and aghas tried to insist that the king should select for government 'only those who have the nobility of race and birth'.[12]

This hostility was one factor that tended to keep these *arrivistes* together, despite rivalries and disagreements. Another was that almost all of them were Sunni by faith and came from the northern part of Iraq. Many also were related by blood or marriage. Thus the Askari and Said groups were closely linked by marriage: Jafar and Nuri as-Said were each married to the other's sister. Jamil al-Midfai had matrimonial ties with the family of Ali Jawdat al-Ayyubi. These ex-Sharifians thus created a new set of networks based on past experience, religion, district, and blood to add to those already dominant in Iraq. Once installed, and with new arrivals in this inner circle, they remained in control of Iraq until 1958, rising and finally dying with the Hashemite monarchy. In the process most of them acquired status and landed wealth, so joining the ranks of the new landed aristocracy. Although some were initially quite radical, in line with the ethos of the Young Turk movement of the pre-1914 period, and some, when in office, proposed modestly radical social reforms, in practice they remained conservative. The main divisions between them arose from the extent of their nationalism, particularly their belief in pan-Arabism, and therefore their attitude to the British. This was to cause the main fissure in their ranks in 1941.

The first great age of the dominance of these ex-Sharifians was from 1920 to the death of King Faysal in 1933, though in fact until 1932 of the 13 appointments to Prime Minister nine were from the sadah and only four from the ex-Sharifian officers, to placate the established upper class. In the early days Faysal relied on them very considerably, much as any new regime relies on its intimate supporters. In the 1920s Nuri was the dominant factor, controlling the army as deputy commander-in-chief and at times holding the Defence Ministry. After 1932 the ex-Sharifians increased their political dominance. Between the first military coup of 1936 and 1941 half of all prime ministerial appointments were from that group, though now there was also one Prime Minister who, as well as being an ex-Sharifian, was also from the 'official aristocracy'. Between 1946 and 1958 Sharifians continued to hold at least 40 per cent of the prime ministerships. From a military standpoint, as late as 1936 the three major-generals, twelve of the senior officers, three of the four brigadiers, and six of the eleven colonels were

---

[12] Batatu, *Old Social Classes*, 322. Chapter 10 provides the best account of the ex-Sharifian officers after 1920.

ex-Sharifians. When Nuri became Prime Minister for the first time in 1930 five of the six seats in the cabinet went to them. His relations with Faysal were not always smooth and cooled after about 1930, but were never hostile. As for the British, ironically in the light of their very close association with Nuri later, in the early years they tended to distrust him, partly at least because of his demand for a much larger and conscript army, which was against British policy.

It was from 1933 and the accession of King Ghazi that the unity of the ex-Sharifians began to be broken. The fracture tended to run along the lines of those who were with Faysal before 1918 and those who joined the ranks once he seemed to be victorious and able to offer a secure future in Syria. Thus Brigadiers Bakr Sidqi and Abd-ul-Latif Nuri, who staged the 1936 military coup and were responsible for the murder of Jafar al-Askari in that year, along with the four younger colonels who were to constitute the so-called 'Golden Square'— Salah-al-Din al-Sabbagh, Kamil Shabib, Fahmi Said, and Mahmud Salman—were all later adherents to al-Ahd and Faysal. By that time, all these men had been developing their own networks of supporters, particularly in the armed forces, a foretaste of the pattern of Iraqi politics from 1958.

2. THE BRITISH RESPONSE, 1914–1932

There were three early factors that were to condition the British experience in Iraq throughout the mandate and beyond.[13]

The first was that the British did not come as deliverers. They were invaders of an Ottoman and Islamic territory who were resented both as enemies of an empire to which the great majority of Iraqis were still loyal and for which very many of them were fighting, and as infidels who were attacking the Caliph. For the Shia majority, who did not accept the concept of a Sunni Caliph, the British were equally hated as non-believers: many of their clerics wanted a theocracy. It is

---

[13] This account of the early years is based mainly on the following: P. Graves, *The Life of Sir Percy Cox* (London, 1941); P. W. Ireland, *Iraq: A Study in Political Development* (London, 1937); E. Kedourie, *England and the Middle East: The Destruction of the Ottoman Empire 1914–1921* (London, 1956) and *The Chatham House Version and Other Middle Eastern Studies* (London, 1970); S. H. Longrigg, *Iraq 1900–1950: A Political, Social and Economic History* (London, 1953); J. Marlowe, *Late Victorian: The Life of Sir Arnold Talbot Wilson* (London, 1967); E. Monroe, *Britain's Moment in the Middle East 1914–1956* (London, 1965) and *Philby of Arabia* (New York and London, 1973); J. Nevakivi, *Britain, France and the Arab Middle East 1914–1928* (London, 1969); A. A. al-Razzafi Shikara, *Iraqi Politics 1921–1941* (London, 1987); D. Silverfarb, *Britain's Informal Empire in the Middle East: A Case Study of Iraq 1929–1941* (New York and London, 1986); P. Sluglett, *Britain in Iraq 1914–1932* (London, 1976); M. A. Tarbush, *The Role of the Military in Politics: A Case Study of Iraq to 1941* (London, 1982); E. Tauber, *The Formation of Modern Syria and Iraq*; C. Tripp, *A History of Iraq* (Cambridge, 2000); Sir A. T. Wilson, *Loyalties: Mesopotamia 1914–1917* (London, 1930) and *Mesopotamia 1917–1920: A Clash of Loyalties* (London, 1931); H. V. F. Winstone, *Gertrude Bell* (London, 1978). Much of the argument follows that in the introduction to Fieldhouse (ed.), *Kurds, Arabs and Britons*.

uncertain how deeply the feeling of Arab nationalism had penetrated Iraq by 1914—certainly not as much as in Syria, but it existed among certain circles and was intensified by the return of the Iraqi officers and others in and after 1920. Probably there was considerable support for the pre-1914 concept of greater autonomy for Arab territories, but not the destruction of the Ottoman empire or its institutions. In short, the British were not wanted and were initially resented. The most they could hope for was reluctant acceptance of their dominant position and some interested collaboration from those who might see benefit in the new dispensation.

The second main factor was the time-span between the first British attack on Basra in November 1914 and the announcement of a new Iraqi state in 1920. There were two main reasons for this. The first was military. After the occupation of Basra, which secured the safety of the Abadan oil refinery—the main objective of the invasion—the Indian Expeditionary Force (IEF) was not authorized to move north and attempt to take Baghdad until April 1915. This then proved a failure: the Indian forces were defeated at Ctesiphon in November and retreated to Kut-al-Amara, where they were besieged until April 1916, finally surrendering to the Turks for lack of supplies and the inability of the army to relieve them. At the end of 1916 the push for Baghdad was resumed, more to relieve pressure on the Russians than because Baghdad was regarded as intrinsically important, and it was not taken until March 1917. Mosul did not fall until November 1918, after the Armistice of Mudros. Hence the British occupation was slow and piecemeal: indeed, significant areas of the country, notably the Kurdish regions in the northeast, were never militarily occupied. This slow progress impeded consideration of long-term objectives and also resulted in an ad hoc and largely unpopular military administration which caused much hardship to the inhabitants.

The third and most important factor was British inability to decide what, if anything, to do with Iraq in the longer term. Here the fission of responsibility between the various British offices of state mentioned above was critical.[14] The basic questions in and after 1917, once Baghdad had been occupied, were as follows. Should all or any part of Mesopotamia be annexed by Britain, perhaps as a protectorate? Should the three vilayets be integrated or dealt with separately? What type of regime should be installed: indigenous or imperial? On these issues there were major disagreements between the India Office and Foreign Office and between men on the spot and in London and New Delhi.

Since the 1914 expedition came from India, and there were no formal instructions from London about the future strategy, the India Office and New Delhi were responsible in the first instance for policy. Initially, it seems to have been assumed that at least the Basra vilayet would remain under British control indefinitely, which meant adding it to those many Arabian territories under some

---

[14] A recent detailed examination of this is by J. Fisher, *Curzon and British Imperialism in the Middle East 1916–1919* (London, 1999).

form of Indian suzerainty. Indeed, almost all the early administrative and judicial innovations were based on Indian practice and officials. But by 1917, after the capture of Baghdad, and in the light both of the Sykes–Picot Agreement and of the 1915 promise to Sharif Husayn, the position looked different. In March 1917 Sir Arthur Hirtzel, secretary to the political department of the India Office, who was to play a major role in the evolution of Iraq policy, was thinking in terms of a movement towards a quasi-indigenous regime. He told the newly created Mesopotamian Committee (MAC), set up to co-ordinate policy between the War, India, and Foreign Offices, that the best strategy was to keep on the ad hoc administrative system set up as the occupation progressed but 'with substitution of Arab for Turkish spirit and personnel. The façade must be Arab. . . . The inhabitants should be formally invited to assume control . . . and the British Officers to be lent should be strictly limited to the minimum necessary as advisers.' He wrote that the army was too keen on its own administrative methods. This was unacceptable as '*vis-à-vis* both of [*sic*] King Hussein and of the Allies they [HMG] are irretrievably committed to the policy of the Arab State, until, at all events, the Arab State has been tried and proved a failure'.[15] Here was the germ of the solution ultimately adopted in 1920. Later in March 1917 Austen Chamberlain, now Secretary of State for India, told the Viceroy that Baghdad was to be an Arab state with a local ruler or government under a 'British Protectorate in everything but name'.[16] This was seen by the MAC as a device to ensure that Baghdad did not fall under Indian rule, along with Basra. But it was uncertain whether this would emerge as the preferred option. A proclamation issued by General Maude, the General Officer Commanding, in Baghdad on 19 March made no mention of an Arab regime there or anywhere, speaking only of liberation from Turkish rule.

A complicating factor was that Lord Curzon, after being in the political wilderness since 1905, was now back in the cabinet as Lord Privy Seal: he was to become Foreign Secretary in succession to A. J. Balfour in October 1919. In 1917 he was determined that there should be no retreat from Baghdad and wanted long-term British control of both Baghdad and Basra, possibly because these were seen as a safeguard against Russian control of land access to the Gulf. He also disagreed with the India Office assumption that Britain would eventually have to give up direct rule in Baghdad.

By the beginning of 1918, with Mosul still not conquered, the future of Iraq was still under debate. By this time the leading role was being played by the man on the spot. Sir Percy Cox, long-serving Indian Political Service officer and expert on Persian and Gulf affairs, had arrived as Political Officer with the IEF in 1914 and in 1917 was created Civil Commissioner to establish a civil administration in Baghdad. His deputy was A. T. Wilson, of the same service, who became Acting Civil Commissioner in 1918–20 while Cox was away in Persia. Also seconded to his

---

[15] *Fisher Curzon and British Imperialism in the Middle East 1916–1919*, 45.
[16] Ibid. 51.

team was Gertrude Bell, famous for her archaeological work in Arabia, as Oriental Secretary. Cox in 1917 wanted to integrate Baghdad with Basra, and was later to fight for the integration of Mosul into a unitary Iraq. Initially he was hamstrung by the need to work through the army and the India Office, and by the feud between Cairo and New Delhi over future strategy, particularly concerning the promises made to Sharif Husayn. But by 1918, his huge experience in an area on which the British were largely ignorant gave him considerable weight on policy decisions.

In February 1918, called back to meet the newly established Middle Eastern Committee (MEC) of the cabinet, which was reconstituted as the Eastern Committee in March 1918, Cox told Curzon that 'Everything depends on a full practical British control of the administration for many years to come.' At a meeting of the MEC he said that this should consist of 'government by a High Commissioner assisted by a Council, formed partly of the Heads of the most important Departments of state, and partly of representative non-official members from among the inhabitants. But the foreign relations of such a government must surely lie in British hands, and it would be practically a British protectorate.' Alternatively there might be a titular native ruler. He was then against a Hashemite ruler, regretting that Mesopotamia was ever part of the McMahon–Husayn negotiations, and setting himself against the strategy of the Cairo Arab Bureau. He did not want Husayn to have any claims outside the Hijaz. The aged Naqib of Baghdad would be the best ruler as most acceptable both in Iraq and to the Muslims of India. Cox thought there was little administrative talent available among the Iraqis, so that 'extensive and close supervision by British officers' would be essential. Balfour accepted this: he thought President Wilson, though hostile to any form of imperial annexation in the Middle East, might accept a British protectorate if he was convinced that there was no feasible alternative. The MEC accepted Cox's arguments and he was told to develop administration in Mesopotamia along these lines.[17]

Cox was then sent to Teheran to relieve the Ambassador, leaving A. T. Wilson as Acting Civil Commissioner, which he remained until October 1920, though Cox was constantly involved in evolving Iraqi questions. He was expected to return and take over control as soon as possible: in November 1919 Curzon told him to return as soon as the mandate for Iraq was fixed (actually at San Remo in April 1920), since the current direct system of government was incompatible with the Anglo-French Declaration of 8 November 1918 which promised 'national governments as administrators deriving their authority from the initiative and free choice of the indigenous populations' in ex-Ottoman territories. By that time, also, the future shape of Iraq had been clarified by the informal agreement between Lloyd George and Clemenceau in December 1918 that, despite the Sykes–Picot Agreement, Britain would control Mosul. Lloyd George's view was that, since the British had done all the fighting in the region, the

---

[17] Ibid. 127–30.

Sykes–Picot Agreement, in so far as it related to Iraq, was no longer relevant. Thus the options were now open, and in London the Eastern Committee was replaced in January 1919 by an informal Inter-Departmental Conference on the Middle East (IDME).

From the end of 1918 to October 1920, British policy on Iraq went through an extraordinarily confused period, and this was a major cause of the crisis of 1920.[18] The underlying reason was that London was reluctant to take any final decisions until the future of Iraq was settled, which was not until the San Remo conference in April 1920. There was also continued friction between all the main London departments, Cairo, and New Delhi. But another major factor was that Wilson in Baghdad was for long not prepared to accept the viability of the type of semi-autonomous Arab regime outlined by Hirtzel in 1917. As an old India hand he had little faith in the ability of Iraqis to run their own affairs. They had never had the opportunity to do so, since all valis and many senior positions had been held under the Ottoman regime by Turks. There had never been a single Iraqi state. There were huge disparities between the Shia and Sunni areas, between urban and rural society, between the riverine lands and the mountainous Kurdish territories. In London the Foreign Office seemed to be thinking in terms of a grouping of indigenous states on the model of the Indian princely states. T. E. Lawrence, who then had great influence, was pressing the claims of the Sharif or one of his sons. In May 1919 Wilson himself favoured a quasi-protectorate for five years with Cox as High Commissioner and no Arab head of state. But Hirtzel disapproved, writing privately to Wilson that 'You are going to have an Arab State, whether you like it or not, whether Mesopotamia wants it or not.' The idea of Iraq as 'the model of an efficiently administered British dependency or protectorate is dead . . . and an entirely new order of ideas reigns'. When Wilson objected to allowing in the Iraqi officers from Faysal's army as possible trouble-makers, he was told by H. W. Young of the Foreign Office that it was essential to bring in and use the Arab nationalists.[19]

The critical fact is that until the summer of 1920, Wilson could get no firm directives from London. Early in 1919 he ordered a plebiscite, with Foreign Office approval, in which local notables were asked three questions that seemed to be consistent with the November 1918 Anglo-French Declaration. Should a unitary state be set up, probably including Mosul? Should this state have an Arab titular ruler? If so, who might be the best candidate? Since local British officers were advised to press for positive responses to the first two of these questions, given that most notables were then anxious to keep on the good books of the occupying power, they got them. But there was no agreement over who might be an acceptable head of state. On this fragile basis, Wilson in April 1919 visited

---

[18] For a detailed account of British attitudes to the future of Iraq in these years see T. J. Paris, *Britain, the Hashemites and Arab Rule, 1920–1925: The Sherifian Solution* (London, 2003), Part II, which examines the process that led to Faysal being placed on the throne as king.

[19] Ibid. 263–5.

London and spelt out his ideas to the IDME. Government should for the time being be in the hands of the High Commissioner without an amir. There would be no central legislature but councils in each of the four proposed provinces, whose members would be elected by the nominated members of a divisional council. The main towns would have nominated Arab governors with British advisers. He got no definite answer, and in the meantime the established wartime direct administration by British officials and subordinate Iraqis continued.

By March 1920, however, still unable to get any firm directive from London, Wilson had decided that his earlier scheme was inadequate. He now proposed to set up a 'Central Legislative Council, with the High Commissioner (when he should arrive) as President, and Arab members in charge of Departments, with British Secretaries'. Again getting no response from London, he set up a committee under his Judicial Adviser, Sir Edgar Bonham-Carter, recruited from Egypt, and who, in February 1919, had argued for an Arab cabinet and senior civil servants under British supervision along Egyptian lines.[20] The committee broadly accepted Wilson's most recent proposals. They recommended postponing nomination of a ruler since it was thought that no Sharifian amir would be acceptable to the majority of Iraqis. Meantime there would be a nominated Council of State under an Arab president but with a British official majority. There should also be a Legislative Assembly whose members would be elected or appointed by local bodies, which in turn would be elected by constituencies of about 50,000, but with special seats for Jews and Christians. Its members could initiate legislation except on tax and constitutional matters, and put written questions. This constitution might last for seven years, after which the British government would set up a commission to inquire into the operation of the system.[21]

These proposals were wired to the India Office on 27 April 1920. That Office was inclined to accept them, but the Foreign Office blocked action until the peace treaty was signed with Turkey and the mandate awarded. Meantime Wilson was forbidden to publicize the proposals. News of the acceptance of the mandate, issued on 28 April, reached Baghdad on 1 May. Wilson could still make no announcement. On 5 May, London issued a formal statement of the need for immediate measures in consultation with the councils and with the approval of local opinion to frame definite proposals for 'creating a form of civil administration based upon representative institutions which would prepare the way for the creation of an independent Arab state of Iraq'.[22] This statement inevitably aroused nationalist opinion in Iraq, which did not know of Wilson's not incompatible scheme, and assumed that he was holding back on disseminating power. Wilson wired for urgent permission to publish the Bonham-Carter proposals to show that action was intended, but did not get permission to do so until 7 June. By that time it was too late. News of the British defeat at Tal Afar was out. Pressure from

[20] Sluglett, *Britain in Iraq*, 33.   [21] Wilson, *Mesopotamia 1917–1920*, 242–7.
[22] Ibid. 249.

Damascus, where the Faysal regime was still in power, and from returning Sharifians increased. When on 2 June, Wilson summoned a group of Baghdad notables, including the surviving fifteen delegates from the last Ottoman parliament, for their views, he was told that there must be a national convention based on Turkish electoral law, to prepare for a national government in line with the Anglo-French Declaration. Wilson immediately wired London to this effect: a constituent assembly would have to be summoned as soon as the mandate was finalized. But by the end of June the main Euphrates revolt was in progress and Wilson's scheme was sunk without trace. By the end of July he capitulated to the earlier concept of a quasi-independent state under a Hashemite head. Hearing of Faysal's deposition in Syria, he wired the India Office suggesting that Faysal be offered the headship of 'the Mesopotamian State'.

The Euphrates revolt may be seen as the Iraq equivalent of the attempted creation of an Arab state in Syria in 1919–20, though it had many differences. The common factors were that such Arab nationalism as existed in Iraq before 1914 had been against centralization and Turkish control and in favour of local autonomy. The main differences were that there was no Iraqi equivalent of al-Fatat or al-Ahd, even though many of the members of the latter were Iraqis, and that Iraq lacked the concentration of highly sophisticated urban notables found in Syria. Another contrast was that the majority of the Islamic population of Iraq was Shia, whereas most Syrians were Sunnis. But the overwhelming common factor was dislike of European occupation, which added to earlier dislike of control by non-indigenous Turks the fact that the new controllers were Christian infidels. Both countries made their bid for freedom in 1919–20, the Syrians first because of the nominal conquest by Faysal and the Northern Army in 1918, the Iraqis later because the British were already in firm occupation. For both the final crisis came in and after July 1920 with the crushing of Faysal's Syrian kingdom at Maysulun by the French, leading to their full control over Syria, and the suppression of the Euphrates rising in Iraq between July and late September.[23]

At that point, however, the similarities stop. The Iraqi rising had two distinct elements. The first, chronologically, was the attempted invasion of Mosul vilayet by forces from Syria.[24] These were led by Iraqi members of al-Ahd whose aim was the incorporation of Mesopotamia into Syria. With support from local beduin, they occupied Dayr al-Zur, which was regarded as the best base from which to stimulate an anti-British rising in Mosul, in November 1919 and occupied Tal Afar, a mere 32 km from Mosul, early in June 1920, killing two British officers and two other ranks. This force was quickly defeated and forced to retire by the British, and the hoped-for Mosul rising never occurred. But the news of British defeats and withdrawal had a dynamic effect in other parts of Iraq and encouraged the far more serious Euphrates rising of July.[25]

[23] For the details of the Syrian experience see Ch. 7, below.
[24] The best account of the invasion is in Tauber, *The Formation of Modern Syria and Iraq*, ch. 7.
[25] A detailed account of the rising is in Ireland, *Iraq*, chs. 13 and 14.

The revolt broke out on 30 July 1920 at Rumaitha, on the Lower Euphrates, nominally as a mob broke into a gaol to release an imprisoned shaykh. But its rapid spread throughout much of the Lower Euphrates region reflected deep-seated resentments at nearly six years of British control. There was a strong religious element. For many Shia in that area 'nationalism meant the erection once again of an Islamic State, with the priesthood in their rightful position'.[26] The Shii ulama played a leading role in mobilizing the tribes and preaching against the infidel. But there were other important secular grievances. Many of the tribes and shaykhs were alienated by much higher levels of taxation; some were hostile because of British reliance on chosen senior shaykhs and the increase in their powers under the Tribal Regulation. In the cities one-time senior officials were resentful because they had either lost their posts or found themselves subordinate to British officials. Many hankered after Turkish rule or alternatively a Muslim regime under a Turkish-led federation. Landlords and tenants were both affected by stricter British taxation and administrative pressures which, as the then British Political Officer, S. H. Longrigg, later put it, were 'pitiless to long-familiar lax-ities'.[27] Inflation rates were high. The military had occupied many of the houses of notables. Post-war retrenchment resulted in the dropping of some infrastructural projects. In short, the rising was a general reaction to the realities of foreign occupation, sparked off by evidence of apparent British military weakness in Mosul, and given a crusading spirit by the clerics.

But it had two main weaknesses. First, there was little support for the rising in the main towns: Baghdad, Basra, and even Mosul, where the Syrians had looked to find strong support, remained quiet. Second, there was no 'national' figurehead to which the rebels could look for leadership and inspiration, as the Syrians had looked to the alien Hashemite, Faysal. The rising was suppressed by October because there were still sufficient British and Indian troops available, despite the start of military reduction, to deal with it. The costs were high on both sides. The British lost 426 British and Indian troops, 1,228 wounded, 615 missing or taken prisoner. A number of Political Officers were killed, including the famous Colonel G. E. Leachman. There were over 8,000 casualties among the insurgents. Perhaps more significant for British policy-makers were the financial costs of the military occupation. For a government then embarked on major post-war retrenchment this was taken as proof that radical changes were necessary to reduce the costs of the mandate.

As in all colonial situations the fundamental question was then how to reduce the costs of British occupation without losing the advantages that control of Iraq was intended to provide. The ideal solution was to set up a client indigenous state whose rulers could claim to be in some sense independent but which also recog-nized the benefits of underlying British influence and would therefore accept some limitation on their sovereignty. This would both reduce local hostility to the

[26] Ibid. 246.   [27] Longrigg, *Iraq*, 113.

alien presence, because it would be to some extent camouflaged, and therefore make it possible to reduce military costs, and at the same time provide Britain with her essential needs. These in the early 1920s were limited to control of Basra and access to Abadan oil, provision of air bases, and a dominant position in the prospective, though still unproven, Kirkuk oil reserves. Relatively minor considerations were the security of British commercial enterprises and the legal position of British nationals, then covered by the Capitulations. All these things might be covered by a treaty with a viable Iraqi government, provided such a government could be set up and was accepted by the majority of those Iraqis who carried political and social weight. There were plenty of models of such situations in the then imperial world, including French-controlled Morocco and Tunis, Malayan Sultanates, Indian princely states, even Egypt before 1914, though Britain had no treaty with the Khedive. The French had had the opportunity to create such a system in Syria in 1920, but had been discouraged by the aggressive tactics of the Syrian (though in fact largely Iraqi) nationalists in crowning Faysal king and rejecting French influence under the mandate. The question in Iraq was how to build a state from the fragments of the three Ottoman vilayets and to find a credible king who would be prepared to play the double role of leader of his people and ally of the British as the mandatory power.

It was perhaps the main achievement of the British in Iraq that they were able to create at least the semblance of an independent monarchical state while retaining their essential interests. The solution had been partly planned by A. T. Wilson as early as 30 July 1920 when, hearing that Faysal had been deposed in Syria, he wired the India Office suggesting that Faysal should be offered 'the headship of the Mesopotamian State'. 'Faysal alone of all Arabian potentates has any idea of running a civilized government on Arab lines.'[28] The evidence suggests, however, that Wilson envisaged Faysal as a purely titular head of state with a predominantly British administration and a gradual injection of Iraqi officials in ministerial positions. Wilson was in any case replaced by Sir Percy Cox as Civil Commissioner on 4 October, and, having just discussed strategy in London, he acted promptly. He had persuaded the British government that the only way to end the rebellion and reduce British costs was to carry out 'a complete and necessarily rapid transformation of the façade of the existing administration from British to Arab'.[29] Here the key word was 'façade'. Cox had no intention of losing control of Iraq: what mattered was how the thing looked. He was in a uniquely strong position to act since the rebellion had been suppressed by Wilson and the Iraqi notables were momentarily ready to do what they were told. The first thing was to create an Iraqi state to replace the current military occupation. He did this by setting up a Council under the Naqib of Baghdad with a number of carefully selected notables and leading Sharifians as nominal heads of the main departments. In November Cox declared that this Council of nine was the provisional national

[28] Wilson, *Mesopotamia 1917–1920*, 305–6.   [29] Graves, *Cox*, 266.

government. The Council planned an Electoral Law for calling a Constituent Assembly which would draw up a constitution. A national army was planned along with a gendarmerie.

It therefore appeared that Cox, at one stroke, had laid the foundations for a modern democratic indigenous state. This, of course, was a mirage. Ultimate power still lay with the British. The High Commissioner, as the Civil Commissioner was now called, had a veto on all Council proposals. Each Arab minister had a British Adviser (on the Egyptian pattern) who was appointed by and was responsible to the High Commissioner. These men could insist on their recommendations to their ministers being accepted if rejection would have serious domestic or international consequences. In practice, since virtually none of these ministers had any experience of government at this level, the Advisers virtually dictated departmental policy. In addition to this control in the centre there were British Political Officers, from 1923 called Administrative Inspectors, who had much the same influence on the local governors (mutasarrifs) of the provinces—liwas. In short, the apparent contrast between Wilson's proposals and the instantaneous creation of an Iraqi state by Cox was largely an illusion.

Yet to complete the new pattern of an Iraqi state it was essential to set up a head of state. This was not easy. There was no Iraq equivalent of the Sharif of Mecca: the nearest parallels were the Naqibs (keepers of the shrine) of Baghdad, Saiyid Abdur Rahman, and of Basra, Saiyid Talib ibn Saiyid Rajab. The former was acceptable and collaborative as President of the Council, but too old to become head of state, while Talib, although Minister of Interior in the new Council, had a notorious reputation as pre-1914 boss of Basra with many murders alleged against him. He was, moreover, a very committed Sunni in a country with a Shii majority. The obvious thing was therefore to import a king, as many of the new states of eastern Europe did in and after 1919. Given the role played by the Hashemites in the Arab rising and the fact that large promises had been made to Husayn in 1915, it seemed reasonable to choose one of Husayn's sons. The question was which of them. Abdullah, the second son, had played the largest role in negotiating the alliance with Britain, but his record in the war was poor. Faysal, however, had become the embodiment of the Arab rising and, having just been ejected from Syria, was available: as was seen above, Wilson regarded him as the logical choice.

The final decision to impose him on Iraq was taken at the Cairo Conference of March 1921, though the decision had in fact been taken in London in December 1920. This was set up by Winston Churchill, who had become Colonial Secretary in January. At the same time Iraq along with Palestine was transferred from India Office and War Office control to a new Middle Eastern Department of the Colonial Office.[30] As War Minister in 1920 Churchill had demanded reduction in the size and cost of British military forces in Iraq and he now set out to achieve

[30] For the transfer of Iraq and Palestine to the Colonial Office see Paris, *Britain, the Hashemites and Arab Rule*, ch. 6.

this in his new role. He chaired the Cairo Conference, whose members included the main service chiefs in the Middle East along with Sir Percy Cox for Iraq, Sir Herbert Samuel as High Commissioner for Palestine, T. E. Lawrence, Gertrude Bell, and Jafar al-Askari, the sole Iraqi representative, one-time Governor of Aleppo and now a leading member of the Sharifian Iraqis who were prepared to collaborate with the British. For Iraq the conference had to take four main decisions: to choose an Arab ruler; to decide how to deal with the northern Kurds; to decide how to reduce British military expenditure; and to arrange for defence after the projected withdrawal of British forces.

The choice of king had in fact been made in December 1920, when Faysal was informally offered the post. He initially refused on the ground that his older brother, Abdullah, had a prior claim. Abdullah had been supported by Curzon at the Foreign Office, but for obscure reasons he was now persuaded by Lawrence to step down. As will be seen in Chapter 6, he was later pensioned off by being made Amir of the newly created Amirate of Transjordan, which was carved out of the Palestine mandate. Faysal was thus chosen on the grounds that he had proved his ability as leader of the Northern Army in the Hijaz and had much experience of international affairs through his negotiations in Paris. It remained to impose him on Iraq, which had no connection with the Hashemite family and had not been involved in the Hijaz campaign, though many of the Iraqi officers who were now returning from Syria knew him well.

The Kurds proved an insoluble problem. The Treaty of Sèvres in 1920 had promised a Kurdish state to be carved out of the regions occupied mainly by Kurds in Iraq and the newly emerging Turkey. By 1921 it was clear that Mustafa Kemal would never accept this, and Cox was convinced that the Kurds within the British occupied area of Iraq, whose northern borders were still unclear, were incapable of forming and running a state. Their future was therefore left uncertain, but their region was to be left in a semi-autonomous condition for the time being.

Much more decisive action was taken over defence. It was decided that British and Indian forces should be run down rapidly and that from 1922 the newly established Royal Air Force, which had demonstrated its utility in dealing with recalcitrant Somalis, should be responsible for both internal and external security. To support the RAF the existing irregular forces known as Levies would be expanded, including the Nestorian Christian refugees from Anatolia known as Assyrians. These would be paid from British funds, while Arab Levies would be paid by the Baghdad government. Thus British defence costs would be greatly reduced, as they were also in Palestine, leaving the two High Commissioners heavily dependent on the collaboration of Iraqis and Palestinians. It was a high risk strategy and was in contrast with that of the French in Syria, who always kept substantial numbers of troops in Lebanon and Syria, many of them from French West and North Africa.

The Conference left Cox to carry out this strategy in Iraq. The first step was to impose Faysal on an apathetic or even hostile people. As a preliminary it was necessary to eliminate the two alternative candidates for head of state. The Naqib of Baghdad, who had earlier strongly opposed a Hashemite ruler, was talked round by Cox and agreed not to stand. Talib was a more difficult problem. He was very ambitious and had a strong political base in Basra. His candidature was supported by his Adviser as Minister of Interior, H. St J. B. Philby. Talib openly supported the candidature of the Naqib of Baghdad, probably hoping to succeed him on his predictably imminent death. On 16 April he made a speech threatening a rising if the British did not appoint the Naqib. The following day he was arrested on Cox's orders after having tea with Gertrude Bell and deported to Ceylon. It was, as Winstone later described it, 'an act of social and political insensibility',[31] and Philby along with many other British officials was outraged. He protested to Cox, and was promptly dismissed.[32] The whole episode was typical of the more arbitrary aspects of British colonial rule and made nonsense of the claim that the Iraqis had a free choice of ruler.

This was made even clearer when Faysal was pushed onto the stage. He was brought to Basra on 23 June and went by train to Baghdad amidst public apathy. On 11 July the docile Council duly and unanimously declared him King. But he had still to be accepted by the people. Between then and August a forceful campaign was mounted to persuade notables in all areas to accept Faysal and Political Officers were instructed to impose maximum pressure. Gertrude Bell, by then a firm supporter of Faysal, applied her considerable influence on the tribal chiefs. The strongest argument in Faysal's favour, at a time when the British were at their most dominant and still had substantial forces available, was that they wanted Faysal. The outcome was a very improbable claim that 96 per cent of those consulted had favoured Faysal: of course no alternative was offered. Thus on 23 August, Faysal was duly enthroned in Baghdad,[33] and became King as a British puppet: as Gertrude Bell, though his strong supporter, put it to the American chargé d' affaires, 'We have carried him on our shoulders.'[34]

From a British standpoint, therefore, Faysal's appointment was intended to establish a 'national' government which would attract genuine Iraqi support, and so deflect anti-British feelings, but would nevertheless be subservient to British interests. As in all imperial situations, this was a very difficult balance to achieve. If Faysal was too subservient to the British High Commissioner he would never gain the allegiance of his subjects. Conversely if he became a genuinely free agent the British position would be eroded. This balancing act depended on two things. First, British rights and obligations would have to be defined, probably in a treaty willingly accepted by the new Iraqi government. Second, it was essential to persuade Faysal, once he was firmly established, to see that it was in his interests to accept British rights and carry his government with him. These became the central issues during the remaining eleven years of the British mandate to 1932.

[31] Winstone, *Gertrude Bell*, 240.
[32] For his later career in Transjordan and Saudi Arabia see Monroe, *Philby of Arabia*.
[33] For a cynical account of the ceremony by a Political Officer who was present see Fieldhouse (ed.), *Kurds, Arabs and Britons*, 96.   [34] Kedourie, *Chatham House Version*, 242.

The immediate need was to negotiate a treaty. In 1921 Britain was in a strong position to obtain one that secured its perceived interests since it had theoretically unlimited powers under the mandate, Iraqi politicians were not yet firmly established or experienced in administration, there were still substantial British forces available, and Iraq could only become formally independent if Britain was willing to testify to the League of Nations that Iraq was fit to become a sovereign state. On the other hand, as in Syria after 1932, there were sufficiently strong nationalistic and Arabist feelings among a minority of the political elite, particularly the ex-Sharifians from Syria, to make it very difficult to find a formula that would satisfy both British demands and Iraqi claims to independence. In particular Iraqi politicians took the view that a treaty could only be between two sovereign states, and that if they signed one it would signify the end of the mandate.

Negotiations over a possible treaty began early in 1922. A draft was accepted by Faysal on 3 October and ratified by the Council on 10 October, both subject to ratification by the projected National Assembly. As in Syria a decade later, the initial draft came from the metropolis.[35] In form it was a treaty between two states but this was an illusion. The draft incorporated many of the articles of the mandate. In addition the King agreed to be guided by the High Commissioner on important international and financial matters and on British interests and would consult him on sound financial policies so long as Iraq had financial obligations to Britain. All gazetted officials who were not Iraqis must be approved by the High Commissioner—in effect ensuring that they were British. Faysal was committed to framing an organic law to be presented to a Constituent Assembly which was to ensure full political and social rights for all irrespective of creed or race. Defence was to be at Iraqi cost after conclusion of the agreement. Britain would assist in the defence of Iraq, training the officers of the new army and providing all imported defence equipment of 'the latest pattern' (later an important issue). The Capitulations were abrogated but courts holding cases affecting foreigners were to have at least one British judge. Iraq was to pay about £588,000 for British public works installations and to accept its share of the Ottoman debt. A separate protocol defined the position of British officials in gazetted posts. They were to be employed and paid by the Iraq government but were to be 'servants of His Britannic Majesty' and answerable to the High Commissioner. The existing system of ministerial and provincial 'Advisers' was retained with different terminology. The treaty was to remain in force for twenty years, though a protocol of March 1923 stated that it would expire when and if Iraq became a member of the League of Nations—that is, fully sovereign—or not later than four years after the conclusion of a British peace treaty with Turkey.

[35] The main clauses of the draft treaty, together with an extensive footnote on its drafting in London, are printed in A. F. Madden and J. Darwin (eds.), *The Dependent Empire, 1900–1948* (Westport, Conn., 1994), 636–8. There it is argued that the original draft came from Churchill in February 1922 and that he persuaded the cabinet to prefer his draft to that of the Foreign Office, drafted by Major H. W. Young.

There was so much in this draft that offended Iraqi and Arab nationalism that it was only accepted by Faysal and the Council on the assumption that it might be amended or rejected by the projected Constituent Assembly. Essentially it imposed a colonial system on a country whose leaders, especially the ex-Sharifian officers, believed they had been fighting for full independence and fulfilment of the Anglo-French promise of November 1918 of self-determination. It is therefore less surprising that it took until 1924 to get it ratified by the Constituent Assembly than that it was ratified at all. Its terms were strongly opposed by the Shii ulama and many in the south. Faysal could not allow himself to be seen to be in favour of it. Cox, followed as High Commissioner by Sir Henry Dobbs from February 1923, dealt with this opposition by a mixture of force, concession, and persuasion. In August 1922 Faysal seemed determined to oppose the treaty, so that the Naqib, who was in favour of it, resigned with his cabinet. At that point Faysal fortuitously developed appendicitis, and while he was away Cox imposed direct rule as before the creation of the Council. To reduce Shia opposition he exiled a number of the most strongly opposed ulama on the grounds that they were Persian. When Faysal recovered in September he had clearly grasped the realities of the situation. He reinstated the cabinet and signed the draft treaty. Opposition was further reduced by the protocol of April 1923 which reduced the duration of the treaty to four years after the signature of a treaty with Turkey. Since the Lausanne Treaty was signed in July 1923, this implied that the treaty would expire in 1927 and made it seem far less significant. The complication here was Mosul. The Turks still claimed that vilayet and its future was left open by Lausanne for the League of Nations to decide. Between 1920 and 1923 the Turks had posed a serious threat to British/Baghdad control over the province, infiltrating with irregular troops and forming alliances with alienated Kurdish chiefs. From the standpoint of Faysal and Baghdad politicians, who were determined to include Mosul in the new state, British help was essential in dealing with this threat. It was not finally removed until 1926 when the League of Nations Council, after sending an investigatory commission, decided to award the province to Iraq. Even so the condition was that there should be a new Anglo-Iraqi treaty, to be in force for twenty-five years unless Iraq was meantime admitted to the League as a sovereign state.[36] This greatly confused the issue and made a second treaty necessary, though in fact the first treaty had been ratified before this decision.

Meanwhile the Council had debated at length and revised the draft constitution of the Constituent Assembly as provided by the Colonial Office. In particular it was decided to retain the old Ottoman system of elections in two stages, whereby all male taxpayers over the age of 21 voted for the secondary electors who in turn voted for the deputies. Four seats were reserved for religious minorities.

[36] For detailed accounts of these frontier skirmishes and how eventually the RAF dealt with them see W. R. Hay, *Two Years in Kurdistan: Experiences of a Political Officer, 1918–1920* (London, 1921); Edmonds, *Kurds, Turks and Arabs*; Fieldhouse (ed.), *Kurds Arabs and Britons*.

Notionally this would produce a democratic system in which the cabinet was responsible to the Chamber of Deputies (the Senate was nominated by the King) and could be forced to resign by a majority vote in the Chamber. Any deputy could propose legislation with the support of ten others, provided it did not concern financial matters. But in fact the system was far from genuinely democratic. The King (under the mandate effectively with British approval) could appoint and dismiss cabinets, summon, prorogue, or dissolve parliament, reject legislation, and issue ordinances while parliament was not sitting. Moreover the double-stage electoral process enabled the government to put great pressure on the final electors to return approved candidates: this had been a key aspect of the final years of the Ottoman regime.

Despite a fatwa banning electoral participation issued by Shii divines, the election to the Assembly duly took place between January and March 1924 and the Assembly met on 27 March. There was little opposition to the electoral law and the constitution, but immediate and strong opposition to the draft treaty. Again Dobbs invoked the threat of force. The treaty was debated in secretive sessions and a number of deputies resigned. Dobbs then threatened that unless the treaty was ratified he would prorogue the Assembly and adopt direct rule under the mandate. The threat worked. The treaty was ratified by 37 to 24 votes with eight abstentions, subject to the proviso that it would not come into force unless Britain could secure Mosul for Iraq. It was significant that a large number of tribal leaders supported the treaty on the assumption that they would benefit from tax remissions and grants of state land, as indeed many did.

Iraq now had a constitution and its modern political life began. But the League of Nations decided in 1926 that a new treaty should be drawn up and that it should run for twenty-five years. This was largely due to reservations by members of the 1925 Mosul Commission about the future treatment of Kurds and other minorities. The Colonial Office was by then anxious to speed up the process of making Iraq independent and ending the mandate, largely for financial reasons (Iraq still received £3.9 million British subsidy in 1927, largely for the remaining military costs), subject to protection of British interests. Negotiations therefore began again in September 1927. This time Faysal proved compliant, provided that independent Iraq had full control over defence and was free to adopt military conscription, which the British had so far blocked. But Faysal now found it very difficult to persuade his politicians to accept even the modified treaty he signed in December 1927. Key objections were over defence costs and the role of the High Commissioner. After two years of haggling the terms of a new treaty were agreed in 1929 and signed in 1930. It is significant that the Prime Minister who finally accepted the treaty was Nuri as-Said, who was to become the main agent of Anglo-Iraqi alignment until his murder in 1958. Its terms were to be critical for British interests in Iraq until the 1950s.

From a British standpoint, the treaty was intended to secure what were regarded as essential British interests in Iraq with minimum cost to Britain.

Britain would recommend to the League of Nations that the mandate would end and that Iraq would become a fully independent member of the League in 1932 'if all goes well' in the meantime. Once independent, Iraq would have an agreed common foreign policy with Britain. There would be mutual help in time of war, including the right of Britain to transport troops across Iraq and the use of two military airfields, to be leased rent-free. Iraq would take over all British responsibilities. Subsidiary agreements specified that Iraq should normally employ Britons in posts held by non-Iraqis and continue to buy its military equipment from Britain. There was to be a new uniform legal system, replacing the rule that there should be British judges in cases affecting British subjects, but there would continue to be British lawyers in specified positions. The High Commissioner would become an Ambassador and British officials would continue in post only where invited by the Iraq government.

The treaty was eventually ratified by the Iraqi parliament in November 1930, against strong opposition, particularly from the Kurds who rightly complained that it made no mention of the autonomy promised in 1922 or of later pledges concerning appointment of Kurds to local official positions and the use of Kurdish in education and public documents. It was to last for twenty-five years, though either party could request modifications. The treaty was then sent to the League's Mandates Commission for approval, where it was minutely examined, particularly since Iraq was the first, and until 1945 the only, mandate to be recommended for independence. British representatives in Geneva consistently minimized obvious problems, particularly those affecting minorities, and played down petitions from Kurds, Assyrians, and others. In June 1931 the Commission reported in favour of ending the mandate provided that guarantees were provided for the interests of minorities, fulfilment of international conventions, financial obligations (for the Ottoman debt), the rights of foreigners, and most favoured treatment for the trade of all League members. It was unanimously approved by the League Assembly in October 1932. Iraq was free.

Two questions arise. First, why, by contrast with France in Syria and Lebanon, was Britain not only prepared but eager to give up her mandate? Second, how much difference in practice did independence make to the position of Britain in Iraq?

These questions are intimately connected. Britain's position in the Middle East as a whole was far more secure than that of France. Still dominant in Egypt and most of the small states of the Persian gulf, with both Cyprus (since 1914) and Aden as colonies, Iraq was not then as important to Britain's strategic position in the region as France conceived its mandates to be in the eastern Mediterranean. If problems arose in Iraq it was possible to bring troops or RAF planes from Egypt or India. Moreover, there had never been a strong emotional swell in British politics of the sort that had induced French governments to demand their share of the Middle East partition. Thus there was no outcry in Britain against the treaty of the sort that arose in France in and after 1936 against the draft treaty with Syria.

Closely related to this was the nature of the Anglo-Iraqi treaty and Britain's relations with the Iraqi regime. Essentially independence did not deprive Britain of any of the important benefits it had had under the mandate. Given the provision of two RAF bases and the right of transit in time of war, Iraq remained a valuable staging post between the Mediterranean and India. Britain held a dominant position in the oil industry. By the later 1920s British interests controlled 47.5 per cent of the shares in the old Turkish Petroleum Company, renamed the Iraq Petroleum Company (IPC) in 1929, and in 1931 this was given a blanket concession covering the whole of Iraq east of the Tigris in the Mosul and Baghdad vilayets. Extensive oil reserves had been discovered in 1927 and it was planned to build pipelines to Haifa and Tripoli, though the oil did not come on stream until 1934. In return IPC agreed to pay large advances on future royalties which were critical for Iraqi finances in that period of international recession. British firms dominated most aspects of the commercial economy, particularly large-scale business in Baghdad and the river steamships. These interests were well protected under the terms of the treaty.

The most obvious change lay in the system of government. The High Commissioner lost his role as effective governor and was replaced by an Ambassador, under the Foreign not the Colonial Office. The many Advisers at the capital and in the provinces lost their directorial and veto powers and many were dismissed, to be replaced by Iraqis. In fact the number of British gazetted officials had been run down progressively from the mid-1920s: from 364 in 1920 to 130 in 1929 and 118 in 1931, of whom 38 had been advisory and 80 executive. The main central departments were taken over by Iraqis, leaving a residue of Britons as civil service advisers. But their influence remained considerable. Few Iraqi ministers still had any experience in the technicalities of their offices or were interested in them: few stayed in office for any length of time to learn the ropes. There were few Iraqi senior civil servants with the highest skills. Thus a core of British senior advisers remained, none more important than Sir Kinahan Cornwallis, who stayed on as Adviser to the very powerful Minister of Interior until 1935. He was then dismissed by King Ghazi, but was replaced by his deputy, C. J. Edmonds, who lasted until retirement in 1945. A parallel evolution took place in the role of the Ambassador. No longer able to veto legislation or acts of the King, he retained much of his influence, provided he was prepared to use it effectively. Remaining in the still-named Residency along with his counsellors and a significant clerical staff, the Ambassador could still exert considerable weight. Although the Ambassador no longer had the ability to call for information as of right, it was accepted that the Adviser to the Ministry of Interior would keep him well informed. This system worked well under the first Ambassador (also the last High Commissioner), Sir Francis Humphreys, until he left in 1935. His successors down to 1941, however, were not old Iraq hands and seem to have lost touch with political realities. Thus the critical army coup of 1936, which changed the whole nature of government in Iraq, apparently took the current Ambassador, Sir Archibald Clark Kerr, completely by surprise.[37] In fact the key to maintaining British influence lay in using the same sort of persuasive skills as were used in Egypt, particularly after the Anglo-Egyptian treaty of 1936. These were fundamental to the sort of informal empire the British were sustaining in the Middle East.

It might thus appear that the British had been successful in their management of the mandate. They could pride themselves in having created a state and possibly a nation out of three fragments of the Ottoman empire. They had built an apparently democratic state where there was no tradition of democracy and established the rule of law which gave equality to all groups. They had finally managed to fulfil the terms of the mandate and transfer their authority to an elected government, while retaining much of the substance of their influence. They might well criticize the French, who had done none of these things and had, indeed, ultimately to be forced by British military force to grant independence to Syria and Lebanon in 1945. Yet there is another side to this picture. The longer-term measure of British success was the nature of the state and society they had created. How justified were the high claims made to the League of Nations in 1929 that Iraq was now in every way fit to become a member of the League? Above all, what was the structure of politics and society? Was this a real democracy? How real were the rights of minorities and indeed of the majority of the population? From a different standpoint, how far did the mandate serve Britain's own interests? Looking ahead, can one see in the mandate period the roots of the militarist autocracy that became endemic in Iraq after 1958?

3. POLITICS AND SOCIETY, 1920–1941

The key to the British approach to creating the Iraq constitution lies in the fact that, uniquely in British imperial history, it was intended to lead to early independence rather than extended imperial rule. This, of course, was consistent with the terms of the mandate; yet there had been no time limit on it. It was largely due to British financial stringency that the decisions of 1921 were taken. The urgent need was then to cobble together a political structure which could operate as a façade for British rule for a short period, at least until a treaty had been agreed and the League of Nations could be persuaded that Iraq was now a viable state with suitable securities for minorities. The need was to construct a mechanism

---

[37] See Fieldhouse (ed.), *Kurds, Arabs and Britons*, 204. Wallace Lyon, an ex-Administrative Inspector and then a Land Settlement Officer, had lunch with Kerr just before the coup and was told that Kerr had contacts only with the then Prime Minister and Nuri as-Said, Minister of Interior. Since these were 'playing ball with him, he didn't bother about anyone else'. About ten days later the coup took place. It has been argued that had the then Ambassador, Sir Basil Newton, been more politically active, the coup of 1941 that might have led to a German occupation of Iraq could have been averted. British influence was then reconstructed by Sir Kinahan Cornwallis, brought back as Ambassador, who was in office until 1945.

which could be wound up and allowed to operate as best it might, subject to observation and correction under the reserved British powers, until the moment of independence. After that it would be left to its own devices.

That being so, the British did not have the time, resources, or indeed the inclination, to undertake fundamental social or political reconstruction. Any political system, though dressed up in the finery of western constitutionalism, would in practice reflect the underlying social realities of the society and its earlier traditions. As was seen above, this, like all other Middle Eastern societies, was a highly stratified society dominated by tribal rulers and land-owners, the urban official aristocracy, and the Islamic clerisy. There was no significant middle class, since the urban business class was small and socially inferior, dominated in Baghdad at least by Jews and foreigners. It had had no experience of representative politics above the level of municipal councils until 1908, and the two-stage electoral system had then enabled the authorities to ensure that the appropriate delegates were chosen. Appointments to official positions, the chief objective of the urban notables, depended on a complex process of networking and patron–client relationships. None of these factors was altered by the British conquest and mandate. The British could only adapt their strategies to the basic social realities; and the Iraqis who drew up the constitution were not interested in liberal innovations. There was only one significant novelty after 1920: the appointment of a King and the closely related influx of the ex-Sharifian officers who had served with Faysal. For the most part these ex-officers came from the middle or lower middle classes of Iraq and under normal condition would have had no significant political or administrative importance. But in the longer term these were to have a dynamic and largely disastrous effect on politics, leading ultimately to the political dominance of the army.

Given the social realities they inherited it is not surprising that, during the British mandate to 1932, there were essentially two political systems in operation. The first was that of the countryside, a system based on the traditional power of the landed classes, the shaykhs, aghas, and other tribal chiefs. The second was the politics of the towns, increasingly dominated by Baghdad. This was the politics of the urban aristocracy, of professionals, wealthy businessmen, and the newer breed of virtually professional politicians, among whom the ex-Sharifian officers played a leading role. The two structures overlapped, but there were functional differences. Few of the landed class were sufficiently literate to hold ministerial posts: according to Batatu, between 1920 and 1936 only two, 1.8 per cent, were tribal shaykhs, and only one of this class, Abd-ul Muhsin as-Sadun, was a Prime Minister.[38] He held this post four times between 1922 and 1929, but he was no mere land-owner. He was an ex-Ottoman officer, member of the Ottoman parliament 1908–18, and an ex-Minister of Justice and Interior. For the majority

[38] Two others, Tawfiq as-Suwaidi and Naji as-Suwaidi, both came from a land-owning family of ulama and ashraf and were sons of a sharia judge. Batatu, *Old Social Classes*, tables 7.2 and 7.3. M. A. Tarbush, in *The Role of the Military*, tables 2 and 3, has different figures, which are quoted below, but this probably results from differing interpretations of 'tribal shaykh'.

of the great land-owners politics centred on their localities and their control over lesser chiefs and their dependants. But they could play an important role in formal state politics because their seats were guaranteed by their control over the electoral process. They were for the most part allies of the British, whom they regarded as protectors of their interests. They could be used to carry critical parliamentary votes, as over the adoption of the organic law by the Constituent Assembly and the treaty. They could also be used as a makeweight against both Faysal and Ghazi. Their most important parliamentary periods were in 1924 and the Constituent Assembly, when representatives of the shaykhs and aghas provided 34 per cent of members, and from 1943 to 1958, when their percentage share never dropped below 31.9, rising to 37.8 per cent in 1954. During Faysal's reign, their numbers were reduced, ranging from 14.8 per cent in 1928 to 20.5 per cent in 1933, mainly because Faysal saw them as allies of the British and used his influence to reduce their importance. Conversely, the late monarchy from 1943 saw them as valuable allies against hostile urban politicians and the now politically very active army.[39] It can therefore be argued that the landed classes provided the mainstay of the British mandate and interest, both in maintaining order in the countryside and in constituting a reliable backing in parliamentary politics.

Yet politics in the conventional sense during and after the mandate was essentially an urban phenomenon, based on the three main cities and increasingly dominated by Baghdad. The question is what sort of political system emerged and how far did it represent and take account of the interests of the mass of Iraqis.

On this there have been two contrasting interpretations. The first, which Elie Kedourie called 'The Chatham House Version', suggests that the creation of a democratic parliamentary system binding the disparate parts of Iraq together was one of the great British achievements. Iraq became the first non-European or European colonial society to have a western-style liberal constitution. If this is correct it would be possible to interpret the complexities of Iraqi political life along conventional western lines as a struggle between principled parties who differed only in their contrasting interpretation of what was best for the nation. It would thus be a matter for surprise and regret that after 1958, Iraq should have become a military despotism and that the interests of Kurds and Shiites should consistently have been subordinated to those of the minority Arab Sunnis.[40]

This, however, has long been rejected as a caricature of the realities of Iraqi politics. The alternative interpretation, in its extreme form put forward by Kedourie, is that from the start post-1920 Iraqi politics were fraudulent. He argued that Iraqi politics flowed from their flawed beginning in the arbitrary imposition of Faysal and British haste to limit their responsibilities. The constitution ratified in 1924 by the Constituent Assembly was notionally democratic, providing one deputy in the lower house for each 20,000 adult male tax-payers. But it was in no

---

[39] Tarbush, *The Role of the Military*, 44–50; Batatu, *Old Social Classes*, tables 6.1, 7.4.
[40] For this general argument see Kedourie, *Chatham House Version*, chs. 9, 10, and 12.

sense democratic in operation. Delegates were virtually nominated by the government of the day through its ability to put pressure on urban and rural notables.
There were no principled parties: parties were put together by notables, often with
high-sounding reforming objectives, but had no intention of altering the status
quo. The fact that between 1921 and 1958 there were no fewer than fifty-seven
ministries, Kedourie wrote, 'argues a wretched political architecture and constitutional jerry-building of the most dangerous kind'.[41] Moreover, this artificial state
was extremely unfair in its treatment of minorities, notably Kurds, Jews, and
Assyrians. Kurds and Shiites were always grossly under-represented in cabinets,
the Chamber of Deputies, and provincial administration. Education policy was
designed to promote Arabic and pan-Arabism at the expense of non-Arab minorities. Land policy favoured the minority of mainly Baghdad politicians and large
land-owners, who were able to amass or expand their estates at the expense of the
peasant cultivators. In short, from the start the state of Iraq was a caricature of
a liberal western state, dominated and exploited by a small elite. It was therefore
no surprise that it ended with the military coup of 1958.

Kedourie was born a Baghdad Jew, and the terrible treatment of his people in
Iraq in and after 1948 may have influenced his views. Yet virtually all subsequent
research and publication supports his argument. On the political system in particular there seems unanimity that this democracy was a farce. Longrigg, who was in
the administration until 1932, wrote later that, while there was no real indigenous
alternative in 1920, given the lack of any traditional ruler, Iraq was not capable of
acting like a western democracy. Hence:

In 1932 the Government of Iraq consisted of a façade of democratic forms behind which
operated the actual power of a small ruling class: a class which contained on the one hand
more than enough figures capable of filling the ministerial posts available, but on the other
too little variety of viewpoint to compete for power by the advocacy of genuinely alternative programmes.[42]

Analysing the character of cabinets and parliaments between 1920 and the military coup of 1936, Tarbush provides details which fully support this analysis. Of
the 59 men who held cabinet appointments in these years only eight (9 per cent)
were tribal shaykhs. Seventy-five per cent came from the three main cities, including
63 per cent from Baghdad. Twenty, over a third, had been Ottoman or Sharifian
soldiers. Within this elite was an inner circle of fourteen men who between them
held 97 (54 per cent) of the 179 ministerial appointments made. Four-fifths of
these were urban notables, nine of them from Baghdad. Of the eleven Prime
Ministers eight came from Baghdad, two from Mosul. From a different standpoint,
the Shia, though constituting 56 per cent of the population, had only 24 per cent
of cabinet posts and provided only two of that inner circle. Cabinets had a very
short life, on average only 8.5 months. Policies and elections played little part in

---

[41] Kedourie, *Chatham House Version*, 239.   [42] Longrigg, *Iraq*, 224.

these changes. No government resigned because it lost the confidence of parliament. Ministries were normally changed because the King, who could dismiss any cabinet at will, wanted to alter the ministerial balance or reward a supporter, or because leading political figures fell out between themselves. A general election was used by the incumbent government to get rid of opponents or reward supporters. When an election was called the government sent instructions to the mutasarrifs (provincial governors) who controlled the electoral system to ensure the election of the desired candidates. Thus in the 1925 election, all but eight of the 88 deputies elected were supporters of the government under as-Sadun. Significantly, this, the first election under the new constitution, reduced the number of shaykhs and aghas in the Chamber of Deputies from 34.3 per cent in the previously British-sponsored Constituent Assembly, to 19.3 per cent. The new urban political class had established its dominance over the rural aristocracy.[43]

All this strongly supports Kedourie's condemnation of the nature of Iraqi politics. Both before and after independence in 1932 they were run by a small elite which had capitalized on the introduction of a quasi-democratic constitution to shuffle office and its rewards between them. In most respects this did not matter very much before 1932 because real power lay with the British who ran the administration and could promote policies or veto what was proposed by the government. Ministries came and went but there were no significant consequences. After 1932, however, these constraints were removed. Thereafter governments were free to do as they pleased, and most of their policies in the later 1930s, particularly over land rights and education, were designed to favour the Sunni elite and the Arabs against the mass of peasants or the minority of non-Arabs. It is therefore not surprising that the army, the new third party (after the crown and parliament) in Iraq, should have had little respect for the politicians. In fact, the creation and rise of the army was the most important single political development in Iraq during the period before the crisis of 1941.

The creation of the army was intimately connected with the position and interests of the ex-Sharifians who came to Baghdad after 1920. As was seen above, the 300 or so of these men had almost all been officers in the Ottoman army, some of whom had deserted or changed colour after being captured by the British. They divide into two groups: those who had supported and fought with Faysal before 1918—these were the inner corps of his supporters—and those who had jumped onto his band-wagon in and after 1918. They had, however, two main virtually uniform characteristics: they were unemployed, and almost all came from the middle or lower middle class, mostly from Baghdad, the northern part of Baghdad vilayet, or from Mosul vilayet. Many were also influenced by the radical reformist ideas of the Young Turks: they believed in strong government from above which would break down ancient shibboleths. Faysal defined this in a confidential memorandum of 1933, shortly before his death.

---

[43] Based mainly on Tarbush, *The Role of the Military*, ch. 3; Batatu, *Old Social Classes*, table 6.1.

The young men of Iraq, who run the government, and at their head a great number of those in positions of responsibility, believe that no consideration should be given to the opinion of fanatics and holders of traditional views . . . and that the country should be driven forward and the people raised to an appropriate level of life without regard to any opinion . . . so long as law and force are the government's and it can coerce all to abide by what it dictates.[44]

This instinct for authoritarian innovation was to have important consequences later on.

But at first the importance of these ex-Sharifians was that they were virtually the only people who unquestioningly supported Faysal. They were, in a sense, his praetorian guard. He gave many of them senior positions in government. Under the mandate they provided 30.8 per cent of Prime Ministers (the sadah most of the rest), and between 1932 and the military coup of 1936 50 per cent. This, and their substantial representation in all cabinets, was deeply resented by many of the landed upper class and the urban notables. Significantly, Jafar al-Askari and Nuri as-Said, both pre-1918 Sharifians and both future Prime Ministers, were appointed Minister of Defence and Commander-in-Chief respectively of the projected but non-existent army in 1920. It was they more than anyone else who fought for the creation of an indigenous and conscript Iraqi army.

This demand was instinctive with these ex-Ottoman army officers who had been trained to believe that a conscript army was the best way to bring together the disparate elements of a far-flung empire. In addition conscription would cost much less than a professional army. The British were consistently opposed to conscription. In 1921 they decided that an Iraqi army must be created to replace the British forces, and also to provide jobs for the otherwise potentially dangerous ex-Sharifian officers. But it was to be relatively small, with a maximum of 15,000, and based on volunteers. It would be backed up by eight squadrons of the RAF, four British or Indian infantry battalions, and the Levies under British officers. Offers of commissions were made to 640 ex-Ottoman officers, who were retrained at a British-run military college. Most newly recruited officers, like the ex-Sharifians, came from the Baghdad area and were Sunnis. But the Sharifians continued to dominate the army: in 1936 twelve of the nineteen senior officers came from their ranks, including all three major-generals, three of the four brigadiers, and six of the eleven colonels.[45] It was initially harder to attract other ranks on the low pay offered; but by 1925 higher pay had led to there being more applicants than places on offer.

Conscription, however, remained a major political issue on the broad grounds of its contribution to the creation of the nation state. Despite their misgivings, the British allowed a conscription bill to be put forward in 1927; it was withdrawn after vehement resistance, especially among the Shia and Kurds: the Shii minister of education resigned over the issue. A new bill was put up and passed in 1934. By

[44] Batatu, *Old Social Classes*, 321.   [45] Ibid. 334.

1936 the army had risen from 12,000 in 1932 to 20,000, two-thirds of it stationed in the Euphrates area where conscription was most detested. At the start this was not an efficient army. Its record in the 1920s and early 1930s against dissident Kurdish chiefs had been poor and the RAF had several times had to rescue military forces. Its first 'success' was to massacre Assyrian civilians in 1933, then, with the first intake of conscripts available, to suppress Shii risings in the Euphrates and a Yazidi rising in the Barzan region in 1935–6.[46]

These operations clearly gave the army leadership confidence in its national role and led directly to the military coup of October 1936.[47] It is tempting to see in the politicization of the Iraqi army in the 1930s parallels with the activities of the Young Officers there in the later 1950s and the earlier military takeover in Egypt. There was indeed some connection between leading army officers and at least overtly reformist politicians: the army could claim that successive governments had been unable to carry through progressive legislation due to the weight of conservative forces in parliament. More specifically there were links between the Ahali group of politicians, formed in 1931 with a mildly socialist agenda, who included the veteran politician Hikmat Sulayman, and senior army officers. The most important of these were Brigadier Bakr Sidqi and Brigadier Abd-ul-Latif Nuri, both from the second generation of Sharifians, as indeed were the so-called Golden Square of colonels who masterminded the 1941 coup. The difference between these army leaders of the 1930s and the rebels of the 1950s was that this earlier generation had by the mid-1930s been absorbed into the upper class of Iraq with substantial properties. They were not social revolutionaries. On the other hand, they were strongly nationalist and pan-Arab, and they had come to despise the rank and file of professional politicians. They were also resentful that successive governments had not provided sufficient money, despite the start of oil revenue in 1934, for the expansionist and modernizing needs of the army. Bakr himself was resentful of the power of the chief of staff, Taha al-Hashimi, backed by his brother, the Prime Minister, Yasin al-Hashimi. Taking advantage of Taha's absence in Turkey, Bakr Sidqi led his army into Baghdad in October 1936, ordering the murder of Jafar al-Askari, who was sent with a message from King Ghazi to persuade him to hold back. This proved a fatal blunder as it made Bakr a marked man for friends of Jafar: he was duly shot by an army officer in August 1937. Meantime, Hikmat Sulayman was installed at the head of a proclaimed reformist government.

Predictably little of this reformist spirit was translated into action. Within a few months it became clear that the reformist plans of leading ministers were disliked by many officers. In the same month that Bakri Sidqi was killed, Sulayman was forced to resign as Prime Minister in the face of an open rebellion by the northern section of the army based on Mosul.

[46] For details of these risings and their suppression see Tarbush, The *Role of the Military*, 102–20.

[47] There is a detailed account of political developments and the army's activities in this period in M. Khadduri, *Independent Iraq 1932–1958: A Study in Iraqi Politics* (1951; 2nd edn. London, 1960), chs. 5–7, on which much of this account is based.

Although its immediate effects were small, the 1936 coup proved a turning point in Iraqi history. Khadduri lists and describes six more army political coups between 1936 and April 1941.[48] Not all were as dramatic as that of 1936 and the most significant of all in 1941. But in effect political change was now dictated by the army, which could indicate to the Prime Minister that he should resign or tell the King—after the death of Ghazi in 1939 the Regent for the young King Faysal II, Abd al-Illah—to change his government or face the consequences. These interventions were sometimes caused by links between ambitious senior officers and related political groups, sometimes by army dissatisfaction with what many officers saw as the self-seeking and inertia of most career politicians. They had little or no effect on what governments did, since the dominant group of army officers were by now integral with the established elite. But they were to prove critical in 1940–1 when war put the strength of the Anglo-Iraqi relationship to the test.[49]

From the death of Hikmat in 1937 the army had been dominated by the seven senior officers who had conspired to kill him. These were Husain Fawzi, Amin al-Umari, Aziz Yamulki, and the so called 'Golden Square' of Colonels Salah-al-Din al-Sabbagh, Kamil Shabib, Fahmi Said, and Mahmud Salman. Initially neither they, nor the then government under Nuri as-Said, who was on good terms with them, particularly over the Palestine issue, was anti-British. When Britain declared war on Germany in September 1939 Nuri quickly complied with the letter of the 1930 treaty: he did not declare war on Germany but broke off relations with it, ejected or interned all Germans, and imposed censorship, curfews, rationing, and all the regulations needed to put Iraq on a war footing. The Golden Square was still supporting Nuri in February 1940, when the other three, older, members of the group seemed set to force the Regent to dismiss Nuri in favour of other leading politicians. They were prevented by the Golden Square, and Fawzi, al-Umari, and Yamulki were promptly retired from the army. But during the spring of 1940, as German forces occupied France and Italy came into the war, the attitude of the Colonels changed. It now seemed likely that Germany would win the war. This would predictably rid them of the disliked British presence, and might, as the one-time Grand Mufti of Jerusalem, Hajj Amin al-Husayni, who had taken refuge in Baghdad, claimed, lead to the end of Zionist power in Palestine.

For some time, however, neither the Golden Square, nor Rashid Ali al-Gaylani, who became Prime Minister again in March 1940, was prepared to break the British connection. Rashid Ali for long wanted careful neutrality in the war, to see what eventually emerged. In the long run it was partly British pressure that forced him and the Square into an overtly pro-German stance. There was a row over British proposals to send Indian troops to Basra, theoretically in transit to Palestine: this was in fact blocked by the Indian government, but Rashid protested

---

[48] M. Khadduri, *Independent Iraq 1932–1958: A Study in Iraqi Politics*, chs. 7–9.

[49] There are many accounts of the events of 1940–2 in the sources listed above. One of the clearest is in Tripp, *History of Iraq*, 94–107.

at the proposal. By this time he was negotiating confidentially with the Italian government, having refused to break off relations with Italy when she entered the war in June. By August he was in touch with Berlin and in October Germany and Italy gave a veiled promise of support for the independence of all the Arab lands after the war, though Germany was not then keen on Iraq breaking with Britain: von Ribbentrop expressly advised against it. But by the end of 1940 the British government came to regard Rashid Ali as a threat. In January 1941 it refused to supply dollars for the purchase of American armaments, a reasonable request since the British were unable to provide the equipment specified in the treaty, though they did not stop the payment of oil royalties. Moreover, it instructed the Ambassador to use all his influence on the Regent to get Rashid Ali out of office.

This was a serious mistake. He was forced out but now dropped his neutrality. On 1 April his military allies forced the resignation of his successor, Taha al-Hashimi, and besieged Baghdad. The Regent refused to accept the order to install Rashid Ali as Prime Minister. He then escaped, along with other members of the government, including Nuri, to Palestine. Since there was no possibility of a legitimate installation of a new government, the army occupied Baghdad, installed Sharif Sharaf, a cousin of the young King Faysal II, as Regent, and made Rashid Ali Prime Minister. He reluctantly accepted a British demand to land troops in Basra, allegedly in transit, and the first of them arrived on 17 April. Rashid then legitimately (since the treaty did not specify the numbers that could be in Iraq at any one time) insisted that no more troops could land until this detachment had gone to Palestine. The British rejected this. They kept the Indian brigade in Basra and flew some troops to Habbaniyah. On 28 April, Cornwallis, just arrived as Ambassador, told the government that three more troopships were coming: they arrived on 29 April. On 30 April, 9,000 Iraqi troops plus artillery and armoured cars massed near Habbaniyah. On 1 May, Cornwallis declared that Britain was at war with Iraq. All British subjects were then interned and the Residency blockaded.[50] It seemed probable that, since there were so few British troops in Iraq, apart from the few in the Habbaniyah RAF base west of Baghdad and those now arriving in Basra, the Iraqis might hold out until effective German support arrived.[51]

Timing was now critical. The Germans had only just completed the occupation of Crete and had warned Rashid Ali that they could not send significant reinforcements for some time. They did, however, send some fighters and bombers, using Syria as a transit base, with the collaboration of the Vichy authorities there. The Italians sent 12 planes and the Vichy authorities ammunition and trucks.

[50] For a detailed and vivid account of conditions in the Embassy during the crisis, including pictures, see Freya Stark (then Oriental Secretary to the Ambassador), *Dust in the Lion's Paw: Autobiography 1939–1946* (London, 1961), ch. 7. See also C. J. Edmonds's diary, Edmonds Papers (see n. 7, above), Box 27/3, paras. 312–490. For an account of the experience of other interned Britons, see Fieldhouse (ed.), *Kurds, Arabs and Britons*, ch. 11 and appendix.

[51] There were some 1,300 RAF servicemen and 100 British soldiers, plus 800 Assyrian Levies in the RAF's Habbaniyah air base.

Had the Iraqi army acted effectively and quickly it might have been able to take over Habbaniyah and block British airborne reinforcement before the main British military build-up could be completed. It would also have made it easy for the Germans to fly in reinforcements. As it was the British took the initiative. Although heavily outmanned, the Habbaniyah commander started an attack on 2 May, and the Iraqi forces began to withdraw as early as 6 May. Why they did so remains a mystery. Tripp writes as if the British military power was overwhelming,[52] but this was certainly not so in early May. The Habbaniyah garrison had no artillery and was very vulnerable to Iraqi artillery. It was not until 18 May that some British and Arab troops, of the Transjordan Arab Legion, arrived after a trek of 800 km across the desert, along with 500 Indian troops flown in from Basra. When the combined force of 1,500, including Assyrian Levies, still with very little artillery, arrived on the outskirts of Baghdad on 30 May there were still some 20,000 Iraqi troops near the city and a further 15,000 in Mosul, who could have been moved down quickly. Yet Rashid Ali, the Colonels, Amin al-Husayni, and many of their political allies left for Iran and some thereafter for Berlin. It is likely that the military indecision stemmed from ministerial uncertainty at the start of May, which Silverfarb argues reflected a split both in the ruling clique and within the army higher command. Moreover, the regime could get little public support. Many Shia were still resentful at the suppression of the Euphrates rising of 1935–6 and some offered to support the British. The Kurds also were resentful that they had obtained none of the autonomy promised in earlier years, that they were grossly under-represented in parliament, and more immediately that an Arab had just been appointed mutasarrif of Suleimaniya, the most Kurdish of all liwas. Shaykh Mahmud, that one-time opponent of the British, offered his services against the Baghdad government. The army also was divided in its attitude. The troops besieging Habbaniyah early in May could have rendered it unusable by destroying its water towers with their artillery had they been determined. Freya Stark explains this anecdotally. She wrote later that 'Johnny Hawtrey [Air Vice-Marshal and Inspector of the Iraq Air Force in 1940] remarked to his ex-pupils how poor their artillery had been against Habbaniyah. . . . They always retorted that, on the contrary, their aim had been *extremely good*, not many of them had wished to destroy us; and this double current through the country . . . was a factor of great though unassessed importance throughout the revolt.'[53]

Whatever the causes, the events of May 1941 ended the first period of politics in independent Iraq and also, until the later 1950s, the dominance of the army over politics. In the short term the British effectively occupied Iraq for the second time, and until 1946 controlled it as they had done during the mandate. The Allied occupation of Syria and Lebanon in June 1941 against resistance by strong Vichy forces secured the northern frontier. In August the Allies invaded

---

[52] Tripp, *History of Iraq*, 105.
[53] Silverfarb, *Britain's Informal Empire*, 131–9; Stark, *Dust in the Lion's Paw*, 128.

Iran in conjunction with the Russians. From later in 1942 Allied successes in the western desert removed the Axis threat to Egypt; and from 1943 Iraq ceased to be of great relevance to the main war.

It was left to the British to reconstruct their informal rule over Iraq.

4. THE REVIVAL, DECLINE, AND FALL OF BRITISH POWER IN IRAQ, 1941–1958

After the crisis of April–May 1941, the British stood in virtually the same position as they had done in 1920. They were military conquerors able to dictate strategies. The main difference was that there was now a well-established constitution with a monarchy and parliament and a range of powerful political leaders, each with his network of supporters in the army and society. For the British, if they wished to reconstitute and preserve their dominant position in Iraq, the need was to construct some new and more acceptable relationship with these indigenous forces, which would provide them with the leverage they wanted and at the same time reduce or eliminate the nationalist resentments at the presence and dominance of a foreign power. The story of their attempt and ultimate failure falls into three time periods. From 1941 to 1946 they ruled Iraq as effectively as they had done under the mandate. From 1946 to 1948 they attempted to negotiate a better long-term relationship, culminating in the failed Treaty of Portsmouth. Finally, from then until 1958, they gradually lost their influence, giving up their formal rights as part of the Baghdad Pact of 1955, but failing to reap the popularity that might have sustained their influence. In 1958 the coup that destroyed the Hashemite monarchy also destroyed the remnants of British influence.

In and after 1941 the British regained virtually full authority to control Iraq. British officials were given authority in key ministries, notably the Ministry of Interior (which controlled the police), railways, roads, currency, and irrigation. British Political Advisers were used to supervise districts, reporting to the Embassy. A primary function was to influence the local notables. C. J. Edmonds, still Adviser to the Minister of Interior, commented that the Embassy had 'pushed its tentacles into the internal administrative machine even more deeply than the High Commission in its later days'.[54] The British also had their military 'area liaison officers' who reported direct to the British military headquarters. Under such pressure successive Iraqi governments had to do as they were told. In point of fact those who held office during these years—Nuri as-Said, who, in or out of office, was the dominant political figure of the next seventeen years, as Prime Minister 1941 to 1944 followed by Hamdi al-Pachachi (1944–6), Tawfiq as-Suwaidi

[54] Quoted D. Silverfarb, *The Twilight of British Ascendancy in the Middle East: A Case Study of Iraq 1941–1958* (New York, 1994), 17. For an account of the activities of these officers see Fieldhouse (ed.), *Kurds, Arabs and Britons*, ch. 12.

(briefly in 1946), Arshad al-Umari (June–November 1946), and Salih Jabr, the first Shii Prime Minister 1947–8—were all old political hands belonging to the Nuri camp. They were prepared to play ball with the British and caused little trouble. More difficult to handle was the Regent, who increasingly wished to exert the sort of influence that Faysal I had had and who was prone to change ministries to suit his immediate political ends.

Probably the most significant achievements of these successive governments were to relax wartime restrictions on political activity and to reduce the effectiveness of the army. In 1943–4 many of those imprisoned in 1941 were released and in 1946 political parties were again permitted. The Electoral Law was changed, ending the two-stage election system. The effect was to increase political activism, which was greatly stimulated by the effects of inflation and poor harvests. The wholesale price index rose from 100 to 614 between 1939 and 1944, due partly to huge British war expenditure of £61.5 million in 1941–3, a shortage of imported goods, and poor harvests, despite a great increase in the acreage under cultivation. The effect on the wage-earning classes was very serious and government attempts to control food prices and use rationing were ineffective. Conversely the land-owning classes did very well, as did black marketeers. These economic developments had a serious effect also on the Kurds, who received little consideration from the Arab officials in Baghdad. Starvation was now added to their long-standing grievances over lack of representation in parliament, government, and administration, and the failure of Baghdad to fulfil its earlier promises of Kurdish officials in Kurdish areas and the use of Kurdish in schools and administration. These grievances fuelled the major Kurdish rising of 1943–5, led by the Mulla Mustafa Barzani.[55] Despite the sympathy many British officials had for the Kurds, they had little for Mulla Mustafa and generally supported the Iraq army's attack on him and his forces.[56]

Perhaps the most serious effect of the Kurdish conflict was to show up the low quality of the Iraqi army. It had never been effective against Kurds in the mountains since most of the conscripts came from Shia in the lowlands. But it was at a very low ebb by the mid-1940s. This was partly due to British inability in the later 1930s and early 1940s to honour their treaty obligations to provide Iraq with the latest military equipment, which was urgently needed for British rearmament, but also to a deliberate policy of running the army down after the crisis of 1941. As General J. M. L. Renton, head of the British military mission in Baghdad, wrote in 1947,

After the collapse of the Revolt [*sic*] and the entry of British troops into Baghdad, the British authorities decided that although it was not possible to disband the Iraqi Army, a policy of weakening it indirectly should be adopted, mainly through the agency of Nuri

---

[55] There is a good account of this in Silverfarb, *The Twilight*, 39–54. See also D. McDowall, *A Modern History of the Kurds* (London and New York, 1997), 290–5.

[56] See Silverfarb, *The Twilight*, 51 for a selection of comments by members of the Residency. Cornwallis called him 'overbearing and tyrannical'; Stewart Perowne 'an egregious brigand'; General Denton, head of the British military mission, 'a cold blooded murderer'.

Pasha. . . . Rations were cut down by 1,000 calories a day below what was considered necessary by the medical authorities for Eastern troops, no clothing or equipment were purchased and by the Spring of 1944 the Army was in rags, with no equipment and no morale.[57]

It was therefore not surprising that the Iraqi army put up such a poor showing against the Kurds: some 14,000 troops and the air force faced some 1,000 men under Mustafa and about 1,300 Kurds of other connections. In fact Mustafa was defeated after three months more by other Kurds, who were bribed to turn against him, than by the army, which suffered some thousand casualties. Thereafter, however, the British, who were about to withdraw their forces once again, were keen to rebuild the Iraqi army, mainly for internal security: it was not deemed competent to take a successful role elsewhere. An urgent need was for modern equipment, particularly tanks, which, under the treaty, only the British were entitled and obliged to supply. But when the Iraqi government negotiated for such equipment in and after 1946 the British government had to reply that Britain had virtually ceased manufacturing military equipment: it had ample war surpluses and was trying to convert industry back to civilian production for export. The Iraqis refused to accept used equipment available in Egypt and it took six months for Britain to organize production in 1947. Meantime the British had attempted to remodel the army. In and after 1944 many senior officers were retired, training was improved, and rations and clothing provided. But the Iraqi army was still under-equipped and in poor condition when it was called to fight in Palestine in 1948–9: in particular it had no tanks.

The importance of all this is that military weakness formed one of the many grievances felt by leading Iraqis against the British at the end of the war. The British withdrew their forces in 1946–7 along with the 'advisory' administrative structure in Baghdad and the provinces. All that remained was the Ambassador, some provincial consuls, and the two air bases. The British were therefore by 1947 back where they had been in 1941. They were, moreover, now extremely unpopular with many sections of Iraqi society, including the armed forces, the more radical nationalist politicians, and the urban mobs, who blamed them for shortages and high prices. It was therefore problematic whether Britain could reconstruct a system of influence which would provide them with what they regarded as the essentials: in particular control of the two air bases, rights of landing and transit, and continued Iraqi membership of the sterling area. In short, could the 1930 treaty, though not due to expire until 1957, be revised and resuscitated to meet new post-war conditions? These were the issues that led to the critical year of 1948 and the failure of the so-called Portsmouth treaty.

[57] Quoted Wm R. Louis, *The British Empire in the Middle East, 1945–1951* (Oxford, 1984), 324. Louis is probably the best source for British policy in Iraq in this period. See also Louis, 'The British and the Origins of the Iraqi Revolution', in R. A. Fernea and Wm R. Louis (eds.), *The Iraqi Revolution of 1958: The Old Social Classes Revisited* (London and New York, 1991), and other chapters.

There is no doubt that the Labour government in Britain in and after 1945 was as keen as any of its predecessors to maintain a dominant British position in Iraq, and indeed throughout the Middle East.[58] As Foreign Secretary Ernest Bevin's concept was one of partnership of equals in which Britain would help Iraq to modernize and to improve the lot of the poverty-stricken majority of the population. But Iraq was strategically critical for Britain in a way it had never really been before, because its airfields now provided crucial staging posts on the route to India and as bases for possible attacks on the Soviet Union. The hope in London was that a revised treaty would provide these advantages, along with secure control of oil supplies and Iraqi membership of the sterling area.

In fact, however, the initiative for a revised treaty came from Iraq, whose leaders began to demand a revision of the 1930 treaty as soon as the war ended in 1945.[59] Negotiations began in 1947 both in London and Baghdad. The air bases were central to the debate. The Iraqis wanted the British air bases to be transferred to Transjordan and Kuwait because these were symbols of continuing British power. This was rejected by London on the grounds of cost (given Britain's then critical financial position) and that these sites would be less useful in terms of the range of aircraft. The Iraqis then suggested that use of the bases should be restricted to time of war, but the British response was that a base that was not in full continuous operation was useless. The Iraqis eventually accepted Bevin's suggestion that the bases should be occupied until the last peace treaties had been signed and an international security organization under the United Nations had been created. The treaty as eventually signed in *HMS Victory* in Portsmouth in January 1948 was surprisingly favourable to Britain. The two air bases were to be used jointly by the British and Iraqi air forces, but would be under full British control. British troop movements were allowed under the ambiguous definition of 'need'. British warships could be sent into the Shatt al-Arab without permission from Iraq. Iraqi war material was to be compatible with that of Britain, so effectively maintaining the 1930 restriction to British sources of supply. Iraqi army officers were to be trained in Britain. There would be a Joint Defence Board with 50–50 membership to plan defence. Britain did, however, make some concessions compared with the 1930 treaty. Consultation on foreign relations was scrapped. The Levies, deeply unpopular in Arab circles, would be disbanded. Iraq would no longer pay the costs of the British military mission and it would no longer be obligatory to employ Britons in civilian posts if non-Iraqis were used. Finally Britain handed over all other military and other installations without charge (by contrast with the charges levied after 1920) and ended the 1936 agreement over staff and equipment on the Iraqi railways.

[58] This is strongly argued by Louis, *The British Empire in the Middle East*, 106–27, 331–6. For the gradual erosion of British control after 1945, though with continuing influence through the Embassy, see M. Elliot, *Independent Iraq: The Monarchy and British Influence 1941–1958* (London and New York, 1996). See also Fernea and Louis (eds.), *The Iraqi Revolution of 1958*, for useful essays on the factors leading to the revolution and the end of British influence.

[59] In addition to Louis, *The British Empire in the Middle East*, this account is based on Silverfarb, *Britain's Informal Empire*, chs. 10 and 11, and Tripp, *History of Iraq*, 118–27.

The treaty gave Britain all that it still wanted in Iraq. In fact it got far too much. The main reason was that it was negotiated by a group of Iraqi politicians of the old guard, with Salih Jabr as Prime Minister but with Nuri as-Said hovering in the wings, who believed that the British connection was vital for their personal position in the face of growing political ferment, and also for the security of Iraq against the communist threat. These British bases would be a safeguard against the feared Soviet attack in support of the Iraqi Communist Party (ICP). It was also unwise for all the heavyweights of the government to be in London when the news broke. It was immediately clear that the treaty was intensely unpopular with all political parties. Particularly unpopular were the continued British use of the airfields and the automatic alliance if either party was attacked. It was also, wrongly, alleged that the treaty would tie Iraq in perpetuity. But in fact the basic cause of the huge outcry manufactured by the opposition political parties was simply political. It was a traditional tactic of such parties to use hostility to Britain to bring down a government that appeared to be subservient to it. In particular the Istiqlal party, many of whose members had been interned in and after 1941, were determined to bring down Jabr. He was a Shia, was accused of favouring his fellow Shia for jobs, and had recently imposed compulsory public purchase of 50 per cent of the wheat crop in order to check black marketeering at a time of shortage. This had infuriated many Sunni land-owners from the northern provinces who had been making fortunes out of concentrating on wheat production.

It proved easy to muster a large public outcry in Baghdad against the treaty. High food prices coupled with the lag of wages behind prices and increased unemployment as the British withdrew, backed by endemic hatred of allegedly corrupt politicians, distrust of a political system always rigged by politicians, and the underlying dislike of any apparent subservience to Britain, made the urban crowds easy to arouse. This had been done by the army in 1936 but not on the scale of 1948. In fact the riots began with student demonstrations against the United Nations vote on Israel in December 1947, and they broke out again on 16 January once the details of the treaty were known. Two years earlier the government, backed by British forces, would have suppressed these riots without difficulty. But now there were no British forces, nor were the leading members of the government present to take decisions. The Regent, after meeting the minor ministers still there and other party leaders, took fright. On 21 January, and without informing the British Embassy, he announced that he would not ratify the treaty. When Jabr arrived back on 26 January he refused to resign and proposed to present the treaty to parliament. The Regent thereupon dismissed him, appointing Muhammed al-Sadr, another Shia, with much the same mix of cabinet ministers. Al-Sadr accepted the Regent's decision and on 4 February told London that the treaty would not be accepted. Anglo-Iraqi relations therefore automatically reverted to the basis of the 1930 treaty.

There are different interpretations of the treaty fiasco and the Regent's reaction. Renton thought the Regent had been justified: his prompt action had 'saved the country from Revolution and anarchy. The alternative would have been to declare Martial Law, and to use the Army to shoot down the rioters in Baghdad and other large towns.' In addition he thought the whole matter had been handled very incompetently by the government, which had done nothing to prepare the public for the treaty and had failed to return to Baghdad in time to argue the case.[60] Others in Baghdad variously blamed weakness on the part of the Regent, ministerial incompetence, the continuing unpopularity of the Hashemites and their British connections, and the ill-fortune that the Palestine crisis coincided with the treaty, arousing much pan-Arab excitement. Perhaps what the episode showed above all else was that the old regime in Baghdad now lacked the strength at a time of nationalistic fervour to act as effective clients of the British. They were still sufficiently well entrenched with networks of supporters in both the army and society to survive; but they were now as never before vulnerable to mass action. The riots of 1948 were not merely an echo of those of 1936 but a precursor of those of 1958.

Yet the political status quo survived, and along with it much of Britain's influence in Iraq. That influence now depended very heavily on the power of Nuri as-Said, who, whether in or out of office during the next ten years, was the dominant force in Iraqi politics. Nuri still believed in the British connection as a safeguard against external threat, now increasingly from the Egypt of Gamal Abd al-Nasser. His own domestic position was based on the networks of supporters he had built up since 1920 and his alliance with the still very powerful landed and official classes. He was ruthless in suppressing popular resistance movements, using martial law, executions, and imprisonment of opponents without hesitation. So long as he retained control British interests in Iraq were secure. Moreover, Nuri had some nationalistic concessions to show for his British alignment. In 1949 Iraq finally escaped British currency control when the Currency Board, characteristic of all British colonial dependencies as the issuer of local currencies tied to the pound sterling, was wound up and replaced by a national currency controlled by the National Bank of Iraq. In 1952, moreover, the IPC accepted the Aramco model of a 50/50 share in oil profits, coupled with provision for up to 12.5 per cent of net production to be given to the government for sale on world markets. As oil prices and production boomed the Iraqi government had unprecedented oil revenues, much of which was used to buy modern armaments and so, hopefully, to keep the army and air force happy. But these were also boom years in Iraq in which a great deal of infrastructural work and some land redistribution was carried out, and some industrialization stimulated by import-substituting measures. Finally, in 1955, the Baghdad pact, initially between Iraq and Turkey, was joined by Britain. This finally abrogated the 1930 treaty. The two airfields were handed over to Iraq in return for air passage and refuelling rights. Britain remained committed to defend Iraq if it was attacked and to train Iraqi forces. By

---

[60] Louis, *The British Empire in the Middle East*, 336–7.

contrast with 1948, this aroused no significant opposition in Iraq: British power ended with a whimper, not an outcry.

Writing in the early 1950s, Stephen Longrigg, with long experience of Iraq, was moderately optimistic about its prospects. In administrative terms the state was now strong and had universal control: 'the administration as an operating and governing machine could by [1951] face comparison with that of any comparable country, and might be thought superior to those of many longer-established nations'. The regime was beneficial, 'with its benevolent and generally popular monarchy vested in an ancient royal house and its not inadequate governmental machinery'. Longrigg thought that Iraq might well take a lead among the Arab nations. On the other hand there were less hopeful omens. The democratic system had no deep roots and was basically unstable. Deputies were not representative and governments normally ignored their views. All 47 cabinets since 1920 had been weak, either falling from internal division or royal disfavour, none due to electoral defeat. There were no strong or long-established parties with consistent programmes to fight elections, which were still determined by the mutasarrifs as in Ottoman times. Nuri was 'the only statesman of international stature'. So the regime could easily be subverted by a military coup. But all these and other weaknesses were inherent in a less-developed country, which was strung between its past and future.[61]

This was a not unrealistic assessment in 1953. Five years later the mould was shattered, and along with it the remnants of British influence. The military coup of July 1958 that killed the King, the Crown Prince (as the Regent had become when Faysal II came of age), and Nuri, along with many of the old guard of politicians, effectively ended the British connection.[62] This time there would be no British alliance with the new regime, as there had been with the notables of Iraq and their new members of the 1920s, the ex-Sharifians. Although many of the Free Officers who carried out the coup were from the same lower middle class as many of the Sharifians, they had a different and much more radical view of life. They were also strongly pan-Arab and admired Nasser and his economic and social strategies. Conversely, Britain was hated as an imperialist and alleged supporter of Israel. Iraq was launched on what can now be seen as a standard trajectory of Middle Eastern military despotism.[63]

[61] Longrigg, *Iraq*, 394–8.

[62] For a detailed analysis of Nuri's role and the genesis of the 1958 revolution see Louis's chapter in Fernea and Louis (eds.), *The Iraqi Revolution of 1958*, 'The British and the Origins of the Iraqi Revolution'.

[63] There is a good account of the nature of successive regimes in Iraq from 1958 to 1999 in Tripp, *History of Iraq*, chs. 5 and 6. Tripp emphasizes the continuity between the techniques of networking of the old regime and that after 1958, in particular the close clan and family relations that underpinned them. Thus, while the governing elite was new and though it virtually destroyed the old social order, its control was no more democratic than that of government under the Hashemites and its methods even more bloody.

How, then, should one assess the character and achievements of the British mandate in Iraq? The final chapter will attempt to compare these with the British role in Palestine and Transjordan and that of the French in Lebanon and Syria. First, however, what light does the present chapter throw on the character of the British position in Iraq? Why did it eventually crumble?

It was emphasized above that the essential fact of Britain's position in Iraq was that it had to be cheap. The huge military costs of 1919–22 were unacceptable. The country would therefore have to be controlled by alliance and collaboration, not military power. The fact that the RAF was put in control of security in 1922 symbolized that this was a new situation in the colonial world, for aeroplanes could intimidate and punish, not rule. At first sight it appeared that the British had managed a difficult conjuring trick. They had set up an apparently indigenous Arab state, found a suitable head of state for it, and persuaded its leaders to draw up a constitution that looked respectably democratic. At the same time this state was committed to accept a form of British over-rule which provided Britain with all the control it needed, almost entirely at Iraqi cost. The treaties of 1924 and 1930 were regarded by nationalists in Syria as models to which they should aspire. In 1932 the League of Nations accepted that the British had fulfilled their mandate and that Iraq was now a viable democratic state providing justice and equality for all its inhabitants. Thereafter, under the 1930 treaty, Britain retained what it regarded as key rights in Iraq, still at minimum cost. Until 1958, and despite the 1941 crisis, Britain remained a dominant influence there, yet Iraq was apparently a genuine sovereign state able to decide its own destiny. It seemed that for once an imperial power had succeeded in combining the classic concepts of imperium and libertas.

Yet this was, of course, largely an illusion. British power had from the start been based on the survival and pre-eminence of the pre-1918 Iraqi upper classes: the landed shaykhs and aghas, along with their client gentry, and the urban aristocracy of service, mostly also large-scale land-owners. They had reluctantly accepted the new men, the ex-Sharifians, as necessary allies along with the monarchy, and these soon acquired the landed estates that entitled them to be classed with the older elites. The result was the perpetuation of the class structure of the Ottoman period and a widening of the gap between the very few property-owners and the mass of the peasantry. By allying with this upper class, whose internal political fissions were of limited significance to them, the British were able to build their own influence on existing networks of power and patronage. This in turn meant that their position depended almost entirely, except for the years of military occupation from 1941 to 1946, on the survival of what Batatu called 'the old social classes'.

This was not, of course, unusual in the wider context of European colonial rule. The difference was that, by contrast with virtually all other such territories, Iraq was officially a democratic state, after 1932 a sovereign state. The basis of Kedourie's condemnation was that this political and constitutional structure was a sham. It took little account of the interests of the Shii majority and almost none of the Kurdish minority. Iraq was run by a minority of the Sunni elite, mostly in and to the north of Baghdad. Until the 1950s little was done to improve the social conditions of the mass of the peasantry. This was largely because the political system could not generate genuine political parties with reformist agendas; and that in turn was due to the fact that Iraq did not develop a liberal middle class of the European type. Socially, it remained divided between the rich and the poor with little or no possibility of the gap being bridged. Thus the British were throughout tied into an *ancien régime*. When it fell in 1958 so did their position.

It is, however, one thing to state these facts, another to apportion responsibility. The reality is that there was only one way in which the British might have made any significant impact on the traditional patterns of Middle Eastern society, common with differences in detail to all the territories that became European mandates in 1920, as also to Egypt and much of Islamic North Africa. That was the course promoted by Sir Arnold Wilson between 1918 and 1920. A prolonged period of effective British rule, even with a figurehead amir or king, might have made something like the impact that British rule had, over a much longer period, in British India or Ceylon. Such a regime might have broken patterns of traditional patrimonialism and prebendalism and established standards of public service similar to those shown by the Indian Civil Service and its post-independence successors. Nationalist resistance to the alien regime might also have generated genuinely representative political parties with a wide social base of the type that developed in India. For reasons suggested above this did not happen. The regime established in and after 1920, though probably an improvement in terms of efficiency and honesty on its Ottoman predecessor, was undeniably unreformed. Its main function and effect was, as Longrigg was later to comment, to create a strong state but not one based on social justice.

That, however, had not been a primary British aim in and after 1920. Individual British Political Officers and Advisers may have tried to impose such values within their limited remits, but they could not have changed the underlying realities of Iraqi society. Conversely, there is no reason to think that a totally independent Iraq—or for that matter Syria—after 1920 would have been very different or better governed. It is very difficult to conceive of how any viable state could have been created in Mesopotamia in and after 1918 if the British had not been there and if the alleged promises to Husayn in 1915 had been fulfilled. Without a British military pressure, there would have been no support for a Hashemite ruler and it is very unlikely that any indigenous leader could have established effective rule over the whole territory. The result might well have been fragmentation into a number of competing and ill-organized states, or conceivably reintegration into the new Turkey. Either way, there would have been no significant change in the structures of traditional society. As it was, while British rule probably had some beneficial effects on Iraq by establishing a single state out of the three Ottoman vilayets, it could not, and did not attempt to, reconstruct

Iraq as a traditional Middle Eastern society, nor protect it from the type of military revolution that was to overwhelm several Middle Eastern states in the 1950s. If anything, by creating a centralized bureaucratic regime which generated an unnecessarily large army, it made the eventual revolution quite straightforward.

This is to suggest that the British mandate and later British influence had a relatively limited effect on the long-term evolution of Iraq. As in virtually all colonial situations the influence of the imperial power was far less than either its supporters or opponents claimed. That is not surprising. It was a cut-price regime with strictly limited objectives. Britain wanted administrative control as well as control over the oil fields. This was part of an integrated economic and political system in the Middle East, which in turn was part of the worldwide British economic and military system. The British hoped that by granting independence earlier rather than later they could continue to remain on good terms with the elites who had ruled Iraq and thus perpetuate Iraq's place in the British system. In this they were successful. The British got most of what they wanted for some forty years and then left Iraq to its own devices. Iraq could then fall into what became the common mould of other revolutionary Middle Eastern states under military regimes, almost as if the mandate had never existed.

4

Palestine: Zionism and the
Genesis of the Mandate

Mandatory Palestine, built from the sanjaq of Jerusalem and two southern sanjaqs of the vilayet, was unique in British imperial history. Hitherto all British dependencies had fallen into two broad categories: colonies of occupation and colonies of settlement. The first, ranging from India and Nigeria to Gibraltar, were held because they were thought to fulfil some of a wide range of economic or strategic purposes. They were controlled but received few British permanent settlers. The second, such as Australia and Canada, were acquired mainly for settlement by Britons. Palestine fitted neither category. It should have been a quasi-colony of occupation, providing the primarily strategic benefits described in Chapter 2. Settlement was not required. Yet it was treated as a colony of settlement. Moreover the settlers were to be non-British Jews, mostly from eastern Europe. It is the purpose of this chapter to explain this apparently irrational fact. Chapter 5 then examines the disastrous consequences down to the end of the mandate in 1948. In each chapter the attitudes of the three main interested parties—Zionists, Palestinian Arabs, and the British government—will be examined in turn.

1. ZIONISM: THE CASE OF THE COLONISTS[1]

There can be no doubt that the Zionist case for a Jewish home, and possibly state, somewhere or other, though not necessarily in Palestine, had stronger moral and physical justification than that of most other modern colonizing movements. The need arose from the condition of the Jews of eastern Europe. In 1900 there were between 12 and 13 million Jews in Russia, most of them in the Russian-occupied parts of Poland, and in Romania. These eastern European Jews constituted some four-fifths of world Jewry, though by about 1914 there were some three million of them in the United States and many in Ottoman territories. Ironically, as the

---

[1] There is, of course, an immense literature on the background and evolution of Zionism, which is reflected in the bibliography. This account is based heavily on D. Vital's impressively researched and balanced trilogy: *The Origins of Zionism* (Oxford, 1975); *Zionism: The Formative Years* (Oxford, 1982); and *Zionism: The Crucial Phase* (Oxford, 1987).

western states adopted policies of assimilation and toleration after the French Revolution, Russia moved the other way. All Jews, unless they had special permission, had to live within the Pale, that part of western Russia that had been Polish before the partition of the late eighteenth century. Although they had legal rights, these did not extend to citizenship, and from 1827 Jews were particularly badly affected by military conscription. Their condition improved under Alexander II, though there was very little assimilation; but after his assassination in 1881 things deteriorated rapidly.

The effective starting point of modern Zionism was the series of pogroms that began in 1881, lasting in the first instance to 1884, then reviving in 1905. These were essentially attacks by poverty-stricken Russian and Polish peasants who could, in the long tradition of anti-Semitism, be persuaded that their economic problems were the responsibility of the Jews as moneylenders, businessmen, shop-keepers, and so on. These pogroms did not cause huge loss of life, but did immense damage to property. Above all they destroyed the confidence of many Jews that in course of time their condition might improve, as that of Jews in most western European states had done. This misery, which intensified from the 1880s to 1917, was the genesis of modern Zionism.

Zionism, however, was not a new phenomenon in the later nineteenth century. Nor was the diaspora simply the result of the final Roman destruction of the Jewish state after AD 132. Jews were already dispersed throughout much of the then known European world and in North Africa.[2] Most became assimilated into the societies in which they lived; but for many the concept of a mystical Return to Israel and of Redemption was deeply felt. Ironically, much of the early enthusiasm for settling Jews in Palestine was in Britain and the United States, and among millenarian evangelical Christians rather than Jews. George Eliot's novel *Daniel Deronda* (1876) expressed a form of Zionism. This British and American idealism was to be very important historically because it was among such Christians that the eventual decision to back the Zionist movement in 1917 was generated.

But in practical terms Zionism grew from the condition of Jews in Russia after 1881. The main issue then facing Jews in the east was whether to leave Russia, and if so where to go. In practical terms those who wanted to leave had to go west, since the Russian state did not attempt to prevent their leaving, moving gradually through Germany and western Europe and finally to the United States. Until legislation in 1921 and 1924 the USA was open to all immigrants, and it was there that most emigrating Jews ended up. But there grew also several organizations that aimed at the colonization of Palestine for a mix of ideological and practical motives. In Romania, independent only since 1878, an organization was set up which, relying on hoped-for largesse from rich Jews in the west, bought land at Zamarin (south of Haifa) in 1882 and sent 228 colonists there. In Russia there

---

[2] For an account of early Judaic influence in North Africa and Egypt see R. Oliver, *The African Experience* (London, 1991), 77–9.

were two early societies. The more intellectually coherent was Bilu, started by students in Kharkov, which aimed to combine emigration with national renaissance and a return to the land in model villages. Its first venture, near Jaffa at Bedara in 1882, proved a failure, but its concept of the settler as pioneer and agriculturalist had a big influence on later Zionism.

Much more durable was Hovevei Zion (lover of Zion). This also had begun as a group of student organizations in Russia without any clear view of their aims; but in and after 1881 it acquired a firm ideological base. This was provided by two men. Moshe Lilenblum came to believe that there was no solution for the Jews in eastern Europe and argued in many articles in Jewish journals after 1881 that, rather than emigrate to America, Jews must have their own country, which must be 'Eretz-Israel', Palestine, 'to which', he argued, 'we have an historic right which has not been lost along with our [lost] rule of the country, any more than the peoples of the Balkans lost their rights to their lands when they lost their rule over them'.[3] In 1882 this call for a Return was developed further by Yehuda Pinsker, a sophisticated German-speaking physician in Odessa, in his *Autoemancipation*. This short pamphlet argued that Jews would always be aliens in any country except their own. This did not necessarily imply a return to Palestine: he had no objection to that, though he thought it unsuitable in many ways. Rather, Jews must find a single fertile territory anywhere to which 'surplus' Jews (those that could not fit into their land of birth) could go. He argued that other countries were busy creating new colonies (this was the era of the partition of Africa), so why should not the Jews do the same?

Pinsker's pamphlet struck a vibrant chord and he was persuaded by Lilenblum and others to set up a central committee in Odessa to promulgate these ideas. By 1888–9 there were some 138 local branches of Hovevei Zion, Hibbat Zion (love of Zion), with perhaps 14,000 members in 1885. Its purpose was to raise funds in order to send small groups of Jewish settlers to Palestine to create farming communities. The organization was weak and its income small; so its main achievement was to create a sense of purpose. Its first general Congress of delegates from the local branches, held in 1884, set up a committee in Odessa and aimed at investigating the possibilities offered by Palestine and probing Ottoman reactions to increased Jewish immigration and land purchase.

By about 1887 Hibbat Zion was in a bad way. It had little money. The Ottoman government had tightened regulations against Jewish purchase of land in Palestine, which could only be done by subterfuge. As late as 1900 the organization had only bought about 50,000 acres in Palestine, of which half was actually used. There were 22 settlements with 705 farms and a rural population of 5,210. The only significant financial support had come from Baron James de Rothschild, head of the French branch of the family, who had become convinced of the need for Jewish settlement in Palestine and paid very large sums, possibly £5,600,000,

---

[3] Vital, *Origins*, 119.

to buy land and stock it, and ran these estates as a great capitalist enterprise through agents, using Arab labour as well as Jewish. This was quite contrary to the ethos of the Odessa group, who thought in terms of small-scale Jewish farms. Though the Odessa society continued to believe in its piecemeal style of operation, its capacity to provide any solution to the problem of Jewry in eastern Europe was seriously in doubt.

This point was made very strongly by the man who became a leading intellectual force in the Zionist movement, Asher Zevi Ginsberg, a self-taught intellectual from a farming background but a brilliant journalist, who wrote under the pen-name of Ahad Ha-Am. After visits to Palestine in 1891 and 1893 he denounced the pathetically inadequate attempts of Hibbat Zion to provide for the needs of the Jews. He could see no practical possibility of a substantial settlement in Palestine. The most that could be hoped for was to establish there a 'spiritual centre' as a focal point for national revival, so that all Jews everywhere could see themselves as part of a single nation.[4]

The relative failure of this early Zionist movement has highlighted and probably exaggerated the achievements of Theodor Herzl as the creator of political Zionism. Herzl was a German-speaking Hungarian Jew, fully assimilated and a leading journalist in Vienna. After five years in Paris, when he felt the force of French anti-Semitism, he was converted to Zionism in 1895. His view was that the Jewish problem was not restricted to Russia, which he had never visited, but was common to all Jews, however apparently assimilated. In 1896 he published his famous pamphlet, *Der Judenstaat*, later translated into most European languages and also into Hebrew. He argued that the need was to create a Jewish state, not to send small groups of settlers to Palestine. He saw many advantages in establishing a Jewish state in Palestine, but at this stage he regarded this as probably impracticable, since it could not contain any significant proportion of European Jewry. The means was to be a Society of Jews which would negotiate with governments for a concession, and a Jewish Company which would be set up as a British-registered chartered company with a large working capital which would create the conditions for the new state.

Here the model was clearly that of the various British chartered companies that had recently taken the initiative in colonizing parts of Black Africa and the Pacific. There was therefore nothing particularly original in the concept of a chartered Jewish colonizing venture. But Herzl and the Zionist Organization that was created at the first Congress at Basel in 1897 faced two problems that had not been faced by these other ventures. First, they had no national government to back them up and if necessary negotiate with the rulers of territories to be colonized. Second, they would have to raise large amounts of capital, and without governmental

---

[4] For a critical account of Ha-Am's later and very critical views on Zionism in practice see Hans Kohn, 'Zion and the Jewish National Idea', in W. Khalidi (ed.), *From Haven to Conquest* (1971; Washington, DC, 1987), 807–39.

backing this was likely to prove difficult. In fact it proved impossible. Herzl's proposal received no support from the great French or British Jewish bankers, and Baron de Rothschild remained obdurate in his opposition. Nor did he get support from the Odessa committee. Nevertheless, he managed to organize a general Congress at Basel in August 1897 and to persuade delegates from Russia and most western states to attend.

The Basel Congress is normally taken as the starting point of the movement that led eventually to the establishment of the state of Israel. In terms of its stated objectives this is certainly true. It was agreed that the Congress should be the 'chief organ' of the movement and should meet regularly, initially every year. It elected an Actions Committee to be based in Vienna, which would act between meetings of Congress.[5] The more difficult part was to determine the objectives of the movement. Although Herzl had used the word 'state' in his pamphlet, and claimed in his diary that 'At Basel I founded the Jewish State',[6] it was accepted that there was no chance of the Ottoman government conceding this in Palestine. It was therefore decided to adopt the formula 'Zionism aims at the creation of a home for the Jewish people in Palestine to be secured by public law'. This was to be achieved by the settlement of Palestine with Jewish farmers, artisans, and tradesmen; the organizing and unifying of all Jewry by means of appropriate local and general arrangements subject to the laws of each country; the strengthening of Jewish national feeling and consciousness; and preparatory moves towards obtaining such governmental consent as would be necessary to the achievement of the aims of Zionism.

These were grand words and huge ambitions. Many Jews thought them over-grandiose, and in retrospect they can be seen in much the same light as other improbable expansionist projects, such as the contemporary dream of Cecil Rhodes for a Cape to Cairo railway. Herzl's scheme depended entirely on persuading the Ottoman government to issue a charter or comparable document that would entitle the Zionists to settle in Palestine with complete security and freedom to run their own affairs: once that had been done they might be able to evolve into a state. Herzl therefore spent the rest of his life, to his early death in 1904, attempting to negotiate at the highest level with the Porte (the government at Constantinople) for such a concession. His main lever was the offer of substantial Jewish financial aid to relieve the chronic indebtedness of the Porte.[7] Meeting consistent resistance there, since the Sultan Abdulhamid had no intention of allowing yet another potentially difficult and possibly pro-Russian community to evolve in his domains, Herzl tried devious routes to influence him. These included attempted access to the Kaiser, the King of Italy, the Tsar, the Pope, and the British

---

[5] There are close similarities here with the Indian National Congress, set up in 1887, though in the Zionist case the membership was from the start restricted to elected delegates, whereas for long the INC had no formal membership.   [6] Vital, *Origins*, 369.

[7] The story is told in detail in Vital, *Zionism: The Formative Years*.

government. Nothing came of these approaches, though the last produced a possible alternative to Palestine.

This was an offer of land in the newly acquired British East African Protectorate. It resulted from contacts with Joseph Chamberlain as Colonial Secretary, who was anxious to promote the colonization of what eventually became Uganda, partly in order to make the railway from Mombasa viable. This offer, which was compatible with Herzl's original argument before he became convinced that only Palestine would be acceptable, became the main issue at the 6th Congress in August 1903. A three-man commission was therefore sent. It reported very unfavourably, and the proposal was finally dropped. But it had split the movement, and a group under Israel Zangwill, a British journalist, set up the Jewish Territorial Organization for the Settlement of Jews within the British Empire. However this proved the end of Zionist attempts to find an alternative to Palestine.

By 1914 it must have seemed that Herzl's project was dead. As Vital commented, 'He had no true successor and no competitors. He left no heirs. He had few true followers. He was, it seems true to say, unique.'[8] The Turks under the post-1908 Young Turk and CUP governments proved even more resistant to approaches than that of the Sultan. It was in the interest of no European power to support Zionism. Moreover, a large proportion of Jews in western Europe and America remained intensely hostile to Zionism, notably the Alliance Israélite in France and the main British Jewish organizations, who were generally satisfied with the integration they had already achieved into the host society. Yet despite failures, the basic Zionist bureaucracy remained intact in Berlin. There were branches in most western countries and a substantial, fee-paying international membership: perhaps 130,000 all told, including 8,000 out of a total of 300,000 Jews in Britain and 12,000 out of some 3 million in the United States,[9] though with a much greater number of non-active supporters. This was Herzl's true legacy. He had created a bond between Jews in many countries and provided a clear objective. Without this it is very unlikely that the completely unpredictable opportunity opened up by the First World War could have been exploited.

Given the inability of the Zionists to make a dramatic breakthrough to establish their 'home', the important question was how successful the Odessa strategy of gradual permeation of Palestine had proved, what obstacles it had met, and what omens it held for the future.

---

[8] Vital, *Zionism: The Formative Years*, 347.

[9] L. Stein, *The Balfour Declaration* (London, 1961), 66–8. Stein's book was written before access was allowed to the official primary sources, then still closed under the fifty-year rule, and was based mainly on Zionist records. But Stein, a Balliol College graduate, was Secretary to the Zionist organization in Britain between the wars and had exceptional access to both information and the still living protagonists of the creation of the Zionist 'home'. His book should be read in conjunction with Vital's *Zionism: The Crucial Phase*, which was based on full documentary access and disagrees with Stein on some key issues.

By 1914 there were some 85,000 Jews in Palestine, of whom about 35,000 had immigrated since 1881 in what are called the first (to 1904) and second (1904–14) aliyah. The majority of Jews were long-term residents with Ottoman nationality, mostly involved with maintenance of Jewish religious observance, particularly in Jerusalem, and supported largely by overseas donations. Of the newcomers only some 13,000 lived in 43 agricultural settlements, many of them supported by Baron de Rothschild.

This was not a very impressive achievement for 35 years of effort, but it was not in fact surprising. There were two main obstacles to larger Jewish immigration.[10] First, Palestine was not in any way a suitable site for large-scale colonization of the conventional kind. It was small. Much of the land was arid mountainous country or marshlands in the flatter regions towards the coast. Although the Arab population was relatively small at between 500,000 and 700,000, it was increasing before 1914 and there was growing pressure on land, much of it driven by large land-owners to increase production of the main grain crops. In no sense, therefore, was Palestine 'vacant' for colonization, though there was uncultivated land in the marshy regions. It is critical that here, by contrast with virtually all modern colonization in the Americas and Africa, land could not be taken by conquest or by payment of minute compensation. It had to be bought: and until the war of 1948 all land acquired by the Zionists was bought, often at an inflated price. Land purchase was helped by the fact that some 75 per cent of land was owned in large blocks by wealthy notables, but since much of it had been bought as a speculation under the revised land regulations of 1858, they would not sell it cheaply. This made colonization an expensive business, since the promoters had not only to buy land, much of it from notables in Syria and Lebanon, but also provide stock and equipment for immigrants, most of whom had no capital and little or no farming experience. In short, there were few countries in the world that were less obviously suited to large-scale European colonization than Palestine, a point much stressed by those Zionists who favoured a settlement somewhere else. It could certainly not solve the problems of east European Jewry.

The other obvious obstacle to Zionist settlement, even on a small scale, was the attitude of the Ottoman government. Although for centuries Jews had been tolerated, along with Christians, under the millet system (whereby non-Islamic religious communities were allowed to practise their own faith and control many aspects of their civil affairs), and excused from military service on payment of additional taxes, from about 1882 the Porte adopted a policy of limiting both land sales and Jewish immigration into Palestine. This was mainly because most immigrants were Russians and this threatened to create a new society hostile to Turkey. The local governors, the mutasarrifs, were therefore frequently ordered to ban

---

[10] The following section is based largely on G. Shafir, *Land, Labor and the Origins of the Israeli–Palestinian Conflict, 1882–1914* (Cambridge, Mass., 1989), and N. J. Mandel, *The Arabs and Zionism before World War I* (Berkeley, 1976).

land sales to Jews and prevent permanent immigration. In this they were largely unsuccessful. Under international agreements 'pilgrims' could not be excluded: they were given a red card on entrance for a limited period, which was supposed to be surrendered on departure, though few such would-be settlers did so. Since most settlers came from Russia they could appeal to their consuls under the Capitulations.[11] Ottoman officials were badly underpaid and were thus open to bribes: few were either efficient or honest. Moreover, land purchases could usually be made in the name of an Ottoman subject. Thus the Jewish Colonization Association (not connected with Zionism) and its Zionist equivalent, the Anglo-Palestine Company, could both buy land that was notionally not for Jewish settlement under the 1867 Land Code. The coming to power in Constantinople of the Young Turks in 1908 and their successors, the CUP, made little difference. The government maintained, as the Sultan had told Herzl previously, that Jewish settlement would be welcome in other parts of the Ottoman Near East, but not in Palestine; though in 1913 the government, desperate for money after the disasters of the Balkan wars, made contacts with the Zionists in the hope of getting a Jewish loan in return for relaxation of the immigration restrictions. But the money could not be found (reflecting the fact that the most affluent western European Jews were still hostile to Zionism); and the negotiation fell through.

It was, therefore, obvious that unless international conditions changed radically, the most that Zionists could hope for was a continued very slow trickle of Jews into Palestine, relying on the porous character of the regime. Nevertheless, in many ways the pattern of later Jewish settlements and their relationship with the Arab population was established before 1914. Above all the foundations were laid for a genuine settler society in that, as in Australia and New Zealand, most of the modern economy was in the hands of the settlers and their income levels were not determined by a market in which they could be undercut by cheaper indigenous labour.

It was not always clear that this principle of 'Hebrew labour' (only Jews to be employed in Jewish-owned enterprises) would become dominant. The early Russian settlers of the 1890s, mostly small traders or artisans with no agricultural experience and little money, attempted subsistence agriculture, copying Arab modes of production, but with little success. Most such settlements died out. Baron de Rothschild therefore attempted to establish large-scale plantations, mostly of grapes and citrus fruit (already highly developed by Arabs in the Jaffa region). These employed both Jewish and Arab labour, but the Jews were paid a higher wage than the Arabs to match their higher expectations. After 1900 de Rothschild stopped subsidizing these plantations, which were handed over to the

<hr />

[11] The Capitulations were agreements made between the Ottomans and leading European states since the sixteenth century which provided special rights for nationals of these states in Ottoman territories, particularly in juridical matters, and also limited the level of import duties. They survived until after the Ottoman defeat in 1918.

Jewish Colonization Association (JCA) to be run on commercial lines. The JCA closed the least profitable plantations and handed most of the rest over to planters on leases. The planters wanted the cheapest labour, which was based on going Arab wage rates, so Jewish settlers working on these estates claimed a division of labour which gave them higher wages, on the largely spurious ground that they had higher skills. They were successful; but since plantation work was seasonal, the Jewish workers did not do well, having, unlike the Arabs, no smallholdings to fall back on. Many Jews therefore left Palestine or moved to the towns, particularly the new (1909) Jewish suburb of Jaffa, Tel Aviv. Clearly the plantation system could not provide the basis for a land-based self-perpetuating Zionist society. Another initiative, by the capitalist planter Aharon Eisenberg, to import Yemeni Jews (Ottoman subjects since the 1870s) to provide a Jewish labour force at the same cost as an Arab one proved a failure. The Yemenis resented having lower wages and poor conditions. As Sephardic Jews they were disliked by the western Ashkenazi Jews, and ultimately most left the plantations and became a rural prole-tariat. The large plantations in turn mostly failed and the Eisenberg estate was bankrupt by 1917. Thus, before about 1908 Jewish 'colonization' really amounted only to the acquisition of land, with very few permanent settlers. Conversely, the main Ottoman and Arab complaint against the Zionists was about land sales, not immigration.

The problem therefore remained of how to establish a viable Jewish farming stock in Palestine. What Shafir calls 'the unintended means: co-operative settle-ment' was worked out after 1907 by the World Zionist Organization (WZO). This amounted to a pure settlement strategy and may have been based on German and Austrian attempts to colonize large estates in Poland and Bohemia after the 1880s: the WZO was based in Germany and Austria until after 1920 and was dominated by German or Austrian Jews. Land purchase and use were controlled by the Jewish National Fund (JNF), but it had little success in organizing settle-ment. In 1907 the Zionist Congress set up the Palestine Office in Jaffa under Arthur Ruppin, leading to the creation of the Palestine Land Development Company (PLDC), a joint stock company copied from the Prussian Colonization Commission. The PLDC's function was to buy land, prepare it for settlement, and provide initial credit. Within this system there was a scheme set up in 1909 for settlement co-operatives on Zionist-owned land, the members to decide whether to maintain the co-operative or to split the land into individual holdings once the initial debts had been paid. Thus for some years it was uncertain whether Jewish agricultural settlement would eventually take the form of small individual holdings or co-operatives.

The outcome was the evolution of the kibbutz, or settlement based on co-operation. The first of these, set up by Ruppin at Degania on the Jordan bank in December 1909, survived and became permanent in 1912. In 1913 the train-ing farm at Kinneret also became a permanent co-operative settlement. Shafir argues that this type of co-operative, which was to become the symbol of later

Zionist settlement, owed nothing to ideology or even Russian socialist concepts. It evolved accidentally from the experience of the settlers under the wing of Mosche Berman and the fact that Degania, unlike Franz Oppenheim's Merchavia 'settlement co-operative', made a profit from its first year. It was not consistent with the earlier plan of Oppenheim for co-operation, since his scheme was to lead to individualization of holdings.[12] This early success led to the creation of 30 more kibbutzim between 1914 and 1918, which contained 446 workers.

Shafir argues that the eventual predominance of the kibbutz in Palestine reflected the failure of capitalist settlement and the WZO's inability to finance this adequately. Conversely, the kibbutz was cheap because the workers accepted a lower standard of living than the Jewish workers in capitalist enterprises. On the other hand the early small kibbutz did not solve the problem of large-scale immigration. The first large kibbutz was Ein Harod, set up in 1922. By then the third aliyah, starting after 1917, had brought a socialist agenda to rationalize the fact of the kibbutz. It then, as Shafir put it, 'became the most homogeneous body of Israeli society: it included almost exclusively Eastern European and North African Jews, and was constructed on the exclusion of Palestinian Arabs'. Though kibbutz members always constituted a minority of Palestinian Jews, they 'became the real nucleus of Israeli state formation'.[13] Their peculiar value, from a Zionist point of view, was that the kibbutzim proved capable of accepting the mass migration of the period after 1919 and again after 1933, while conducting social experimentation and remaining a viable and relatively attractive institution throughout the mandatory period. Above all, they provided the basis for a pure settlement colony, immune to competition from Arabs in the labour market, until the conquests of 1948 made it possible to extend their exclusion generally throughout Israel.

In Shafir's view this development of an exclusive Jewish labour market, first by 'the conquest of labour' (differential wage rates), then 'autonomous labour' (the kibbutz), both embodied in the Histadrut (the General Federation of Jewish Workers in Eretz Israel, set up in 1920), was critical for the formation of an exclusive Jewish state of Israel. Above all, it transformed what might have been a mixed society into a pure settlement colony in which, after 1948, Jews from North Africa and the Middle East replaced Arabs at the bottom of the social and industrial pyramid. In short, the essential features of the eventual Israel were laid before 1914.

But this is to look thirty years ahead. It is only teleology that makes it possible to reach this conclusion. In 1914, and even as late as early 1917, it seemed much more likely that these tiny Jewish colonies, then harbouring only about 12,000 people out of a Jewish population of around 85,000, and occupying about 2 per cent of the total land area of Palestine, might eventually be absorbed into the generality of the Palestinian population. On the map their settlements look extensive, with concentrations near the Sea of Galilee and near Jaffa. But most of these were

<hr />

[12] Shafir, *Land*, 165–81.   [13] Ibid. 184.

very small and still struggling. A reasonable prediction was that the Jews would continue to constitute a millet, along with the many other religious minorities of the Ottoman empire, clinging to their distinctive religious customs and perhaps preserving the peculiar collectivism of their new rural settlements, but in no sense forming a 'nation', still less a state, as Herzl had projected. It was only because the Ottomans chose to ally themselves with the Central European powers in 1914 and were ultimately defeated, and because the British chose to take control of Palestine and, quite unpredictably, to underwrite the Zionist project, that Israel became a possibility. Thus the key to ultimate Zionist success lay in the circumstances of the Balfour Declaration of 1917, which will be examined later.

But the history of western colonization cannot deal only with the initiatives of the colonizers. It is equally necessary to consider the condition of the indigenous population and their attitude to the slow seepage of Jewish immigrants and their land purchases before 1914. How far was Zionism made possible by the passive or active collaboration of the Arab people, both Muslim and Christian?

2. THE ARAB STANDPOINT

Nowhere, in the whole course of modern European overseas expansion, has the attitude of the indigenous peoples to foreign intrusion been united or unambiguous. For the most part foreigners were judged on the evidence. In many cases the newcomers were welcomed because they brought goods or skills that were clearly valuable. In some they were seen as valuable allies in local power struggles. Conversely, indigenous collaboration was often critical, particularly in the supply of food, for the survival of the earliest settlers. Often, when some part of the host society fell out with the colonizers, others would fight on their side. Thus it was in no sense certain how the Arabs would view the small trickle of eastern European refugees and the organizations which offered to buy their land in the thirty years after 1881.

It is obvious, but very important for the attitude of Palestinian Arabs, both Muslim and Christian, to the Jewish influx, that, by contrast with that of many earlier native Americans, tropical Africans, and South Sea Islanders to foreign incursions, neither Europeans nor Jews were in any sense a novelty. That is, they were not respected on the grounds of unfamiliarity or because they came from a superior civilization and possessed skills such as literacy. Their main potential asset was money. Some land-owners and peasants were happy to unload unwanted land at an enhanced price. Many peasants were also glad to find a market for their products and labour in the struggling early settlements. The main early hostility came in the towns, where local notables, bankers, artisans, and tradesmen feared increasing competition from Russian Jews whose background lay in these fields. In sum, by about 1908 there was no enthusiasm for Jewish immigration, and a growing fear of Zionist intentions.

Perhaps the main contrast between the incoming Jews and the indigenous population lay in social structures. In common with most of Syria and also Iraq the society of both the vilayet of Beirut and the sanjaq of Jerusalem was dominated by urban elites who had gained influence as the village shaykhs had lost it during the nineteenth century, and had benefited from the land reforms of the Ottomans to build up large rural estates, worked by a dependent peasantry. In Jerusalem there were three main and very competitive families: the al-Husaynis, the al-Khalidis, and the al-Nashashibis, which played a major role during the mandate period; but there were comparable families in most of the other major towns. These families dominated the Ottoman administrative system of these areas and also its intellectual and religious life. Also among the notables were some important Christian families of various church affiliations, but led by the Patriarch of Jerusalem, head of the Orthodox church. The Christians tended to be among the best-educated section of Arab society and, at least at first, as hostile to Jewish competition as the Muslim majority.

This hierarchical and decentralized social structure was to be pitted against the totally different structures of Zionism, with its centralized western-style committees and funding and its commitment to a single Jewish quasi-state. But in 1914 that competition could not have been foreseen. In fact, after the Young Turk revolution of 1908 and its successor regime, the Committee for Union and Progress (CUP), it seemed likely that restrictions on Jewish immigration and land purchase would be intensified. In particular, since the Palestinian deputies to the new Ottoman parliament were all Arab notables, and since after 1908 these were increasingly hostile to Jewish land purchase (rather than immigration as such), pressure would be placed on the Ottoman government to tighten regulations. In June 1909 questions on the subject were raised in the Ottoman parliament for the first time.

Meantime hostility to Zionism was increasing in Palestine. In the Galilee region there were outbreaks of violence between settlers and local peasants over disputed land rights, and it was alleged that the peasants were encouraged in this by the local CUP branch in Tiberias. Conversely there were attacks on the CUP on the false ground that it was dominated by Jewish and Masonic elements. Some local newspapers were now strongly anti-Zionist, notably the Haifa paper *al-Karmel*, edited by Najib al-Khuri Nassar, who in 1911 also published a book, *Zionism: Its History, Object and Importance*, and the Jaffa paper *Falastin*. Both editors were Christian, but their approach differed. *Falastin* adopted a local Palestinian patriotic line, while *al-Karmel* was in favour of Ottoman patriotism. In Damascus and Lebanon several Muslim papers were hostile to Zionism, but also hostile to Christianity and anti-European, though some Christian papers in Damascus defended Zionism. Typical accusations made against the Jews were that they claimed divine right to Palestine; that they exploited the Capitulations; that they were disloyal to the Ottoman regime; that they had too much land already; that they did not integrate but had political aims and used national symbols as if a quasi-state. When the mutasarrif of Jerusalem, Muhdi Bey, a CUP supporter, gave permission in 1912 for a Jewish land-settlement scheme, he was first forced to retract by the Porte, and then recalled.

It is true that in 1913 there seemed briefly to be some chance of a rapprochement between Arabs and Zionists.[14] The Arab Decentralization Society of Cairo thought it might use the possibility of Zionist loans to the cash-strapped Ottoman government to extract concessions to Arab claims for local autonomy in Arab provinces and a larger proportion of Arabs in senior administrative posts. An Arab conference in Paris in June 1913 seemed moderately favourable to the idea and it was supported by the Jewish editor of the Constantinople journal *Le Jeune Turc*. This negotiation came to nothing, but in 1913–14 the Porte, still hoping for Jewish money, relaxed some controls against Jewish immigrants; the vali of Beirut thought Jewish immigration useful; and the new mutasarrif of Jerusalem was also favourable to it, despite local Arab opposition. But this moment passed. By 1914 there was a general reaction against Zionism among Turks, Muslims, and Arab Christians in both Palestine and other parts of the Ottoman empire. In Palestine anti-Jewish feeling among the younger educated Arab elite was growing, and there was recurrent violence against Jewish settlements in the north.

This escalating hostility to Zionism in Palestine is very important for grasping the significance of the Balfour Declaration of 1917 and the subsequent history of the British mandate in Palestine. Seen in the general context of European imperialism and expansion, Arabs in Palestine were exceptionally well informed about the character and intentions of the colonizing force before it achieved the official status it was given in 1917 or became deeply entrenched, and were deeply hostile to it. There is no possible doubt that, if the British had attempted to get the views of the Arab population, presumably by discussing the matter with the notables, they would have been told very strongly that Zionism was not welcome and that Jewish settlement on a large scale would be strongly resisted. Of course no such investigation was made. The Balfour Declaration was issued on 2 November 1917, a month before Jerusalem was occupied, and a year before the conquest was completed. There was clearly no opportunity to consult the indigenous population in advance; and this was never considered, any more than it had been before the secret agreement for the partition of the Ottoman empire in 1916, the Sykes–Picot Agreement. In short, the British treated Palestine as a mere territory to be allocated as they found convenient, exactly as they and other imperial powers had done for the past centuries. It should therefore cause no surprise that Palestine proved probably the most difficult of all British dependencies to govern and caused more problems than any other part of the post-1918 partition of the Near East. It is, therefore, critically important to discover why this most experienced of imperial powers should have acted in this apparently irrational way.

---

[14] The details are ibid., chs. 7 and 8.

3. THE GENESIS OF THE BALFOUR DECLARATION

There are basically two main general explanations or narratives in the literature on the origins of the Balfour Declaration, with a third that may be described as tactical.

The first asserts that the British government was persuaded of the moral claims of the Zionists to possession of Palestine as their one-time homeland. Since the matter was not previously debated in parliament nor ventilated publicly, this explanation would suggest that this momentous commitment was made because a very small group of senior politicians succumbed to the arguments of an equally small Zionist pressure group within the same political and social establishment. This would therefore constitute a classic example of 'insider' politics which took no necessary account of the broader national or international issues at stake. This was in fact the first explanation to be widely accepted and was documented by Leonard Stein in his book *The Balfour Declaration*, first published in 1961. It is important historiographically that this and similar explanations were written before the public records were opened for this period. This sets them apart from accounts published after the archives for the period were opened in the later 1960s.

The second dominant narrative is based on later and more detailed consideration of the then available official and private records. It suggests that the Balfour Declaration and the whole British strategy was based on a highly sophisticated, perhaps cynical, perception of the national interest by the 'official mind' in London. In this account Zionism becomes neither the seducer of British statesmen nor the motor of the Declaration, but the tool of British policy. Briefly, the British came to see Zionism as a convenient means of resolving the problem created by the projected 'international zone' of Jerusalem in the Sykes–Picot Agreement. Zionism was to ensure that neither France nor Russia gained access to an area regarded as critical for the security of Egypt, itself the guardian of the route to India and the East.

The third, 'tactical' explanation was also current from early days and may be seen as more relevant to the timing than the genesis of the Declaration. This suggests that, at that dire period of the war, it came to seem vital to attract the support for the Allies of the mass of Jews in Russia, particularly because that state was by then (and just before the November Revolution) under a new and allegedly Jewish-dominated regime. Since most Russian Jews had hitherto been pro-German and the Zionist headquarters were in Berlin, whose government was thought to be supporting the Zionist cause in Palestine, it seemed important to persuade them that the Allies were their true friends and so induce them to use their influence to keep Russia in the war. Similar considerations applied to the United States, where the huge number of immigrant Jews had been predominantly pro-German. America was already in the war against Germany, though not against the Ottomans; but a declaration of this type might strengthen the hand of President Wilson in the war effort and also induce American Zionists to persuade him to favour British claims to Palestine.

It is proposed to consider the first two of these possible explanations of the Balfour Declaration in turn: the third will be embedded in these narratives.

There was an underlying sympathy in Britain with Jewish aspirations in Palestine that dated at least to the 1840s, when Palmerston, influenced by strong contemporary evangelical faith in the concept of the Return and possible conversion of the Jews to Christianity, showed some interest in the idea of a Jewish settlement in the Ottoman empire.[15] But in 1914 there was no strong support in Britain for Zionist ambitions in Palestine. Indeed, the close connection between the WZO in Berlin, the German government, and the Ottomans aroused considerable suspicion in Britain, especially because Russian Jewry, understandably, was strongly pro-German because hostile to the Tsarist regime.

The outbreak of war in 1914 and the fact that the Ottomans joined Germany changed the situation radically because for the first time it opened the question of the future all the Ottoman possessions in the Near East. On 11 November 1914 (six days after the Porte had declared war) Asquith, as Prime Minister, stated that the Ottoman empire would be broken up after defeat. Palestine would therefore be a major issue because of its proximity to Egypt, now made a protectorate for the first time and regarded as the key to British communications with India and the east. On the same day Herbert Samuel, the archetypal rich assimilated British Jew, a Balliol College man and a Liberal Cabinet minister, discussed the future of Palestine with Lloyd George, then Chancellor of the Exchequer and a potential successor to Asquith. David Lloyd George had been brought up in a devout Bible-reading nonconformist tradition in Wales and seems to have had romantic ideas about the future of Palestine based on the Old Testament of the Bible rather than contemporary conditions. He is alleged to have told Samuel that he was 'very keen to see a Jewish state established' in Palestine.[16] Early in 1915 Samuel, possibly under the influence of Lucien Wolf, head of the Special Branch of the Conjoint Committee of British Jewish organizations, which were strongly anti-Zionist, appeared to step back from the aim of a Jewish state. In two cabinet memoranda of January and March 1915 he argued that, in view of the presence of a large Arab population, there should not be a Jewish state. Britain should rather declare

---

[15] This account of the growth of British interest in Zionism before 1917 is based mainly on Stein, *Balfour*. According to A. M. Lesch, *Arab Politics in Palestine 1917–1939: The Frustration of a Nationalist Movement* (Ithaca, 1979), 53, in 1923 Stein showed his moderation in arguing for 'a permanent *modus vivendi* with the Arabs by means of Arab participation in Jewish undertakings and the admission of Arab students to the Technical Institute of the Hebrew University in Jerusalem'.

[16] Stein, *Balfour*, 103. See also J. Grigg, *Lloyd George: War Leader, 1916–1918* (London, 2002) for a detailed discussion of Lloyd George's views.

a protectorate over Palestine and Jews should be allowed

To purchase land, to found colonies, to establish educational and religious institutions, and to co-operate in the economic development of the country, and that Jewish immigration, carefully regulated, would be given preference, so that in course of time the Jewish inhabitants, grown into a majority and settled in the land, may be conceded such degree of self-government as the conditions of that day might justify.[17]

This appears to constitute Samuel's considered view of what Jewish immigration to Palestine should do: it was not Zionism, but if carried out might lay the foundation for a Zionist state. It is remarkably close to the 1917 Declaration. In 1915, however, there was no chance of Britain adopting such a policy. Asquith was against it, Lloyd George only interested in 'the Holy Places', Haldane mildly interested, and Grey, as Foreign Secretary, keen but cautious. It was to take nearly three years for the government to make a commitment along these lines, and even then it was necessary for sustained pressure to be brought by insiders on then new Lloyd George government, for a decision to be taken.

The key word here is 'insiders'. It was critical that by 1917 Britain was ruled and its policies decided by a small war cabinet, formed by Lloyd George in December 1916. This concentrated all war strategy in the hands of, initially, five men: Lloyd George, Lord Curzon, A. Bonar Law, Arthur Henderson (representing the Labour Party), and Viscount Milner. Jan Smuts, Sir Edward Carson, and G. Barnes (replacing Henderson) joined during 1917. There were, of course, still departmental ministers outside this cabinet, including Balfour as Foreign Secretary and Edwin Montagu as Secretary for India. Never in modern times had the decision-making process in Britain been concentrated in so few hands; and it was by concentrating on such people that the Zionists were able ultimately to achieve their objectives.

Much of the credit for this conversion has conventionally been given to Chaim Weizmann, the classic example of an outsider who learnt how to penetrate the citadel of power. Weizmann was a Russian Jew who was educated in Germany and migrated to Britain in 1904 as an academic chemist at the University of Manchester, acquiring British nationality in 1913. He had been an active Zionist from youth, was elected to the Zionist Congress of 1913 as one of the two British members, and became Vice-President of the Zionist Federation in Britain. But he was not a top Zionist nor a member of its Executive. He might have remained at the periphery of policy had he not in 1915 been appointed Chemical Adviser on acetone supplies, critical for munition production, which took him to London and put him in close touch with Lloyd George as Minister for Munitions. Even so, he relied very heavily on C. P. Scott, the most famous editor of the *Manchester Guardian*, then the leading Liberal newspaper. Weizmann knew Scott in Manchester and in September 1914 converted him to the Zionist cause. This coincided with Scott's parallel conversion from being an anti-imperialist and against

---

[17] Stein, *Balfour*, 110.

war to adopting a strong imperialist position on the Middle East. By April 1915 he was in favour of unilateral British control over Palestine as the key to Egypt and Iraq. The Zionist objective fitted well into this scenario. From 1915 to 1917, Scott acted as an essential intermediary between Weizmann and Lloyd George.

The two other critical members of the elite which engineered the 1917 Declaration were A. J. Balfour and Lord Rothschild, together with his circle. Balfour, nephew of the great Lord Salisbury and his successor as Conservative Prime Minister from 1902 to 1905, had met Weizmann in Manchester before 1906 and became highly sympathetic to the Zionist cause. His kinsman, Lord Robert Cecil, who was Under-Secretary of State at the Foreign Office, was another Weizmann convert.

Another centre of early British Zionism was the senior branch of the British branch of the Rothschild family. This was split over Zionism, but Nathan Rothschild, who became the first professing Jew to enter the House of Lords in 1885, and Walter, who succeeded him in 1915, were strong Zionists. Closely connected with them were Lady Crewe (Lady Margaret Primrose), daughter of Lord Rosebery by his wife Hannah, born a Rothschild, and her brother Neil Primrose.

To a great extent all these and others connected with them may be seen as theoretical Zionists in the sense that they did not know Palestine and were moved by ethical or idealistic motives. Sir Mark Sykes, who was to be very important in 1917, was a different case.[18] He had travelled widely in the Near and Middle East before 1914, so had far more knowledge of the area than most of his contemporaries in London, and was a Conservative MP from 1911. After 1914 he was working with Lord Kitchener, then Secretary for War, but recently Consul-General and then High Commissioner in Cairo and still involved in Middle Eastern affairs. Sykes negotiated the Sykes–Picot Agreement of 1916 in which part of Palestine was to be designated an international zone, mainly to keep it out of French control. In 1916–17 he was attached to the war cabinet, then to the Foreign Office, and was widely influential in government circles. Sykes seems initially to have been an anti-Semite on the common grounds of hostility to the alleged international Jewish high finance, but was persuaded in 1916 by Samuel that Zionism was different. He saw no incompatibility between the aims of Arab nationalism, in which he believed strongly, and those of Zionism. Stein suggests that Sykes may have seen the presence of a strong Jewish element in Palestine as ensuring a pro-British bloc there, since the Sykes–Picot Agreement had left the danger of French occupation; but that he never conceived of a Jewish state, rather of 'the realization of the ideals of an existing centre of nationality, rather than boundaries or extent of territory'.[19] By 1918 he was becoming worried at Zionist chauvinism. But in 1916–17 he was a very active and valuable ally of the group that were to press the government to make a formal commitment to Zionist aims.

---

[18] A great deal has been written about Sykes. See in particular E. Kedourie, *Into the Anglo-Arab Labyrinth* (1976; 2nd edn. London, 2000) and his *England and the Middle East: The Destruction of the Ottoman Empire 1914–1921* (London, 1956).   [19] Stein, *Balfour*, 283.

In 1917 Sykes was joined in London by Ormsby-Gore as an understudy. He had been converted to Zionism by Aaron Aaronsohn, a distinguished agronomist who had been in Egypt to organize Zionist intelligence in Palestine.

The climax to this secretive planning came during 1917. In January and early February 1917 Sykes, although a government official, had a series of private meetings with Weizmann, Samuel (no longer a minister), and Gaster in which the Zionists produced what proved to be the first real draft of the eventual Declaration. This proposed

Palestine to be recognised as the Jewish National Home, with liberty of immigration to Jews of all countries, who are to enjoy full national political and civic rights; a charter to be granted to the Jewish Company; local government to be accorded to the Jewish population; and the Hebrew language to be officially recognized.[20]

But before such a proposal could safely be launched at the war cabinet the ground had to be cleared with British allies. This was certain to be difficult because the Sykes–Picot Agreement, of which Weizmann and other Zionists did not then know, stood in the way and France had by no means given up hope of controlling 'southern Syria'. There were also Greece and Italy, with their Middle East interests under Sykes–Picot, and beyond them Russia.

France was the most important of these. Nahum Sokolow, as the senior Zionist who happened to be in Britain,[21] talked to Picot in London, but Picot refused to admit to the existence of Sykes–Picot or to make any concessions to the Zionists. Sykes therefore followed him to Paris, and in February warned him that he would have to expect British dominance in Palestine, given the military situation and the forthcoming campaign, largely by British, Indian, and Australian troops. Picot appeared shaken by this breach of their Agreement. But the campaign continued. Sokolow and Sykes put further pressure on the Quai d'Orsay in April, and in June Sokolow got a letter from Jules Cambon, Secretary-General of the French Foreign Ministry and brother of Paul Cambon, French Ambassador in London, which stated that 'it would be a deed of justice and of reparation to assist, by the protection of the Allied Powers, in the renaissance of the Jewish nationality in that Land from which the people of Israel were exiled so many centuries ago'.[22] That was as far as Paris was prepared to go at this stage, and it is clear that Cambon's wording did not commit France to a British protectorate: France might equally have become the pro-moter of the Zionist cause. In December 1917, even after the British occupation of Jerusalem, Stephen Pichon, Minister for Foreign Affairs, still argued that Palestine should be internationalized; and in February 1918 Pichon said he was 'very happy to confirm that there is complete agreement between the French and British

[20] Stein, *Balfour*, 369.

[21] Sokolov was a well-known Russian journalist, writing in Hebrew, and a member of the WZO Executive.

[22] Stein, *Balfour*, 416. It is quoted in full in I. Friedman, *The Question of Palestine, 1914–1918* (London, 1973), 162.

Governments concerning the question of a Jewish establishment in Palestine'.[23] It is significant that the French version of this used the term 'un établissement juif', which Sokolow conveniently translated as 'a Jewish national home'. It was therefore quite unclear what the French position would be. But from the British Zionist standpoint Cambon's original letter was taken as enough to justify any British declaration provided that did not specifically mention British control.

Meantime, the Zionists needed at least neutral statements from the other Allies. Early in 1917 Sokolow therefore went to Rome, where he got a neutral statement from the Vatican, provided the Holy Places were safeguarded, and a vaguely favourable response from the Italian government. High-level soundings made by Justice Louis Brandeis, the leading Zionist in the United States and very close to President Wilson, in April and May 1917 also produced neutral results. Robert Lansing, Secretary of State, was hostile, but President Wilson was said to be 'vaguely sympathetic'. The United States, which entered the war against the Central Powers in April 1917, was not at war with the Ottomans, so had no formal status in deciding the future of their empire. But by September 1917, Brandeis could assure the London Zionists that Wilson, on whom he had been working, was now in entire sympathy with the current draft (by Rothschild) of the proposed declaration. On 16 October Wilson said that he concurred in the latest draft of 4 October (by Milner and Amery: see below), but this was not to be stated publicly until he knew the American Jewish reaction.

There remained Russia, now with its post-revolutionary provisional government. Tchlenow, who was sent to report, thought it might be favourable to Zionism, but not necessarily to British control of Palestine; and the possibility of a separate peace with the Ottomans meant that the secret treaties (not disclosed until after the Bolshevik takeover in November) would become ineffective. Even Jewish and Zionist attitudes in Russia were mixed. Jewish meetings in Petrograd in June 1917 and a Zionist meeting in Copenhagen in July, while wanting Jewish settlement in Palestine, were reluctant to commit themselves to British or French unilateral control.

This was not important. By the autumn of 1917, the Zionists in Britain deemed that there were no serious obstacles to a final assault on the war cabinet. The Foreign Office, now under Balfour, therefore encouraged the Zionists to prepare a draft of their proposal. Between July and 31 October, this went through four drafts, though based on the earlier draft of February. These drafts are printed as an appendix to this chapter. In the process of revision significant changes were made. In the original Zionist draft, the key phrases were 'the national home of the Jewish people' and that the government 'will discuss the necessary methods and means with the Zionist Organization'. In different words these ideas were retained in the Balfour draft of August, though the mandatory 'will discuss . . . with the Zionist Organization' was softened to 'will be ready to consider any suggestions . . . which

---

[23] Stein, *Balfour*, 590.

the Zionist Organization may desire to lay before them'. In the subsequent Milner draft (when Lloyd George and Balfour were away), 'the national home' was changed to 'a home for the Jewish people in Palestine'. A critical change was made in the Milner–Amery draft of 4 October. For the first time account was taken of the interests of non-Jews and of the concerns of British Jews that a Jewish home in Palestine might adversely affect the status of Jews in other countries. These changes were retained in the final draft of 31 October. Thus the final draft was very much less Zionist than any previous draft. It committed the government only to 'favour' and 'use their best endeavours to facilitate' 'a national home' and it reserved the rights of non-Jewish inhabitants. These reservations were to be very important in later interpretations of the Declaration and the British mandate.

This final draft was approved by the war cabinet on 31 October. But, although the majority were clearly in favour, it did not go through on the nod, nor was there unanimity in British opinion. Outside the cabinet, Anglo-Jewish reactions to the Milner–Amery draft of 4 October were either hostile or neutral. Claude Montefiore, President of the Anglo-Jewish Association, objected to 'national home' on the ground that most Jews already had national homes. Sir Leonard Cohen, President of the Jewish Board of Guardians, and Sir Stuart Samuel MP were also hostile. Within government Lord Curzon tried to block the proposal altogether: Palestine could not hold many Jews. Initially he said he would only support it if the formula 'equal civil and religious rights with the other elements of the population, and to arrange, as far as possible, for land purchase and settlement of returning Jews' was included.[24] But, as he was the only member of the war cabinet to oppose, he eventually withdrew his objection. A much tougher fight was put up by Edwin Montagu, now Secretary of State for India. Montagu was a son of the first Lord Swaythling, head of the rich and ultra-orthodox family that founded the banking and exchange firm Samuel Montagu & Co., who had close contacts with Russian Jewry. Montagu opposed Zionism both on the standard Anglo-Jewish grounds and also from the standpoint of his Indian office. He rightly saw that Indian Muslims would be outraged by Jewish domination of Palestine. But he was in a minority of one in governmental circles. The cabinet approved the final draft on 31 October and the Declaration was sent to Lord Rothschild on 2 November. It was addressed to him because he had sent the original Zionist draft in July, because Sokolow was an alien, and because Weizmann was junior to him in the Zionist hierarchy. It is unlikely that so important a statement of government policy had ever before been directed to a private citizen.

It is, therefore, possible to construct a convincing explanation for the Balfour Declaration in terms primarily of the conviction of the group then in power in Britain, given that strategic considerations were by late 1917 largely neutral. It has been seen that Lloyd George, Milner, and Balfour were keen Zionists, and George Barnes, the Labour member of the cabinet, supported it on the basis that the

---

[24] Stein, *Balfour*, 545.

Labour Party's official statement of August 1917 was that 'Palestine should be set free from the harsh and oppressive government of the Turk, in order that this country may form a free State under international guarantee, to which such of the Jewish people as desire to do so may return and may work out their own salvation, free from interference by those of alien race or religion.'[25] Hence the strong sentiment of the great majority of the cabinet was to create a Jewish homeland.

Nevertheless, why this was so remains conjectural. A possible explanation is that the British middle and upper classes were brought up to admire three ancient civilizations: those of Greece, Rome, and the Jews. In the case of Lloyd George and Barnes this school and university background was replaced by nonconformist religious upbringing. Britain had actively supported Greek independence and the unification of Italy in the nineteenth century, and it seemed equally natural now to support a revival of the glories of ancient Israel. Given the military and diplomatic situation late in 1917, there no longer seemed any strong obstacle to indulging these sentiments. There may have been marginal practical inducements to make the Declaration at that point. There was some fear that Germany might come out with a similar statement, though in practice this was blocked by Turkish obstruction. Conversely, a commitment of this kind might stimulate Jewish opinion in both Russia and the United States, hitherto mostly pro-German because of hatred of Russia, to support the Allied war effort. Certainly Balfour at the time used the propaganda argument; but in February 1918 he denied that he and Lloyd George were bidding for this Jewish support. Rather they were influenced by a 'desire to give the Jews their rightful place in the world, a great nation without a home is not right'.[26] Moreover, it is very important that the Declaration was silent on two vital issues. It did not indicate British control of Palestine, which might have been expected had the 'home' been intended as the basis for British territorial claims. Nor did it promise a 'state' of Palestine, merely a 'home' 'in Palestine'. Although Lloyd George seems always to have intended some form of British control, Balfour for long preferred international or United States control; and in view of continued French claims to Syria, including Palestine, this had to be left open until the Peace Conference. As to the future form of the 'home', the Zionists kept this discreetly imprecise. In fact they, along with Balfour, assumed that in the long run Palestine would become a Jewish state by process of immigration At the time this could not be stated publicly, though in December 1917, Gaster spoke of 'an autonomous Jewish Commonwealth' and in December 1918, Weizmann told Balfour that the aim was a Jewish Commonwealth as Jewish as England was English, but with 'many non-Jewish citizens'.[27] At the time, however, these obvious aspirations, based on Herzl's doctrine, were kept under cover. Moreover, under whichever regime Palestine was placed, provided the terms of the Declaration were observed the Zionists were clear that they could work out their own destiny, as indeed eventually they did.

[25] Ibid. 475.   [26] Ibid. 552.   [27] Ibid. 553.

We must now consider the alternative, 'strategic', explanation of the Balfour Declaration and the subsequent British claim to a mandate over Palestine, which follows from the account given in Chapter 2 of the complex diplomacy of the years before 1917.

The case has perhaps been put most strongly by the Israeli historian Mayir Vereté, originally in an article published in 1970, but reproduced in a later collection of his essays.[28] His primary concern was to demolish the myth that Weizmann and his collaborators took the initiative and talked the British government into making a promise they would not otherwise have made. His argument was that 'the British wanted Palestine—and very much so—for their own interests, and that it was not the Zionists who drew them to the country . . . neither was it the Zionists who initiated the negotiations with the government, but the government that opened up negotiations with them . . . had there been no Zionists in those days the British would have had to invent them'.[29]

This was a very challenging revisionist statement which would necessarily change one's whole interpretation of the genesis of the mandate. I propose first to summarize Vereté's argument, without recapitulating the diplomatic material contained in Chapter 2, then to use other sources to see how far it can be sustained.

Palestine had been a British concern, Vereté argues, ever since the occupation of Egypt in 1882. By 1900 the British had forced the Sultan to withdraw his forces north from the Suez canal. They had surveyed the land as far north as Acre, blocked a French scheme for extending the French-owned railway to El-Arish, and in 1914 got German recognition that Palestine lay within a British sphere of interest. In 1915 the de Bunsen Committee accepted the view, put forward by Sykes, but probably representing Kitchener's views, that both western and eastern Palestine, from the line west–east from Acre to Dar'a and south to Aqaba and the Egyptian frontier, lay within the sphere of British interests. Two basic reasons were given for this. First, Britain needed control of a continuous corridor between the Mediterranean and the Persian Gulf, so that reinforcements could be brought quickly from Britain against a Russian threat from the north. Second, the British 'could scarcely tolerate' that the French should have the borders of their parallel future sphere of interest along the canal, the Arabian peninsula, and the Persian Gulf.

It was on this basis that Sykes negotiated the Palestinian elements of the Agreement with Picot. In view of the deep French emotional commitment to 'la Syrie intégrale', which they deemed to include the sanjaq of Jerusalem, the best he could do was to reserve southern Palestine from Acre–Dar'a to a line north of

    [28] M. Vereté, 'The Balfour Declaration and its Makers', *Middle Eastern Studies*, 6/1 (January 1970), reprinted in N. Rose (ed.), *From Palmerston to Balfour: Collected Essays of Mayir Vereté* (London, 1992), ch. 1, hereafter Vereté. See also Friedman, *The Question of Palestine*, which develops a similar argument but places more emphasis on the British need to gain the support of Jews in Russia and the United States.   [29] Vereté, 3–4.

Gaza for an international regime, while the area east of Jordan and between Gaza and the Egyptian frontier would lie in the British sphere of interest with a putative Arab ruler. This had been cleared in advance by Sykes with the Cairo authorities and it was believed that the promise made to the Sharif of Mecca by McMahon in his letter of 24 October 1915, which was to be the cause of endless controversy, was consistent with this. It will be remembered that, in order to persuade the Sharif to create a diversionary rising in Arabia, he was promised that Britain would favour the establishment of an Arab kingdom covering much of the Turkish-controlled parts of Arabia, Mesopotamia, and Syria. The exclusions, however, were critical for Palestine: 'The districts of Mersin and Alexandretta and portions of Syria lying to the west of the districts of Damascus, Hama, Homs and Aleppo cannot be said to be purely Arab and should be excluded from the proposed limits and boundaries.' British acceptance of Arab claims was also restricted to 'those portions of the territories wherein Great Britain is free to act without detriment to her Ally, France'.[30] Cairo reckoned that, on either of these two grounds, Palestine could not be promised to Sharif Husayn. Yet it was equally important that it should not be claimed by France. Hence, Sykes had had to resort to making the sanjaq of Jerusalem and part of the vilayet of Beirut an international territory, presumably under some form of condominium, like that between Britain and France in the New Hebrides. Since this might involve the Russians as well as the French it was only slightly better than allowing France to claim it, as she later did, as part of Syria.

Vereté demonstrates that there was a continuous thread of British official determination to gain control of Palestine from the start of the war with the Ottomans. Thus on 28 December 1914 Ronald Storrs, Oriental Secretary in Cairo, wrote to Kitchener's secretary, Colonel Fitzgerald, for transmission to Kitchener in London, as follows:

With regard to Palestine, I suppose that while we naturally do not want to burden ourselves with fresh responsibilities such as would be imposed upon us by annexation, we are, I take it, averse to the prospect of a Russian advance Southwards into Syria, or a too great extension of the inevitable French Protectorate over the Lebanon, etc. . . . A buffer State is most desirable, but can we set one up? There are no visible indigenous elements out of which a Moslem Kingdom of Palestine can be constructed. The Jewish State is in theory an attractive idea; but the Jews, though they constitute a majority in Jerusalem itself, are very much in a minority in Palestine generally, and form indeed a bare sixth of the whole population. . . . Would not the inclusion of a part of Palestine in the Egyptian Protectorate with the establishment at Jerusalem of a mixed Municipality chosen from a large number of elements and granted wide powers be a possible solution?[31]

Vereté moreover quotes Sykes, after his return from Moscow with Russian acceptance of the Agreement in 1916, as telling the war cabinet why he thought Britain

---

[30] The text of the critical parts of the letter is printed in Kedourie, *Labyrinth*, 97.
[31] Vereté prints only part of this letter on p. 27, n. 2. The fuller version is in Kedourie, *Labyrinth*, 34.

should demand Palestine, both western and eastern. 'It is most important that we should have a belt of English controlled country between the Sherif [*sic*] of Mecca and the French.'[32]

Vereté argues that, so far as this Agreement related to Palestine, Sykes had been reluctant to concede so limited a British interest—to an exclusive control only of the Acre–Haifa area—plus a vague international control of the rest of southern Palestine. This in fact left it open for France, at the eventual peace conference, to claim the whole of Palestine as part of Syria. Others, including Captain Reginald Hall, Director of Naval Intelligence, were worried by this, and Hall wrote a critical memorandum in March 1916. It was at this point, so the argument goes, that British official circles began to become interested in the Jews, though not necessarily the Zionists, as a possible solution to the Palestine question. Sykes may have discussed the issue with Hall and, though not a Zionist at this stage, may have thought that if Britain encouraged Jewish immigration, this would strengthen British claims against those of Russia and France. But in the final version of the Agreement there was no mention of Jews or Zionism.

It was also at this point, early in 1916, with the war apparently going against the Entente and the bulk of Jews both in Russia and the United States strongly in favour of Germany (because of their hatred of the Russians), that the idea of using Palestine to gain Jewish support internationally seems to have been born. Vereté traces the idea to a private letter from the USA late in 1915 and a dispatch from McMahon in Cairo which reported that a non-Zionist Jew, Edgar Suares, had suggested that 'with a stroke of a pen, almost, England could assume to herself the active support of the Jews all over the neutral world if only the Jews knew that British policy accorded with their aspirations for Palestine'. This interested the Foreign Office, which consulted Grey, as Foreign Secretary. Hugh Obeirne of the Office was deputed to write a minute for Sykes to take to Russia on his mission to get Russian approval for the Agreement, which suggested that the Zionist option would have 'tremendous political consequences'. Grey ordered that Cambon, the French Ambassador in London, be told 'that Jewish feeling which is now hostile and favours a German protectorate over Palestine might be entirely changed if an American protectorate was favoured with the object of restoring Jews to Palestine'. Cambon was not impressed; but the Foreign Office persisted and was now ready to press on France and Russia the idea that, with the support of the Allies, Palestine might eventually become something like a Jewish commonwealth.[33] Thus appeal to international Jewry was added to strategic concerns and remained in harness until the end of the war.

Vereté admits[34] that much of this argument before early 1917 is conjectural, but suggests that the limited evidence demonstrates that many in Britain were unhappy with the Sykes–Picot arrangement and were looking for an alternative,

---

[32] Vereté, 6. There is no date or reference to this quotation.
[33] Ibid. 12–13 and the very extensive n. 7.   [34] Ibid., n. 8, pp. 32–3.

which might be an American rather than a British protectorate. This seems to have changed with the accession of Lloyd George's new ministry in December 1916 and the start of the main British push from Sinai early in 1917. Lloyd George was an 'Easterner' and as a fundamentalist Protestant believed in the return of the Jews as a precursor of the millennium. Moreover, from at least early 1915 he was determined that Palestine should fall within the British sphere of interest and should not be controlled by an international condominium. Military occupation coupled with Zionist immigration seemed the surest way of achieving both objectives.[35] The outcome was the series of talks between Sykes, Weizmann, and Sokolov early in 1917, but on the initiative of Sykes, not the Zionists. The primary need was to obtain French acquiescence, and Sokolov was instructed to make visits to France and Italy to obtain French and Italian agreement to the Zionist programme and their preference for a British protectorate. The French were not prepared to give up their political claims to greater Syria, but at least offered 'sympathy' for the Zionist cause. This was later to be a very important bargaining counter. Meantime Sykes had left to become Political Officer attached to the British army in Palestine, visiting Paris on the way; and Lloyd George told him at a cabinet meeting that it was important to secure 'the addition of Palestine to the British area [in the Sykes–Picot Agreement]' and also to ensure the development of the Zionist movement 'under British auspices'.[36] Sir Ronald Graham of the Foreign Office minuted this to Lord Hardinge, then the Permanent Under-Secretary, on 21 April 1917: 'the Prime Minister insists that we must obtain Palestine and . . . Sir Mark Sykes proceeded on his mission with these instructions. . . . His Majesty's Government are now committed to support Zionist aspirations. Sir Mark Sykes has received instructions on the subject from the Prime Minister and Mr Balfour and has been taking action both in Paris and Rome.'[37]

The argument, then, is that as early as April 1917, and before the Zionists had submitted the draft that eventually evolved into the Balfour Declaration in July, the British government was determined not to allow any French or Russian presence in Palestine under the Sykes–Picot internationalization proposal, and that they in effect enrolled the Zionists as their agents on the ground. As Curzon (who was not in any sense a pro-Zionist) put it in a sub-committee of the Imperial War Cabinet on 19 April, 'the Zionists in particular would be very much opposed' to any other solution. In short, the basic reason for British support for the Zionists was that at least those in Britain were determined that Britain rather than France or the hated Russia should be their protectors in Palestine. Conversely, once this argument had been established and publicized, it became essential for the British to adhere to it: having mobilized the Zionists to support their claims against

[35] This is strongly supported by Grigg, *Lloyd George*, ch. 19. In particular he writes: 'His conception of the Jews in Palestine was that they would form a lively, distinct community within the British Empire' (p. 350), and 'But in the end Lloyd George stuck to his concept of a British Palestine, to which, as he believed the Zionist experiment would be accessory' (p. 357).   [36] Vereté, 19.
[37] Ibid., n. 13, p. 35.

Sykes–Picot (and possibly also against the McMahon promises to Husayn), they were stuck with them. This largely explains the whole course of action from then until the granting of the mandate in 1922.

Thus, from April 1917 to the publication of the Declaration on 2 November, the only issue remaining was its precise terms. Vereté suggests that the delay may have been due to the possibility of an early peace with the Ottomans; and by 3 September Lord Robert Cecil, Parliamentary Under-Secretary at the Foreign Office, was urging Balfour to get on with it because otherwise Zionists in America might lose confidence in British intentions. A month later, Balfour pressed for a decision because 'the German Government were making great efforts to capture the sympathy of the Zionist movement'. On 31 October, at the crucial cabinet meeting, Balfour said that 'he gathered that everyone was now agreed that from a purely diplomatic and political point of view it was desirable that some declaration favourable to the aspirations of the Jewish nationalists should be made'. He argued that this would have very favourable propaganda effects and Curzon, though still sceptical, agreed.[38]

Vereté concludes that the huge attention devoted to the negotiations with Zionist leaders, and even the extent of pro-Zionist sentiment among British politicians, is largely beside the point. Sentiment alone would not have produced the commitment to Zionist immigration. It was convenient that after the Declaration leading politicians were emotionally committed to Zionism, and this made it certain that the Jews would get considerably more official help than the phrase 'view with favour the establishment in Palestine of a National Home for the Jewish People and will use their best endeavours to facilitate the achievement of this object' implied. But this was not decisive: 'it was sheer interest in all its aspects that was the decisive motive in making the government resolve on viewing with favour, and lending support to Zionist aspirations'.[39] Of course, once the commitment was made the British were stuck with it. Since the French had not agreed to waiving their interests under the Sykes–Picot Agreement, the fact that the Zionists wanted British control of Palestine became the main British bargaining counter.

But Vereté's argument has one important corollary. Whereas in Stein's and other conventional accounts it would appear that a small coterie of senior British politicians and officials had imposed on both Britain and the Middle East a policy that had never been debated in parliament and therefore expressed only the personal preferences of this small in-group, this interpretation makes the Declaration the outcome of considered official concern that had evolved since 1914 that Palestine must not be allowed to fall into unfriendly hands. It was the product of the Robinson–Gallagher concept of 'the official mind' and expressed the perceived interests of the nation.

How far do other accounts support this interpretation? It seems that many, particularly the more recent of them, do. But so did that of an actor in the process of 1917–18, Leo Amery. Amery had worked with Milner as part of his 'Kindergarten' in South Africa after 1902, and was brought into a vaguely defined position as assistant to Maurice (later Lord) Hankey as Secretary of the War Cabinet. In Stein's account, Amery played a major role in pressing for the Balfour Declaration and its later implementation. Yet in his memoir, published in 1953, he wrote of his original attachment to Zionism as follows:

I confess that my interest was, at first, largely strategical. I was keen on an advance into Palestine and Syria on military grounds, and the idea of consolidating that advance by establishing in Palestine a prosperous community bound to Britain by ties of gratitude and interest naturally appealed to me. I already had doubts as to the permanence of our protectorate in Egypt, and the solution which I then advocated . . . was that we should confine our direct strategic control to the Suez Canal and to the area between its Asiatic bank and the Palestine border, thus interfering as little as possible with the internal independence of our neighbours, but providing a central pivot of support for our whole Middle Eastern policy, as well as assuring the effective control of our sea and air communications with the East.

But it was not long before I realized what Jewish energy . . . might mean for the regeneration of the whole of that Middle Eastern region . . . which in the course of centuries had gone derelict beyond hope of recovery by its own unaided resources . . . Most of us younger men who shared this hope were, like Mark Sykes, pro-Arab as well as pro-Zionist, and saw no essential incompatibility between the two ideals.[40]

Further evidence of pre-Zionist British interest in Palestine is reflected in other modern studies of the period and problem. Thus, according to Andrew and Kanya-Forstner, in their seminal *France Overseas*, as early as December 1915, when in the process of negotiating with Picot, Sykes was determined to establish British interests in Palestine, since he regarded it as crucial as providing access to the Mediterranean from Baghdad. He would have preferred that it be incorporated with Egypt, but had to compromise with French determination to preserve their claim to Syria by arranging for southern Palestine to be an international regime of some sort, but with British controlled enclaves at Haifa and Acre. In 1917 the Zionists were seen in Britain as the way to provide Britain with the essential legitimacy to alter the Sykes–Picot Agreement. Weizmann conveniently rejected the idea of an international regime, and so gave the British their best bargaining counter. Ultimately, in December 1918, Clemenceau verbally conceded Palestine, along with Mosul, to Lloyd George.[41]

David Vital, in the last volume of his well-balanced history of Zionism to 1917, defined four main factors that influenced the decision to issue the Balfour

---

[40] L. S. Amery, *My Political Life*, Vol. 2: *War and Peace 1914–1929* (London, 1953), 115–16. It is interesting that, despite saying that in 1953 he still had hopes for the acceptance of Israel by Arab states, he said almost nothing about the problems of Palestine during his period as Colonial Secretary from 1925 to 1929.

[41] C. M. Andrew and A. S. Kanya-Forstner, *France Overseas: The Great War and the Climax of French Imperial Expansion* (London, 1981), 94–5, 126–30.

Declaration.[42] In first place, he put the desire for security. By the time of Lloyd George's accession to power in December 1916, 'old British reservations about a French presence in Palestine had finally mutated into an explicit (but still secret) determination to establish fully-fledged British control over the country'. Curzon's Committee on the Terms of Peace recommended on 28 April 1917 that:

> To ensure this it is desirable that His Majesty's Government should secure such a modification of the [Sykes–Picot] agreement with France of May 1916 as would give Britain definite and exclusive control over Palestine and would take the frontier of the British sphere of control to the River Leontes [i.e. the Litani] and north of the Hauran. Turkish rule should never be restored in Palestine or Mesopotamia.[43]

Earlier, on 3 April 1917, in their instructions to Mark Sykes, when about to leave as Political Officer with the British army invading Palestine, Lloyd George and Curzon had made the connection between the control of Palestine and the Zionists very explicit.

> They impressed on Sir Mark Sykes, the difficulty of our relations with the French in this region and the importance of not prejudicing the Zionist movement and the possibility of its development under British auspices. . . . The Prime Minister suggested the Jews might be able to render us more assistance than the Arabs. . . . [He] laid stress on the importance, if possible, of securing the addition of Palestine to the British area. . . . [He] suggested that Sir Mark Sykes ought not to enter any political pledges to the Arabs, and particularly none in regard to Palestine.[44]

What Sykes and others wanted, in fact, was something to balance the 'sentimental' French claim to 'la Syrie intégrale', without trying to claim Palestine as a British possession and so creating a crisis within the Entente. This was where the Zionists came in: they could provide a balancing 'pretension' under which Britain could exert effective control over Palestine.

Vital then went on to outline other supporting factors at the top level of British politics. There was sympathy with the plight of Jews in eastern Europe, the main source of Balfour's eventual Zionism: Vital suggests that Balfour's Zionism 'was at heart of a philosophical character and essentially detached from considerations of direct policy and interest'. A second factor that stimulated interest in Zionism was concern at the role Jews played in Russia and the United States. Finally, Vital suggests that, even if briefly, there evolved a wider movement in Britain which came to see Zionism in the same way as the British had in the past seen the movement for Greek independence and Italian unification. This suggested that the Jews would not merely be tools of British imperialism but desirable allies: that the Zionist cause was intrinsically worthwhile. Such feelings gave warmth to what might otherwise have been a cold-blooded strategy of exploiting Zionist ambitions and the pro-British stance adopted by those in Britain (by contrast with that majority in Germany).[45]

---

[42] Vital, *Zionism: The Crucial Phase.*   [43] Ibid. 211–12.   [44] Ibid. 213.
[45] Ibid. 214–23.

Similar arguments were used by Isaiah Friedman, another Israeli historian of this period. Thus in one book he suggested that '[Zionists] alone could present a British claim to Palestine in a more favourable light and negate the accusations that Britain was an expansionist power'. Sentiment was important: '[Balfour] felt passionately on two things; one was the need to maintain friendship with the United states, the second was Zionism. Schooled in Jewish history and civilisa-tion, he regarded the destruction of Judea by the Romans as "one of the great wrongs" and "a national tragedy for the Jews", which the Allied Powers were attempting to redress.' But to balance this moral imperative both the Foreign and War Offices saw things dispassionately. 'There was a combination of motives rather than one which led to the final decision, but what dominated was the desire for security.'[46] In his other book on early Zionism Friedman demonstrated at length how favourable in principle the German government was to both Jews and Zionists during the war: that despite their limited ability to prevent Turkish brutalities in Palestine, their influence saved the Zionist settlements there throughout the war, and that as early as 1915 Berlin was anxious to promote Zionist strategies, provided this did not cause a rupture with Constantinople. Thus instructions to the Consulate in Jerusalem in November 1915 stated:

It seems politically advisable to show a friendly attitude towards Zionism and its aims. Efforts should be made to respect as far as possible, the sensitivity, if any, of the German Jews, particularly those connected with the Hilfsverein who, without justification, behave as if interest in the Zionist movement implies a direct prejudice to their own position.'[47]

In 1917 much of the German press was favourable to Zionist ambitions and was urging the government to back Zionist objectives, provided that these were com-patible with continued Turkish sovereignty in Palestine. The British government was well aware of these German moves and may have taken them more seriously than did Berlin. Friedman writes:

In London it was assumed that if articles in the German Press of almost every political shade were speaking with the same voice then those articles must have been inspired and stimulated by the German Government and reflected its thinking. The British were under the firm impression that the Germans were courting the Zionists and might at any moment publicly identify themselves with the Zionist cause. How deeply rooted was this belief is shown by the fact that Balfour felt obliged to warn the War Cabinet that 'the German Government were making great efforts to capture the sympathy of the Zionist Movement'.[48]

In fact, as Friedman, says, the German government was not prepared to commit itself to a Zionist Palestine; but pressure on it continued. In November 1917, as a response to the Balfour Declaration, Ludwig Haas, a Jew but not a Zionist and

---

[46] Friedman, *The Question of Palestine, 1914–1918*, 289–91.

[47] I. Friedman, *Germany, Turkey and Zionism, 1897–1918* (1977; 2nd edn. New Brunswick, 1998), 265. The Hilfsverein was the German organization representing non-Zionist Jews and was therefore the equivalent of the French Alliance Israélite and the British Anglo-Jewish Association and other bodies.   [48] Ibid. 327–8. There is no date or reference provided for Balfour's comment.

then both a member of the Reichstag and head of the Jewish department of the civil administration in German-occupied Poland, was pressing the Ministry of the Interior to make a comparable declaration in favour of unrestricted Jewish immigration and colonization in Palestine, on the understanding that the immigrants would comply with Ottoman laws and disclaim separatist aspirations. This, he argued, would help to relieve the needs of Jews in east Europe.[49] Although it is impossible to measure how much such information influenced the British government in adopting the Balfour Declaration, it is likely that it carried some weight.

Finally, a minute by W. E. Beckett, Legal Adviser to the Foreign Office, written in January 1939 in the context of belated publication of the McMahon–Husayn correspondence in response to demands by the Arab delegation to the Palestine conference in London, summarized the then accepted official view of the importance of the Declaration for British control of Palestine.

At the time when the McMahon letter was written France was claiming the whole of Syria. . . . Therefore at the time that these words were written H.M.G. [*sic*] did not know whether she would be free to act without detriment to the interests of France in any portion of Syria and, if these words meant anything, they meant that the assurance only applied to areas in Syria with regard to which H.M.G. eventually obtained a free hand as a result of the peace settlement, and it is true that the French claims to Palestine or the French claim for an international administration of Palestine were only withdrawn after the Balfour Declaration had been accepted by the allies, and therefore H.M.G. only got Palestine subject to the Balfour Declaration. But this does not alter the fact that it was H.M.G. who took the initiative as regards the Balfour Declaration and thus secured this fetter on their hands which, unless the interpretation of the first part of the McMahon letter is correct, H.M.G. should never have done.[50]

Elie Kedourie, who quotes this minute, argues that in fact the British were not excluded from creating a separate jurisdiction in Palestine by the terms of McMahon's letter of 24 October 1915; but this opinion demonstrates that the official mind in London was still in 1939 imbued with the idea that it was only the Balfour Declaration that opened the way for British control of Palestine, and that they could not therefore go back on their commitment.

In fact, from the end of 1917 to the London and San Remo Conferences early in 1920, whose function was for the Entente to agree to advise the Supreme Council on the terms of peace with Turkey, and even later until the final award of the Palestine mandate to Britain by the League of Nations in 1922, Britain was indeed 'fettered' by the Declaration. The main problem was that, despite Clemenceau's verbal cession of Palestine to Lloyd George in December 1918, the French government, under strong pressure from colonial interest groups, remained very reluctant to concede this, particularly under the new government led by Millerand from January 1920. At San Remo, the French tried to insist on an

---

[49] I. Friedman, *Germany, Turkey and Zionism, 1897–1918* (1977; 2nd edn. New Brunswick, 1998), 375.   [50] Kedourie, *Labyrinth*, 270.

international mandate in line with Sykes–Picot, and also opposed the terms of the Balfour Declaration being written into the mandate. But Lloyd George was adamant; and finally the British were awarded the Palestine mandate. In addition the ancient protectorate France claimed over Catholic Christians in the area was abolished. Later in April 1920 the Supreme Council agreed on the terms of the mandate. The mandatory should be responsible 'for putting into effect the declaration originally made on the 8th [*sic*] November 1917 by the British Government, and adopted by the other Allied Powers, in favour of the establishment of a national home for the Jewish people, it being clearly understood that nothing should be done which may prejudice the civil and religious rights of existing non-Jewish communities in Palestine, or the rights and political status enjoyed by Jews in any other country'.[51] Moreover, the critical terms of the Balfour Declaration, particularly 'the establishment in Palestine of a National Home for the Jewish people' and the caveat concerning the rights of non-Jews, were written into the terms of the formal mandate issued by the Council of the League of Nations on 24 July 1922.[52]

It therefore seems clear that the main driving motive for the British in issuing the Balfour Declaration was to ensure that no potentially hostile country controlled Palestine. Vereté was right to see the Zionists as ancillary to this purpose. Conversely, the commitment did not stem from the sudden conversion to Zionism of a small coterie at the top of British politics, but from the more conventional assessment by the 'official mind' of British strategic interests. Nevertheless, as will be seen in the following chapter, it is important for what followed that most of those in London who formulated Middle Eastern policy during the next two decades took the moral commitment very seriously. Despite the few who already by 1918 had begun to fear the consequences, including Lord Robert Cecil and Lord Curzon, belief in the essential rightness of the creation of a Jewish home became embedded in the official mind. Thus, whenever serious problems in Palestine seemed to indicate that the mandate would not work and that perhaps changes should be made in its terms, officialdom responded by insisting that it was inviolable. In the 1930s it was often argued that if changes were made or the mandate surrendered, the French would step in. It was not only officials who took this view. As the debates of 1939 over the proposals in the White Paper for strict limitation of Jewish immigration (which are discussed in the following chapter) were to show, the sense of commitment was very deep in all political parties. Since by that time it had become abundantly clear that there was no hope of peaceful coexistence between Jews and Arabs, it is important to examine why, quite apart from the strategic argument, the British political class committed itself so enthusiastically to the Zionist cause that they even built into the mandate a promise that Britain

[51] Quoted Stein, *Balfour*, 661.
[52] The main clauses of the text of the mandate are printed in A. F. Madden and J. Darwin, *The Dependent Empire 1900–1948* (Westport, Conn., 1994), 605–7.

would 'facilitate' Zionist aspirations and also a provision that 'An Appropriate Jewish Agency shall be recognized as a public body for the purpose of advising and co-operating with the Administration of Palestine'.[53] Why should London have deliberately built into its regime a commitment to support Zionist enterprise along with an intrusive body of this kind which would necessarily limit the freedom of action of the mandate government and which had no parallel in earlier British colonial practice?[54]

The answer seems to be that, once the principle of British control for strategic and political reasons had been accepted, the optimism expressed by people such as Amery, in the quotation above, became dominant. Zionists were now seen as dynamic Europeans who as colonists would bring energy, skills, and capital to a 'derelict' region. Moreover, it seems likely that for most of those involved in Britain their image of Zionists was that of the few very able Anglicized Zionists they knew, notably Weizmann, whose loyalty to Britain seemed unassailable. Thus, future Zionist colonizers, who would come mostly from Russia or Poland, were granted honorary British characteristics. They would perform the same civilizing functions as recent British settlers in British East Africa or the Rhodesias, or earlier in New Zealand or Australia, were believed to have done. Few probably thought far enough ahead to realize that such settlers, particularly those with no British connections, were very unlikely to act as loyal supporters of the raj once it ceased to serve their own interests, and still less likely to accept the rights of other residents.

The obverse of such assumptions was, of course, that the native inhabitants of Palestine were seen as uncivilized and non-progressive, and therefore not entitled to serious consideration. This is rather surprising given the British commitment to the Arab nationalist cause and their creation of Arab states in Iraq and Transjordan. Moreover, this was certainly not the attitude of most of the Cairo authorities who had developed the pro-Arab strategy during the war and those who were then landed with the job of administering Palestine. The explanation may be that to most Britons who were not directly involved in the area, the Arabs were those of the desert, embodied in the Northern Army led by Amir Faysal. Conversely there seems to have been a general unstated assumption that the inhabitants of the Mediterranean coastal area were not true Arabs, but 'Levantines' of mixed race and little importance. Their decadence seemed to invite improvement by more sophisticated and harder-working settlers. Thus the mandate can be seen as perhaps the last British venture in the colonization of a 'backward' territory, though largely by non-British settlers.

[53] The main clauses of the text of the mandate are printed in A. F. Madden and J. Darwin, *The Dependent Empire 1900–1948* (Westport, Conn., 1994), 606.

[54] Most of the original American colonies and a number of 'settler' colonies after 1783 had constitutions which embodied representative legislatures. This was because it was believed that British common law entitled such settlers to the rudiments of British constitutional and legal rights. But I know of no earlier example of a statutory advisory body distinct from the legislature in a non-settler colony.

The success of the mandate, which will be examined in the following chapter, therefore depended on the accuracy of three fundamental British assumptions: that Palestine was 'open' for colonization by the West; that the Zionists would become and remain loyal British supporters; and that it would be possible for the British to hold a balance between the two main elements in the population, persuading them to live in harmony. By 1939, and in fact long before, all three had been proved false, and the British were left to face the consequences of their own misjudgement.

APPENDIX: SUCCESSIVE DRAFTS AND FINAL TEXT OF THE BALFOUR DECLARATION

A. ZIONIST DRAFT, JULY 1917

1. His Majesty's Government accepts the principle that Palestine should be reconstituted as the national home of the Jewish people.
2. His Majesty's Government will use its best endeavours to secure the achievement of this object and will discuss the necessary methods and means with the Zionist Organization.

B. BALFOUR DRAFT, AUGUST 1917

His Majesty's Government accept the principle that Palestine should be reconstituted as the national home of the Jewish people and will use their best endeavours to secure the achievement of this object and will be ready to consider any suggestions on the subject which the Zionist Organization may desire to lay before them.

C. MILNER DRAFT, AUGUST 1917

His Majesty's Government accepts the principle that every opportunity should be afforded for the establishment of a home for the Jewish people in Palestine and will use its best endeavours to facilitate the achievement of this object and will be ready to consider any suggestions on the subject which the Zionist organisations may desire to lay before them.

D. MILNER–AMERY DRAFT, 4 OCTOBER 1917

His Majesty's Government views with favour the establishment in Palestine of a national home for the Jewish race and will use its best endeavours to facilitate the achievement of this object, it being clearly understood that nothing shall be done which may prejudice the civil and religious rights of existing non-Jewish communities in Palestine or the rights and political status enjoyed in any other country by such Jews who are fully contented with their existing nationality [and citizenship].

Words in square brackets added later.

E. Final text, 31 October 1917

His Majesty's Government view with favour the establishment in Palestine of a national home for the Jewish people and will use their best endeavours to facilitate the achievement of this object, it being clearly understood that nothing shall be done which may prejudice the civil and religious rights of existing non-Jewish communities in Palestine or the rights and political status enjoyed by Jews in any other country.

Source: L. Stein, *The Balfour Declaration* (London, 1961), 664.

5

Palestine: The British Mandate, 1918–1948

It is arguable that Palestine was the greatest failure in the whole history of British imperial rule. The mandate committed Britain to develop 'self-government'. In the event, Palestine never had self-government in any form: it was ruled by the British through the most autocratic of colonial systems—governor, executive council, nominated advisory council, and no legislative council. Moreover, when the mandate was given up in 1948, there was no government to which power could be handed over. This was unique. In every other British dependency, except for Hong Kong in 1997, power was handed over to an elected government along with a viable set of administrative institutions; and in Hong Kong, although there was no elected government in the normal sense, government was well established. When the British left Palestine in May 1948, journalists asked the Chief Secretary, Sir Henry Gurney, what would happen to the government and its offices when the British left Jerusalem. He replied, 'I shall put them [i.e. the keys of his office] under the mat.'[1] In short, the British, after thirty years, had failed to create a viable indigenous government of any sort and could only evacuate the country and leave its future to be decided by civil war.

Why was this? The easy answer is that, given the complexities of the situation they inherited and their commitments under the Balfour Declaration, 'The British mandate in Palestine was perhaps doomed from the start.'[2] But this is to see events backwards. It is also to assume that it was impossible in a colonial situation to persuade two different religious societies to live in some degree of peaceful cohabitation. There were many British, and indeed other European possessions, in which there were two or a large number of conflicting groups willing to accept

[1] W. Khalidi, *Palestine Reborn* (London, 1992), 76. Wm R. Louis in *The British Empire in the Middle East 1945–1951* (Oxford, 1984), 530, quotes Sir Alan Cunningham, the last High Commissioner, as writing: 'In the end the British were blamed for not having handed over to anyone, whereas, in point of fact, there was nobody to whom to hand over.' In his diary, Sir Henry Gurney noted: 'The Police locked up the stores (worth over £1 million) and brought the keys to the UN [commission], who refused to receive them. I had to point out that the UN would be responsible for the administration of Palestine in a few hours time (in accordance with the UN November resolution) and that we would leave the keys on their doorstep, whether they accepted them or not; which they did.' Quoted in A. Shlaim, *Collusion Across the Jordan* (Oxford, 1988), 219.
[2] B. Wasserstein, *The British in Palestine: The Mandatory Government and the Arab–Jewish Conflict 1917–1929* (1978; rev. edn. Oxford, 1991), 241.

the inevitability of cohabitation and even to collaborate in a single state system. It is true that such systems were most durable under the imperial umbrella and that many broke down during or after the process of decolonization. But at least in all these places the British, French, and even technically the Belgians, left some form of government in place. In Palestine the British merely evacuated.

Moreover, at the start, and indeed until perhaps 1929, many in Britain and Palestine were optimistic about the possible outcome.[3] (Sir) Ronald Storrs, then Governor of Jerusalem, reflected this optimism in a speech he made in Britain in 1921. While no one was more aware of the problems created by the conflicting interests of incoming Zionists and resident Arabs, he made the following statement:

In Jerusalem there meet, and have met for centuries, the highest interests of the three great religions of the world. . . . I do not dare to prophesy . . . but I do dare to believe that what has happened before may happen again, and that if we can succeed in fulfilling, with justice, the task that has been imposed upon us by the will of the nations, and if we can reconcile or unite at the source the chiefs and the followers of those three mighty religions, there may sound once more for the healing of the nations a voice out of Zion. If that should ever be, not the least of England's achievements will have been her part therein.[4]

This may have been rhetoric, putting the best face on an impossible problem. But it probably expressed the early optimism of many British administrators in Palestine that they would somehow manage to overcome the obvious problems of dealing with so divided a dependency. This, after all, was what the British were expert at. They had set themselves the problem and had insisted that the League of Nations write their obligation into the mandate. They did not give up until 1947. Why, then, did they fail here so uniquely? Were they, in the words of Sir Douglas Harris, Special Commissioner in Palestine in February 1945, merely 'ploughing sand'?[5]

There are three possible approaches to this question, based on each of the three main actors: the Arabs, the Zionists, and the British. Any one of these might have blocked the road to an agreed inter-communal settlement. It is therefore proposed to examine the position and actions of each of these in turn, in that order, even though this will result in some overlapping and repetition.

1. THE ARABS

It was seen in the previous chapter that long before the creation of the mandate there was strong anti-Zionist feeling among Arabs, both Muslim and Christian, in Palestine. This was increased by the behaviour of the Zionist Commission under

---

[3] Some were not. Thus Lord Curzon, while accepting the fact of the Balfour Declaration, minuted on 20 March 1920: 'The Zionists are after a Jewish State, with the Arabs as hewers of wood and drawers of water. . . . I want the Arabs to have a chance and I don't want a Hebrew State.' D. Ingrams (ed.), *Palestine Papers 1917–1923* (London, 1972), 96. I owe this quotation to David McDowall.

[4] R. Storrs, *Orientations* (London, 1937; 2nd edn. 1943), 385. Storrs commented in this later edition that 'not excluding 1919 and 1936, I see no reason to recant'.

[5] Quoted in N. Shepherd, *Ploughing Sand: British Rule in Palestine* (London, 1999), 226.

Chaim Weizmann which arrived in Palestine in March 1918, well before the final conquest of the country, and acted as if the Balfour Declaration had already been implemented and a mandate set up. They demanded that the military government, the OETA (Occupation of Enemy Territories Administration), should make Hebrew an official language equivalent to Arabic, and that Jews should be appointed to official posts. These requests were granted, though demands for a Jewish mayor of Jerusalem and for Jews to provide half the members of the town council were rejected. On 2 November 1918 a parade of Jews in Jerusalem celebrated the anniversary of the Balfour Declaration. This triumphalism reflected the Zionist assumption that they had been given the keys to Palestine. The reaction of the Arabs was immediate and forceful. They began to organize as they had never done under Ottoman rule.[6]

They were, of course, largely ignorant of the techniques of public protest as they existed in the West. Their chosen method was to form associations which could organize petitions to the OETA. The first of these in 1918–19 was the Muslim–Christian Associations (MCA). Given the social structure of the society, it was inevitable that these should be led by local notables in each region. Thus in Jerusalem the natural leaders were Musa Kazim al-Husayni, mayor of the city and member of the very rich and influential Husayni clan, and Arif Hikmat al-Nashashibi, head of the *awqaf* (religious endowments). But the OETA forced both to stand down as they were public officials, so the leadership in Jerusalem was taken by Arif Pasha al-Dajani, member of the third dominant clan. Similar branches were established in many other Palestinian towns, again headed by local notables, some Christian but most Muslim. These associations got together to present petitions, first to OETA and then to the Crane–King Commission that visited Palestine in 1919 on behalf of the victorious powers to ascertain local opinion.

The arguments they used then remained virtually constant until the end of the mandate. They claimed that Palestine belonged to the Arabs by right of continual occupation since at least the Arab conquest of AD 634. There were some 512,000 Muslims as against 61,000 Christians and 66,000 Jews, the Jewish population having been seriously reduced during the war. Jews owned only 1 per cent of the land and constituted 7 per cent of the population. Moreover, the Arabs claimed that the Allies had promised them freedom as a nation. This was implicit in the Anglo-French Declaration of 7 November 1918 promising self-determination to all people freed from Ottoman rule. Moreover, article 22 of the League of Nations Covenant promising recognition of 'independent nations' was assumed to apply to Palestine. After the ejection of Amir Faysal from Syria in 1920 there was added the argument that Palestine was excluded from the mandate system under the

---

[6] The following account of Arab organization is based mainly on the following: Y. Porath, *The Emergence of the Palestinian-Arab National Movement, 1918–1929* (London, 1974); Y. Porath, *The Palestinian-Arab National Movement: From Riots to Rebellion, 1929–1939* (London, 1977); A. M. Lesch, *Arab Politics in Palestine, 1917–1939: The Frustration of a Nationalist Movement* (Ithaca, 1979).

terms of the McMahon–Husayn correspondence of 1915, which had excluded from Arab rule only 'portions of Syria lying to the west of the districts of Damascus, Hama, Homs and Aleppo'.[7] Conversely, the Jews had no right to Palestine. The arrival of penniless Zionists had bad economic effects. Many Zionists were communists, and their social habits were obnoxious to Arabs.

To pull all these local associations together and thus exert some influence on the British, in whose good intentions many Arabs were then still confident, the MCA held a series of congresses between 1919 and 1928. In December 1920, the Third Congress set up an Arab Executive Committee (AE), initially to organize a deputation to London in 1921. The Arabs wanted this body to be recognized by the government, since July 1920 under Sir Herbert Samuel as High Commissioner, as a balance to the Zionist Commission and later the Jewish Agency. Samuel refused, on the ostensible ground that the AE was not representative, but actually because it refused to accept the validity of the Balfour Declaration, though in 1923 he tried to organize an Arab Agency parallel to the Zionist Agency. He failed because the Arabs would not accept it on the terms offered, and no similar agency ever existed.[8] The AE attempted to put its case against the mandate and Zionist immigration to Winston Churchill when he visited Palestine in March 1921, after the Cairo Conference. Predictably, since he was and always remained a staunch Zionist, it failed. So also did the first Arab delegation to London later in 1921.

The delegation, after much disagreement, consisted of four Muslim notables, one Greek Roman Catholic from Haifa, one Greek Orthodox from Jerusalem, and two secretaries, only one of whom could speak English. Although Samuel refused to give this delegation official status, the Colonial Office under Churchill used the opportunity to discover what chance there was of an accommodation. Their negotiations provide a clear indication of the limits of the positions adopted by both parties. Churchill wanted to discuss the possibility of setting up some form of legislative council, as was virtually universal in British dependencies. But it was not to be a conventional legislative council since this would have had legislative powers, subject to governor's veto, which would have created the danger that it would attempt to obstruct the Zionist project. His proposal was that it would have advisory functions only. The Colonial Office wanted it to be mostly elected with some nominated members, but all administrative powers were to be retained by the High Commissioner.

The delegates, on the other hand, were determined to have a proper legislative council. They demanded a 'native' (i.e. Palestinian) government responsible to an elected parliament. They also, predictably, demanded annulment of the

---

[7] The claim was delayed until after 1920 because it was thought that Faysal knew that it was false. For the most detailed analysis of the question see E. Kedourie, *Into the Anglo-Arab Labyrinth: The McMahon-Hussayn Correspondence and its Interpretations, 1914–1939* (1976; 2nd edn. London, 2000), which argues at great length that, despite imprecise geographical description, there was no British intention of including Palestine in the promised Arab state under the Sharif.

[8] For the details of this proposal see Wasserstein, *The British in Palestine*, 127–30.

commitment to a 'national home' for the Jews, the cessation of Jewish immigration until the new government was set up, enforcement of Ottoman laws, and free association with Arab neighbours. What they wanted was the type of regime set up in Iraq in 1920, in which there would be indigenous ministers with British advisers. This in turn was unacceptable to London, but the Colonial Office kept discussions going for nearly a year, possibly to keep these men out of Palestine during the period of demonstrations likely in April 1922, following the major riots during the Nebi Musa festival of April 1920. The office made a number of ameliorative suggestions, but none dealt with the key issue of control of Jewish immigration, and all were rejected by the delegation. It is, however, important that the delegates were not unanimous. Three of them (two Christians and one Muslim) wanted to negotiate further on the powers to be exercised by a possible legislative council. They were finally recalled by the Arab Executive after the issue of Churchill's White Paper of 3 June 1922, formalized as an Order in Council in August, which for the moment blocked further discussion.

The White Paper was based on discussions held with Samuel in London in May 1922, and its three main principles were to dominate British policy in Palestine for nearly a decade. While reasserting the British commitment to a Jewish national home, it promised that Palestine would not become a Jewish state and that Arabs would not be subordinated to Jews. Second, there would be a legislative council which could control the rate of immigration in conjunction with the British government. Third, the rate of immigration would be based on 'economic absorptive capacity', a phrase that would have long influence. Until a legislative council was elected, government would be in the hands of the High Commissioner, an executive council consisting of the High Commissioner and senior British officials, and an advisory council consisting initially of British officials and nominated Arab and Jewish members. This last was to be replaced by an elected legislative council.

The failure of this attempt to create an elected legislative council, the centre of Samuel's strategy, proved a major turning point in the history of the British mandate. It was a key element in his approach to making the mandate work that Arabs and Jews should meet in a common assembly and discuss major issues, even if only in an advisory, rather than a legislative, capacity. Seen in the larger context of British imperial history, legislative councils had been a crucial means of transferring power from the executive to representatives of the colonial population, even if the transition from official to non-official majority, and then to a government responsible to the legislature, was in most cases slow.[9] Samuel's scheme called for elections on the Ottoman two-stage system, which would result in a council of eight Muslims, two Christians, and two Jews, roughly in line with the then population, plus eleven officials. No one was enthusiastic about this. The Zionists considered a boycott, but eventually decided to co-operate. But the Arabs proved

[9] Nor was the process irreversible, as the history of Malta and Ceylon (Sri Lanka) shows.

irreconcilable. In 1922 the AE proposed to block the planned census, essential for the elections, but were bullied into withdrawing their opposition. Despite negotiations with Arab leaders, who demanded a number of concessions as the price of supporting the election,[10] the AE decided on an election boycott, which was publicized from mosques throughout the country.

The boycott was overwhelmingly successful. Only 107 out of a possible total of 663 Muslim secondary electors stood. In the first stage only 18 per cent of qualified Muslims voted, plus 5.5 per cent of Arab Christians, and 50 per cent of Jews. Those Arabs who voted were mainly from areas dominated by notables hostile to the then AE, in Jerusalem, the Ramleh, and Galilee. It was clearly impossible to proceed to the second stage of the elections and Samuel suspended the legislative council scheme 'for the time being'. In fact, although further schemes were introduced, all fell on Arab resistance or Colonial Office veto. In 1923, after the election fiasco, Samuel attempted to set up a nominated advisory council (the previous one having died with the new White Paper constitution) but, although he managed to recruit some important men, once the news came out most of them were forced to resign by orchestrated Arab criticism. In 1926 the AE negotiated with the Acting Chief Secretary of the government, Eric Mills, over a possible bicameral elected legislature. This was immediately vetoed by the incoming High Commissioner, Lord Plumer, on instructions from London, as giving too much power to the Arabs.[11] In 1929 Plumer's successor, Sir John Chancellor, pressed the Colonial Office, now under the Labour minister Lord Passfield, to reopen the question, suggesting an entirely nominated council with an official majority of one as against ten Muslims, three Jews, and two Christians. He got the agreement of some Arab notables, including Musa Kazim al-Husayni, but even he was doubtful whether he could sell the idea to the AE; and in the event the idea was made impracticable by the Wailing Wall crisis. Sir Arthur Wauchope revived the idea in 1935, suggesting a complicated mix of officials and elected and nominated unofficials. This was killed by the outbreak of the 1936 Arab strike and subsequent rising. The result was that Palestine under the British never had an elected legislature and the Arabs never got any training in western political forms.

How important this was in the failure of the mandate has been much debated. On the one hand, despite initial Arab hostility, it is possible that taking part in a common institution might have reduced the distrust and hostility between the two sides. It is possible, also, though unlikely given the hierarchical structure of Arab society, that members might have been elected outside the narrow bounds of

[10] These included an agreed annual limit on immigration, more Arab officials, an Arab amir to rule Palestine, and an Arab majority in the legislative council, the balance to be nominated. See Wasserstein, *The British in Palestine*, 121–2.

[11] Plumer came from being Governor of Malta, where the elected legislature was a constant thorn in the flesh of the government. Its constitution of 1887 was repealed in 1903, reissued in 1921, suspended again in 1930, revalidated in 1932, suspended in 1933, and revoked in 1936. Limited representative government was established in 1939 and responsible government in 1947, only to be revoked in 1959 before full self-government was set up in 1961, leading to independence.

the AE and the power structure controlled by Amin al-Husayni and his Supreme Muslim Council. At least the Arabs might have obtained some experience of western-style representative government, and there was talk of a committee of council to debate immigration quotas. As against this, both Porath and Lesch argue that such a council would not have worked. Lesch states that the council would merely have been a forum for protest because it was not responsible and because control of the thing that mattered most to Arabs, Jewish immigration and land purchase, would have been out of the council's control. Porath agrees, mainly on the grounds that immigration and the mandate would have been out of the council's purview and it would not have been able to control the administration.[12]

Whatever the answer, the fact is that from 1922 until the end of the mandate, Palestine was governed as the most austere British crown colony, with all power, and therefore responsibility, limited to the High Commissioner, his council, and his officials. The question then is how the government dealt with the Arabs, in particular how it attempted to create that structure of patron–client relations essential to ensure some degree of collaboration in all colonial situations.

In effect, the government set up two parallel sets of relationships, one for the Zionists (which will be examined in the following section) and one for the Arabs. Both were outside the formal structure of the mandate government. For the Arabs, the key British decision was to attempt to use the Muslim hierarchy as its main lever on Arab society. To do this they fixed the appointment of Amin al-Husayni as mufti of Jerusalem (the British gave him the title of Grand Mufti, though this was not traditional) in 1921 and then enabled him to become president of the newly created Supreme Muslim Council. These decisions proved critical for the success of the British mandate.

Any such appointments were bound to be intensely controversial, given the rivalry between competing Muslim notable families. The al-Husayni family was one of the richest and most influential in Jerusalem, but by no means the only such family. Amin was selected partly because three of his family had held the post of mufti in the earlier twentieth century, but still more because Amin's elder brother, Kemal, as mufti, had been a very important collaborator with the British in 1917–20, and had, unprecedentedly, been appointed *qadi* and head of the central *awqaf* council. Kemal died in March 1921 and the complicated procedure for electing his successor under Ottoman law started. The prescribed electoral council, consisting of local imams, ulama, and elected members of the city coun-cil, duly met and put forward three names for the choice of the government. Amin al-Husayni, though not qualified as an alim, stood and came fourth. One of these three was persuaded to withdraw, after which Samuel appointed Amin as mufti.

This was a most improbable choice.[13] Amin was not a qualified alim or shaykh. He had been trained in Istanbul as a 'tarbush wearer' (administrator), then, after

[12] Lesch, *Arab Politics*, 196; Porath, *The Emergence*, 156–8.

[13] For Amin's background and career see T. Jbara, *Palestine Leader: Hajj Amin al-Husayni, Mufti of Jerusalem* (Princeton, 1985). The book is uncritical of Amin but contains useful information.

being invalided out of the Ottoman army in 1916, took a minor civil service post in Jerusalem. Along with the al-Husayni clan he was pro-Hashemite after 1915, hoping for the unification of an independent Syria and Palestine. He was alienated by the Balfour Declaration and the visit of the Zionist Commission in 1918, and was active in the anti-Zionist riots of 1920. He was tried and condemned to ten years' imprisonment but escaped to Syria. In September 1920 he returned to Jerusalem under Samuel's general pardon. The main thing in his favour was that he was a Husayni, since the clan had been strong supporters of the British since 1917, and would keep the post of mufti in that family. In addition he was clearly very clever. In April 1921 he promised Samuel that if appointed he would support the British administration and ensure that there was no repetition of the 1920 riots. Samuel's senior officials were divided on the issue. The Assistant Chief Secretary, E. T. Richmond, was in favour, while the Chief Secretary, Wyndham Deedes, and the Legal Secretary, Norman Bentwich (a pro-Zionist British Jew), were against. Samuel seems to have decided that Amin's 'extremism' would be modified by high office. Perhaps more important, it was necessary to balance the appointment as mayor of Jerusalem of Raghib Bey Nashashibi in May 1920, in succession to Musa Kazem Pasha al-Husayni, so that these two leading notable families would not feel slighted.[14] Finally, Samuel thought it essential that there should be strong Muslim leadership in control of the *awqaf* revenues and the sharia courts to offset the autonomy enjoyed by the Zionists.[15] The riots of May 1921 seemed to make such measures even more important.

In pursuit of this objective, Samuel went much further than merely making Amin the 'Grand Mufti' of Jerusalem. In August 1921 Samuel told a conference of ulama that he wanted to set up a body representing the country's Muslims to control religious endowments and the superior sharia courts.[16] This would be elected by the existing secondary electors to the defunct Ottoman parliament, though the dismissal of *qadis* (sharia judges) was to be in the hands of the government. The conference accepted this idea and drew up rules for the election. It was decided in January 1922 that this Supreme Muslim Council (SMC) would consist of a president (who would be 'permanent'), plus two members from Jerusalem sanjaq and one each from Nablus and Acre. The Nashashibis fought hard against the election of Amin as president and failed.

The role of Amin and the SMC was initially rather vague. It was unclear whether the president had to be elected every four years, along with the other four members of the SMC. So also were the powers of the SMC and the means of changing its rules. In the event the practical result was that control over Muslim affairs, including the *awqaf* revenues and the sharia courts, was given to Amin al-Husayni. In addition to his salary as mufti he received something over £50,000

[14] Musa al-Husayni was told to resign by Storrs because he had taken part in the riots. See Storrs, *Orientations*, 390–1.
[15] Jbara suggests that Samuel may have been influenced by Storrs, though there is no mention of this in Storrs's *Orientations*.   [16] Porath, *The Emergence*, 194.

a year from the *awqaf* endowments. This, along with his huge influence on the appointment of religious leaders, and the ability to make grants to mosques, schools, and other Muslim purposes, enabled him to build up a range of clients far wider than those the Husayni clan could provide. Thus he could reward allies in supporting areas, while those in opposition, such as in Hebron and Haifa, did badly. Moreover, the mosques became very important as a symbol of his influence, and a pulpit from which attacks could be made on his opponents. In short, in selecting Amin as its main client, the government effectively lost control over Islamic affairs. According to Porath, 'The impression was . . . that, in the eyes of the Government, the Mufti of Jerusalem and President of the SMC was in fact the official representative of the Palestinian population.'[17]

Whether Samuel and the Colonial Office recognized just how significant this was is uncertain. It is clear that, after the riots of 1920 and 1921 and the recognition of the Zionist Assembly in 1920, they thought they should do all they could, short of rescinding the Balfour Declaration, to demonstrate to the Arabs that the government was impartial as between religious communities. This attempt at a balancing act was taken one stage further in 1923 with the proposal for an Arab Agency to parallel the local Zionist Executive, set up to replace the 1918 Zionist Commission and to fulfil the requirement of article 4 of the mandate that there should be a 'Jewish Agency'. The proposal was made late in 1923, as it became obvious that the Arabs were not prepared to take part in the legislative council elections or the nominated advisory council. The Agency was to consist (unlike the Jewish Agency) of members nominated by the High Commissioner. It would have the right to confer with the government on all matters affecting the non-Jewish population, including Jewish immigration. But it would come into effect 'only as an agreed settlement to which both parties are prepared to adhere'.[18] This proved impossible to negotiate: even those opposed to the Arab Executive refused to accept nomination. Thus, Amin and his SMC emerged as the only formally recognized representative of Muslim Arab society, and remained so until it was reconstituted during the Arab rebellion of 1936–8.

This fact is critical for understanding the history of the mandate. The British had chosen as their intermediary with the majority Arab population a leading member of one of the competing notable families. They had gambled on both his ability to control anti-Jewish feeling and his loyalty to the regime. In a colonial situation such gambles were always hazardous, though there were many places where they worked for long periods. The trouble in Palestine was that the British had bound themselves by the Balfour Declaration and the mandate not to make the one concession that really interested the majority of Palestinians—the cessation of Jewish immigration. Thus, they could twist and turn, but ultimately they were faced with the alternatives of surrendering the mandate or facing irreconcilable majority opposition.

[17] Ibid. 201.   [18] Quoted Wassserstein, *The British in Palestine*, 127.

Yet, for the moment, the strategy of alliance with Amin al-Husayni and the SMC seemed to pay off. Between 1921 and the Wailing Wall riots of 1929 there was no significant threat to British control. For this there were two main reasons. First, the level of Jewish immigration and land purchase was far smaller than had been expected, or than the British supporters of Zionism hoped for. Between 1919 and 1924 the total was never more than about 8,000 a year. It rose briefly from 1924 to 1926, mainly because of the partial closing of the United States to east Europeans in 1924, then dropped severely in 1927 and 1928, with a net emigration, and rose only to about 5,000 in 1929.[19] Despite the principle of 'economic absorptive capacity' adopted in 1922 and various government rules about land purchase this was in fact primarily due to the poverty of the Zionist Organization, which nearly went bankrupt in the later 1920s. Thus there was much less pressure on Arabs and it began to seem possible that, as Samuel had hoped, the Zionist impact could be absorbed without major social conflicts.

The other main reason for the limited effectiveness of Arab hostility to the mandate and its pressure on the government before 1929 was the splitting of the nationalist movement into a number of internecine parties, many of them hostile to both the AE and the SMC. This is where the Arabs most obviously differed from the Zionists, who, though also divided into parties, never seriously challenged the control of the Agency. It is clear that, in a 'traditional' society, where power was highly localized in the hands of a number of leading families of notables, it would have been extremely difficult to sustain a centrally organized anti-Zionist movement, particularly in the face of the failure between 1919 and 1923 to obtain any concessions from the British. Moreover, the contrasting fortunes of the leading families in Jerusalem provided a basis for factional divisions. There the long-established al-Husayni and al-Khalidi families were in conflict with the recently risen Nashashibis for the places now in the gift of the British. Such conflicts were repeated in the provinces.[20]

The result of such factional divisions was the growth between 1921 and 1929 of what is normally described as an opposition to the AE, the SMC, and the al-Husayni group. Briefly between 1921 and 1923 there was the National Muslim Association, hostile to the Christian element in the MCA and in close touch with the Zionists. It was mainly based in the northern areas, which resented the dominance of the Jerusalem-based AE and SMC. It supported the elections to the legislative council in 1923, then died from internal conflicts and a reduction in Zionist subventions. Its main successor was the Palestinian Arab National Party, led by the main anti-Husayni elements, opposing the AE with comparable nationalistic and anti-Zionist arguments. In addition there was much opposition from village shaykhs who resented loss of control to the urban notables and the SMC, and who formed a number of localized organizations.

[19] Quoted Wassserstein, *The British in Palestine*, table on p. 160.
[20] See Porath, *The Emergence*, 210–13 for a Namierite analysis of provincial family conflicts.

Given the absence of a legislative council in whose elections these groups could have challenged the dominant Husaynis, the main target of opposition groups was control of or influence on the SMC and the AE. The peak of their success came in 1926 when, after a great legal battle, the government appointed two opposition members along with two Husayni supporters to the SMC, though this left Amin al-Husayni with a casting vote. In 1927 opposition groups had considerable success in local municipal elections, the only elective process in Arab Palestine, winning in most provincial towns and making gains in Jerusalem. Such developments weakened the AE and coincided with a decline in anti-Zionist fervour, encouraged by the dramatic decline in Jewish immigration. In 1928 these trends came to a head in the Seventh Congress, which saw a closing of the Arab ranks. The AE was reorganized with 48 members, including a number from the opposition groups. The Congress showed renewed interest in the possibility of a legislative council, and even considered accepting the mandate. There remained, however, a younger radical element under Hamdi al-Husayni of Gaza which opposed any accommodation with the Zionists or the government and promoted pan-Arab rather than Palestinian nationalist objectives.

In retrospect, 1928 may be seen as potentially the best opportunity for some form of settlement between the Arabs, the Zionists, and the British. The reformed AE began negotiations with the High Commission. Unfortunately there was then a hiatus at the top. Plumer retired in July and his successor, Sir John Chancellor, did not arrive until December. He immediately announced publicly and advised the Colonial Office that some form of legislative assembly should be set up. Again there was a hiatus. Leo Amery, as Colonial Secretary (and a keen Zionist), was not interested, but his successor in the minority Labour government of Ramsay MacDonald, Lord Passfield (Sidney Webb) proposed the creation of a nominated legislative council to consist of ten Muslims, three Jews, and two Christians, with an official majority of one. This was secretly agreed to by the leaders of two of the main factions in the AE, Musa Kazim al-Husayni and Raghib al-Nashashibi, who agreed to serve if appointed. But Musa thought it unlikely that he could sell this to the AE and SMC because a similar proposal had been rejected in 1923. This was never put to the test. The Wailing Wall riots of August 1929 ended all such projects.[21]

The nominal issue in the riots was the extent of Jewish rights to have access and pray at the wall, the last remnant of Herod's temple. They held that these rights included bringing religious furniture, chairs, and a screen to divide men from women. The Arabs had for long challenged these claims, maintaining that the area belonged to Muslims and that any concessions to Jews were customary and defined by Ottoman regulations of 1911, which the British were committed to maintaining on the principle of the status quo. As redefined by Amery in 1928,

---

[21] There are detailed accounts of the riots and their antecedents in Wasserstein, *The British in Palestine*, 222–34, and Porath, *The Emergence*, 258–72. See also C. Townshend, 'Going to the Wall: The Failure of British Rule in Palestine, 1928–31', *Journal of Imperial and Commonwealth History*, 30/2 (May 2002), 25–52. 'Acephalous' means without a chief or ruler.

this permitted only access by Jews, not the bringing of their equipment. There had been rumbles over these issues since 1917, but on 15 and 16 August 1929 there were massive Jewish demonstrations, including members of the Jewish BETAR, an extremist youth group connected with the Jewish Revisionist Party of Vladimir Jabotinsky, from Tel Aviv. The rights and wrongs of the question are esoteric and unimportant from the present standpoint. The significant fact is that they demonstrate the very strong undercurrent of popular feeling since the events in Jerusalem were quickly followed by major riots and much bloodshed elsewhere, notably in Hebron, where a community of long-established non-Zionist Jews were slaughtered. Altogether 133 Jews and 116 Arabs were killed in a week of violence. The British were unequipped to cope with it. There were virtually no British military forces and only about 292 British police in the whole of Palestine. Troops could be and were imported from Egypt and Transjordan, but too late to be useful. Moreover it happened that both Chancellor and the Palestine Zionist Executive were out of the country, so that both government and the Yishuv (the Jewish settler community) were, to use Wasserstein's term, 'acephalous'.[22]

It is unclear just why these festering communal hostilities should have erupted to this extent at this moment. Porath argues that the crisis was engineered by Amin after a year of intense propaganda run by him in support of the Muslim claims to these holy places and against alleged plans by the Jews to rebuild their temple. He suggests that Amin saw the crisis as a way of re-establishing his and the SMC's dominance of the Arab cause in the face of the relative moderation of the reformed AE and the success of rival notable groups. On the other hand the Shaw Commission of 1929, after very intensive investigation and legal argument, concluded (with one dissentient) that 'the Mufti of Jerusalem must stand acquitted on charges of complicity in or incitement to the disturbances'.[23]

Whatever the rights and wrongs of the case it is clear in retrospect that 1929 marked another watershed in Palestine's history during the mandate. On the Arab side the most important fact was the decline and eventual death (in 1934) of the Arab Executive. Its last significant achievement was to send yet another delegation to London in March 1930 consisting of six leaders of the main factions in the AE to negotiate on the whole range of issues. Their demands were virtually unchanged from 1920. They wanted a national Palestinian government with British technical advisers, on the Iraq pattern, an end to Jewish immigration and land sales to Jews, and more Arabs in the higher levels of the civil service. This last was a significant grievance and reflected Arab suspicion that the British favoured Zionists. In the later 1920s Arabs provided only some 40 per cent of men in the senior civil service. No Arab was ever appointed head of a department or as a district commissioner. The highest level they attained was as assistant heads of central departments or district officers. The classic case is that of George Antonius, an Orthodox Christian educated at Victoria College, Alexandria and King's College,

Cambridge, whose blocked career in Palestine and alienation are described in Chapter 1.

The Labour government in Britain predictably refused all the main demands of the 1930 delegation. But Passfield's White Paper of 1930 was influenced both by the views of Chancellor and the Reports made by the Shaw and Hope Simpson Commissions into the riots and their causes (March and October 1930). These emphasized the impossibility of indefinite Zionist immigration due to land short-ages and dispossession of Arab peasants. The White Paper, foreshadowing that of 1939, emphasized the dual British obligation under the mandate to both Jews and Arabs. It suggested that restrictions must be placed on Jewish immigration and land sales and that a legislative council was desirable in the longer term. This was the best result any Arab delegation had so far obtained, and the AE was in favour of accepting the proposals. But, typically of British dealings with Palestine, these pro-posals were quickly blocked by Ramsay MacDonald. The details will be examined in the third section of this chapter. In brief, Weizmann, appalled by the possibility of limited immigration, exploited his close links with the inner circle of politicians to persuade Ramsay MacDonald to publish a letter, initially drafted by the Zionists, which was then read in the House of Commons. This stated that there would be no limit on immigration other than that implied by Churchill's 1922 for-mula of 'economic absorptive capacity'.[24] This 'Black Letter', as the Arabs came to call it, remained the basis of British policy until 1939 and constituted probably the most important single element in the rise of Arab resistance and violence.

The most obvious and immediate result was that the moderation shown by the recent AE was discredited. Its income dried up, due mainly to the refusal of the notables, who alone could afford to support it financially, to pay up. The final blow was the death of Musa Kazem al-Husayni in 1934. The AE did not meet again after August of that year. Its place was taken by a number of largely new and mostly more radical organizations. The SMC was now increasingly and overtly political as Amin al-Husayni emerged as a would-be international Islamic leader, though Amin continued nominally to support the British government and in 1930–2 came to terms with the incoming High Commissioner, Sir Arthur Wauchope, who provided money to improve the SMC's straitened finances. In reaction to the rise of these new and potentially more radical groups the more conservative notables formed new parties.

Thus, by mid-1935 there were at least six organized Arab political parties and the Arab movement was hopelessly fragmented. Meantime the threat to Arab Palestine was greatly increased by the rise of Jewish immigration. For the first time since the mid-1920s this became really significant after 1933 and the rise of anti-Semitism in Germany. Between 1922 and 1936 the Jewish population had risen from 83,000 to 370,000, that is from 11 to 27.7 per cent of the population.

[24] The details of this devious negotiation are in N. A. Rose, *The Gentile Zionists: A Study in Anglo-Zionist Diplomacy, 1929–1939* (London, 1973), ch. 1. See also Tom Segev, *One Palestine Complete* (London, 2000), 335–41, for an excellent analysis of the whole White Paper/Black Letter fiasco.

By 1939 it was to rise to 31 per cent. Meantime Zionist land purchases had also increased. By 1939 they had risen from about 650,000 dunams in 1914 to perhaps 1,420,205 dunams in 1939, a dunam being about a quarter of an acre. The big purchases had been in 1925, 1929, 1934, and 1935. In relative terms this amounted in 1940 to only about 5 per cent of the total land area. The significant fact was the change in the character of these purchases. Between 1891 and 1900 42.7 per cent of Jewish land purchases were in small lots from the fellahin, but between 1901 and 1927 the sales by fellahin became very small, never more than 4.3 per cent and 5,095 dunams (about 1,200 acres), or less. The majority of early land sales were by non-Palestinians in Syria or Lebanon, which accounted for 86 per cent in 1923–7. But after 1928, while such sales by non-Palestinians or large-scale Palestinian owners continued, there was a big rise in sales by the fellahin, to 16,940 dunams in 1928–32 (18.3 per cent) and 9,265 dunams in 1933–6 (22.5 per cent of total sales). The explanation of this shift is that before the later 1920s, the bulk of land sales were in the desolate or half-desolate areas in the coastal plain and the Jezreel and Jordan valleys, mostly not owned by Palestinians and with relatively few tenant farmers, which were preferred by the Zionists as suitable for citrus farming. Thereafter the Jews increasingly bought land owned by Palestinians, the smaller owner-occupiers often selling to clear debts or raise funds for investment in the balance of their properties. Even so, these sales hardly affected the more densely populated mountainous areas—only 3 per cent between 1930 and 1935. Yet there were adverse effects on many small Arab farmers. Some sold all their land and became penniless, usually drifting to the towns, where most found only casual work. Generally owners who sold to the Zionists were evicted. The numbers are uncertain because the official register of landless Arabs used very restrictive criteria: Porath thinks only 'a few thousand'. But there were areas where the effect was quite significant. In the early years there was little Palestinian outcry about these sales, and leading Arab families, despite the official Arab line, were as eager to sell at enhanced prices as the external land-owners. But from the later 1920s, land sales increasingly affected populated districts and this was when and why this became a serious political issue.[25]

It was in fact from about 1930 that the Arab national movement began seriously to exploit the land issue, and did so largely for political rather than economic or social reasons. From 1930 to 1935, Amin al-Husayni ran a propaganda campaign to persuade Arabs not to sell land, with very little result. Successive High Commissioners wanted power to ban or control all land sales, but this was vetoed under the terms of MacDonald's 'Black Letter'. Wauchope intended to introduce legislation to stop the ejection of tenant farmers, without banning sales by owner-occupiers, but this was blocked by the outbreak of the strike in 1936.[26]

[25] These statistics are taken from Porath, *The Palestinian-Arab National Movement*, 81–90.

[26] This may have been influenced by provincial legislation in British India. See e.g. V. Damodaran, *Popular Protest, Indian Nationalism and the Congress Party in Bihar, 1935–1946* (Delhi, 1992); P. Reeves, *Landlords and Governments in Uttar Pradesh* (Bombay, 1991).

So land alienation and eviction of the tenants became a staple of the radicalized politics of the early 1930s.

But it was much less emotive than the huge increase in Jewish immigration. Ironically, this immigration, much of it now by relatively wealthy and educated German Jews, rather than penniless Poles or Romanians, also produced a boom period of investment and economic development in Palestine. This, however, was accompanied by intensified limitation of work in Jewish-controlled enterprises to 'Hebrew' labour at higher wages than were available to Arabs, and this became a major grievance with the increasing number of landless Arabs in the major towns. By late 1935, there was a general sense of crisis, intensified by the assassination in November of Shaykh Izz al-Din al-Qassam in Haifa. Al-Qassam was a Syrian, a fundamentalist Islamic puritan, member of the Haifa Istiqlal, organizer of the Young Men's Muslim Association, which was drilled in military style, and importer of illegal arms. He appears to have been organizing an anti-Zionist rising in Haifa, and after a Jewish pioneer was killed, al-Qassam and others were killed by the Jews. Although al-Qassam had close connections with Amin al-Husayni, it seems unlikely that Amin was directly concerned in this attack.

It was clear to most British officials in Palestine by the end of 1935 that Arab opinion had been seriously radicalized and that some outbreak of violence was expected. The general strike of 1936 marked the end of what may be called the mendicant period of Arab attempts to block the Zionist strategy and the start of physical action. It began in April 1936 with a number of local assassinations of Jews by Arabs in Tel Aviv, Jaffa, and other towns, leading to the creation of local Arab committees. The Nablus committee called for a general strike, to last until Britain carried out the Arab demands in full. This was endorsed by the five main political parties, who were then joined by Istiqlal leaders to form what became known as the Arab Higher Committee under the presidency of Amin al-Husayni. Hurewitz described this AHC as 'the first executive body of the local national movement to function smoothly'.[27] Its membership balanced the various groups of notables: in addition to Amin al-Husayni, two each from the Husaynis, Nashashibis, and Istiqlal, and one each from the other three organizations. Its stated aims were to force the British to suspend Jewish immigration, to forbid sales of Arab land to Jews, and to replace the mandate by a national government responsible to a representative council. Conversely, all talk of negotiation on the proposed legislative council disappeared. This was the first serious Arab challenge to British authority and policy, and was explicitly aimed at Britain rather than the Zionists.

The crisis began with the assassination of two Jews on 15 April 1936. It then developed into a widespread strike by Arab car drivers and merchants, mainly in the towns and especially Jaffa. As a strike its extent was patchy. Arab peasants were not much involved, the major industrial enterprises went on working, and many

[27] J. C. Hurewitz, *The Struggle for Palestine* (New York, 1950; 1976), 68.

Arab office-holders stayed at their posts. The strike had limited economic effects. Zionist enterprises were largely self-contained, and, with government permission, Zionists built a wharf at Tel Aviv to compensate for the closure of Jaffa. Arab workers suffered the most, particularly stevedores, fruit farmers, and others involved in the commercial economy. More important was the resort to violence. This began in the towns but spread to the countryside, particularly the more mountainous areas, where, initially, small guerrilla bands, very poorly armed with old rifles and often defunct ammunition, ambushed Jews and also British soldiers, police, and officials. These attacks were seldom co-ordinated; but in August Fawzi al-Qawuqji, an ex-Ottoman officer then serving in the Iraqi army, arrived with some Iraqi and Syrian solders, and attempted to impose a unified, and very brutal, control over these rebel groups. He had limited success, but the British found it very difficult to suppress or control these attacks. Initially there were virtually no British forces in Palestine, which was still under RAF command: a cavalry regiment, two companies of armoured cars, and one squadron of RAF planes. The police force, consisting of both Arabs and Jews, was quite unreliable, each segment defending its own people. As High Commissioner, Wauchope, though an army general, refused to sanction martial law or effective reprisals. It was not until September 1936 that the British cabinet decided on firmer measures. More British troops were sent out, rising to 20,000 by the end of September. RAF control was replaced by army command under Lieutenant-General J. G. Dill, and Wauchope was authorized to declare martial law—which in fact remained in suspense.

Up to this point the AHC and Amin al-Husayni officially refused to be involved in the rising, though in fact Amin was probably secretly supporting it. By August, probably for fear of losing his influence, Amin became less cautious; but by September it was clear to him that the British now meant business. They were prepared to send a royal commission to investigate, the first since 1930, but insisted that the violence must first end. There were signs of a split in the AHC and much hardship among Arabs. The AHC therefore followed up earlier offers of mediation from Abdullah of Transjordan and Nuri as-Said of Iraq. It arranged for identical letters to be sent from Iraq, Saudi Arabia, and the Yemen, which arrived on 11 October and urged the Palestinian Arabs to stop the violence and to have faith in 'the good intentions of our friend Great Britain, who has declared that she will do justice'.[28] On the same day the AHC issued a statement calling on the Arabs to put an end to the strike. By the end of October much of the guerrilla activity had died down, the British had surrounded most rebel bands, and many of those from other countries, including Qawuqji, were allowed to go home. The royal commission, under Earl Peel, left for Palestine on 5 November.

This was another major turning point in the history of the mandate. It was the first time Arab states had intervened in the Palestinian problem. Whatever the commission might recommend, the fact that it had been appointed by a British

[28] J. C. Hurewitz, *The Struggle for Palestine* (New York, 1950; 1976), 71.

government still deeply committed to the mandate, and that its terms of reference were very wide—to examine the underlying causes of the 'disturbances', 'to ascertain whether, upon a proper construction of . . . the Mandate, either the Arabs or the Jews have any legitimate grievances', and 'to make recommendations for [the] removal [of such grievances] and for the prevention of their recurrence'—was itself revolutionary.[29] There were parallels here with the Iraq situation in 1920 when the much larger revolt, though also dealt with by some 20,000 British and British Indian troops, led to the creation of the state of Iraq and the elevation of Faysal as King the following year. The main difference, of course, was that in Palestine the British and the commissioners remained fettered by the terms of the mandate. Hence the most that they could do was to recommend palliatives that might satisfy Arab desire for some degree of autonomy at the same time as the Zionist claim to freedom of immigration and their concealed determination to build an independent Zionist state. Their report, which was published in July 1937, after an exhaustive investigation and the belated decision of the AHC to give evidence, is generally regarded as the best analysis of the Palestinian problem, then or later.

The basic conclusion of the commissioners was that the mandate as originally envisaged was unworkable because the assumption that the Arabs would acquiesce in the creation of a Jewish national home in view of the material benefits it might produce had proved false. Given the consistent rejection by the Arabs of political coexistence, there was no chance of providing the 'self-government' promised in the mandate: a legislative council had been rejected by the Arabs but, if accepted and made fully representative, with real powers, the result would be a ban on Jewish immigration. Hence the conclusion was that the mandate as envisaged was unworkable. Equally unacceptable were the AHC's proposal that Palestine become an Arab state, with no guarantees for the Jewish minority, and the Revisionist Zionists' claim to a Jewish state, including Transjordan. The only solution the commissioners could envisage was partition of Palestine into two states, one Jewish and one Arab. If this was unacceptable, the only palliatives they could offer were that Jewish settlement should be concentrated in the plains; that Jewish immigration should be restricted to a maximum of 12,000 a year for at least five years (a precursor of the White Paper of 1939); and that there should be very much tougher governmental controls, possibly including martial law. The report provided a draft map indicating a possible division of Palestine. This gave the Jews the whole of Galilee, the Jezreel Valley, and the coastal plain to a southern point halfway between Jaffa and Gaza. The Arab state would comprise the rest, plus Jaffa, and would be incorporated with Transjordan, though Jerusalem, Bethlehem, and a corridor joining them with Jaffa, would remain under the British mandate. Britain would also control an enclave near the port of Aqaba and, temporarily, the towns of Safad, Tiberias, Acre, and Haifa. Both the proposed

[29] Ibid. 72.

states would sign preferential defence and commercial treaties with Britain on the lines of the 1930 Iraq treaty. The Arab state would receive income from the Jewish state (presumably in respect of customs duties on goods in transit to the interior) and would get a grant of £10,000,000 from Britain.

It was evidence of the decline in the political weight of the old British coalition of 'gentile Zionists' by 1937 that the new Chamberlain government issued a White Paper simultaneously with the publication of the report. This accepted its argument on the grounds that, given the 'irreconcilable conflict' between Jews and Arabs, partition 'represents the best and most hopeful solution of the deadlock'.[30] In fact, the British Zionists, who, as always (since they had inside information on discussions in the cabinet and the relevant ministries), had advance information of the Peel proposals, were split on the recommendations. Weizmann, who had been in Palestine while the commission was taking evidence, was in close contact with (Sir) Reginald Coupland, a member of the commission, Beit Professor of Colonial History in Oxford, Fellow of All Souls College, and hence in touch with the powerful group of politicians who were also Fellows, often known as the Cliveden set.[31] Coupland, who drafted the report and provided much of the historical sweep, was probably the most determined of the commission on the importance of partition. He appears to have convinced Weizmann, who was initially against it because it would limit the area of Zionist Palestine, that partition was the best available solution. Weizmann accepted in private, while always stating in public that Zionist acquiescence would depend on the precise area allotted to the Jews. He carried support for partition at the Zionist Congress in August 1937, against the opposition of those who stuck to the claim for the whole of biblical Palestine, though only on the understanding that the Zionist Executive would negotiate 'the precise terms for the proposed establishment of the Jewish State'. Meantime the British Zionists were also split, but the policy makers of 1917 and 1922 were no longer in office. Churchill rejected partition, demanding the continuation of his 1922 'absorptive capacity' formula. Attlee, as leader of the now very small Parliamentary Labour Party, which was committed to the full Zionist programme, Sir Archibald Sinclair, leading Liberal, and Lord Wedgwood, a lifelong pro-Zionist, all spoke strongly against partition. But Leo Amery, also a long-time Zionist, accepted it. The report was attacked in both the Lords and the Commons, where a motion was passed that the issue should be taken to the League of Nations Mandate Commission. This in turn proved unenthusiastic, but passed the question to the League Council. By the time this had met in mid-September 1937 the British government had already decided to send a 'technical' commission to investigate the practicality of partition; so the League Council reserved judgement.

The result was that from this time the Zionists, or at least a majority of them, were prepared to consider some form of partition, subject to a more satisfactory

30 J. C. Hurewitz, *The Struggle for Palestine* (New York, 1950; 1976), 76.
31 Much of the detail on these negotiations is taken from Rose, *The Gentile Zionists*, ch. 6.

division of territory. But the Arabs never did. Although on 3 July, before the publication of the Peel report, the National Defence Party, led by the Nashashibis, had disassociated itself from the AHC, it rejected partition. The rest of the AHC did so much more forcefully. It claimed that the Peel proposal would give the Jews seven-eighths of the Arab-owned citrus groves, would create an economically non-viable Arab state, dispossess large numbers of Arabs in the Galilee region, and result in such pressure on the small Jewish state that it would eventually be forced to expand. The AHC laid down four principles for a settlement: recognition of Arab right to independence in Palestine; the end of the experiment in a Jewish national home; the abrogation of the mandate, to be replaced by a treaty between Britain and Palestine as a sovereign state; and the immediate end of Jewish immigration and land purchases pending negotiation and the conclusion of a treaty. The Arabs never budged from this stand. Moreover, they persuaded the leading Arab states to protest against Peel; and at a conference held in September 1937 at Bludan, in Syria, delegates from Egypt, Iraq, Lebanon, Syria, and Palestine agreed to support the Palestine Arabs against partition and for full independence. Thus the battle lines were set.

In fact, although the British were already beginning to back down from Peel, leading to the appointment of the Woodhead Commission, which was to report on the technical possibilities of partition, and eventually to kill it, that report was not available until November 1938. Meantime, in the face of intensified British measures against guerrilla activity, the revolt had broken out again. It was marked by the assassination of L. Y. Andrews, an acting district commissioner, on 26 September 1937. This persuaded the High Commission to act. In the absence of Wauchope, always reluctant to take firm measures, his deputy, William Battershill, took action. Under new regulations issued on 30 September, he declared the AHC and its local committees illegal, deposed Amin al-Husayni from his post as president of the SMC (oddly, he never seems to have been replaced, though the SMC itself survived under close British supervision), and issued warrants for the arrest of six members of the AHC who were regarded as 'morally responsible' for the outbreak of renewed violence. Jamal al-Husayni escaped to Syria. The other five were deported to the Seychelles. Amin al-Husayni was not indicted, but, afraid he would be imprisoned, managed to escape to Lebanon. This did the British little good. Amin reconstituted an AHC in Lebanon, where the French kept him under house arrest but refused to extradite him, and organized the renewed revolt.

The revolt of 1937–9 was in many ways similar to that of 1936 and was carried out mainly by small bands of irregulars in the mountains. At their peak there may have been 9,000–10,000 active rebels, 3,000 full time, the rest mostly part-time peasants. Amin attempted to control them from Beirut through a Central Committee of the AHC in Damascus, but was never able to create a centralized command structure. The rebels depended, as before, on funds from the wealthy Arabs, and were extremely harsh on those who did not contribute. In fact in some respects this became a civil war of a most brutal kind. The rebels appear to have had no social ideology, and used the opportunity to pay back old grudges. The main sufferers were other villagers, who were forced to contribute money and goods to the armed bands. In the process the rebels alienated a large part of the Arab population and created vendettas that lasted a generation. These divisions were very obvious in 1948 and seriously weakened the Arab resistance to Zionist attack. For their part the British for the first time took draconian measures.[32] Suspected rebels were tried in military courts and some executed. By the end of 1937, some 800 Arabs were in prison. Significantly the government came to rely heavily on the Jewish community, increasing the number of Jewish constabulary from 3,500 to 5,000, and turning a blind eye to the operations of the illegal Jewish Haganah organization. From 1938, Jews were enrolled in Special Night Squad units under Colonel Orde Wingate whose function was to attack Arab irregulars and defend the oil pipeline from Iraq that passed through Galilee. By the summer of 1938 a great part of Palestine was under threat from the guerrillas. But in October 1938 Sir Edmund Ironside, Chief of the British General Staff, arrived to review the situation. He approved the sending of a new British division, made possible by the decline of European tensions after the Munich Agreement between Chamberlain and Hitler. By the spring of 1939 the revolt had virtually been suppressed. Much of Palestine was in deep economic depression, there was vast unemployment among both Arabs and Jews, and many villages had been destroyed.

It was at this point that the British for the first time seriously reviewed the future of the mandate. There were two main considerations. On the one hand, with the rise of European dangers and formation of the German–Italian Axis, which led to much anti-British Axis propaganda in the Middle East, the whole British position in that area seemed increasingly insecure. This will be discussed in Section 3 below. On the other hand, the Woodhead Commission had reported that it could see no satisfactory way of partitioning Palestine. Although the report was not finalized until November 1938, its substance was known to the British government some time earlier. In October 1938 an interdepartmental committee in London had already suggested that the Balfour Declaration had been a mistake. No Jewish state was acceptable. But as an Arab state was equally inconceivable, British rule must continue. Thus revolt and terrorism had been successful. As Hurewitz put it, 'The sponsors of the Arab revolt had thus won two major political victories by the fall of 1938. After the first phase of the uprising London admitted that the Palestine Mandate was unworkable. . . . Now the second phase of the rebellion was followed by the scuttling of the partition scheme, even before any attempt was made to implement it. These events taught the lesson that the use of violence as a political weapon produced results which otherwise

---

[32] There is a graphic anecdotal account of the British retributive measures in Shepherd, *Ploughing Sand*, ch. 5.

appeared unobtainable.'[33] From then until later in 1939 the trend in Britain was towards effectively discarding the core of the Zionist commitment.

In fact this change of British direction was by no means solely due to the Arab rising and was influenced by the international situation: this will be examined later. From an Arab standpoint the immediate issue was whether to attend the conference proposed by London which would include not only Zionists and Palestinian Arabs but for the first time representatives of Egypt, Iraq, Saudi Arabia, Transjordan, and the Yemen. The Palestinian Arab problem was to decide who should represent them. London banned the attendance of Amin al-Husayni, who nevertheless claimed that the reconstituted AHC in Beirut, to which the five exiled members were joined after being released from the Seychelles, was the only body qualified to do so. This was rejected by the Nashashibi-led National Defence Party, now involved in a blood-feud with the al-Husaynis. Eventually both bodies compromised. Two NDP delegates were included in the Arab delegation, which, in conjunction with the Arab states, issued a majority statement of their programme on 17 January 1939. There would be no direct negotiations with the Zionists. All Zionist immigration and land purchase must be stopped. Palestine must become an independent Arab state in a treaty relationship with Britain. As suggested by the Egyptians, Palestine would be cantonized to provide local autonomy in the Jewish majority areas, Hebrew would become the second public language, and the civil rights of Jews would be guaranteed. This was contested by the NDP, which did not insist on immediate independence, accepted limited immigration, and wanted a local legislature.

Predictably, given the totally opposed platforms of the Arabs and Jews, the series of meetings, held separately between British officials and the two delegations, at St James's Palace between 7 February and 17 March 1939 produced no agreement. As a result Britain imposed its own solution. The White Paper issued on 1 May 1939 was based on previous British fall-back plans. In ten years' time a Palestinian state would be set up which would have treaty relations with Britain. Jewish immigration would be restricted to 75,000 over the next five years, 25,000 of them irrespective of 'absorptive capacity', since 1922 the bedrock of British policy as defined by Churchill, and thereafter to be subject to Arab veto. An advisory council would be set up which might possibly evolve into a representative legislative council. Land sales would be decided by the High Commissioner.

The British reasons for making this decision and the domestic reactions will be considered later. But it is clear that the White Paper constituted the first major reversal of the principle of the mandate. While the mandate itself had not been abrogated, the principle of an inherent right of Jewish immigration had been suspended and made ultimately subject to Arab consent. The White Paper then became the basis of British rule in Palestine until 1947. The Arabs had thus won their first significant victory since 1917. It had been at terrible economic and

---

[33] Hurewitz, *The Struggle*, 93.

social cost. But, ironically, the war made possible an Arab economic revival.[34] The huge British expenditure, directed by the Middle East Supply Centre in Cairo, pumped millions of pounds into the Palestinian economy. Despite inflation, real wages rose substantially. Arab businessmen were able to invest in new industrial ventures. The number of Arab workers in the cash economy rose markedly, along with Arab trade union membership. The fellahin were floated off their indebtedness. The White Paper had lifted the immediate threat of huge Jewish immigration and the government strictly controlled land sales to Jews. In fact these years constituted some sort of golden age for Arab Palestine.

Unfortunately, prosperity did not result in the evolution of a united and mass-based Arab political movement. With Amin al-Husayni exiled, after 1941 in Germany and acting as an Axis propagandist, and with Jamal al-Husayni in Southern Rhodesia, there was an opportunity for the old opposition to form an effective national leadership. They did not do so. Political parties were banned by the British until the end of 1942. Then the leaders of the old Istiqlal party, notably Ahmad Hilmi Pasha Abd al-Baqi, Awni Bey Abd al-Hadi, and Rashid al-Hajj Ibrahim, all three of whom had become directors of the Arab Agricultural Bank, renamed the Arab National Bank, re-emerged as potential leaders of a national Arab coalition. Although pro-Axis in the 1930s, the party now became tactfully pro-British. It did not formally resurrect the Istiqlal name, but in November 1943 attempted to organize a conference of all the pre-war parties in Jerusalem to form a united front against the threat of revision of the White Paper. Characteristically of Arab politics, they failed. The presidents of the old National Defence (Nashashibi) and National Bloc Parties turned up, but the heads of the quiescent Reform and Youth Congress parties did not, nor did any of the mayors known to be Husayni supporters. The sole practical achievement of 1943 was to set up the Arab National Fund to support the anti-Jewish movement.

In response to these efforts, the Husayni faction reconstituted itself in April 1944 as the Palestine Arab Party. It was based in Jerusalem under the acting presidency (because Jamal was away) of Tawfiq Salih al-Husayni, Jamal al-Husayni's older brother. The PAP immediately distanced itself from the Istiqlal leaders, who restricted their demands to full execution of the 1939 White Paper. By contrast the PAP was maximalist. They demanded independence for Palestine 'within Arab unity'; the establishment of an Arab government over the whole country; and the dissolution of the Jewish National Home. But the PAP, although by September 1944 already the most powerful Arab party, was only one party and was unable to provide a united Arab leadership. As Hurewitz commented, 'the leadership of the national movement was still being determined on a personal basis'.[35] Thus in 1944–5, the Arab community was still divided. In addition to the Istiqlal and PAP leaders, the one-time leaders of the old National Bloc and Youth

---

[34] Much of the following material is based on Hurewitz, *The Struggle*, chs. 8, 14, and 16.
[35] Ibid. 186–7.

Congress parties reconstituted their parties, while Raghib Bey Nashashibi of the National Defence and Dr Husayn Fakhri al-Khalidi of the Reform Party continued to act as party leaders without formally reviving their party names. The nearest these six groups came to collaboration was for their leaders to meet informally in their own homes. When the European war ended in May 1945 there was still no Arab unity or organization. Meantime Arab communists had formed the League of National Liberation.

This disunity worried the Arab states that were in process of forming the Arab League in 1944–5. In 1944 Jamil Mardam, newly emerged as the President of British-liberated Syria and a leader in the movement for Arab unity, talked the leaders of Istiqlal and the Husaynis into sending Musa al-Alami, a member of the Husayni clan, as representative observer to the Alexandria conference that led to the establishment of the Arab League in February 1945. The conference duly supported the Palestinian Arab claim to independence; and the Pact of March 1945 provided for formal representation of the Palestine Arabs on its Council, with Musa al-Alami as their representative. Late in 1945 the League decided it would have to knock Palestinian heads together to safeguard the Arab position there as Britain seemed likely now to reconsider the long-term future of the mandate. Mardam, now President of the League Council, was sent to Jerusalem, and in the course of one week was able to impose on the Palestinian Arabs what they had been unable to achieve in three years of negotiations. A new Higher Committee was established. Five of the twelve seats were allocated to the PAP, thus giving the Husaynis the largest single bloc, and one seat each to the heads of the other five pre-war parties. Musa al-Alami and Ahmad Hilmi Pasha Abd al-Baqi were also included. The HC was no more able than before to control the various factions of which it was constituted, but at least it provided an official spokesman of the Arab community and was recognized as such by both the Arab League and the Palestine government in January 1946.

Thereafter, the Husayni faction gradually gained full control over the Arab movement. In 1946, after it became clear that the Palestinian parties could not effectively combine through this HC, the League Council ordered the dissolution of both the Higher Committee and the Istiqlal-led Higher Front, formed after disputes within the Council. In their place there was to be an Arab Higher Executive (HE) with Amin al-Husayni, now in Egypt, as chairman, Jamal al-Husayni as vice-chairman, Dr Husayn Fakhri al-Khalidi, head of the defunct Reform Party, as secretary, and Emile al-Ghuri, secretary of the PAP, and Abd al-Baqi as the other members. By January 1947 the HE had been expanded to ten, eight of them belonging to the PAP. Thus, during the crisis of 1947–8, the Palestinian Arabs were led once more by the Husayni family, while those groups not included in it remained alienated. It was in this still disorganized state that the Palestinian Arabs faced and failed to cope with the crisis of 1947–8. It is, however, important for what followed in 1947–8 that the Palestinian Arabs were now, for the first time, effectively dominated by the states of the Arab League. It was to the League that supporters of Amin al-Husayni, as the chief claimant to lead an independent Arab-dominated Palestine, looked for support against the Jews. Thus there was no effective internal defence organization or strategy comparable to that of the Zionists. As clients the Palestinians looked to their external patrons to protect them, and this proved ultimately disastrous.

In accounting for the failure of the Arab national movement before 1947 to organize a united and effective resistance to British and Zionist policies, Lesch suggests the following contributory factors.

The society was highly stratified vertically and localized horizontally. Primary allegiances were to the family, clan, village, and religious sect. The population was largely illiterate, with limited horizons. Peasants defended their own land, but could not coordinate their efforts throughout the country, much less respond to a threat in another district. Antagonisms among villages and clans and rivalries among elite families attenuated the effectiveness of political institutions and limited the possibility of unified action. The landed elite could mobilize villagers through its patron–client ties, which had the benefit of ensuring rapid mobilization, but had the weakness of perpetuating social cleavages. Although the community shared the same ultimate political aspirations and fears, they were unable to structure a movement to work consistently and effectively towards those goals. Thus the mass rebellion degenerated into feuding among villages and families and the political elite adhered to maximalist goals even though it lacked the power to realize them.[36]

Lesch, however, continues by arguing that these weaknesses alone would not account for the total failure of the Arabs. The neighbouring Arab states had closely comparable social structures and internal division; yet they had by the 1930s obained some degree of autonomy (in the case of Iraq nominal sovereignty, in that of Syria and Lebanon the promise of independence). She rejects the suggestion that the Arabs, by rejecting the offer of a legislative council in 1922–3, threw away the best chance of gaining some influence over British policy and using politics as a lever, as happened in many other British dependencies. In 1922 the future of the mandate was still uncertain and acceptance of a council including Jews would have compromised the Arab claim to sole control of Palestine. Thereafter Britain rejected all Arab proposals for a representative council since this might obstruct the Zionist programme. In short, given the British commitment to Zionism and its superior military power, a combination that had no exact parallel in British imperial history, there was nothing the Arabs could have done to prevent the Yishuv (the Jewish community in Palestine) taking root. By the 1940s the Jews, though still in a numerical minority, were sufficiently strong and, as will be seen, well organized, to be able to block any major concession the British might offer to the Arabs. By 1947 the outcome could no longer be decided by Arab actions, nor indeed British policy, but had passed to international actors, above all the United States. In short, the failure of Arab attempts to secure their aims was not due

[36] Lesch, *Arab Politics*, 235.

primarily to their internal weaknesses, though these became critical in 1948, but to the determination of Britain to block them.[37]

2. THE ZIONISTS

The main problem facing the historian of Zionism in Palestine between 1917 and 1948 is exactly the obverse of that concerning the Arabs. For the Arabs it is to explain why they lost their patrimony: for the Zionists why they were successful in establishing not merely a 'national home' but the state of Israel. There is, of course, a vast literature on this.[38] The short answer is that until about 1944, Zionist achievements were made possible by the British in that they stuck to the Balfour Declaration, even as modified by the 1939 White Paper, and refused to allow the Arabs to block Jewish immigration. But this by itself will not explain the extent of the Jewish achievement, and in particular their ability during the crisis of 1945–8 first to force the British to give up the mandate and the proposed single state of Palestine, and then to defeat the combined, though in fact very disorganized, forces of the four main Islamic states of the region. For that it is necessary to look at the nature of the Zionist organization and the reasons for its strength. The British component of this explanation will be considered in the following section. Here the emphasis will be placed on the Zionist economic and political achievement before 1945.

The basic economic and social achievement of the Zionists was to create a dynamic western-style society and economy attached to but distinct from that of the Arabs. Its central aim was autonomy. Already, before 1914, as was seen in the previous chapter, the settlers established the principle that Jews should be paid higher wages than Arabs for the same work. After 1917, this was extended: as far as possible only Jews should be employed in Jewish-owned enterprises. This was less a version of apartheid than a determination to provide work for the flood of new arrivals, and it became increasingly important as the numbers increased. In 1919

[37] Ibid. 235–8. It is significant that the British never, except in the Thirteen Colonies in 1776–83, failed to overcome an indigenous rebellion in their colonies. Even in 1942, they were able to suppress the Quit India movement while fighting a losing war against both the Axis and the Japanese. By these standards, Arab resistance in Palestine was a minor problem.

[38] Among the books listed in the bibliography, the sources most reflected in this account are: N. Bethell, *The Palestine Triangle: The Struggle between the Jews and the Arabs, 1935–1948* (London, 1979); M. J. Cohen, *Palestine and the Great Powers, 1945–1948* (New York, 1978); M. J. Cohen, *Palestine: Retreat from the Mandate. The Making of British Policy, 1936–1945* (London, 1978); Hurewitz, *The Struggle*; E. Karsh, *Fabricating Israeli History* (London, 1997); E. Karsh (ed.), *Israel: The First Hundred Years*. Vol. 1: *Israel's Transition from Community to State* (London, 2000); Wm R. Louis, *The British Empire in the Middle East, 1945–1951* (Oxford, 1984); M. Rodinson, *Israel—A Colonial Settler State?* (New York, 1973); N. A. Rose, *The Gentile Zionists*; A. Shlaim, *Collusion Across the Jordan* (Oxford, 1988); A. Shlaim, *The Politics of Partition: King Abdullah, the Zionists and Palestine, 1921–1951* (Oxford, 1990); N. Shepherd, *Ploughing Sand*; B. Wasserstein, *The British in Palestine*; B. Wasserstein, *Britain and the Jews of Europe 1939–1945* (Oxford, 1979).

there were only about 65,000 Jews in Palestine: a decline from the 85,000 of 1914. This had increased to about 400,000 by 1936. There had been some 280,000 legal immigrants given visas by the British, plus an unknown number of illegal arrivals. The peak years were 1933–6, marking the start of the Nazi anti-Semitic drive, when 166,000 settlers arrived. Although the British determined the number of visas, the Jewish Agency (an arm of the World Zionist Organization), which was set up in 1929, allocated them as it saw fit. The Agency maintained recruitment offices in all the larger European cities, showing a preference for young healthy men with agricultural or industrial skills. In fact Khalidi (admittedly writing from an Arab standpoint) has argued that, far from aiming to rescue downtrodden and endangered east Europeans, the Zionists wanted only tough potential pioneers. He also suggests that the Rabbinical leaders in Poland were against mass emigration to Palestine as 'all forms of Zionism are to us [unclean]'.[39] This selectivity, of course, was typical of many other colonizing ventures and was similar to the policy adopted by the British Colonial Land and Emigration Board of 1840, and later agents of the settler colonies in recruiting emigrants. The result was that by 1936 more than 85 per cent of Jews in Palestine were under 45 and the average age 27. The great majority of them were east European Ashkenazim, rather than the Sephardim of the Mediterranean and the Middle East.

The majority of these immigrants, most in any case from European urban areas, settled in the towns, particularly Tel Aviv, initially a suburb of Jaffa but by 1936 a large and exclusively Jewish city of about 150,000. Yet it was a key element in the ideology of Zionism that Jews, having been denied ownership of land in Europe for centuries, should develop as a farming community. This required land, and that was expensive since, before 1948, all Jewish land had to be bought, not conquered.[40] While, despite their protestations, most large Arab land-owners, in Palestine as well as Syria and Lebanon, were happy to sell at enhanced prices, the expansion of Zionist land-ownership was relatively slow. Thus, while the Jewish population increased by about 400 per cent, land-ownership grew by only 200 per cent, from 110,000 to 308,000 acres by 1936, or a mere 4.6 per cent of the total land area. Yet on this land the number of village settlements grew very considerably: from 44 villages with 12,000 Jews in 1914 to 203 villages with 98,000 inhabitants by 1936. These were mostly in the areas south-east of Jaffa, in the coastal plain between Jaffa and Haifa, in the Jezreel Valley, and in east Galilee. This land was mostly bought and controlled by the Jewish National Fund (JNF, a subsidiary of the WZO), which also provided initial working capital and equipment (through the Palestine Foundation Fund) and expert technical advice from its research stations. This was a far cry from the cash-starved settlements of the later nineteenth century. The main product of these villages, especially in the

---

[39] Khalidi, *Palestine Reborn*, 38–9.

[40] This constituted a contrast with most other European colonizing ventures, in which much land was simply acquired by force or bought at notional prices. The Jews had to pay the market price until the conquests of 1948.

coastal plain, was citrus fruit, which implied a form of capitalist agriculture with paid workers. By 1936, Jewish capitalists had invested some $75 million in these groves and they provided the largest part of Jewish exports. But elsewhere, and especially after the drop in the market value of citrus exports in 1936, the JNF encouraged self-sustaining mixed farming, either in collective (kibbutzim) or co-operative units. There were 82 of these in 1936 and they were increasing.

Parallel with this agricultural expansion there was a substantial industrial development. Many of the immigrants were artisans from eastern Europe and until the mid-1930s the typical industrial enterprise was a small hand-craft firm. But from the mid-1930s, with increasing immigration from central Europe by wealthy capitalists, much larger industrial enterprises developed. Jewish industrial employment rose from 4,750 in 1920 to 28,616 in 1936 and the total product from $12 million to $43 million. Most of these manufactures were for local consumption: the only large-scale export product was salt from the Dead Sea, controlled by a Jewish company. In support of all this, the Jews developed their own infra-structural institutions. The Anglo-Palestine Bank, the official bank of the Jewish National Home, was second in importance only to Barclays, banker for the government and agent for the Palestine Currency Board that handled the currency.[41] The Zionists also invested heavily in transport, though the railways, inherited from the Turks, remained out of their control and inadequate for a dynamic western economy.[42] But they did provide and own the first electricity supply for the whole of Palestine except for Jerusalem. In short, the Jewish settlers had created a partially autonomous and dynamic, though still small, settler economy by the mid-1930s, when the Arab revolt put most things on hold. As the British had expected, they injected western technology into a less-developed country.

A key element in this development was the growth of western-style trade unionism. Stemming from the pre-1914 concept of 'the conquest of labour', a central element in Zionist economic strategy was the exclusive employment of Jews in Jewish farms and industry. Drawing on their European experience, the Jews were quick to establish trade unions. At the end of 1920 the General Federation of Jewish Labour was established, which by the mid-1930s had some 87,000 members, representing three-quarters of the Jewish labour force. But this Federation, commonly called the Histadrut, was more than a mere federation of unions. In its own right it promoted a wide variety of productive co-operatives, some 770 by 1936. It had become the second largest employer of labour after the government.

The autonomy of the Zionist settlement was further extended in social and educational services. The Agency provided hospitals, clinics, and child welfare

[41] This was part of a system set up by the British before 1914 to provide currency for the dependencies. Its key elements were that the dependency must cover its currency by securities or gold held in Britain and that the local currency was at par with the pound sterling. Thus the Palestine pound (£P) replaced the original Turkish pounds and the Egyptian pounds used during the early occupation.
[42] See W. Rothschild, 'Railways in Israel: The Past and the Future', in Karsh (ed.), *Israel: The First Hundred Years*, i. 144–57.

stations. They ran medical research laboratories to counter endemic diseases such as malaria and tuberculosis, which received only very small subsidies from the government. Education was provided by a Hebrew University in Jerusalem, and a network of teacher training and technical colleges, secondary and primary schools, all of which used Hebrew as their main language and inculcated patriotic Zionist values. But the society was not entirely homogeneous. While there was no landed gentry, since most Jewish land was owned by the Agency, and until the later 1930s no large capitalist industry, there was a class of outsiders. These were mainly Sephardic Jews from the Middle East who were more likely to speak Arabic than Hebrew, remained largely illiterate, and were seldom members of a trade union. They remained a sub-class and their numbers were greatly increased from the early 1950s.

All this was in many ways typical of the social and economic structures of other settler societies of the nineteenth and early twentieth centuries. Where Zionism differed was in its extraordinarily complicated political structure and the relationship between the settler society and the international organization that lay behind it. This flowed from the original Zionist conception of 1897. The Jewish nation worldwide was a single entity. The Palestine settlement was only part of it. The ultimate authority remained the WZO with its biennial meetings and its elected General Council, Executive, and President. The Executive's role was to carry out decisions of the WZO. From 1919 to 1935 its headquarters were in London, having previously been in Berlin, presumably because Weizmann, as President until 1931 (he was re-elected in 1935), was its dominant figure. In 1935 it transferred to Jerusalem. In 1929, after five years of debate, another subordinate organization was created. The Jewish Agency for Palestine was set up to enlist non-Zionist support for the National Home as a Jewish cultural and religious centre. This also had its Council, and Administrative Committee and an Executive of forty, which had its main offices in Jerusalem and was responsible for ensuring that WZO policies were carried out. Thereafter the Agency was the dominant factor in Zionist policy and by the mid-1930s it was predominantly Zionist. With the WZO President also President of the Agency, this was no great problem, though after the resignation of Weizmann as President of both bodies in 1931 following an adverse vote by the Zionist Congress, much of his previous control over the Agency was lost. In his absence, David Ben-Gurion, leader of Mapai, the Palestine Labour party, built up a majority of votes on the Agency Executive and became Chairman of it. Two of his supporters, Moshe Shertok (later called Sharett) and Eliezer Kaplan, became respectively heads of the Agency's Political and Treasury departments. Thereafter, until Weizmann was finally removed from his Presidency by the WZO Congress in January 1946, Ben-Gurion built up his power base in Palestine, and on many issues opposed Weizmann. Thus the Agency became the mainspring of Jewish enterprise.

The role played by the WZO and the Agency in the colonization of Palestine had no exact parallel in European colonization, though the limited control exercised by the European-based headquarters of companies such as the British, French, and Dutch East India companies and colonizing companies in Australia and New Zealand, along with earlier American colonizing ventures, had some similarities. The power of the Zionist worldwide organizations was essentially based on the fact that it was they, through their very large number of supporters, especially in the United States, that financed the Yishuv. But the settlers also had their own institutions, closely related to these international organizations. Settlers had votes for the WZO Congress, but they also had votes for the Yishuv's Assembly.[43] This had started informally with elections in 1920 but was formalized by the government in 1927 as an Elected Assembly. It was elected by all Jews aged over 20 with at least three months' residence and had to meet at least once a year. It delegated authority to a National Council, which in turn nominated an Executive. The Assembly was elected on a preferential single party-list system, which made for a multiplicity of parliamentary factions. In practice, by the mid-1930s, the various labour parties connected with the Histadrut, of which Mapai was the largest, controlled local Zionist policy. The main ideological, though at that stage not politically serious, opposition came from the New Zionist Organization, led by the Russian-born Vladimir Jabotinsky, who in 1935 formally resigned from the WZO. He and his followers, known as Revisionists and much of whose support came from Poland, challenged the relative moderation of Zionism as expressed by Weizmann; and, though Jabotinsky himself was expelled from Palestine by the British in 1929, his few supporters there argued for much tougher measures against the British.

Thus, by the mid-1930s, the Palestine Jews not only virtually controlled the Agency but had their own parliament and executive. They were indeed a state within a state. Moreover, they possessed one other attribute of a state—a private army. This, the Haganah (defence), was strictly illegal. It began in 1920 as a means of defending outlying Jewish settlements against Arab attacks during the period of riots. The government turned a blind eye to it, partly because there was no adequate police system and very few troops. By the mid-1930s it consisted of some 10,000 armed and trained men, and another 40,000 available for rapid mobilization. It was to play an important role during the Arab revolt, when the British recruited Jewish settlers to protect the railways, oil pipeline, and border security fences and, as will be seen, an even more vital one during the Second World War.

In retrospect it is clear that the Zionists' relations with the British went through four main phases after 1918. During the first, to the publication of the Peel Commission report in 1937, they were confident of British support for their strategy of maximal immigration leading, though this was never stated, to eventual Jewish domination of the whole of Palestine. The second phase began with the publication of Peel. Zionist reaction was generally favourable, though there were

---

[43] There is another parallel here with the assemblies set up in early colonial America, even while ultimate authority might rest with the company, promoter, proprietor, or the crown.

those who, like Zabotinsky, insisted on Zionist control of the whole of Palestine. It ended with the publication of the White Paper of 1939, which killed partition and set limits to Zionist immigration. The third phase began with the outbreak of war and strong Zionist support for the war effort against the common British and Jewish enemy. The final phase began in 1944 with continued British support for the White Paper principles, leading to acute and increasingly violent Zionist hostility to Britain, which eventually forced the British to return the mandate to the United Nations and evacuate Palestine.

During the first phase the main support for Zionist strategy was the strength of the pro-Zionist political lobby in Britain. The focal point of this strategy was Weizmann in London. As President of the Zionist Organization for most of the time (except 1931–5) and a confidant of British ministers and many politicians, he could be relied on to ensure that the terms of the Balfour Declaration were observed. This inside track put successive High Commissioners in a difficult position. As Wauchope remarked in 1936, when he had had a phone call to the effect that Weizmann was going to see the Prime Minister to protest at the existence of an Arab Strike Committee, 'The thing is I have never met the PM and I don't suppose I ever shall. Weizmann can go in there when he wants to.'[44] Although the strength of British establishment support for Zionism waned later in the 1930s, it was still strong in 1938–9. Neville Chamberlain was a Zionist, but the only strong Zionist in his cabinet in 1938–9 was Walter Elliott. He, however, played a vital role in leaking relevant cabinet decisions and discussions to Mrs Blanche ('Baffy') Dugdale, niece of Lord Balfour, who in turn leaked them to Weizmann. Nevertheless, the continuing strength of Zionism among the British political class was shown by the vote on the White Paper in May 1939, when the government had a majority in the Commons of only 89 as against its theoretical majority of 250. In short, until 1937 all the Zionists had to do was to ensure that the promise of 1917 was kept. In course of time the process of immigration would give them effective control over the whole of Palestine, which, to some, implied also Transjordan.

It was during the second phase that Zionist confidence in this British bulwark for their strategy faltered. Weizmann was fully informed about the proposal for the Peel Commission from the start. He was initially, at least in public, against the proposed partition, since that would limit the size of the eventual Israel. But in private he said that the Zionist reaction would depend on how much land the Zionists were given and under what conditions. Although much of the Zionist movement was against the Peel proposals, Weizmann defended partition at the 1937 Congress in principle, though not the small area allotted to the Jews by Peel. Partition was attacked root and branch by Jabotinsky and the Revisionists, who insisted that the whole of Palestine, plus Transjordan, must become Jewish.

[44] Shepherd, *Ploughing Sand*, 186, quoting Ralph Poston, Wauchope's private secretary, in a television interview of 1976.

Ben-Gurion also was initially against partition, but came round to the principle by July 1937. Ultimately the Congress authorized Weizmann and the Executive to negotiate on 'the precise terms for the proposed establishment of a Jewish State [*sic*].'[45] Thereafter some form of partition became central to the majority Zionist creed, subject to how it was worked out.

The opportunity for Zionist manipulation seemed to come with the appointment of the Woodhead Commission later in 1937. This was in principle a 'technical' body, instructed to report on the economic, social, and political feasibility of partition. The Colonial Office, then under the pro-Zionist William Ormsby-Gore, was now wedded to partition, and tried to insist that the Peel principles should be upheld. If not, the report should say so confidentially. The Foreign Office, however, for reasons that will be examined later, was against partition and insisted that Woodhead be given a free hand. The Commission took a long time in investigating and reporting. Meantime, Malcolm MacDonald, son of Ramsay, had been appointed to the Colonial Office in May 1938. Given his past support of Zionism (he had acted as middle-man in 1931 to persuade his father to issue the 'Black Letter' modifying Passfield's White Paper), it was not surprising that Blanche Dugdale thought that 'this is probably the best appointment that would [*sic*] be made from the Jewish point of view'.[46] MacDonald was not allowed a preview of the report, which was not finalized until October 1938 nor published until November.

In the event, the Commission provided three alternative partition proposals. Their preferred plan 'C' also gave the Jews the smallest area, and would have reduced the Zionist state to a mere 400 square miles northward along the coastal plain from Tel Aviv. But the Commissioners were divided on this: two had serious reservations. The general impression given by the Report was that none of these three, nor any other possible plan, was feasible. In effect they said that partition was impracticable. MacDonald had already reached this conclusion. He had started to move away from partition early in 1938 on the grounds that, given Arab resistance and the renewed violence, it would be impossible to enforce it. After moving to the Colonial Office, he had several meetings with Weizmann to see what alternatives might be acceptable. Weizmann, however, now a deeply committed partitionist, refused to budge. He had taken his stand and was vulnerable to attack within the Zionist movement if he changed course. Moreover, in July 1938 the military arm of the Revisionist Party, the Irgun Zvai Leumi (National Military Organization, hereafter Irgun), decided to end the principle of self-restraint against Arab attacks on Jews that had been laid down by the Agency. It carried out a series of reprisals, the most significant of which was the explosion of land mines in the Arab fruit market of Haifa, which killed 74 and wounded 129 people. Such acts of violence continued during the following year, although

[45] Rose, *The Gentile Zionists*, 141.   [46] Bethell, *The Palestine Triangle*, 38: no attribution.

denounced by the Jewish Agency. This was the forerunner of the much more extensive and anti-British campaign of the same organization and its offshoots after 1945.

Under these conditions it was not surprising that, although in March 1938 Chamberlain had assured Weizmann that 'We are all committed to partition',[47] when the report was considered in cabinet in November, it was clear that partition was dead: only Elliott still supported it. It was decided to hold a round table conference in 1939 to debate alternatives. Weizmann was as usual well informed on cabinet decisions, and although still wedded to partition, immediately adopted his own fall-back position. 'The struggle . . . before them was a struggle of their rights under the Balfour declaration and mandate . . . especially their right to immigration, subject only to economic capacity, without any political limitations—avowed or hidden.'[48] This was the position maintained by the large Zionist delegation of 44 at the St James's Conference which opened in London on 7 February 1939.

It was not, of course, really a round table conference since Jews and Arabs refused to meet formally. In fact MacDonald and his officials held bilateral talks with each delegation, with representatives of the Arab states also present for the Arab meetings. MacDonald had by February worked out his proposed formula, and this was what he tried to get accepted by both sides. Essentially this was that there could be no Arab or Jewish state. There would continue to be a single territory under British mandate. As to immigration, MacDonald played with two alternatives. One was for a build-up of Jews to a maximum of 40 per cent of the total population over ten years, implying an 11 per cent increase over the 1939 Jewish population, after which future levels of immigration would be up for discussion between Zionists and Arabs. Alternatively, he suggested that there should be an Arab veto on immigration after the ten years. Meantime land sales to Jews would be limited to the coastal area and reduced in number. An advisory council might be set up on a parity basis, despite disproportionate populations: this was a sop to the Jews, who had demanded parity in the past.

Predictably, neither Arabs nor Jews would accept this. Weizmann maintained that control of immigration was impossible in the long run and on 17 February the Zionist delegation formally rejected all proposals. The nearest they came to an accord was on 18 February when, in private discussions with MacDonald, Ben-Gurion suggested that there should be a Jewish state 'within a semitic federation', coupled with partition along Peel lines and temporary limits on immigration for five years with no eventual Arab veto. The Zionists attempted to use their very large following in the USA to bring pressure to bear on MacDonald, but failed. On 13 May, after the conference had ended and before the White Paper (whose details are outlined in Section 3 below) was published, Weizmann went to a meeting

[47] Bethell, *The Palestine Triangle*, 37, quoted from N. A. Rose (ed.), *Baffy* (London, 1973).
[48] Rose, *The Gentile Zionists*, 173.

at MacDonald's country house in a last-minute attempt to influence the terms of the White Paper, due out four days later. He failed. MacDonald later recalled that Weizmann told him: 'Malcolm, your father [who had died eighteen months previously] must be turning in his grave at what you are doing.'[49]

This marked the end of the second phase of Anglo-Zionist relations and of the honeymoon period. Weizmann returned to Jerusalem. Irgun immediately started a terrorist campaign. They blew up the Palestine broadcasting station at the moment when the White Paper was due to be broadcast, then killed a Jewish policeman, fired shots in Arab areas, and put bombs in public telephone booths, Arab houses, and the Department of Migration. The best hope of the Zionists, however, lay in the League of Nations. Britain was forced, under the terms of the mandate, to present the White Paper to the League's Mandates Commission. The League Commission duly reported to the League Council that the White Paper policy was 'not in accordance with the interpretation which . . . the Commission had placed upon the Palestine mandate'. Four of the seven Commissioners added that 'they did not feel able to state that the policy of the White Paper was in conformity with the mandate, any contrary conclusion appearing to them to be ruled out by the very terms of the mandate and by the fundamental intentions of its authors'.[50] This was an advisory report: what might have happened had it been considered by the League Council is uncertain, though Britain might well have been forced to modify the White Paper. In the event the outbreak of war prevented this; and under the succeeding United Nations Charter decisions of this kind were to be left to the mandatory.

What might have developed in Palestine from 1939 had war not broken out is unclear. The Zionist organization was split over its strategy. Essentially, apart from the Revisionists, the movement was divided between Weizmann and Ben-Gurion. Weizmann, despite his disappointment over the White Paper of 1939, remained committed to the British alliance and had to hope that a change of government might lead to a reversal of policy. In fact the fall of Chamberlain in 1940 and his replacement by Churchill, one of the most fervent pro-Zionists from the start and vehement critic of the White Paper, promised well. Malcolm MacDonald was soon removed from the Colonial Office and eventually dispatched as Governor-General of Canada after the death of Lord Tweedsmuir (John Buchan). Thereafter there could be hope of a reversion to a pro-Zionist strategy. But in Jerusalem Ben-Gurion had been building up his strength in the movement. His Mapai party, representing the Labour movement and the Histadrut, had had a majority on the Jewish Agency Executive since 1933 (when Weizmann was not President of the WZO), and from 1935 Ben-Gurion had been Chairman of the very important Agency Executive. He saw the White Paper as evidence of the total failure of Weizmann's strategy of collaboration with the British and thereafter determined

[49] Bethell, *The Palestine Triangle*, 67. There is no attribution for this quotation, but it may have been the result of personal contact between Bethell and MacDonald.

[50] Hurewitz, *The Struggle*, 105–6.

both to get rid of Weizmann and to achieve an independent Zionist state, including if possible Transjordan. He also came to see that his strongest card lay in the six million or more Jews in the United States rather than in the goodwill of the British Zionists.

The outbreak of war, however, changed the situation. Britain's war against the Axis was necessarily also the Zionists' war against anti-Semitism. Hence the third phase of the mandate, lasting from September 1939 to 1944, saw an overtly enthusiastic Zionist support for the British war effort, despite the fact that the British put into effect elements of the White Paper policy. Immigration was rationed and land sales restricted to the coastal strip between Haifa and south of Tel Aviv, though urban properties were still open for Jewish purchase. No land sales were allowed in the mountain areas of maximum Arab occupation, or in Gaza and Beersheba. Meantime, the proposed advisory council was not set up. There was much debate over this between the British authorities, but the blowing up by Jewish terrorists in Haifa harbour on 25 November 1940 of a refugee ship, the *Patria*, which was to transport illegal Jewish immigrants to a British colony, created such a wave of feeling that the plan was scrapped. Arab enthusiasm for a council gradually declined thereafter as their interests shifted to the concept of Arab unity.

Meantime, the Jews pressed very hard for the creation of a Jewish army or military formation. This was generally opposed by all the British departments concerned, partly for fear of alienating the Arabs, but also because of the danger of training Jews as soldiers who, after the war, would be capable of fighting the British army.[51] From July 1940, and mainly because of Churchill's insistence, it was decided that Jews and Arabs could be recruited into six companies of up to 1,000 men in each, to be part of the East Kent Regiment, always called the Palestine Buffs. Since few Arabs volunteered, the number was later reduced to 500. But this was not what the Jews wanted, which was a separate Jewish army under its own flag. Under pressure from Weizmann, and after serious disagreement with Ben-Gurion over the composition and role of these troops, it was decided in principle by cabinet on 10 October 1940 that the Jewish Agency be authorized to recruit 10,000 Jews to form separate units of the British army, not more than 3,000 to come from Palestine. This was not announced, and there was long consultation and disagreement between the British departments and the military commanders in the Middle East. Meantime many Jews enrolled individually in the British forces. It was not until July 1942, with the North African situation critical, that London eventually authorized the creation of a Palestine Regiment, to be recruited by the British authorities, not the Jewish Agency. The parity principle was dropped: this would be a Jewish regiment. But it was not armed for front line service, due partly to lack of adequate equipment. It was not the army the Agency wanted. Meantime Jewish demands for the raising of 10,000

---

[51] There is a detailed account of this issue in Cohen, *Palestine: Retreat from the Mandate*, 98–124.

extra armed Jewish special urban police were rejected: only an additional 1,500 rural special police were to be raised.

The Zionist demand for their own army was not satisfied until September 1944. On Churchill's insistence a Jewish Brigade was then created which was able to fly its own flag. It saw service in Italy and Germany and after the end of the war proved valuable in helping to deal with displaced Jews. Thereafter the returning ex-service Jews proved a significant element in the formation of a Zionist army. They were, however, probably much less significant than the hugely expanded Haganah, which had grown to over 100,000 by October 1941 and had been well armed for local defence by the British. The Irgun Zvai Leumi was also well prepared, though quiescent until 1944. A breakaway offshoot of Irgun, the Lehi (Lohamei Herut Israel), had only a few hundred members, mostly from eastern Europe. Under their leader Abraham Stern they regarded Britain rather than Nazi Germany as their main enemy. They began their career of murders and terrorism in 1941. Stern himself was shot by British police early in 1942, but the 'Stern gang', as they came to be called, survived and were to play a major role after 1944. By contrast, the significance of the Brigade and its flag was mainly psychological: it was the first visible concession made by the British to the principle of Zionist nationality, though this did not entitle the Palestine Jews to recognition as a state by the United Nations.

Meantime far more important political developments had taken place within Zionism. Early in 1942 both Weizmann and Ben-Gurion were in America. Ben-Gurion attempted to use the opportunity to dethrone Weizmann, whom he regarded as too moderate and too committed to negotiation with Britain. His aim was to harness American Jewry behind his cause. As Shertok had written in 1939, 'there are millions of active and well-organised Jews in America . . . they could influence public opinion, but their strength is not felt since it is not harnessed and directed at the right target'.[52] Partly to counter Ben-Gurion's militancy, Weizmann published an article in January 1942 in which he made the first public (though always implicit) Zionist demand for a Jewish Commonwealth over the whole of western Palestine. Some of his supporters then organized a conference of several hundred Zionists at the Biltmore Hotel in New York in May 1942, which produced a statement that came to be known as the Biltmore Programme. This had three main provisions. Palestine must be opened for immigration; the Jewish Agency must be given control of immigration and have the authority to develop the country; and after the war Palestine should be established as a Jewish Commonwealth integrated into the structure of the democratic world.[53] Although this was essentially a Weizmann position, Ben-Gurion became its foremost advocate. In the process he changed what had originally been a moderate and imprecise formulation, that allowed for continuation of the British role for the interim, into

---

[52] Quoted Khalidi, *Palestine Reborn*, 44.
[53] The text of the declaration is in Hurewitz, *The Struggle*, 158.

hard dogma. He returned to Palestine, campaigned for adoption of his interpretation of Biltmore as the new Zionist strategy, and eventually got the Inner General
Council (which, though consisting entirely of Palestine Jews, was acting for the
inoperative Zionist Congress) to accept the programme. This constituted the first
major step away from acceptance of the concept of a bi-national Palestine, though
it was opposed by many Zionists who believed in this and by others who saw that
it could only be achieved through partition. From then until 1948 it remained the
objective of the Zionist movement.

Meantime Ben-Gurion made his major attempt to unseat Weizmann as
President of the WZO. In America he tried, unsuccessfully, to persuade local
Zionists that Weizmann must go because he was acting too autocratically, particularly over the question of a Jewish army. He failed there, and again during the next
two years in Palestine, despite repeated threats to resign from the Executive of the
Jewish Agency. Weizmann survived until he lost the election as President at the
first post-war WZO Congress. But in fact the initiative had already passed to Ben-
Gurion and the political forces within Palestine. It was there that vital decisions of
1944–8 were to be taken, and by 1943 the majority of the Yishuv had already come
to see total independence as essential and were ready to fight Britain to achieve it.
That was the main change in Zionist strategy that occurred during the war.

The fourth and final stage in the saga of Zionism developed between 1944 and
1947. The dominant fact was now the power and determination of the terrorist
organizations, Irgun and Lehi. These had different strategies. Irgun, now led by
the recently arrived Polish Jew, Menachem Begin, always maintained that, while
its purpose was to force the British to create a Jewish state, its method was to
destroy buildings rather than take lives, though this did not always work out in
practice. Lehi, by contrast, was prepared to assassinate British officials of all types.
From the standpoint of the Jewish Agency and Ben-Gurion this was a serious
liability, since they still depended on Britain and, increasingly, on America to give
them what they wanted. As Jewish indignation against news of the Holocaust in
Europe penetrated Palestine, the terrorist organizations became more active. In
August 1944 an attempt was made to kill the High Commissioner, Sir Harold
MacMichael, in an ambush. It failed, though an ADC was seriously wounded. In
September a British police officer, Tom Wilkin, exceptional among the Palestine
police in that he knew Hebrew, had a Jewish mistress, and was close to Haganah
circles, was shot by Lehi. Then on 6 November 1944 Lord Moyne, then Minister
Resident in Cairo and believed by many Jews to be unsympathetic to the plight of
Jews in Europe, was murdered in Cairo by members of Lehi, now called Freedom
Fighters. This act had serious consequences. It ended the current British plan for a
revival of partition and for the first time checked Churchill's Zionist enthusiasm.
Jewish society was split over these and other terrorist actions. Many clearly supported them, as was reflected in the great difficulty the British had in obtaining
information or catching terrorists. On the other hand, the Jewish leadership was
very concerned that their movement was being taken over by assassins. Despite

internal disagreement, the Agency under Ben-Gurion decided to take control. Between the end of 1944 and early 1945 it used Haganah forces, particularly the Palmach, a specialist force created by the British, to deal with selected Irgun and Lehi terrorists, often collaborating with the British police and using British gaols to hold those they wanted out of action. But the collaboration was highly selective. The British police complained that they were seldom given information on the really important Irgun men, and that those whose names they were given were often men the Agency wanted out of action.

This period of relative collaboration between the Agency and the British, often called the 'hunting season' or *saison*, lasted into early 1945. Irgun and Lehi attacks then started again, probably in reaction to alleged British reluctance to help displaced Jews and survivors of the Holocaust in Europe. By September, Haganah was again prepared to ally with the terrorists, spurred by news that the British would only allow some 1,500 Jewish immigrants a month, whereas President Truman was by then pressing Attlee to admit 100,000 Jews at once: the Zionists were always well informed of such notionally confidential matters. While terrorists continued to destroy property and kill British servicemen, the Anglo-American Commission was investigating the situation. Its report on 20 April 1946 rejected partition but among another things recommended the immigration of the 100,000. Had the British accepted this and allowed in a substantial number early in 1946 it is possible that the Jewish Agency and the mass of the Yishuv might have been prepared to reject terrorism. In the event Attlee and Bevin refused. In their view this would have been unjust to the Arabs and would have destroyed their whole Middle Eastern strategy. They also believed that Britain had the option of suppressing terrorism. As a result the British government insisted that the price of the 100,000 immigrants would be the disarming of the Jews. From then until 1948, whatever their formal protestations, the Jewish Agency and the Vaad Leumi (the Jewish Assembly) were prepared to back the terrorists, while the great majority of the Yishuv either supported them or failed to give any help to the British. The outcome was a guerrilla war that ended with the British deciding to give up the mandate.

The British were, in fact, very badly equipped by tradition and experience to handle a guerrilla war against such highly organized and technically skilled opponents, many of them trained by the British in guerrilla tactics and the use of explosives during the Second World War. This was very different from the Arab Revolt of the previous decade and from the many small wars the British had fought in Africa: a nearer equivalent was the war in South Africa from 1899 to 1902, which had also proved very difficult to win without the use of collective punishments. Although they eventually had 100,000 soldiers and 20,000 armed police in Palestine, these were ineffective unless the British were prepared to adopt Nazi or Soviet methods of destruction. They might, for example, have bombed Tel Aviv, as they had bombed Arab villages in the 1930s and in Iraq in the 1920s. But they never did so. In India they had never, before 1942, faced serious armed opposition and terrorism since the Mutiny of 1857. The nearest the British came to adopting their Indian strategy of large-scale imprisonment of Jewish activists was in June 1946. Then British forces undertook intensive house-to-house searches in Tel Aviv, occupied the Agency, seized vast numbers of files (though they had difficulty in translating these from Hebrew), and arrested some 2,700 Jews, almost all from Agency supporters. Most were later released, though three members of the Agency Executive and about 700 others were kept in detention. The Jewish riposte was rapid. On 22 July, with Haganah approval, Irgun blew up part of the King David Hotel, then largely used by the administration. Although this had not been intended, since an attempt was made to give warning and get the building evacuated, there were some 91 deaths. These included 41 Arabs, 28 British, 17 Jews, and five others.[54] This in turn led to very extensive but ineffectual British punitive actions. For its part the Agency condemned the King David bombing and broke off relations with Irgun. But there was little that it could do without losing the support of the mass of the Jewish settlers. Its capacity, and indeed will, to act as 'moderates', always the British hoped-for support in a colonial situation of this type, was therefore very limited.

Perhaps the last attempt at compromise by the Agency and moderate Zionists came later in 1946. On 28 October 1946 Ben-Gurion told Weizmann that he would accept either partition, if a large enough area was allocated to the Jews, or a return to the mandate with unlimited right of Jewish entry. On 20 November Abba Hillel Silver, a leading American Zionist, told Bevin in New York that there would be no difficulty in arranging a partition, if the British and Americans backed it: the Arabs would simply accept a *fait accompli*. This clearly demonstrated how little Jews understood the Arab position. A key test of the Jewish position was now whether or not to send a delegation to the resumed London Conference in January 1947. Weizmann, who never gave up his belief in the ultimate honesty of Britain, made this a condition of his standing for continuation as President of the WZO at its Congress in Basel. Although he made an impassioned speech in favour of negotiation and against violence he was defeated and his candidacy automatically lapsed. No Zionists officially attended the conference, nor did any Palestinian Arabs. The moderates were thus defeated. Early in 1947 Lehi and Irgun violence became much more intense. Huge-scale illegal immigration of Jews continued, and the British were getting a very bad and embarrassing international reputation for the methods they used to turn back immigrant ships and deal with their occupants. British attempts to control terrorism were severely handicapped by limited intelligence and the regular leaking of their plans through Jewish clerks in British offices. In February 1947 the British government announced that it was surrendering its mandate to the United Nations.

But this did not let the British off the hook. Until the United Nations decided what to do, Britain had to maintain the mandate. The fifteen months that followed, before the final British withdrawal on 15 May 1948, were the worst during the

---

[54] There is a detailed account of the bombing in Bethell, *The Palestine Triangle*, ch. 6.

whole two and a half decades of British rule. Although the Agency, and nominally at least Haganah, disapproved of violence, they were intent on maximizing the rate of illegal Jewish entry and importing arms for the predictable future struggle with the Arabs. Haganah in particular organized repeated attempts to bring in immigrants. Many such attempts failed, but the inevitable brutality of the British attempts to stop them, which climaxed with the Royal Navy boarding the *President Warfield* (renamed *Exodus*) later in 1947,[55] gave the British a very bad name internationally and significantly reduced the British will to continue. But for long, the Agency had little hope of a satisfactory decision from the United Nations. What they wanted was partition and a Jewish state, and it seemed very unlikely that they would get either. It was not until 15 May 1947 that some hope emerged when Andrei Gromyko, the Russian delegate to the United Nations, announced, at the special session of the General Assembly that opened on 28 April, that, in view of what they had suffered in Europe, the Jews were entitled to found their own state. The Soviet motive may have been to eliminate a British, and therefore assumed anti-Soviet, base in the Middle East; but this at least made partition seem conceivable.

The United Nations Special Committee on Palestine, UNSCOP, spent five weeks in Palestine. The Arabs refused to meet it officially but their views were obtained unofficially. Predictably they were against partition and demanded an Arab state in which there would be toleration for Jews. The Agency, however, put its case for partition skilfully and indefatigably, led by Moshe Shertok and David Horowitz.[56] In its report of 31 August 1947 UNSCOP recommended, by a majority of seven to three, that Palestine should be partitioned into Arab and Jewish states, with a permanent UN trusteeship for the Jerusalem area. The minority, consisting of the delegates from India, Iran, and Yugoslavia, proposed a three-year continuation of the mandate under the UN, after which there would be a federal government of Arab and Jewish states with Jerusalem as the federal capital. Apart from this the main difference lay in the areas allocated to the two sides. The majority proposal gave the Jewish state a far larger area than that of Peel in 1937. And in particular it allocated the whole of the Negev to the Jews.

For the Zionists this represented their most important victory since the 1917 Balfour Declaration, even though for the Revisionists and other radicals it would give less than the biblical Zion they demanded. Before UNSCOP invited Agency opinion on the matter, the Agency had debated its attitude in New York. Ben-Gurion initially proposed that a small Jewish state be set up in those areas where the Jews predominated, the rest of Palestine to continue under UN trusteeship, with free Jewish immigration, 'until such time as that part was ripe for independence as a Jewish state'.[57] After much further debate in Jerusalem, which showed continuing basic divisions, the Agency reached the conclusion that it

---

[55] There is a detailed account of the *President Warfield* case ibid., ch. 10.

[56] There is a good analysis of influences operating on the Committee in Louis, *The British Empire in the Middle East*, 466–77.   [57] Cohen, *Palestine and the Great Powers*, 263.

should continue to claim the whole of Palestine, while privately conceding that it would accept a satisfactory partition. This was conveyed by Ben-Gurion to UNSCOP on 4 July, and remained the Zionist position to the end. Thereafter the Zionist problem was to ensure first that the final version of the UNSCOP report provided a favourable partition, and then that the United Nations General Assembly accepted its recommendations. In fact the final version of the partition map was slightly less favourable to the Jews than the original version, but it was still acceptable. The remaining hurdle was the General Assembly.

It was at this point that the Zionists were able to bring their greatest ally into play. This was the six million or so Jews in the United States and their political influence on an indecisive White House.[58] After considerable indecision, and following the Soviet support for partition on 13 October, Truman decided to back partition. As a result the whole force of American diplomacy, supported by its then unique capacity to give or withhold economic favours, swung behind partition. Small member states of the UN were seduced or bullied into promising to vote for partition. As David Horowitz wrote: 'the United States exerted the weight of its influence almost at the last hour, and the way the final vote turned out must be ascribed to this fact.'[59] In its own way the vote of 29 November 1947, which by a narrow margin provided the necessary two-thirds majority of the General Assembly, was to prove as crucial for the future of the Middle East as the Balfour Declaration of November 1917.

It remained, however, quite unclear how partition was to be carried out and what was to succeed the unitary mandate state. The arrangement was that a five-member Palestine Commission named by the United Nations should arrange a peaceful transfer of power to the two new states. In fact the Commission never did anything. This was partly because it was not ready to operate until January 1948, partly because (for reasons discussed in Section 3) the British refused to co-operate with it in transferring administrative power. As a result the outcome was determined by force of arms. The moment the partition resolution had passed guerrilla war broke out between Jewish and Arab communities. The Arab League refused to recognize the validity of the partition and prepared to fight to prevent the creation of a Jewish state. For their part the Jews, far better prepared than either Palestinian Arabs or their allies, mobilized for war.

The final phase of the Jewish fight for Israel, and also of the British mandate, began immediately after the UN resolution. The situation was dominated by three main factors. First, a UN Assembly resolution was not binding. It was advisory and many believed that it had no legal justification.[60] Hence, the eventual

---

[58] The most detailed analysis of the evolution of American policy at this stage is in Louis, *The British Empire in the Middle East*, Part IV, ch. 6. See also Cohen, *Palestine and the Great Powers*, ch. 11.

[59] Louis, *The British Empire in the Middle East*, 586.

[60] See the arguments put forward at length by sub-committee 2 of the General Assembly (acting as an ad hoc committee) on 11 November 1947. It must be said, however, that the members of this

General Assembly vote, procured by the Truman administration, apparently largely for domestic political reasons,[61] had no binding force. It was never rescinded but equally it was never adopted by the Security Council. Since the US State Department began to backtrack on partition in December 1947, and thereafter pursued a policy of creating some form of UN trusteeship, it was uncertain whether the partition resolution would stand.

Second, it was immediately clear that the UN lacked any means of enforcing its vote, even if it was not overruled. Despite the terms of its charter, the organization had no military force and no power to compel its members to support its decisions. Since, moreover, any proposal for intervention would have required a unanimous vote in the Security Council, this was very unlikely to happen in view of the USSR's stated position in favour of partition.

Finally, the British, with a very large army in Palestine and the only state in a position to enforce the terms of the partition, flatly refused to do so. Britain had abstained in the General Assembly vote, and Ernest Bevin, as Foreign Secretary, was determined that no more British lives should be lost in mediating between embattled Jews and Arabs. Britain had handed the problem to the UN and was concerned both to pull out by the stated date of 15 May 1948 and not to alienate the Arab states in the process. Clement Attlee's government was, in fact, determined to adopt the same strategy as in India in 1947, though without going through the process of getting an agreed territorial partition before Britain quitted.

These facts are critical for understanding the course of events between November 1947 and the end of 1948. Both Arabs and Jews in Palestine faced the prospect of a Hobbesian state of nature in which power was the only relevant factor. This fact determined the new Zionist strategy. Hitherto official Zionism, including the Agency, had been meticulous in observing the rules, apart from encouraging illegal immigration, which they regarded as legitimate under the mandate. Now their protector, the British, had opted out: they could no longer rely on British arms to contain Arab fury. They had to fight to save the nation. This was the main justification for the strategy they were to adopt, which changed them from peaceful settlers under international law to an occupying force ignoring legalities.

It is in any case arguable that it was the Arabs, not the Jews, who first rejected a peaceful partition along the lines set out by UNSCOP. The war effectively started with Arab attacks on Jews and Jewish settlements. On 8 December a large Arab force attacked a suburb of Tel Aviv and outlying settlements were mostly cut off. The Arabs controlled most of the main roads, and threatened Jewish access from Tel Aviv to Jerusalem. In Galilee the so-called Army of Liberation under Fawzi al-Quawuqji posed a serous threat, though its attacks on northern Jewish settlements

sub-committee represented 6 Arab states, Afghanistan, and Pakistan, all Muslim countries. See W. Khalidi (ed.), *From Haven to Conquest* (1971), no. 63, pp. 645–95.

[61] There are detailed accounts on how this was managed ibid., nos. 65–8; Cohen, *Palestine and the Great Powers*, ch. 11; Louis, *The British Empire in the Middle East*, Part IV, ch. 6.

were mostly unsuccessful. On the other hand, the Arab League was reluctant at this stage to intervene directly and gave little support to Amin al-Husayni in his attempts (from Lebanon) to set up an Arab army and stop refugees from leaving Palestine. Moreover the Arabs had no central organization to co-ordinate the various local militias. As in 1936 their effectiveness was seriously limited by localization and internal divisions.

Nevertheless, until perhaps March 1948 it was unclear how the struggle would end and what proportion of Palestine the Jews would be able to secure. As late as March 1948 the British thought the Jews might lose Galilee and the Negev but hold on to the coastal strip. By that time, however, the Jews had begun to build up their forces for an aggressive, not a defensive campaign. In January, Yigael Yadin, chief of operations, began planning full mobilization and an attacking strategy. Arms were being bought in Europe, though the main flow did not come until after May 1948, and then mainly from Czechoslovakia, paid for by dollars provided by American supporters.[62] A major factor in the Zionists' favour during this early period was that Abdullah of Jordan, whose Arab Legion with its British officers was the most effective military force on the Arab side, was prepared to collude secretly with the Zionists in the partition of Palestine, provided that he got control of at least the central area adjacent to his state. He made a secret agreement that he would not attack the areas allocated to the Jews by the UN with Golda Meyerson (later Meir), a senior member of the Agency's Political Department, on 17 November 1947, on the understanding that the Jews would respect his claim to part of Arab Palestine.[63] This 'collusion' in fact continued until May 1948, when Abdullah was at last forced by the pressure of the Arab League to go through the motions of attacking the Jews, though his only serious military action was to defend the Arab sector of Jerusalem.

The main Jewish counter-attack started early in April under the new Haganah Plan D, or 'Dalet'.[64] Its aim was 'To gain control of the area allotted to the Jewish State and defend its borders, and those of the blocs of Jewish settlements and such Jewish population as were outside those borders, against a regular or pararegular enemy operating from bases outside or inside the area of the Jewish State.'[65] This implied that the prospective state of Israel, actually declared at midnight on 14 May 1948, would ignore the limits set by the UN. In the classic mode of all conquering and colonizing enterprises, Israel would take what it could

[62] See Khalidi, *Haven*, no. 70 for a detailed account of how these arms were bought and moved to Palestine. Much of the *matériel* was abandoned Second World War equipment, both Allied and German. It was mainly paid for by American Jewish money: at least $79 million in 1947 and $106 million in 1948. Ibid., app. V.

[63] For details see Shlaim, *Collusion Across the Jordan*, 110–17, 140–3. Shlaim provides the most detailed and convincing account of Jewish–Jordanian relations throughout the whole period, though some Jewish historians regard his interpretation as dangerously revisionist. Abdullah's negotiations with the Agency are described in Ch. 6, below.

[64] For a detailed account of 'Dalet' see Khalidi, *Haven*, no. 71, from a later account by Lieut.-Col. N. Lorch, an Israeli commander, in 1948.   [65] Ibid. 756.

get. Moreover, and equally important for the future, the Jews now dropped the long-stated claim that Jewish ownership and control did not mean deprivation of Arabs. In 1918, Weizmann, speaking in Jaffa, had said that 'It is not our objective to seize control of the higher policy of the province of Palestine. Nor has it ever been our objective to turn anyone out of his property.'[66] Similar statements had been made by Weizmann and many others since 1918. Moreover, until 1948 every bit of landed property held by the Jews had been paid for, though in many cases they had evicted Arab tenants. Such moderation was now cast aside. The Jewish forces had two objectives: to occupy as much land as possible and to clear it of Arabs to make way for the predicted huge influx of Jewish settlers.

In terms of territory the Jews had made their greatest advance before the end of the mandate. Before 15 May, the Haganah had made massive incursions in western Galilee, in the Jaffa area, and to the west of Jerusalem. Tiberias, Haifa, Jaffa, and Safed had been occupied and Acre was isolated. By 20 April the Arab blockade of Jewish Jerusalem had been broken. Thereafter, during the short periods of open war in between truces imposed by the UN, they greatly expanded their territory, so that by the armistice terms of 1949 Israel was immensely larger and more integrated than in the UNSCOP or any previous partition plan.

Another innovation was that the Jewish forces were for the first time attacking and destroying Arab villages and ejecting their inhabitants. The most notorious example was Deir Yasin. This undefended Arab village, near Jerusalem, had signed a non-aggression pact with the Jews. Yet on 9–10 April Irgun and Stern Gang men attacked the village and killed 245 villagers, some only after they had been paraded in triumph in the streets of Jerusalem.[67] This atrocity was immediately disavowed by the Agency and Haganah. Yet it did as much as any other Jewish action to make sure that what was later to be called 'ethnic cleansing' took place in Arab Palestine. Already there had been a huge outflow from major towns such as Jaffa and Haifa. Now Arabs everywhere began to flee the terror. In the course of 1948–9, some 650,000 Arabs became refugees, some in Lebanon, some in Syria, many in what was to become the West Bank, then held by the Arab Legion. In principle the Jews accepted the continued ownership of Arab property in the occupied areas, and after 1949 there were long negotiations over the right of these *émigrés* to compensation. But in practice the Jews held what they conquered. In a few weeks they had acquired much more than during half a century of patient purchase.

---

[66] Ibid. 187.

[67] There is a vivid account of the massacre and its aftermath by Jacques de Reynier, head of the International Red Cross delegation in Palestine, ibid., no. 72. A comparable, though less bloody, attack was made by the Palmach on the neighbouring village of Kolonia on 12 April, described later with delight by a British Jewish journalist who then worked for the *Daily Herald*. Arabs also committed massacres in revenge: the worst example was in the Etzion bloc of four settlements, south of Jerusalem, whose Jewish settlers had been attacking the Arab Legion. The Legion took Kfar Etzion on 13 May, and handed the 127 settlers over to Arab villagers. All but three of these were killed. But settlers in the other three Etzion settlements were taken by the Legion to Jordan, where they remained safely until the armistice of February 1949.

Erskine B. Childers, an Irish journalist, wrote in 1961 that by then 80 per cent of Israel's land surface had been abandoned by Arabs, plus 25 per cent of all standing buildings, and 50 per cent of citrus fruit holdings, some 33 per cent of Jews were then living in the property of absentee Arabs. This was irreversible. In August 1948 Israel's Foreign Minister, Moshe Sharett, replied to a request by Count Bernadotte, the UN Mediator, for information concerning Jewish policy on the refugees:

On the economic side, the reintegration of the returning Arabs into normal life, and even their mere sustenance, would present an insuperable problem. The difficulties of accommodation, employment, and ordinary livelihood would be insuperable.[68]

That was a mere five months after the first major Jewish push.

This is not the place to recount the course of the war of 1948–9. In terms of the time spent fighting it was very short. Backed at last by Security Council threats of sanctions for non-compliance, Bernadotte was able to negotiate a four-week truce starting on 11 June. Fighting broke out again as soon as that period was over, and after six days the Security Council again ordered a cease-fire. This officially came into force in Jerusalem on 16 July and elsewhere on 18 July. But in fact the fighting in and around Jerusalem never really stopped, and during each truce period the Israelis were, via their contacts in Soviet-controlled eastern Europe, able to evade the UN embargo on arms imports, which seriously inhibited the fighting capacity of the Arab forces. Israel thus became stronger over time as the Arabs were defeated and were unable to recoup their losses. The last major fighting took place in October 1948, when Israeli forces defeated the Egyptian army in the south and occupied the whole Negev. Thereafter prolonged negotiations under UN auspices eventually produced a series of armistice agreements in 1949 that decided the borders of Israel until the war of 1967.

In retrospect it may seem inevitable that the Zionists should triumph. But it was only the huge influx of settlers during the 1930s and immediately after 1945 that gave them the numbers to do so. Until then they had depended entirely on the British shield against the great majority of Arabs.[69] But once British policy was no longer in line with Zionist aspirations, that is from 1945, when the British attempted to maintain the general policy of the 1939 White Paper, the Jews turned against the hand that had protected them. They then fought two wars. From 1945 to early 1948 they fought against the British, then against the Arabs. Their methods in the first struggle were those of terrorism and their main agents the Irgun and the Lehi/Freedom Fighters/Stern Gang. However much the Agency might officially deplore their actions, it was in fact their guerrilla tactics which

[68] Ibid., no. 79; quotation from p. 802.
[69] As Tom Segev has written, 'The Jewish community in Palestine was entirely dependent on the willingness of the British administration to protect it and aid its development. The Jews' power to impose themselves on the British Empire, against its own interpretation, thus derived from a false image that was conditional on the willing belief of the British.' T. Segev, *One Palestine Complete* (London, 1999), 337.

persuaded the British that it was no longer worth their while to maintain 100,000 troops in Palestine and accept the considerable human and financial costs involved. This ranks as one of the major defeats in British imperial history, comparable perhaps with that by the Thirteen Colonies in 1776–83 and the fall of Singapore in 1942. The reasons for this will be considered in the final section.

As to the course of the war against the Arabs that followed the defeat of Britain, Israel's victory must be attributed partly to the efficiency of the newly embodied and equipped Israeli army, but still more to the incompetence and division of the Arab forces.[70] There was never an effective single Arab command. Abdullah of Jordan was more opposed to Amin al-Husayni and his AHC than to the Jews. The Syrian and Lebanese forces achieved almost nothing.[71] The Iraqi army duly occupied that part of the West Bank north of the area controlled by the Arab Legion and were never seriously defeated; but their eventual pull-out forced Abdullah to make major territorial concessions that caused huge hardship to the evicted villagers.[72] The Egyptians, who should have constituted the greatest Arab military force, did little more than occupy the Gaza Strip and part of the Negev and attempt to support Amin in the creation of an autonomous Arab Palestine.[73] Landis has summed up the essential weakness of the Arab war effort as follows:

In many ways it is helpful to view the struggle in Palestine as an inter-Arab conflict, which the Israeli forces ably exploited to conquer Palestine. Though the Arab armies did not openly fight each other, their actions were mutually destructive because they refused to cooperate and wilfully stood by as Zionist forces destroyed one Palestinian militia and Arab army after the next. The mutual enmity and distrust of the two Arab blocs— the Hashemite bloc and the Egyptian, Saudi, and Syrian bloc—not to mention the Palestinian forces under the command of Hajj Amin al-Husayni, was greater than their desire to keep Palestine from the Jews. The Arab governments each pursued their own national interests and so were unable to formulate a common plan of battle against the Zionists.[74]

---

[70] R. Khalidi, 'The Palestinians and 1948: The Underlying Causes of Failure', in E. L. Rogan and A. Shlaim (eds.), *The War for Palestine* (Cambridge, 2001), follows much the same argument based on Arab disunity as is suggested here. But he also emphasizes that the Palestinian Arabs were never given a 'national' organization comparable to the Jewish Agency which might have provided better control and planning. This, however, ignores the fact that they were offered a parallel, though not self-selected, Arab Agency by Samuel in 1923, and refused it.

[71] For the Syrian war effort see J. Landis, 'Syria and the Palestine War: Fighting King Abdullah's "Great Syria plan" ', in Rogan and Shlaim (eds.), *The War for Palestine*, 178–205. Landis argues that President Shukri al-Quwwatli and his Prime Minister, Jamil Mardam, both old-time Syrian politicians from the National Bloc (see Ch. 7), were aware that the Syrian army was too small and weak to fight effectively and were primarily concerned to prevent Abdullah of Jordan from using the war to obtain both Palestine and Syria. Hence the Arab Liberation Army, financed by members of the Arab League and based in Syria, rather than the Syrian army, was made to take the most active part in the 'Syrian' war effort.

[72] For details of this see Shlaim, *Collusion*, 400–25 and map on p. 413. For reasons why the Iraqi army did so little fighting in 1948–9 see Charles Tripp, 'Iraq and the 1948 War', in Rogan and Shlaim (eds.), *The War for Palestine*, esp. 137–9, 145.

[73] For the disasters of the Egyptian campaign and the related Arab disunity, see F. A. Gerges, 'Egypt and the 1948 War', ibid. 151–77.   [74] Landis, 'Syria and the Palestine War', 200.

This Arab military failure proved merely the first of three, each of which further limited and weakened Arab Palestine. But ultimately responsibility for the disaster of Palestine must lie with the British, to whom we must now turn.

3. THE BRITISH IN PALESTINE, 1918–1948

Many aspects of the British role in Palestine during the mandate have been described in the earlier sections of this chapter. Here it is proposed mainly to examine briefly the reasons behind the shifts in British policy.[75] These fall into four main periods. First, from 1918 to 1936, British policy, despite a short-lived vacillation in 1930, was based on the terms of the mandate. The second phase, from 1936 to 1939, reflected the Arab revolt and, after a flirtation with partition along the lines proposed by the Peel Commission, ended with commitment to a unitary territory in which Zionist aims were circumscribed. The third phase, during the war and down to 1945, saw an attempt to maintain the principles of the 1939 White Paper, made easier during the war by Zionist collaboration. During the final phase, from 1945 to 1948, the British decided to abandon the hopeless task of maintaining neutrality as between embattled Jews and Arabs and to hand the problem over to the United Nations. What factors conditioned these changing British positions?

During the years between the final conquest of Palestine in 1918 and the outbreak of the Arab Rising in 1936, British motives for staying in Palestine and facing the multiple problems this caused had two main foundations, both closely connected with the original motives for claiming the mandate. Probably the more important of these was strategic. As was suggested in the previous chapter, the British government regarded Palestine as critical for the security of its control of Egypt, itself vital for the route to India and the East. After 1919, French intentions in the Middle East were still suspect, and the mandate was seen as the main legal basis for British power in Palestine. Hence it was essential to satisfy the League of Nations that the terms of the mandate were being observed, and this was reflected in the response of interested parties to the White Papers of 1930 and 1939 and the submission of the latter to the League Mandates Commission. Dealing with recalcitrant Jews and Arabs was a price Britain had to pay for this security, just as dealing with even more difficult people in other parts of the empire was the price of dominion.

The second continuing factor was the force of philo-Zionism in the British political elite. So long as the generation that had supported the Declaration in

[75] There are surprisingly few general histories of the British government in Palestine, particularly before 1936. For the earlier period I have relied heavily on B. Wasserstein, *The British in Palestine*, his *Herbert Samuel: A Political Life* (Oxford, 1992), and Shepherd, *Ploughing Sand*. For the later period, Rose, *The Gentile Zionists*, Cohen, *Palestine: Retreat from the Mandate* and his *Palestine and the Great Powers*, Bethell, *The Palestine Triangle*, and Louis, *The British Empire in the Middle East*.

1917 was around this provided Zionism with an apparently impregnable shield. Successive Prime Ministers from David Lloyd George, Ramsay MacDonald, and Stanley Baldwin to Neville Chamberlain were all, in varying degrees, Zionist supporters. So were many leading office-holders, such as Winston Churchill, William Ormsby-Gore, and Leo Amery. Anthony Eden, as Foreign Secretary from 1935–8 and 1940–5, was a rare exception at the higher level of politics. Each of the three main political parties was committed to the Declaration, so Arab hopes that a change of government in London might prove favourable to their claims were fruitless. At the fringes of this consensus there were very active propagandists, notably Lord Wedgwood. In the 1920s and 1930s he was promulgating an idea that dated back to at least 1917, when, even before the Balfour Declaration was made, Herbert Sidebotham, a British journalist, argued that a Zionist-controlled Palestine might become a British Dominion, along with New Zealand, Australia, Canada and South Africa, and safeguard British interests in the Middle East.

The greatest victory won by these Gentile Zionists was over the Passfield White Paper of 1930, which, after the reports of the Shaw and Hope Simpson Commissions into the Wailing Wall riots, proposed limitation on both Jewish immigration and land purchase. Passfield (Sidney Webb) was then Colonial Secretary and took seriously the evidence that unlimited immigration and land sales could result in continuous and escalating inter-communal violence. To the Zionists and their supporters this was to go against holy writ. The Gentile Zionists mobilized. A letter was sent to *The Times* signed by Baldwin, Amery, and Austen Chamberlain, but organized by Blanche Dugdale, attacking the proposal as incompatible with the mandate. There was some party animus involved here, since the White Paper was issued by a Labour government backed by the Liberals, but it had wide support. The result, notoriously, was that Ramsay MacDonald agreed to a conference between leading ministers and Zionists. The Zionists failed in two of their main aims, which were to get Palestine transferred from the Colonial Office to the Foreign Office and to get a joint Agency/cabinet committee to enable them to bypass the Colonial Office. But MacDonald agreed to write a letter to the Zionists, which was read to the House of Commons and so became a formal statement of government intentions. It promised that the restrictions suggested in the White Paper would not be enforced. This remained the official government position until the White Paper of 1939 and made possible the huge surge of Jewish immigration during the 1930s which in turn enabled the Yishuv to challenge British power after 1945.

Restrained in this way by British official commitment to the letter of the mandate, the administration in Jerusalem found itself with very little room to manœuvre. Between 1918 and 1920 the military government under OETA was very aware of Arab hostility to the Zionists, then in their most triumphalist phase. Using the status quo principle, the OETA attempted to block or slow up Zionist immigration and land purchase and refused to recognize Hebrew as an official language of Palestine. Few Jews were appointed to official posts. This attempt to soften the impact of conquest and Jewish expectations on Arab opinion was quickly ended after pressure was brought by Zionists on the London government. General Sir Arthur Money and General Sir Gilbert Clayton both resigned in 1919, as Chief Administrator and Chief Political Officer respectively, after pressure was put on them to favour the Zionists. They were replaced by General Sir Harry Watson, who was (wrongly) thought to be a pro-Zionist, and Colonel Meinertzhagen, who certainly was. Ronald Storrs, then Governor of Jerusalem, had hoped for the senior post but was blocked on suspicion that he was not sufficiently pro-Zionist. In short, the views of the men on the spot, many of them in favour of an Arab-oriented strategy, could not stand up against the influence of the Zionists in London.

Their continuing influence was demonstrated in 1920 by the appointment of Sir Herbert Samuel as first High Commissioner of a civil governent. As a major promoter of the Balfour Declaration and close friend of Weizmann, he was regarded by the Zionists as their man. So also was General Wyndham Deedes, another passionate Zionist from the evangelical camp, as Civil (later Chief) Secretary. These appointments and the end of the military administration were intended to inaugurate a normal colonial regime in Palestine: they were parallel with the establishment of a civil government in Iraq in the same year under Sir Percy Cox (see Chapter 3). Samuel immediately set about expediting the Zionist programme of immigration and land purchase. But he was also aware of the importance of gaining Arab confidence, particularly in the light of the riots of March–April 1920. He pardoned Arabs convicted for their part in the 1920 riots, including Hajj Amin al-Husayni. He set up an advisory Council consisting of eleven officials and ten non-officials (four Muslims, three Christians, and three Jews—so giving a majority of Arabs). He offered to recognize the Executive Committee of the Arab Congress of December 1920 as equivalent to the Zionist Executive in London and the Zionist Commission in Jerusalem, which was regarded as an official body and sent copies of its minutes to the High Commissioner. But Samuel made it clear that such recognition was contingent on Arab acceptance of the terms of the draft mandate. This the Arab Executive refused. Thus the terms of the mandate proved at the very start an absolute barrier to the creation of some form of Arab executive organization that might have enabled them to match the Jews in their direct access to government.[76]

This failure was repeated in 1922–3 when Samuel made his greatest effort to integrate the Arabs into a single political system. Following normal British colonial practice he proposed, after much debate and modification, the creation of an elected legislative council of 22 members, eleven officials, the rest elected on the old Ottoman franchise system. Of those elected at least two were to be

[76] For a recent study of Samuel as High Commissioner see S. Huneidi, *Broken Trust: Herbert Samuel, Zionism and the Palestinians* (London, 2001). After a very detailed examination of the evidence Huneidi rejects any claim (as in Wasserstein's study) that he was impartial as between Arabs and Jews. See in particular p. 230 for a summary of her argument.

Christian and two Jewish. This was Samuel's grand design to involve all parts of the community in a single representative body. No subjects were reserved (as in other colonial constitutions), but no ordinance passed by the assembly might be repugnant to the terms of the mandate. That is, the assembly might discuss Jewish immigration but could not attempt to block it.

The results on the Arab side were seen earlier in this chapter: the great majority boycotted the elections and the whole enterprise had to be called off.

In fact, in retrospect it is obvious that 1923 marked the final failure of the Palestine mandate. There was no longer any chance that Jewish immigration could be made compatible with the rights of the Arabs. Why, then, was the mandate preserved to 1948? In the shorter term there were two main explanations. First, the mandate was still regarded as the only firm justification for British control of Palestine. A British cabinet committee of 1923, after the collapse of the proposed elections in Palestine, decided that there was 'no way of reversing the policy without throwing up the mandate, and this might lead to the occupation of Palestine by France, Italy or Turkey'. To which Curzon, then Foreign Secretary, added the concept of British honour:

It is well nigh impossible for any Government to extricate itself without a substantial sacrifice of consistency and self-respect, if not of honour. Those of us who have disliked the policy are not prepared to make that sacrifice. Those of us who approved the policy throughout would, of course, speak in much less equivocal terms.[77]

The second reason was more pragmatic: until 1929 the mandate was made to work. As has been seen, in 1922 Winston Churchill, since 1921 Secretary of State at the Colonial Office, to which Palestine was then transferred from the Foreign Office, issued a White Paper which interpreted and subtly modified the harshness of the mandate. It pointed out that the Balfour Declaration did 'not contemplate that Palestine as a whole should be converted into a Jewish National Home, but that such a Home should be founded in Palestine'.[78] Moreover, while maintaining the principle of the right of Jewish immigration, Churchill established the concept of 'economic absorptive capacity' in the Order in Council of 1922. This enabled the government to decide how many visas should be issued (though not their allocation, which was left to the Agency). It was also empowered to control land sales in the interests of the Arab cultivators. These emollient interpretations of the mandate were coupled with a major decline in the rate of Jewish immigration. Apart from the two years 1925 and 1926, and despite the limitations now placed on immigration to America, in these years more Jews went to the States than to Palestine. And although Jewish land-ownership doubled between 1917 and 1929, in absolute terms this remained very small. The main factor here was the poverty of the Zionist Organization in the later 1920s: it could simply not afford to finance large-scale immigration and land purchase.

---

[77] Wasserstein, *The British in Palestine*, 127.   [78] Ibid. 118.

The six years after 1923, ending with the Wailing Wall riots of 1929, were therefore among the quietest in the British occupation of Palestine. This enabled them to withdraw most of their military forces. This interlude ended with the riots but in some sense revived from 1931 to 1936. The two communities existed side by side with little contact. The Zionists continued to run their own quasi-state while the Arabs, kept docile by Amin al-Husayni, remained resentful but quiescent. It was as if these were two millets under the old Ottoman system.

In both periods the British administration undertook quite extensive social engineering, though with very limited funds and no British subsidies.[79] A serious effort was made to sort out land-ownership. Attempts by successive High Commissioners to limit land sales and prevent eviction of peasants, using the 1922 Order in Council and subsequent local ordinances, had little effect as Palestinian land-owners continued to evade them. Attempts were made to provide health facilities and schools for Arabs (the Jews ran their own much superior hospitals and educational establishments), though with limited success. In short, Palestine resembled many British Crown Colonies in this period, in that poverty restricted development projects and little thought was given to its longer-term future.

The second stage of British policy, if the muddled reactions of the period can be described as a policy, began with the 1936 riots and ended with the White Paper of 1939. In this period there were two main and to some extent incompatible influences on British thinking. The first was the Arab rising, which suggested that there was no possibility of continued inaction. Solutions had to be looked for. The rising also reinforced relations with the Jews. They now played the role of loyal British subjects, supporting the Jerusalem government, and providing armed forces to counter the Arabs. They did this, of course, in their own interests, but for the moment the British were forced back onto a pro-Zionist strategy.

The other and entirely contrary influence was the threat of war in the Middle East and the effect this had on British relations with the independent or partly independent Arab states. The failure of League sanctions against Italy during its invasion of Ethiopia in 1935–6, and the subsequent drift of Italy into the Axis with Germany, showed that British control over the eastern Mediterranean was at risk. Palestine was now increasingly seen not merely as a buffer for Egypt, but also as a potential land and air link between the Mediterranean and Iraq. For the first time also the attitudes of the hitherto largely discounted Arab states (Iraq, Saudi Arabia, the Yemen, Egypt) now became important. Since they were all in varying degrees hostile to Zionism and supportive of the Arab cause in Palestine, it became a main Foreign Office policy to involve them in the Palestinian question and, as far as possible, to placate them. This in turn implied an anti-Zionist policy in Palestine.

During these three years the British attempted to square this circle. In 1936 they continued to use military means to suppress the Arab rising, while offering a royal

<hr />

[79] See Shepherd, *Ploughing Sand*, chs. 3 and 4 for a useful summary of government enterprises.

commission as soon as the rising was over. In September 1937 the Arab rulers made their first successful incursion into Palestinian affairs by accepting the suggestion of Amin al-Husayni to offer mediation. This enabled the AHC to call off the strike without loss of face and led to the arrival of the already prepared Peel Commission. Thereafter these Arab states could legitimately claim some standing in Palestinian affairs and were to have an important influence on them to the end of the mandate.

The Peel Commission report, by recommending the partition of Palestine into Jewish and Arab states, at last broke the mould of the Balfour Declaration, admitting that a single polity was impossible. The British bureaucracy was divided over the issue: the Foreign Office strongly against, the Colonial Office, under Ormsby-Gore, possibly because of his close links with the Zionists, in favour. The Zionists also were divided. Many of the British Gentile Zionists were against it because it would limit Jewish expansion and the scope for immigration. It implied the failure of the mandate. The Revisionists under Jabotinsky were absolutely hostile to Peel because it would limit Jewish expansion. Weizmann was prepared to consider it in principle, provided the land allocation was negotiable, and persuaded Ben-Gurion to support this stance at the Zionist Congress of August 1937. As a result the Zionist Executive was authorized to negotiate 'the precise terms for the proposed establishment of a Jewish State'.[80]

At this point the Foreign Office, aware of intense Arab hostility to partition, and under Anthony Eden, an anti-Zionist, began to dominate British policy. Using the revival of Arab terrorism and the murder by Arabs of the British administrator Lewis Andrews in September, the Office was able to insist on the creation of yet another commission under Sir John Woodhead. The Woodhead Commission took its time and its report was not available until October 1938. By that time, Ormsby-Gore had been replaced in March 1938 as Colonial Secretary by Malcolm MacDonald, son of Ramsay, and regarded as a keen Zionist. But when the report was eventually released it became clear that it was not favourable to those Zionists who wanted partition. Woodhead suggested three alternative patterns of partition, all giving the Jews less land than Peel, but in fact concluded that none was viable. It would be impracticable to creat two autonomous and economically viable states out of Palestine.

That gave the Foreign Office the lever it wanted to sink Peel and please the Arab states, particularly Ibn Saud, whose position in the Red Sea was thought to be of critical strategic importance. On 9 November 1938, the cabinet decided to publish Woodhead and announce that it no longer supported partition.[81] But that would leave all issues undecided, so it also stated that a round table conference would be held to consider future options.

This St James's Palace Conference met officially from 7 February to 17 March 1939. There was, in fact, no round table, since Palestinian Arabs, Jews, and

[80] Rose, *The Gentile Zionists*, 141.
[81] In March 1938 Chamberlain had reassured Weizmann that 'We are committed to partition'. Ibid. 37.

representatives of the Arab states refused to sit at the same meeting: the British delegation therefore met separately with each of them. The Palestinian Arabs were led by members of the AHC, momentarily combining Husayni and Nashashibi factions. These had previously met in Cairo with representatives of the Arab states—Saudi Arabia, Egypt, Iraq, Transjordan, and the Yemen—in January. Their presence at the conference was immensely significant of Foreign Office determination to keep them on side: probably no comparable conference in British imperial history had included third parties to take part in deliberations over the future of imperial policy. Their agreed position was that there must be an end to Jewish immigration, land purchases, and the mandate. Palestine must become a sovereign Arab state, though with guarantees for the rights of others. The Zionist delegation, led by Weizmann and Ben Gurion of the Jewish Agency Executive, also included heads of Jewish communities in Britain and the United States, thus maintaining the concept of a single worldwide Jewry. These also had co-ordinated their position with the Assembly of the Yishuv. They would demand full maintenance of the Balfour Declaration, including immigration and land purchase rights.

Since these positions were immutable it was clear even before the conference started that no agreement would be possible. But the British were accustomed to such colonial impasses: only recently, between 1930 and 1932, they had gone through the tedious routines of three Indian Round Table Conferences on future political development. Given the impossibility of any agreement between British, Congress, Muslim League, and Indian princely objectives, they had decided unilaterally what they would do. The outcome was the Government of India Act, 1935. This was Malcolm MacDonald's approach. Even before the conference met, he had drawn up his reserve plan, which went through many adjustments, and had varying detailed prescriptions. Basically Britain would have to remain in Palestine due to strategic factors: war was almost certain. Partition was impracticable, so that some form of unitary government under British control was necessary. Most other things were negotiable. There were two particular issues to be decided: first, the rate and size of Jewish immigration and whether the Arabs should have any control over it; second, the form of government, and in particular whether there should be some type of representative assembly. After two months of wrangling over these issues MacDonald issued his White Paper of May 1939, whose details were outlined above. Having told the delegations on 15 March what it was likely to contain, he knew that none would be entirely satisfied. Although the Arabs had got much less than they demanded, in fact they had got much of what they asked for. On the other hand the Jews were outraged. Weizmann's reaction was that he must 'commit the Zionist movement to a policy of non-cooperation with Great Britain'.

The White Paper provided for a Palestinian state, neither Jewish or Arab, within ten years which would have treaty relations with Britain. If this was postponed Britain would consult not only with the League of Nations but also with the Arab states represented at the conference: another extraordinary admission of the standing of third parties in an imperial issue. There would be no Jewish veto on this, as had been discussed at the conference. Jewish immigration would be restricted to 75,000 over five years, of which 25,000 would be admitted irrespective of the principle of 'economic absorptive capacity'. Thereafter there would be an Arab veto on further immigration. Land sales would be restricted to the coastal strip and would be at the discretion of the High Commissioner. After much discussion concerning a move to 'self-government', there would be merely an advisory council, which might evolve into a legislative council with elected members. In short, the British killed the Zionist dream of a Jewish state and projected an eventual mixed state in which the Arabs would have a permanent numerical majority. Although there would be continued Jewish immigration this put paid to Herzl's Zionist project and emasculated, though never actually disavowed, the Balfour Declaration.

The 1939 White Paper marked the end of the second period of the British mandate. The third period lasted for the duration of the war, to the summer of 1945. From the British standpoint, the White Paper performed its intended wartime function. Although the Husayni faction in the AHC rejected its terms as unacceptable, the Nashashibi faction was prepared to accept it as the best on offer. Arab terrorism stopped almost completely early in 1939. The Arab states, the main concern of the British government, also accepted it for the time being. Though during the war strong elements in Iraq and Egypt were attracted by Axis propaganda, the only serious repercussions came in Iraq in 1941, when the Rashid Ali and army factions attempted to throw off British supervision and side with Germany. But Ibn Saud remained firm on the British side. As for the Jews, the fact of German anti-Semitism forced them to swallow their resentment and back the Allied cause. It was not until 1944 that the Revisionist military groups, Irgun and Lehi, stepped up the terror campaign that was to lead into the fourth and last phase of the mandate between 1945 and 1948.

British policy during the war period in fact divides into two. From 1939 the Axis threat to the Middle East made it more than ever essential to keep the goodwill of the Arab states: hence the White Paper had to be treated as gospel. Meantime Palestine enjoyed relative peace and considerable prosperity due to the influx of money via the Allied Middle East Centre in Cairo. But from late in 1942 conditions changed. The defeat of the Germans in North Africa and the survival of the Soviets greatly reduced the danger of an Axis attack on Palestine. Moreover, with the United States now in the war, American attitudes became very important. America had now, in fact, become the main centre of Zionism, and the Biltmore Programme of 1942, with its commitment to a Jewish state in Palestine, became a focal point for the politics of American Jewry which neither Roosevelt, nor his successor Truman, could ignore. Meantime, the Americans had greatly increased their economic stranglehold on the Middle East, mainly through control over oil concessions. Another relevant factor was that the immigration quota fixed in the White Paper was due to run out in 1944. This meant that, unless the rules were changed, there would be no further immigration without Arab consent, just as it became clear that a vast number of Jewish survivors from the Holocaust would want to enter Palestine.

For all these reasons, the British government began reconsideration of the White Paper in July 1943. Churchill did not regard his government as committed to the 1939 White Paper. Between then and December 1943 a sub-committee of cabinet discussed possible variants on the Peel and Woodhead partition plans. Its membership inclined it towards partition and to Zionist demands. The chairman was Herbert Morrison, Home Secretary, and other members were Leo Amery (Secretary of State for India), Colonel Stanley of the Colonial Office, Sir Archibald Sinclair, Liberal and Minister for Air, and R. K. Law, Permanent Secretary of the Foreign Office. All these except Stanley and Law were committed Zionists, as was Churchill, instigator of the sub-committee, who had picked its members. The committee considered many and varied points of view, but concentrated mainly on a revised partition plan produced by Amery. The military mind, represented by the Chiefs of Staff, the Cairo command, and Lord Wavell as Viceroy of India, was determined that Britain must retain control of an undivided Palestine. It would be the only base in the eastern Mediterranean, other than Cyprus, that did not depend on the goodwill of an Arab state. Eden at the Foreign Office and R. G. Casey, the (Australian) Minister of State in Cairo, both opposed partition vehemently.[82] The Foreign Office concentrated attack mainly on Amery's proposal that the Jews should be allocated the Negev in place of those parts of Galilee which they would have had under the Peel scheme, mainly due to the likely Arab repercussions. Casey and Stanley preferred the White Paper principles, but if partition was essential wanted the area allocated to the Jews reduced. Eventually a revised partition scheme was worked out and got support from a majority of the committee. Casey wrote a dissenting paper and the Foreign Office remained hostile to any change in the White Paper.

Partition was thus back on the agenda. The sub-committee's scheme was accepted by the cabinet in January 1944 as being 'as good as any that could be devised',[83] but they decided to shelve further consideration until after the American elections later that year, and also until after the end of the European war.

There then occurred one of those unpredictable events that change the course of history. On 6 November 1944 Lord Moyne, Deputy Minister of State in Cairo and one-time Colonial Secretary, was assassinated by the Stern Gang in Cairo. He was regarded by them as an anti-Semite and anti-Zionist but still more as a symbol of the hated British empire.[84] This proved fatal to the cause of partition and ended a period of relative collaboration between the British and the Jewish Agency in

---

[82] Eden minuted on 6 September 1943 that 'Mr Amery has never been right on any subject that I can recollect from Palestine to the League of Nations'. Cohen, *Palestine: Retreat from the Mandate*, 165.   [83] Ibid. 172.

[84] For Lehi motives see Bethell, *The Palestine Triangle*, 181.

Palestine. Although the Agency denounced the assassination and most Jewish settlers applauded the hanging of the killers in Cairo, Churchill was for the first time alienated from the Zionist cause.

If our dreams for Zionism are to end in the smoke of assassins' pistols and our labours for its future to produce only a new set of gangsters worthy of Nazi Germany, many like myself will have to reconsider the position we have maintained so consistently in the past.[85]

Cabinet discussion of the partition scheme was immediately suspended. But, as the 1939 immigration quota ran out, action became essential. In February 1945 Stanley demanded some decision, still favouring some version of the latest partition proposal. But by then the balance of influence had shifted against partition. In Jerusalem MacMichael had been replaced by Lord Gort, and in Cairo Casey by Sir Edward Grigg. Grigg was against partition and favoured an Anglo-American solution of the Palestine problem. There should be a new international body which would frame a new mandate or trust which would limit British responsibilities but leave Britain effectively in control. The establishment of the Arab League had radically changed the balance of forces in the Middle East, and partition would prove entirely unacceptable to the League. This position was supported by the British Ambassadors in the Middle East, though not by Stanley.

It was at this point in the debate that the European war ended and the coalition government in Britain was dissolved. Churchill became head of a caretaker government until the general election of July 1945 which returned a Labour government under Clement Attlee. The new government lacked experience in Middle Eastern affairs and did not feel committed either to its recent thinking in the coalition government or to the White Paper. This was the start of the fourth and final phase of British policy on Palestine that lasted until the final British evacuation in May 1948.

In point of fact 'policy' is again too strong a word to use for this period.[86] The essential fact was that for the first time since 1917 the British had very limited freedom of action. They were now hedged in by six main constraints.

First, the Americans had moved into the Middle East during the war. They had huge oil interests and regarded the area as part of a global security system that could no longer be left to the British. Moreover the huge numbers of Jews in the United States, particularly in the politically important New York, put great pressure on the President and the parties to placate domestic Zionists. As Truman said to some Arab diplomats, 'I am sorry, gentlemen, but I have to answer to hundreds of thousands who are anxious for the success of Zionism; I do not have hundreds of thousands of Arabs among my constituents.'[87] With Congressional elections in

---

[85] Cohen, *Palestine: Retreat from the Mandate*, 179.
[86] This section is largely based on the following: Cohen, *Palestine and the Great Powers*; Louis, *The British Empire in the Middle East*; Bethell, *The Palestine Triangle*; Khalidi, *Palestine Reborn*; Hurewitz, *The Struggle*; Shlaim, *Collusion*; Shepherd, *Ploughing Sand*.
[87] Khalidi, *Palestine Reborn*, 50.

the fall of 1946 and Presidential elections in 1948, this domestic political consideration had an important, perhaps decisive, effect on American policy. It tended to sideline the American State Department, which took a more balanced view of the various forces in play in Palestine, and it frustrated the British Foreign Office, now led by Ernest Bevin.

A second new factor was the evolution of the Arab League, established with British support in 1945. While it was not an alliance its members were solidly behind the Arab cause in Palestine and by 1945 five of them were members of the United Nations. Britain regarded good relations with states such as Iraq and Saudi Arabia as central to its Middle Eastern strategy and had to take their views into account on every aspect of Palestinian policy. Their demand was consistently for a single Arab state in Israel, with guarantees for the rights of minorities, including the near half-million Jews.

Third, the situation in Egypt was by this time uncertain. The Egyptian nationalists were determined to modify the 1936 Anglo-Egyptian treaty and to get British forces out of Egypt, ultimately including the Canal Zone base. This cast Palestine in a new light. If Britain could not rely on Egypt as its main military base for the Middle East and for security of the route to India and the East, perhaps Palestine might act as a substitute. Between 1945 and 1947 the British Chiefs of Staff played with this idea and for long insisted that Britain must retain the mandate as the basis for its control of military facilities in Palestine. This in turn implied maintaining the principles of the 1939 White Paper and avoiding partition. It was not until August 1947, and after the failure of the negotiations for the revision of the Egyptian Treaty, that Sir Orme Sargent of the Foreign Office stated that elite's revised conclusion that:

The political advantages of withdrawal [from Palestine] outweigh the strategic advantages of maintaining limited strategic rights under an Ordinary Trusteeship, or even of maintaining our present strategic facilities under the Mandate if contrary to expectation the [United Nations] Assembly would agree to a continuation of the Mandate. In neither case could we expect to maintain such facilities for any long period.[88]

Fourth, by 1945 the two terrorist organizations of the Zionists were far better placed to make British control of Palestine difficult and costly in terms of lives and money. While the Agency and the Haganah officially disapproved of their actions and occasionally attempted to control them, in practice and increasingly Irgun and Lehi went their own way. As the British were forced to adopt counter-measures, the Jewish population increasingly supported the terrorists. By 1947 even 100,000 British troops in a country with a population of some two million and the size of Wales were unable to control the situation. This was in marked contrast with the position in 1936–9, when some 20,000 troops were able to control the Arab rising.

Fifth, the international system was now increasingly dominated by a two-power structure mediated through the new United Nations. The USSR had

[88] Cohen, *Palestine and the Great Powers*, 41.

begun to show great interest in the Middle East and might support either the Jews or the Arabs, according to its assessment of the advantages to be obtained. Moreover, the Russians could use the UN as a tool of diplomacy, given their control over a number of its eastern European members. In 1947 their influence proved decisive in the UN vote for partition of Palestine and in 1948 they encouraged the Czechs to sell critical military supplies to the Zionists.

Finally, there was the condition of Britain itself. For the British these were bad years. The Americans ended Lease Lend immediately after the Japanese war ended in August, leaving Britain with a huge deficit on international trade until its industries were re-geared from war-production, little income from the few of its pre-war foreign investments that had not been sold to pay for American munitions before 1941, and huge overseas debts. Although Britain's armed forces were still very large, demobilization was taking place and its military capacity dwindling. Although British instincts were still those of a world power, its ability to maintain this role was in fact limited. In this situation the need to maintain so large a military force in Palestine and the costs involved—some £30 to £40 million a year by 1947—were too great a burden. Moreover, for the new Labour government reduction of imperial burdens was a major aim. Britain was to cut the Indian knot in 1947 after nearly two centuries of occupation, even at the cost of huge disruption and loss of life. If India, famously the jewel of the empire, was to be scuttled, then why not Palestine, much of whose strategic function was to help protect the route to India?

Given these constraints, it is not surprising that between 1945 and 1948 the British were unable to settle on and impose any considered strategy in Palestine. For most of the period their fall-back position remained that of the White Paper of 1939. This had the virtue that it pleased the Arab states, kept the Palestine Arabs quiet, and preserved British strategic rights. But it came under immediate attack from the Americans. On taking office as Foreign Secretary Ernest Bevin inherited a letter sent by Truman to Churchill, before he lost office.[89] This stated that

The drastic restrictions imposed on Jewish immigration by the White Paper of May, 1939, continue to provoke passionate protest from Americans most interested in Palestine and in the Jewish problem. They fervently urge the lifting of these restrictions which deny to Jews . . . entrance into the land which represents for so many of them their only hope of survival.[90]

This marked the start of a continuous American campaign. By August, Truman had endorsed a figure of 100,000 Jewish immigrants, which stemmed from a report by Earl G. Harrison, the American representative on the Intergovernmental Committee on Refugees, who had been sent to Germany in June to report on the condition of displaced persons (DPs). This endorsement was on a Zionist

---

[89] According to J. Wheeler-Bennett's *King George VI: His Life and Reign* (London, 1958), it was the King who had persuaded Attlee to appoint Bevin rather than Hugh Dalton, because of the latter's well-known pro-Zionist views. Quoted Bethell, *The Palestine Triangle*, 201–2. Dalton became Chancellor of the Exchequer instead, but played an important role in later Labour cabinet debates on Palestine.   [90] Cohen, *Palestine and the Great Powers*, 55.

initiative, and the figure of 100,000 probably came from a demand made by Weizmann to Churchill in November 1944 for 1.5 million immigrants over fifteen years. Ironically, there were then only some 50,000 Jewish displaced persons in Europe: had the British given them all immigration certificates the Zionist campaign for a state to house immigrants would have been severely weakened. The British refused: and during the winter of 1945–6 the Jewish underground smuggled thousands of Jews from eastern Europe west to the Allied DP camps in Germany and Austria, so that by mid-1946 over 250,000 were in these camps. As a result, the figure of 100,000 immigrants became totemic as a minimal first step in the relief of this pressure and remained perhaps the most important issue between all parties for the next two years. This was also the first main intervention by Truman into Palestinian affairs, and typically the report was leaked rather than stated openly.

The immigration question and the figure of 100,000 now became the main Zionist preoccupation and the ground for terrorist attacks in Palestine. Conversely, it was vital for the British to avoid so large an inrush because it would be incompatible with the White Paper and would alienate the Arabs. They had also, particularly in view of the current negotiations for an American loan, to keep the United States on side. Their strategy was therefore to avoid an immediate answer and to play for time, in the hope that some compromise would result. Hence, against a backdrop of escalating Irgun and Lehi violence, they negotiated. The first step was the setting up of an Anglo-American Commission early in 1946 to report on the immigration question. This had six British and six American members of mixed attitudes. It started work in Washington, visited the DP camps in Europe (where they found the Jews well primed to say that virtually all wanted to go to Palestine), and then went to Palestine. There the Higher Committee boycotted them while the Zionists pressed vehemently for the now sacred 100,000 immigrants at once. Meeting in Lausanne to draft their report, the Commission divided into three. Four of the Americans supported the 100,000 and a single bi-national state under UN trusteeship. Five Britons (excluding the Oxford academic, now a Labour MP, Richard Crossman) agreed with the unitary state but wanted the 100,000 immigration to be contingent on the Jews giving up their formidable armaments. The other three wanted partition but made the 100,000 the pressing need. Their collective report in April proposed that visas should be issued at once so that 100,000 immigrants could enter by the end of 1946. They also wanted restrictions on land purchase lifted. These together spelled the end of the White Paper principles. They were more vague on the structure of government. The mandate would have to continue until a new trusteeship was set up under the UN. Ideally there should be representative elective government with neither Jews nor Arabs dominant. Crossman saw this as a device for enabling the assumed Zionist 'moderates' to regain control.

Reactions to this report were mixed. The Zionists were divided, Ben-Gurion insisting on partition and a Jewish state. Truman, without consulting the State

Department, announced publicly on 30 April 1946 that he endorsed the 100,000 and free land purchase principles and was delighted that this would abrogate the 1939 White Paper. The Arab League damned the report out of hand. The British considered that the key lay in whether the USA was ready to co-operate in and to help to pay for implementing the report, and also to provide troops. Cabinet decided on 29 April that the report could only be implemented if 'illegal organizations' in Palestine were disarmed and if the Americans shared the military and financial costs. On 1 May, cabinet reconsidered this position in the light of Truman's statement the previous day. Attlee told the Commons that the British would investigate American willingness to collaborate and would make no immediate decision.

This investigation took place in June 1946, when an American team of bureaucrats led by H. F. Grady, an American career diplomat, went to London to discuss matters with a British team under Sir Norman Brook, Secretary of the cabinet. It became clear that the Americans were not prepared to offer any military help: the Chiefs of Staff (COS) had told Truman that there were no troops available. They also warned him that implementation of the report against the will of the Arab states might seriously endanger the whole western position in the Middle East. Hence all that Truman authorized his team to offer was that Palestine should not become either a Jewish or an Arab state; that the USA would make a grant in aid of $25–50 million for the resettlement of the 100,000; and that he would ask the International Bank for development funds for the Middle East as a whole. He made no attempt to deal with the constitutional settlement or the wider Middle East repercussions. This was not enough for the British. It would involve too great a cost in terms of both troops and money. The cabinet also ruled out the earlier Anglo-American committee's report as bound to alienate the Arabs. They therefore fell back on a Colonial Office proposal for 'cantonalization' of Palestine. This had been considered and rejected by the Peel Commission in 1937 but had been lurking in the Colonial Office mind. It was reconsidered by cabinet in September 1945, put anonymously to the Anglo-American Committee early in 1946, and was now put forward by Sir Douglas Harris of the Colonial Office. This was partition under a different name and with limited ethnic independence. It would have left most local matters to Jewish and Arab cantons but reserved common matters, including defence, railways, customs, and telegraphs, to the central power. The centre would initially deal with immigration and security, but these would eventually devolve to the provinces. The British would control this central government along with the Jerusalem area and the Negev for the time being. The British pointed out that this scheme had the merit that it might evolve into either a unitary state (as the Anglo-American committee had wanted), or into a federation, or into two separate sovereign states. From a British point of view, given current negotiations for military withdrawal from Egypt, it would also leave strategic control in their hands. But implementation would depend on both Jewish and Arab acceptance.

Reactions in the American team were initially favourable, mainly because the scheme smacked of partition. There was debate over the boundaries for the cantons, but the main disagreement was over the timing of the immigration of the 100,000, the British insisting that the immigration should begin only after acceptance of the scheme by all parties. These were the essentials of the eventual Morrison–Grady report, so called because Herbert Morrison was acting as Foreign Secretary while Bevin was ill. Surprisingly even Truman seemed at first to approve. But, typically of the whole course of events, he then came under intense American Zionist pressure to reject it because immigration of the 100,000 was contingent on Arab acceptance. To escape from this dilemma Truman got the six members of the earlier Anglo-American team to meet with the Grady team of experts to thrash out the differences between their proposals. Since the six carried the greater political weight they felt able to denounce the latest proposals: this gave Truman a convenient escape route from his earlier approval. On 30 July, even before the joint committees met, the British Ambassador was warned that Truman was unlikely to endorse the Morrison–Grady report. The following day Rabbi Abba Hillel Silver, the leading American Zionist, boasted in public that the Zionists had forced the President to pull back. Meantime, in Britain also there were reservations about the Morrison–Grady scheme.[91] It was unlikely to be acceptable to the Arabs, especially since it would include mass immigration, and was incompatible with their stated objective of a single Arab Palestine. In short, the most the scheme might do was to provide a breathing space and a basis for further negotiations.

These began on 9 September 1946 at the first session of the London Conference. It was attended only by representatives of the Arab states: the Zionists had refused to attend unless Morrison–Grady was dropped and the Conference concentrated on partition.[92] For their part the Arab League, after the meeting at Bludan in June, rejected the Morrison–Grady cantonal system and demanded full maintenance of the 1939 White Paper. They also demanded the end of the mandate, leading to a single independent state; a democratic government to be established after a constituent assembly had met; the Jews to have minority civil rights and political status according to population; and no more Jewish immigration until the Palestine government was set up. The new state would sign an alliance treaty with Britain. Full provisions would be made for access to the Holy Places. Bevin rejected the ban on immigration and reserved his position on the other points. On 2 October the Conference was adjourned.

Before that could meet again Truman had muddied the waters by his notorious Yom Kippur statement of 4 October. After summarizing the Morrison–Grady proposals and the counter Zionist demand for 'a viable Jewish State in control of its own immigration and economic policies in an adequate area of Palestine

---

[91] So called because Herbert Morrison was then acting as Foreign Secretary during Bevin's illness.

[92] For the complicated Zionist internal debate that led to this and their divisions see Cohen, *Palestine and the Great Powers*, ch. 7.

instead of in the whole of Palestine', plus the immediate issuance of immigration certificates, he made the following statement.

From the discussion which has ensued it is my belief that a solution along these lines [i.e. the Zionist proposals] would command the support of public opinion in the United States. I cannot believe the gap between the proposals which have been put forward is too great to be bridged by men of reason and goodwill. To such a solution our Government would give its support.[93]

Hedged though it was by the hint of compromise, which had been inserted by Dean Acheson, Undersecretary at the State Department, in a first draft that had been written by two Zionists, this was clearly seen both in America and London as a Presidential commitment to the Zionist cause of partition, and also as the product of the need to propitiate Jews for the forthcoming Congressional elections. It is arguable that Truman did not intend to commit himself at this stage to partition and a Zionist state. But the statement was welcomed by Zionists on the assumption that he did; though Silver suspected that, once the electoral credit had been cashed, Truman might drop his support. But in London the statement was read as an unconditional support for the Zionist position and led to violent reactions there. In December the defeat of Weizmann's proposal at the Zionist Congress that a delegation be sent to the London Conference when it resumed, which he made the condition of his remaining President of the Congress, committed the Zionists to non-collaboration and the unconditional demand for partition. Taken with the earlier Arab demands this signified the effective end of the British attempt to negotiate a compromise along Morrison–Grady lines. It also marked the end of any constructive British policy on Palestine based on agreement between the parties.

In late October 1946, Bevin had told the British cabinet that only three options now remained. Britain might attempt to impose a solution which was acceptable to one or other party. It might surrender the mandate and withdraw, though this would harm its strategic position and world standing. Finally it might adopt a scheme of partition which might provide for the Arab section to be merged with Transjordan, although this would be opposed by both the League and the HC. When cabinet met on 22 January it did not reach a conclusion but left the options open.

The resumed Conference met between 27 January and 6 February 1947 and predictably also failed to reach any conclusion. The Zionists were again not officially at the Conference because of the defeat of Weizmann at the Congress, but were in London for discussions. They were in fact in a dilemma since they knew that their maximalist demands, on the Biltmore line, would be totally unacceptable. They therefore temporized, asking for full implementation of the original mandate, though they later outlined, with careful imprecision, their territorial aims in a partition. Bevin turned both proposals down flat. Instead he put

---

[93] Ibid. 163.

forward the provincial autonomy scheme with additional powers for each community. For their part the Arab states stuck to their original demand: a unitary state and no more immigration.

Having failed to get any agreement or compromise, the British cabinet on 2 February formalized its own final plan. There would be a five-year period of trusteeship to prepare for self-government, giving the greatest amount of autonomy and hoping to persuade both societies to collaborate. Immigration would continue at 4,000 a month for two years, thus nearly providing the now symbolic 100,000. Thereafter immigration would be determined by the High Commissioner on the old principle of absorptive capacity. Land sales would be controlled by the local authorities. In the event of disagreement the United Nations would be asked to arbitrate.

There was nothing new in this formulation. It was an amalgamation of various demands: the Arabs' for a unitary state, the Jews' for immigration, the Defence chiefs' for continued control. It did not, however, fully satisfy the Chiefs of Staff. They disliked the five-year limitation, wanting a review rather than termination, then with a possible extension to ten years. The Chiefs of Staff, in fact, still regarded Palestine as essential to British strategic positions in the Middle East. They were confident that they could constrain Jewish terrorism. Their aim was an eventual unitary state with a defence treaty with Britain. They argued that if the issue was put to the UN there would be no majority for partition, so Britain would be left to run a unitary state. In fact there is no evidence that the Defence experts ever decided that Palestine was expendable or that it could not be held. It was the politicians and public opinion who decided that the price of control was too high.[94]

This final British position was flatly and predictably rejected by both sides when it was put to them on 12 February. On 14 February, Bevin proposed to cabinet that the matter be referred to the United Nations in the hope that the threat would produce 'a more reasonable frame' and a compromise. This was opposed by Dalton and Shinwell, both now partitionists, and also by the Chiefs of Staff on both the normal strategic grounds and also because British military morale would suffer if they were no longer defending a clear position. But it is important that the cabinet agreed to submit the issue to the United Nations for advice—not at this stage to give up the mandate. If finally no acceptable scheme emerged Britain could then simply surrender the mandate and could not be held responsible for the consequences by either Jews or Arabs. As Bevin told the House of Commons on 18 February,

We have decided that we are unable to accept the scheme put forward either by the Arabs or the Jews, or to impose ourselves a solution of our own. We have, therefore, reached the conclusion that the only course now open to us is to submit the problem for the judgement of the United Nations. . . . We shall explain that the Mandate has proved to be unworkable in practice and that the obligations undertaken to the two communities in Palestine have

[94] For details see Louis, *The British Empire in the Middle East*, 444–7, 456–7.

been shown to be irreconcilable. We shall describe the various proposals which have been put forward for dealing with the situation. . . . We shall then ask the United Nations to consider our report, and to recommend any particular solution.[95]

Churchill's response was favourable, though he criticized the government for delay.

Are we to understand that we are to go on bearing the whole of this burden, with no solution to offer, no guidance to give—the whole of this burden of maintaining law and order in Palestine, and carrying on the administration, not only until September [the next meeting of the UN General Assembly], which is a long way from February, not only until then, when the United Nations have solved the problem, to which the right hon. Gentleman has declared himself, after 18 months of protracted delay, incapable of offering any solution? How does he justify keeping 100,000 British soldiers in Palestine, who are needed here, and spending £30 million to £40 million a year from our diminishing resources upon this vast apparatus of protraction and delay?[96]

From one who had supported the Zionist programme and the mandate from the start this was a devastating admission of British failure.

The nine months that followed Bevin's announcement were among the worst in the British experience in Palestine. As Churchill had pinpointed, the British were now left to sustain the tatters of the White Paper, and in particular the control over immigration, in the face of increasingly severe terrorist attacks by Irgun and Lehi. Two special events affected British and international attitudes. On 30 July two British sergeants who had been captured by Irgun were hanged in reprisal for the execution of three Irgun men caught in their attack on Acre prison. This outraged British opinion and convinced many that the mandate must be wound up on any conditions. Then during July and August there was the long-running and widely reported saga of the Jewish ship *Exodus*, carrying 4,500 Jewish displaced persons who had no entry visas from Marseille to Palestine. After an extended tussle with Royal Naval vessels, the passengers were eventually taken back to North German camps. But there was widespread international condemnation of the alleged brutality of British methods which had a significant influence on the eventual United Nations decision.[97]

Meantime, in April 1947 the United Nations, in response to the British message, had held a special session of the General Assembly, which set up a Special Committee on Palestine (UNSCOP) to investigate and report. This consisted of eleven members from relatively minor states with Ralph Bunche as secretary. Long before it could report Andrei Gromyko, Soviet delegate to the UN, announced to everyone's surprise that the USSR would support a single bi-national state, but that if that proved impossible, it would accept partition. Since everyone had expected that the Soviets would adamantly oppose partition as part of their general anti-Zionist stance, this opened up new diplomatic vistas. Once in action,

[95] Cohen, *Palestine and the Great Powers*, 223.   [96] Ibid. 227.
[97] For a detailed and vivid account see Bethell, *The Palestine Triangle*, 318–43.

UNSCOP soon found the same problems as the British had done for so long. The Zionists formally demanded the whole of Palestine, in line with the Biltmore Programme, but also indicated privately that they would consider an adequate partition. The Arab League, meeting UNSCOP in Beirut, demanded a unitary Arab state with no special rights for Jews, all laws to be non-discriminatory. The Amir Abdullah formally supported the League's line to UNSCOP, but told London privately that he would accept partition if the Arab part was attached to Transjordan.[98] The HC was not consulted, but Musa al-Alami, ex-associate of the Mufti, suggested that Amin al-Husayni would reluctantly accept partition provided he was put in control of the Arab part. The British administration in Jerusalem of course avoided any statement of opinion, but had in fact already decided that partition was inevitable.[99]

UNSCOP withdrew to Geneva to prepare its report, which was ready by the deadline of 31 August 1947. Its members were unanimous that the mandate must be ended and the Palestinians be given independence. Eight of the eleven proposed that Palestine be divided after two years, beginning on 1 September 1947, during which 150,000 immigrants would be admitted. They provided a map showing the proposed division. Compared with the Peel Commission map the main differences were that the proposed Jewish state would now include most of the Negev, but would exclude western Galilee. Nor would there be a permanent British enclave including Jerusalem and Jaffa, though Jerusalem itself would become a permanent UN trusteeship under unspecified control. There would be two states linked by a treaty of economic union and constitutions with guarantees for minorities. The minority of three (India, Iran, and Yugoslavia, each with Muslim concerns) proposed instead a federal state after a three-year period of international control by the UN.

These reports were considered by the United Nations General Assembly, constituting itself into an ad hoc committee, which in turn divided into two sub-committees, each to consider one of the UNSCOP reports. They reported on 19 November.[100] Sub-committee one recommended partition on the grounds that no compromise between the various parties was possible. They proposed that partition should take place on 1 May 1948, when the mandate would be ended and the British would withdraw. Thereafter, the UN would supervise the partition. Sub-committee two rejected partition, challenged the UN's competence to partition Palestine, and recommended a unitary state. Its proposals were voted down by 29 to 12 with 14 abstentions on 24 November. The main sub-committee

[98] For details of Abdullah's secret negotiations with London see Shlaim, *Collusion*, esp. pp. 93–4, 101–2, 135–9. It was only in February 1948 that Bevin gave Abdullah, via his Prime Minister, informal encouragement to occupy those parts of Arab Palestine allocated to the Arabs by the UN Assembly in November 1947. See also Ch. 6, below.

[99] There are interesting parallels here with the League of Nations Mosul Commission of 1925 in Iraq.

[100] For the details of the two sub-committees' recommendations and the debate over them see Cohen, *Palestine and the Great Powers*, 284–92. For the report of sub-committee two, see Khalidi, *Haven*, 645–95.

then tackled the other report. It amended but finally accepted the report by 25 to 13 with 17 abstentions. Since this ratio, if repeated in the General Assembly, would not provide the necessary two-thirds majority, it led to intense lobbying in which Truman cast his weight behind partition, and his agents twisted arms to get client states to vote in the desired way. On 29 November the General Assembly voted 33 to 13 with ten abstentions (including Britain) for partition.[101]

While all this was going on the British had reassessed their position, particularly since a possible failure in the Assembly to get a two-thirds vote on the UNSCOP recommendations would leave the future open. By September 1947 no clear line of agreement had emerged. The Colonial Office was now convinced that partition was inevitable, but wanted the map redrawn so as to leave fewer Arabs in the Jewish zone. The Foreign Office was determined that Britain should not overtly support partition because of the bad effect this would have on Arab allies. The Chiefs of Staff still clung to their view that Palestine was a critical strategic base. Their preference was for continuing British trusteeship and, if that was rejected, a unitary state with a defence treaty with Britain. If partition was chosen Britain should make a treaty with one of the resulting states.

From this medley of options, cabinet on 20 September decided to accept Bevin's memorandum of 18 September. Bevin argued that the majority UNSCOP proposal was unfair to the Arabs and should be opposed. Against the Chiefs of Staff he held that, since the Security Council had, in August, rejected Egypt's plan to abrogate the 1936 treaty, on which British military rights were based, there was no immediate need to hold Palestine for this purpose. If the Palestinian Arabs resisted partition it would be madness for the British to attempt to suppress them. The unitary plan put up by the minority UNSCOP report was impracticable. That left only withdrawal. Its benefits were clear. It would save British lives and large sums of money, and it would not alienate the Arabs, who at this stage were confident that they could crush a new Jewish state. Britain should therefore tell the UN that, if no compromise was possible, it would pull out on a stated date. This gained general cabinet approval for the reasons Bevin proposed it; moreover the current evacuation of India seemed to provide a good example of withdrawal without commitment to either party.

This decision was announced in the UN on 20 November 1947. Britain would not transfer any authority to either Jews or Arabs while the mandate lasted, nor allow a UN commission any authority there. On the final vote on 29 November, Britain was one of the ten abstentions and one of nine out of the seventeen who had abstained on 25 November in the sub-committee of the Assembly who stuck to their position.[102] There remained the problem of winding up the mandate as

[101] For details of this notorious pressure see Cohen, *Palestine and the Great Powers*, 292–9; Louis, *The British Empire in the Middle East*, 478–93; Khalidi, *Haven*, 709–22.

[102] The tenth was Greece, which had been persuaded by the Arabs not to give in to American pressure. The seven who switched from abstention to support for partition were France (who was threatened with losing American aid if it did not), Belgium, Haiti, Liberia, Luxemburg, Netherlands, and New Zealand.

the two Palestinian sides geared up for war. Despite the race riots in India in 1946–7, there was no exact parallel in British imperial history since there was to be no formal transfer of power to anyone. On 11 December government announced in the Commons that British civil rule would end on 15 May 1948, though the final military withdrawal would be phased until 31 July to allow for the withdrawal of the estimated 150,000 tons of military stores, which were urgently needed in Europe in view of the Soviet threat. In March 1948 it was decided to try to speed up the military withdrawal, but to leave the date for ending civil government unchanged. Meantime, Britain refused to allow the UN partition commission to enter Palestine for fear that this would spark off Arab resistance: only a small advance party was allowed in during April, and then, since this had no executive authority, it was unable to achieve anything. As early as January 1948 elements of the civil administration were run down or closed: the supreme and assize courts of law were inactive, the general post office closed down, and many administrative departments were short-staffed. In short the mandate was ending in disorganization.[103] Meantime, the British refused to allow either Jews or Arabs access to official archives or to transfer any administrative functions. This may look like, and has been criticized as, simply bad temper, demonstrating British bitterness at the ignominious retreat to Haifa. In fact it was a deliberate part of the policy of neutrality. To have handed the administrative offices and records in Jerusalem to anyone would have compromised British neutrality.

British resolve to evacuate was tested early in 1948 by a swing in opinion in America against what was clearly going to be a very uncertain partition.[104] In February UNSCOP told the Security Council that it was clear that, without UN military intervention, partition could not be carried out along the lines proposed. Since military and domestic political considerations prevented the USA from providing this military intervention, on 21 February the State Department advised Truman that the issue should be taken back to the UN General Assembly to consider some form of trusteeship. Truman accepted this provided it did not involve the USA reneging on its commitment to partition. But when the Americans suggested to the Security Council on 24 February that the UN should set up a five-man commission to report on whether developments in Palestine constituted a threat to 'keeping the peace', which might entitle the UN to intervene within the terms of its charter, this got little support and died. In March the Americans, worried by the then apparent inability of the Jews to match Arab militancy, again made a move, this time to get Palestine put under the Trusteeship Council of the UN, which would set up an administration in Palestine to last until the Jews and Arabs agreed on a future constitution. This was, typically of American political life, incompatible with a private pledge made by Truman to

[103] But Shepherd, *Ploughing Sand*, 237–8, gives examples of British officials continuing with even trivial bureaucratic tasks and issuing ordinances: for example, one 'preventing the setting up of a lido or any dance-floor in the neighbourhood of the Sea of Galilee'. Ibid. 237.

[104] There are full details of this in Cohen, *Palestine and the Great Powers*, ch. 13.

Weizmann on 18 March that he would recognize a Jewish state the moment the mandate ended. The British refused to have anything to do with the trusteeship proposal; and in any case by mid-April it was clear that the Zionist crisis was over. The Jews therefore also rejected the trusteeship proposal and proceeded with their victorious campaign.

It was at this stage that the British role inevitably became most inglorious. Primarily concerned to withdraw in good order to their enclave in Haifa, they were not prepared to intervene between Arabs and Jews or to prevent massacres. Both sides accused the British of partiality, but this probably cut both ways and was the result of decisions by relatively junior local British officers. Perhaps the most serious British failure was the decision to evacuate Haifa on 24 hours' notice, which enabled the Jews to massacre or eject the great majority of the remaining Arabs. In the event there were few British casualties, but vast amounts of military stores had to be left behind. On 15 May, the British ended their mandate, and Truman announced that the United States would recognize the state of Israel. Palestine was left to find its destiny in blood.

Walid Khalidi, the Palestinian historian and active participant in the events of 1945–8, called the British record in Palestine 'perhaps the shabbiest regime in British colonial history'.[105] It is difficult to disagree with this verdict, but the essential question is why it was so.

In retrospect it seems clear that the British position in Palestine was, from the start, based on serious misjudgement as well as gross self-deception. As was argued in the previous chapter, most of those who were responsible for the 1917 Declaration and who pressed for the mandate knew little of Palestine. They had no conception of the hostility of Palestinian Arabs to Jewish immigration and land purchase before 1914. Most seem to have regarded them as decadent 'Levantines' who were unable to develop their own country. What they needed was an injection of skills and the western work-ethic. It was the classic western attitude to an allegedly backward people, and differed little from the view taken by the British and other Europeans of the societies of Black Africa and the Pacific during the partition of the world before 1914. Britons in Cairo, and later in Palestine, knew better. Most respected Arab values and were extremely critical of the Zionist commitment. But they were consistently overridden. It was not until 1939 that a senior British politician was prepared to face up to the realities of the Palestinian situation, and by then the situation was beyond repair.

Why did the British adopt and then hang onto their Zionist strategy for so long? It was suggested in the previous chapter that there were two main explanations for the original adoption of the pro-Zionist programme. The first was ideological— conversion to the Zionist ethic—the other political and strategic—concern to control an area critical to the defence of Egypt, coupled with the tactical desire to

---

[105] Khalidi, *Palestine Reborn*, 76.

get the support of Jewry in Russia and America in the war against the Germans. The evidence in this chapter suggests that the Zionist cause remained dominant among the British elite until at least 1939. It was a long-standing commitment of the Labour Party, accepted by the Liberals, and influential among many Conservatives. In this respect it has a parallel in contemporary attitudes to India where there were similarly deep entrenchments, particularly among Conservatives. It is ironic that Churchill, hammer of projects for self-government or Dominion status for India in the 1930s, should also have remained a vehement Zionist until the terror after 1945. Moreover, until the mid-1940s Zionists were still widely regarded as allies of Britain, as reflected in the Seventh Dominion movement led by Lord Wedgwood. In short, Zionism retained a persuasive power in the British political establishment that the parallel pan-Arab movement never achieved. It was with a great sense of guilt that many people, such as Malcolm MacDonald, eventually decided that they must abandon the cause.

Apart from conviction politics, the other main reason for retaining the mandate and therefore commitment to Zionism in some form was, of course, the continuing importance of Palestine to British strategy and world power. Until the Second World War suspended the League of Nations, giving up the mandate was still thought to open the gates to French or other intrusion. Even after 1945 the mandate was thought to remain the main British claim to occupation. As has been seen, the British defence establishment never viewed the evacuation of Palestine as an acceptable option. This was partly related to uncertainties in the Egyptian situation, and hence the security of the Canal Base, and partly to the concept of continuous British access through Palestine, Transjordan, and Iraq to the Persian Gulf. Even the evacuation of India in 1947 did not seem to blunt this appetite. Nor did the difficulty of dealing with terrorists in Palestine. The military mind was closed on the issue.

The parallel question is why the British did so little to support the Arab cause. This, after all, had been a major element in their Middle Eastern strategy during the First World War, and it remains arguable that the commitment to the Sharif Husayn in 1915 covered also Palestine.[106] One possible answer is that until the later 1930s the British lost interest in Arab nationalism. Iraq was first a mandate, then tied to Britain by treaty. Saudi Arabia seemed a docile client state. Egypt was tied by treaty and held by the British army. While there had been much sympathy for Palestine Arab claims before 1936, though never as much as there was for the Jews, the fact that Arabs had consistently refused to collaborate in any of the political schemes developed after 1920, and then attacked the British administration fiercely for three years from 1936, had lost them much of this support. At all times the divisions between the various Arab factions discouraged British officials from relying on them for government or the security organizations: Arab police were notoriously unreliable in sectarian clashes. This attitude changed fundamentally

[106] This, of course, was long debated, particularly in 1939 over the White Paper. The strongest statement of the case against the commitment is in Kedourie's *Labyrinth*.

in the later 1930s as the threat from the Axis developed and the need to secure the support of the now more powerful Arab states grew. Hence the White Paper of 1939 and the determined British attempt to stick to its limitation on Jewish immigration and land purchase until 1947. But there was never a possibility that the British would so far renege on the mandate as to give the Arabs the one thing they wanted, which was sole control over their own country. By the later 1930s, and still more after 1945, this was no longer feasible: there were too many Jews there and they had too much support from America. The best the British could have done was to agree to police the creation of an Arab state following partition. But since the Arab League and the Palestinian Arabs were resolutely opposed to partition, this was never a possibility. One must conclude that the Arab cause went largely by default, but also that in most respects the Palestinian Arabs and their Arab League allies were their own worst enemies, and never more than in 1947–8, when they attempted to overthrow the UN partition scheme and then lost much of the territory that would have created an Arab state.

But in the last resort the tragedy of Palestine, in 1948 as still in the early third millennium, was the responsibility of the British. Seen in the broadest terms, Palestine was one of the many territories round the world whose character and ethnic mix was fundamentally changed by British colonization. The readiness to transport or allow the movement of diverse ethnic groups from one place to another to suit British or British settler interests created fundamental disparities in many countries. In some places a degree of accommodation between groups was arrived at; in others the new arrivals continued to dominate; in others again after decolonization the settlers were ejected or persuaded to leave. Palestine was exceptional only in one respect: the settlers and the indigenous inhabitants were from the start absolutely determined that there should be no accommodation and neither, before 1948, was able to establish dominance over the other. The British mistake was to nurse a Zionist invasion at a time when the concept of the 'trust' was already raising doubts about the role of settlers in Africa, to the point at which the Jewish settlers were strong enough to take over. Palestine can best be seen as a classic late example of the European imperialism of the later nineteenth and early twentieth centuries, whose effects it has proved impossible to unravel.

6

Transjordan, 1918–1956

Transjordan was in many ways the most remarkable of the post-1918 European mandates.[1] Its origins were unplanned. No one had contemplated creating it as a political unit, let alone a future state, during the long negotiations that ended with the allocation of mandates in 1922. It had no historical unity under the Ottomans, consisting in the early nineteenth century of three districts connected with Palestine and Syria. The population of perhaps 225,000 in the early 1920s was relatively homogeneous, predominantly Arab and Sunni Muslim, though there were a number of Circassians, also Sunni Muslim, especially in Amman, and under 10 per cent of Christians of the standard Middle Eastern denominations. About 54 per cent of the population was 'settled' in the few towns and many villages, the rest nomadic, divided into four main tribal groups. The southern section of the region was essentially part of the Hijaz, the northern part of Syria. Its only obvious frontier was the Jordan valley to the west, but there were very close links between central Transjordan and Palestine. In short, given the plasticity of the region after 1918, it might have ended up as part of mandatory Palestine, since it fell within the area allocated to Britain and was technically part of the Palestine mandate, or being divided between Syria and the Hijaz. Thus, no one in 1918 could reasonably have predicted that the area would become a state, still less that it would be the only

[1] The best general account of the history of Transjordan to 1951 remains Mary Wilson, *King Abdullah, Britain and the Making of Jordan* (Cambridge, 1987). Another useful general history is K. Salibi, *The Modern History of Jordan* (London, 1993), though this is not based on primary sources. For the late Ottoman period the best source is E. L. Rogan, *Frontiers of the State in the Late Ottoman Empire: Transjordan 1850–1921* (Cambridge, 1999), which emphasizes the impressive constructive achievements of the Ottomans in that area before the First World War. Other more specialized works used in writing this chapter are: U. Dann, *Studies in the History of Transjordan 1920–1949* (Boulder, Colo., 1984) and *King Hussein and the Challenge of Arab Radicalism: Jordan 1955–1967* (Oxford, 1989); Y. Gelber, *Jewish–Transjordanian Relations, 1921–1948* (London 1997); Wm R. Louis, *The British Empire in the Middle East 1945–1951* (Oxford, 1984); B. Maddy-Weitzman, 'Chafing at the Bit: King Abdullah and the Arab League', in A. Susser and A. Shmuelevitz (eds.), *The Hashemites in the Modern Arab World* (London, 1995); J. Nevo, *King Abdallah and Palestine: A Territorial Ambition* (Basingstoke, 1996); I. Pappé, 'British Rule in Jordan, 1943–56', in M. J. Cohen and M. Lolinsky (eds.), *Demise of the British Empire in the Middle East: Britain's Responses to Nationalist Movements 1943–55* (London, 1998); R. Satloff, *From Abdullah to Hussein* (New York, 1994); A. Shlaim, *Collusion Across the Jordan* (Oxford, 1988) and *The Politics of Partition: King Abdullah, the Zionists and Palestine, 1921–1951* (Oxford, 1990); P. J. Vatikiotis, *Politics and the Military in Jordan: A Study of the Arab Legion 1921–1957* (London, 1967); Wm R. Louis and R. Owen (eds.), *A Revolutionary Year: The Middle East in 1958* (London and New York, 2002); T. J. Paris, *Britain, the Hashemites and Arab Rule, 1920–1925: The Sherifian Solution* (London, 2003).

monarchical state created after the First World War in the Middle East to remain one into the twenty-first century, ruled moreover by the same dynasty.

Transjordan had one other unique feature. It was the only Arab mandate or state that had a continuously close relationship with the Zionist enterprise from its early days, and after 1948 with Israel. That relationship was not always amicable but it was always fundamental to Transjordanian existence. It is a moot question whether the survival of the Hashemite regime there owed more to Britain, as mandatory until 1946 and provider of subsidies until 1956, or to the Zionist Agency, which provided much needed additional funds from the early days until 1948 and 'colluded' with Transjordan over the partition of Palestine in 1948–9. Conversely, the Zionists owed a great deal to Transjordan as provider of essential information on British intentions until the crisis of 1948, and then as observer of the United Nations partition plan. This was a symbiotic relationship which differentiated Transjordan from all other contemporary Arab states and reflected both geographical realities and the *realpolitik* of King Abdullah.

Israel and Transjordan had one common feature: both states were essentially autochthonous. While each of them grew up under British overlordship, and could not have survived their early days without that support, they alone among the ex-Ottoman mandated territories established themselves by their own efforts. Faysal was imposed on Iraq and neither Syria nor Lebanon was able to create an Arab state once the Faysal kingdom was destroyed by the French in 1920. But the Zionists and Abdullah built from the ground upwards. The Hashemite achievement has been summarized, perhaps over-generously, by Salibi in these terms:

Starting virtually from scratch, and working against an amazing array of local and regional odds, the Hashemite monarchy in Amman has managed to create a civil society and political community seen by many as models of their kind in the Arab world. At the same time, a country which began as one of the poorest in the Arab world has come to stand in the front line of Arab development, mainly through the efforts of its human resources [*sic*] under the guidance of a patient and enlightened leadership....

Once regarded as the most precarious of the Arab states, the Hashemite Kingdom of Jordan also managed to devise a formula for its existence whereby it could have stability and stride towards democracy at the same time.[2]

In this account it is proposed first to outline the genesis of Transjordan as an entity from 1918, emphasizing the influence of Britain as mandatory, then to examine the complexities of its relations with the Zionists to 1949, and finally to survey the fortunes of the regime to 1956 and the final break with the British connection.

1. THE BRITISH CONNECTION

In November 1918, when the British forces, allied with the Hashemite Northern Army, entered Damascus, the British had no particular plans for the Trans-Jordanian area through which Faysal's troops had moved up the line of the Hijaz railway.

---

[2] Salibi, *Modern History*, 274.

Although the borders had not been demarcated it was clear that it fell within the areas allocated to Britain in the Sykes–Picot Agreement, backed up by the later agreement that Palestine would become a British mandate. The French, at least, accepted that it did not fall within Syria as then allocated, though supporters of the 'Syrie intégrale' project thought it ought to do so. Technically it fell within the Palestine mandate, though to the east it could have been incorporated into Iraq and the southern area might have been taken by Ibn Saud in his campaign to obliterate the Hashemite kingdom of the Hijaz. On the other hand, seen from London, the area had strategic significance as a route from the Mediterranean to Iraq and the Gulf, and to keep France away from Palestine and Egypt. Clearly, it had to be kept under British control, one way or another.

The question no one had answered by 1920 was the best way of doing this. The Foreign Office, under Curzon, had so far avoided any commitment but was thinking of putting in Zayd, the youngest of Husayn's sons, as nominal ruler. Herbert Samuel, having just taken over as High Commissioner in Palestine, wanted to incorporate it into the Palestine mandate, probably with a view to Zionist colonization in what had been historically part of Judah. The War Office took a negative view: whatever happened they must not be obliged to keep significant numbers of troops there. A compromise was reached. Samuel was to send some political officers as advisers to the local notables: in August 1920 he visited Salt and promised that there would be no incorporation with Palestine, no military conscription, and no disarmament. This was welcomed by the local notables as a security against French threats. Samuel left behind six British officers, one of whom, a Captain Brunton, was to organize a small Arab force consisting of 75 mounted gendarmes and 25 machine-gunners. This in turn was soon taken over by Lieutenant-Colonel Frederick Peake, sent to command the gendarmerie. This was the nucleus of what was later called the Arab Legion, the mainstay of the Hashemite state.

This might have become the basis of a loose British control over the area along the lines of many frontier regions in other colonies. It would have remained part of mandatory Palestine and might well eventually have been absorbed into the area designated as a home for the Jews. There would have been no one central government but a number of local administrations run by committees of local notables with British advisers. In fact this did not happen: Transjordan emerged as a unitary state. But it is at least arguable that until quite late in the day, perhaps until 1936 or even 1941, the region was still seen as an anomalous frontier zone of uncertain future, dependent on British subsidies and British military and civil officers. The difference was that it came to have a single nominal ruler rather than half a dozen local polities. This was the achievement of the Amir Abdullah.

Abdullah, as was seen above, was the second son of the Sharif Husayn. He had played a leading role in the negotiations that led to Britain backing the Hijaz rising and had been seen as the effective heir of the Sharif because of the weakness of his older brother, Ali. But from 1917 his reputation had suffered. Sent to besiege Medina in 1917 he had sat there inertly, accumulating British money and armaments for his intended campaign to expand the Sharifian empire to the east, into Aser and the Yemen, when the time was ripe, and also as a defence against the imperialism of the Saudis. Meantime his younger brother, Faysal, had led the Hijaz expedition with T. E. Lawrence; and it was Faysal who was sent to Paris to negotiate on behalf of the Sharifian claim to the Arab kingdom. Then Abdullah met his greatest defeat. A campaign against the Saudis in the Khurma oasis over entitlement to taxes by the Sbay tribe, which began in 1918, ended in his decisive defeat and near capture at Turaba in May 1919. For the Hashemites this marked the beginning of their eclipse by the Saudis that ended with the destruction of their Hijaz kingdom in 1925. For Abdullah it meant that his ambition for an Arabian kingdom was dead. Moreover, his relations with his father were now very poor, so there was no future for him in Mecca. He had to look elsewhere.[3]

One possibility was Iraq, whose future in 1920 was still uncertain. In March 1920, at the general congress in Damascus which elected Faysal as King of Syria, the large contingent of Iraqis present elected Abdullah King of Iraq. This of course was not in their gift but in that of the British. During 1919 Abdullah had been seriously considered by the relevant British departments as a possible future ruler of Iraq, the common and generally condescending opinion being that, if there was to be a titular ruler with no real power, Abdullah would do. A. T. Wilson, as Acting Civil Commissioner in Iraq, was ordered to conduct a poll as to Abdullah's acceptability.[4] Wilson, who wanted direct British administration for the time being, arranged matters so that the answer from the Iraqi notables was negative. This effectively ended Abdullah's hope of the kingship of Iraq. By July 1920, however, conditions had changed. The French had ejected Faysal from Damascus and the risings in Iraq made it seem necessary to install some Arab ruler. This might have been Abdullah's chance; but opinion in London and Baghdad preferred Faysal as far more sophisticated and proven in battle. Abdullah was still without a future.

His response was to fall back on what became the central object of his life, the kingship of Syria, which, he always maintained, had been promised to his family by the British in 1915. By July 1920 this was probably a hopeless ambition since the French had just decided to eliminate the Hashemite monarchy there and, though they had no concrete plans, to establish some form of direct rule. Nevertheless Abdullah, having fallen out with his father, set off up the partially destroyed Hijaz railway with a number of armed supporters, variously estimated at between 500 and 1,000, and about £90,000 on 27 September 1920 and arrived at Maan on 21 November. By then he had only about 300 supporters but managed to get on good terms with the local shaykhs and tribal leaders, and also

[3] See Paris, *Britain, the Hashemites and Arab Rule*, ch. 8, for details and the whole of Part III for the course of events between 1920 and 1925.

[4] Wilson, *King Abdullah*, 41–2, provides a range of British opinions of Abdullah's fitness for the post, all of which were disdainful but tended to think his indolence and other negative qualities would make him an acceptable figurehead.

attracted a number of largely urban nationalists who had left Syria or Palestine and were from the more nationalistic north-west of Transjordan. There he remained until February 1921. He was fortunate that by then the British government was moving towards a 'sharifian' solution to the government of both Iraq and Transjordan. It had been decided in principle to impose Faysal on Iraq and it seemed convenient to try out Abdullah as ruler of Transjordan, still part of mandatory Palestine but excluded from the area covered by the Balfour Declaration as a home for the Jews. With British backing Abdullah was invited by a delegation of Arab notables, plus Mazhar Raslan, the mutasarrif of Salt, who had previously been hostile, to move to Amman. He arrived there on 2 March 1921.

But his future there was still entirely uncertain. It was debated at the Cairo Conference, where his claims were opposed by Wyndham Deedes, the Civil Secretary of Palestine, and also by T. E. Lawrence, who thought Abdullah might still be invited by the French to become a nominal ruler of Syria, with the danger that he might carry Transjordan with him into union with Syria. On the other hand, it might be difficult to dislodge him from Amman and some ruler had to be found. Churchill, as Colonial Secretary with responsibility for the Palestine mandate, therefore told the London authorities that something might be made of Abdullah. He summoned him to Jerusalem in March and had three days of discussions with him. The outcome was that Churchill offered, and Abdullah accepted, the position of ruler of Transjordan on a six months' probation with a British subsidy of £5,000. No British troops were to be stationed there. It was left to Abdullah to make what he could of this ungenerous settlement.

His future was not really decided until he visited London late in 1922. Meantime T. E. Lawrence had visited Amman, now becoming the effective capital of the territory, to investigate conditions. In a report of January 1922 he recommended that Abdullah be allowed to stay with a minimum of British supervision. His grant was to be increased, but was to be paid to a British representative due to suspicion of Abdullah's profligacy. The area under his control could be increased gradually into southern Arabia, presumably to Aqaba.[5] Lawrence still had great influence, and this report may well have protected Abdullah against the continuing hostility of the Foreign Office under Curzon and of the Palestinian government under Samuel, who wanted to incorporate Transjordan into the Palestine mandate and so open it to Zionist settlement.

The future was mapped out during Abdullah's invited visit to London between October and December 1922. By then the mandate system had been clarified, Faysal was on the throne of Iraq, and the French were in effective control of inland Syria. Abdullah asked for 'full independence', the exclusion of Transjordan from the implications of the Balfour Declaration, territorial extension to give him a Mediterranean port (a demand he was still making in the early 1940s), and direct communication with the Colonial Office, rather than through Jerusalem. He was

[5] Dann, *Studies,* 43.

given verbal assurance that he would be Amir of an independent administration, and an annual subsidy of £150,000. The first call on this and internal revenues was to be the cost of the Reserve Force under Peake, now to be called the Arab Legion and to be raised to 1,300, and the salaries of the British officials.[6] But none of this was confirmed or published until Abdullah had agreed to the arrest of at least one of those Syrians accused by the French of the attempted assassination of General Gouraud, the High Commissioner of Syria, or of Sultan al-Atrash, the leader of an anti-French rising in Jabal Druze. Accepting the advice of H. St J. Philby, his newly appointed political officer, in succession to Albert Abramson, Abdullah co-operated. Al-Atrash surrendered and the French were duly impressed. Their Commander Arlebosse, head of the political section in Damascus, is reported to have commented of Abdullah, 'Si ce type-là avait été à Damas à la place de Faisal, il serait là jusqu'à maintenant.'[7] That is, he was thought to be the pliant collaborator the French might have been able to work with. The result was to remove the last obstacles to formal recognition by London. In May 1923 it was announced that

Subject to approval of the League of Nations, His Britannic Majesty's Government will recognise the existence of an independent Government in Trans-Jordan, under the rule of His Highness the Amir Abdullah ibn Husain, provided such government is constitutional and places His Britannic Majesty's Government in a position to fulfil their international obligations in respect of the territory by means of an agreement to be concluded between the two Governments.[8]

This 'Assurance' appeared to give Abdullah a reasonably firm basis for his rule. In fact his position was unstable and conditional on his satisfying British objectives. Thereafter there would always be tension between Abdullah's very strong instinct to be independent and the British view that he was their subordinate agent to administer a territory under their responsibility. The first main crunch came in 1924. By then Philby had been replaced as British representative by (Sir) Henry Cox (in April 1924), a regular soldier who had served in the Sudan before 1914 and more recently as governor of Nablus in Palestine. Cox had none of Philby's admiration for Arab modes of government.[9] Even before his arrival in Amman, Clayton, as Chief Secretary in Jerusalem, was considering the possibility of replacing Abdullah by his brother Ali on the ground that Abdullah was financially profligate, using too much of the subsidy to placate tribal leaders in the traditional Arab style. There were other grounds for distrust. The Amir appeared altogether too smooth in his relations with British officials to be trusted. More important, politics at Amman seemed to be dominated by Arab nationalists,

---

[6] There was, however, a great deal of haggling between the Transjordan team, the Colonial Office, and the Foreign Office over the precise terms of the arrangement. See Dann, *Studies*, 47–71. Dann reproduces drafts submitted by Rikabi Pasha on behalf of Abdullah on 1 December and a Colonial Office draft of 15 December, ibid., 72–5.

[7] Quoted Wilson, *King Abdullah*, 74.   [8] Ibid. 75.

[9] Philby went on to work for Ibn Saud. For his career see E. Monroe, *Philby of Arabia* (New York and London, 1973).

many of the Istiqlal party and refugees from Syria who were thought to be disloyal to Britain and likely to cause trouble with the French in Syria. Another problem was the visit of the Sharif Husayn to Amman in January 1924, which was designed to demonstrate that Transjordan belonged to his kingdom of the Hijaz. He went so far as to declare that the Maan region, with its sea outlet at Aqaba, was a vilayet of his kingdom. All in all it would fall to Cox, as a traditional British colonial administrator, to tighten British control of Transjordan.

Cox immediately took control. He insisted on Rida Pasha al-Rikabi, Chief Adviser in Transjordan in 1922–3 and with whom Abdullah had fallen out, being recalled from Syria and appointed Chief Minister.[10] While Abdullah was away on the haj for two months from June 1924 Cox seriously suggested that he should not be allowed to return. The Colonial Office rejected this as too complicated but authorized a tough ultimatum to Abdullah. This was prepared by Clayton and delivered to Abdullah on his return in August 1924. Six conditions were defined if he was to remain Amir. Two related to control over the armed forces, which were to be under the Air Officer Commanding in Palestine. A further two demanded the immediate expulsion of seven named Syrian nationalists. The fifth insisted on the abolition of the Tribal Administration Department, which reflected Peake's hostility to the beduin. Finally, Abdullah must accept full British control of his finances. A written acceptance of these conditions was demanded.

It is critical for the history of Transjordan and the survival of Abdullah that, when bluntly presented with these demands on his return, he accepted without argument.[11] Abdullah demonstrated that, for all his improbable ambitions, he was first and foremost a realist. Since he depended almost entirely on the British, not only for money but also for security, as had been demonstrated by the fact that on 14 August the RAF had had to disperse the last of the Wahhabi raids towards Maan, he accepted the situation. Thereafter he used his great skill at evading obstacles rather than approaching them head on, and in this way was able to survive and ultimately to increase his independence: it is an interesting question whether he might have been able to survive by these evasive tactics had he become nominal ruler of French Syria.

During the next half a dozen years after the crisis of 1924, the Transjordanian system and Abdullah's relations with Britain settled down into much the same form as they were to keep until the 1940s. The idea of a genuinely independent state had been buried. Abdullah was now in much the same subservient position as rulers of princely states in India or in Northern Nigeria. He was nominal ruler of the country but he was obliged to do as the British representative—from 1927 given the

[10] Al-Rikabi came from a Damascus family of notables. He had served in the Ottoman army, held a series of senior administrative posts, including Governor of Medina, ending as a general in the Ottoman army. In 1918–20 he had been military governor and chief of the council of state in Syria under Faysal, then took refuge in Transjordan. After serving in Transjordan until 1926 he became a significant political figure in Syria, having come to terms with the French. Given his past it is not surprising that Abdullah did not like him.

[11] There is a verbatim account of the interview by Cox and Abdullah's immediate acceptance in Dann, *Studies*, 89–90.

more dignified title of Resident—dictated. His finances were controlled by Alan Kirkbride, brother of Alec Kirkbride, the later Resident. He was perpetually short of money, which was to have a major influence on his relations with the Zionists. Under British pressure Abdullah provided no help to the Syrian rebels in 1925–6, which might once have seemed his opportunity to achieve his Syrian ambitions. The result was that he lost his credentials as leader of the Arab nationalist movement. The reward for his obedience came in 1928 with a formal Agreement with Britain comparable to the Anglo-Iraqi treaties of 1924 and 1926. The 1928 treaty, which had been under consideration for two years, basically ratified the status quo. It defined British rights, which included control over foreign affairs, the armed forces, communication, and public finance, leaving Abdullah free only to spend his civil list, which was kept low. There was no mention of 'independence' and the main reward Abdullah received was the continuation of the British subsidy, which went mostly on the cost of the Resident and his staff, and the Arab Legion, which was now regarded as effectively part of the British armed forces.

The Legion was in a sense the core of the state: without it there would have been no state.[12] In the 1920s it had been drawn almost entirely from the sedentary population: it was not until the 1930s that the beduin were recruited. In 1926 it numbered some 1,500; but in that year the Transjordan Frontier Force (TJFF) was set up to protect the frontiers. This was paid for largely out of the Palestine budget and was under the command of the High Commissioner, with 700 men and British officers. To balance this the Legion was reduced to under 900 men, still under Peake and other British officers. It now became essentially an internal security force. It was only in 1930 that a new Desert Mobile Force was set up under J. B. Glubb, who had been a political officer in Iraq and specialized in relations with tribal groups. It consisted entirely of beduins and soon became highly professional, the most effective part of the Legion. Moreover, Glubb, by contrast with Peake, got on well with Abdullah and understood how best to deal with an Arab notable, particularly a beduin chief. By 1939, when Glubb succeeded Peake in command of the Legion, its total complement was 1,600, 800 of whom were combat troops. They were to play a decisive role in the future of Transjordan.

Once the Agreement had been fixed Transjordan had to be given a constitution, predicted in the 1923 Assurance. Until then government was technically that of the Amir and his executive council, chosen by him, but heavily influenced by the Resident. There was now to be a legislative council of 21, of whom 14 were elected, two appointed tribal chiefs, the Chief Minister, and four others appointed from the executive council. The Chief Minister acted as president of the council and did not normally vote. Elections continued to be under the two-stage Ottoman system, which enabled the government to bring pressure on the second-stage electors to choose their preferred man. This gave Abdullah some control. He could appoint or dismiss the non-elected members and influence the elections in the

---

[12] The standard account is still Vatikiotis, *Politics and the Military*, on which this account is based.

same way as government in Iraq could influence elections, through his contacts with the notables. Moreover the Amir could summon and dissolve the council, which was not responsible to the legislature. In fact, throughout Abdullah's life, politics and government were run by him and a small group of loyalist politicians whom Satloff calls 'the king's men'. These were for the most part not indigenous Transjordanians but Syrians, Circassians, and Palestinians. They competed for office and sometimes built so-called political parties. On occasion they might act against Abdullah. But for the most part they stuck to him and he to them. He constructed his cabinets from them, rotating offices from time to time. But until after 1948 his ministries had very little relationship with the membership of the legislature or with political parties. Provided that he kept in with his British Resident and the High Commissioner in Jerusalem, Abdullah could rule much as he wished.[13]

On this basis Transjordan survived with little change until the Palestinian crisis of 1936. Abdullah ran domestic politics under the watchful eye of the Resident. Meantime the British attempted standard colonial development strategies with limited funds. Between 1928 and 1933 an assessment of tax liabilities was carried out and land taxes made uniform throughout the country. Starting in 1933 a survey of land-ownership began, following the model of Egypt and Iraq. The object was to determine individual rights which had been left uncertain under the Ottoman land registration schemes, and also to attempt to prevent the accumulation of large estates at the expense of peasants. Only the Aijun district in the north had been completed by 1939, when the survey was suspended. Much progress was also made in bringing the beduin tribes under effective control through the Beduin Control Board. The beduin role in the state expanded greatly with the creation of the Desert Patrol under Glubb. By 1939 beduins provided more than half the total of the Arab Legion and were the most loyal of all army regiments to the Amir.

2. ABDULLAH, PALESTINE, AND THE ZIONISTS

For Abdullah, Palestine presented a major problem but also significant opportunities. As a Hashemite he regarded it as part of the Arab kingdom allegedly promised to his father in 1915. Palestine, along with Syria, was always part of his expansionist designs: he was, after all, 'A Falcon trapped in a canary's cage'.[14] He necessarily had close connections with the Palestinian notables, and, as has been seen, many of his officials and ministers were Palestinian. Ultimately he was bound to align himself with their Arab nationalists. On the other hand, the Hashemites were not

---

[13] There are many similarities with the position in Iraq, particularly with the role of the ex-Sharifian politicians. But the Iraqi kings included local notables in their governments far more than did Abdullah.　　　　　[14] The title of ch. 1 of Shlaim's *The Politics of Partition*.

anti-Semite. In January 1919, while pursuing his diplomacy in Paris, Faysal had come to an agreement with Chaim Weizmann to encourage Jewish settlement in Palestine. There was, however, a proviso, written by Faysal as a codicil to the agreement, which made it invalid: 'Provided the Arabs obtain their independence as demanded . . .'.[15] Abdullah shared this view. Zionists could bring skills and capital which the Arab world seriously lacked. Provided they accepted a subordinate role in an Arab state or states they were welcome. Abdullah throughout favoured a revival of the Ottoman millet system which allowed non-Islamic groups to live as self-regulating communities under Arab rule: he was still promoting this idea in the critical period after 1945. There was, therefore, a basic tension between these two strands of Abdullah's thought and situation. On the one hand his family history bound him to support Palestinian Arab demands for an independent Arab-dominated state in Palestine. On the other hand he wanted to gain the greatest benefits from Jewish enterprise. It was not until the Palestinian revolt of 1936 that the incompatibility of these two objectives became evident.

Until then, Abdullah played the Zionist card quite strongly. To Zionists, Transjordan had a double significance. In the longer term it was part of the unadmitted but certainly hoped-for greater Zionist state to include all of biblical Israel. In the short term it offered economic and business opportunities and the possibility of buying additional land for settlers in the fertile Jordan valley. In the mid and later 1920s the Zionist movement was too short of money to indulge in large-scale land-buying or immigration. Moreover, British regulations banned the sale of land in Transjordan to Jews. But in 1927 the Jewish-owned Palestine Electric Company was allowed to buy some 1,500 acres at the junction of the Zarqa and Jordan rivers to build an electric power plant for both Palestine and Transjordan. In the same year, the Russian Jewish chemical engineer A. M. Novomeysky obtained a concession for his Palestine Potash Company to set up a plant at the southern end of the Dead Sea. For a country as poor and as primitive economically as Transjordan, these were important assets, though some more committed anti-Jewish elements there refused to use Jewish electricity. After 1929, encouraged by the growth of the land settlement scheme, the attraction of Jordanian land for Jews increased.

Unintentionally, the Colonial Office encouraged Abdullah to attract Jewish settlement. As a reward for his efficiency in suppressing support for the Arabs in the 1929 Wailing Wall crisis, it encouraged the Transjordan legislative council to give Abdullah three blocks of state land to develop, plus a grant of £3,000 to do so. One estate, the most valuable, was leased to Zayd al-Atrash, brother of the Druze leader, and a partner for an annual rent of £150. The other two estates were in the Jordan valley, one potentially valuable, the other of little immediate potential. In 1933 Abdullah made a deal with the Jewish Agency about the second of these whereby the Agency got an option on the lease for 33 years at £500 for six months, with the right of renewal. This option was continued indefinitely and was

---

[15] Quoted P. Mansfield, *The Arabs* (1978; 3rd edn. London, 1992), 182.

regarded by the Agency as a political bribe to keep Abdullah on their side.[16] Since Abdullah's civil list was then only £18,000, this was a significant addition to his very small private resources. In 1937 A. H. Cohen, of the Agency's Joint Bureau for Arab Affairs, who had been largely responsible for the constant clandestine contacts between the Agency and Abdullah since 1929, estimated that in the previous five years Abdullah had received £10,000. Meantime, other Transjordanian land-owners were making similar deals. With the great increase in Jewish refugees and their capital from Germany in and after 1933, it seemed likely that this process might continue and result in significant Jewish settlements east of the Jordan once such settlement was allowed.

A major obstacle, however, to this détente between Abdullah and the Jews was the attitude of Palestinian Arabs, both inside Transjordan and in Palestine. There were by 1933 a large number of Palestinian Arabs in Amman and Abdullah then began to increase their share of top ministerial posts. His aim was to become the prospective ruler of Palestine, along with Syria, and for this he needed the support of Palestinian Arab leaders. His problem was the division of Palestinian nationalists into competing groups. Initially, in 1921, Abdullah had supported Amin al-Husayni and persuaded Samuel to give him a pardon for his part in the anti-Jewish riots. But later that year Abdullah felt that he was slighted by Amin when he excluded him from talks with Samuel, and thereafter relations were poor. They did not, however, become overtly hostile until after 1936. Given this situation Abdullah's natural allies in Palestine were the Nashashibi clan, who, in competition with the Husaynis and their control of the Supreme Muslim Council, saw Abdullah as a potentially valuable ally. Moreover, they shared with him the view that collaboration with the British was a necessary means of achieving Arab objectives. By the 1930s the Nashashibis were urging the unification of Palestine and Transjordan under British protection, with Abdullah as King.

By the time of the 1936 Arab strike, Abdullah thus had a significant though informal role in Palestinian politics. The strike gave him the opportunity to transform himself from a minor Arabian princeling with ideas beyond his station to a significant player in Middle Eastern politics. Until then, the British had not accepted that he had any part to play in Palestinian affairs: in 1934 the High Commissioner considered that he had no 'body of opinion' behind him.[17] But in 1936 the strike gave him the opportunity to intervene. In May, members of the Arab Higher Committee visited Amman to ask for mediation. Abdullah's advice was to call off the strike and send a delegation to London to argue their case. This they refused. Abdullah saw that the only way to end the strike without complete loss of face by the Arabs was to persuade the Zionists to make some concession on immigration. His opportunity came in July when the Colonial Secretary, Ormsby-Gore, in a statement to the House of Commons, was understood to have suggested that immigration

---

[16] In 1932 Abdullah had received £2,000 as a deposit for the lease of this same Ghawr al-Kibd estate from a Swiss company, pending investigation into its possibilities. The lease was never taken up but Abdullah kept the money.   [17] Salibi, *Modern History*, 135.

might temporarily be suspended if the strike was called off. This gave Abdullah an opening. He had for years been in close touch with the Agency, using Muhammad al-Unsi, originally a Lebanese from Beirut and his secretary and general factotum, as clandestine intermediary. It was through him that the various financial deals had been arranged, and also through him that Abdullah provided the Agency with vital information on British and Arab intentions. In May 1936, Abdullah sent al-Unsi to Jerusalem to suggest to the Agency that they suspend immigration to Palestine for a few years, diverting it to Transjordan. He also asked for a subvention of £500. He got the money, but the Agency strongly rejected the proposed check to immigration. This led to a marked cooling of relations between Amman and the Agency, but, as always happened in this period, each side depended too much on the other for it to lead to a breakdown. On 28 July, Abdullah sent al-Unsi back to persuade Moshe Shertok (later Sharett), head of the political department of the Agency, to suggest to the strongly Zionist Ormsby-Gore that some concession should be made to the Arabs. Again this came to nothing. In August he tried, and failed, to persuade the AHC to suspend the strike on the expectation that immigration would be halted. Amin al-Husayni was determined that Abdullah should be kept out of the situation. In fact, when Nuri as-Said, then Foreign Minister of Iraq, took the initiative on behalf of his state, Saudi Arabia, and the Yemen, to persuade the AHC to suspend the strike so that the Peel Commission could start working, Abdullah initially refused to back them, disgruntled because he regarded that intermediary role as his own. But eventually he joined with the three states in the published appeal to the AHC of 11 October, after which the strike was called off.

Abdullah had succeeded in giving official support to the Arab cause, while maintaining his links with the Zionists. This was duly recognized. In January 1937 Aharon Cohen summarized the services Abdullah had rendered to the Zionist cause.

Upon the disturbances' outbreak, the Amir's [*sic*] revealed his true friendship with us. During that period the Political Department had direct contacts with the Amir's palace. The latter supplied it with information on the bedouin tribes, the government and Transjordan's political circles. The department, too, provided the Palace with intelligence on the Palestinian Arabs and helped the Amir to carry the financial burden of keeping Transjordan quiet. Abdullah was quite active in restraining clans who had wanted to infiltrate into Palestine and join the terrorists. He prevented the terrorists' leaders from attacking Naharayim. He arrested several Arabs who had tried to smuggle arms into the country, and confiscated their weapons. The Amir played a central part in these disturbances by his endeavour to mediate between the government and the Arab Higher Committee. Prior to every meeting... he used to consult us. In the wake of the conferences, he conveyed to us the gist of his talks with the Arab leaders and with the British authorities.[18]

There could be no better testimony to the skill with which Abdullah had played his few cards, nor of the closeness of his relations with the Jewish Agency. His alleged 'collusion' with the Zionists ten years later should come as no surprise.

[18] Quoted Gelber, *Jewish–Transjordanian Relations*, 99.

The Peel Commission gave Abdullah another chance to influence events. Since the AHC initially boycotted the Commission, Abdullah was the first Arab spokesman they met. His advice was that Britain should observe the terms of the mandate by setting up a representative legislative council and that he favoured a united Palestine under his rule which would have a treaty with Britain. Jewish sources were told, in one of the invariable leaks of British confidential information they received, that he had also recommended a maximum Jewish population of 35 per cent of the Arab population. He said that he would be willing to accept Jewish settlers in Transjordan provided they had no special privileges. The Commission, however, rejected these suggestions. In its report, as was seen in Chapter 5, it recommended partition of Palestine. But it did propose that the Arab section should be attached to Transjordan. Although this was less than he had hoped for, it became Abdullah's immediate objective. But the proposal, and his enthusiasm for it, isolated him from all other Arab groups and states, whose stated aim, then, after 1945, and into the twenty-first century, remained the creation of an integrated Arab state of Palestine.

It also necessarily forced him closer to the Zionists, who were to accept the concept of partition as a starting-point for further expansion. During the two years 1937–9 and the renewed Arab revolt, Abdullah remained quietly in Amman, becoming even more dependent on the Zionists for funds. In 1938 he became increasingly afraid of the threat of the Arab nationalists to his own position. Nevertheless his recommendation to the Woodhead Commission was that the whole of Palestine should be incorporated into Transjordan, with autonomous cantons for the Jews. This implied a swing towards the Arab nationalist position and he made a public statement in July 1938 which was explicitly anti-Zionist. This, he explained to the Agency, was a necessary tactic to placate Arab nationalists, and this was understood. But at the St James's Palace conference of 1939, where Abdullah was represented by his veteran minister, Tawfiq Abu al-Huda, Transjordan fully supported the resultant White Paper which dropped partition and restricted both Jewish immigration and land purchases. For this he was rewarded by the British with increased subsidies. Conversely it destroyed the basis of collaboration with the Zionists, though the exchange of information continued secretively.

The outbreak of war in 1939 changed everything. Above all, it made Abdullah and Transjordan more important. From a British standpoint, the Arab Legion now became a valuable military force: it was expanded and the subsidy increased. It played a critical role in the Baghdad crisis of 1941. Close contacts with the Agency were resumed. Abdullah became the key source of information on British policy and Middle Eastern politics for the Zionists. But on both fronts these good relations soured after 1941. From a British standpoint, Abdullah's constant pressure to be able to take over Syria once the Vichy regime there had been removed was a major complication. By 1942 London was once again thinking of a possible replacement to improve relations with the Free French. In 1942 Churchill rejected the proposal from MacMichael, the High Commissioner, to make

Abdullah King of Transjordan after the war. Meantime, links with the Agency became much less close, though they were never broken. The creation of the Arab League in 1945 reduced Abdullah's international significance.

The end of the war in 1945 again changed all positions. It also ushered in the period of Abdullah's greatest significance to Palestine, Britain, and the Zionists. Ernest Bevin, as the new Foreign Minister, wanted Abdullah's agreement to the operations of the Anglo-American Committee on Palestine. Abdullah was invited to London in February 1946 and by March a new treaty had been drawn up and signed. Transjordan would now be recognized as an independent state: the mandate was over. The treaty provided for perpetual peace and friendship. Britain would continue the subsidy for the Legion on condition of extensive British military facilities. The treaty gave both the Americans and the Soviets an excuse for not recognizing the new kingdom of Transjordan. The Americans held back because of strong American Zionist pressure, on the ground that this would bar their claims to the region beyond the Jordan, and they did not recognize Jordan or agree to its joining the United Nations until 1949. By then Israel was no longer so hostile to Abdullah and the USA wanted Britain to agree to *de jure* recognition of Israel and the simultaneous admission of both states to the UN.[19] The Soviets saw the treaty as proof that Transjordan was merely an imperialist agent, but they also agreed to UN entry in 1949. Transjordan thus achieved roughly the same position as Iraq had had since 1932, an independent state tied to Britain by defence and financial agreements.

This, however, was merely the later crowning symbol of Transjordan's post-war rise to significance. Between 1945 and 1949, despite the British treaty, Abdullah was distrusted or hated by virtually all those involved in the Palestinian question. The British Foreign and Colonial Offices regarded him as a loose cannon. Some members of the Arab League distrusted him as being too much under British influence, while others hated him as a Hashemite with dangerous ambitions to take over Syria and possibly Iraq: indeed, during the critical period from 1946–9, these Arab states were as much concerned to prevent Abdullah from gaining Palestine as they were to block the emergence of Israel. In the two years after 1946 Abdullah had therefore to work his way back on to good terms with the Arab states by nominally opposing partition of Palestine. He disagreed with the proposals of the Anglo-American Committee in 1946, particularly their recommendation for immediate immigration certificates for 100,000 Jews. At the Bludan meeting of the League later in 1946 he toed the current Arab line against partition of Palestine, though both Britain and the Agency knew that in fact he favoured partition. When the UNSCOP committee arrived Abdullah carefully avoided making any positive statement to them. Once they had recommended partition and this had been accepted by the United Nations Assembly in November 1947, Abdullah had overtly to follow the standard League policy in rejecting it. He was thus morally committed to the League's campaign against a potential Israel.

[19] Dann, *Studies*, ch. 7.

All this posturing as a genuine Arab nationalist inevitably affected Abdullah's close relations with the Zionists. In 1945–6 there was a temporary cessation of close contacts between them. But the relationship was too strongly symbiotic to be broken. By mid-1946 the Zionists were prepared to accept partition, rather than the greater Israel of the Biltmore Programme. That meant that they had to decide who would take responsibility for the Arab section of the country, and the choice essentially lay between Transjordan and Egypt. In August 1946 Elias Sasson of the Agency's Political Department, and one of its most able negotiators, met Abdullah twice. It was secretly agreed that Abdullah would support partition provided he obtained what was later called the West Bank. To encourage him he was paid £5,000, though Abdullah had asked for £25,000. It was also arranged that confidential contacts between Amman and the Agency should in future be handled by Dr Shaukat Seti, Abdullah's Turkish doctor, following the death of al-Unsi. The following month, September 1946, Abdullah told Shertok that his envoy to London, Samir al-Rifai,[20] would press Bevin to agree to partition, and also that Abdullah should take over Syria. Shertok agreed with both: the Agency then thought that Abdullah's control of Syria would block British plans for Palestine.

Throughout the critical period between February 1947 and the United Nations vote for partition in November, Abdullah walked a tightrope, avoiding overt commitment to partition while nominally supporting the League's demand for a united Arab-controlled Palestine. Contacts with the Agency were intermittent, but on 17 November 1947, twelve days before the critical United Nations vote on partition, Golda Meyerson (later Meir) as acting head of the political department of the Agency, went to meet Abdullah secretly at the Naharayim electricity plant.[21] Although Abdullah was taken aback by having to deal with a woman, he made his position clear. Ideally he would like to incorporate Palestine in a Transjordanian state, possibly also including Syria, the Jews to form an autonomous republic within that state. When it was clear that this would not be acceptable to the Zionists, he retreated to the position that he would aim to occupy any areas allotted to the Arabs in Palestine, but respect those given to the Jews. He also provided much information on the League's plans and preparations. For their part, although they refused to make any formal commitments, the Jewish delegation accepted that Abdullah, rather than the Arabs under Hajj Amin, should occupy the Arab parts of Palestine. Shlaim summed up the deal as follows:

Abdullah secured Jewish agreement for annexing the populated Arab part of Palestine adjacent to his kingdom. Mrs Meir, inexperienced though she was, returned home with what amounted to a non-aggression pact with one of the leading Arab states. The ruler of that state and the master of the Arab Legion had promised that he would never attack the

[20] Prime Minister 1944–5, 1947, 1950–1.
[21] There are detailed accounts of this meeting in Gelber, *Jewish–Transjordanian Relations*, 235–7, and Shlaim, *Politics of Partition*, 92–100.

Jews or join with other Arabs in frustrating the establishment of a Jewish state. What is more, he was prepared to consider a formal pact embodying the terms of collaboration between Transjordan and the Jewish Agency.[22]

This informal agreement was to be the foundation of all Transjordanian–Jewish relations during the next two years. At times Abdullah appeared to deviate from it and, under the compulsion of his Arab relationship, to fight against the Jews. Yet both sides always knew that this was the underlying reality of their relationship.

The United Nations vote of 29 November for the partition of Palestine along the lines proposed by UNSCOP put this understanding to a severe test. Abdullah appeared to vacillate: no one knew which way he would go. Early in 1948 he was permitting recruits and equipment to pass through his state to the Arab Liberation Army set up by the League. Then he tried to stop this flow in order not to alienate the Jews, but found this impossible and politically unwise. Meantime he had secured an informal British agreement to his project to take over the West Bank to match the understanding with the Agency. On 7 January 1948 his Prime Minister,[23] Tawfiq al-Huda, had a private interview with Bevin in London: the only other person there was Glubb, acting as translator. The official British position was that after their withdrawal on 15 May 1948, what happened in Palestine was none of their business. On the other hand, it was obvious that British attitudes might be critical at any future peace settlement. Bevin had been well briefed. Tawfiq outlined Abdullah's plans, emphasizing that he proposed to send troops into those areas of Palestine designated Arab before the end of the mandate to ensure that the Jews did not get there first. Because the matter was so sensitive no formal record was made of Bevin's response. According to Glubb, it was 'It seems the obvious thing to do', and then again, 'It seems the obvious thing to do ... but do not go and invade the areas allotted to the Jews.' Bevin's own minute merely stated that he would study the statement. But he telegraphed Sir Alec Kirkbride, since 1939 Resident in Amman, then called Minister, and Ambassador when Transjordan became independent in 1946, that he was satisfied with al-Huda's assurances about Abdullah's intentions.[24]

Abdullah now had two very informal assurances from the only two powers that could effectively block his strategy of taking as much as possible of Palestine: the Jews because they could almost certainly defeat the Legion if they determined to do so, the British because it was their money and arms that made the Legion the most effective non-Zionist military machine in the region. The Foreign Office, moreover, was now keen that the Negev should be annexed to Transjordan to provide certain access between Egypt and Iraq via Transjordan. But there were technical problems. The Legion was led by British officers as well as being paid for by Britain. What would be their status if the Legion marched into Palestine in contravention of the UN's resolution?

---

[22] Ibid. 100.   [23] The term Prime Minister replaced Chief Minister in 1939.
[24] Louis, *The British Empire in the Middle East*, 372; Gelber, *Jewish–Transjordanian Relations*, 255.

The meeting with Bevin was a well-kept secret: even the Agency's normally impeccable access to British information (via their clerks in the High Commission and elsewhere) was lacking. Moreover, there was no direct communication between the Agency and Amman for a couple of months after February 1948. The Agency was very keen to re-establish contact, but Abdullah was then playing a very complicated game. On the one hand he prevented the Legion from actively protecting Arabs against the Jewish onslaught, or from attacking the Jews, except in the Etzion bloc on 12–13 May, just before the end of the mandate, where Jewish forces were blocking the vital road between Jerusalem and the Suez canal base. On the other hand, Abdullah was outraged by Jewish treatment of Arabs in the areas they occupied, and in particular by the notorious Deir Yasin massacre of 9 April 1948. Abdullah was obviously slipping into the strategy of the League. The Agency was very worried about this, as indeed was Abdullah. A highly secret meeting was arranged by Abraham Rutenberg of Naharayim. On 12 May, Meyerson, disguised as an Arab woman, went to talk to Abdullah in a last-minute attempt to avoid open war between them. Abdullah made it clear that, as protector of the Palestinians, he could not abandon them. Given Jewish military aggression he could not adhere to his earlier promises. There was no compromise possible. Meyerson reported to the Agency:

We met in friendship. He looked troubled and his face was distraught. He did not deny that there had been talks and understanding between us on a mutually acceptable arrangement, namely, that he would take over the Arab area, but now he is only one among five. This was his proposal: a united country with autonomy for the Jewish area. After one year this would become one country under his rule.

Meyerson, of course, had to reject this.[25] The era of good relations seemed to be over for good. On 15 May, the Legion invaded Palestine.

From then until the armistice of 1949 Abdullah was nominally fighting as part of the Arab League against the Israelis.[26] At times the fighting was in earnest; but by contrast with the other Arab states, Transjordan's objectives were tightly limited. Abdullah wanted to retain as much as possible of the Arab parts of Palestine that his Legion had occupied, and was always prepared to do a deal with the Jews to achieve this. On several occasions his agents discussed possibilities confidentially with Israeli agents.[27] Gelber summarizes the relationship as follows.

Sasson's two meetings with Abdullah in August 1946 had resulted in an unwritten agreement to partition Palestine between the future Jewish state and Transjordan. This understanding constituted the basis for further contacts between both sides until Abdullah joined the Arab coalition and invaded Palestine on 15 May 1948. Even then the King was careful that his army should not cross the frontiers of the Jewish state. With one exception (the raid on kibbutz Gezer on 10 June 1948) all the then encounters between the Arab Legion and the Israel Defence Forces took place within the area intended for the Palestine

25 Gelber, *Jewish–Transjordanian Relations*, 281.   26 See ch. 5 for details of the war.
27 The details of these contacts are in Shlaim, *Politics of Partition*, chs. 10–19.

Arab state or within the Jerusalem enclave which was supposed to be international and which was not included in the agreement.[28]

This conclusion is fully borne out in Shlaim's *Collusion Across the Jordan*. In his own devious way, Abdullah squared the circle between his Arab nationalist obligations and his need to propitiate the Zionists.

3. TRANSJORDAN, ISRAEL, THE ARAB LEAGUE, AND BRITAIN, 1948–1956

In April 1949, Jordan (as Transjordan was called in the new constitution of 1947) signed an armistice with Israel after very long secret negotiations. The effect was an informal recognition by the only power capable of accepting or rejecting Jordan's occupation of what came to be known as the West Bank. The Arab League resolutely refused to accept this, maintaining the fiction of an All-Palestinian government led by Amin al-Husayni based in Gaza. To offset this threat and acquire some legitimacy for his occupation of eastern Palestine, Abdullah held two congresses to mobilize Palestinian Arab opinion in his favour. The first, in Amman on 1 October, was a relatively small affair, but that on 1 December in Jericho consisted of some 3,000 Arab notables, many compelled to attend by the army. The congress proved difficult to handle and resolutions were passed in favour of a united Palestine under Abdullah as King. Eventually the published resolutions were drawn up by a rump committee which declared that the congress had recognized a united 'Arab Hashemite Kingdom', with Abdullah as King. A royal decree of 6 January 1949 incorporated the occupied area into Transjordan, at least in Jordanian law. This was the state that existed until 1967. It was, however, a precarious kingdom. The West Bank (as the area west of the river Jordan came to be called) was not mentioned in the Jordan–Israel armistice of April 1949. Nor would the Arab League formally recognize the annexation: the furthest it would go was to accept annexation as 'a practical consideration' and for Abdullah to 'hold this part as a trust until a final settlement of the Palestine question [was] realised . . .'.[29] Hence Abdullah's rule there remained ad hoc rather than *de jure*.

The incorporation can be seen in two ways. On the positive side, it partially fulfilled Abdullah's territorial ambitions. It brought into his kingdom a very large number of Palestinians with education and technical skills it had not possessed. It increased Jordan's weight in the outside world, and made it seem more significant to Britain as its main external supporter. On the other hand, expansion changed the nature of the old Jordanian state and created fundamental problems for its regime. It has been estimated that some 518,488 refugees from the Israeli-occupied areas of Palestine had gone to the West Bank and Jordan (about 100,000 to Transjordan). They settled, mainly in relief camps, among the 433,000 natives of the West Bank

[28] Gelber, *Jewish–Transjordanian Relations*, 283.   [29] Quoted Nevo, *King Abdallah*, 198.

and 476,000 Transjordanians. This caused serious social and financial problems, softened by United Nations funds and organizations. More serious were the political problems. Early in 1949 Abdullah tried to sort some of these out. In February 1949 he offered Jordanian citizenship to all Arab Palestinians, who would otherwise have been stateless. This also, of course, gave them political and legal rights in his kingdom. In March he set up a civil government under a governor in the West Bank to replace the previous military government. In May he eliminated the various barriers to goods and vehicles between the East and West Banks. He also then put three Palestinians in his cabinet. In December, Abdullah announced that he had taken over all the rights and obligations Britain had held in Palestine under the mandate. At the beginning of 1950, preparations began for elections to a united parliament which took place in April 1950, still under the old two-stage process. The total number of members of parliament was increased; all males over 18 could vote in the first stage; but only half the total number of seats was allocated to the West Bank, though it contained twice the total population of the East Bank. This was an obvious indication that Abdullah saw the danger of the situation. It was clear that the West Bankers in general were much more hostile to Israel, the United States, and Britain than most Transjordanians. They were also more radically Arab Nationalist. Even by 1950, there were cells of the newly developing Arab nationalist parties in Syria operating in Transjordan, notably the Baath Arab Socialist Party of Damascus. Moreover, most West Bankers disliked the power of the Arab Legion, now expanded, the main agent of royal control, whose main front-line troops were beduin. The new breed of politicians wanted far more influence on government than was traditional in Transjordan, where parliament traditionally had very little control over the king's government.

It is impossible to predict how Abdullah might have dealt with this very difficult situation. In the event he was shot by an Arab gunman when on a visit to Jerusalem in July 1951. The motives for the killing remain obscure, and were not elucidated by the elaborate trial of those accused of plotting it. The important question was whether this quasi-state, constructed personally by Abdullah over a period of thirty years, could survive him. For some time this was unclear. There was uncertainty about the royal succession, since the elder son, Talal, was thought to be mentally unstable, and his younger brother, Nayif, unsatisfactory. It was at this point that what Satloff calls 'the king's men', the core of the old regime, swung into action, led by Kirkbride, who was recalled from leave in Britain to handle the crisis, but retired later that year. A new government was formed under Tawfiq al-Huda. Talal was declared fit to rule, and was brought back from a sanatorium in Switzerland so as to thwart the ambitions of both Nayif and the Iraqi branch of the Hashemite family. This implied a collective regime of top notables who expected to handle Talal as a *roi fainéant*. This lasted until August 1952, when parliament declared him deposed and he was sent into exile, first in Egypt, then for the rest of his life in Istanbul. A regency council was set up until Talal's son, Husayn, came of age in May 1953.

So far, the transition from the autocracy of Abdullah to a collective regime had gone remarkably smoothly. Al-Huda inherited the autocratic approach of Abdullah. He used the Legion to deal with any resistance, manipulated elections, and imprisoned opponents without trial. But political trouble was brewing. The new constitution of 1952 for the first time made the government responsible to parliament. An adverse vote by two-thirds of the lower house (the upper house was nominated) could force a government to resign. Moreover, Kirkbride's successor as Ambassador, as the one-time Resident became after 1946, lacked Kirkbride's very long experience of Jordanian affairs: he had, after all, been there even before Abdullah. With him British influence also declined. The treaty, renewed in 1948, and the British military presence continued, along with the subsidy. In London there were contrasting views as to the future British role in Jordan. The army wanted more British troops there as part of its general Middle Eastern strategy. On the other hand the Foreign Office wanted to reduce them because of their bad effect on Britain's relations with the Arab League states. For its part the Amman government no longer regarded itself as part of the British imperial defence system. The treaty of 1948 was now seen as a defence of Transjordan (since the treaty did not apply to the West Bank) against an Israeli attack: the British had already blocked a threatening Israeli move towards Aqaba. Thus, while, as seen from London, Jordan remained a British quasi-dependency, integral to its broader Middle Eastern defence and political system, and relying almost entirely on the British subsidy to maintain its Legion, in Amman Britain was no longer seen as a virtual metropolis.

In any case the ideological high ground was now being taken by Egypt, particularly after the military coup of 1952, and by nationalist politicians in Syria. The so-called 'liberal experiment' of 1954, when the then Prime Minister, Fawzi al-Mulqi, for the first time allowed elections to a new parliament to be conducted with virtually no governmental intervention, produced a lower house which reflected very strong Baath and pan-Arab influences and was hostile to the monarchy: parliament had rapidly to be suspended. Fawzi was sacked and replaced by al-Huda, representing the old guard of 'king's men', and the traditional system of political manipulation. New elections in 1954 were accompanied by riots. Every possible technique was used to produce a docile parliament, including tactical distribution of the Legion to swing elections. They succeeded, but the public mood was very hostile to the regime. By 1954 Nasser, now dominant in Egypt, saw Jordan as a dangerous element of the British position in the Middle East, and the Cairo radio channel, 'Voice of the Arabs', broadcast constant attacks on the Hashemite regime, both there and in Iraq.

It was in 1954 also that the future of Jordan, and in particular its connection with Britain, became tied in with Anglo-Egyptian negotiations over the future of the Suez canal base and the Anglo-Egyptian Sudan, and the parallel British attempt to build up the 'northern tier' alliance that was formalized in the Baghdad Pact. The canal base issue was resolved in July 1954, the last British troops leaving it in March 1956. But the other issue now became critical. An agreement between Turkey and Pakistan reached in 1954 escalated as Iraq, Iran, and Britain all joined the agreement in February 1955. For Iraq, as was seen in Chapter 3, this meant the end of the British presence and the abrogation of its rights there. The British were keen that Jordan should join the pact, and the outcome would be decisive for the future of the Anglo-Jordanian connection and possibly also of the Hashemite monarchy.

For the young and inexperienced Husayn this proved a major turning point. Early in 1955, al-Huda, as Prime Minister, was keen to join. Husayn at that stage was not, and in May, al-Huda was dismissed. But after the notorious Czech arms deal by Nasser in September and under a hail of vituperative attacks by 'Voice of the Arabs', he came round to favouring it, along with his new Prime Minister, Said al-Mufti, an East Bank Circassian and a 'king's man'. Jordanian opinion was bitterly divided. The cabinet was split, members from the West Bank strongly opposed. Most Palestinians on both Banks were violently hostile. The struggle now lay between Britain, Nasser, and the other Arab League states. The British, still determined late in 1955 to sustain their Middle East military and diplomatic position, sent General Templer, the hero of the Malayan emergency, to persuade Jordan to join the pact. His main lever was an offer to increase the subsidy from £10 million in 1955 to £16.5 million in 1956 and thereafter £12.5 million. But bribery was not enough. Templer's style was too abrasive and he alienated much potentially pro-British opinion. His visit resulted in violent riots on both sides of the Jordan, suppressed by the Legion, but a serious warning to Husayn. It proved one of the worst tactical blunders in British treatment of a Middle Eastern ally. It reflected British underestimation of the strength of pan-Arab feeling and the force of Cairo's influence.

For Husayn this was a critical moment. He changed his prime ministers several times, eventually appointing the veteran Samir al-Rifai on 8 January 1956. Jordan refused to sign the Baghdad Pact, after which Cairo dropped its vituperative radio campaign and the Saudis withdrew their threat to occupy Aqaba. Husayn appears at this point to have decided to wind up the British connection as the price of his survival. This was done by stages. The first was to dismiss Glubb as commander of the Legion. The underlying reasons for this remain obscure. Husayn had not the same close relationship with Glubb that Abdullah had had, and his presence, and that of the many British officers of the Legion, was a constant stimulus to popular resentment. There may also have been some pressure from the group of 'Free Officers' (aping the Egyptian group before the coup of 1952) whom Husayn met while at Sandhurst in 1952. There were more immediate differences of opinion. Glubb was opposing the transfer of the police force from the Legion to the Ministry of Interior. He had demanded the dismissal of some 20 Arab officers on the ground that they were dabbling in politics: the Legion was then the least politicized military force in the Middle East. Husayn had committed Jordan to attack

Israel if Egypt and Syria did so, and Glubb's position on this was suspect. Whatever the reasons, the dismissal indicated that Husayn was now a clever politician and master in his own house. Glubb's contract was due to expire on 31 March 1956. Instead, to make a populist point, he was dismissed on 1 March and given 24 hours to clear out. The remaining British officers in the Legion left later in 1956.

Yet the close connection with Britain remained, and the subsidy was crucial for Jordan's survival. The nine months after March 1956 were serious for Jordan. The quality of the Legion deteriorated as inexperienced Arab officers took over and many beduin left in disgust at being controlled by townsmen, who were increasingly politicized and depended on their constituency networks for power. The elections of October were uniquely unmanaged by the government, and the National Socialist Party (NSP) emerged as the largest single group. Sulayman al-Nabulsi was their leader and, reflecting the new character of Jordanian politics, Husayn made him Prime Minister. Al-Nabulsi was not particularly socialist, but he and his party were strongly anti-western Arab nationalists who wanted close links with Egypt and Syria. They demanded abrogation of the British treaty. Moreover they were anxious to reduce Husayn to the role of a limited constitutional monarch. The party's policy statement was announced without having been previously agreed with Husayn.

By now Husayn had acquired some experience and political finesse. To save the monarchy he had to go with the tide for the moment. In October 1956 Jordan joined the Egyptian–Syrian military pact and avoided involvement in the Anglo-French–Israeli attack on the canal. But the problem of the subsidy remained. On 19 January 1957 Jordan signed the Arab Solidarity Agreement with Egypt, Syria, and Saudi Arabia, part of whose conditions was that these three states would together replace the British subsidy of £12.5 million for ten years. But Husayn rightly distrusted this promise: in the event only the Saudis ever paid up. Even before the Agreement was signed he had asked informally whether the United States, following the announcement of the Eisenhower Doctrine of containing communism in the Middle East on 5 January 1957 (adopted by Congress on 7 March 1957), would provide financial support.

With this double expectation, Husayn felt able to end the British relationship. Negotiations, initiated on the formal request of the new British Ambassador, Charles Johnson, began on 4 February and were completed on 13 March. There were no serious problems. The British agreed to withdraw all their forces from Jordan (as they had done from Iraq in 1955) within six months (in fact some were still there in 1957). Jordan agreed to pay £4.25 million over six years for stores and facilities (this was never paid). Britain exonerated Jordan from £1.5 million of debts relating to the 1948 war. The only significant survival was the British defence obligation, which, as will be seen below, was acted on in 1958 by landing airborne British troops at Amman when Husayn faced a possible domestic coup, thought to be backed by the newly formed United Arab Republic of Egypt and

Syria. In that year of great danger for the Hashemite monarchy, moreover, British officers were brought back to help train the Legion.[30]

The abrogation of the treaty in 1957, however, marked the formal end of the British connection. Severance was made possible by the promise, initially, of Arab subsidies, and when these failed fully to materialize, by American subsidies. In this sense the United States had taken over Britain's role. But the underlying reason for the break was Husayn's realization early in 1957 that overt links with the west were a serious threat to the survival of his dynasty. He had to appear to be a fervent pan-Arabist: moreover, since the Egypt–Syria axis was then closely related to the USSR, on 2 April Husayn, despite his generally anti-communist stance designed to win American support, agreed to a link with Moscow: it never came to anything. Ultimately all this stemmed from the incorporation of the West Bank. The relatively small and generally very loyal Transjordan people had been swamped by Palestinians who regarded the West, and particularly the United States, as the source of their misfortunes, and were determined to align Jordan with Nasser's Egypt and the Baath regime in Syria. For many of them the Hashemite regime was a main obstacle. Husayn's tactic in 1956–7 was to adopt the guise of a genuine Arab patriot and so ride out the storm. By 10 April 1957 he appears to have thought that the crisis was over. He then dismissed the al-Nabulsi government, perhaps because it had produced a list of leading officials thought to be hostile to the government, most of whom were Hashemite loyalists, for retirement, possibly also because it was thought to be connected with a short-lived blockade of Amman by the 5th Armoured Car Brigade, under Captain Nadhir Rashid.

But the crisis was not yet over.[31] A Syrian army brigade was then at Irbid, presumably ready to strike if a coup took place. On 13 April the army commander, Ali Abnu Nawar, demanded that NSP member, Nabib al-Nimr be appointed Prime Minister. To gain time Husayn agreed and appointed an acceptable cabinet. The same day what may have been an attempted coup was led by the same Captain Nadhir Rashid, based at the Zerqa barracks near Amman. This was strongly opposed by the beduin troops, led by their NCOs. Husayn appeared and rallied his supporters. If there were plans for a coup, which is uncertain, they were poorly planned. Satloff suggests that there were three elements involved with different objectives: junior officers who may have planned to attack the palace; senior officers allied with radical politicians who wanted to coerce the king into political submission; and the beduin, who took the initiative against their own officers before Husayn appeared. In any case the crisis justified Husayn in sacking al-Nimr and appointing Dr Husayn Fakhri al-Khalidi, ex-mayor of Jerusalem, a man with equally impeccable nationalist credentials, as Prime Minister on 15 April. The reaction came on 22 April, when the nationalists held a 'Patriotic Congress' at

---

[30] For a detailed account of the British intervention and its diplomatic circumstances see Wm R. Louis, 'Britain and the Crisis of 1958', in Louis and Owen (eds.), *A Revolutionary Year*, 61–76.

[31] For detailed accounts of the crisis period 1947–8 see Satloff, *From Abdullah to Hussein*, chs. 9 and 10; Dann, *King Hussein and the Challenge of Arab Radicalism*, chs. 3–8.

Nablus, always the centre of Palestinian Arab radicalism since the 1930s. This demanded federation with Egypt and Syria, full application of the liberal 1952 constitution, the dismissal of officials hostile to the party, and a general strike to be held on 24 April. That day al-Khalidi was dismissed. On 25 April martial law (politely called 'emergency administration') was declared.

But before that, Husayn had taken precautionary measures. Starting on 14 April the army command was purged and the Chief of Staff went to Damascus and defected. On 24 April members of the old loyalist political corps were summoned to the palace to plan operations. A curfew was imposed in all the main towns, policed by beduin troops. On 26 April loyalists were appointed to six military governorships. On 28 April parliament was prorogued. That day the United States promised a $10 million subsidy to add to the Saudis' £2.5 million and a grant of $250,000. Later in May Husayn asked for, and got, the withdrawal of the Syrian troops, though the final break with Egypt and Syria did not occur until July 1958.

Husayn had survived without external help, despite the danger from the Syrians and Egyptians. There were still substantial numbers of British troops in the country—they did not finally leave until July 1957—but they were not asked to take any action. The British government quietly observed and approved Husayn's actions. Thus the most significant aspect of this critical period was that Husayn and his loyalist supporters, particularly the beduin troops of the Legion, had solved their own problems. For Jordan, 1957 can be compared with 1920, when Abdullah had arrived uninvited to establish his own dynasty there, and, as he hoped, also in Syria. But, as in 1921, Jordan had to pay a price. Husayn's action to free himself from the dominance of his own radical Palestinian nationalists backed by the pan-Arabists in Egypt and Syria had left him effectively, and dangerously, dependent on America and Britain. This was primarily for money—the Americans increased their subsidy to $30 million in May 1957 and also provided military equipment—but also for military action in emergency. Indeed, Jordan now depended largely on the new American Middle Eastern strategy. When the United Arab Republic was formed in February 1958, Britain and America began to plan military action should the UAR attack Jordan, now seen as an important element in the western position in the Middle East, though Amman did not know of this. Husayn heard of the planned army plot of July 1958 from Washington, which heard of it from the usual impeccable Israeli sources. The plot was to assassinate Husayn in conjunction with UAR intervention and to join Jordan to the UAR. Husayn initially appealed to his Hashemite relations in Baghdad, and, ironically, it was the 20th Iraqi brigade that was on its way to help him that chose instead to kill the Hashemites and Nuri as-Said and set up a republic. That left Husayn isolated. He appealed to the United States and Britain as a threatened nation under the United Nations Covenant. United States marines duly arrived in Lebanon, and British paratroopers, along with American planes carrying oil, went to Amman, having obtained Israeli permission to over-fly its territory. On 21 August the United Nations General Assembly passed a resolution calling on all Arab states, without name, to 'abstain from any action calculated to change established systems of government'. There was no invasion and no assassination.

The British troops left in November 1958, along with the American marines. Husayn was once again on his own, though now dependent on American aid. Jordan's future lay in its relations with the Arab states and Israel. Relations with his still revolutionary Palestinian subjects remained tense, but despite assassination attempts, Husayn survived. In August 1965 he made a treaty with the Saudi government, a milestone in the relations between the Hashemite and Saudi families. By 1966 relations with Egypt and Syria were deteriorating, partly due to Husayn's refusal to allow the newly established Palestine Liberation Organization to raise taxes in the West Bank. Yet in 1967 he decided to ally with the League states. The overt reason was the Israeli attack on Samu (south of Hebron) in retaliation for the death of three Israeli soldiers from land mines. This certainly infuriated Husayn, but it remains unclear why he should have joined the ill-fated attempt to drive the Jews out of Palestine. It may have been a sense of obligation to his fellow Arabs. Was it because he was afraid of being swept away by the tide of Palestinian fury if he abstained? He may have been over-impressed by Egyptian claims to be invulnerable. It is even conceivable that he was confident of retaining his East Bank, and felt that his dynasty would be safer without the West Bank. Abdullah had felt obliged to ally with the other Arabs in 1948, but then he had his informal guarantee from the Jews that if he did not attack them, they would not attack him. In 1967 Husayn had no such safety net. Nor was Britain prepared or indeed able to help. In two days the Israelis occupied the whole West Bank that Abdullah had so carefully protected. Jordan was now once again Transjordan.

Yet the Hashemite dynasty survived into the twenty-first century. Until 1956 it did so mainly because the British backed it, thereafter because the Americans did. But neither could or would have saved it from its own internal enemies, just as they did not save the Hashemite dynasty in Iraq. Hashemite rule survived because of the determination and flexibility of Abdullah and Husayn in the face of domestic conflict and international threat, and also because the Israelis, until 1967, kept to their agreements. But ultimately Jordan survived because of the quality and loyalty of the Arab Legion, which, alone among Near Eastern Arab armies, remained for the most part loyal to the monarchy. That tradition of military loyalty may well have been the greatest gift of the British to Jordan.

7

Syria and the French, 1918–1946

There are two major questions central to any study of the French mandate in Syria (and also of Lebanon) between 1918 and 1946.

First, why were the French so determined to get political control over what they initially described as 'la Syrie intégrale', and why, by contrast with the British in Iraq, did they never voluntarily concede independence to it?

Second, why, despite the fact that Syria was the centre of Arab nationalism before 1914 and was the first Arab territory to declare itself an independent state between 1918 and 1920, did it prove a relatively docile French dependency for so long?

The answer to the first of these questions lies in the labyrinthine structure of French domestic politics and interest groups before and after 1918: ironically the latter included the same Lyon silk manufacturers who had worked for annexation of Tonkin in the 1880s. It was these who in each case enabled a small minority of activists to seduce the Republic into undertaking, and later refusing to give up, these unrewarding imperialist strategies. To investigate this involves examining in more detail the complexities of French diplomacy before 1918 and then the evolution of political and administrative hierarchies which came to have a vested interest in continuing the mandate indefinitely.

The answer to the second question lies in the complexities of the Syrian social structure, which alone made it possible for the French to make some form of compromise with the social elite of notables, who in turn provided sufficient collaboration to make the alien regime viable. It will therefore be necessary to examine the position of the Syrian notables and how they saw their interests under the French regime.

Both questions must be examined in detail. Although in Chapter 3 the social structure of Iraq was examined first, here French policy will take first place. The reason is that in Syria the French initially knew very little about the society with which they had to deal and their strategies were evolved on the basis of their earlier colonial traditions and prejudices. It was only after nearly a decade that they started to remould political structures to take account of the specifics of Syrian society, and more particularly of its notables.

1. THE FRENCH IN SYRIA: AIMS AND METHODS

The motives for French imperial expansion from the 1870s have been much debated and studied. The general consensus appears to be that, although extremely complex, it stemmed largely from reaction to defeat by Prussia in 1870–1, which stimulated nationalists to look for compensation overseas, coupled with a longer-running resentment that the British had pre-empted France's imperial role between the 1750s and 1850s. Trafalgar was always a deep wound in national pride. Thus the search for national prestige, rather than for concrete economic or strategic benefits, fuelled by jealousy of the continuing expansion of the British empire and, after 1880, also that of Germany, was the underlying motive for French expansion.[1] This, of course, is a gross over-simplification. There were many interest groups in France which either pressed for colonial annexations or exploited and argued for them once annexed. These included the navy, the main source of annexation in the east and Pacific, the army, which flourished on colonial campaigns in time of European peace, missionary societies, and special economic interests, such as the Marseille shipping and trading firms and the Lyon silk weavers. But perhaps the most vociferous and typically French drive for colonies came from nationalist societies, of which the Société de Géographie (founded in 1821) was the pioneer. As will be seen, much of the demand for control over parts of the Ottoman empire in the early twentieth century came from comparable pressure groups with specific objectives, usually very small in number but influential because their members were at or near the seat of political power.

The potential influence of such pressure groups was greatly increased by the structures of French public life.[2] Parliament had little part in the making of foreign policy and was seldom told of even major alliances, such as that with Russia in 1894. It was highly fragmented and ministries usually lasted for short periods. It was rare for any one politician to hold office for more than a few months, though some did: thus Stephen Pichon was Foreign Minister 1906–11 and again in 1912–13 and 1917–20. This gave huge power to the bureaucracy, but that also was fragmented. Colonial affairs were divided between the Quai d'Orsay (Foreign Office), the War Office, the Ministry of Marine, and the relatively new Colonial Office, which was very much a junior party in the period before 1918 and badly organized. Each had its own fiefdoms: thus Algeria was an army matter, while the Middle East came under the Foreign Office. The nearest French public life came

[1] This, at least, is the argument of Henri Brunschwig, doyen of French imperial historians in the mid-twentieth century, in *French Colonialism 1871–1914: Myths and Realities* (1960; English edn. London, 1966).

[2] There is an excellent analysis of the way in which the armed forces could obtain governmental approval and financial support for overseas expansion in S. Kanya-Forstner, *The Conquest of the Western Sudan: A Study in French Military Imperialism* (Cambridge, 1969). See also R. Girault, *Diplomatie européenne et impérialismes.* I. *1871–1914* (Paris, 1979), ch. 1.

to possessing a body of continuous thinking on imperial (as other) matters, lay in the permanent officials of the major departments, who were the embodiment of the Robinson–Gallagher concept of 'the official mind'. Given the weakness of most ministries and the ignorance of the majority of ministers, these men could in effect make policy. Moreover, if they became attached to a particular line of policy, here relating to the future of the Ottoman empire, they could virtually decide strategy. If, moreover, such men were personally attached to specialized pressure groups, either though conviction or interest, they could act as the medium through which otherwise improbable or even irrational policies became those of the Republic. It is along these lines that it seems necessary to explain the otherwise inexplicable French drive into the Near East after 1914.[3]

The largest pressure group on imperial affairs in the early twentieth century was the Parti Colonial, founded in 1894 on a broadly nationalistic platform. It acted as an umbrella organization for a considerable number (perhaps fifty) of smaller, more specialized groups. Among these were several with scientific interests in the Middle East. The most important was the Comité de l'Asie Française (CAF), whose members included Philippe Bertelot, Robert de Caix, François Georges-Picot, Jean Gout, and Pierre de Magerie. Other influential societies included the Comité de l'Orient (CO, to which Pichon belonged), and the Comité de Défense des Intérêts en Orient (CDIO). Originally much of the interest of these societies had lain in the Far East; but by 1914 it was clear that little more could be achieved there. In 1914 colonial enthusiasts were therefore ready to concentrate on Africa, fuelled by success in Morocco in 1911, which to some extent dispelled the anger over Fashoda, aiming to take over German territories in both West and East Africa. The entrance of the Ottomans into the war provided another potentially fertile field for their expansionist efforts in the Near East.

France had, in fact, very limited established interests in the Ottoman empire. The main and powerful stake was cultural and religious. There was a close connection between the Catholic church in France and the Maronites of Mount Lebanon: France had been party to the international agreement on the future of the Mountain in 1861. There were French Catholic missions and schools there and in Syria which aimed to indoctrinate pupils with French language and culture.[4] This was central to the much-discussed French 'civilizing mission', there as well as in the French overseas empire. This influence was strong long before France acquired its mandates, and was to survive the end of its political control there into the twenty-first century. The French, moreover, had the right to protect Catholics in Palestine. They had been one of the first European states to establish treaty relations with the Ottomans: they had established trading rights under the

---

[3] Much of the following argument is based on C. M. Andrew and A. S. Kanya-Forstner, *France Overseas: The Great War and the Climax of French Imperial Expansion* (London, 1981).

[4] In the nineteenth century, France was competing with Russia in missionary and educational work in Syria, Lebanon, and Palestine and this had established an important sense of possession among French Catholics in rivalry with Russian Orthodox missions.

Capitulations as early as 1535. France had only some 13 per cent of Ottoman foreign trade in 1914 but had subscribed 60 per cent of the Turkish public debt (one reason why after 1918 France demanded servicing of the debt by the Turkish state and its one-time Arabian possessions) and had provided some 40 per cent of private capital investments in the empire. France had financed several of the railways in the Palestine area and was involved in financing the projected Berlin to Baghdad railway. France was an important market for Lebanese silk. All this convinced many French imperialists that France had a prior claim on Syria and Lebanon should they come onto the market. On the other hand, it is arguable that French influence was on the decline by 1914. The Catholic protectorate had become less significant after 1904 and the break with the Vatican over French anti-clerical legislation, and there was a drop in the number and influence of French schools and missions.[5]

This in fact stimulated rather than depressed interest among the specialist pressure groups. From about 1911 there was an increasing demand among these circles for a greater French influence in the Ottoman empire. Within the CAF there was fear that the Lebanese would concede France's privileged position under pressure from the Young Turks and that the British and Americans were gaining influence in Beirut. These fears led to the creation of the CDIFO in 1911: it was absorbed into the CAF in 1913. Since 1908 the Amis de l'Orient, founded by the Maronite *émigré* Shukri Ghanem and the Greek Melchite Georges Samné from Damascus, had been active in Paris. Mostly consisting of Syrian and Lebanese *émigrés*, it had attracted some French colonialists, including Georges Leygues, Lucien Hubert, and Etienne Flandin, the two latter becoming leaders of the 'Syrian Party' in Paris after 1914. In 1912 Ghanem founded the Comité de l'Orient to press for French interests in Lebanon. Ghanem was a romantic Arabist and play-writer who had great influence with the Quai d'Orsay. But in fact he was largely out of touch with contemporary Arab opinion in Syria, which was better represented by al-Fatat. When a Lebanese separatist movement arose in 1912 in response to the Balkan wars, the French government accepted that France might have to provide support. There was also fear of British interference in Lebanon and Syria; but in 1912 Sir Edward Grey, as Foreign Secretary, promised that this would not happen.

With this assurance French policy in 1914 was to postpone the break-up of the Ottoman empire as long as possible, while retaining French claims to primacy in Syria as a sphere of influence. The government backed the Arab Congress held in Paris in 1913 which demanded devolution in the Arab countries. When it became clear that Istanbul would not honour the promises made to the Congress, the Quai d'Orsay's reaction was that France must not be directly involved. Good relations with the Porte were more important. This led to the Franco-Turkish

---

[5] See W. I. Shorrock, *French Imperialism in the Middle East: The Failure of Policy in Syria and Lebanon 1900–1914* (Madison, 1976).

agreement of April 1914 which virtually determined the future spheres of influence in the Near East. In fact, Germany had got the lion's share: France had even had to concede German control over Alexandretta, essential for the Baghdad railway project. Thus in 1914 French policy on the future of the Ottoman empire was contradictory. On the one hand, official policy was to continue to support the empire. On the other hand, strong pressures existed for French claims to Syria. Even Bompard, French Ambassador in Istanbul, who believed that French control over Syria would cause more trouble than it was worth, accepted that France would not be able to accept the loss of prestige if the Ottoman empire was partitioned and Syria went to another power, presumably Britain.

Once war was declared with the Ottomans in November 1914, these conflicting French objectives had to be made compatible. The French expansionists were still divided. Théophile Delcassé, as Foreign Minister, though in general terms an imperialist and expansionist, was opposed to claiming Syria for France. The CAF also opposed formal partition of the empire, preferring division into spheres of influence. But Etienne Flandin and Georges Leygues starting planning for partition and French control over the whole of Syria. In this they were supported by the French minister in Cairo, Albert Defrance, who was determined to block the known plan hatched there by Kitchener and Storrs for British dominance in the Red Sea. Indeed, from this time on the main French aim in the Middle East was to prevent Britain from taking Syria, Lebanon, and Palestine, and possibly also northern Iraq, which was closely connected with Syria and had oil prospects. The French problem was that, over-extended on the western front in France, they could never muster sufficient military forces to take a dominant role in any part of the Middle East until 1920; nor was the French navy capable of large-scale activity. Thus the French were furious that the British and Dominion forces predominated in the Gallipoli campaign of 1915–16. Yet in November 1914, once the Marne battle front was stabilized, activists in France, led by Flandin in the Senate and Leygues in the Chamber, along with some leading politicians such as Alexandre Millerand, then Minister of War, and from 1920 Prime Minister, hatched a plot to send a French expedition to Syria. Delcassé would have none of it: but, as Andrew and Kanya-Forstner comment, 'The imperial ambitions of Britain and the southern dominions [*sic*] thus provided the colonial party with the unanswerable argument of national prestige to buttress their otherwise unappealing expansionist demands.'[6]

The French were therefore left with diplomacy as their only weapon, based on the fact that the British would be very reluctant to strain the entente now that war was on. Their strategy was to obtain formal commitments from Britain, and also Russia, on the assumption that the Ottoman empire would be divided once the Allies had defeated it. In February 1915 Grey and Delcassé agreed informally that France would have a prior claim to Syria and Alexandretta, though Delcassé

---

[6] Andrew and Kanya-Forstner, *France Overseas*, 70.

thought only of spheres of influence. The serious planning for partition was started in March 1915 by the Russians, who feared they might lose the prospect of gaining Istanbul and the Straits if the planned Gallipoli invasion was successful and demanded that these be allocated to them. Grey accepted the demand in principle provided British objectives were achieved. Delcassé was initially horrified by the demand: he wanted Russia to have merely a sphere of influence there. He eventually accepted the Russian demand on condition that France had a sphere of influence in Syria 'including the promise of the gulf of Alexandretta and Cilicia to the Tauris mountains': that is, broadly the colonial activists' aim of 'la Syrie intégrale'. Characteristically of French public life, he told the French cabinet only what Russia had demanded and commented that France had to accept it because the British had done so. The cabinet, let alone the French parliament, never saw the reply to Russia.

Delcassé had gone so far partly because the British had done so, to ensure that the Russians remained in the war, but also to placate the vociferous colonial activists. These, led by members of the CAF and particularly Georges-Picot (hereafter Picot), now campaigned strongly in parliament and the press for French control, not merely a sphere of influence over the whole of Syria, including Palestine. In May 1915 parliament accepted a report prepared by Flandin which (improbably) maintained that Syria was essential for the defence of the Maghreb, and that it was already effectively French in language and culture. This reflected the peculiarity of the whole French position on Syria and the Middle East. Few of those involved (excepting Picot) had any direct experience of the Near East and had grossly exaggerated conceptions of its wealth and of Arab attitudes to France. The Syria they wanted was partly mythical: their primary aim to express the glory of the Republic and to fend off assumed British ambitions, about which many in France were paranoid. But it was on this flimsy basis that Picot, assigned to London to advise Cambon as Ambassador, persuaded him to agree that Picot should negotiate the partition of the Middle East with Britain.

The course of those negotiations was outlined in Chapter 2. The outcome was the formal (though secret) ratification of the Sykes–Picot Agreement on 15 and 16 May 1916. But these were only preliminary arrangements: what France actually got was dependent on the fortunes of war and her ability to maintain her claims in later negotiations. The primary aim of colonial activists now became control of the whole of 'la Syrie intégrale'. They therefore concentrated on propaganda and continuous pressure on successive French governments. This, indeed, became the main function of the many closely interrelated pressure groups that were formed between 1916 and 1918. Their main problem was that Clemenceau was not interested in colonies: for him the Rhine was the only thing that really mattered. In November 1917 he had told Lloyd George that 'he did not want Syria for France', but that he would accept a protectorate there if it was offered to 'please some reactionaries'.[7] He was prepared to give Britain a free hand to negotiate with

---

[7] Ibid. 151.

Turkey over peace terms. This indeed culminated in his secret verbal agreement with Lloyd George in December 1918 by which Britain was to get mandates over Palestine and Mosul in return for France getting a free hand in Syria and Cilicia. Typically of the way diplomacy was then being carried on, neither the French or British Foreign Offices was consulted or informed about this critical deal, which effectively destroyed the Sykes–Picot Agreement. Paradoxically, by that time Clemenceau had recognized that, even if he did not want Syria or Palestine, both the British and many of his own French politicians did. Hence in 1919–20 he cynically used concessions in the Middle East to get his way on other issues in negotiation with Britain.

But from the standpoint of the French colonial activists, backed only by their own supporters, Lyon, Marseille, and the French Catholic church, Clemenceau had failed the Republic by giving up Palestine and Mosul. It may be some indication of the extent to which their propaganda had penetrated French national conscious-ness that in January 1920 Clemenceau was defeated as a candidate for the Presidency and then resigned as Prime Minister, to be replaced by Millerand and his 'Bloc national'. The new government and parliament demonstrated a far greater interest in the empire as a whole and particularly in Syria. With Albert Sarraut, ex-Governor-General of Indo-China, as Minister for Colonies and strong representation of the colonial lobbies, the new government reflected a strong, though short-lived national belief that colonies would be the salvation of a country devastated by war. One result was much greater French determination in dealing with allies and also with nationalists. At the San Remo Congress in April 1920 the French insisted on getting mandates for Lebanon and Syria and a share in Mosul oil. Palestine was now a lost cause, though the French tried to insist on continuation of the Catholic protectorate. They lost, and also had to accept the Zionist clause in the Palestine mandate. Thus the dream of 'la Syrie intégrale' under French control died, and France was also later forced to concede Cilicia to the resurgent Turks under Mustafa Kemal.

But, shorn of its more grandiose elements, the French dream of a Middle Eastern empire had become a reality. This was the more surprising because France had done very little to obtain it. It was British, Dominion, and Indian troops, with limited support from Faysal's Northern Army, that had conquered Iraq, Palestine, and Syria. In 1919 the British still controlled all these areas. Two things safeguarded the French claims. Britain was determined to preserve the entente in Europe, even though Curzon and others now saw France as the main enemy in the Middle East. Above all, perhaps, by 1919 the British recognized that they lacked the resources to hold Syria and Lebanon, as well as Iraq and Palestine. By September 1919 Lloyd George had to acknowledge that there was a serious military over-stretch, now that demobilization was under way. He then decided to evacuate Syria in November, leaving it open whether the French stepped in or made a deal with Faysal as its governor under the military occupation. By that time he had also reduced the British subsidy to Faysal by 50 per cent as part of the British attempt to reduce military expenditure. This left the newly established Hashemite state of Syria poverty-stricken but, for the first time, without any external rulers: there were already French forces in Beirut, so Lebanon was prospectively under French control. It remained to see how France dealt with this situation.

The important thing is that, despite huge financial costs and the lack of sufficient military forces until Cilicia was settled in 1920, there was never any serious question of France not taking up its inheritance. The costs were indeed high: 50 million francs in 1919, 165 million in 1920 for the Quai d'Orsay alone, plus 525 million for the War Ministry's activities in Syria and Lebanon. The original civil estimates for 1921 soared to 1,200 million francs, but were pared down to 800 million. Syria was never to come cheap: it was estimated in 1936 that France had so far spent some 4 billion francs on the Syrian mandate.[8] Syria provided few benefits in return, except to specific groups such as the Lyon silk firms, the Marseille traders, army and navy officials, civil servants, shareholders in the railways, and religious organizations. The chief reward was status as a major European and Mediterranean power. This had been the objective of the minority of enthusiasts who had campaigned for Syria after 1914 and it remained the main reason for staying there. As Andrew and Kanya-Forstner summarized the point, 'For most colonials—and most Frenchmen—the most important issues at stake in the Middle East were the intangible considerations of national prestige and France's civilizing mission.'[9]

Even so, the French had to decide how to deal with their new possessions. Lebanon, which is examined in Chapter 8, was always seen as distinct from inland Syria: it had been so designated both in the Sykes–Picot Agreement and in the McMahon correspondence with Husayn in 1915. The French conception of 'Syria' had always been based on Mount Lebanon, with its dominant Maronite population, Catholic missions, western universities, and other institutions. It was also the only part of the new French empire that was predominantly in favour of French control. It would always be the main French power base, even though they complicated their position there by expanding Mount Lebanon to include Beirut, Sidon, Tyre, Tripoli, and the Biqa Valley, all predominantly Islamic and difficult to run in harness with the Maronite Mountain. But inland Syria was an altogether different question. Despite its significant Christian population it had few ties with France. It had no historic unity and contained large and potentially hostile minorities, such as the Alawites in the north and the Druzes in the south. In 1919–20 the French had no clear idea of the nature of this society, though the colonial enthusiasts had propagated the idea that its inhabitants would welcome French rule. What they knew of it came mostly from Catholic missions and from contacts with Greek Catholics in the Hawran and Jabal Druze. French consuls in Damascus were also very active, travelled a lot, and sent enthusistic reports of

<hr>

[8] Ibid. 228, 245.   [9] Ibid. 239.

Syrian attitudes. It was from this limited knowledge and these misconceptions that most of the problems of French rule over the next quarter of a century were to stem.

In 1919, when the French were at last able to muster sufficient forces in Lebanon to be able to contemplate positive action in Syria, they had essentially two main options. On the one hand they could accept the fact of the Syrian state set up under Faysal and base their control on some form of indirect rule. Alternatively they could establish some form of direct control, even though there might be some devolution of power to Syrians in subordinate units. The first of these options had been the choice of Clemenceau. Late in 1919 he had made a secret agreement with Faysal. This provided that France would accept and guarantee the independence of Syria as defined by the Paris Conference and as it was to be established by the San Remo Conference in April 1920. Syria would accept the French mandate, relying entirely on French military and economic help, and France would arrange Syria's foreign policy. Syria would recognize the independence of Lebanon under French mandate. The Druze of the Hawran would form a separate unit connected with Syria. Arabic would be the official language, though French would be taught in the schools. Damascus would become the capital. The High Commissioner would reside in Aleppo as 'the Representative of the Mandatory State'.

These conditions were remarkably similar to those imposed on Iraq by the British later in 1920, though the French had a ready-made Syrian ruler whereas the British had to construct one for Iraq. It is an interesting question whether this might have provided a working basis for French control over Syria. In the event it was made invalid by two things. First, Clemenceau was replaced in January 1920 by Millerand, whose government was far more interventionist. Second, when Faysal reported this confidential deal to his supporters in Damascus, al-Fatat, by then in full control, forced him to drop it. They made him summon back the Syrian Congress, which had met in July 1919, and on 7 March 1920 Congress declared the unconditional independence of Syria. The following day Faysal was reluctantly declared King of the 'United Syrian Kingdom', to include Palestine and the Lebanon. An official Syrian government was immediately set up in Damascus.

This was a challenge which the French could not fail to accept. General Gouraud, who arrived in Beirut late in December, did not know of Clemenceau's offer to Faysal, but, as a veteran of the Moroccan campaign, he had little sympathy with the pretensions of indigenous regimes. As early as 29 December 1919 he sent a telegram to the Quai d'Orsay which set out his views.[10] First,

The divisions of Syria, which should help us to organize it in a way that is both practical and favourable to our interests, are already very useful in containing the movement

---

[10] The material that follows is based on the chapter by W. Kawtharani, 'Le Grand-Leban et le project de la Confédération Syrienne d'après des documents français', in Y. M. Choueiri (ed.), *State and Society in Syria and Lebanon* (Exeter, 1993), 46–61. Translations are my own.

organized against us. It would be deplorable, both now and in the future, to efface these [divisions] within the unity of a Sharifian authority which in the eyes of the people incarnates their hostility towards us and which sees an understanding with us merely as a temporary contrivance in contradiction of the principles on which it was based....

Syria itself does not force us to make any concessions. The Sharifian government... is for us no more than useless and even a nuisance.[11]

That was the authentic voice of the colonial administrator with experience of dealings with the Sultan of Morocco. At the Quai d'Orsay there was a similar view which in some respects mirrored that of Hirtzel in the British India Office, which were seen in Chapter 3. In May 1920, after Faysal had been declared King of Syria, M. Baryeton of the Quai d'Orsay minuted as follows:

From now onwards it is necessary to consider the regime which will follow our occupation and will allow us to maintain our position with reduced military resources. It will be necessary to ensure that it is understood there that our military action has a definite objective so that the reduction of our forces does not appear to imply weakness....

The need is for an indigenous façade which is reasonably consistent, behind which we can operate without direct responsibility and in the way and under the circumstances which we judge useful....

The possibility of an Arab dynasty reigning over a united Syria being excluded, it would seem that there would be no danger in leaving the various ethnic groups, by themselves or with help requested from us, to establish the framework of their national autonomy....

The main difficulty lies in the constitution of the native political organizations, not only those foreseen in the repeated declarations of the Allies and implied by the principle of the Mandate, but above all essential in the development of our policy in the East.

His solution, based on his reading of Ottoman history and the concept of state and nation, was as follows:

In those territories once part of the Ottoman empire... the opposition between these secular notions of state and nation generated an anarchic spirit and made it impossible for the people to opt for small ethnic and regional groupings. This condition is favourable for us by making a general opposition difficult; but too great an encroachment may place us in an embarrassing legal position.

It will therefore be essential to make a study of those ethnic groups which may as soon as possible constitute the first regional autonomous units....

To carry our policy, it is necessary that Syria organizes itself. And to ensure that a unitary Syria does not establish itself from the top, it is urgent that a federative Syria starts to establish itself from the bottom.[12]

In this comment there are clearly two dominant concepts. First, Syria should be divided into segments to block nationalist sentiment and action. Second, there should be an indigenous façade behind which the French would pull the strings: this was almost precisely the strategy adopted by the British in Iraq from 1920

---

[11] *State and Society in Syria and Lebanon,* 46–7.   [12] Ibid. 47–8.

onwards. The difference was that, after some initial playing with the idea of a federative system, the British, led by Cox, settled for a unitary state, initially only excluding part of Kurdistan. Thereafter the French never changed their minds: Syria would be ruled as a group of states under the control of the High Commissioner.

The remaining issue was how many states, on what basis they should be organized, where the capital should be, and their relationship with Lebanon. In a key dispatch from Millerand to Gouraud of 6 August 1920, presumably drafted by the Quai d'Orsay, a first decision was to separate Lebanon from the rest of Syria. Lebanon had 'in every way shown its unshakeable desire for complete independence under the French mandate: it does not want to enter directly into the Syrian confederation, seeing itself as more cultivated and mistrusting the Muslim majority of the country'. Lebanon might, however, choose to attach itself to Syria once the French had controlled it successfully. As for Syria, Millerand excluded the Hijaz and the region east of the Euphrates, which required special treatment. The core of Syria might then be divided into eight 'autonomous' units, each with different organizations, according to local circumstances. In any case there would have to be a single customs regime since Syria depended on the Lebanese ports. As to the central government of the High Commissioner, there should be a federal council. Its members would be nominated by the governments of the states, not by the people, and its functions would initially be purely consultative, But eventually the President of this council along with some directors ('always controlled by the High Commissioner') might acquire some executive powers. Conversely there was absolutely no case for a representative parliamentary system. This would not 'reflect the present state of the public education of the country. The object of the mandatory regime is to consider the organization of Syria realistically, in conformity with the interest of the mass of the population and not of particular groups with political pretensions.'[13]

The details changed, but this conception of the French role in Syria did not. It was based on a profound distrust of Arab nationalism, which Paris did not understand, and more broadly on the long traditions of French colonial rule, which had never (except in the special case of the four *anciennes colonies* enfranchised by the French Revolution) allowed elective politics. At the start Millerand's concept of many small states, which he defended on the grounds that bigger states would be less manageable than small states, was challenged by Gouraud. It would in fact encourage the idea of a united Syria because the units would be non-viable. Conversely, 'it would be easy to maintain the balance between three or four States big enough to be self-sufficient and needing to compete with each other. This rivalry is already evident between Damascus and Aleppo. In practical terms it would also be inconvenient to burden these small isolated States with administrative expenses out of proportion with their limited importance.'[14] Gouraud got his

[13] Ibid. 48–54.   [14] Gouraud to Millerand, tel., 20 August 1920, quoted ibid. 56.

way. Initially, four 'states' were established: the Alawites[15] in the north, Aleppo, Jabal al-Druze, and Damascus; Alexandretta was treated as a separate region. In 1922 all but the Jabal al-Druze were united in a single federation, but in 1924 the Alawites of 'Latakia' were again detached, leaving a central federal core based on Damascus.[16]

Far more important than the pattern of states was the French approach to running this society and their relations with the indigenous Arabs. Did they observe either the letter or the spirit of article 1 of the mandate for Syria and Lebanon, which had demanded that

The Mandatory shall frame within a period of three years from the coming into force of this mandate, an organic law for Syria and the Lebanon.

This organic law shall be framed in agreement with the native authorities and shall take into account the rights, interests and wishes of all the population inhabiting the said territory. The Mandatory shall further enact measures to facilitate the progressive development of Syria and the Lebanon as independent states. Pending the coming into effect of the organic law, the Government of Syria and the Lebanon shall be conducted in accordance with the spirit of this mandate.

The Mandatory shall, as far as circumstances permit, encourage local autonomy.[17]

The answer is clearly that they did not. First, on a technical point, no organic law was established within the three years. The French did not summon a constituent assembly to draw one up until late in 1927, and then refused to accept six important articles of the Assembly's draft.[18] The Assembly's draft purported to give Syria many of the essentials of a sovereign state, subject to the mandate, in much the same way as the Iraqi constitution of 1924. But this resulted in an outcry in Paris. Since the Assembly refused to compromise, it was suspended. In 1930 the High Commissioner issued decrees which put elements of the 1928 constitution into effect, but it was heavily modified to safeguard French powers and interests. It did not operate until 1932, when at last Syria had an elected president and parliament. It was the first and very limited French step towards the creation of Syria as an 'independent state'.

[15] The Alawites were members of the Nusayri sect, which had a strong Shii doctrinal strain, and had inhabited the mountainous areas of north-west Syria even before the Ottomans took over. The name was coined by the French as 'Alouite'. See A. Hourani, *Minorities in the Arab World* (London, 1947). The Druzes were an entirely endogamous community, probably starting in Egypt, whose religion was an eclectic mix of Islamic, Christian, Greek, and pagan concepts. They were another tough mountain group which had survived four centuries of Turkish rule and were more or less left to themselves.

[16] The Alawites and the Jabal Druze were incorporated into Syria in 1936, detached again in 1939, but reincorporated with Syria in 1942.

[17] Quoted S. H. Longrigg, *Syria and Lebanon under French Mandate* (London, 1958), app. D, 376.

[18] These declared the unity of Syria, Lebanon, Palestine, and Transjordan; stated that Syria would have its own national army; and gave the elected President of the Republic the power to conclude treaties, declare martial law, receive ambassadors, and grant pardons. See P. A. Shambrook, *French Imperialism in Syria 1927–1936* (Ithaca and Reading, 1998), 19–21.

This reluctance to transfer any real power to indigenous Syrians was the hallmark of French rule there throughout. Khoury suggests that the ethos of the mandate was transferred from Morocco, along with many of the early French officials.[19] These included Gouraud, General de Lamothe as Delegate in Aleppo, Colonel Niéger and his successor General Billotte in the Alawite territory, and General Georges Catroux, the first Delegate in Damascus. At the Quai d'Orsay Robert de Caix also had served under Marshal Louis-Herbert Lyautey in Morocco, then as Secretary-General under successive High Commissioners in Syria until 1924. The key to understanding the early French strategy in Syria thus lies in how the French had dealt with Morocco and also Tunis. The main point is that, by contrast with French policy in West Africa, in these North African protectorates the French had adopted a strategy then called 'association'. Lyautey described his Moroccan system

as the economic and moral penetration of a people, not by subjection to our forces or even to our liberties, but by a close association, in which we administer them in peace by their own organs of government and according to their own customs and laws.[20]

The implication of this was that they retained their indigenous rulers—Sultan of Morocco, Bey of Tunis—along with indigenous senior officials, but that these were controlled by the High Commissioners and Delegates. In the provinces, the French had left tribal chiefs in position, again controlling them with French officials. Thus those who came to Syria with North African experience were accustomed to maintaining at least a façade of indigenous government; whereas those coming from West Africa were bred in a policy of direct rule through French officials, with Africans as mere subordinates.

This was not, in fact, very different from the British indirect rule tradition, with its Indian princes, Malayan Sultans, and Northern Nigerian chiefs. Moreover, as was seen in Chapter 3, it was close to the system evolved in Iraq after 1920. The difference lay in the British tradition of legislative councils in virtually all colonies not under such indirect rule. Even though these were at that time mostly nominated and had limited powers, the assumption that local legislation was made by bodies in some sense representing local interests was fundamental. Moreover in some places such councils had evolved into genuine elected legislatures. In short, the British colonial tradition was in essence progressive, though until the middle of the twentieth century the rate of progress was extremely sluggish.

The French, despite their republican culture, had no such tradition. Apart from the *anciennes colonies*, which could send representatives to the French parliament, there were no representative electoral systems, nor did their nominated councils have any real powers. The Moroccan system was essentially static, a device for attracting support from local notables, not a path to political progress. One of

---

[19] S. Khoury, *Syria and the French Mandate: The Politics of Arab Nationalism 1920–1945* (London, 1987), ch. 3.   [20] Ibid. 56.

their major mistakes in dealing with both Syria and Lebanon was to assume that what worked in Morocco would work in these far more sophisticated Near Eastern communities which, moreover, had had some experience of representative government under the reformed Ottoman system of the post-1908 period. Equally importantly, the French largely ignored the force of pre-1918 Arab nationalism and the fact that Syria had briefly formed an autonomous state under Faysal from 1918 to 1920. Admittedly, in 1922 Gouraud created a federal council to cover all the mandated territories except Lebanon and the Jabal Druze. It had fifteen members appointed by the French from the Damascus, Aleppo, and Alawite administrative councils. Its president was elected by the members. But this was a mere shadow of a representative system. In 1923 the new High Commissioner, General Weygand, decided to set up a more genuinely representative system in each of the then three states. These representative councils were elected on the old Ottoman two-tier system (which was opposed by the nationalists, who wanted a single-tier system). The delegates to these councils in turn elected five delegates to a federal council, This looked like a quasi-democratic system. But in fact these councils had very little real power. As will be seen below, they acted mainly as a means of expressing anti-French hostility and complaint, as any similar body with no real authority was bound to do. Their main result was to generate a system of political factions which were later to have some importance.

As a nominal step towards a more representative system, in 1925 the states of Damascus and Aleppo were united into the state of Syria. The President was to be elected by the new united Representative Council and would appoint a cabinet of five to head the main departments along with senior officials. All these were, however, subject to approval by the High Commissioner and all departments were to have controlling French advisers. Thus, while the new state of Syria had an indigenous façade, all real power remained with the French. But in any case, after the second elections to the council in 1925, the incoming French High Commissioner, Henri de Jouvenel, unable to find anyone deemed suitable to head a notional Syrian government, suspended the constitution. Syria reverted to direct rule. It was not until 1928 that another, and more fundamental, attempt was made to establish a representative system of government in Syria.

Meantime, Syria was governed by the French with minimal indigenous collaboration. The administrative structure from 1920 onwards was as follows.[21] At its centre, in Beirut, was the High Commissioner, responsible to Paris for both Syria and Lebanon. He was appointed by and was responsible to the French Ministry of Foreign Affairs, the Quai d'Orsay, but in practice was largely free to act as he chose. He did not have to get approval from any Syrian organization for his actions: he could issue decrees (*arrêtés*) and had final veto power. Nor was he tightly controlled by Paris, and only reported to the Quai d'Orsay intermittently: this was in marked

---

[21] The following summary is based on S. Joarder, *Syria under the French Mandate: The Early Phase, 1920–1927* (Dacca, 1977), 70–3; Khoury, *Syria and the French Mandate*, 77–85.

contrast with British colonial practice. His subordinate was the Secretary-General, the equivalent of the British Colonial Secretary, and like him and unlike the High Commissioner, usually a long-serving official who got to know the territory well. He had the role of a permanent secretary in a European department of government and, in the conditions of the 1920s in Syria, was the effective chief minister. The role was essentially established by Robert de Caix, as Secretary-General until 1924, when he became the French representative on the Mandates Commission of the League of Nations. Another very important central organization was the Services Spéciaux, an information department which dealt with intelligence, press censorship, propaganda, and the Sûreté Générale. These Special Services were staffed by French officials, mostly with excellent knowledge of Arabic and indigenous societies. The most important branch was the Service des Renseignements, the intelligence service, some one hundred strong, who were spread around the country and reported on every aspect of local life, particularly political movements. Also in Beirut were the main governmental departments—public security, education, public works, beduin affairs, and the Common Interests, which handled a wide range of public services common to both Syria and Lebanon, such as customs, postal services, telegraphs, and concessionary companies.

This was the powerhouse of the French administration. At the higher levels it was exclusively French: there was no system of indigenous ministerial heads for the whole mandate such as was set up in Iraq in and after 1920. In the capitals of the individual states it was different. In these there were, from the start, appointed Syrian governors and Syrian ministers. But at their side were always French officials appointed and paid for by the High Commissioner. Each Governor had a Delegué or Representative with a substantial staff (more than twenty in Damascus in 1921) of French officials who were attached to the various departments. The Representative had a veto on decisions taken by the Governor: disagreements were reported to the High Commissioner, whose decision was final. Similarly the departmental officials had a veto on policy. Further down the hierarchy, the indigenous administrators of districts—sanjaqs—had French officials at their elbows, known as Joint Delegates. Again, they had to approve the proposals of the mutasarrifs: disagreements were referred to the State's Delegate and ultimately to the High Commissioner. All these officials were paid by Beirut; but in addition there were French officials who were appointed at the request of the local authorities and paid for from state funds. Typically these might be Commissioners of Police or Chief Administrators of municipalities. In 1926 the total number of French direct and indirect agents was 316, 117 paid for by the states, plus 109 officials paid for jointly, mostly in the customs service.

This structure of French administrators and advisers ensured that France ruled Syria as effectively as any colony. No significant decision could be taken at any level without French approval. It is important, however, to see this in perspective. This French system was remarkably similar to the British system in Iraq, even in the numbers involved. In 1926 there were some 300 French advisers: in that year there were some 360 British gazetted officials in Iraq. The totals may not be directly comparable, depending on how their roles were defined. But the system of advisers in central ministries and state/provincial governments was almost identical. The main difference lay in the façade. In Baghdad all the main departments had ministerial heads: notionally policy was theirs, even if it had to be cleared with an adviser. This never happened in Syria. The most important departments in Beirut were always under exclusive French control: it was only in the states that something approaching a British ministerial system was introduced in 1932. Thus, while the newly independent Iraqi government of 1932 could adopt a conventional ministerial system, recasting the few remaining British advisers as conventional permanent secretaries of departments, Syria had no such easy transition.

Another important difference between the Syrian and Iraqi experience lay in the armed forces. In Syria in 1921 there were 70,000 regular soldiers in the Armée du Levant, many of them North Africans, Senegalese, and Madagascans, plus some Foreign Legion battalions, a few artillery batteries, and engineer and aviation corps from France.[22] This was immensely larger than the British and Indian forces in Iraq even in the 1920 crisis. The costs were huge, and after 1921 the number of regular troops was reduced to some 15,000, though increased during the crisis of 1925–7. Even so this was far larger than the post-1921 British military force in Iraq, which was almost eliminated and security handed over to the RAF. Until 1926 the costs were met almost entirely by France, but thereafter the states were forced to pay 24 per cent of the costs, representing about one-third of total public revenues, drawn mostly from their share in the Common Interests.[23] Nevertheless, the costs to France were also huge. By 1939 France had spent some four billion francs out of total expenditure in Syria of five billion on defence.

In addition to the regular Army of the Levant, the French raised a local force, the Syrian Legion (Troupes Spéciales). It had about 6,500 men in 1924 but had risen to more than 14,000 by the mid-1930s. The majority of officers were initially French, but by the mid-1930s there were 201 Syrian and Lebanese officers out of a total of 378. This army was always a volunteer force, both officers and men drawn largely from ethnic or religious minorities, including Armenian and Kurdish irregulars. As in Iraq few notable families were represented in the officer corps, so that the army provided a career open to talent for the petty bourgeoisie. Again, as in Iraq, this had the long-term result that the army after independence came to see itself as an agent for social and political reform ready to overthrow the traditional social and political structure.

---

[22] Syrian and Lebanese Arabs were mortified and felt humiliated at being lorded over by Black African troops.

[23] It must be remembered, however, that British India had to pay all the costs of the Indian Army, including those of the British regiments stationed there, apart from the costs of overseas wars, until the late 1930s. This represented some 30 per cent of Indian government expenditure.

The French mandate state of the 1920s was, therefore, essentially a military state, based on superior force rather than consent. Dissent was met with arrest or exile through special military tribunals headed by French officials. But there were other more specific areas in which the French gave cause for legitimate complaint by Syrians and fodder for nationalist protest.

First, there was the system of justice. For the most part the old Ottoman civil and sharia courts and laws were maintained, though French judges had the power of inspection. But in matters affecting foreigners the French ignored article 5 of the mandate which had ended the special juridical status and courts for foreigners under the Capitulations. From 1923 any foreign national engaged in a civil or commercial case could have it tried in a court presided over by a French judge or judges, the cost to be borne by the states' budgets.[24]

Second, the French took full control over the *Awqaf,* the organization of Islamic charitable endowments (*waqfs*). The High Commissioner now appointed the Controller-General who chaired the Supreme Muslim Council which controlled these endowments and could veto its decisions. While there was clearly need to reform this institution, the fact that it was now directly controlled by an infidel and that perhaps 5,000 Muslim ulama stood to lose their income if the government disapproved of their attitudes became a standing grievance. By contrast in Palestine the British had not directly interfered with either the election of the President of the Supreme Muslim Council in Jerusalem or his decisions on use of funds. Indirectly connected with this invasion of Muslim proprieties was the fact that the French transferred the Syrian section of the Hijaz railway to a French company in 1924. This had been the only railway in Ottoman Arabia not owned and run by foreign companies and had symbolized the autonomy of the haj route for Muslims. This remained a Syrian grievance throughout the mandate.

Third, French currency and financial strategies proved highly controversial. Inevitably, since this was the policy of all colonial powers, the Syrian and Lebanese currencies were pegged to the metropolitan franc at a fixed rate of £S1 = 20 francs, to replace the Egyptian pound established by the British after 1918. This created two problems. First, the exclusive right of currency issue was given to a private French bank, the Banque de Syrie et du Grand Lebanon, which became also the sole deposit holder of public funds. The use of metropolitan-linked currencies was standard with all imperial powers in the twentieth century. The problem with franc currencies was that the French franc depreciated heavily between 1920 and 1926 and again between 1936 and 1939. This stimulated Syrian and Lebanese exports but also gave French imports a great advantage over those from harder currency areas. The main sufferers were importers from outside the franc zone and salaried officials in Syria and Lebanon. One inevitable result was the smuggling of gold to Baghdad or Palestine, seriously depleting Syrian gold reserves. As to the bank, it had very limited reserves and followed a most conservative lending

---

[24] A similar system was in fact established by the British in Iraq until 1932.

strategy, with bad effects on local businesses in need of credit. Another limitation on economic growth was the fact that the state governments, although from 1923 running revenue surpluses, were inhibited from using these for development investment: an average of 32 per cent of state revenues went on security.

All in all, therefore, the French regime in Syria in the 1920s, and in many respects until 1939, was a particularly austere version of modern colonial rule. On the economic side it was designed to maximize French benefits. Almost all public concessions were to French companies. Markets were manipulated to benefit French firms and individuals. Yet it seems likely that, on balance, France spent more on Syria and Lebanon than it obtained from the mandate. There was inadequate protection for Syrian manufactures, even though from 1927 import duties were raised to 25 per cent for League of Nations members and to 50 per cent to others. The result (as elsewhere in the Middle East, including Iraq) was a continued decline in artisan manufacture, virtually halving between 1913 and 1937, which produced a drift to the towns and mass urban unemployment, providing a ready-made supply of agitators to be manipulated by indigenous politicians. Thus there was never any lack of grievances for nationalist politicians to exploit, and given the nature of French rule the blame could always be placed on them. In Syria and the other states after the fusion of Aleppo and Damascus in 1925 there was serious discontent throughout the mandate period. Yet only in the period 1925 to 1927 was there a serious threat to French control, and that was largely focused on the Jabal Druze. This suggests two alternative, though in fact interrelated, explanations. First, that the French learnt from the hostility of the early 1920s and liberalized their regime. Second, that sufficient of the leading Syrian notables and politicians were prepared to collaborate with the French, despite their underlying nationalist objectives. It is proposed first to examine the French strategies from the later 1920s to 1939, then in the following section to consider the question of Syrian nationalism and the nature of the response to French rule.

For the French and Syria (which will now be understood as the amalgamated states of Damascus and Aleppo, excluding the Alawite region (Latakia), the Jabal Druze, and Alexandretta), the Druze rising of 1925–7 and its wider extension provided much the same incentive to create a viable indigenous state as the Iraq risings of 1920 had for the British.[25] The revolt had been very expensive in both money and military lives and the obvious need was for something similar to the British system in Iraq: an indigenous government and a treaty that would still provide the mandatory with whatever rights it felt necessary. The question was whether the French could match the realism of the British strategy in transferring sufficient power to satisfy indigenous politicians while retaining both a guiding hand and control of key factors in Iraq.

A start was made with the arrival in October 1926 of Henri Ponsot as High Commissioner. He was only the second High Commissioner not to be a military

[25] Much of the detail that follows is based on Shambrook, *French Imperialism*; Khoury, *Syria and the French Mandate*; Longrigg, *Syria and Lebanon under French Mandate*.

man and the first professional diplomat from the Quai d'Orsay. He served until 1933, the longest tenure of any French High Commissioner in Syria, and Lebanon. He had wide colonial experience, including North Africa, and accepted that concessions to nationalist demands were necessary. On the other hand, he was realistic in what he knew Paris would accept: every step would need to be carefully negotiated. He was fortunate in his timing. There was general exhaustion in Syria, and in October 1926, following a press statement by Colonel Catroux, Delegate to Damascus and a man trained by Lyautey in Morocco, that France planned an organic law (*statut définitif*), a group of leading notables had announced that they were prepared to collaborate. As will be seen in the following section, these men formed the nucleus of what from 1932 came to be called the National Bloc and were to dominate Syria politics until 1945. On 25 October 1926 they stated that 'we believe in the necessity of *collaboration* based on the reciprocity of interests and on the determination of mutual obligations'.[26]

To seize this unprecedented opportunity Ponsot announced elections for a Constituent Assembly to draw up an Organic Law which the League of Nations Mandates Commission was demanding to fulfil the terms of the mandate. The elections followed the traditional two-stage pattern, though the primary elections were based on the district (qadha) rather than the sanjaq to prevent urban nationalist politicians from dominating the larger units. Meantime it was necessary to appoint a new Syrian government. Since April 1926, with the formal ending of the period of direct French administration, the Syrian government had been led as Prime Minister by Damad Ahmad Nami, a Circassian from Beirut who acted as a French collaborator. He formed a cabinet which, surprisingly, included three nationalists and made some sensible suggestions concerning future relations with France. The cabinet had split over French insistence that it take full responsibility for the final suppression of the Druze rising and the three nationalists had been replaced by more conforming politicians. Nami had headed three governments by early 1928 and looked as if he might become the French standby head of government. But by 1928 he had alienated many, particularly republican-minded nationalists, by his campaign to be made King of Syria. Ponsot wanted a Syrian government to oversee the elections that had more credibility with the moderate nationalists. On 2 February 1928 Nami was induced to resign, and was replaced by Shaykh Taj al-Din al-Hasani.

Shaykh Taj was to become the central all-purpose French ally in Syria for the next four years. His main claim lay in the fact that his father was the most distinguished Sunni divine in Syria and he was regarded by the French as a moderate. As early as 1926 Jouvenel as High Commissioner had considered appointing him Prime Minister. Negotiations had broken down over Taj's insistence on the reunification of Syria with those parts of Lebanon that had been attached to the Mount Lebanon in 1920 by the French, an essential element in the nationalist position.

[26] Khoury, *Syria and the French Mandate*, 248.

Now Ponsot chose him to succeed Nami as possibly the best compromise between the more extreme nationalists and the discredited French collaborators. Taj was shrewd and a survivor with good political sense. He was also expert in the use of political patronage: he was said to have packed the Syrian bureaucracy with notables who were his supporters and friends. He survived as Prime Minister until 1932; was reappointed in 1934 for nearly two more years; and in 1941 was made President of Syria by the Free French. He died in 1943. He may be seen as the archetypal colonial collaborator, but he had one major drawback: he could not command the support of the bulk of indigenous nationalists and had to depend largely on French backing. Meantime it was his duty to oversee the elections.

Ponsot regarded these as critical for the French position in Syria. In December 1927 he had written to the Quai d'Orsay that 'We must seize this occasion and choose: either we continue to practice a policy based above all on our military force, or we make a definite attempt to come to terms with the nationalist opposition and let it eventually come to power.'[27] To create a suitable public mood he allowed in a number of exiled politicians, though excluding Dr Abd al-Rahman Shahbander, Shukri al-Quwwatli (later to play a very important political role), and Sultan al-Atrash. For the election Taj formed a temporary alliance with the leading nationalists, the future Bloc. In Damascus they were very successful, getting seven of the nine elected members of the Assembly. Aleppo returned nationalists to all nine seats. But the French had worked hard in the rural areas to get moderates returned: only 22 of the 70 members were nationalists, all from urban electorates. On the other hand it was these urban members who understood parliamentary tactics and they were able to dominate the Assembly from the start: they were able to get two of their members, Hashim al-Atasi and Ibrahim Hananu, elected respectively as President of the Chamber and Chairman of the Committee to draft the constitution. That committee of 25 also had a predominantly nationalist membership. The crucial question was now whether they would produce a draft that was acceptable both to nationalist Syrian opinion and to the French government.

When the draft had been completed during the summer of 1928 it became clear that it was not. The draft of 115 articles essentially defined a constitutional system based on that of the French Republic without its Senate. There was to be a single chamber, universal male suffrage, four-yearly elections, and religious equality for all except for the President, who must be a Muslim. All that was harmless. But there were six articles that were to prove the main obstacle to Syria acquiring some form of independence comparable to that of Iraq. The most controversial was article 2, which stated that Syria, Lebanon, and Palestine were 'one and indivisible'. To the French, who were committed to an independent separate Greater Lebanon, this was, and remained throughout the next decade, completely unacceptable. So, at least for the time being, was article 110, which stated that

---

[27] Shambrook, *French Imperialism*, 11.

Syria was to have its own national army. Four more articles were anathema to Paris. The President was to be able to act as head of an independent state. He could conclude treaties with foreign powers, declare martial law, receive ambassadors, and grant pardons.

The reaction of Paris was predictable. In its present form the constitution was unacceptable, partly at least because it was incompatible with the terms of the mandate. But the main reason was that it would have denied France that effective control over Syria that the colonial activists had fought for since 1914. Once the Assembly had voted to accept the draft in full, Ponsot suspended it for two successive three-month periods. After the nationalists then rejected a French compromise article, he prorogued it indefinitely in February 1929. It did not meet again until 1932, and meantime Taj and his government continued under close French supervision. It remained to be seen whether any compromise could be worked out.

From 1929 until 1939 two main issues dominated French policy on Syria. First, what constitution should Syria have? Second, how to draw up a treaty as the basis for independence. Over both questions hung French determination not to lose effective control while making whatever concessions were necessary to avoid serious resistance.

The constitutional issue had been resolved, at least overtly, by Ponsot, by 1932. He persuaded the Quai d'Orsay to accept the core of the draft 1928 constitution, shorn of the objectionable six articles, in the hope that this would make it possible to draw up a treaty acceptable to the League of Nations. On 22 May 1930 he announced six decrees which established constitutions for Syria, Lebanon, Latakia, and the Jabal Druze. The Syrian constitution was basically that drawn up by the Constituent Assembly but without the six articles and with ten additional articles which effectively protected French control and banned any action contrary to the mandate obligations. Elections to a new assembly were postponed to some date at the end of 1931. The League accepted this strategy. French authorities spent the year's grace preparing the ground for elections that favoured France. In November 1931 Ponsot decided to act. He dismissed Taj as Prime Minister, dissolved the still prorogued parliament, set up a nominated Consultative Council of governmental supporters, and appointed Tawfiq al-Hayani to act as Secretary-General for Syria and run the government.[28] On 7 December 1931 the Council was told that elections would start later that month and would end by 5 January 1932. A treaty would be negotiated with the new parliament and government.

The French took these elections seriously because they wanted to establish a moderate parliament and government which would accept their position. Great

---

[28] Al-Hayani was a professional administrator, member of a notable land-owning family of Aleppo, with official experience under the Ottomans and then mutasarrif of the Hawran. Athough officially neutral he was thought to be secretly favourable to the nationalists.

pressure was placed on leading notables and the second-stage electors to support pro-governmental candidates, and also on non-Muslims in the Aleppo constituencies. The end result was that, of 69 deputies elected, 14 could be regarded as nationalists and members of or connected with the now designated National Bloc.[29] It remained to elect a President for the Syrian Republic and a government. After much haggling in the Chamber, Ponsot backed Muhammad Ali al-Abid and he was elected by a majority of four over Subhi Barakat. Al-Abid was a large land-owner, a member of a Damascus family of merchants and land-owners, an archetypal Syrian notable of the type that had been in Ottoman service for generations. He had worked in the Ottoman Foreign Affairs ministry and had been Ambassador to Washington before 1908. He was then dismissed by the Young Turks and went into exile in Paris. He returned to Syria in 1919 but kept out of politics. From a French standpoint he was an ideal collaborator, possibly the richest man in Syria with wide political influence, pro-French, and a man of western culture. Abid then appointed Haqqi al-Azm, another Damascus notable, a close connection, and the first Governor of the Damascus state from 1920 to 1922, as Prime Minister. Thus two stalwart supporters of the French connection held the two highest posts. It remained to appoint the cabinet.

Here the French were more cautious. Having installed two clearly collaborative notables in the top posts, they saw the need to make a concession to nationalist opinion and also to balance the regions. The three men appointed were Salim Jambart, Mazhar Raslan, and Jamil Mardam. Jambart was a wealthy Greek Catholic merchant from Aleppo who called himself a Liberal Constitutionalist. Raslan came from a middle-ranking landed family in Homs, had served in the Ottoman administration, and then joined Faysal in 1919. After July 1920 he moved to what became Transjordan and formed a short-lived autonomous Arab government in Salt and Amman. After heading two governments under Abdullah he returned to Syria in 1924 and was implicated in the Druze rising. He was exiled until the amnesty of 1928 and became a member of the moderate wing of the National Bloc. Mardam was a relatively young (38) member of a wealthy absentee land-owning family in Damascus, was educated in Paris, and had been a member of the radical People's Party under Faysal. He had been a member of what became the National Bloc since 1928 and was to have the most significant political role in pre-1946 Syrian history. If anyone was likely to fight for the principles of the 1928 draft constitution it was Mardam. Al-Azm and, these three men headed the seven main departments of government (two each apart from Jambart), which indicated how little actual control of business such ministers had and how much they depended on their French advisers. For them a ministry provided status and patronage, not the opportunity to direct strategy. Again the parallel with Iraq is obvious.

The main function of this new government and parliament, from a French standpoint, was to put through a treaty comparable with that between Britain and

---

[29] Khoury, *Syria and the French Mandate*, 374, has 17 National Bloc members.

Iraq of 1930 which could then be presented to the League of Nations Mandates Commission. The moment was exceptionally favourable because the French government of Edouard Herriot of the radical left was keen for a settlement. The treaty was to be based on a draft prepared by the Quai d'Orsay in 1931, though this was concealed: allegedly the terms were drawn up by Ponsot and Al-Abid, who had been authorized to negotiate by the Chamber. The most extraordinary feature of these negotiations was that initially the cabinet was not shown any written version of the proposed treaty. Ponsot read out the twelve main articles to cabinet on 16 November 1932, and they accepted them in principle, reluctantly since they did not include unity of all the Syrian provinces bar the Mount Lebanon. By 22 November Ponsot had the verbal agreement of the cabinet and this was reported, again verbally, to Geneva to demonstrate that France was making progress. But at no point was the list of attached conventions, which contained the guts of the remaining French rights in Syria, revealed. As stated to the cabinet the treaty would divide the mandated territories into three zones. The treaty zone would cover only Syria. Greater Lebanon, the Alawite region of Latakia, and the Jabal Druze would remain under the mandate, though Ponsot concealed the fact that the Syrian treaty would not cover the second and third of these. When Ponsot reported this to Geneva he refused to be precise about how independent either zone might be under the treaty. Indeed, the Quai d'Orsay report stated that 'It is obvious that contrary to the Italian and German delegates in Geneva [to the Mandates Commission] France can grant independence to the former territories of Syria at different dates and in different forms', while publicly affirming, that both Syria and Lebanon had an 'international vocation'.[30] This did not, however, satisfy the Mandates Commission, which reported to the League Council that all the Syrian segments should become independent at the same time and that Syria should not be cut off from the Mediterranean by a separate Lebanon.

The unity question now became central to the negotiations, as it had been in the constitutional negotiations of 1928. On 2–4 February 1933 Ponsot at last published his statements to the Mandates Commission, minus their discussion and report to the League Council. The Bloc, which had been split over the whole issue for some time, held a conference at Aleppo and on 19 February issued a statement.

Syrian nationalists, anxious to achieve the rights and interests of their country, proclaim to the people of the coast and the interior, their unwavering attachment to the principle of national unity. No treaty is to be signed and no negotiations are to be undertaken with France except on this basis.[31]

Mardam nevertheless attempted to maintain confidential negotiations with Ponsot, but by late March 1933 had reached the limit of what Paris would allow Ponsot to concede. He resigned from his Bloc and official positions on 20 April 1933.

---

[30] Shambrook, *French Imperialism*, 105.   [31] Khoury, *Syria and the French Mandate*, 386.

Al-Azm formed a new cabinet dominated by two 'Liberal Constitutionalists' and, with the Bloc members absent, managed to get a vote of confidence in his government. Meantime, Ponsot had attempted to keep discussions going by concentrating on four critical issues: the Common Interests, which provided 88 per cent of the Syrian budget; protection of minorities; a possible timetable for independence—the French wanted a four-year period; and unity. But Paris ordered him to stick to the letter of the draft treaty and get a 'yes' or 'no' answer. When parliament went into recess at the end of May 1933 nothing had been achieved.

May 1933 also marked the end of Ponsot's period as High Commissioner: he was moved to Morocco. He had attempted to square the circle of French and nationalist intransigence by splitting the nationalists and persuading some of them to collaborate. He failed because Paris refused any compromises: despite changes in French governments the Quai d'Orsay remained wedded to its determination to sustain French power in Syria and Lebanon and refused to follow the British in Iraq in gambling on the goodwill and collaboration of an independent Syria. On the issue of unity, moreover, they could rely on the hostility of the Alawites, the Jabal Druze, and the majority in Greater Lebanon to unity with Syria.[32] The original strategy of dividing to rule held firm.

Ponsot was succeeded in October 1933 by Comte Charles de Martel, another career diplomat, ex-Ambassador to Tokyo and an autocrat by nature. In October 1933 he was instructed by Paris to restart negotiations on the treaty with the government before parliament met. On 16 November the government, under great pressure, did so. Two days later, de Martel published the terms of the treaty, adding that rejection by parliament would show that Syria was not yet ready for independence. It was also stated that two critical protocols that would define military, economic, and juridical matters remained to be dealt with. The Alawites and Druzes were to remain separate from Syria. Parliament had meantime met and debated the treaty. The nationalists violently attacked, and on 21 November managed to get a vote against the treaty despite an attempt by the Delegate, Weber, to read out an edict of prorogation. Weber refused to accept the legality of the vote and suspended parliament for four months. The treaty was technically dead.

It had been killed by intransigence on both sides. The nationalists were unrealistic in trying to insist on the integration of Syria with the Alawite Territory and the Jabal Druze, neither of whom wanted this, and on the recovery of the pre-1920 Syrian qadhas of Lebanon. For their part, the French had been devious and vague

[32] The attitude of the Druze notables to Syria was, however, mercurial and mixed. They had oscillated between Turks and Sharifians between 1916 and 1918, then between the Sharifians and French. Within the Atrash clan there were some who were consistently hostile to the French, notably Sultan al-Atrash, a consistent ally of Abd al Rahman Shahbandar. But rival and mostly minor families became increasingly nationalist and favourable to Syria. This variety of behaviour, of course, resembled patterns in other Middle Eastern mandates. Those with something to lose stuck with the status quo. Outsiders with nothing to lose supported a more radical line. I owe this point to David McDowall.

on several key matters, including their future military role, the continuation of French magistrates and advisers, and the Common Interests. Clearly, France was not prepared to adopt the Anglo-Iraqi model, even though that had left Britain with control of what seemed most important to it.

The two years from 1934–6 constitute a sort of interregnum in Syrian political history. De Martel's attitude, common among colonial administrators, was that most of the problems of the recent past stemmed from a minority of rabble-rousing nationalists and that the majority would be happy to get on without political excitements, provided improvements were made in their economic conditions. In a note he wrote in September 1934 he said that

A government of experienced Syrian notables can efficiently administer the country without them [i.e. the nationalists] and that in concert with the Mandatory Power, such a government can introduce practical legislative and administrative reforms which will later produce a form of Franco-Syrian collaboration that guarantees the interests of both countries.[33]

His strategy in these years was to avoid summoning parliament and to restructure the whole administrative and governmental system. The basis would be elected councils in the sanjaqs (Damascus, Homs, Hama, Aleppo) with representatives of the Damascus central government along the same lines as in Alexandretta. These in turn would send representatives to a central council which, together with the President and government, would manage national affairs. This council would have limited powers, particularly over finance. On this basis a new Syrian constitution could be constructed without any formal announcement or definition.

This system was never established, but it demonstrates de Martel's approach. In November 1934 decrees were issued which suspended parliament *sine die*, this being blamed on the extremism of the nationalists. The Quai d'Orsay agreed to maintain the non-parliamentary regime for the moment while the defence question was discussed with the Commander of the Armée du Levant and the Chief Naval Officer in Beirut. Draft conventions covering this and other key questions could be attached to the draft treaty. The Syrians would then be left with a choice: 'weighing up—with regard to the independence offered—the price of the conditions inscribed in the treaty'.[34] In September de Martel and Taj went to Paris to finalize the draft new constitution of 103 clauses, which incorporated de Martel's concept of sanjaq councils. This was to be promulgated by France to avoid embarrassing the Syrian government in December–January 1935–6, to be followed by elections two months later.

This never happened, because of a complex set of not necessarily related developments between December 1935 and early 1936. Externally riots in Cairo led to the British starting negotiations for a new Anglo-Egyptian treaty, which stimulated Syrian activists. The Bloc, now more united and with Mardam back in

---

[33] Shambrook, *French Imperialism*, 157.   [34] Ibid. 168.

the fold, took the opportunity to restate its maximum demands for a treaty. There were repeated public demonstrations in Damascus and on 20 January 1936 the government arrested Fakhri al-Barudi, a leading Bloc member, and Sayf al-Din al-Mamun, leader of the Nationalist Youth movement. Further riots, organized by the Nationalist Youth, led to arrests and bloodshed, and on 27 January Mardam called for a general strike, to last until the constitution was restored. Syria was almost completely paralyzed for the next month. De Martel's reaction was to imprison Mardam and Nasib al-Bakri and to exile other Bloc leaders. But he also dismissed Taj as President and installed Ata Bey al-Ayyubi, a moderate Damascus notable though respected by the nationalists, as Prime Minister, along with a new cabinet which included three moderate nationalists. De Martel believed that the frequent riots were caused by students rather than the respectable notable nation-alists. He told the new government that France intended to proceed with the treaty and that it would encourage the other sanjaqs to accept unity, provided they retained local autonomy. Between 29 February and 2 March 1936, de Martel held meetings with Hashim al-Atasi, President of the Bloc, and the al-Ayyubi cabinet to find an emollient formula. This produced a bland public statement signed by al-Atasi. The unity issue would be analysed. A Bloc delegation would go to France with de Martel to discuss the future. The rights provided by the treaty would 'not be inferior' to those given by the 1930 Iraq treaty. A return to normal parliament-ary life should now be possible.

Whatever the outcome, this was a major change in the French position. There appear to have been two likely causes. First, there was fear that disorder would spread from the towns to the countryside. Second, the French government was now, briefly, headed by Albert Sarraut, veteran colonial administrator and Minister for Colonies, and was prepared to adopt a softer line than its predecessor led by Pierre Laval, even though the new Foreign Minister was that dyed-in-the-wool colonial activist, Pierre-Etienne Flandin. The deputation, led by al-Atasi, Mardam, Sadallah al-Jabiri, and Faris al-Khuri of the Bloc, and two technically expert Syrians left for Paris with de Martel on 22 February amid general rejoicings and the suspension of rioting and strikes. The Bloc had salvaged its reputation by extracting concessions from the French through its proclaimed strategy of 'hon-ourable co-operation' rather than political abstention and violence. They knew that even a treaty along the Iraqi lines would leave France with considerable power in Syria and that independence would come in stages (as in Iraq), but this was acceptable.

The delegation was away for six months. Their negotiations fell into two phases, divided by the change of government in France in April.[35] During the first phase, in negotiations with Flandin's officials, the Syrian delegation was not

---

[35] Technically the government was not replaced until the start of June for constitutional reasons, though it lost its majority in the elections of 26 April. Discussions were therefore suspended during May.

accorded official status as not representing the government, so discussions took place in the Levant Office of the Quai d'Orsay, and included de Martel. In these, the French position moved very little. General Gamelin at the War Ministry initially insisted that France must retain its full military position in Syria and Lebanon, including military control of the main towns, Latakia, and the Druze. On unity, the French insisted that Latakia and the Druze must remain autonomous for the duration of the treaty: their only concession was that the governors of these sanjaqs should be appointed by the President of the Syrian Republic rather than by the High Commissioner. On the military front, it was conceded that the army would no longer occupy the main towns but would remain in Latakia and the Druze and in the Homs–Tripoli zone to ensure the security of the pipeline from Iraq. France would retain responsibility for religious minorities, a symbol of its Catholic protectorate. There was some clarification of the 1933 draft treaty and its protocols, which still formed the basis of the French bargaining position; and on 6 May the delegates were for the first time shown a copy of the complete draft of the treaty. There seemed no prospect of any radical shift in either side's position.

The second phase, from the effective inauguration of the Popular Front government of Léon Blum in June 1936 until the fall of that administration in 1937, proved to be the most optimistic in the French mandate in Syria. The government was believed to be the least imperialist since 1918 and Pierre Viénot, appointed Under-Secretary of State at the Quai d'Orsay, was a moderate socialist who accepted that the mandate was transitory and that it was essential to accept the reality of Syrian nationalism. But there were still limits to how much he and the ministry would concede. Before talks began he had assured a Lebanese delegation that Greater Lebanon would remain and would not be incorporated into Syria. Moreover, the ministry had its own in-built official strategy and was under continuous pressure from military and colonialist pressure groups. There was only a limited room for concession and manœuvre.

Viénot met the delegation for the first time on 26 June 1936 and meetings continued until September. There was vigorous debate over the standard key issues, but for once both the Bloc and the French were prepared to make some concessions to obtain agreement. It was agreed that Latakia and the Druze were be incorporated into Syria once the High Commissioner had got their consent. They were to have considerable autonomy comparable to that of Alexandretta, but their Governors would be appointed by the Syrian President.

The treaty itself, modelled on that of Iraq, was bland: it was to operate for 25 years after acceptance by the League of Nations, again on the Iraqi model. Its teeth lay in the now agreed military conventions, five protocols and eleven letters.

The miliary convention stated that France would help to defend Syrian independence. Syria would raise and maintain an army of one infantry division and a cavalry brigade. France would keep two military air bases (again the Iraqi model) and would have port and transport rights to support these and their garrisons.

These garrisons, of undefined size, would be stationed in the Alawite and Druze districts for five years after the treaty came into force.

Lebanon was not mentioned as a separate state, but the Common Interests were to be retained and the distribution of revenues negotiated between Syria and Lebanon.

Finally, there was to be a three-year transitional period during which the Syrian troops (the Troupes Spéciales) would be handed over to the Syrian government's Ministry of Defence, French troops would withdraw to the zones allocated to them, the Special Services would be wound down, the price to be paid for French installations negotiated, and a Syrian Foreign Affairs Ministry and overseas delegations established.

The treaty was initialled by Viénot and al-Atasi on 9 September 1936 in the presence of the French Prime Minister and the Syrian delegation. It remained to be ratified by both French and Syrian parliaments. It appeared that France had resolved the Syrian problem only four years after Britain had ended its control of Iraq. The news caused general rejoicing in Syria, though there was some complaint from the Patriotic Front and Abd al-Rahman Shahbander in Cairo that it was too favourable to France. Some Alawites and Druzes feared the effects of eventual incorporation into Syria, but negotiations later in 1936, and strong French pressure, persuaded both territories to accept promises of autonomy similar to that of Alexandretta. Elections to parliament in November produced a Bloc landslide. Al-Atasi was elected President, Mardam Prime Minister, and a cabinet dominated by the Bloc appointed. On 22 December, de Martel and the Syrian government signed the treaty and it was ratified unanimously by parliament.

Two questions need to be examined. First, why had the French made apparent concessions leading to the treaty? Second, would the new system work? Both depended on France ratifying the treaty so that Syria could become technically independent, and meantime on the French acting in the spirit of the treaty and allowing Syria to act as a genuine state despite residual French rights and powers.

The answer to the first question is that Paris had never really changed its attitude to Syria: the concessions were superficial. The Quai d'Orsay and the War and Navy ministries were determined to maintain effective control as part of their strategic view of the Mediterranean and Near East: Shambrook considered that France wanted to maintain the mandate 'primarily for strategic reasons', particularly in view of the rise of the Italian threat in the Mediterranean and North Africa.[36] Backing this stance were the same vested interests as had fought for the mandate before 1920: clerics, businessmen, imperialist activists. From the early 1930s the French had no intention of accepting a treaty that would lead to genuine Syrian independence, any more, in fact, than the British then had of conceding independence to India or of relinquishing effective control over Iraq. The notional concessions made in 1936 were the result partly of France having

---

[36] Shambrook, *French Imperialism*, 247.

underestimated the force of nationalist feeling in Syria, particularly among the young, which made some apparent concessions desirable, and to a limited extent the accident of the Popular Front government of 1936. Even so, Syria would remain far from independent or autonomous.

Second, whether the new system would work depended on two things: first, whether the Bloc government could deal with a host of serious domestic problems—economic depression, the effects of the Palestinian rising, secessionary tendencies in Latakia and the Druze, and above all the effects of French devaluation of the franc in 1936, which had devastating effects in Syria, whose currency was still tied to the franc; and second, whether France would ratify the treaty and so sustain the Bloc's credibility.

The second of these proved more intractable. Once the revised treaty had been published in France all the predictable forces were mobilized against it. The Blum government fell in June 1937 and the incoming Daladier government had no sympathy with colonial nationalists. The colonial party and its allies renewed the standard arguments against Syrian independence. France must maintain its influence in the region. France must remain a Muslim power to block pan-Arabism in North Africa. The Lebanon must be protected against Syrian irridentism. The religious minorities in Syria must be protected against Sunni dominance. Commercial and banking interests must be protected. The route to the East must be secured to prevent a British monopoly. Naval and air bases were critical for French power in the eastern Mediterranean. Under such pressures Paris persuaded Mardam to go to Paris in November 1937 to discuss modification of the treaty and its connected documents. In December he exchanged letters with the Quai d'Orsay which guaranteed the rights of minorities and continued French collaboration in a range of technical services. These concessions caused riots in Damascus and resulted in the subsequent resignation of Shukri al-Quwwatli as Minister of Defence and Finance over the renewal of the Banque de Syrie's monopoly concession. Mardam returned to Paris in August 1938 to confirm these and other concessions[37] and in return Daladier's government promised to submit the treaty to the French parliament for ratification, to come into effect in September 1939. It did not do so. In December 1938 the Syrian parliament rejected all the amendments agreed by Mardam since the agreed 1936 draft. In February 1939 Mardam and his Bloc government resigned.

This marked the effective end of the drive for Syrian independence through a treaty. On the one hand the Bloc had lost much of its reputation through failure to negotiate successfully; on the other France was now determined to regain control in the light of the probable war with Germany and Italy. Already, France had sacrificed the sanjaq of Alexandretta in order to wean Turkey from the Axis: it was

[37] These included the use of the French language in education along with Arabic; permanent French officials in senior posts; and French protection of the rights of minorities, particularly Christians.

formally incorporated into Turkey in June 1939 after three years of negotiation and political manipulation.[38] The threat of war also affected French policy on Syria. In January 1939 Gabriel Puaux, another long-serving French diplomat, had been appointed High Commissioner with a brief to reimpose direct French rule by gradually destroying the parliamentary system. In this he was helped by the fragmentation of the Bloc into three main factions and the failure of successive governments appointed by President al-Atasi after Mardam's resignation. In July 1939 Puaux issued four decrees which suspended the Syrian constitution and set up a Council of Directors of departments as the government and legislature under Bahij al-Khatib, a Syrian bureaucrat. Al-Atasi resigned as President. Latakia and the Druze were given greater autonomy and there was direct French control in the Jazira, the sanjaq in the extreme north-east of Syria on the Iraqi border. The British Consul in Damascus provided a cynical epitaph to the era of Bloc rule:

The amount of rope that the French authorities allowed the Syrian nationalists in power between December 1936 and December 1938 sufficed for the Nationalist bloc to hang itself in the eyes of most Syrians. The Bloc has disintegrated into emulous political factions, whilst the bulk of the population has had a surfeit of political intrigue and place-hunting. The French political officers have skilfully played on all the chords. It may therefore be guessed that there will be little or no dangerous internal anti-French reaction.[39]

These were hard words, and this condemnation of the nationalists as incompetent will have to be weighed against French intransigence in the following section. But there can be no doubt that the French had never been prepared to concede effective independence to Syria. Indeed, if Syria is seen in the broader context of French imperial history, it was no exception. Looking ahead, the French only left Syria and Lebanon in 1945/6 under British military pressure. They fought long and hard in Indo-China until they were defeated. They fought a brutal war in Algeria until de Gaulle decided to leave in 1963; and then, as in Tunis and Morocco in the previous decade, it was on condition of accepting treaties that left France with significant benefits. Decolonization in West Africa after 1960 followed the same pattern of qualified independence. In short, it would have been entirely contrary to French imperial traditions to give Syria independence except on French terms. While this is also true of the British in Iraq before 1932, the difference lay in the nature of the reservations built into the treaty. The British were prepared to gamble on limited residual rights, the French were not.

[38] The details are in Khoury, *Syria and the French Mandate*, ch. 19. Essentially the Turks, who had been forced to renounce Alexandretta at the Treaty of Lausanne in 1923, even though ethnic Turks constituted the largest single element in the population, became worried that under the 1936 draft Franco-Syrian treaty the sanjaq would be fully incorporated into Syria. Long negotiations involving the League of Nations led to an artificial Turkish majority in the sanjaq's assembly and creeping Turkish military and administrative control. The loss of the sanjaq was a further source of discredit for the Bloc government.
[39] Col. Gilbert MacKereth to Lord Halifax at FO, 3 July 1939, quoted Khoury, *Syria and the French Mandate*, 580.

The rest of the French regime in Syria must be dealt with briefly. After the defeat of France in 1940, the Vichy regime attempted to retain control of Syria. The new High Commissioner, General Dentz, a Vichy supporter, provided the Germans with airport and other facilities in April–May 1941 to provide support for the Rashid Ali regime in Iraq. Although this had limited effect, a German occupation of Syria remained possible; and this persuaded the British that Vichy must be thrown out of Syria. A joint British and Free French attack was launched via Lebanon and Iraq in June 1941. The Vichy forces fought hard but were defeated. The Armée du Levant was allowed to go home, leaving the Troupes Spéciales plus the Allied forces.

But if Syrian nationalists expected that this would at last provide independence or self-government they were wrong. De Gaulle was as firm a believer in France's imperial mission as any French imperialist. In September 1940 he had hoped to establish a Free French base in Syria, taking over the Armée du Levant, then numbering about 70,000. This was impracticable. His associate, General Catroux, with his long experience of Syria and then in Cairo, had issued a statement promising Syrian independence subject to treaty before the 1941 invasion. But de Gaulle refused to back an Anglo-French declaration to guarantee Catroux's promise; and after the armistice of 14 July 1941 an exchange of letters with Oliver Lyttelton, the British Minister in Cairo, confirmed French control. As the price of retaining close relations with the Free French at a time of great British miliary weakness, Lyttelton stated that Britain had no desire to encroach in any way upon the position of France. 'Both Free France and Great Britain are pledged to the independence of Syria and Lebanon. When this essential step has been taken ... we freely admit that France should have the predominant position in Syria and Lebanon over any other European Power.'[40] This position was repeated by Winston Churchill in a parliamentary statement in September 1941; but he also stressed that the British expected the French to concede accelerating self-government in Syria leading to independence. 'We contemplate constantly increasing the Syrian share in the administration. There is no question of France maintaining the same position which she exercised in Syria before the war ...'.[41] He envisaged a Franco-Syrian treaty similar to the Anglo-Iraqi treaty of 1930.

That was precisely what de Gaulle intended to do. He announced that France had resumed 'entire sovereignty' (though that was never the content of the mandate) over Syria and Lebanon and proceeded to treat the British occupying forces as French guests. The Free French controlled the Troupes Spéciales, the police, the public services, the economy, and communications. There was endless bickering between Catroux and General Edward Spears, the British representative in Syria and Lebanon, over the promise of independence. Finally, in 1943 the French announced that the 1936 constitution was reinstated and that parliamentary

[40] Quoted A. H. Hourani, *Syria and Lebanon: A Political Essay* (London, 1946), 245.
[41] Ibid. 246.

elections would be held. They were predictably won by the reinvigorated Bloc, now called the Nationalist Party. Shukri al-Quwwatli, who had been allowed back after a long exile under British pressure, became President and appointed a Bloc cabinet. He proceeded to dismiss or second a number of collaborating officials for fear of a French coup. The situation was now peculiar. In many respects Syria and Lebanon were virtually independent and at the start of 1944 control of the Common Interests and other common services was transferred to their governments. Both states accepted the separation of Greater Lebanon from Syria. Both the USA and the USSR recognized Syria and Lebanon as independent. On the other hand the French still maintained that the mandate was in force and that it would be made effective once France had the military force. The Troupes Spéciales would not be transferred until a treaty was signed. Conversely, the Nationalist government refused to contemplate a treaty with France until the mandate was withdrawn. Churchill, out of touch with Arab nationalism, still thought that an Iraqi-type treaty was desirable and possible, despite the advice of both Spears and the British Ambassador in Cairo, Lord Killearn, who thought the Arab world, now led by the British-backed Arab League, would be outraged if France was allowed to impose its own terms for Syrian and Lebanese independence.

The crunch came in 1944–5. De Gaulle, now with a French base and resources, sent the first of an intended army of occupation: 900 Senegalese troops arrived in Beirut on 6 May 1945. With these behind him the French representative, General Begnet, listed French conditions for final evacuation and transfer of the security forces to the Syrian government. These included the standard post-1936 demands: commercial and cultural primacy for France; transport facilities from the ports to military and airforce bases; and continued control of the Troupes Spéciales. Both Syrian and Lebanese governments rejected all of them and there were general strikes and riots in both Damascus and Beirut. The French retaliated by bombarding mosques and the parliament building in Damascus and caused much other destruction. The Troupes Spéciales were disarmed because likely to support the Syrian government, or defected. At this point the British, whose troops in Syria had been held back in barracks, intervened. Terence Shone, the British Minister in the Levant, persuaded Churchill that there must be intervention. The British commanding officer, General Paget, was ordered to take command of all Allied troops, which included those from France. The French troops were ordered back to barracks, despite Begnet's refusal to accept the order. British troops took over control.

Thereafter French power gradually ebbed away. The Troupes Spéciales were transferred in July 1945. Intense diplomacy eventually led to the simultaneous withdrawal of French and British forces from Syria and Lebanon, which was essential to convince the French that the British were not taking over, and was completed in August 1946, in parallel with the final withdrawal of British troops from Iraq. No treaty was signed with either Syria or Lebanon. The mandate simply lapsed, though technically it might have been transferred to the new

Trusteeship Council of the United Nations, along with other mandates, had this been politically possible. It was not: there would have been no support for France in the UN. The Americans in particular were extremely hostile to French colonial rule, in Syria as throughout the world, which they regarded as far more exploitative and less progressive even than that of Britain. Thus, by a supreme irony, the French were left with no formal rights (though much cultural and religious influence) in Syria and Lebanon, whereas the British retained their treaty rights in Iraq until 1955.

Final failure should not, however, obscure the fact that France had maintained effective control over Syria, along with Lebanon, for two and a half decades after 1920. Throughout this period they had been faced with apparently strong nationalist movements which demanded independence. In Iraq the British had conceded independence after twelve years, in 1932. The French never found it necessary to do so until they were forced by the British in 1945. The question then remains why this was possible. Was it merely the fact of superior military force which could suppress dissent? Or did the underlying reason lie in the nature of Syrian society and its effects on the character and strength of the nationalist movement? This is the problem to be considered in the following section.

2. SYRIAN SOCIETY AND THE NATIONALIST MOVEMENT

The basic paradox concerning Syrian dealings with the French is that, on the one hand, Damascus, and to a lesser extent the other main Syrian towns, had been the centre of Arabism before 1914 and the basis of Faysal's Syrian kingdom from 1918 to 1920, yet, on the other hand, they came to be dominated by collaborative Syrian politicians who adopted a strategy of 'honourable co-operation' with the French after about 1928. It was this collaboration that made it possible for France to retain control over Syria until 1939 and to spin out negotiations for independence with relatively limited reliance on military force. It will be argued that the explanation lies in the structure of Syrian society and in particular in the social and political dominance of the indigenous notables who came to see that their position was to some extent secured by the French against potentially dangerous domestic social forces. In this respect Syria therefore resembled Iraq.[42]

The history of Syrian nationalism and its response to the French falls into five main periods. From 1918 to 1920 it was expressed in the Faysal kingdom. From

[42] The following section is based mainly on the following: P. S. Khoury, *Urban Notables and Arab Nationalism: The Politics of Damascus 1880–1920* (Cambridge, 1983); Khoury, *Syria and the French Mandate*; Shambrook, *French Imperialism*; Joarder, *Syria under the French Mandate*; J. A. Gelvin, *Divided Loyalties: Nationalism and Mass Politics in Syria at the Close of Empire* (Berkeley, Los Angeles, and London, 1998); D. Pipes, *Greater Syria: The History of an Ambition* (New York, 1990); A.-K. Rafeq, 'Arabism, Society and Economy in Syria 1918–1920', in Y. M. Choueiri (ed.), *State and Society in Syria and Lebanon* (Exeter and New York, 1993).

1920 to 1927 it produced repeated acts of physical resistance culminating in the Great Rebellion of 1925–7. The third period, from 1928 to 1933, marked the start of what may be called collaborative politics in which the notables formed what became known as the National Bloc and negotiated for a treaty. That period ended in 1933 with the failure of the treaty negotiations and led to three years of increasingly radical nationalism activity. The fourth period, from 1936 to 1939, saw the political dominance of the National Bloc and the closest that it or Syria came to real 'honourable co-operation' with the French, which in turn was ended by the second failure to secure a treaty. The last, from 1939 to 1946, saw the return of the Bloc to office in 1943 and its final, though short-lived victory in Syrian independence.

As in Iraq, the key to understanding Syrian politics lies in its social structure. In common with other Middle Eastern countries this was dominated by clans of notables, many of which had risen to wealth and influence since the mid-nineteenth century as Ottoman land regulations allowed the accumulation of large estates and growing trade generated wealth for grain producers and merchants. In his seminal *Urban Notables*, P. S. Khoury defined the two main categories of Syrian notables. First there were the land-owning scholars, members of the clerical orders and their families who held both religious and secular positions and were very wealthy, sometimes through holding tax farms. The leading Damascus families included the Al-Ajlanis, represented in the first of these periods by Ata al-Ajlani, the al-Ghazzis, the al-Kaylanis, the al-Hasibis, the al-Jazairis, and the al-Bakris. All these played an important role in early twentieth-century politics. Second there were non-scholarly land-owning and bureaucratic families, some of them merchants, who had acquired land, government appointments, and wealth. The most significant of these were the al-Azms, the al-Abids, the al-Yusufs, the Mardams, the al-Quwwatlis, the al-Shamas, and the al-Barudis. Khoury argues that in the early twentieth century, these families dominated Damascus politics and wealth within a larger Damascus elite numbering perhaps 62, which included social and economic climbers who were extending their resource bases by getting government appointments and contracts. The other main towns had similar elites, though not normally as large or as powerful. For all of them the key to influence lay in creating vertical links of patronage and clientage and horizontal links with other elite families. The patronage system depended on the availability of disposable jobs and favours: hence the acute rivalry between clan leaders for the right to appoint to posts in the official system, even well down the social and administrative scale. Each main city therefore consisted of a number of fiefdoms which were jealously guarded.

It was argued in Chapter 1 that this rivalry within the Syrian urban elites (though mostly land-owning they almost always resided in the cities, leaving their estates to be run by agents) was the key to the positions they adopted on the issues of Arabism and the future of the Ottoman empire before 1914. Briefly, the top strata, who had been most successful in obtaining official positions and patronage, remained Ottomanists, while the less successful and to some extent younger notables became in some sense nationalists who wanted decentralization. The test of their attitudes and the extent of their nationalism came with the Hijaz rising and the formation of Faysal's Syria after 1916.

In 1915 it was thought in some Allied quarters that Syria might form the basis for an Arab rising against the Turks: that indeed was what Cairo was told. But the Turks took effective preventative action. Having found files listing members of al-Fatat and al-Ahd in the French consul's office in Beirut, leading members who had not managed to flee were tried and executed, thus becoming martyrs to the Arab cause. The Arab military forces in Syria were moved to other fronts and replaced by Turkish troops. When Husayn nevertheless started the rising in 1916, Syrian reactions were mixed. Most of the Northern Army officers were captives or deserters from the Ottoman army and were Iraqis or Hijazis rather then Syrians. Most Syrian notables hedged their bets and retained their offices under the Ottoman regime. Some saw the rising as treason, despised the beduin troops, and distrusted Hashemite ambitions.

Once Damascus had been taken in 1918, of course, Syrians had to change allegiance, despite continuing dislike of the Hashemites. It was a Syrian committee of local notables set up in Damascus by the retreating Ottomans, including Amir Abd al-Qadir and his brother the Amir Said al-Jazairi, that surrendered the city. These had expected to be appointed to continue to rule the city. Instead, T. E. Lawrence appointed Shukri al-Ayyubi, a member of another notable Damascus family, a one-time high Ottoman army officer and now a close confid-ant of Faysal, as Acting Military Governor. The Jazairi supporters took to the streets, calling for a holy war against Faysal as a British stooge. They were defeated and Abd al-Qadir killed. This rising reflected deep-seated resentment among not only the Jazairis, then the dominant local family, but also a much wider group of notables. Thus the Faysal regime began with considerable alienation among local notables, even though they now found it prudent to appear to collaborate with it. This fact was fundamental to what happened during the following two years and eventually influenced the attitude of Syrian notables to the French.

Faysal, in fact, largely ignored the local notables and appointed his supporters, many of them Iraqis, to top positions. Most of these lacked administrative experience and many were corrupt. The new state was initially dominated by al-Fatat, which was expanded to include many of those who now jumped onto the nationalist bandwagon. These included Ali Rida al-Rikabi, military governor of Damascus, and some younger notables such as Jamil Mardam, Nasib al-Bakri, Ahmad Qadri, and Shukri al-Quwwatli. Early in 1919, al-Fatat set up a front organization, the Party of Arab Independence (*Hizb al-istiqlal al-Arabi*). Another influential and also overlapping organization was the Arab Club, set up late in 1918 expressly to counter Faysal's negotiations with the Zionists, though then supportive of the Hashemite cause. Filiates of this Club were set up in the other main cities. They differed in structure and were largely autonomous. Thus the Aleppo branch had distinct interests and was not keen on the Faysal government, resented job preferences for the Sharifians, and had pro-Turkish tendencies.

Although not united, these notable-controlled organizations dominated the elections to the first Syrian Congress of June 1919, held under the old Ottoman two-stage electoral system, which predictably returned largely notable represent-atives, those from Damascus mainly from the old guard, who were less than enthu-siastic about the Hashemites and the nationalists. Nevertheless, the Congress, proved to be strongly nationalistic and demanded total and unqualified Syrian independence, by contrast with Faysal's possibly coming to terms with the French, as he attempted to do in December 1919 with Clemenceau. Reacting against the extremist tone of the Congress, Faysal then set up a Council of Directors to replace the military rule, staffed by his loyalists and headed by al-Rikabi, whose aim was to 'take steam out of the Syrian Congress' without having to disband it.[43] Thereafter conditions in Syria took a turn for the worse. In September the British, after their agreement with France, announced that their forces would be with-drawn from Syria and that their subsidy to Faysal would be halved. Left in the lurch, Faysal then negotiated the deal with Clemenceau. When this came out in January 1920 there was an outcry among Syrian nationalists. Al-Fatat rejected it. Faysal then saw the need to woo the older notables for the first time. In January 1920 he set up the National Party (*al-Hizb al-Watani*), based on the more nation-alistic notables including Sami Pasha Mardam-Beg, Muhammad Arif al-Quwwatli, Ata al-Ayyubi, and Badi al-Muayyad. While nominally nationalist and demanding full Syrian independence, in fact this conservative and pragmatic group recognized that a compromise with France along the lines of Faysal's still-undisclosed agreement with Clemenceau was inevitable. Contacts were made with French agents.

Meantime, however, more radical organizations were evolving. In September 1919 Yasin al-Hashimi, an ex-Ottoman soldier, an Iraqi, although President of Faysal's new Council, who was hostile to Faysal and the now dissolving Northern Army, attempted to set up a volunteer defence force of 12,000 and an autonomous Committee of National Defence. He was kidnapped and exiled to Palestine by the British, and thereafter had an important career in Iraq. But the creation of volunteer defence groups continued and was supported by the Arab Club of Iraq. These were often led by notables who armed their clients and retain-ers, sometimes to demonstrate their status. Some time after September 1919 there developed the Higher National Committee (HNC). Initially a loose coalition of leaders of Damascus militia groups, it organized elections to an all-Syrian HNC. These elections were genuine since the HNC wanted wide public support. According to Gelvin the HNC recast traditional structures of power in four main ways.[44] It asserted the primacy of elected representatives over traditional leaders. It forced notables to compete with political upstarts. It took over power from urban

---

[43] Quoted Khoury, *Urban Notables*, 88.   [44] Gelvin, *Divided Loyalties*, chs. 1 and 2.

notable families. And it reduced the neighbourhood power functions of notables. The HNC set up elected local branch committees to organize support, raise money, and control the militias. When Faysal returned from Paris in January 1920 he attempted to control or suppress the HNC, particularly its militias. The HNC, now led by Shaykh Kamil al-Qassab, responded by forming executive agencies to provide some limited control over the local committees. It absorbed a number of family and trading networks, and performed some 'governmental' functions, including policing. It developed links with some guerrilla forces and beduin. Parallel with the main HNC was the Committee of National Defence, which under the nominal authority of the HNC raised local militias which involved many leading citizens. But over time, splits emerged between elements in these committees, particularly over the increasing popular control of them and over the activities of guerrilla groups, notably those organized by Ibrahim Hananu of Aleppo.

These developments, stemming largely from the weakness and poverty of Faysal's government as the British withdrew both military and financial support and as Syria experienced serious economic and fiscal problems, implied the erosion of the power of the older generation of top-level notables. Initially, from 1918, the Faysal government attempted to widen its own support base by a sustained propaganda campaign. Schools, colleges, artisan guilds, and other groups were organized to take part in patriotic demonstrations and public ceremonies. Public holidays were created to mark crucial events in the nationalist calendar, such as the outbreak of the Hijaz rising, the Syrian martyrs of 1915 and 1916, and the occupation of Damascus in 1918. Subsidized, and censored, newspapers and theatrical performances were used to propagate patriotic ideas. But by the later part of 1919 these governmental enterprises were increasingly taken over by the committees and escaped governmental control. The tone now became populist rather than traditional, the links horizontal rather than vertical, reflecting previously untapped lodes of popular feeling. In short, the crisis was sapping the roots of traditional political and social hierarchy.

All this was reflected in the reconvened Syrian Congress of March 1920. This rejected the reported deal with Clemenceau, demanded full independence for a Greater Syria, to include Palestine and Lebanon, rejected a Jewish home in Palestine, and forced Faysal to dismiss his Council of Directors. Initially a new cabinet was formed under al-Rikabi, but in May Faysal was forced to replace him by Hashim al-Atasi, a notable from Homs and later Syrian Prime Minister, along with a cabinet of the more extreme leading nationalists, including Dr Abd al-Rahman Shahbandar as Minister for Foreign Affairs. In short, even before the French occupation of July 1920 Syrian politics were escaping from the control both of the traditional older notables and of the new Hashemite regime.

In the short term, these trends towards a more populist, even quasi-democratic, political structure in Syria were quashed by the French. In preparation for a possible deal with the French, Faysal, closed the HNC offices on 12 July and its leaders fled abroad. Increasing anarchy in Damascus induced the government to impose martial law and other restrictions, which alienated many and inclined some towards French rule. The militias proved useless against the French army, which crushed an ad hoc Syrian force at Maysalun. The French then tried many nationalist leaders, mostly *in absentia*, and imprisoned minor committee leaders and others accused of brigandage. The French in turn engaged in intensive propaganda and organized pro-French demonstrations. There was some resistance to the French forces in Damascus and guerrilla activity elsewhere, but essentially the Faysal regime died with a whimper.

This did not, however, imply that it had no longer-term consequences. First, the nationalist programme of an independent Greater Syria enunciated by the Congress of 1920 became the basis of all Syrian nationalist politics until 1945, and many of the leading radical politicians were to play a major role in the anti-French movements of 1920–5, culminating in the rising of 1925–7, and again in the period 1936–9 in negotiations with France.

Second, and critical for the argument that follows, the political mobilization of the period before 1920 had threatened the dominant position of the leading notable families, particularly their older and most powerful members. The only group who welcomed the French were notables who had been sidelined under the later Faysal regime. In Damascus the French maintained in office Ala al-Din al-Durubi, a moderate nationalist and notable from Homs, and a supporter of the French, who had been appointed Prime Minister by Faysal just before the end, along with his cabinet of like-minded conservative notables from Damascus, including Abd al-Rahman al-Yusuf, Badi al-Muayyad, and Ata al-Ayyubi. Al-Durubi and al-Yusuf were killed by outraged nationalists on 20 August, but the tradition of collaboration by a section of the notables had been established. Both the surviving members of this government were to have important political careers under the French and their families remained moderate supporters of the French regime. Thus the second main inheritance from the Faysal years was that some of the more moderate notable families, seeing the danger of a threat from the more extremist and socially inferior elements to their traditional status, decided that it was worth collaborating with the French. This did not necessarily mean that they ceased to be nationalists; rather that they preferred to follow the route of negotiation and collaboration rather than confrontation. This was the root of both the concept of 'honourable co-operation' and the strategies of the National Bloc after 1928.

But before such strategies could become effective Syria had to go through a period of revolt and the suppression of resistance to French rule between 1920 and 1927. This second phase fell into two periods. First, from 1920 to 1923 there were risings among the Alawites in what the French called Latakia, in Aleppo, and in Damascus and other main towns. These risings had effectively been suppressed by 1923, but resentment continued to simmer. The major rising came in 1925, based on the Jabal Druze but involving much of the rest of the combined state of

Damascus and Aleppo. This 'Great Revolt' was suppressed by 1927, and the new period of non-violent politics then followed.

The Alawite resistance had litle to do with Syrian or Arab nationalism or the French. The Alawites were the Nusayri, a syncretic Islamic sect related to the Shia branch of Islam called *Alouites* by the French.[45] They lived in the mountains behind the port of Latakia in northern Syria and, in common with many other Middle Eastern mountain peoples, had maintained their quasi-independence throughout the Ottoman period. They were untouched by Arab nationalism; but once the French had occupied Latakia in November 1918 and began to move into the interior a resistance movement arose under Shaykh Salih al-Ali which accepted help from the Damascus government under Faysal. They also received help from the Turks, then fighting the French in Cilicia. This ended with the Turko-French Agreement of October 1921 and the Alawites surrendered. Shaykh Salih was eventually pardoned but lived only to 1926. The interest of his revolt was that, while not a nationalist in the normal sense, he had seen the value of co-operating with genuine Syrian nationalists in support of his basic desire for continued local autonomy.[46] The French then decided that what they called the state of Latakia should remain separate from the rest of Syria, along with Alexandretta and the Jabal Druze.

The next main anti-French resistance was in Aleppo. This was very different from that in Latakia, based on the second largest city in Syria and led by sophist-icated Arab nationalists who resented the influence of Damascus. It was organized by Ibrahim Hananu, a one-time Ottoman bureaucrat and land-owner who had joined the Faysal army in 1916 and joined al-Fatat in 1919. He was appalled by the verbosity of the 1919 Congress and its lack of effective action, and returned to Aleppo to mobilize more effective defence against the French. He founded a League of National Defence as a guerrilla force, and the Arab Club of Aleppo, which disseminated Arab nationalist ideas. The revolt in fact began as a rural rising in 1919 but was joined by urban nationalists after the French occupation of the city in 1920. It was heavily dependent on Turkish arms, men, and money: moreover Aleppo had always been more closely connected economically and culturally to Turkey than to southern Syria. With the French Senegalese forces occupying Aleppo the revolt became a guerrilla war and there was a serious pos-sibility that Hananu's forces would control much of north-western Syria. From late 1920 Turkish supplies gradually dried up and by April 1921 the rising had been contained by a reinforced French army. Hananu escaped to Transjordan in July 1921 but was captured by British police in Jerusalem and handed over to the French. He was tried in 1922 and surprisingly acquitted of organizing rebel bands, brigandage, murder, and the destruction of public utilities. He remained

[45] See Hourani, *Minorities in the Arab World* for the Alawites and also the Druze.

[46] There are many points of similarity here with Kurdish resistance to Baghdad rule in the early 1920s. In both cases these were mountain tribes which resented all forms of external interference and received help from Turkish irregulars.

an important nationalist leader until his death in 1935. His guerrilla bands had given up by the autumn of 1921. As a revolt the movement was eventually killed by the French agreement with the Turks that year.

With these two risings suppressed the French were free, with a large military force, to impose effective control over Syria. As was seen above, they were able to install collaborating notables in top positions. In Aleppo Kamil al-Qudsi, member of one of the grand Aleppine land-owning families, was made Governor with a Council of Directors of proven pro-French collaborators. Al-Qudsi followed normal practice under the Ottomans of appointing some sixty members of his family to official posts. He was supported in his pro-French role by a faction headed by Shakir Nimat al-Shabani, from the same land-owning/bureaucratic class, an ex-colonel in the Ottoman army who had lived in Europe and had strong French sympathies. In 1919 he had founded the Democratic Party of Aleppo, which co-operated with the French once they had occupied Aleppo but retained contacts with anti-French nationalists. He was to have a long and important political career under the mandate. France thus had a significant political base in Aleppo, though it was always a minority and many of the local notable families remained extremely hostile to those given office, partly from ideology, but also for traditional reasons of competition for official posts.

In Damascus, surprisingly given its nationalist record before 1920, there was very little resistance to French occupation. Most of the leading nationalist leaders had left or been imprisoned, the nationalist organizations had disintegrated, and there was no chance of Turkish support as in Aleppo. The French appointed the Damascus notable, Haqqi al-Azm, as Governor. Al-Azm, member of one of the most powerful of the local clans, had been an Ottoman official, joined the nationalists in 1912 after losing a rigged election to the Istanbul parliament, lived in Cairo, and belonged to the Decentralization Party. After 1914 he supported British policy in Arabia but fell out with the Hashemites in 1917 and was one of the first Syrian nationalists to support the French. In 1918–20 he was unable to mend fences with Faysal and tried to form his own anti-monarchical party. He was unpopular even with the non-nationalist notables of Damascus as a turncoat. But as Governor, though without any real administrative functions, he had the patronage to build up a block of supporters, including his own Azm and Muayyad relatives. The French refused to allow him and his departmental heads any freedom of action, but his faction's support helped them to maintain effective control over Damascus.[47]

This initial quiescence in the main cities ended in 1921 when an amnesty allowed most of the earlier nationalists to return from exile. Among them was Abd al-Rahman Shahbandar. Although from a merchant rather than land-owning family, he had married into the Azm clan. Unlike them he was no collaborator.

[47] It is worth remembering that in Iraq as well as in Syria there was very little urban resistance to the foreign occupation in the critical early years. In both cases this was largely due to the conservatism of the notables, who saw the need to come to terms with the new rulers and could then control the urban masses.

After training as a doctor, he had left for Cairo in 1916, co-operated with the Arab Bureau, and returned to Syria in 1919 as a nationalist supporter of Faysal. In 1920 he again took refuge in Egypt, but returned after the amnesty in 1921. He then helped to organize the Iron Hand Society, a highly secret nationalist group comparable in some ways with the earlier al-Fatat, which was pledged to work for Syrian independence and against the collaborating Azm government. The return of Charles Crane, of the 1919 King–Crane Commission, on a short visit to Damascus on 5 April 1922 provided the excuse for holding public meetings, organized by the Iron Hand Society, in safety from the French police. At these a wide range of grievances were put to Crane on the unfounded belief that the United States might do something about French rule. But when Crane left the French cracked down. Shahbandar and four other Iron Hand leaders were arrested. This sparked the first major riots in Damascus. On 8 April, 10,000 marched through the streets, including students, nationalists, religious leaders, and quarter bosses with their gangs. The parade was dispersed by French troops with many arrests and injuries, but was repeated on a larger scale on 10 April, this time with three Syrians killed, many injured, and more arrested. By 12 April the French had re-established control, but a pattern had been set. For the rest of the mandate the French were liable to be faced with large-scale urban demonstrations and the closing of all shops and businesses. The Iron Hand had demonstrated that nationalist protest was possible and that it could mobilize vast numbers for civil disobedience. Moreover, there were parallel movements in other main towns. In Aleppo an offshoot of the Iron Hand, the Red Hand, was formed by Sadallah al-Jabiri, who came from one of the leading notable families. It was not as effective as the Iron Hand but demonstrated that these new tactics of urban mobilization were adaptable to all major towns.

By May 1922 the Iron Hand had been effectively destroyed after the French were tipped off about its headquarters and membership. Many further arrests took place, including Jamil Mardam and Nazih Muayyad al-Azm, Shahbandar's brother-in-law. Some were given long prison sentences, others exiled. But in Damascus at least the ground had been laid for future co-operation between urban nationalists and rural rebels during the Druze rising of 1925–7. Moreover, these events had convinced the French that the collaboration of a small part of the local Syrian elite was not sufficient: a wider basis for their rule was needed. This led to the political reforms of July 1922 and June 1923. As was described above, the first of these set up the Federal Council consisting of fifteen appointees from the three Administrative Councils of the states of Damascus, Aleppo, and Latakia while the second created elective Representative Councils in each state, whose deputies would nominate their delegates to the Federal Council. Despite their limited powers, these bodies provide some insight into the role of the notables in this first essay in elective politics under the mandate.

In Damascus, four parties (though not well organized and more accurately groupings) evolved, though only three were prepared to take part in the elections.

The first was led by Haqqi al-Azm and Badi al-Muayyad, and consisted of notables allied with the Azms. The second was led by Rida al-Rikabi, now back after a period in Transjordan and prepared to ally with the French. These were regarded as government parties. The third, under Fawzi al-Ghazzi, from a land-owning/scholarly family, and Wathiq Muayyad al-Azm, who had fallen out with the pro-French Azms, was regarded as in opposition, Their demands were moderate: unification of Syria, and an amnesty for all political prisoners, but not the end of the mandate. The fourth group, led by the Iron Hand, was unable to bark because its leaders were mostly in prison or exile. Its stated aims were the end of the mandate and complete independence for Syria, its strategy to call for a boycott of the elections coupled with closure of shops and businesses. The elections were heavily managed by the French in favour of the 'government' parties, with very low turn-outs in Damascus and Aleppo. In Damascus the Azm faction won most of the seats, in Aleppo the supporters of the collaborating Subhi Barakat, already President of the Federal Council. In the Alawite state ten of the twelve seats went to French-backed notables. Barakat was then elected President of the new Federal Council, and Badi al-Muayyad, a rival, consoled with the Presidency of the Damascus Representative Council. Neither state nor federal councils had much political power, but they demonstrated the continuing dominance of the local notable families with French backing. But the Federal Council took two important decisions in January 1924. It rejected a Banque de Syrie proposal that it should continue to be free to issue paper currency without backing; and it declared that the Federation was replaced by a Syrian Union.

This in fact was in line with current French thinking, largely due to the financial problems of the small individual states. In June 1924 General Weygand, the High Commissioner, announced the fusion of Damascus and Aleppo. Latakia and the Druze would remain distinct, though Alexandretta would join the new Syrian state. The new united Syrian constitution came into force in 1925, and the new High Commissioner, General Sarrail, for the first time gave permission for the creation of political parties. The immediate result was the establishment by Shahbandar, who had been allowed to return from abroad following his imprisonment, of the People's Party. By June 1925 it had some thousand members, most from the traditional land-owning class plus others from mercantile and professional groups. It remained essentially an elitist organization and was a coalition rather than an integrated party. Its stated objectives were predictably moderate and were to become the staple of the later National Bloc. There must be a united Greater Syria, including Lebanon. There must be personal liberty and freedom, the protection of Syrian industries, and a unified educational system. The party would operate by 'legal means'. The party was strongly secularist: this was Syrian, not Islamic nationalism. Against the People's Party was the Syrian Union Party, led by Barakat to counter Shahbandar, and it consisted mainly of people collaborating with the French. But in fact the contrast between these parties was not fundamental. Both were led by Syrian notables and supported by the local elites.

However, before the elections, due to start in October 1925, could be completed, the Druze rising began. In February 1926 the new High Commssioner, Jouvenel, had suspended the constitution and imposed direct French rule. It is therefore impossible to know which faction of the elites of Aleppo and Damascus would have won a dominant position in the new Syrian Assembly.

The Druze rising of 1925, and the Great Revolt which it sparked off, was one of the major turning points in modern Syrian history. The Jabal Druze was one of those many pockets of religious autonomy found throughout the Middle East. The Druze were an entirely endogamous community which arose in Egypt in the eleventh century. Their religion was an eclectic mixture of Islamic, Christian, Greek, and Pagan beliefs. They were essentially a tough mountain group, resembling the Maronites of the Lebanon and the Kurds elsewhere, who had survived four centuries of Turkish rule and had been more or less left to themselves. They formed a number of clans of varying status, of which the dominant clan were the Atrash. Early French strategy had been to allow continued autonomy and to make an alliance with the head of the Atrash clan, Salim Pasha, as Governor. Apart from a limited amount of guerrilla activity, which had connections with Damascus nationalists, the Druze caused little trouble to the French.

Things changed after 1922 with the appointment of Captain Gabriel Carbillet as Commandant. He was an energetic official from French West Africa who set about making infrastructural reforms with great energy. He also aimed to improve the lot of the peasants through land tenure reforms. This alienated many of the local notables, including the Atrash clan. Ironically, on the death of Salim al-Atrash in 1923, disagreement between the members of the clan over the succession resulted in the majlis (the local council) electing Carbillet as Governor, which was a complete break with the established principle of an indigenous figurehead. In the spring of 1925 the Atrash clan, expressing general disillusionment with Carbillet's rule, sent a delegation to Beirut to complain and ask for his dismissal. As High Commissioner, Sarrail instead sent him on leave. In July his second replacement, Major Tommy Martin, warned Beirut that the Atrash clan were planning a major rising. Three Atrash chiefs then arrived in Damascus at Sarrail's invitation to discuss their grievances. Incredibly, they were arrested and exiled. This was the final catalyst of the rising. Sultan al-Atrash, who had wisely refused to go to Damascus with the delegates, united the Atrash clan and organized a major rebellion against the French.

In isolation, though a serious military threat since there were then relatively few French troops in Syria and they were certain to face the normal problems of fighting a fierce and well-armed mountain people, this rising might not have been serious. Its importance stemmed from the fact that it sparked off risings in Damascus and other major Syrian cities. These were to some extent the result of serious economic hardships caused by droughts, bad harvests, and, in the case of Aleppo, obstructions to its traditional economic links with Turkey. But they also reflected the continued nationalist feeling and the survival of urban resistance organizations. The Damascus radicals, led by Shahbandar's People's Party, were ready to revolt if the Druze could provide sufficient military support. By August 1925 a number of defeats of French troops provided the necessary stimulus: the Damascus radicals made an alliance with the Druze. A Druze advance to Damascus was, however, held back and the French arrested many suspected Damascus nationalists. Those who escaped moved to the Jabal Druze and there set up in September what they claimed was a national government whose aim was independence for a Syria which included Lebanon. By the end of 1925 large parts of Syria were in revolt, and the rebellion was not finally suppressed until 1927.

This was a genuine nationalist rebellion, comparable in many ways with the Arab rising in Palestine from 1936 to 1939. But its leaders had limited aims. According to Khoury,

They did not seek to overturn the French-controlled system of rule; rather they sought something less, the modification of the existing system and the relaxation of French control. Their real objective was to shift the balance of power between themselves and the French back in their own direction so as to restore their traditional influence over local politics—an influence which the French had undercut both in the nationalist towns and in the Jabal Druze.[48]

Yet, even though the Jabal Druze leaders had traditional aims, they adopted new tactics and alliances with the towns that cut across the normal lines of class, religion, and district.

In fact, between, September 1925 and mid-1926 there were major risings in Hama, Damascus, and Aleppo, but none in the Alawite state or Alexandretta. In each place there were different alliances between a section of the local notables, bosses of the quarters, and large sections of the working class. Most of the fighting was between guerrilla bands and French regular and irregular troops. The French were extremely brutal in their suppression and there was substantial loss of life and destruction of property.[49] By the summer of 1926 there were some 50,000 French troops in Syria and the risings were crushed. By the spring of 1927 the only remaining pockets of resistance were in Hama and in the Jabal Druze, and the neighbouring al-Laja region. Sultan al-Atrash was forced to take refuge in Saudi Arabi.

Who in Syria had supported and who opposed the rising? The main French collaborators were the Alawites and inhabitants of Alexandretta, who valued French protection. Two minorities also backed the French, the Circassians and the Armenian refugees who depended on French goodwill. Neutrals included most Syrian Christians and some absentee land-owners. The latter were typical of the Syrian notable class in that they preferred to sit on the fence and keep their options open, attempting to act as mediators. They included Rushdi al-Safadi, Ata al-Ayyubi, Shamsi al-Malki, Ahmad al-Hasibi, Anwar al-Bakri, Umar al-Abid,

---

[48] Khoury, *Syria and the French Mandate*, 165–6.
[49] There is a detailed account of this ibid. ch. 7.

and Said al-Jazairi. Conversely, other notables were among the three main groups who kept the revolt going. Some of these were in the lineal descent from notables who had been anti-Ottomanists before 1914, had later backed Faysal, and remained ideologically anti-French and in favour of a united independent Syria. But by the mid-1920s other notables with limited ideological ideas had been alienated by a number of aspects of French policy. Many had failed to obtain official posts from the chosen French collaborators. Many more had been affected by a doubling of the land tax and its more efficient collection. The French policy of land registration threatened their control over the peasantry. Thus, while there remained a gulf between these and the actively nationalistic notables, during the revolt a much wider section of the class backed it in varying ways and degrees.

The two other main groups, some of whose members supported the revolt, were merchants and peasants. The merchant class was divided. Most Christians hedged or supported the French. But many Muslim merchants, often closely related to the land-owning notables, supported the rebels. They were alienated by growing European penetration, especially by French companies, and by French monetary and tariff policies. As to the peasants, many feared the effects of land reform on their way of life, were affected by the growing capitalization of agriculture (though this had started long before the French), and hated the richer village heads, the mukhtars, who could exploit them and had often collaborated with the French. There were, moreover, many landless peasants who welcomed the chance to join one of the rebel bands.

Was this, then, a nationalist revolt? For most people loyalties were still personal—to the family, clan, quarter of a town, a village, or a religion—rather than to a nation. But the nationalists were able to convince many of the masses that the French were to blame for their immediate and often acute economic and financial problems. The largely secular nationalism promoted by the nationalist minority was able, briefly, to canalize these grievances against the French. As Khoury put it, 'Nationalism provided a handy mechanism by which to express grievances.... It was presented as a cure-all for all sorts of economic and social ills across a broad spectrum of society.'[50]

The third phase of Syrian nationalist politics began in 1927. With the Great Revolt suppressed and many of the more radical notables in exile or in prison, the way was open for the more moderate or time-serving notables to re-establish their position. What line they should adopt was heavily influenced by the group of *émigrés* in Cairo, many of them wealthy, who had formed the Syrian–Palestine Congress in 1921 to lobby in Geneva for an independent Syria and Palestine and who operated as a sort of government in exile. Its Executive was closely connected with the Party of Syrian Unity, set up after 1918 as a successor to the Cairo-based Party of Administrative Decentralization. The Executive consisted largely of representatives of many of the major Syrian notable families, but it was always

[50] Ibid. 217.

divided in purpose. The original President, Michel Lutfallah, a very rich Greek Orthodox Christian, was closely connected with the Hashemite dynasty and was pro-British. A close colleague was Shahbandar, who spent much of his repeated exiles in Cairo. It was Lutfallah who financed Shahbandar's People's Party. Opposed to them in many ways was Shakib Arslan, a Druze radical from Lebanon. He had been strongly in favour of the Young Turks, and was anti-British and anti-Hashemite. Closely connected with him were Shaykh Rashid Rida, and Ihsan al-Jabiri. Rida was elected Vice-President of the Congress executive, so could balance Lutfallah. These factions and their supporters fought for dominance in the Executive and over policy in Syria. By 1925 Lutfallah's group had been weakened by the defeat of Husayn in Arabia by Ibn Saud. In November 1925 Arslan had a private interview with Jouvenel in Paris before he left for Syria at which he proposed conditions for future Franco-Syrian collaboration. These were more than France would accept: independence, reintegration of the Alawite territory with Syria, and a plebiscite for those parts of Greater Lebanon attached in 1920 to choose whether to rejoin Syria. Given these concessions, the Syrians would give France exclusive economic rights and strategic bases. No nationalist had previously conceded so much, and it produced a major rift in the Cairo Executive. This generated the Jerusalem Committee, under Shukri al-Quwwatli, another anti-Hashemite (though he had held office under Faysal), with close relations with the Saudis, who was exiled by the French in 1920. By 1927 the Cairo Congress had virtually split, with two competing Executive Committees.

At this point, and with the return of effective French control in Syria, some of the Cairo exiles began to realize that their best strategy might, after all, be to come to some sort of agreement with the French. Their aim was to govern alongside the French until the mandate was ended. The opportunity came with the statement reported above, by Catroux in July 1927, that France might contemplate an organic law and devolution of power to Syrians, along with integration of the Druze and Alawites with Syria. In October 1927 Lutfallah was at last ousted as President of the Congress Executive; and on 25 October a conference of Syrian and Lebanese nationalists in Beirut, organized by the Congress, while regretting the limitations of Catroux's announcement, made a very important statement:

We are certain that in France the nation supports our national cause and desires to re-establish confidence between us. The sentiment of justice of the French people is evidence of this and we believe in the necessity of *collaboration* based on the reciprocity of interests and on the determination of mutual obligations.[51]

These words, reflecting a new realism after the defeat of the revolt, marked the beginning of a new era of Syrian politics.

The most visible sign of this was the evolution of a loose coalition of Syrian notables into what eventually came to be known as the National Bloc. This began

---

[51] *Syria and the French Mandate*, 248.

with seven of the fifteen of those who attended the Beirut conference in 1927, and they became the core of the Bloc: Ihsan al-Sharif from Damascus, Najib al-Barazi and Abd al-Qadir al-Kaylani from Hama, Ibrahim Hananu and Abd al-Rahman al-Kayyali from Aleppo, and Mazhar Raslan and Hashim al-Atasi (conference President) from Homs. In 1928, when the French issued a partial amnesty, others joined the group, including Fawzi al-Ghazzi, Lutfi al-Haffar, and Faris Khuri from Damascus, Husni al-Barazi from Hama, and Sadallah al-Jabiri of Aleppo. Conversely, the fact that Shahbandar and others of his People's Party, along with members of the Istiqlal Party (mostly in Transjordan), were excluded from the amnesty and therefore still abroad meant that the Bloc could evolve without their opposition along non-revolutionary lines. At a second conference in 1928 in Damascus it was announced that the coalition (hereafter the Bloc, even though the term was not used until 1932) would compete in the elections to the Assembly. By this time the original seven had been joined by others who became stalwarts of the Bloc: Fakhri al-Barudi, Zaki al-Khatib, Ahmad al-Lahham, Afif Sulh, Faiz al-Khuri, Muhammad al-Nahhas, and Jamil Mardam from Damascus; Tawfiq al-Shishakli from Hama; and Ahmad al-Rifai, Abd al-Qadir al-Sarmini, Hasan Fuad Ibrahim Pasha, and Jamil Ibrahim Pasha from Aleppo.[52]

Analysis of this group throws much light on the character of Syrian nationalism and on the social structure of politics. Of the leading members of the Bloc, 90 per cent were Sunni Muslims. All came from the main cities (50 per cent from Damascus, 30 per cent from Aleppo). Most were well-educated, in Istanbul, Beirut, or Europe. Nearly two-thirds came from the land-owning/bureaucratic or land-owning/scholarly classes, another quarter from more or less wealthy merchant families, the rest mostly from the unpropertied functionaries. There were exceptions, but most of these men were in their middle age in the 1920s. Some had belonged to the secret societies before 1914, more had joined al-Fatat during the Faysal era, and several had held important offices under Faysal. Thus the Bloc was a direct descendant of the pre-1914 nationalistic societies. Like them it consisted mostly of Syrian notables who were always ready to protect their social and political position while claiming to represent the interests of the 'nation': though whether this nation was the whole Arab people or merely Syria was uncertain.

The strategy of 'honourable co-operation' with the French, the stated aim of the Bloc from 1927 to 1939, was born out of defeat. The suppression of the Great Revolt demonstrated that military confrontation was not only pointless but also destructive of property and lives. The alternative was to demonstrate, both to the French and to the broader enfranchised class of Syrians, that this group could strike a viable balance between maintaining the crusade for independence and providing efficient administration if given office. To do this the Bloc had to discredit two categories of Syrian politicians: on the one side the 'moderates' and collaborators who had provided most indigenous office-holders since 1920, men

---

[52] Ibid. 248–9.

like Taj; on the other the more extreme nationalists, represented by the People's Party, who were not prepared to compromise with the French on any conditions. Their task was made possible by the shift in French strategy that was outlined above. They now recognized the need for Syrian collaborators who could command wider support than those they had used previously. Thus the Bloc presented France with the opportunity to achieve a settlement along Iraqi lines. The problem was that they were unable fully to exploit it.

The Bloc thus emerges as the lineal descendants (often, of course, the same men) of those who had wanted a moderate compromise between external authority and local self-rule under the late Ottoman empire. They remained essentially secular in outlook, while observing Islamic forms. They had no systematic social or economic programme. They did not attempt to organize mass support among the peasantry, though they were adept at mobilizing urban support in demonstrations, using their clan systems of patronage. They were committed to parliamentary tactics, confident that they could manipulate the electoral system to provide adequate, if not majority, support in the Chamber. This seemed to most notables the safest way to achieving Syrian independence without losing control over society.

There was, however, one major obstacle to achieving their aims by collaboration with the French. This was the need to maintain their nationalist credentials. The 1932 Congress of the Bloc in Homs, which first declared the Bloc a political organization, defined its primary aim. This was a commitment to form an independent Greater Syria. In deference to reality it no longer stood by the terms of the 1928 draft constitution, which had stated that 'the Syrian territory separated from the Ottoman state constitutes a single indivisible unit and any arbitrary division that has occurred from the end of World War I [*sic*] is meaningless'. Instead the 1932 Congress stated that the Bloc stood for the complete unity, territorial integrity, and independence of Syria, with the proviso that Lebanon could 'decide her own political fate within her pre-1920 borders'—that is, shorn of Beirut and the other maritime provinces attached to the Mountain by the French. That was a concession to reality, but it was not enough. Along with other French reservations, the territorial imperative was to plague all negotiations for a treaty until 1939 and had not been realized by the time of full independence.[53]

Since the Bloc was to play so important a role in Syrian politics it is necessary to outline its structure and organization as set up in 1932. There was a Permanent Office of seven, elected by the Council (the Office plus 31), which in turn was elected by Congress. There were to be regular meetings of Congress, which was seen as the means by which large numbers of supporters could be mobilized at

---

[53] *Syria and the French Mandate*, 262–5. There was a parallel here with the attitude adopted by the main Arab organizations in Palestine, both before and after partition in 1948, which, by refusing to accept the terms of the mandate or the United Nations decision of 1947, blocked any possibility of a settlement that included a Jewish homeland.

need. In practice the Bloc was run by the Permanent Office. Although this makes the Bloc appear to be a modern, structured, western-style national political organization, in fact it was very different. It was 'national' in only a restricted sense in that it had limited contacts in the Alamite state and the Druze, and with those parts of Greater Lebanon that the Bloc claimed for Syria. Nor was it an integrated organization. It was a loosely constructed coalition of landlords, merchants, and middle-class professionals. It provided horizontal links between the vertical networks of patron–client relationships which were the foundations of Syrian society. It was therefore vulnerable on two fronts. During the 1930s its power in the cities was gradually weakened by the growth of modern mass political organizations which displaced the old patron–client structure. Then, in common with many other colonial nationalist parties, it could retain its cohesion and *raison d'être* only so long as it was the main front organization in the struggle with France. Once that was over it lost its influence and structure.

Yet during the decade after 1928 it was the Bloc that dominated Syrian politics and took Syria closer than had ever seemed possible to a satisfactory treaty with France and independence. Its members had two main aims, which were not necessarily compatible. First, as nationalists, they had to use every possible device, short of insurrection, to force the French to concede acceptable terms for independence. Second, however, they wanted power for themselves and the patronage that went with it in order to maintain their systems of clientage. They had also to fight off potential threats to their near-monopoly of organized political power from new or revived rival organizations, possibly from lower classes in the towns. The nearest they came to achieving their objectives was between 1936 and 1938. Thereafter they were all but destroyed by the impossibility of squaring the circle.

The Bloc's first taste of power came in 1928 with the new Assembly. Despite much bribery and intimidation (probably on both sides), the Bloc got seven of the nine Damascus seats and all nine of those in Aleppo. Despite having only 22 of the 70 seats the Bloc was immediately dominant because most of the rest were held by men from rural areas who were not politically organized. As a result two Bloc members were elected to the two critical posts: Hashim al-Atasi as President of the Chamber and Ibrahim Hananu as Chairman of the Committee to draft the new constitution, most of whose other members were also of the Bloc or committed nationalists. The result, as was seen above, was a draft constitution which included six articles that set out the basic Bloc and nationalist position. Then from 1929 to 1932 there was no Assembly, and the Bloc had lost its main theatre for political drama.

Their opportunity came in 1932 under the constitution announced by Ponsot in 1930. The French used the normal electoral devices to return 'moderates' and supporters. In Aleppo, which had returned the entire Bloc list in 1928, the Bloc's candidates were withdrawn once it was clear that the government's list, mainly from the very moderate northern Liberal Constitutionalists party organized by Subhi Barakat, could not be beaten. But in the other main towns the Bloc did well, and there were 17 nationalists in the new Assembly of 69. These were not sufficient to dominate the elections to the top posts. Muhammad Ali al-Abid, from one of the richest and most distinguished Damascus families but not a party man, was elected President of the Republic, and he appointed Haqqi al-Azm, one of the longest-serving pro-French notables, as Prime Minister. But, probably on the instigation of the French, al-Abid appointed two Bloc members to cabinet posts: Mazhar Raslan and Jamil Mardam, along with a moderate Aleppine Liberal Constitutionalist, Salim Jambart. This was as near as the French had gone so far in recognizing the need to reflect electoral results and parliamentary strength in min- isterial posts. It remained to be seen whether the Bloc could convert this limited success into an acceptable treaty negotiation.

Circumstances were confused. On the one hand, the new French government under Herriot had instructed Ponsot to make progress towards a treaty. On the other hand, the Bloc was going through a period of intense unpopularity, partly because it had supported the managers and owners of the local textile industry in a strike for higher wages. In October, when parliament met, the Bloc was so unpop- ular with the crowds that only one of its deputies other than Raslan and Mardam dared attend. The division within the notable factions was made clear when Barakat was re-elected Speaker and Shakir Nimat al-Shabani, formal head of the Liberal Constitutionalist party, complained that there were two nationalists in the cabinet. At a conference in Homs early in November the Bloc, now joined by the previously very hostile nationalist, Shukri al-Quwwatli, enemy of Mardam, patched up differences and it was agreed that delegates would attend parliament and adopt what al-Atasi publicly described as 'a policy of conciliation'. The Bloc then succeeded in getting the support of the Liberal Constitutionalists to autho- rize the President to negotiate for a treaty. This appeared to be a major triumph for the moderate wing of the Bloc. The Syrian notables seemed at last to have arrived at a more or less common front.

The treaty negotiations were, however, handicapped before they started by statements made by Ponsot in Geneva. France would retain the mandate over the Alawites, the Jabal Druze, and the Greater Lebanon even if a treaty gave Syria independence. This was inconsistent with one of the Bloc's fundamental princ- iples. A conference at Aleppo, which was a hardliner centre under Hananu, denounced the French position: no member of the Bloc was to negotiate on those terms. Mardam, always ready to compromise, attempted to negotiate privately with Ponsot. He made no progress. Hananu insisted that he resign from the cabinet, which he and Raslan did, overtly in protest against French intransigence, though in fact because the Bloc leadership was determined they should go. The government was reformed without its Bloc members. The treaty negotiations came to a halt at the end of 1933.

The episode throws much light on the politics of the notables in the post-1928 era. First, the Bloc, despite all its conferences and agreements, was anything but united. It was basically divided between a more radical northern wing based on

Aleppo and dominated by Hananu, and a more flexible Damascus grouping led by Mardam. This was a regional as well as dogmatic division, and emphasized that the Bloc remained merely an unstable coalition. Second, the Liberal Constitutionalists were an ad hoc party largely created by the Delegate, Lavastre, to take the steam out of the Bloc in the north. Its leaders were Subhi Barakat, the arch city boss, and al-Shabani, and its members included an impressive list of northern notables, many of whom had held high office under the French. Their common denominator was willingness to work with the French, while overtly proclaiming the now standard objectives of independence and unity. Their success in the 1932 elections was largely due to French manipulation of the first-stage voting, and as a party they soon lost their coherence. Third, the fact that there were so many notables who were prepared to take office irrespective of the issues involved demonstrated that the old division between notables who regarded office as the main objective and those who were firm nationalists survived from pre-1914 days.

But the days when the notables in the great cities had a monopoly of high politics were ending. In 1933, and partly as a response to acute economic problems and unemployment, the League of National Action was formally established. It was not a specifically Syrian organization and grew out of the highly secretive pan-Arab Arab Liberation Society which had branches in Iraq and Palestine.[54] In Syria its first leader was Abd al-Razzaq al-Dandashi, a lawyer and member of a powerful landed family based in Tall Kalakh. He was convinced pan-Arab nationalist and extremely hostile to the Bloc's strategy of co-operation with the French. His followers were mainly urban professionals, many from the merchant class, but lacked the power-base of the Bloc and other notable politicians. The League built up a following in all the main cities, except for Aleppo. To compensate for its lack of traditional client support it concentrated on getting recruits in the youth organizations, particularly the Boy Scouts. In this the League came up against the Nationalist Youth organization, founded in the late 1920s and run by Fakhri al-Barudi as a training ground for Bloc supporters. The result was a competition in most of the big cities between the two organizations for members in the secondary schools and the law school in Damascus. The League tried to organize itself as a modern western-style political party. Its appeal was to a generation younger than that of the main Bloc leaders, and its propaganda more radically nationalist and pan-Arabist. Yet it lacked the material and social strength of the Bloc. During the 1930s, therefore, the League tended to act in collusion with the Bloc, while forcing the Bloc to take account of its radical aims. In short, while the politics of the notables remained dominant, there were new organizations representing other social strata of which the Bloc and other more conservative politicians now had to take account. This was to influence attitudes to the next round of treaty negotiations during the fourth period after 1936.

[54] There are details of the background and wider influence of the Society in Khoury, *Syria and the French Mandate*, 400–6.

The movement by the notables towards using the youth organizations and the urban mob as a political weapon became clear early in 1936, perhaps influenced by the example of the Wafd in Egypt. On 20 January, the French foolishly closed the National Bloc office in Damascus and arrested two Bloc leaders. The Bloc then organized demonstrations, which led to shooting by the French troops, with two dead. At that point the Bloc lost control of the situation, which was taken over by the student leaders, mostly from the League of National Action. Until 27 January, in an attempt to regain control, Mardam called formally for a general strike, though this had already been in effect for a week. The strike lasted for 36 days and was more complete even than that during the Great Revolt, extending to all the main towns. The French responded with martial law, very many arrests, including Mardam and Nasib al-Bakri, and many deaths. The crisis lasted until 2 March. Meantime de Martel, probably on orders from Paris, had replaced Shaykh Taj as President and installed a more moderate but not nationalist government under Ata al-Ayyubi. Al-Ayyubi met the Bloc leaders and, presumably with French approval, it was announced by Hashim al-Atasi, the Bloc President, that he and a Bloc delegation would proceed to Paris to negotiate a treaty, and that political prisoners would be released. On 3 March the Bloc declared that the strike was over.

Paradoxically, because the strike was not really the work of the Bloc, it enabled the Bloc to resume control of the nationalist movement in Syria. The fact that the strike had been officially called by the Bloc, and that it had proved capable of controlling the mobs, using its structure of patron–client relationships, demonstrated that the notables were still in command. As the British Consul in Damascus reported to London, 'a notable feature of the general strike . . . was the remarkable degree of obedience shown to the leaders and the powers of organization and command that these leaders displayed in controlling the crowds'.[55] This feature was critical: the Bloc and the notables as a whole might well have lost control over the urban forces they had encouraged, and it reflected the continuing hierarchical structures of urban society. The Bloc's triumph seemed complete with the apparently successful negotiations in Paris and the initialling of the draft treaty in September. With this momentum the Bloc was able to dominate the general elections in November 1936. Hashim al-Atasi was elected President of the Republic, Mardam as Prime Minister with a Bloc cabinet. The Bloc then followed standard Middle Eastern practice. The central and regional governments were packed with Bloc supporters, including the governorships of Latakia and the Druze. It seemed that, though still under French mandate, the Syrian nationalists could harvest the fruits of political victory as freely as any government in independent Iraq.

It is, however, important that the electoral victory was won in part by the use of new weapons that stemmed from recent experience of techniques of urban control. While the Bloc leaders were in Paris, their colleagues in Syria developed a new and more sinister supporting organization from the Nationalist Youth. This

[55] *Syria and the French Mandate*, 463.

was the Steel Shirts, copied from similar organizations in Italy and Germany, and paralleled by paramilitary organizations in Lebanon, the Phalanges, the White Shirts, and the Najjada. They were organized in Damascus by Fakhri al-Barudi, who dreamt of developing a national army. By the end of 1936, there were some 15,000 members in Damascus and the other main towns. They wore grey uniforms, marched, used the fascist salute, and became a dominant influence among the young, mainly students and the petty bourgeoisie. They were financed by subscriptions and by payments from a range of merchants and large companies. These troops were used by the Bloc to demonstrate its influence among the young. More seriously, the Steel Shirts were extensively used during the 1936 elections. They helped to bring voters in from the countryside and demonstrated widely in support of Bloc candidates. How significant their support was in the electoral success of the Bloc is impossible to estimate. But it is clear that by 1936 these notable politicians had begun to turn from their traditional dependence on the clientage system and the urban quarter bosses. It was a pointer to the later effects of having a national army which was outside the control of the notables and developed its own mind.

The two years from 1936 to 1938 marked both the apogee of the rule of the notables who formed the National Bloc and the start of its downfall. As with all indigenous collaborators in a colonial situation, Mardam and his party were in a cleft stick. On the one hand, they had to depend on the continued good faith of the French. Their credibility depended on their success in using the 'honourable co-operation' technique to get what the French had promised: an acceptable treaty leading to independence. On the other hand, they had to maintain control over the divided people of Syria and its outlying provinces. By the end of 1938 it was clear that they had failed on both counts.

The most serious failure stemmed from French backsliding, as was described above. The final refusal of the French parliament in December 1938 to agree to ratify the treaty effectively destroyed the Bloc's position. Even before that the Bloc's support had been seriously weakened by the concessions Mardam had been forced to make in his visits to Paris in 1937 and 1938. These eroded elements in the draft treaty on minority rights, provincial decentralization, the use of French advisers and experts, French oil rights, the teaching of French in schools, and the tenure of the Bank. Although these concessions were sweetened in 1938 by Paris bringing forward the transitional period to independence to 30 September 1939 if the treaty was ratified, they were used by opponents of the Bloc to discredit it, led by Shahbandar, now intermittently back in Syria and leading the anti-Bloc Constitutional Group. Moreover, in February 1938 al-Quwwatli resigned in protest against the leaked news of the 1937 concessions, starting what eventually became a serious fragmentation of the leading Bloc members.

Another major blow to a party pledged to the unity of an independent Syria was the French cession of Alexandretta to Turkey. The Turks had renounced all claims to the sanjaq at the Treaty of Lausanne in 1923 and made no move until

1936. Then the news of the Syrian treaty, which included the unification of the state of Syria and the four autonomous sanjaqs—Alexandretta, Latakia, the Druze, and Jazira—caused an outcry among the 39 per cent who were ethnic Turks that they would lose their position. Ankara then took up the protest, and in 1937 the League of Nations mediated a compromise which was embodied in a Franco-Turkish treaty. Alexandretta would remain autonomous with its own parliament. Turkish would remain the official language, but Syria would control foreign relations, customs duties, and currency. The agreement was denounced by the Damascus government but was immutable. Thereafter, increasing friction between the various ethnic groups in Alexandretta led to another Franco-Turkish treaty in March 1938 which allocated the ethnic Turks 22 of the 40 seats on the sanjaq's new parliament. This Turkish-dominated parliament and its entirely Turkish ministry then legislated effectively to bring Alexandretta under Turkish control. The sanjaq was renamed Hatay and in June 1939 the French, anxious above all to prevent Turkey joining the Axis, agreed to cede that part of their mandate to Turkey.

The loss of Alexandretta was a serious blow to the Bloc's prestige. So also were developments in the other three autonomous sanjaqs. These were all to be integrated into the Syrian Republic by the terms of the treaty, and decrees issued by the High Commissioner in December 1936 had put that into effect. All now sent delegates to the Syrian parliament and governors were appointed by the Damascus government. There were still, however, French troops in each sanjaq. In each place opinions on integration were divided and in each local political struggles broke out after 1936. The worst of these took place in the Jazira, resulted in considerable bloodshed, and had to be put down by French troops. All this was a serious blow to a Bloc government which professed the essential unity of all Syria. In 1939, with the Syrian constitution suspended, the High Commissioner issued decrees placing all three provinces effectively under direct French rule.

These things, along with the failure of the treaty negotiations, contributed to the fall of the Bloc as the dominant Syrian party. Al-Quwwatli, the strongest critic of Mardam's concessions, resigned in February 1938 and there were other defections. The Aleppo Bloc was alienated and internally divided. By the end of 1938 the Bloc was divided into four groups: those still supporting Mardam; the al-Quwwatli faction, which included the industrialist Khalid al-Azm and others of importance; a third group led by Faris al-Khuri; and a fourth led by the Bakri brothers and Faiz al-Khuri. As the Bloc disintegrated, other groups emerged into prominence. The Arab Club, equally elitist, was both anti-French and pro-German, and was in touch with German authorities. It was shut down in 1939 by the French, as was the League of National Action, which had continued to attack the Mardam government. More influential than either was Shahbandar, amnestied in 1937. Returning, he reinvigorated the Party of National Unity, set up in 1935, which had denounced the proposed treaty on the ground that it prolonged French control for 25 years after independence. Although Shahbandar did not stay long in Damascus before returning to Cairo, he galvanized the opposition to both the treaty and Mardam and provided a focal point for opposition leaders.

Aware of his growing political weakness, Mardam made as an excuse for resigning in February 1939 on a nationalist issue, a decree issued by the High Commissioner on personal status affecting the religious communities, so going out of office as a political martyr. He was followed by a series of short-lived ministries, and there was much public disorder and many strikes. These were fomented by Puaux's announcement in May, after a visit to Paris, that negotiations for a treaty could be renewed provided the Syrians accepted the concessions offered by Mardam. This was widely rejected; and in July, while parliament was adjourned, Puaux issued the four decrees suspending the constitution. The first era of Bloc domination and quasi-self-government for Syria was over.

But this was not the end of the regime of the notables, nor even of the Bloc. Divided they might be, yet they had retained the two essentials of political power in Syria: their wealth and their ability to control or mobilize the masses in the towns. In this last period after 1939, even under wartime conditions, the French could not do without their collaboration. In 1939–40 Puaux saw advantages in getting the support of Shahbandar, who was vociferously anti-Axis and also a political enemy of the Bloc. He was assassinated, for no apparent reason, in June 1940, and leading Bloc members were alleged to have been involved. These included Mardam, Lutfi al-Haffar, and Sadallah al-Jabiri, who escaped to Iraq. The assassination shattered Shahbandar's loose party and left the Bloc the only significant political group. Now led by Shukri al-Quwwatli, who adopted a quali-fied pro-Axis position, on the assumption that the Germans were more likely than the French to grant full independence, it maintained opposition to French rule and organized strikes early in 1941.[56] This did not get the Bloc back into office. But in April 1941, in order to reduce opposition, the new High Commissioner, General Henri Dentz, set up a legislative council under Khalid al-Azm, member of the dominant Damascus family, a moderate nationalist but with no Bloc associ-ations. Ironically, however, because the appointment of al-Azm and the council was clearly the outcome of the Bloc's strikes, the Bloc was ready to support him.

The Allied invasion of Syria and the end of Vichy rule cleared the way for the return of the Bloc and notable power. De Gaulle, of course, had no intention of giving Syria independence: his aim was to prepare for renewed negotiations for a treaty under the conditions demanded by Paris in 1937–8. But meantime he and his Delegate-General Catroux needed Syrian collaborators. Moreover the French were under pressure from the British Foreign Office to restore the constitution and hold elections. The 1936 constitution was reinstated in September 1941 and a cabinet installed, though with no elections. The French were unable to recruit

[56] In this respect al-Quwwatli resembled Rashid Ali, who, as was seen in Ch. 3, saw the Germans as likely to end Iraq's continuing ties with Britain.

Hashim al-Atasi and others of the old Bloc, so they appointed that old war-horse of French rule, Shaykh Taj, as President. His cabinet consisted of a group of notables who were not Bloc members, but included Hasan al-Hakim, one-time ally of Shahbandar as Prime Minister, and other well-established moderates. Al-Hakim could not long work with Taj, and he was replaced by two successive collaborating notables in 1942 and January 1943. Thus for nearly two years the Free French ruled as the French had done for most of the period before 1939, with an appointed cabinet of no political alignment.

The final phase of political domination by the notables of the Bloc began in 1943 and lasted some five years. Al-Quwwatli and Mardam were allowed back late in 1942 under British pressure, and in January 1943, after the death of Taj, the French announced that elections on the basis of the 1939 constitution would take place in July. The Syrian parties immediately began to gear up. Al-Quwwatli renamed the Bloc the Nationalist Party (though here still referred to as the Bloc) and refurbished the old alliances with the leading Bloc notables. In the July elections the Bloc won a sweeping victory. The new government was a replay of the old Bloc governments. Sadallah al-Jabiri was Prime Minister, Jamil Mardam Foreign Minister, and others included Lutfi al-Haffar, Abd al-Rahman al-Kayyali, Khalid al-Azm, and Mazhar Raslan. When the parliament met, al-Quwwatli was elected President. The old elite was back in power.

But it now faced opposition of a new type from politicians outside its patronage system and some from other social groups. Most of these parties were small but some were to have longer-term significance. The Youth Party, lead by Akram Hawrani of Hama, from a land-owning family that had lost its land and wealth, stood for social reform, and was the first to raise the issue of peasant poverty and insecurity in a parliament that had always ignored issues of this kind. Small new groups were the Baathists, the Communists, and the Muslim Brothers. The Baath Party (Renaissance) did not take that name until after 1945, but was led from 1943 by Michel Aflaq, a former schoolteacher in Damascus. Although a Christian, and French-educated, he promoted a vision of an ideal Arab movement that was essentially based on Islam and opposed dangerous European influences. A parallel small party was the Communist Party under Khalid Bakdash, again composed mainly of minor professionals and a few organized industrial workers. Its strength had grown during the war as it championed the need of the working class in relation to food prices. The Muslim Brethren, founded as a party in 1944, emerged from two decades of conservative Islamic campaigning by shaykhs and ulama against the introduction of western modes of dress for women and in general the weakening of Islamic traditions, which had generated a large number of small pressure groups. It was led by Shaykh Abd al-Hamid Tabba of al-Gharra, who was elected to parliament in 1943 and had supported al-Quwwatli. He expected the new government to legislate in line with his conservative Islamic principles, and was outraged that the government repressed riots in May 1944 against a proposed ball at which Muslim women would not wear the veil.

These were in 1944 merely portents of a more fractured political system that would eventually challenge the dominance of the Bloc and the notables. But until 1949 the old guard were safely ensconced in power and office. It was they who negotiated with the Free French until 1945 and, with essential British support, insisted that the French evacuate and hand over all authority and facilities. They became the first government of a genuinely independent Syria. Ironically their last great achievement under the mandate—the transfer of the Troupes Spéciales from French control in 1945—was to lead to the destruction of the reign of the notables. The Troupes Spéciales had been recruited by the French largely from the minority communities, Alawites, Druzes, Armenians, Circassians. They did not come from the ranks of the notables, who, as in Ottoman times, despised military service. By 1945 the majority of their officers were Syrian, and, like those in the Iraqi army, they came mostly from the petty bourgeoisie who saw the army as a path to social improvement. They were also easily infiltrated by radical politicians. At the same time, after independence the senior officers were mostly appointed from Sunni and upper-class backgrounds, probably as part of the system of political patronage.[57]

It was ultimately this army that ended the rule both of the Bloc and, in the longer term, that of the notables. In 1948 the miserable showing of the Syrian army in the fight for Palestine discredited the government, then under Jamil Mardam, and outraged the army, which blamed the politicians for their failure. In December 1948 Mardam resigned and Husni az-Zaim, as Chief of Staff, took over control. Initially he intended to maintain normal constitutional government and persuaded that veteran Bloc politician and minister, Khalid al-Azm, to form a government. Army and government, in the face of widespread public agitation and disorder, eventually fell out. On 30 March 1949 az-Zaim staged a coup, forced the resignation of both President and Prime Minister, dissolved parliament, banned political parties, and made himself President after a referendum in which he was the only candidate. So, though with some short-lived gestures in the direction of new liberal constitutions and civilian rule between 1949 and the union with Egypt in 1958, ended both the rule of the Bloc and the era of democratic constitutionalism in Syria.

It is now possible to provide tentative answers to the two questions posed at the beginning of this chapter.

To the first question, why the French wanted to control Syria and why they had eventually to be forced out of it, the answers have already been suggested. Expansion into the Ottoman Middle East formed part of a French nationalist drive to maintain the Republic's international position, along with a range of French established interests, and to avoid being excluded by the British. Once

[57] There is a useful analysis of the recruitment patterns of the Troupes Spéciales (Special Forces), later the Syrian Army, in N. van Dam, *The Struggle for Power in Syria: Sectarianism, Regionalism and Tribalism in Politics, 1961–1978* (London, 1979), 39–44.

there, a complex of emotions and interests made it difficult for any French government to back out even as far as the British had done in Iraq by 1932. Emotions were important, particularly those associated with religion and the concept of the civilizing mission. Of the vested interests perhaps those of the armed forces had become the most important by the later 1930s: Syria and Lebanon had come to be regarded as vital for preserving French power in the eastern Mediterranean. Of these Lebanon, with its major ports and naval facilities, was the more important: hence the continuous opposition to Syrian demands for unification. In this respect French attitudes resembled those of the British military after 1945 in Palestine and Iraq. But a major consideration was the price France had to pay for staying there. Had there been further major risings comparable with the Great Revolt, or the Palestinian rising of 1936–9, France might have had to reconsider its options. Hence the critical factor was the ability of France to maintain political control at relatively small military and financial cost; and this leads into the second question, why Syria, and also Lebanon, which will be considered in Chapter 8, proved more docile than their early protestations and claims for independence would have led one to predict.

The argument in the second section of this chapter suggests that the key to the relative docility of the nationalists in Syria lay in the attitudes of the notables. There is a paradox here. On the one hand many, perhaps the majority, were nationalists in the sense that they honestly wanted an independent and sovereign Syria. But there were fundamental reservations in their pursuit of this aim. As a class, though that is probably not an accurate term for so diverse a grouping, their primary aim was preservation of their status. They were therefore strongly against any major changes in the basics of their society, such as land-ownership, from which most of them derived their wealth and influence. Although the French started a widespread land survey and attempted to sort out the complexities of land-ownership, they made no attack on the large estates or on absentee landlords. On the whole the economic impact of France was favourable to the notables, particularly improved communications.[58] Thus French rule may be regarded as a conservative factor. It preserved the social structure and with it the status of the notables, the urban merchants, and other established groups. It was only where the status quo seemed to be threatened, as in Latakia and the Druze, that there was serious resistance by the notables.

Yet the notables were deeply divided between different shades of nationalism. How far these divisions were essentially dogmatic and how far tactical is debatable. Some notables were undoubtedly deeply committed nationalists, such as Shahbandar, others seemed to shift with the tides. In effect there was a continuous spectrum of notable politicians, from those who had no objection to French rule, were culturally affiliated to France and so in a sense *évolués*, and were prepared to

---

[58] Longrigg, with long administrative experience in Iraq before 1932, gave a favourable general assessment of French economic achievements between the wars. See Longrigg, *Syria and Lebanon under French Mandate*, 271–83.

collaborate under all circumstances, to those who opposed it tooth and nail, but were willing to negotiate for independence under acceptable conditions. French rule was possible because shrewd administrators could play these various factions off against each other, always able to find docile collaborators to hold high offices when more fractious politicians became too difficult. Above all, the French possessed the same asset once held by the Ottomans: they could distribute office and with it all the power and perquisites that provided. Thus in many ways the politics of the mandate resembled those of the years before 1914, and notables were similarly divided between those who held office and those who wanted it. There were some sea-green incorruptibles who would never be seduced by French patronage, as there had been before 1914, but they were probably a small minority. In this sense the French therefore simply played the same role as their Turkish predecessors, and the notables reacted in much the same way. Unfortunately for France, their collaborators came to be outnumbered and outgunned by the nationalists, after which French rule became impracticable except at vast military cost.

Perhaps the most significant aspect of the French mandate was that it preserved the status quo, particularly of the upper class. The Faysal regime might well have led to radical changes: the mandate did not. Thus, while the notables might complain, they received most of the rewards of office that they might have obtained under an independent regime. The supreme irony is that after two and a half decades of struggling for independence, once it came in 1945 the notables had very little time left. In both Iraq and Syria it took exactly four years from independence for the army to destroy their political domination in the military coups respectively of 1936 and 1949. It is ironic also that in Iraq the regime of the old notables was given a new lease of life from 1945 to 1958 as a result of the second British wartime occupation. In Syria there was no reprieve. The age of army-based radical regimes had come to stay. In retrospect, therefore, the mandate constituted the last golden age of social and political power for the Syrian notables.

8

Lebanon and the French, 1918–1946

The modern history of Lebanon began in 1920, when the French, the prospective mandatory, created a state which they called Le Grand Lebanon, Greater Lebanon. Since this state had no historic unity its later development depended on whether this amalgam of Ottoman districts and religious sects could hold together and generate a sense of common nationhood. Because this was necessarily largely a political process, much emphasis in this account will be placed on political structures and developments. It is proposed here to divide the study into two sections: first the establishment of the mandate and its background, second the operation of the mandate to 1945.

1. THE FORMATION OF LEBANON TO 1920

Lebanon in its modern form had never been a state or even a defined geographical region. It had always constituted part of an empire, since the sixteenth century that of the Ottomans.[1] The region included in the new state of Greater Lebanon by the French in 1920, corresponding with contemporary Lebanon, consisted of a composite of largely tribal societies with their own clans and highly competitive rulers. The Mountain, the main Maronite area, was populated by a mosaic of powerful land-holding kindred groups with a large subservient peasant society beneath it. These kindred groups evolved a hierarchy of power. Among the Druzes, the Jumblatts and Arslans vied for pre-eminence but were immensely

[1] Here I am following K. Salibi in *A House of Many Mansions: The History of Lebanon Reconsidered* (1985; London, 1988), and E. D. Akarli, *The Long Peace: Ottoman Lebanon, 1861–1920* (London and New York, 1993), which provides the best detailed account of the politics of the Mountain before 1914. Other basic texts used in this account are: A. I. Baaklini, *Legislative and Political Development: Lebanon, 1842–1972* (Durham, NC, 1976); Y. M. Choueiri (ed.), *State and Society in Syria and Lebanon* (Exeter, 1993); D. C. Gordon, *Lebanon, the Fragmented Nation* (London, 1980); J. Entellis, *Pluralism and Party Transformation in Lebanon: al-Kata'ib 1936–1970* (Leiden, 1974); A. H. Hourani, *Syria and Lebanon* (Oxford, 1946); M. C. Hudson, *The Precarious Republic: Political Modernization in Lebanon* (New York, 1968); S. H. Longrigg, *Syria and Lebanon under French Mandate* (London, 1958); K. S. Salibi, *The Modern History of Lebanon* (London, 1965); N. Shehadi and D. H. Mills (eds.), *Lebanon: A History of Conflict and Consensus* (London, 1988); M. Zamir, *The Formation of Modern Lebanon* (Ithaca, 1985); M. Zamir, *Lebanon's Quest: The Road to Statehood 1926–1939* (London, 1997).

dependent on the loyalty of a plethora of smaller kindred groups which tended to form two loyalty groups based on mythical descent from pre-Islamic kindreds: the Qays and the Yamani. In the Muslim areas annexed to the Mountain in 1920, most notably the Shii Biqa and the south, very large landlord families emerged in the second half of the nineteenth century, usually families that had acquired tax-farmer status. They lorded it over large estates.

Lebanon was deeply divided. In terms of religion there were Christian Maronites (in communion with Rome), Druzes, Shia, Sunnis, and several smaller sects including Greek and Catholic Orthodox. Economically and socially the area ranged from the arid Mountain region to the richer agricultural Biqa Valley and Baalbek, and to the highly commercial seaports of Beirut, Tyre, Sidon, and Tripoli. The nearest the whole area had come to unity was under the Maronite Shihab dynasty, appointed as tax farmers by Istanbul from 1711 to the 1840s. These Amirs had used their tax authority to establish something approaching a single polity, tied together by deals with local tribal notables, over the Mountain, the Jabal Shuf, the Jabal Kisrawan, and eventually Jabal Lubnan. In some sense Lebanon acquired a coherent shape in this period, and this created the concept of Lebanon as a proto-state.

This era, known as the Imarah, ended in the 1840s after the Egyptian invasion and occupation of 1831 and the breakdown of the system of group alliances. Struggles for power developed between the Maronites and the Druze of the Mountain. There were civil wars in 1841, 1845, and 1860: the last of these resulted in the death of more than 10,000 Christians and made 100,000 homeless. The Ottomans were persuaded, under strong western pressure, to intervene. The western powers backed the demand of the Maronites to become a separate administrative unit, and this was fixed by the Règlement Organique of 1861, guaranteed by Britain, France, Russia, Austria, and Prussia. The Maronite section of the Mountain was made into an autonomous sanjaq or mutasarrifiya within an Ottoman vilayet: from the 1880s this was the vilayet of Beirut. The area of the sanjaq was never precisely demarcated but covered some 2,600 square kilometres. Critically, it excluded both the four main ports and also the fertile Biqa Valley and Baalbek. It therefore consisted essentially of the economically weak mountain districts and had to depend on imported wheat and other foodstuffs. Hence the irredentist demand for more territory and for access to the great commercial ports, and so for a Greater Lebanon.

But it was the political structure that gave the Mountain its peculiarity and was to have a critical effect on later political development. Under the Règlement there was to be a mutasarrif (governor) who was appointed by the Porte, but who had to be approved by the European powers, and by convention was a Christian. The sanjaq had its own council, administration, and budget and a French-trained militia. As compared with other Ottoman provinces it had tax privileges and its inhabitants were exempt from military conscription. The most important feature of this system was the powers and composition of the Administrative Council. Its powers were quite extensive. They included the raising of taxes, supervision of expenditures, the construction of roads and public facilities, and acting as a review body for the election of the village leaders. This was exceptional in Ottoman sanjaqs and reflected the influence of the five supervising powers. More important for the future was the composition of the Council. Of its twelve (later thirteen) elected members, initially four were Maronites, three Druzes, two Greek Orthodox, and one each Greek Catholic, Mutawalli (Shia), and Sunni. This ratio was imposed on the sanjaq by the Powers and was intended to prevent a Maronite domination. Conversely, the pattern of representation, and indeed the whole Règlement, was from the start challenged by the leaders of the Maronite church. They had three main objections.

First, they wanted representation proportional to numbers, which would have given the Maronites a built-in majority. Moreover, the four Maronite members were elected by the people, not nominated by the church, as they had been before 1861.

Second, although the older feudal structures had been dismantled, the Governors adopted the standard Ottoman ploy of appointing amirs and shaykhs to the higher administrative posts as governors of districts and other official positions. This had the effect of keeping the older feudal families in power, though now as bureaucrats rather than autonomous rulers.

Third, the Maronite hierarchy deeply resented the fact that the boundaries of the sanjaq were substantially smaller than those of the earlier Imarah, though in fact they exaggerated the size of the older Lebanon.

Two of these aspects of the 1861 settlement—a multi-confessional council and a territorially restricted sanjaq—were to become dominant features of Lebanese history before and after 1920.

The Administrative Council had a profound influence on the political structures and politics of Lebanon to the end of the mandate and beyond. It gave the Mountain an exceptional experience, probably unique within the Ottoman system, of elective politics: thereafter Lebanon was always to be intensely political. The distribution of seats by confession, although altered later to approximate more closely to population, was to remain fundamental, along with the principle that individual electorates would return members from different faiths.[2] This was embodied in the 1926 constitution, which, apart from the abolition of the Senate in 1927, was to remain the basis of Lebanese political life to the 1970s. The fact that the Council had administrative responsibilities generated a class of administrators of considerable ability. The continued involvement of the local landed classes ensured general support: between 1920 and 1939 52.15 per cent of deputies were landlords, as compared with 18.03 per cent for lawyers and 23.9 for other professionals. Thus, exceptionally within the Ottoman empire in the Middle East, the Mountain was accustomed to a large degree of self-government. The result was that, once these traditions had been transferred to the Greater

[2] For the changing distribution of seats by confession after 1920 see Baaklini, *Legislative and Political Development*, table 1, p. 85. For the continued political domination of the landlords see table 2, p. 86.

Lebanon of 1920, the territory was much more difficult to control by the mandatory power than one like Iraq or even Syria, which had no similar quasi-democratic tradition and in which the notables were generally able and willing to control government and politics in the interests of the mandatory.

The other major aspect of the Règlement was that it established a deeply felt resentment at the boundaries set. The aim of those who established the regime was to provide a Christian majority to prevent more sectarian massacres, even though this was not reflected in the Council. This made it necessary to cut off three main regions which had been more or less included in the Imarah: the western coastal region with the main ports, the Biqa Valley and Baalbek with fertile agricultural land to the east of the Mountain, and the Jabal Amil and Jabal Akkar to the south and north. From the moment the new sanjaq was created, this truncation became a major grievance with many Maronites. They demanded the incorporation of all these areas in what they regarded as the 'natural geographical borders' of their sanjaq. There were a variety of reasons for this. There were many Christians (though few Maronites) in Beirut and the Biqa Valley, who, it was claimed, wanted to join the Maronites. Economics were crucial. The Mountain was a poor region unable to feed itself: it needed agricultural land to become viable, particularly in view of the decline in silk exports in the later nineteenth century. Its businessmen wanted wider markets. The sanjaq needed a seaport, particularly as Beirut, its natural point of access to the Mediterranean, was a separate sanjaq and there were customs barriers between the two sanjaqs. Moreover, Beirut was the main banking and business centre for Lebanon, indeed for much of the eastern Mediterranean. The need for more territory was supported by the figures for emigration, mainly of Christians: between 1900 and 1914 some 100,000 Lebanese, a quarter of the population, left for America, Egypt, West Africa, and South America. A larger Lebanon would be better able, it was claimed, to support its growing population.[3]

Zamir, however, argues that the main impulse towards a Greater Lebanon was a Maronite demand for independence. This had been expressed as early as 1876 by Yusuf Karam, a middle-class Maronite, who had the support of the Maronite Patriarch. He rebelled in the hope of becoming Governor, was defeated and exiled. But he became an icon of Maronite expansionists. In 1908 a book by Bulus Nujaim, under the pen-name M. Jouplain and published in French for European consumption, demanded both an expanded and autonomous Lebanon. Moreover, Nujaim appealed to France, as one of the signatories of the 1861 Règlement, to intervene.

This was very significant. Whereas most French claims in the Middle East had little historical basis, their links with the Maronites were genuine and long-established. These dated to the Crusades and, more recently, the French adoption of the Capitulations in 1535 and specific protection of the Maronites established in 1649, which had been restated repeatedly since then as part of the wider French

[3] Zamir, *The Formation*, 15.

claim to a protectorate over Roman Catholics in the Middle East. Some 6,000 French troops had landed in Beirut in 1861 to suppress the civil war. Thereafter France remained the conceived saviour of the Maronites and the means to achieve their objectives. It is very important for what followed that the Maronites, and some other Christian groups in Lebanon, were the only indigenous people in the Middle East who not only welcomed but actually invited European control after 1918. For them France came not as an infidel invader but as a Christian saviour. The only comparable group were the Zionists, for whom, though in quite different circumstances, Britain played the role of protector and promoter. The result in both Lebanon and Palestine was similar: a deeply divided society and civil war.

But before the mandate, Lebanon had more than half a century of effective autonomy. After the ratification of the Règlement in 1864, there were no major changes in the structure of government. But the coming to power of the Young Turks in 1908 and the restoration of the 1876 Ottoman constitution stimulated Maronite demands for more autonomy, as it had done elsewhere in the Ottoman Middle East. In September 1908 a so-called Liberal Party demanded an increase in the Council's powers, new elections to it, tax reductions, and dismissal of corrupt officials. They besieged the Governor's house, and to forestall riots he dismissed the Vice-President of the Council and some other officials. But the Mountain was split over whether to take part in elections to the resuscitated Ottoman parliament. Broadly the division was between the Maronites, who feared that an Ottoman parliament would be the precursor of greater centralization and loss of the Mountain's autonomy, and the other Christian denominations, plus the Muslims and Druze, who supported participation, in the converse hope that this would reduce Maronite domination. In the end the Maronites persuaded a majority of the Council to vote against participation: the Mountain was one of the few sanjaqs in the empire not represented in the Ottoman parliament before 1914.

The subsequent Ottoman strategies of greater centralization and control were predictably resented in the Mountain. Some of these were common to the empire as a whole, including the introduction of identity cards and military service for non-Muslims. While Christians in the Mountain were still exempt, the many who had moved to other parts of the region were not. Istanbul, moreover, refused to meet the budget deficit, as specified by the Règlement. A specific grievance was Istanbul's refusal to allow the sea town of Junieh, within the Mountain's territory, to be used as a port in order to bypass Beirut. The Council then appealed to the protecting powers, and particularly France, for support. This proved successful. In December 1912 the Liberal Union government in Istanbul approved a new proto-col. The powers of the Council were increased, an additional Maronite member attached, the electoral system changed, and two ports were authorized, Junieh for the Maronites and Nabi-Yunis for the Druzes.

But by this time, with French encouragement, such concessions no longer satis-fied the Maronites: they wanted a Christian state under French protection. France became more overtly interventionist and the Council acquired unprecedented predominance under the new Governor, Ohanes Pasha. For the first time, political parties evolved, though mostly very small and consisting mainly of lawyers and journalists. There was also a proliferation of Lebanese organizations overseas in Paris, Egypt, and America, whose members were often more nationalistic than the Lebanese at home—in particular the Comité Lebanais in Paris, led by Shukri Ghanem and Georges Samné, who linked up with the wider French colonial activists in the Comité Central Syrien to demand French control of Syria. On the Lebanese coast, especially in Beirut, there were many Orthodox Christians who wanted to join the Mountain as a defence against their Muslim neighbours.

The Muslims, particularly the Sunnis, were divided over the whole issue. Most saw themselves as integral with Syria and some saw the Maronite demand for French protection as a form of treason to the Ottoman empire. They wanted autonomy and decentralization, but not independence. In Beirut some Muslims resented the growing Christian population which dominated the commercial sector. There was growing anti-French sentiment, partly due to French dominance of much of the modern economy of Lebanon. But after the military disasters of the Balkan wars, there was a significant coming together of Sunni and Christian notables in Beirut, demonstrated by the Reform Society, which wanted autonomy for the existing vilayet of Beirut, which included the Mountain, and which proposed an assembly and executive committee on which Muslims and Christians would have had parity. Although the new vali of Beirut banned the Society in 1913, this collaboration between Muslims and Christians continued and was reflected in the joint Christian–Muslim delegation sent to the Arab Congress in Paris that year. Thus it would be wrong to suggest a fundamental division between Christian and Muslim notables on the coast. They were, after all, all Arabs with many common interests. The main dividing factor was their attitude to France.

The war intensified this division. Both Christians and Muslims suffered under the rule of Jemal Pasha but they differed in their hope for the future. While many Muslims saw hope in the British and eventually supported the Faysal regime in Syria, most Christians, and especially the Maronites, who suffered most and whose Council was suppressed, saw salvation in France and were violently hostile to Faysal. For them an enlarged Mountain under French protection now seemed the only basis for security. By 1919 the Patriarch Hawayik, who had suffered severely during the war, was ready to lead his Maronite community in a demand for a Greater Lebanon under France.

It was, however, far from certain that the Maronites would achieve their aim.[4] That France was determined to acquire effective control over western Syria, including the whole of what became Greater Lebanon, was demonstrated by both

---

[4] The following summary is based mainly on Zamir, *The Formation*, ch. 2, and C. M. Andrew and A. S. Kanya-Forstner, *France Overseas: The Great War and the Climax of French Imperial Expansion* (London, 1981).

the Sykes–Picot Agreement of 1916 and by the McMahon–Husayn correspondence of 1915: Lebanon clearly lay to the west of the districts specified as part of the prospective Arab kingdom. But whether Lebanon would constitute merely part of a greater Syria under some form of French tutelage or would be separate from inland Syria remained in doubt until 1920 and the San Remo Conference. The French arrived in Beirut in October 1918 after a new Anglo-French agreement that OETA West (Lebanon) would have a French civil administration. Beirut then became their main operational centre. There was never any question of their ceding control of the coastal areas to the British. But whether Lebanon would be separated from Syria once the French took over the inland areas from the British—after November 1919—remained uncertain. As late as April 1919 Clemenceau agreed with Faysal that, if Faysal accepted a French mandate over the whole of Syria, Lebanon would be included in 'a federation of local communities'. Even Robert de Caix, later a key player in Lebanon and a strong French imperialist, discounted Maronite demands for separation and independence. In 1926 he wrote that there was little hostility in 1919 to an agreement with Faysal. But

One only felt that we could not honourably hand over to the Sharif our long-term clients, but it seemed that, in guaranteeing Lebanon against excessive tendencies to [Syrian] unity . . . one would do what was necessary. For the rest, one was perfectly content with the limited autonomies to be given to these minorities which were one of the objects of Wilsonian policy.[5]

This attitude was vehemently attacked by the Maronites. They sent a delegation of seven members of the Administrative Council to Paris in December 1918, later (in August 1919) replaced by the Patriarch Hawayik, which allied with Shukri Ghanem and the Comité Central Syrien, though this meant support for a general strategy of French control over Syria rather than for a specific Lebanese objective. Initially neither embassy had much impact. But after Hawayik had presented a paper to the Peace Conference on 27 October 1919, detailing Lebanon's claim to complete independence under French mandate, French attitudes began to change. This followed Clemenceau's September agreement with Lloyd George, which left him with a much freer hand. On 10 November 1919 Clemenceau sent Hawayik a letter which for the first time formally accepted Lebanon's claim to be separate from Syria, though the boundaries were not then stated. This decision reflected both strong pressure from vested interests and activists and official assessment of the value of Lebanon to France as a main focus of her power in the eastern Mediterranean. The agreement between Clemenceau and Faysal on 6 January 1920 left the boundaries of Lebanon to the Peace Conference but included Sidon, Tyre, and other parts of southern Lebanon. On the other hand, they excluded Tripoli, Akkar, much of the Biqa and Baalbek: this was not the Greater Lebanon of Maronite fantasy.

[5] Quoted Zamir, *The Formation*, 61, trans. D. K. F.

The resignation of Clemenceau and the accession of Millerand in January 1920 radically changed the situation. So also did the growing aggression on the part of the Syrian government and Syrian guerrillas, answered by intensified French military action. Meantime, the inhabitants of what was to become Greater Lebanon, according to the investigations of the King–Crane Commission of 1919, were deeply divided over its future. On the Christian side almost all Maronites and Greek Catholics supported a French mandate and separation of Syria and Lebanon. The Greek Orthodox were divided, but feared Muslim dominance if Lebanon was united with Syria. Almost all Sunnis wanted incorporation in an independent Syria. The Druze, led by the two most powerful Druze families in Lebanon, the Jumblatts and the Arslans, were strongly against a French-dominated Lebanon. The Shii Mutawallis of Jabal Amil in the south were afraid of both the Sunni and the Christians, and wanted a loose connection with Syria. Clearly no solution to the limits of Lebanon could command general acceptance.

In the end, once the San Remo Conference had allocated the Syrian and Lebanese mandates to France, it was General Gouraud, the first High Commissioner, who decided the issue. There was, however, no unanimity among the French administration in Beirut. Robert de Caix, as Secretary-General, and others with local knowledge were strongly against a Greater Lebanon. De Caix thought only the Biqa Valley and the Jabal Akkar in the north, both mainly Christian, should be attached to the Mountain at once. Beirut and Sidon should remain separate for the time being and Tripoli become part of Syria. Beirut was too big and heterogeneous to be part of the Mountain, and might overbalance the rest of Lebanon. It should become an autonomous municipality, but serve as the main port of Lebanon. Sidon might form the focus of a small Mutawalli state, though closely linked with Lebanon. All this was designed partly to avoid the danger of interconfessional conflict within an extended Mountain, partly to serve French interests by cutting off the more positively Muslim areas of Lebanon from the Muslims in Syria. All these segments would be linked in a loose Lebanese federation.

De Caix sent these proposals direct to the Quai d'Orsay on 17 July 1920, even before the occupation of Damascus. They were approved and sent to Gouraud by Millerand on 6 August as a guide to policy. But Gouraud, a devout Catholic, did not accept de Caix's arguments. He was a strong supporter of the Maronite demand for a Greater Lebanon and underestimated Muslim hostility to being incorporated with the Mountain. He also overestimated the size and importance of Christian groups in the predominantly Muslim areas. Even before he heard from Paris he annexed the Biqa Valley to the Mountain on 3 August. Under continuous pressure from Gouraud and from Christian groups Millerand finally gave in. On 21 August he authorized the incorporation of all the areas demanded by the Maronites, while warning that the inclusion of Beirut and Tripoli might cause problems: they should have considerable autonomy. On 1 September Gouraud issued decrees creating the Greater Lebanon of the Maronite dream.

The establishment of Greater Lebanon was to have consequences in some respects comparable to those following the Balfour Declaration in Palestine, though of course there were no significant foreign settlements in Lebanon. In both, a foreign power established a state that was fundamentally divided and in which there might ultimately be no single nation. Again, the motives of France were as mixed as those of Britain in Palestine, which were discussed in Chapter 4. In each case there was a strong religious element. The conservative and Catholic right in France, with its long connection with the Maronites, saw this as an opportunity to establish what they expected to be a predominantly Christian society and to protect the Maronites from the assumed threat of Islam. Moreover, many felt some gratitude to the Lebanese Christians for their activity in mobilizing French opinion after 1914 to demand French control of Syria. There was much sympathy for the sufferings of the Maronites during the war. Such sentiments paralleled those in Britain who favoured a home for the Jews in Palestine. But, as for Palestine, there were also more practical considerations. French determination to control Syria, which had now to be seen as a resentful dependency, made it more important to have full power on the coast. A Syria without direct access to the sea was likely to be more docile than one that controlled Beirut and Tripoli. If Lebanon was enlarged it would be a more viable French partner than the poverty-stricken Mountain could be. Moreover, since France was determined to match British power in the eastern Mediterranean, a Lebanon dominated by loyal Christian collaborators would provide a solid base for French military and naval forces. Thus, Greater Lebanon was expected to serve both ethical and practical purposes.

The question was whether it would become a stable society, and possibly a nation. The odds in favour of this were in fact better than they were in Palestine. Virtually all the inhabitants of the new Lebanon of whatever confession were Arabs and spoke Arabic, despite the preference of the intelligentsia for French. They shared a common culture: as was seen in Chapter 1, the revival of Arabic and the cult of Arabism initially evolved in Lebanon. There had been common ground in the resistance to Turkish centralization policies after 1908. In Beirut in particular there was much interplay between the various Christian sects and Muslims. In the Mountain there had been half a century's experience of a multi-sectarian legislature with considerable collaboration between Maronites and Druzes. The question was whether such earlier experience in a small Lebanon could be extended to the new Greater Lebanon.

The main danger, of course, came from the fact that much of the area now annexed to the Mountain was occupied by Sunni and Shii Muslims who had expected to be part of a Muslim Syria. Until 1920 Christians had constituted about 79 per cent of the sanjaq, of whom over 58 per cent were Maronites, along with relatively few Sunnis and Mutawallis but 11 per cent Druzes.[6] In 1921 the proportions were radically different. Maronites were still the largest single group

---

[6] These and the following statistics are taken from ibid., table 3.1, p. 98. Statistics have been rounded up.

with 33 per cent but along with Greek and Catholic Orthodox and a few other Christians constituted 55 per cent. Sunnis were not over 20 per cent, Mutawallis 17 per cent, and Druzes 7 per cent, making a total of 45 per cent Muslims. By 1932 the Christian proportion had declined to just 51 per cent, and Maronites to 29 per cent, compared with Sunnis at 22 per cent. Moreover, despite the Maronite claims, Christians did not constitute a majority in any of the newly annexed territories. The Christian segment was further reduced by an absolute decline in Maronite numbers, the result largely of emigration. Clearly this was not going to be the Christian-dominated entity of French imagination.

Equally significant was the huge contrast between the Mountain and much of the rest of the new Lebanon. First, the political experience of the Mountain, with its elective Council, was very different from that of the other regions, which had had only advisory councils with little power and only elections to the Ottoman parliament after 1908 as an introduction to electoral politics. Second, there were profound differences in social structure. The Mountain consisted largely of independent farmers and a few land-owning notables, with the Maronite church as the largest land-owner. By contrast, the typical Middle Eastern social structure of large land-owning notables and tenant farmers remained the norm in most Sunni areas in the Jabal Akkar to the north and among the Mutawallis in the Biqa Valley and the Jabal Amil to the south. Third, the new areas were more closely linked to inland Syria than to the Mountain. Finally, most of the religious sects were concentrated in particular areas, so tended to retain their differences.

At its birth, therefore, there was no common identity in the Greater Lebanon, and no instinct to become a nation. A substantial proportion of the population, predominantly Muslim, conceived itself to be part of Syria as under Faysal in 1920 and resented both the French mandate and imposed unification with the Mountain. These were not, however, insuperable obstacles to the evolution of a nation state. Time and common experience might soften sectarian acerbities. Elites of different persuasions might, especially in larger towns such as Beirut, find common cause: there was already much interaction between Sunnis and the Orthodox Christians there. But perhaps the most important factor was politics. All states with complex confessional and other fractures have either to accept that a dominant group have permanent control or to devise political forms that provide reasonable access for minorities and a balance of interests so that no part feels excluded. In both Iraq and Syria the Sunni element achieved a dominant position, though for different reasons. In Lebanon only the Maronites might have achieved that position, and they would undoubtedly have wished to do so. But both the complexity of the society and French policy prevented this. Maronites could be no more than the first among equals. Their power would depend on how well they could play the game of favoured clients of the mandatory and use their sophisticated knowledge of electoral politics to acquire the fruits of power. In fact, the future of Lebanon as a nation state would depend very largely on how a political structure contrived to minimize sectarian resentments could be made to work.

2. POLITICS AND NATION-BUILDING, 1920–1945

The political life of Lebanon under the mandate began in 1921. It was not, in fact, until then that the separation of Lebanon from Syria was finally established after a period of debate within French circles. In 1920 the Commissioner dissolved the old Mountain Council and then set up an Administrative Council. The important fact was that the old principle of confessional seats survived. The new council of seventeen had six Maronites, four Sunni, three Greek Orthodox, one Greek Catholic, two Mutawallis, and one Druze. These were all appointed by the High Commission and were carefully selected as supporters of France. The Council had very limited powers but demonstrated the same sense of autonomy as the old Mountain Council. It was, in any case, merely an interim arrangement. In March 1922 de Caix put out two decrees concerning future arrangements. The first defined the Representative Council. This was to have thirty delegates and would be elected for four years by 'general suffrage'. Its most important feature, which was to become fundamental to Lebanese politics, was retention of the confessional principle. The allocation of seats was based on the 1921 census and gave ten seats to Maronites, six each to the Sunnis and Mutawallis, four to the Greek Orthodox, two to the Druze, and one each to Catholics and minorities. Thus there would be seventeen Christians to fourteen Muslims. But the electoral system was carefully designed to prevent straightforward confessional voting. There were six electoral districts, deliberately large so that the French could influence the results. Each district would choose a specified number of deputies from each of the confessional communities, but every deputy had to be elected by the whole electorate, using the old Ottoman two-stage system. This encouraged collaboration between candidates of different sects to persuade voters to vote across confessional lines.[7] De Caix, who drew up the scheme, justified it on the grounds that

it is the rite, the confessional community, that constitutes the real nationality of Lebanon. The idea of the Fatherland, that is, the union of all in a common temporal or social ideal, cannot at the moment prevail against the barriers that divide the many religious groups. Even the two main groups, Christian and Islamic, subdivide into various schismatic rites, which form quite separate nations. Moreover each nation claims for itself its own proper right to influence the destiny of the country. It follows that the only just basis for a government must be provided by an exact measurement of the members of these different groups. Until such time as there evolves a common interest among these particular interests, the country can only be run by a policy of division correctly proportioned among the various elements which compose it.[8]

This decree was generally welcomed. The other decree, which defined the powers of the Council, was not. The Council was to have only advisory power and

---

[7] This was in marked contrast with the system of voting in British India, where there were separate electorates for different confessions. This tended to harden sectarian political divisions.

[8] Quoted Zamir, *The Formation*, 142–3, trans. D. K. F.

could not initiate legislation. The Governor (French, by contrast with the indigenous governors of some of the Syrian states) or the High Commissioner could initiate legislation, ignore or reverse Council decisions, draw up a budget if the Council failed to do so, and adjourn or dissolve the Council at will. This caused a huge outcry, reflected in Lebanese circles in Paris and elsewhere; but de Caix justified the decision on the ground that this was merely a transitional arrangement. This general resentment was reflected in the elections. Most Sunnis abstained and only one-third of the electors in Beirut voted. The result was that all six elected Sunnis were pro-French. But the first Council, in the three years of its life before it was dissolved in 1925, established what became important conventions. All the three elected Council Presidents were Maronites. The Vice-Presidents were Sunnis, the Secretaries a Mutawalli and a Greek Orthodox. The Council acted mainly as sounding-board for grievances and a training for politicians but came to be seen as a symbol of national autonomy. It also began the process of incorporating leading Muslim politicians into the new secular state.

But the Sunnis were far from ready to accept their inclusion in Greater Lebanon, and during these three years they campaigned hard for a return of the newly attached territories to Syria. They were not, however, united on this: there were some, supported by many Greek Orthodox, who wanted Beirut to be made an independent city, others who demanded an independent coastal zone. These demands were blocked by France, and by 1924 the pressure had diminished. By that time, however, a new problem developed under the new High Commissioner, General Maurice Sarrail, appointed by the new French government of the 'Cartel des Gauches'. Sarrail, an anti-clerical Mason, was initially welcomed by the Sunnis as one who might reduce the Maronite hegemony. Sarrail did, indeed, warn the Maronite Patriarch that he would oppose any intervention of his church in political affairs. Sarrail then attempted to gain popularity by announcing that a new Governor would be appointed, that he would be a Lebanese, and would be chosen from three names put up by the Council. The leading candidate proved to be Emile Eddé, then President of the Council. Despite the fact that the French-educated Eddé had made his political career as a strong supporter of the French mandate, he was obnoxious to Sarrail because he was a Maronite and suspected of wanting to promote Christian domination.[9] Sarrail vetoed his candidacy, tried to persuade the Council to choose his preferred French candidate, Léon Cayla, the Governor of the Alawites, and when this failed, dissolved the Council. He then appointed Cayla. This resulted in an outcry in Lebanon, particularly from the Maronites, who had always regarded France as the defender of their interests. It was also severely criticized in French political and official circles. But Sarrail and Cayla attempted to carry on with an anti-sectarian programme so as to lay the foundations for a secular state. They proposed the creation of a secular unified educational system, which, after much Maronite

---

[9] There is a good summary of Eddé's career in Zamir, *Lebanon's Quest*, 70–4.

opposition, was eventually blocked. Similarly, a proposal to end both the allocation of seats in the Council along confessional lines and the two-stage electoral process was opposed by both Maronites and Muslims, and was vetoed by Paris. One major change, however, was made. While the six electoral units remained, the administrative structure, including taxation and justice, was remodelled. There were now eleven units, which cut across confessional lines.

In June and July 1925 elections to a new Representative Council were held. As usual the High Commission did all it could to influence the process, using the appointed Secretary-General, Habib al-Saad, a long-serving Maronite politician who had been president of the old Administrative Council of the Mountain, then of the original French Council and finally of the Representative Council, to arrange matters. He did so effectively. Only thirteen of the old members were re-elected and prominent Maronites such as Eddé were not. On the other hand, there was increased interest and involvement among Sunni notables, who were prepared to collaborate with Sarrail on the assumption that he was the first High Commissioner not to be a fervent supporter of the Maronites and that a share of power would benefit their community. It was the beginning of what was to become intensive Sunni engagement in Lebanese politics. While the new President of the Council was Musa Namur, a Maronite, the Sunni notable Omar Dauq became Vice-President with a Greek Orthodox and a Mutawalli as Secretaries. The docile new council then re-elected Cayla, rather than an indigenous candidate, as Governor until the new constitution was prepared.

The new Council was due to prepare a constitution. But before it could do so the Druze revolt, examined in Chapter 7, broke out in Syria. This had serious effects on Lebanon. Militarily Zayd al-Atrash's invading force occupied Mount Hermon and the Wadi al-Taym in October 1925, hoping for support among the Druze of southern Lebanon in order to establish a combined Druze state. On 10 November they occupied Hasbaya, the main Druze centre in the area. But on 11 November a small Druze force under Hamza Darwish attempted to occupy the nearby Maronite village of Kawkaba and about thirty Maronites were killed before the village was looted and set on fire. This terrified the Maronite commuity, which remembered the massacre of 1860, and prevented any Maronite–Druze collaboration. In fact many Maronites were provided with arms by the French, though, along with other armed groups, they engaged more in looting and terrorism against Druze villages than in actively opposing the invaders. Successful defence of the citadel town of Rashaya by French troops on 20 to 24 November marked the end of the serious threat to Lebanon, after which a delegation of Lebanese Druze went to Beirut to declare their loyalty to the mandate. But looting by Druze guerrillas continued in the Biqa Valley for much of 1926 with considerable loss of life and property among the predominantly Christian, but also Druze, inhabitants.

Politically, the main effect of the invasion was to stir up confessional rivalries and to revive Syrian demands for reintegration of Tripoli and the Biqa with Syria.

This received considerable support among Sunnis on the coast and a formal petition was presented to the new High Commissioner, Henri de Jouvenel, who arrived early in December after the dismissal of Sarrail in October, by a group of Sunni notables. This revived hostility to the Greater Lebanon was carried over into the discussions on the new constitution. Conversely, investigation made by Jouvenel into the attitude of Tripoli and other areas to their possible return to Syria outraged the Maronites. In short, the Druze invasion and Jouvenel's attempts to find a solution to the annexed territories combined to deepen confessional divisions and to undo much of the integrative developments of the previous five years.

The new constitution was promulgated on 23 May 1926. It is not at all clear who were its authors or just how extensively the Lebanese were consulted. In May 1925 a French deputy, Auguste Brunet, was sent to Beirut and he discussed possibilities with a wide range of local notables and politicians. The Druze revolt occurred while this process was going on and intensified demands from the Lebanese Representative Assembly that it should take part in the preparation of the constitution. The revolt also influenced Paris, which decided to accept this demand. Jouvenel was instructed to allow the Council to debate and draft a constitution.

It did so for some six months between December 1925 and May 1926. A drafting committee of twelve, with balanced confessional membership, was set up which in turn appointed a sub-committee of five under a Greek Orthodox chairman, to prepare a draft. This sent questionnaires to representatives of each community. The general consensus was that Lebanon should be a republic with a parliament of two houses, the ministers to be responsible to parliament, and that confessional representation should continue. In a hurry to get the constitution through before he returned to Paris on 27 May, Jouvenel instructed the Council to convene on 19 May as a constituent assembly. It then debated the draft for four days and on 22 May approved it, along with protocols defining the powers of the mandatory and relations with Syria, which had been drawn up by the French. On 23 May Jouvenel formally promulgated the new constitution. Under pressure from Jouvenel, on 26 May the old Council, now called the Chamber of Deputies, held a joint meeting with the newly appointed Senate (chosen along conventional confessional lines) and elected Jouvenel's choice for President of the Republic, the Greek Orthodox and proven pro-French Charles Dabbas. With the formation of a cabinet under the Maronite, Auguste Adib Pasha, who had long administrative experience both in Egypt before 1918 and in Lebanon, as Prime Minister, the process was complete.

This constitution with some adjustments, such as the abolition of the Senate in 1927, was to survive into the later twentieth century. It represented the conclusion of the first main stage of nation-building. As it emerged in 1926, parliament had two houses. The Senate had 16 members, seven of them appointed by the President of the Republic, nine elected for six years. The Chamber of thirty was elected for four years. Both elections were on the old two-stage system with universal male suffrage. Jointly the two houses elected the President, dealt with motions of confidence in the government, and approved budgets. Executive power lay with the President, who was elected for three years in a joint session of both houses. A second term was permitted. He had very extensive powers. He could appoint a Prime Minister and ministers, dissolve parliament provided he could get a three-quarters majority of the Senate, and initiate constitutional revision. The other ministers were individually responsible to parliament. As to the sectarian balance, article 95 guaranteed that 'the sects shall be equitably represented in public employment and in the composition of the Ministry', though article 12 stated that 'every Lebanese shall have the right to hold public office, no preference being made except on the basis of merit and competence', while article 27 stated that 'a member of the Parliament shall represent the whole nation'.

A year after this had been approved the system was changed. The new High Commissioner, Ponsot, took the opportunity of a crisis over the budget to strengthen the executive and end the two-house system. This was not simply a French strategy: there was a widespread feeling that the constitution already needed revising, though there were political aspects to this. To avoid accusations of French manipulation Ponsot entrusted revision to the President, Charles Dabbas, and his Prime Minister, Beshara al-Khuri. With Ponsot they hammered out proposals which were sent to Paris and approved. The Senate and Chamber would be amalgamated into a house of 45—thirty elected and fifteen nominated by the President. The President would have increased powers independent of parliament, which included passing laws, initiating constitutional revision, and financial freedom. Predictably, these proposals aroused general resistance in both houses, since they would significantly reduce parliamentary control over the executive. After months of intensive negotiation a heavily amended draft was agreed. The main concession was that all existing members of both houses would initially sit in the new combined house, so that no one had to undertake the expensive process of standing for election. Other innovations were that ministerial responsibility was to be collective, not individual, that a no confidence motion required a two-thirds majority (increased to three-quarters in 1929), and that the President could impose a budget if the parliament failed to pass one. Four (rather than three) ministers might now be deputies.

This was, and was intended to be, a presidential constitution, markedly different from that of the French Third Republic, in which the Prime Minister was head of the government, and far closer to that of the United States or, for that matter, the French Fifth Republic. The justification was that already politics in Lebanon were demonstrating that a legislature lacking coherent political parties would not manage affairs efficiently and was too prone to factional obstruction. If France was to allow the Lebanese to run their own affairs, provided French interests were protected, it was essential that they should do so efficiently. Conversely, of course, concentrating so much power in the hands of a President made it more possible for France, provided the High Commission could influence his election and policies, to exert control. One thing, however, was certain. From then on the main prize in Lebanese politics was the presidency. It became a central Maronite aim to ensure that the President was one of them, so that they were in effective control.

The first general election after the new constitution came into effect was in 1929, and this was the real test of how politics would now work. One thing that had not changed was the confessional allocation of seats. As in the past, the first-stage electors voted for members of an electoral college in each of the 1922 districts. In the second stage, the delegates voted for the actual delegates from lists of those who had received a majority in the first round. The quotas for elected members were the same as in the earlier Chamber, to which a proportionate number of nominated members would later be added by the President. In an eventual Chamber of 45, thirty would be elected, the rest nominated, and the total for each confession would be in the same proportion. Thus, whereas in 1926 there had been ten Maronites, six Sunnis, five Mutawallis, four Greek Orthodox, four Druze, one Catholic, and one representative of minorities, there would now be the same proportion of elected members for each confession but an addition of fifteen nominated to maintain the same ratios, except for the minorities, which still had one deputy. This system had the beneficial result that it encouraged candidates from different sects to organize themselves on joint lists, since a successful list was one whose members had secured the most electors from all sects. Thus there was likely to be as much if not more competition between would-be delegates from the same sect within a given district as between the sects. Conversely, it made for collaboration between politicians of different sects. In short, it was the list that mattered.

The preparation of these lists had begun long before the elections. Thus, in the south, which was dominated by feudal families, the two leading clans, the Azads and the Zeins, made deals to fill the six seats allocated to the electorate. The list was headed by two Mutawallis, led by Yusuf al-Zein, and two other Shia. There was one Sunni and two lesser-known Maronite and Greek Catholic candidates. All were duly elected. In the Biqa the three leading Shia clans agreed to maintain the balance of power between them. The final list included Shia from these families (another would be nominated), one Maronite, one Greek Orthodox, one Greek Catholic, and one Sunni. There was much more competition in the north for the one Maronite seat there. It was even more intense in the Mountain where there were no large feudal families to arrange matters, though the church played a large part. There were major divisions within the Druze community, which complicated the preparation of lists. In the event only 37 per cent of the potential electorate voted in the first stage, lowest in the Sunni areas, due to the Sunnis' official rejection of the constitution, and in Tripoli, highest in the Mountain and the Shiite areas, where the great lords got their dependants out to vote for their list. The second stage was marked by a great deal of physical intimidation of the electors and much bribery. It left communities deeply divided.

The elections convinced Ponsot that Lebanon was not ready for parliamentary democracy, and there was a widespread feeling among the younger intelligentsia that politics was corrupt and government inefficient. Politicians were in it only for personal profit and all governments used office mainly to provide appointments and rewards for their supporters. The public service was grossly overstaffed, but politicians were too deeply engaged in the patronage competition to agree to reforms. Thus in 1929, when Emile Eddé as Prime Minister attempted to close some hundred state schools as being weak and unnecessary, there was a huge outcry in parliament and in the country, led by Muslims who complained that these were mainly for Muslim students. They were backed by Muslims in Palestine and Syria. Dabbas, as President, felt it was too dangerous to back the project and in March 1930 Eddé gave up and resigned office.

This defeat reflected what was to become the central feature of Lebanese politics for the next decade and later. This was the struggle between rival Maronite factions for the presidency. The two main contenders were both Maronites, and this implied a serious split in their ranks. The first was Eddé. He was a Damascus-born Maronite, though never a religious enthusiast, son of a dragoman (interpreter) to the French consul. He was educated at the Jesuit College in Beirut and in France. From 1912 he was legal adviser to the French consulate and married into a wealthy Greek Orthodox family. During the war he had taken refuge from possible conscription in Egypt, returning in 1919 as political adviser to Georges-Picot. He then formed an alliance with his future main opponent, Beshara al-Khuri, and his banking ally, Michel Chiha, to form the Progressive Party, aiming to secure Lebanese independence under French mandate. He was appointed to the Administrative Council in 1920 and elected to the Representative Council in 1922. He established a lucrative legal practice and invested successfully in property. He would thus appear to have been the ideal collaborator for the French administration. In fact, High Commissioners and other officials tended to distrust him as potentially too powerful, especially as he had direct links with the Quai d'Orsay. Moreover, he consistently opposed the fact of a Greater Lebanon, arguing for the return of Tripoli and the Biqa to Syria. Eddé never developed a strong political base in the Mountain: his base was Beirut. But he was a very powerful politician in his own right, strongly supported by the influential newspaper *L'Orient*, and could not be ignored by either the French or other politicians.

His main opponent became Beshara al-Khuri. This was ironic since Khuri had originally been an Eddé protégé and ally.[10] Unlike Eddé he came from an elite Mountain family and was a cousin of Bishop Abdallah al-Khuri, who was a strong supporter. His early experience paralleled that of Eddé and he worked in the latter's law office. By marrying a sister of Michel Chiha, he allied with a powerful and rich Beirut banking family, which financed his political career. He became the

[10] There is a good and balanced portrait of al-Khuri and his ally Michel Chiha ibid. 33–43, on which this summary is based.

leader of a bloc of powerful Maronite families which included Charles Amoun and Camille Chamoun and was to be the core of the Constitutional Bloc established in the 1930s. In an autobiography published in 1961, al-Khuri portrayed himself as a committed nationalist who struggled for full Lebanese independence and wanted close co-existence with Muslims. In fact, however, he served the French loyally, holding a series of senior legal appointments in the early 1920s and only becoming hostile to the High Commission when it backed Eddé for the presidency in 1936.

These two, and their backers, dominated political warfare from the mid-1920s to the 1950s. As in Iraq and Syria, there were few major issues of principle that divided the antagonists. Nor were groups divided along simple confessional lines. Since there was a built-in Christian preponderance, all Presidents were Christian, but there evolved a convention that the Prime Minister would be a Sunni and other senior positions would be allocated to other sects. Moreover, the list system in elections made for interconfessional collaboration. Hence notables from all communities learnt to co-operate in the pursuit of office and therefore patronage, power, and wealth. This did not necessarily imply an end to sectarian divisions. For most Maronites the fundamental aim was to preserve Greater Lebanon, while to most Muslims, particularly in Tripoli, it was to be rejoined with Syria. But during the mandate this was never a realistic possibility. Thus, since all these leading politicians formed part of a social elite, to whom social reform, including land redistribution, was unthinkable, the only possible focus for political activity, apart from possession of office, was independence from France.

Yet the distinctive feature of political life in Lebanon, as compared with Iraq or Syria, was that the achievement of independence through a treaty never became a major focus for politicians and a rallying cry for nationalism as it had done in those countries. The reason is, of course, that while in both Iraq and Syria obtaining a treaty and thus formal independence was a great uniting crusade, despite differences over the precise content, in Lebanon independence was a highly divisive issue. The matter first became urgent in 1930 with the conclusion of the Anglo-Iraqi treaty. Ponsot then pressed Paris hard for similar treaties for Syria and Lebanon. In the end it was French rather than Lebanese initiative that produced a treaty in 1936.

When the issue was first seriously debated in 1931 it was the French army and naval officers who were most opposed to a Lebanese treaty on the grounds that France must maintain full control over the major ports, just as they opposed a Syrian treaty which gave Syria control over Latakia and Alexandretta. In November 1931 Ponsot was instructed in Paris that the treaty policy was not to apply to these areas or the Jabal Druze. But the issue was clearly only dormant, and from then until 1936 it was much debated in Lebanon. There was a basic division between Christians and Muslims, but both communities were divided on the question and were heavily influenced by their approach to relations with Syria.

On the Muslim side, there were three main standpoints: those who accepted Greater Lebanon so long as Muslims had full equality; those who demanded immediate and full union of the Muslim areas with Syria; and those who were prepared for independence provided the Maronites broke their close ties with France. The first of these positions was represented by the Tripoli political boss, the Sunni, Muhammad al-Jisr, who had already had an important political career under the mandate and was later to become Prime Minister. He genuinely believed that the coastal Sunnis were better off within Lebanon than within Syria. He would therefore support a treaty that provided adequate protection for Muslims. The second group were represented by al-Jisr's main Tripoli rival, Abd al-Hamid Karameh. Also a Sunni, he was always vehemently against the mandate and Greater Lebanon, and in favour of the annexation of Tripoli to Syria, which he believed would be best for the Tripoli economy. The third position was held by Riyadh al-Sulh from Sidon. As a long-term opponent of the French and close ally of the National Bloc in Syria, he might have been expected to support return of the Muslim areas to Syria. In fact he wanted to preserve Greater Lebanon on the grounds that a smaller state would perpetuate Maronite dominance. He was therefore in favour of independence for Greater Lebanon on the assumption that it would eventually be dominated by Muslims, after which the Maronites, bereft of their dependence on France, would take their place as equals in a multi-sectarian state within the larger context of pan-Arabism. It was his concept that eventually won out. In 1943, as Prime Minister in one of the rapidly rotating ministries of the period, he thrashed out with members of the Constitutional Bloc under al-Khuri, then President, the so-called National Pact, which formed the basis for coexistence in Lebanon until the crisis of 1975. This was an unwritten gentleman's agreement by which Muslims accepted the existence of Greater Lebanon as part of the pan-Arab world, but on condition that by convention there should be a fair allocation of official and political roles between the sects.[11]

If the Muslims were divided, so also were the Christians. One group of Maronites, led by Eddé, argued for a treaty that would maintain the French mandate but allow for the transfer of Tripoli, the Biqa, and Jabal Amil to Syria. Eddé was opposed in his own paper, *L'Orient*, by Habib Bustani, a Maronite intellectual, who wanted a treaty providing for the maintenance of Greater Lebanon, on the assumption that the various sects would eventually learn to live peaceably together. Since this represented a basic split in Christian attitudes, it would have been very difficult to establish anything like a united front in negotiations with France.

In fact, it was not until 1936 that the Lebanese were forced to do so, and then only because France wanted to settle a Lebanese treaty to be presented to the League of Nations along with that of Syria. The Quai d'Orsay, led by Viénot and de Martel as High Commissioner, prepared a draft in Paris in conjunction with heads of the armed forces. The draft was based on that for Syria, though without any economic protocols. On 13 November, a mere month after negotiations began, de Martel and Eddé signed the treaty. It was then approved by all but one

[11] See Salibi, *A House of Many Mansions*, 185–8 for an account of the terms of the Pact.

of the delegates to the Assembly, reduced, since the suspension of the constitution in 1932 and the introduction of a new temporary constitution in 1934, to 25 members.

In common with the Syrian treaty, the Lebanese treaty was never ratified by France. But long before that the futility of the Lebanese political system had been clearly demonstrated, and along with it French belief that the Lebanese were not ready to have full independence.

The crisis began in 1931 with a struggle for elections to the presidency, due in 1932. The initial conflict was between the Eddé and al-Khuri factions of the Maronites: Eddé had been forced to resign in 1930 and had been succeeded as President by the flexible Charles Dabbas, another Maronite. Both factions engaged in intensive coalition-building, but neither seemed able to achieve a dominant position, partly because the new Patriarch of the Maronites, A. P. Arida of Tripoli, lacked the capacity to impose his will on the Maronite factions. The result was that in August 1931 a third contender entered the lists: Muhammad al-Jisr, the Sunni from Tripoli. Al-Jisr had held high office in the past and was a clever and ambitious politician, previously allied with the al-Khuri faction. But he was a Sunni, and that created a major problem which tested the non-sectarian character of the 1926 constitution.

There was nothing in the constitution to bar a Muslim from the office, but from both a Maronite and a French perspective such an election would be inconsistent with their concept of a Christian Lebanon in which other religions were tolerated. Moreover, al-Jisr was in contact with al-Sulh in Syria and therefore suspected of supporting reversion of the annexed parts of Lebanon. But Paris could not overtly veto al-Jisr's candidacy. Hence, on 9 May 1932, Ponsot dissolved parliament, suspended the constitution, and appointed Dabbas, the existing President, as head of state. France had reimposed direct rule in all but name.

From a French standpoint, this was justified by belief that the 1926 constitution had done little more than provide a playground for the local politicians, plus the opportunity to exploit the wealth of the state for their personal gain and patronage. They had done little or nothing to tackle the very severe economic and fiscal problems resulting from the global recession. Thus, in 1929 official salaries absorbed some 75 per cent of all state revenues in Lebanon, as contrasted with 45 per cent in Syria; and in 1930 Eddé's resignation had resulted largely from his proposal to economize on education.[12] He had achieved some other savings, but they were relatively small and inadequate. Ponsot regarded the constitutional suspension as an opportunity to do what the politicians failed to do. Between 1932 and 1934, he issued decrees to enforce significant economies, reducing the number of officials in all branches of the public service and the salaries of those who remained: even French officials took a temporary 10 per cent salary cut. All of this was intensely unpopular, coupled as it was with large-scale unemployment.

[12] Longrigg, *Syria and Lebanon*, 200 n. 1.

The modified 1926 constitution came back into effect in January 1938, with elections held late in 1937. But before then a sinister new political development had taken place, the foundation of paramilitary youth militias in 1936. The first of these, the White Shirts, was the youth wing of the party L'Unité Libanaise, which was established in June 1936 by Tawfiq Awad with the backing of Eddé. It was a nationalist party of Maronites supporting Lebanese independence and opposing Syrian claims to Lebanon. A parallel organization was the Phalanges. This was another Maronite organization, founded by Pierre Gemayel and others, which included supporters of both al-Khuri and Eddé and aimed to preserve the integrity of Greater Lebanon. They began activities with demonstrations in Beirut in November 1936 to counter Muslim demonstrations against the treaty and the Lebanese state. They were better organized than the White Shirts and attracted a large number of Christian youths from the Mountain and the Christian sectors of Beirut. After 1937 they adopted a more overtly anti-French stance and demanded an end to the mandate. Against these two Christian militias there was the Muslim Najjada. It was formed in 1936 from Muslim Scout groups to counter the activities of the Christian militias. It marched in the Muslim quarters of Beirut with the Syrian flag calling for unity.

Late in 1937, with elections in prospect, these militias began to come to grips. The government became worried. On 18 November 1937, with the prospect of a major Phalanges rally on 21 November, the Minister of Interior (under pressure from the High Commission) issued a decree dissolving these three organizations and banning all such paramilitary formations, on the grounds that their functions were no longer athletic and that their religious affiliations made them a danger to a multi-confessional society. There was a violent outcry from the Maronites and on 21 November, when police attempted to break up a now illegal Phalanges march in Beirut, there were casualties and many arrests. This in turn provoked a general strike in Beirut and parts of the Mountain. Though nominally suppressed, both the Phalanges, later known as the Kataib, and the Najjada continued to meet and organize in private. They emerged into the open again after 1943 and were to play a very dangerous role in post-1965 Lebanon.[13] Kataib was legalized as a party in 1943, after which it changed its name to Hizb al-Kataib, then in 1952 to the Lebanese Social Democratic Party. It became a dominant force in and after 1958 with a group of members of parliament. By the 1970s it may have had some 65,000 members, 80 per cent Maronites, with a militia of about 10,000. Most members were lower middle class. After 1969 the Kataib became the main opponent of the Palestinians in Lebanon and it was they who were largely responsible for the struggles of 1975. They, along with the Najjada, which also survived into independence, though with less importance, were perhaps the first concrete evidence that, at grass roots, the model of a multi-confessional society had not taken root.

[13] There is a useful summary of the history of the Phalanges/Khataib to the mid-1970s in Gordon, *Lebanon, the Fragmented Nation*, 150–3. For a fuller sociological analysis see Entellis, *Pluralism and Party Transformation in Lebanon*.

The 1937 elections inaugurated what proved to be the last phase of Lebanese parliamentary government under the revised 1926 constitution before the Second World War. The elections were fixed by de Martel, Khair al-Din al-Ahdab, the Sunni ally of Eddé, and al-Khuri. These allocated seats, both elective and nominated, between 'government' and the Constitutional Bloc, in such a way as to produce a reasonably balanced confessional house. The seven-member government reflected confessional balances, as did subsequent governments. Eddé, whose term as President had been extended for a further three years, now had little power and was more a formal head of state: real power lay with al-Ahdab and al-Khuri. But despite the careful sectarian balance in parliament and government, there remained much bitterness among Sunni and Shii Muslims. They regarded those Muslims who had taken office as time-servers and collaborators with the French. The interconfessional government was regarded by many as a cover for continued Maronite dominance. Although it was now becoming an established convention that the Prime Minister would be a Sunni, as all three were to be between 1937 and 1939, this resentment continued.

In any case, Lebanese constitutionalism had a short life. France was now primarily interested in the probability of war, after the Austrian Anschluss of March 1938. Lebanon was seen as a vital naval and military base, and the support of the Maronites crucial for the French position there. In January 1939, de Martel was replaced by Gabriel Puaux, another career diplomat, whose intended function was to prepare Lebanon for war. It had already been decided in Paris not to ratify the 1936 treaty. The Syrian constitution had been suspended in July 1939, the Lebanese constitution was suspended after war had broken out on 21 September. Eddé was appointed head of state with Abdallah Bayhum, a Sunni, as Secretary. But all real power now lay with the High Commissioner: it was as it had been in 1920.

The later history of the mandate must be summarized briefly, since in many ways it reflected that of Syria as summarized in Chapter 7. The period falls into three phases: from 1939 to May 1941; from then until late 1943; and from then until 1945–6.

After the fall of France in June 1940, Lebanon remained under the Vichy government, which insisted on its full neutrality. Hostility to Britain increased greatly after the destruction of the French fleet in Oran on 3 July, when Vichy broke off relations with Britain and the authorities in Beirut rejected British suggestions that they should join in the anti-German war. Puaux, as High Commissioner, was covertly pro-British, but he was replaced in November 1940 by the fervently pro-Vichy General Dentz. The Armée du Levant also remained staunchly pro-Vichy. Politics, in a very restricted form, remained as factional as before. On 5 April 1941 Eddé was forced to resign as President and was replaced by Alfred Naqash, an elderly Maronite, former judge, and warranted French supporter, as head of state rather than President, along with a conventional mixed cabinet. It seemed that Lebanon, along with Syria, would sit out the war under French control.

This changed fundamentally in April–May 1941, under the stimulus of the Rashid Ali revolution in Iraq and German designs on the Middle East after their defeat of Greece and the occupation of Crete. Vichy, despite its nominal neutrality, instructed Dentz to provide full facilities for the German air force and authorized him to send munitions to the Baghdad government. British diplomatic agents were sent away to Palestine. The Lebanese airfields were vital to German aircraft on their way to Baghdad but, as was seen in Chapter 3, they arrived too late to have an impact on events. After the fall of the Rashid Ali regime at the end of May the British had to decide what action to take, since the German threat remained. They were reluctant to occupy Syria and Lebanon because they were short of troops and aircraft and their policy towards Vichy was ambivalent. Moreover de Gaulle was strongly against British action without Free French forces to take over. Nevertheless, for fear of a German invasion, General Wavell, as Commander-in-Chief Middle East, started planning for a joint British and French invasion on 25 May. On 8 June, pamphlets were dropped over Syria and Lebanon promising, in the name of both Britain and Free France, that both would become 'free and independent', and on the same date a three-pronged attack went in. The Vichy forces, whom de Gaulle had hoped would transfer to his side, fought hard until 14 July, and in the end only about a fifth of the French Armée du Levant joined the Free French: the rest were allowed to return to France. De Gaulle was then reluctant to accept the armistice terms offered, and it was not until 24 July that he and Oliver Lyttelton, British Minister of State in Cairo, agreed terms for the occupation. The British were to be in military control, but the French would be responsible for all civil government. They would also control the Troupes Spéciales.

Thereafter, the French reasserted their authority and largely ignored the promises made of independence. Although very short of experienced staff, they reverted to the post-1939 regime. Alfred Naqash remained as President with an appointed multi-confessional government, and was succeeded in June 1942 by Sami al-Sulh, of the great Sunni family. Change came in March 1943. Catroux then announced that the 1939 constitution would be re-established once elections had been held, though parliament would be reduced to 55 members, 30 Christian and 25 Muslims. Elections took place and parliament met on 21 September. It elected Bishara al-Khuri as President, thus ending Eddé's hopes of a return to power. Riyadh al-Sulh was appointed Prime Minister. It was they who worked out the unwritten gentleman's agreement known as the National Pact which was outlined above and was to constitute the basis of Lebanese political life into the 1960s. Lebanon was to remain an Arab country. The Maronites would hold the Presidency, control security, and command the prospective army, and Sunday would remain the official Sabbath. But the Prime Minister would always be a Sunni, and there would be a fair distribution of top appointments between the sects. The ratio of Christians to Muslims in parliament would be fixed at six to five, with multi-member constituencies and reserved sectarian seats. It was a major psychological turning point in Lebanese history: the dominant Muslim sect had at last accepted the existence of Greater Lebanon. From their point of view Lebanon was now independent: it remained to persuade the French that this was so.

The Free French government, however, proved as reluctant to concede independence as pre-war French governments. Controlled by the French National Committee in Algeria, it refused to transfer effective power without a treaty reserving French interests. The crisis, conventionally known as 'les Evénements', began in November 1943, when the Lebanese parliament adopted amendments to the constitution which removed all reference to the mandate, reasserted the sovereignty of Lebanon, made no mention of any residual French rights or functions, and ended the use of French as an official language. Jean Helleu, as High Commissioner, reacted violently. On 11 November, he arrested al-Khuri and all but two members of the government (who went into hiding), suspended the constitution, and appointed the pliant Eddé as head of state. This caused an outcry. There were riots and strikes throughout Lebanon, the British and Americans were outraged and put great pressure on the French in Algiers. De Gaulle attempted to support Helleu's actions, but eventually Catroux was sent to Beirut to make peace. Helleu was withdrawn and all his decrees cancelled except that vetoing the constitutional amendments, this being regarded as a critical symbol of the continuing mandate. Al-Khuri's government was reinstated along with parliament and the constitution.

From then on the French control gradually withered away and France made little attempt to block the transfer of power until 1945. In December 1943, by a tripartite agreement between the Free French, Syria, and Lebanon, a range of French-controlled functions, including the customs, were taken over by the two states. In January 1944, the Common Interests were placed under a joint Higher Council of Lebanon and Syria, and during 1944 most remaining public services were divided and transferred. In 1944 both the United States and the USSR recognized Lebanon, along with Syria, as independent states, and in early 1945, when both had declared war on Germany and Japan, they were admitted to the United Nations and joined the newly formed Arab League. But the Troupes Spéciales remained under French control, along with French schools and some religious charities. Moreover, a large number of French officials remained in office. That was as far as the French were prepared to go unless a treaty was signed with France; and this both Syrian and Lebanese governments refused to do. When the crunch came in May 1945 there was no Lebanese equivalent of the French military action in Damascus, but the Lebanese reactions to renewed French demands for a treaty were much the same as those of Syria. On 21 June 1945, the Lebanese government joined with Syria in denouncing all remnants of French authority, and in July the Troupes Spéciales were at last divided between the two states and transferred. The last French troops left in August 1946, leaving only a staff to liquidate assets. But, whereas Syria left the franc zone, Lebanon remained within it, a last remnant of the Maronite attachment to France. Thereafter, Lebanon was free to go its own way. The political parties reverted to their normal rivalries. Revolving ministries contained much the same mix of dominant political figures from the limited range of those regarded as capable of ministerial functions. Lebanon was launched onto its multi-confessional independence.

The danger with making any assessment of Lebanese history and the effects of the French mandate is that the events of 1975 and thereafter cast too long a shadow. In retrospect it might seem that all roads inevitably led to the civil war and virtual disruption of the Lebanese state and society. This is clearly wrong. After independence Lebanon enjoyed some two decades of unprecedented prosperity and, apart from 1958, very little dangerous internal friction. The major domestic crisis of 1958 stemmed largely from dissatisfaction with the activities of Camille Chamoun as President, who was thought to have broken the terms of the 1943 Pact and to be aiming at an unconstitutional second six-year presidential term. The disturbances were also related to the Revolution in Iraq and the potential revolution in Jordan. The immediate crisis was dealt with by United States Marines, but in the longer term it was resolved by General Fouad Chehab, Commander-in-Chief of the 6,000-strong Lebanese army. He was elected President that year. Although a Maronite he was able to re-establish the conventions of the Pact and was largely responsible for the relative stability of Lebanon during the following decade.[14] It was probably the influx of Palestinian refugees and militias after 1967 that more than anything else destroyed the equilibrium created by the National Pact. Yet the events after 1975 demonstrated that the underlying fissures of that society were real and potentially lethal.

There are basically two ways of explaining these fissures: the effects of the French mandate, and the underlying realities of Lebanese society. These will be considered briefly in turn.

First, the effects of the mandate. It was suggested above that Lebanon was unique among the post-1918 Middle Eastern mandates, indeed among non-settler colonies generally, in that the largest segment of what became the Greater Lebanon, the Maronites, strongly welcomed the French presence. For them France was the Christian saviour, their guarantee against being submerged in an Islamic sea. No imperial power could have inherited more enthusiastic collaborators. These clients were not, of course, uniformly co-operative, any more than earlier European settler communities had been. But their underlying loyalty was assured until, at least, the events of 1943.

France reciprocated this loyalty. For France Lebanon was the jewel in its new Middle Eastern empire. Syria was a necessary burden, but Lebanon provided much that the colonial activists wanted. It was a showcase of the 'civilizing mission' exemplified in the plethora of French-language schools and missions and the widespread attachment of the educated Lebanese to the French language and culture. Beirut became virtually a French city. Lebanon provided considerable opportunities for French investment, particularly in infrastructure and banking. Lebanon after 1920 acquired a modern infrastructure, mostly built, or owned and run by French companies. Moreover, in Lebanon France acquired the facilities for a major Middle

---

[14] For a useful account of the Lebanese crisis of 1958 see the chapter by WM. R. Louis, 'Britain and the Crisis of 1958', in WM. R. Louis and R. Owen (eds.), *A Revolutionary Year: The Middle East in 1958* (London and New York, 2002), 45–53, and also other chapters in this book.

Eastern naval and military power, with a great naval base in Beirut and army stations throughout the territory. In this sense Lebanon was to France what Iraq was to Britain, a major element in its determination to constitute a great power.

But the main stated purpose of the mandate was for France to train the Lebanese in the skills of modern self-government, leading to independence. In this they had a contradictory record. On the one hand, the French provided Lebanon with a modern, liberal constitution which attempted to square the circle of conflicting confessional groups. They also held the hands of successive inexperienced politicians and governments, providing the official backing they needed and taking over when indigenous ministries failed. They prevented the Maronites from completely dominating state institutions and attempted to integrate the various communities through the balanced confessional political system. Few colonial powers ever made such a consistent attempt to prepare a subject people for self-government.

As against all this France was responsible for what was to become the central problem in Lebanese politics and society. By the incorporation of a large minority of Sunni and Shii Muslims into the new territory the French placed enormous pressure on the political institutions they set up. This was not, of course, as extreme a problem as that in Palestine. As was suggested above, the fact that the Lebanese were almost all Arabs and spoke Arabic, and that Beirut had been the cradle of the Arab cultural 'awakening', made it not impossible that a single political 'nation' would emerge. But the odds were against it, particularly because of Syrian insistence on the return of the annexed territories and the close links between many Lebanese and Syrian politicians. This was seen early on by such informed observers as de Caix and Henri de Jouvenel. It was seen also by Emile Eddé. Had the predominantly Sunni Tripoli and the Biqa Valley been returned to Syria, Syrian irridentism would have been defused and the Christian nature of the residual Lebanon reasserted. The remaining Muslims might have resented this, but might more readily have been absorbed into a Lebanese nation. French resistance to such proposals stemmed partly from reluctance to offend the intransigent Maronites, partly from determination to prevent Syria from having a Mediterranean coastline. Although the 1943 National Pact cemented Sunni acceptance of the Greater Lebanon, the fact that the confessional ratio was by then probably (in the absence of a new census) very nearly balanced meant that the political future remained in doubt. Over time, the Muslims would predictably achieve a majority, and then the whole fragile balance between the communities would be upset. In short, it is arguable that the worst thing the French did in Lebanon was not to postpone independence and continually interfere in Lebanese politics, but to create a plural society.

That said, however, the second question remains. Why, given the existence of a political system, inherited from the old Mountain, that was carefully designed to integrate confessional communities, did this not lead to a more integrated Lebanese society, and to a political nation? Was this due, not to French strategies but rather to deep-rooted fissures in Lebanese society? To suggest answers to this question, it is proposed to examine the views of three historians or commentators, to whom reference has been made in this account, on the strengths and weaknesses of the Greater Lebanon created by the French mandate: a British one-time Iraqi administrator and scholar, S. H. Longrigg, writing in the later 1950s, before any crisis seemed likely; Kamal Salibi, a Protestant Lebanese scholar, publishing in 1988; and the Israeli historian, Meir Zamir, writing in the later 1990s.

Longrigg, with long experience of administration in Iraq before 1932 and writing in 1957, put a lot of blame for instability on the character of Lebanese politicians of all groups and confessions. There, as in Iraq and Syria, the political leaders 'were deficient in political and constitutional experience, and excelled in criticism and opposition but were new to responsibility. . . . Finally, they spoke with no single voice; not only various parties, various degrees of moderation or extremism confronted the Mandatory [*sic*] . . . but various communities and enclaves throughout the territory insistently claimed special treatment and refused assimilation.'[15] Such politicians never formed parties with consistent objectives. They were intent on the achievement of power and the benefits it could bring to their own following and community. Thus politics, which were intended to generate a single political nation, in fact merely intensified sectional and factional conflicts.

Of these three writers, Salibi was closest to the subject.[16] As a member of a very small minority of Protestant Christians, though from the Mountain, with a Ph.D. from London University, and as a professor at the American University of Beirut, he could be described as a Lebanese nationalist who could take a dispassionate view of the country's problems. His analysis of the Lebanese situation was far more complex than that of Longrigg.[17]

The basic problem with the Greater Lebanon was that the political structures designed to minimize sectarian frictions operated only at the higher level of those from all sects who were able and willing to take part in the political game. Despite initial Muslim resistance to integration of the Muslim majority areas, by the later 1930s leaders of the non-Maronite communities were increasingly integrated into the complex political structures and formed governments with non-Muslims. This culminated in the 1943 National Pact. But this acceptance of the need for intersectarian collaboration in the running of a unitary quasi-secular state (the only non-Muslim state in the Middle East apart from post-Mustafa Kemal's Turkey) did not penetrate far down the social structure. As Salibi wrote,

The potential for violence had its strongholds in the mountains, where a full heritage of political rancours and interconfessional suspicions remained entrenched, most notably between the Christians and the Druzes of the Shuf Mountains [south-east of Beirut]. Here, as in other rural regions, latent tribalism rallied around traditional or emerging chiefs who alone were trusted political representatives. Violence, however, had a strong presence in the

[15] Longrigg, *Syria and Lebanon*, 366.
[16] There is a useful thumbnail sketch of Salibi in Gordon, *Lebanon, the Fragmented Nation*, 229–32.
[17] The following is based mainly on ch. 10 of Salibi, *A House of Many Mansions*, 182–99.

coastal cities too, where Sunnite Muslims felt highly insecure and continued to nurse feelings of resentment against the Christian ruling establishment, awaiting the opportunity when the tables could be politically turned. In the capital, Beirut, Sunnite Muslims and Christians, by the late 1930s, were already facing one another in organized gangs brandishing the banners of Arabism and Lebanism respectively.[18]

Beirut was the best hope of national integration. It was the dynamic centre of an increasingly service-based economy, which could act as 'the clearing house for political differences', where Muslim politicians such as al-Jisr from Tripoli could take a leading part in politics, and where the presence of non-Maronite Christians in dominant economic positions could act as a buffer between Sunnis, Shiites, and Maronites. It was in this quasi-neutral environment that the best hope for the emergence of a secular nationalism lay.

A great deal therefore depended on whether the elite politicians who ran the political system in Beirut could agree to form non-dogmatic parties whose objectives were the national, rather than sectarian interests. In fact this never happened. The complicated electoral system, inherited from the Mountain, which was intended to provide an acceptable balance between different sectarian communities, made it virtually impossible for any political group to promote any line of policy that affected vested interests. Hence what was perhaps the key issue, the unification of civil law in a single system of state courts, as in Turkey, was blocked by the preservation of sectarian codes. Thus, the Sunni and Shii religious courts continued to be based on the Sharia, while the Christians and Druzes had separate codes enacted by the national parliament. Moreover, every citizen had by law to belong to one of the recognized religious communities, which resulted in two identities, one national, one religious. Although there were calls on both sides of the confessional fence for the secularization of society, this was largely dishonest. There was considerable secularization among the westernized groups and many of all persuasions argued for political secularization, ending the confessional electoral system. But this would only have been possible if there had been also social secularization, and at the grass roots this was unacceptable. Moreover, confessionalism was a very valuable tool for politicians who had no other ideological pull on their potential supporters. It is very significant that the last census in Lebanon was taken in 1932 by the French, and even that was suspected of being manipulated to show a Christian majority. The Maronites thereafter always refused a census for fear that it would show that demographic change had eliminated the majority on which the whole artificial political system was based.

Thus, Salibi concludes, the very political game on which the viability of Greater Lebanon was based, was a fraud.

The plain fact was that most of the Lebanese, no less than their leaders, were more concerned with the game than with the national interest, and their wild clamours encouraged the leaders to play the game hard, and way beyond the limits of safety. . . . By the early

[18] Ibid. 182.

1970s, the Lebanese political game was already degenerating into a general brawl in which external as well as internal parties freely participated. The worst fears of Michel Chiha were about to be realized: Tradition, in Lebanon, was rapidly ceasing to be effective as the means to protect the country from the violence that would destroy it.[19]

Finally, there is Meir Zamir's assessment of 1997.[20] As an Israeli historian who had done fundamental research in French, British, and Israeli archives and has written the two most detailed accounts of Lebanese political history since the nineteenth century, Zamir is well qualified to take an informed and dispassionate view. In his assessment of the weakness of the Lebanese state he examines three factors: the French influence, the underlying social structures, and the operation of the political system.

France, he argues, did much for Lebanon, its favoured Middle Eastern possession. It defended its post-1920 territorial integrity, gave it a complicated constitution designed to minimize sectarian friction and to prevent the Maronites from exploiting their dominance, and did a great deal to create the economic structures that made Lebanon the economic powerhouse of the Near East. On the other hand French policy on Syria created fundamental instabilities. By refusing to return the annexed provinces they ensured that Syrian nationalists would remain hostile to the very existence of Lebanon, despite the National Bloc's acceptance of the frontiers in 1936. That hostility in turn encouraged Muslim politicians to look to Syria rather than Beirut and to demand that Lebanon become part of an Arab Middle East rather than an outpost of western Christianity, which was how the Maronites saw it. Confronted by the pull of Muslim Syria and pan-Arabism, it was very difficult for the majority of Islamic Lebanese to feel fully integrated into their own state and society.

Second, whatever the French might do, and irrespective of the ingenious constitution, there were indigenous forces in Lebanon which made it very difficult for the political system to achieve its integrative purpose. Zamir wrote:

While the constitution provided for Western institutions, Lebanese political culture was, in reality, largely determined by traditional forces. What emerged was a unique mix of the experience accrued from practising a parliamentary democracy, and the successful penetration of the new state institutions by the primordial forces at work within Lebanese society—community, feudalism and kinship. Paradoxically then, while Lebanon appeared to be the most Westernized country in the Arab Middle East, it retained more features of Ottoman society and politics than any other state in the Fertile Crescent.[21]

The third factor, closely related to the second, was what Zamir calls 'political feudalism'. This was distinct from confessional conflict. The effect of the constitutional system, and in particular the large powers given to the President, who was always a Maronite, gave the Maronite political elite access to state institutions and wealth that they could not have had otherwise. This enabled the leading

---

[19] Salibi, *A House of Many Mansions*, 199.
[20] This is based mainly on ch. 5 of Zamir, *Lebanon's Quest*.   [21] Ibid. 245.

Mountain elites to form political coalitions to exploit the new opportunities. Into this system were drawn leading Muslim and Druze families, whose support was necessary for the Maronites because of the electoral system. Thus political feudalism became entrenched in Lebanon, just as it was in Iraq and Syria. This political class saw that it was in its interest to perpetuate political confessionalism because it was the basis of its claim to office and its rewards. Thus, as Zamir put it, 'the Lebanese state became not only a corporation of "communities" but of "beys" '. By the 1930s this had resulted in the consolidation of political clans, first those led by Eddé and al-Khuri, then, after 1943, others led by Muslim notables. Hence, the post-1918 vision of Lebanon as a liberal democratic state unique in the Middle East was transformed. In its place evolved a society dominated by competitive interest groups which used the apparatus of the state to pursue their own interests. Zamir described this as a 'merchant republic'.[22]

The conclusion must, therefore, be that the attempt to transform Lebanon into a nation state failed. This failure was unusual. In the standard literature on nationalism it was often argued that a sense of nationality preceded and probably caused the evolution of a nation state. That was the conventional pattern in Europe, where peoples with a common language, culture, and history which were under the rule of alien empires first felt and expressed their sense of common interest and ultimately, when conditions were ripe, transformed this into a nation state. Conversely, of course, there were places where statehood preceded a sense of common nationality, which might have to be deliberately and artificially fostered by groups dominant in the state. Greater Lebanon certainly did not fit the first model, except so far as the Maronites were concerned. They indeed had a strong sense of community and regarded themselves as a nation. In this they were no different from the many other minority communities in the Ottoman Middle East before 1914, notably the Kurds and Armenians, who were promised statehood by the Treaty of Sèvres in 1920. The Maronites were more fortunate than they because it was in the interests of France to give them a state. Their basic mistake was to be greedy, to demand the incorporation of the coastal Islamic areas into their state. As has been suggested, France, for its own reasons, gave it to them, though the more far-seeing French administrators saw that this was a mistake. The result was that Greater Lebanon was a nation only in the eyes of the Maronites and some of their Christian allies. For the rest of the population it was an imposed state dominated by the Maronites in which they felt less at home than they had been when they were part of an Ottoman vilayet. There was a state, but it was not a nation state.

Whether it might have become a true nation state over time is unpredictable. As has been seen, there were powerful forces at work within Lebanon working in that direction. But they were operating at the top, not at grass roots. It was in no one's interests to campaign for a truly secular state. Thus Lebanon remained what

[22] Ibid. 245, 247.

in Ottoman terms would have been a collection of millets. Under the Ottoman umbrella this was a viable situation, since the imperial power could hold the balance. It was viable also under the French mandate. But it demonstrated its vulnerability once Lebanon became truly independent. Then there was no over-lord to keep the balance.

This is not, of course, to say that the disaster of Lebanon after 1975 was entirely due to these internal fissures. There are many other nation states with profound internal divisions and lacking even the common language and culture of Arab Lebanon which manage to maintain unity. Lebanon was unfortunate in that it was a very small state, with around 785,000 inhabitants in 1932 and an estimate 2.4 million in the mid-1960s, backed by much larger and more powerful states, all of them, except for Israel, uncompromisingly Islamic. The pull of Islam was very strong for very many of the Lebanese, and with the crisis over Palestine after 1948 it was virtually impossible for Lebanon to escape its backlash. Nevertheless, it is difficult to avoid the conclusion that a political unit of that kind, lacking any general sense of community, was better off under the protection of a greater power, whether it was the Ottoman empire or France.

PART THREE

CONCLUSIONS

9

Conclusions

The central question faced in this book has been the effect the mandates held by Britain and France had on the one-time provinces of the Ottoman Empire in the Middle and Near East. It is now necessary to summarize these effects.

This is, in fact, extremely difficult to attempt because it implies a comparison. Whatever Britain and France did must be considered in relation to what might, theoretically, have happened if they had not taken control of these provinces in the form of mandates. What were the alternatives?

One hypothetical possibility, of course, is that the situation might not have arisen: Istanbul might not have declared war in 1914. In that case it seems certain that the Ottoman empire in the Middle East would have survived and that all the existing trends and tensions outlined in Chapter 1 would have continued to work themselves out. It is now widely thought that, with all its limitations, and despite the brutal treatment of Armenians and other minorities, which was to some degree distorted and exploited by Allied propaganda during and after 1914, the Ottoman empire in its modernizing form might have been the best available guardian of the interests of the Arab Middle East.

Once war had started in November 1914, however, there were only three possible outcomes. First, some or all of these Arab provinces might have remained within an Ottoman or Turkish empire, if, after defeat, it had been allowed to keep them. Second, these countries, once cleared of Ottoman/Turkish control, might have been given immediate full independence, either as a single Arab state under the Hashemites, as was allegedly promised in the McMahon letter of October 1915, or as a group of states, as was promised in the Anglo-French declaration of November 1918. Finally, of course, they could have been, as in fact they were, taken over by the victorious powers as quasi-colonies.

By 1918 the first of these alternatives was no longer a possibility. As with the German colonies elsewhere, too much Allied blood had been shed and too many expectations aroused for the Allies to contemplate giving up what they had just captured. Hence, the only real alternatives after 1918 were that the Allies might honour their commitments of 1915 and 1918 to the Arabs or that they would maintain control. Since it has been a staple of Arab nationalist rhetoric ever since that Arabs were perfectly capable of taking over their countries without European interference once free of the Turks, and that the League of Nations' classification of these societies as 'not yet able to stand by themselves under the strenuous conditions of the modern world' was an insult to their competence, it is worth reviewing the evidence to see how this alternative to the mandates might have worked out. Would the Arabs have done well or better if the British and French had simply withdrawn?

One possibility can be ruled out. Sharif Husayn's dream of a single Arab kingdom stretching from the Mediterranean to the Yemen was beyond all probabilities. The Hashemites were a small Hijaz dynasty, though of distinguished Islamic pedigree. Before the Hijaz campaign the most they could hope for was survival against Ibn Saud and possibly conquests towards the Yemen. They could arouse no loyalty in Mesopotamia—Faysal had to be imposed on an indifferent people by the British in 1921—and there was little enthusiasm for them in Palestine or Syria, except among those who believed the independence of Syria depended on supporting Faysal in Damascus. How, given a free choice, the alternative division of Arab territories might have taken place is impossible to tell. Syria, excluding the Maronite Mountain but including Palestine, was a reasonably coherent group of vilayets with common interests and there was a strong sense of a proto-Syrian nation by 1918. It might have held together. There was no similar sense of cohesion in the three vilayets of Mesopotamia. Given a vote they might well have opted to become separate states. So also might the Kurds, though their sense of nationality was complicated by the fact that they were divided between Mosul, Anatolia, Syria, and Iran and was not as well developed as Arab nationalism elsewhere. As for the Hijaz, it was likely that in due course the dynamic Ibn Saud would take it over from the Hashemites, as indeed he was to do in the mid-1920s, then controlling territory as far as the eastern borders of Palestine, including much of what became Transjordan.

The key question, however, concerns the probable character of governments in whatever political units emerged. The best concrete evidence is what happened in Syria in the short period of Faysal's regime there between November 1918 and July 1920, when the French took over. The evidence summarized in Chapter 7 does not suggest that the Faysal regime would have been stable or efficient.[1] Longrigg gave the regime a moderately favourable assessment:

Never stable nor truly efficient, never in the prevailing conditions able to do much for its subjects, the Administration had nevertheless shown abundant vitality, an excellent comprehension of local conditions, a willingness to decentralize, toleration of all communities without rancour or fanaticism, and the possession of a considerable number not merely of competent military officers but also of civil administrators. Moreover, the Arab national

---

[1] I. Friedman, in *Palestine: A Twice-Promised Land?* (New Brunswick, 2000), 211–16, argues that the post-1918 Damascus government was impossibly inefficient, and quotes a range of British and other observers to support this assertion. For a contemporary comment by one who was devoted to the Arabs, see Gertrude Bell's report of May 1920 that Damascus was in chaos. 'The bazaars are . . . standing still, there is no government in Syria'. Quoted T. J. Paris, *Britain, the Hashemites and Arab Rule, 1920–1925: The Sherifian Solution* (London, 2003), 70.

movement upon which the State and monarchy were based was a strong political force, which had been gathering pressure for a generation, enjoyed all the powerful appeal of emotional patriotism, was conversant with the spirit of the times in other countries, had been strengthened by its wartime martyrs, was fully confident in its own capacity, and had had good reason, based on the Allies' wartime and post-war promises, to expect that its claim to independence would not be opposed.[2]

But, quite apart from the French threat, there were serious internal weaknesses. Longrigg pointed to two of the most important. First,

the [national] movement . . . was still limited to a small political class and to such following as this could partially or temporarily inspire; it did not include—and Faysal's own supporters did not include—the totality even of the Muslim instructed classes, since a proportion of these were for varying reasons tepid or hostile to his cause, while a proportion felt also that a temporary foreign mandate in some form was necessary to the consolidation, progress, and enrichment of their country.

Second, the nationalists

suffered from an incomplete knowledge of the politics, forces, and methods of the international world; they lived in a closed and emotional region of hopes, general principles, and enthusiasms; they had by temperament and training no adequate conception of the necessary gradualness, the indispensable compromises, the need for the conciliation and retention of friends, the recognition of politics as truly 'the art of the possible', by which alone the weak can hope for political success.

Hence the Congress's refusal to contemplate any possible compromise with the French that might have resulted in some form of autonomy under Faysal.[3]

If the Syrians were indeed so unready to face the realities of independence, the probability of success elsewhere was far less. Syria had been handed to Faysal as more or less a unit and a going concern by the British at the end of 1918. It had been conquered, and the conquering Northern Army, plus British forces until the end of 1919, was still there to back up his regime. Greater Syria was the most politically sophisticated region of the Ottoman Middle East. What might have happened in other areas had they been given the self-determination promised in 1918?

One possible answer is that, lacking a central indigenous authority, once the occupying forces withdrew, the hard core of remaining Ottoman officials and the local notables would have taken control. Some of the best evidence for this is in what became Transjordan. There, as was seen in Chapter 6, once the Northern Army had passed through on its way to Damascus, groups of local notables in the towns and tribal leaders in the beduin areas automatically formed juntas to organize life. These ran the area for nearly two years, before the British sent British officers to advise the notables. Had the British not occupied Palestine, and thus had an interest in what happened over the Jordan, these local authorities might well

---

[2] S. H. Longrigg, *Syria and Lebanon under French Mandate* (London, 1958), 105.
[3] Ibid. 105–6.

have continued to run the area, possibly forming a federation or other means of collaboration. They would, however, have been vulnerable to the northward thrust of Ibn Saud, had not Abdullah pre-empted this and obtained British protection for his rule. The point, in any case, is that Allied withdrawal would not have left a void. The building blocks of autonomous administration already existed.

The Iraqi position was very different, but the same principle applies. Each of the three vilayets had its own structures of authority and groups of notables who had run affairs under the Ottoman valis. In Basra it was predictable that the Naqib, Saiyid Talib ibn Saiyid Rajab, its pre-war boss, would take control. In Baghdad the notables, led by the Naqib Saiyid Abdur Rahman, would have taken over. In Mosul much the same would have happened, though, with strong pro-Turkish influences, the province might well have opted to be incorporated in the post-1922 Turkey. The problem in the north was the Kurds, who wanted to run their own affairs but were incapable of durable collaboration. Predictably there would have been endemic quarrels and fighting between the main tribes, and fragmentation into regional blocs. Thus, Mesopotamia would probably have split into its component parts. How relationships between them would have evolved is uncertain, but it is very unlikely that a unitary Iraq would have emerged. On the other hand, unless there were incursions from Syria, there is no reason to think that British withdrawal would have been immediately catastrophic, even though Gertrude Bell, with her very wide experience of local society, and before her conversion to the rule of Faysal in 1919, had notoriously stated in 1915 that 'the Arabs cannot govern themselves'.[4]

The general conclusion must, therefore, be that, while mere withdrawal of the British and French from the Ottoman provinces after 1918 would not have resulted in a political vacuum, neither would a group of well-constructed indigenous states have emerged fully-fledged. The Arabs were perfectly capable of running their own local affairs and all the basic building blocks of administrative and judicial control existed. But these were only on a provincial level. With Ottoman and Allied control suddenly withdrawn, these regions would probably have fragmented. Thus there would have been no state system and probably a great deal of confusion and rivalry. The main case for the mandates was that, if used as the theory proposed, as a short-term device for creating viable states out of groups of Ottoman provinces, the mandatories could do for the Arabs what it would have been very difficult for them to do for themselves. But of course this would have implied a very disinterested approach by Britain and France. We must, therefore, finally consider how they approached their mandates and whether they pursued the best interests of their temporary subjects.

It is, of course, evident from earlier chapters of this book that disinterest was not a primary feature of the Allied attitude to the Ottoman empire. Britain and France were determined to obtain what advantages each desired. Their objectives

---

[4] Quoted E. Burgoyne, *Gertrude Bell from her Personal Papers 1914–1926* (London, 1962), 31. Bell, of course, later changed her mind and in 1919 became a strong supporter of Faysal as a possible king of Iraq.

were therefore primarily selfish. For Britain, these included control of at least Basra as a security for the oil interests in Persia and for the route to the East. A marginal early concern was for the still unproven oil reserves at Kirkuk and for the safety of the important British import–export trade up the Tigris. Thus, strategic and economic interests combined to determine that the British would keep at least Basra and Baghdad vilayets: Mosul was at first uncertain. To the west, Palestine was a major objective, initially to keep either the Ottomans or possibly the French from access to the Suez canal and Egypt, later as a home for the Jews. For the French, as has been argued, the impulses were more complicated. There was a strong nationalistic drive to establish their military and naval power in the eastern Mediterranean, and this was supported by the influential Catholic lobby in France which wanted to help their fellow Catholics in Lebanon. There again there were powerful economic interests—investors, bankers, traders, monopolists—who demanded French control of Syria and Lebanon. In short, British and French motives were characteristic of the medley of motives that constituted late nineteenth- and early twentieth-century European imperialism.

The question, then, was what form of western control would best satisfy these various interests. Before 1917, protectorates would have been the normal method, as had been used in much of tropical and North Africa since the 1870s. Protectorates offered the advantage that they were not necessarily permanent and in their early form commonly involved leaving indigenous rulers and their political structures in place, thus avoiding the expense of a full-blown colonial administration. But once the United States had joined in the European war, anything as overtly imperialistic as a protectorate was ruled out. The mandate was the weasel word that would appear to combine the reality of effective western control with the ethics of President Wilson. On paper at least, a mandate was expected to be a vehicle for the advancement of a mandated territory. Article 22 of the Covenant of the League of Nations justified the mandate system on the ground that the ex-Turkish and German colonies being taken over were 'inhabited by peoples not yet able to stand by themselves under the strenuous conditions of the modern world'. It was therefore right that 'the tutelage of such peoples should be entrusted to advanced nations who, by reason of their resources, their experience, or their geographical position, can best undertake this responsibility . . . as Mandatories on behalf of the League'. As to the ex-Ottoman territories, some had 'reached a stage of development where their existence as independent nations can be provisionally recognized subject to the rendering of administrative advice and assistance by a Mandatory until such time as they are able to stand alone. The wishes of these communities must be a principal consideration in the selection of the Mandatory.' Mandatories must make an annual report to the Mandates Commission of the League, which would report to the League Council.

The key words in this prescription, since there was never any chance that the Arabs would have any choice of mandatory, were 'administrative advice and assistance'. They implied a very light control, leading to full autonomy and becoming 'independent nations'. The argument of this chapter has been that this, in fact, was what the ex-Ottoman territories needed. They were competent to run their own affairs as municipalities or relatively small provinces, but they were not equipped to form viable nation states. To become in any sense nations they had first to be formed into states, which might then generate the sense of common and exclusive interest that might eventually make them also nations. This, at least, each of the mandate powers achieved. Four of the five territories examined in this book (Palestine excluded) became states with some of the normal western state equipment. Did that imply success? Longrigg, who had seen the birth of the Iraq mandate from within and later studied Syria and Lebanon, suggested that there were three critical tests of such a success.

First, there must be 'cordial goodwill between the Mandatory and mandated'. Second would be 'the effective and fairly rapid consolidation . . . of full-self-government and self-reliance, this to include a suitable Constitution (if possible self-evolved), sound political institutions and methods, a competent administration, a viable economy'. This would have to be accompanied by significant economic and health improvements, better justice and security, 'all to be achieved by the benevolent precept and example of the agents of the Mandatory'. Finally, and not before any initial goodwill had evaporated, the mandate must be made a free nation.[5]

These are rather pompous prescriptions, but they cover much of the ground. How far does the evidence in this book suggest that either of the two European states fulfilled anything like these expectations? What were the longer-term consequences of what they did or failed to do?

On the face of it the British came fairly close to meeting some at least of Longrigg's criteria, at least in Iraq and Transjordan. In Iraq they had established a central government by 1920, gave it a king in 1921, and allowed the local politicians considerable scope in defining their constitution and laws. They had secured Mosul for Iraq against Turkish pressures and largely neutralized the capacity of the Kurds to act as a permanently threatening frontier. They negotiated a treaty which led to Iraqi independence and membership of the League of Nations in 1932. Along the line they had done a good deal to improve infrastructure and train men to run a national army. Their technique had been to act as advisers behind the indigenous rulers at all levels. On the face of it this was seen by many to be a reasonable attempt to satisfy the demands of the mandate.

In Transjordan, also, the British achieved a remarkable amount. This was no proto-state, merely a fragment of Palestine, Syria, and the Hijaz brought together as a convenient entity under the pliant authority of the Amir Abdullah. No one expected it to have a future in 1919. Yet it emerged with a system of government and laws that was precisely adapted to local circumstances; and ironically it was the only one of the mandates to retain both its original territory and dynasty into the twenty-first century.

---

[5] Longrigg, *Syria and Lebanon*, 363–4.

These may be regarded as the up-sides of the British mandatory experience. Postponing the question of Palestine, what were the obvious down-sides, particularly in Iraq? There were, perhaps, four.

First, the autonomy of both Iraq and Transjordan, even after each became independent, was largely a fiction. For all practical purposes, until 1932, Iraq was run by its British advisers, just as Egypt had been. This enabled the rapidly changing central governments and local governors to avoid real responsibility. Governments did not have policies, and ministers seldom bothered to master the problems of their departments, which in any case changed hands very rapidly. Even after 1932, the remaining advisers at Baghdad continued to influence policy and the more able and active British Ambassadors could continue to exert great influence: symbolically the Embassy continued to be called and thought of as the Residency. Hence, politics in Iraq were largely a farce, a playground for the ambitious who could use office for personal and faction advancement. These were not the characteristics of a genuinely responsible polity.

Second, as was emphasized in Chapter 3, the British relied very heavily on the local notables. Indeed, they increased their social and political influence. Since the indigenous notables, expanded by the early influx of Hashemite supporters and later other social risers, had a common interest in preserving the social status quo, and particularly the land distribution structure, there was a virtual standstill in terms of social development until 1958. This was indeed an *ancien régime* given new life by the imperial power. But once that power was removed the social structure was certain to collapse, as it did after the end of the British-supported monarchy in 1958. Though of course this was not unique to Iraq, since the same thing was to occur in many Middle Eastern countries after the Nasser regime was born in Egypt in 1952, in Iraq it was largely a British responsibility.

Third, the British proved seriously inadequate in protecting minorities in Iraq. On the national level, they did little to offset the dominance of the minority Sunni over the majority of Shia Muslims. Iraq became, and was until 2003, a Sunni state. Moreover, the British failed to fulfil the many promises they or the Iraqi government they controlled had made to give the Kurds some degree of autonomy and national status. The Kurds, and also the Assyrians, were left in 1932 defenceless against the centralizing and Arabizing strategies of Baghdad. The Assyrians were virtually eliminated or left for Syria, but the Kurdish problem remained unresolved into the twenty-first century.

Fourth, whatever the rhetoric of Iraqi independence in 1932, the British resolutely maintained their military control through possession of the military airfields and naval facilities until 1955. Iraq remained a quasi-military dependency. As against this the Iraqi army that was built up after independence, notionally along British lines and with British equipment, was neither efficient as a military force nor reliable as an arm of government. This was not in fact the fault of the British, who had resolutely refused to allow military conscription until after independence. But they failed in their training to instil the principle of military neutrality in politics as it existed in Britain. The effect was that this proved to be the first politically-impregnated army in the Middle East. From 1936 to 1941, and again after 1946, all governments came to depend on the army. It should have come as no surprise in 1958 that the Free Officers, by then following the Egyptian model, should have decided to pull down the monarchy and reconstruct a new state and society in their own image.

Finally, however, and most important, the first of Longrigg's tests was not met in Iraq: there was never general 'cordial goodwill'. From the start most Iraqis, excluding minorities, wanted the British to leave. A few welcomed the British presence, mainly because it was thought to serve their interests, and there were many personal linkages. But the great majority disliked them as conquerors and infidels. They put up with the mandate, and then residual British powers and rights under the treaty, because they had no alternative. But the outburst of 1948 reflected deep residual popular dislike. There had been no conquest of hearts and minds.

The British achievement in Iraq was, therefore, mixed. They created a state with reasonably efficient western-style administrative and political institutions. They handed over power in Iraq before they did this in any non-settler British dependency. At the same time, they maintained the advantages they had looked for in Iraq from 1918. All this showed cleverness. On the other hand, they pre-tended to the League in 1931 that Iraq was a genuine democracy in which the rights of all, including minorities, were secure. This was false. The state they left was a strictly patrimonial society in which a small, rich minority of land-owners, politicians, and tribal rulers were able to exploit the assets of the society. Whether in fact the British as short-term mandatories could have done very differently is another question. But this was certainly not the genuine democracy the League was led to believe.

Palestine, of course, must be regarded as the major British failure. This, as was argued in Chapters 4 and 5, was the result of a mix of strategic ambitions and misguided philanthropy. Britain wanted to control the territory as a defence of Egypt against France in Syria. Zionism, though sincerely believed in by many leading Britons, was a convenient excuse for a British mandate rather than the international zone planned in Sykes–Picot. No attempt was made to discover what the resident Arabs thought about a home for the Jews in their country, though in fact this was quite obvious. Initially the British, as represented by Sir Herbert Samuel, the first High Commissioner, seem genuinely to have thought that some form of cohabitation would be possible between Zionist settlers and the indigenous Arabs and that this could be developed through common legislative agencies. That this would be impossible was shown by Arab refusal to take part in the first elections to a legislative council in 1923: there could be no political solu-tion. Thereafter, the British spent more than two decades attempting to find a way out of the dilemma they had created for themselves. In the end they had to give up and walk out. It was probably the most ignominious failure of its kind in British imperial history, the first time that Britain ended its rule without leaving an established government behind it.[6]

While the basic fault lay with the British, it must be said that intransigence on the part of both the majority of Arabs and the Zionists was an important contributory factor. Then, and still until the twenty-first century, the Arabs refused to accept the reality of a Jewish community or later of an Israeli state. Their refusal to do so was dogmatic, expressing partly the dominant concept of an Arab nation but also rejection of the known intention of the Zionists ultimately to form a Jewish state in which the Arabs would form a minority. Whether such a condominium would have been viable is unpredictable, depending on the goodwill of both communities and in particular victory for those in the Zionist leadership who were willing to accept Arabs as an integral part of their society and state. In fact, however, such men were in the minority in the Zionist leadership. Their vision remained that of Herzl: there must be a Zionist state and, as Ben-Gurion saw it, there would be no room in it for non-Jews. The events of 1948 demonstrated that ethnic cleansing, not collaboration, was the Zionist strategy.

The British record as a mandatory was, therefore, very mixed. Ironically it was most successful in the least considered territory, Transjordan, apparently successful in Iraq, in that it was given independence as a going political organism within a decade of the mandate being formally transferred, and a disaster in Palestine, where an attempt at social and political engineering led to the creation of the greatest single source of continuing instability in the Middle East.

On the face of it, the French record as mandatory was even less successful. Except among the Maronites and some other Christian groups in Lebanon, there was never any 'cordial goodwill'. That was to be expected, given the circumstances of the French occupation. There were collaborators and time-servers, but few even of those welcomed the French presence. Nor was there a 'fairly rapid consolidation . . . of full self-government'. On the contrary, the main charge must obviously be that the French made very little attempt to promote or expedite the formal independence of either Syria or Lebanon. Rather, they haggled for decades over the terms of an independence treaty and had eventually to be forced by the British to evacuate without one in 1945–6. Subsidiary charges have been that they did little to train indigenous officials, gave undue preference to French economic interests, and imposed an artificial and unrealistic division between the different components of Syria and Lebanon. Above all, they failed to give Syria a proper education in responsible self-government and perpetuated a confessional basis for politics in Lebanon. These accusations would add up, if true, to a statement that the French did not fulfil the obligations imposed by their mandates.

---

[6] The partition of India in 1947 might be seen as a previous example in that the British did not police the division and the transfer of populations. But there was a constituted government in what became India and adequate administrative agencies in Pakistan, which soon formed its own government.

In some degree all these are justifiable accusations. But the two most significant defects of French policy, as compared with that of Britain in Iraq, were territorial division and failure to allow the development of true self-government.

The policy of division, as was seen in Chapter 7, was integral with the original French approach to the mandate. The fragmentation of Ottoman Syria was based partly on genuine belief in the incompatibility of the various components of Syria—Druzes, Alawites, urban Arabs, beduin, Maronites, Shiites—partly on the French colonial tradition of ruling by division. In Syria itself this had some justification, as the attitude of both Alawites and Druzes to inclusion into a unitary Syrian state demonstrated. But the separation of the Islamic coastal areas as part of Lebanon was, as de Caix and others predicted, a great mistake. The outcome was that Syria emerged after 1945 as a unitary state with very little experience of unity, while Lebanon was left to overcome the intrinsic problems of confessional conflict.

In the political field the basic French handicap was that they had no tradition of self-government in their colonies. It was against all their instincts to allow possibly inexperienced or incompetent local politicians to blunder on and to use politics to feather their nests. Hence the continuing primacy of French officials at all levels and conversely the irresponsible attitude of many Syrian and Lebanese politicians, who knew that whatever they did the French would adjust things. It must, however, be said that this differed only in degree from British techniques in Iraq and Transjordan. In all these countries government was probably better and more honest than it might otherwise have been. But the longer-term result was that political parties in Iraq, Syria, and Lebanon (they barely existed in Transjordan by 1946) could afford the luxury of not developing consistent strategies or taking major responsibilities. This made them extremely vulnerable to attack by groups outside the restricted political arena, notably those in the army, on the grounds that they were self-seeking and non-progressive.

Indeed, in a longer-distance view, the main feature of both British and French rule was that they depended on the established social classes and helped to perpetuate their dominance. In effect they inherited and maintained the Ottoman system of ruling through landed and urban elites. This was true even in Arab Palestine, where the British attempted to use the Islamic hierarchy to control the Muslim population. Given the social structure of all these societies there was, in fact, no alternative. The consequence was that, however much these elites might complain at alien domination, in fact it worked very much in their favour. The political systems imposed on them enabled them to control electorates and share the rewards of office between them. Conversely, it enabled them to preserve social and economic hierarchies. Hence, it could be argued that the period of mandates was one of virtual social standstill in all these territories, indeed that it was the last golden age of the indigenous elites. Only after independence were the forces of dissent and the demand for radical change able, mainly through the armies, to express themselves.

To revert to the alternative options for the future of the Ottoman territories outlined at the start of this chapter, it becomes clear that after 1918 some system of foreign control was the only real possibility. While a rejuvenated Ottoman or Turkish empire might have been the most desirable, this was never on the cards: the Allies were determined to keep what they had taken. Nor was it certain that the Arab countries would have been prepared to revert to control by Istanbul.

Equally implausible is the argument that, if the Allies had stuck to their promises and allowed immediate self-determination to all the occupied territories without any strings attached, this would have produced a group of viable nation states.

We are therefore left with the conclusion that, once the British had occupied the Ottoman Middle East, there was no real alternative to some form of continued foreign control. In principle the mandate system was therefore the best available option, best simply in that it was defined as temporary and advisory. But how well did it fulfil its defined function of preparing these societies to become independent nation states?

Its most positive achievement was that it created a system of states with viable western-type governmental institutions with the potential to develop into nations. This made it possible for Britain and France to hand over their responsibilities with a good conscience. But these were mere states, not truly nation states. Since all were cobbled together they contained many essentially incompatible elements and unresolved conflicts.

First, within the new states, particularly in Syria and Iraq, the British and French left ruling elites whose attitudes remained those of an unreconstructed patrimonial society, but who now had weapons of political control undreamed of by the Ottomans. Briefly, these old elites were able to exploit their new power in their own interests. But within a few years these same weapons of control were seized by other social groups, led by the military. The outcome was the militaristic despotisms of the later twentieth and early twenty-first centuries.

Second, the mandates bequeathed dangerous international instability. By fostering Zionist power in Palestine, the British created not only an irreconcilably divided country but also, in the resultant state of Israel, a standing insult to the Arab world which was to become the main cause of conflict throughout the Middle East. Parallel to this, though on a smaller scale, the French created a Greater Lebanon with deep and unbridgeable confessional divisions. This fission in turn became connected with the Palestinian issue after 1967 and added to the profound instability of the whole region.

It is, however, necessary to make a distinction between these two consequences of the mandates. The first was in no sense peculiar to the British and French policies in the Middle East. In virtually every non-settler western colony, imperial rule was necessarily based on the collaboration of the ruled, so that the imperialists took over the hierarchical patron–client social structures they inherited and on which their rule was based. Equally, when they left, they bequeathed dangerous power to the old and new elites who succeeded them. The autocracies of Black Africa and many other ex-colonies in the Third World have a genetic relationship with those of the Middle East and stem from the same imperial policy of building quasi-western political structures on indigenous social foundations. Hence, it can be said that the mandates differed from other European forms of imperialism mainly in their brevity. In every case a main effect was to shore up indigenous elites and social structures, leaving the resolution of these disparities until after the imperialists had withdrawn.

By contrast, although there were many other examples of plural societies created by the imperial powers in their own interests in other parts of the colonial world, with serious domestic consequences after the imperial umbrella was removed, it is arguable that none has created as much misery and international instability as that imposed on Palestine. British policy there must stand as one of the greatest errors of judgement in western imperial history.

The conclusion must therefore be that, although the mandates, or some comparable form of western rule, became inevitable once Ottoman rule had been destroyed, they did not fulfil the expectations of those idealists who drew up the guidelines for the system. This was, of course, predictable. Britain and France were there for their own purposes, strategic, economic, ideological. Mandatory control gave Britain strategic control of much of the Middle East until 1955 and France power in the Eastern Mediterranean for some thirty years. Both reaped extensive and still continuing economic advantages, and much of their cultural influence survived their withdrawal, particularly that of France. It was no part of their ambitions to undertake that fundamental social and political reconstruction that might, in the longer term, have generated truly democratic and stable societies. They left when it was no longer convenient to stay; and in leaving they left behind a multitude of unresolved tensions and potential conflicts. The mandates sowed dragon's teeth that were eventually to grow into the complex of tensions and despotisms that constitute the contemporary Middle East.

Select Bibliography

GENERAL: MIDDLE EASTERN HISTORY AND ARAB NATIONALISM

ANDERSON, B., *Imagined Communities: Reflections on the Origin and Spread of Nationalism* (London, 1983).

ANTONIUS, G., *The Arab Awakening* (London, 1938; 1945).

CHOUEIRI, Y. M., *Arab Nationalism: A History* (Oxford, 2000).

COHEN M. J., and KOLINSKY, M. (ed.), *Demise of the British Empire in the Middle East: Britain's Response to Nationalist Movements, 1943–55* (London, 1998).

DAWN, C. E., *From Ottomanism to Arabism: Essays on the Origins of Arab Nationalism* (Urbana, Ill., 1973).

DAWISHA, A., *Arab Nationalism in the Twentieth Century: From Triumph to Despair* (Princeton and Oxford, 2003).

FISHER, J., *Curzon and British Imperialism in the Middle East 1916–1919* (London, 1999).

FRANKLIN, D., *A Peace to End All Peace: The Fall of the Ottoman Empire and the Creation of the Modern Middle East* (New York, 1989).

GOMAA, A. M., *The Foundation of the League of Arab States* (London, 1977).

GRIGG, J., *Lloyd George: War Leader, 1916–1918* (London, 2002).

HAIM, S., *Arab Nationalism: An Anthology* (Berkeley, 1962).

HELMREICH, P., *From Paris to Sèvres: The Partition of the Ottoman Empire and the Peace Conference of 1919–1920* (Colombus, Ohio, 1974).

HOURANI, A., *Arabic Thought in the Liberal Age* (1962; rev. edn. Cambridge, 1983).

—— (ed.), *The Emergence of the Modern Middle East* (Berkeley, 1981).

—— *Europe and the Middle East* (London, 1980).

—— *A History of the Arab Peoples* (London, 1991).

—— *Minorities in the Arab World* (London, 1947).

JANKOWSKI, J., and GERSHONI, I. (eds.), *Rethinking Nationalism in the Arab Middle East* (New York, 1997).

KEAY, J., *Sowing the Wind: The Seeds of Conflict in the Middle East* (London, 2003).

KEDOURIE, E., *Democracy and Arab Political Culture* (London, 1994).

—— *Into the Anglo-Arab Labyrinth: The McMahon–Hussayn Correspondence and its Interpretations, 1914–1939* (1976; 2nd edn. London, 2000).

—— *Islam in the Modern World* (London, 1980).

KENT, J., *British Imperial Strategy and the Origins of the Cold War, 1944–49* (Leicester, 1993).

KHALIDI, R. I., *British Policy towards Syria and Palestine, 1906–1914* (London, 1980).

—— *et al.* (eds.), *The Origins of Arab Nationalism* (New York, 1991).

KRAMER, M., *Arab Awakening and Islamic Revival: The Politics of Ideas in the Middle East* (New Brunswick and London, 1996).

LOUIS, WM R., *The British Empire in the Middle East, 1945–1951* (Oxford, 1984).

—— and OWEN, R. (eds.), *A Revolutionary Year: The Middle East in 1958* (London and New York, 2002).

MADDY-WEITZMAN, B., *The Crystallization of the Arab State System* (Syracuse, NY, 1993).

MONROE, E., *The Mediterranean in Politics* (London, 1938).

OWEN, R., *The Middle East in the World Economy, 1800–1914* (London, 1981).

PODEH, E., *The Quest for Hegemony in the Arab World: The Struggle over the Baghdad Pact* (Leiden, 1995).

PORATH, Y., *In Search of Arab Unity* (London, 1986).

SUSSER, S., and SHMUELEVITZ A., (eds.), *The Hashemites in the Modern Arab World* (London, 1995).

TAUBER, E., *The Arab Movements in World War I* (London, 1993).

—— *The Emergence of the Arab Movements* (London, 1993).

TIBI, B., *Arab Nationalism: A Critical Enquiry* (1971; Eng trans. London, 1981).

YAPP, M. E., *The Near East since the First World War* (London, 1991).

ZEINE, Z. N., *Arab–Turkish Relations and the Emergence of Arab Nationalism* (Beirut, 1958).

—— *The Emergence of Arab Nationalism* (Beirut, 1966).

OTTOMAN EMPIRE

AHMAD, F., *The Young Turks: The Committee of Union and Progress in Turkish Politics, 1908–1914* (Oxford, 1969).

DADRIAN, V., *Warrant for Genocide: Key Elements of Turko-Armenian Conflict* (New Brunswick and London, 1999).

FRIEDMAN, I., *Germany, Turkey and Zionism* (Oxford, 1977).

HALE, W., *Political and Economic Development of Modern Turkey* (London, 1981).

HOURANI, A., 'The Ottoman Background of the Modern Middle East', in K. H. Karpat (ed.), *The Ottoman State and its Place in World History* (Leiden, 1974).

KAISER, H. (ed.), *Marsovan 1915: The Diaries of Bertha B. Morley* (Reading, 1999).

KAYALI, H., *Arabs and Young Turks: Ottomanism, Arabism and Islamism in the Ottoman Empire, 1908–1918* (Berkeley, 1997).

KEDOURIE, E., *England and the Middle East: The Destruction of the Ottoman Empire, 1914–1921* (London, 1956; rev. edn. 1987).

KENT, M. (ed.), *The Great Powers and the End of the Ottoman Empire* (London, 1984).

KIESER, H.-L., 'Les Kurds alévis face au nationalisme turc Kemalist' (Occasional paper, Amsterdam, 1993).

LEWIS, B., *The Emergence of Modern Turkey* (Oxford, 1968).

MCCARTHY, J., *The Ottoman Peoples and the End of Empire* (London, 2001).

MACFIE, A. L., *The End of the Ottoman Empire, 1908–1923* (London and New York, 1998).

MANSFIELD, P., *The Ottoman Empire and its Successors* (London, 1973).

OSCAN, A., *Pan-Islamism, Indian Muslims, the Ottomans and Britain, 1877–1924* (Leiden, 1997).

PALMER, A., *The Decline and Fall of the Ottoman Empire* (London, 1992).

SHAW, S. J., *History of the Ottoman Empire and Modern Turkey: Empire of the Gazis* Cambridge, 1977).

—— and SHAW, E. K., *History of the Ottoman Empire and Modern Turkey. Vol. 2: Reform, Revolution and Republic: The Rise of Modern Turkey 1808–1970* (Cambridge, 1977).

TRUMPENER, U., *Germany and the Ottoman Empire, 1914–1918* (Princeton, 1968).

WEIKER, W. F., *Modernization of Turkey* (New York, 1981).

ZÜCHER, E. J., *Turkey: A Modern History* (London, 1993).

IRAQ

BASSAM, T., *Arab Nationalism: A Critical Enquiry*, ed. and trans. M. Farouk-Sluglett and P. Sluglett (London, 1981).

BATATU, H., *The Old Social Classes and the Revolutionary Movements of Iraq* (Princeton, 1978).

BELL, LADY (ed.), *The Letters of Gertrude Bell* (London, 1927).

BRADY, J., *Eastern Encounters: Memoirs of a Decade 1937–1946* (Braunton, Devon, 1992).

BURGOYNE, E., *Gertrude Bell from her Personal Papers 1914–1926* (London, 1961).

BUSCH, B. C., *Britain, India and the Arabs 1914–1921* (Berkeley and London, 1971).

CHALIAND, G., *The Kurdish Tragedy* (London and Princeton, 1994).

COHEN, S. A., *British Policy in Mesopotamia 1903–1914* (London, 1976).

DARWIN, J., *Britain, Egypt and the Middle East: Imperial Policy in the Aftermath of War 1918–1922* (London, 1981).

—— 'An Undeclared Empire: The British in the Middle East, 1918–1939', *Journal of Imperial and Commonwealth History*, 27/2 (1999), 159–76.

DODGE, T., *Inventing Iraq: The Failure of Nation Building and a History Denied* (London, 2003).

EDMONDS, C. J., *Kurds, Turks and Arabs* (London, 1957).

ELLIOT, M., *Independent Iraq: The Monarchy and British Influence 1941–1958* (London and New York, 1996).

EPPEL, M., 'The Decline of British Influence and the Ruling Elite in Iraq', in M. J. Cohen and M. Kolinsky (eds.), *Demise of the British Empire in the Middle East: Britain's Response to Nationalist Movements, 1943–55* (London, 1998), 185–97.

FAROUK-SLUGLETT, M., and SLUGLETT, P., *Iraq since 1958: From Revolution to Dictatorship* (London and New York, 1987).

FERNEA, R. A., and LOUIS, WM R. (eds.), *The Iraqi Revolution of 1958: The Old Social Classes Revisited* (London and New York, 1991).

FUCCARO, N., *The Other Kurds: Yazidis in Colonial Iraq* (London, 1999).

GRAVES, P., *The Life of Sir Percy Cox* (London, 1941).

HAJ, S., *The Making of Iraq 1900–1963* (Albany, NY, 1997).

HAMILTON, A. M., *Road through Kurdistan: The Narrative of an Engineer in Iraq* (London, 1937).

HAY, W. R., *Two Years in Kurdistan: Experiences of a Political Officer, 1918–1920* (London, 1921).

HOURANI, A., 'Ottoman Reform and the Policies of Notables', in W. R. Polk and R. Chambers (eds.), *Beginnings of Modernization in the Middle East* (Chicago, 1968).

IRELAND, P. W., *Iraq: A Study in Political Development* (London, 1937).

IZADY, M. R., *The Kurds: A Concise Handbook* (Washington, DC and London, 1992).

JAWAD, S., *Iraq and the Kurdish Question 1958–1970* (London, 1981).

KARSH, E., 'Reactive Imperialism: Britain, the Hashemites, and the Creation of Modern Iraq', *Journal of Imperial and Commonwealth History*, 30/3 (Sept. 2002), 55–70.

—— and KARSH, I., *Empires of the Sand: The Struggle for Mastery in the Middle East, 1789–1923* (Cambridge, Mass., 1999).

KEDOURIE, E., *The Chatham House Version and Other Middle-Eastern Studies* (London, 1970).

KEDOURIE, E., *England and the Middle East: The Destruction of the Ottoman Empire 1914–1921* (London, 1956).

KELIDAR, A. (ed.), *The Integration of Modern Iraq* (London, 1979).

KENT, M. (ed.), *The Great Powers and the End of the Ottoman Empire* (London, 1984).

—— *Oil and the Empire: British Policy and Mesopotamian Oil 1900–1921* (London, 1976).

KHADDURI, M., *Independent Iraq 1932–1958: A Study in Iraqi Politics* (1951; 2nd edn. London, 1960).

KIRISCI, K., and WINROW, G. M., *The Turkish Question and Turkey* (London and Portland, Oreg., 1997).

KIRK-GREENE, A., *On Crown Service: A History of HM Colonial and Overseas Civil Services 1837–1997* (London, 1999).

LANGLEY, K. M., *The Industrialization of Iraq* (Cambridge, Mass., 1967).

LONGRIGG, S. H., *Iraq 1900–1950: A Political, Social and Economic History* (London, 1953).

MACDOWALL, D., *A Modern History of the Kurds* (London and New York, 1997).

MARLOWE, J., *Late Victorian: The Life of Sir Arnold Talbot Wilson* (London, 1967).

MONROE, E., *Britain's Moment in the Middle East 1914–1956* (London, 1965).

—— *Philby of Arabia* (New York and London, 1973).

NEVAKIVI, J., *Britain, France and the Arab Middle East 1914–1920* (London, 1969).

OLSON, R., *The Emergence of Kurdish Nationalism and the Sheikh Said Rebellion, 1880–1925* (Austin, Tex., 1989).

OMISSI, D., *Air Power and Colonial Control* (Manchester, 1990).

PARIS, T. J., *Britain, the Hashemites and Arab Rule, 1920–1925: The Sherifian Solution* (London, 2003).

ROTHWELL, V. H., *British War Aims and Peace Diplomacy* (Oxford, 1971).

—— 'Mesopotamia in British War Aims 1914–1918', *Historical Journal*, 13/2 (1970), 273–94.

SASSOON, J., *Economic Policy in Iraq 1932–1958* (London, 1987).

SHIKARA, A. A. AL-RAZZAFI, *Iraqi Politics 1921–1941* (London, 1987).

SILVERFARB, D., *Britain's Informal Empire in the Middle East: A Case Study of Iraq 1929–1941* (New York and London, 1986).

—— *The Twilight of British Ascendancy in the Middle East: A Case Study of Iraq, 1941–1958* (New York, 1994).

SIMON, R. S., *Iraq between the World Wars: The Creation and Implementation of a Nationalist Ideology* (New York, 1986).

SLUGLETT, P., *Britain in Iraq 1914–1932* (London, 1976).

SOANE, E. B., *Through Mesopotamia and Kurdistan in Disguise* (London, 1912).

STARK, F., *Dust in the Lion's Paw: Autobiography 1939–1946* (London, 1961).

STORRS, Sir R., *Orientations* (London, 1937; 2nd edn. London, 1943).

TARBUSH, M. A., *The Role of the Military in Politics: A Case Study of Iraq to 1941* (London, 1982).

TAUBER, E., *The Formation of Modern Syria and Iraq* (Ilford, Essex and Portland, Oreg., 1995).

TRIPP, C., *A History of Iraq* (Cambridge, 2000).

WARNER, G., *Iraq and Syria 1941* (London, 1974).

WILSON, Sir A. T., *Loyalties: Mesopotamia 1914–1917* (London, 1930).

—— *Mesopotamia 1917–1920: A Clash of Loyalties* (London, 1931).

WINSTONE, H. V. F., *Gertrude Bell* (London, 1978).

PALESTINE

AMERY, L. S., *My Political Life*, 3 vols. (London, 1953).

BAIN, K. R., *The March to Zion: United States Policy and the Founding of Israel* (Austin, Tex., 1979).

BENTWICH, N., *Mandate Memories 1918–1948* (London, 1965).

BETHELL, N., *The Palestine Triangle: The Struggle between the Jews and the Arabs, 1935–1948* (London, 1979).

BEGIN, M., *The Revolt: Story of the Irgun* (Tel Aviv, 1964).

CHARTERS, D. A., *The British Army and Insurgency in Palestine, 1945–1947* (Basingstoke, 1989).

COHEN, A., *Israel and the Arab World* (Boston, 1976).

COHEN, M. J., *Churchill and the Jews* (London, 1985).

—— *Palestine and the Great Powers, 1945–1948* (New York, 1978).

—— *Palestine: Retreat from the Mandate. The Making of British Policy, 1936–1945* (London, 1978).

CROSSMAN, R., *Palestine Mission: A Personal Record* (London, 1947).

EGREMONT, M., *Under Two Flags: The Life of Major-General Sir Edward Spears* (London, 1997).

EL-AWASI, ABD AL-FATTAH, M., *The Muslim Brothers and the Palestine Question, 1928–1947* (London, 1998).

ELPELEG, Z., *The Grand Mufti: Haj Amin Al-Husaini* (London, 1993).

EPPEL, M., *The Palestine Conflict in the History of Modern Iraq: The Dynamics of Involvement, 1928–1948* (London, 1994).

FRIEDMAN, I., *Germany, Turkey and Zionism, 1897–1918* (Oxford, 1977; 2nd edn. New Brunswick, 1998).

—— *The Question of Palestine, 1914–1918: British–Jewish–Arab Relations* (1973; new edn. London, 1992).

—— *Palestine: A Twice-Promised Land? I. The British, the Arabs and Zionism, 1915–1920* (New Brunswick, 2000).

GILBERT, M., *Exile and Return* (London, 1978).

HOURANI, A., *The Emergence of the Modern Middle East* (London, 1981).

HUNEIDI, S., *A Broken Trust: Sir Herbert Samuel, Zionism and the Palestinians* (London, 2001).

HUREWITZ, J. C., *The Struggle for Palestine* (New York, 1950; 1976).

KAMEN, C., *Little Common Ground: Arab Agriculture and Jewish Settlement in Palestine, 1920–1948* (Pittsburgh, 1991).

KARSH, E., *Fabricating Israeli History* (London, 1997).

—— (ed.), *Israel: The First Hundred Years*. Vol. I: *Israel's Transition from Community to State* (London, 2000).

KAYYALI, ABD AL-WAHHAB, *Palestine: A Modern History* (London, 1978; 2nd edn. 1981).

KEDOURIE, E., and HAIM, S. G. (eds.), *Palestine and Israel in the 19th and 20th Centuries* (London, 1982).

KHALIDI, W., *Palestine Reborn* (London, 1992).

LESCH, A. M., *Arab Politics in Palestine, 1917–1939: The Frustration of a Nationalist Movement* (Ithaca, 1979).

LESCH, A. M., *Origins and Development of the Arab–Israeli Conflict* (Westport, Conn., 1998).

LOUIS, WM R., *The British Empire in the Middle East, 1945–1951* (Oxford, 1984).

—— and STOOKEY, R. W. (eds.), *The End of the Palestine Mandate* (London, 1986).

MANDEL, N. J., *The Arabs and Zionism before World War I* (Berkeley, 1976).

MARLOWE, J., *The Seat of Pilate* (London, 1959).

MILLER, Y., *Government and Society in Rural Palestine, 1920–1948* (Austin, Tex., 1985).

MORRIS, B., *The Birth of the Palestinian Refugee Problem, 1947–1949* (Cambridge, 1988).

—— *1948 and After: Israel and the Palestinians* (Oxford, 1990).

—— 'Revisiting the Palestinian Exodus of 1948', in E. L. Rogan and A. Shlaim (eds.), *The War for Palestine* (Cambridge, 2001).

MUSLIH, M. Y., *The Origins of Palestinian Nationalism* (New York, 1988).

NAHI, B. M., *Arabism, Islamism and the Palestine Question 1908–1941* (Reading, 1998).

OWEN, R. (ed.), *Studies in the Economic and Social History of Palestine: The Nineteenth and Twentieth Centuries* (Carbondale, Ill., 1982).

PAPPÉ, I., *Britain and the Arab–Israeli Conflict, 1948–1951* (London, 1988).

—— *The Making of the Arab–Israeli Conflict* (London, 1992).

PARKES, J. W., *The Emergence of the Jewish Problem, 1878–1939* (London, 1946).

PORATH, Y., *The Emergence of the Palestinian-Arab National Movement, 1918–1929* (London, 1974).

—— *The Palestinian-Arab National Movement: From Riots to Rebellion, 1929–1939* (London, 1977).

RODINSON, M., *Israel—A Colonial-Settler State?* (New York, 1973).

ROGAN, E. L., and SHLAIM, A. (eds.), *The War for Palestine: Rewriting the History of 1948* (Cambridge, 2001).

ROSE, N. A., *The Gentile Zionists: A Study in Anglo-Zionist Diplomacy, 1929–1939* (London, 1973).

—— (ed.), *From Palmerston to Balfour: Collected Essays of Mayir Vereté* (London, 1992).

RUBIN, B., *The Arab States and the Palestine Conflict* (Syracuse, NY, 1981).

SAMUEL, M., *Harvest in the Desert, 1917–1948* (Philadelphia, n.d.).

SEGEV, T., *One Palestine Complete: Jews and Arabs under the British Mandate* (London, 2000).

SEIKALY, M., *Haifa: Transformation of an Arab Society, 1918–1939* (London, 2000).

SHAFIR, G., *Land, Labor and the Origins of the Israeli–Palestinian Conflict, 1882–1914* (Cambridge, Mass., 1989).

SHEPHERD, N., *Ploughing Sand: British Rule in Palestine* (London, 1999).

SHERMAN, A. J., *Mandate Days: British Lives in Palestine, 1918–1948* (London, 1997).

SHLAIM, A., *Collusion Across the Jordan* (Oxford, 1988).

—— *The Politics of Partition: King Abdullah, the Zionists and Palestine, 1921–1951* (Oxford, 1990).

SMITH, B., *The Roots of Separatism in Palestine: British Economic Policy 1920–1929* (London and New York, 1993).

STEIN, K. W., *The Land Question in Palestine, 1917–1939* (Chapel Hill, N.C. and London, 1984).

STEIN, L., *The Balfour Declaration* (London, 1961).

STORRS, SIR R., *Orientations* (London, 1937; 2nd edn. London, 1943).

SYKES, C., *Cross Roads to Israel* (London, 1965).

VITAL, D., *The Origins of Zionism* (Oxford, 1975).

—— *Zionism: The Formative Years* (Oxford, 1982).

—— *Zionism: The Crucial Phase* (Oxford, 1987).

WASSERSTEIN, B., *Britain and the Jews of Europe 1939–1945* (Oxford, 1979).

—— *The British in Palestine: The Mandatory Government and the Arab–Jewish Conflict, 1917–1929* (1978; rev. edn. Oxford, 1991).

—— *Herbert Samuel: A Political Life* (Oxford, 1992).

ZWEIG, R. W., *Britain and Palestine during the Second World War* (Woodbridge, 1986).

TRANSJORDAN

ABDULLAH, KING, *Memoirs of King Abdullah of Transjordan* (New York, 1950).

ALON, Y., 'Tribal Shaykhs and the Limits of British Imperial Rule in Transjordan, 1920–46', *Journal of Imperial and Commonwealth History*, 32/1 (Jan. 2004), 69–92.

ARURI, N. H., *Jordan: A Study in Political Development* (The Hague, 1972).

ASHTON, N. J., 'A "Special Relationship" Sometimes in Spite of Ourselves': Britain and Jordan', 1957–73, *JICH* 33/2 (May 2005), 221–44.

BAKER, R., *King Hussein and the Kingdom of the Hijaz* (Cambridge, 1979).

COHEN, A., *Political Parties in the West Bank under the Jordanian Regime 1949–1967* (Ithaca and London, 1982).

DANN, U., *King Hussein and the Challenge of Arab Radicalism: Jordan 1955–1967* (Oxford, 1989).

—— *Studies in the History of Transjordan, 1920–1949* (Boulder, Colo., 1984).

DEARDEN, A., *Jordan* (London, 1958).

GELBER, Y., *Jewish–Transjordanian Relations, 1921–1948* (London, 1997).

GERSHUNI, I., 'King Abdullah's Concept of a Greater Syria', in A. Sinai and A. Pollock (eds.), *The Hashemite Kingdom of Jordan and the West Bank* (New York, 1977).

GLUBB, SIR J. B., *A Soldier with the Arabs* (London, 1957).

KIRKBRIDE, SIR A., *From the Wings: Amman Memoirs 1947–1951* (London, 1976).

LOUIS, WM R., *The British Empire in the Middle East 1945–1951* (Oxford, 1984), ch. 9.

LUNT, J., *Glubb Pasha: A Biography* (London, 1984).

MADDY-WEITZMAN, B., 'Chafing at the Bit: King Abdallah and the Arab League', in S. Susser and A. Shmuelevitz (eds.), *The Hashemites in the Modern Arab World* (London, 1995).

MISHAL, S., *West Bank/East Bank: The Palestinians in Jordan 1949–1967* (New Haven, 1978).

MORRIS, J., *The Hashemite Kings* (London, 1959).

NEVO, J., *King Abdallah and Palestine: A Territorial Ambition* (Basingstoke, 1996).

PAPPÉ, I., 'British Rule in Jordan, 1943–56', in M. J. Cohen and M. Lolinsky (eds.), *Demise of the British Empire in the Middle East: Britain's Responses to Nationalist Movements 1943–55* (London, 1998).

PARIS, T. J., *Britain, the Hashemites and Arab Rule, 1920–1925: The Sherifian Solution* (London, 2003).

PLASCOV, A., *The Palestinian Refugees in Jordan, 1948–1967* (London, 1981).

PORATH, Y., 'Abdallah's Greater Syria Programme', *Middle Eastern Studies*, 30/2 (1984), 172–89.

ROGAN, E. L., *Frontiers of the State in the Late Ottoman Empire: Transjordan 1850–1921* (Cambridge, 1999).

SALIBI, K., *The Modern History of Jordan* (London, 1993).

SATLOFF, R., *From Abdullah to Hussein* (New York, 1994).

SHLAIM, A., *Collusion Across the Jordan* (Oxford, 1988).

—— *The Politics of Partition: King Abdullah, the Zionists and Palestine, 1921–1951* (Oxford, 1990).

SINAI, A., and POLLACK, A. (eds.), *The Hashemite Kingdom of Jordan and the West Bank* (New York, 1977).

SUSSER, A., *Jordan: Case Study of a Pivotal State* (Washington, DC, 2000).

—— and SHMUELEVITZ, A. (eds.), *The Hashemites in the Modern Arab World* (London, 1995).

TROELLER, G., *The Birth of Saudi Arabia: Britain and the Rise of the House of Saʿud* (London, 1976).

VATIKIOTIS, P. J., *Politics and the Military in Jordan: A Study of the Arab Legion 1921–1957* (London, 1967).

WILSON, M. C., *King Abdullah, Britain and the Making of Jordan* (Cambridge, 1987).

SYRIA

ANDREW, C. M., and KANYA-FORSTNER, A. S., *France Overseas: The Great War and the Climax of French Imperial Expansion* (London, 1981).

CASEY, LORD R., *Personal Experience 1939–1946* (New York, 1962).

CATROUX, GENERAL, *Dans la bataille de Mediterranée* (Paris, 1949).

CHOUEIRI, Y. M. (ed.), *State and Society in Syria and Lebanon* (Exeter and New York, 1993).

COMMINS, D. D., *Islamic Reform: Politics and Social Change in Late Ottoman Syria* (New York, 1990).

GELVIN, J. L., *Divided Loyalties: Nationalism and Mass Politics in Syria at the Close of Empire* (Berkeley, Los Angeles, and London, 1998).

HOURANI, A. H., *The Emergence of the Modern Middle East* (London, 1981).

—— *Syria and Lebanon: A Political Essay* (London, 1946).

JOARDER, S., *Syria under the French Mandate: The Early Phase, 1920–1927* (Dacca, 1977).

KHALIDI, R., *British Policy towards Syria and Palestine, 1906–1914* (London, 1980).

KHOURY, P. S., *Syria and the French Mandate: The Politics of Arab Nationalism, 1920–1945* (London and Princeton, 1987).

—— *Urban Notables and Arab Nationalism: The Politics of Damascus 1880–1920* (Cambridge, 1983).

LONGRIGG, S. H., *Syria and Lebanon under French Mandate* (London, 1958).

PIPES, D., *Greater Syria: The History of an Ambition* (New York, 1990).

RUSSELL, M., *The First Modern Arab State: Syria under Faysal 1918–1920* (Minneapolis, 1985).

SEALE, P., *The Struggle for Syria* (London, 1965).

SPEARS, SIR E., *Fulfilment of a Mission* (London, 1977).

TAUBER, E., *The Formation of Modern Syria and Iraq* (London, 1995).

TIBAWI, A. L., *A Modern History of Syria, including Lebanon and Palestine* (New York, 1969).

ZEINE, Z. N., *The Struggle for Arab Independence: Western Diplomacy and the Rise and Fall of Faysal's Kingdom in Syria* (Beirut, 1961).

LEBANON

AKARLI, E. D., *The Long Peace: Ottoman Lebanon, 1861–1920* (London and New York, 1993).

BAAKLINI, A. I., *Legislative and Political Development: Lebanon, 1842–1972* (Durham, N.C., 1976).

CHOUEIRI, Y. M. (ed.), *State and Society in Syria and Lebanon* (Exeter, 1993).

ENTELLIS, J., *Pluralism and Party Transformation in Lebanon: al-Kata'ib 1936–1970* (Leiden, 1974).

FAWAZ, L. T., *Merchants and Migrants in Nineteenth Century Beirut* (Cambridge, Mass., 1983).

GORDON, D. C., *Lebanon, the Fragmented Nation* (London, 1980).

HOURANI, A. H., *Syria and Lebanon* (Oxford, 1946).

HUDSON, M. C., *The Precarious Republic: Political Modernization in Lebanon* (New York, 1968).

LONGRIGG, S. H., *Syria and Lebanon under French Mandate* (London, 1958).

OWEN, R. (ed.), *Essays on the Crisis in Lebanon* (London, 1976).

SALIBI, K. S., *A House of Many Mansions: The History of Lebanon Reconsidered* (Beckenham, 1985).

—— *The Modern History of Lebanon* (London, 1965).

SHEHADI, N., and MILLS, D. H. (eds.), *Lebanon: A History of Conflict and Consensus* (London, 1988).

ZAMIR, M., *The Formation of Modern Lebanon* (Ithaca, 1985).

—— *Lebanon's Quest: The Road to Statehood 1926–1939* (London, 1997).

Index